Seventh Edition

INTERNATIONAL MANAGEMENT
MANAGING ACROSS BORDERS AND CULTURES

TEXT AND CASES

Helen Deresky

Professor Emerita, State University of New York–Plattsburgh

Prentice Hall

Boston   Columbus   Indianapolis   New York   San Francisco   Upper Saddle River
Amsterdam   Cape Town   Dubai   London   Madrid   Milan   Munich   Paris   Montreal   Toronto
Delhi   Mexico City   Sao Paulo   Sydney   Hong Kong   Seoul   Singapore   Taipei   Tokyo

*To my husband, John, and my children, John, Mark, and Lara,
for their love and support*

Editorial Director: Sally Yagan
Editor in Chief: Eric Svendsen
Acquisitions Editor: Jennifer M. Collins
Editorial Project Manager: Susie Abraham
Director of Marketing: Patrice Jones
Marketing Manager: Nikki Jones
Senior Marketing Assistant: Ian Gold
Project Manager: Renata Butera
Operations Specialist: Renata Butera
Creative Art Director: Jayne Conte

Cover Designer: Suzanne Duda
Manager, Rights and Permissions: Beth Brenzel
Image Coordinator: Craig A. Jones
Manager, Cover Visual Research & Permissions: Karen Sanatar
Full-Service Project Management: Shiji Sashi
Cover Art: iStockphoto.com
Composition: Integra Software Services
Printer/Binder: Edwards Brothers
Cover Printer: Lehigh Phoenix, Hagerstown
Text Font: Times 10/12

Credits and acknowledgments borrowed from other sources and reproduced, with permission, in this textbook appear on appropriate page within text.

Microsoft® and Windows® are registered trademarks of the Microsoft Corporation in the U.S.A. and other countries. Screen shots and icons reprinted with permission from the Microsoft Corporation. This book is not sponsored or endorsed by or affiliated with the Microsoft Corporation.

Library of Congress Cataloging-in-Publication Data

Deresky, Helen.
  International management : managing across borders and cultures / Helen Deresky.—7th ed.
     p. cm.
Includes bibliographical references and index.
ISBN-13: 978-0-13-609867-6 (alk. paper)
ISBN-10: 0-13-609867-3 (alk. paper)
1. International business enterprises—Management.   2. International business
enterprises—Management—Case studies.   3. Industrial management.
I. Title.
HD62.4.D47 2011
658.049—dc22

2009048763

10 9 8 7 6 5 4 3 2

Prentice Hall
is an imprint of

PEARSON

www.pearsonhighered.com

ISBN 10:   0-13-609867-3
ISBN 13: 978-0-13-609867-6

BRIEF CONTENTS

Comprehensive Cases   405

Integrative Section   432

CONTENTS

PREFACE

SEVENTH EDITION CHANGES

- *Over 50% of the content of this book is new to the seventh edition*
- **Comprehensive cases:** *All 12 of the comprehensive cases are new and current.*
- **Chapter-Opening Profiles: Nine of the 11 Chapter Profiles are new,** keeping two favorites
- **Chapter-Ending Cases: Six of the nine chapter-ending cases are New; three favorites have been updated.**
- **NEW**: Integrative Case: The International Committee of the Red Cross: Managing Across Cultures
- Two of the eleven Comparative Management in Focus sections are new, and the rest have been revised and updated.
- Five of the eleven Management Focus boxes are new.
- Added NEW coverage of the Global Financial Crisis and its effects on strategy throughout.
- **70% increase in coverage of developments in globalization and its growing nationalist backlash – in particular resulting from the global financial crisis**
- **100% increase in coverage of emerging market economies – in particular China and India.**
- **Added NEW coverage of South Africa**
- **Added NEW section on strategies for emerging markets.**
- **Added NEW section on strategies for SMEs**
- **Added NEW section on Value Creation in alliances.**
- **Added NEW sections on "born global" companies and on the CAGE strategy model.**
- Added NEW section on the "global mindset of leaders," and expanded coverage of expatriate assignments.
- Cut out some "old" sections and exhibits, and pruned sections on work motivation.
- Added NEW research data on expatriate assignments and relocation.

The seventh edition of *International Management: Managing Across Borders and Cultures* **Prepares students and practicing managers** for careers in a dynamic global environment wherein they will be responsible for effective strategic, organizational, and interpersonal management. While managing within international and cross-cultural contexts has been the focus of this text since the first edition, the seventh edition portrays the burgeoning level, scope and complexity of international business facing managers in the twenty-first century. The seventh edition explores how recent developments and trends within a hypercompetitive global arena present managers with challenging situations and guides the reader as to what actions to take, and how to develop the skills necessary to design and implement global strategies, to conduct effective cross-national interactions and to manage daily operations in foreign subsidiaries. Global companies are faced with varied and dynamic environments in which they must accurately assess the political, legal, technological, competitive, and cultural factors that shape their strategies and operations. The fate of overseas operations depends greatly on the international manager's cultural skills and sensitivity, as well as the ability to carry out the company's strategy within the context of the host country's business practices.

In the seventh edition, cross-cultural management and competitive strategy are evaluated in the context of global changes—the expanding European Union (EU), the increasing trade among the Americas, and the rapidly growing economies in Asia—that require new management applications. In the seventh edition we have added focus on how rapidly developing economies, in particular China and India, present the manager with challenging strategic decisions in an increasingly "flat world," as posited by Thomas Friedman. Throughout, the text emphasizes how the variable of culture interacts with other national and international factors to affect managerial processes and behaviors. In addition, the growing competitive influence of technology is discussed throughout the text. Concerns about Corporate Social Responsibility (CSR) and Sustainability while operating in global locations are addressed at length.

This textbook is designed for undergraduate and graduate students majoring in international business or general management. Graduate students might be asked to focus more heavily on the comprehensive cases that conclude each part of the book and to complete the term project in greater detail. It is assumed, though not essential, that most students using *International Management:*

Managing Across Borders and Cultures, Seventh Edition, will have taken a basic principles of management course. Although this text is primarily intended for business students, it is also useful for practicing managers and for students majoring in other areas, such as political science or international relations, who would benefit from a background in international management.

SEVENTH EDITION FEATURES

- **Streamlined text** in eleven chapters, with particular focus on global strategic positioning, entry strategies and alliances, effective cross-cultural understanding and management, and developing and retaining an effective global management cadre. The seventh edition has been revised to reflect current research, current events and global developments, and includes company examples from the popular press. In Chapter 1, we introduce trends and developments facing international managers and then expand those topics in the context of the subsequent chapters. For example, we discuss developments in globalization and its growing nationalist backlash—in particular resulting from the global financial crisis. We discuss the effects on global business of the rapidly growing economies of China and India and other emerging economies such as those in Africa, and the expansion of the EU; the globalization of human capital; and the escalating effects of Information Technology and the global spread of e-business. We follow these trends and their effects on the role of the international manager throughout the book. For example, in Chapter 6 we focus further on strategies for emerging markets, while also dealing with changing strategies to respond to economic decline around the world and an increasing level of nationalism in some industries; we have a section on "Using E-Business for Global Expansion" as well as discussing "born global" companies. In Chapter 7, we added a section on strategies for SMEs and a new section on "Value Creation in Alliances." We have condensed some research material in Chapter 3, while adding a new cultural profile on Latin America and expanded the one on Germany. In Chapter 2 we lead into another contemporary topic gaining increasing attention—that of CSR (corporate social resposibility) with a new opening profile, "Primark's Moral Maze," and a comparative section on Human Rights in China. We added focus in the HR chapters, 9 and 10, on Strategic Human Resources Management, and additional coverage on managing expatriate assignments as well as knowledge transfer. We have condensed the research on work motivation in Chapter 11 and added new research on the "global mindset" of leaders. Other revisions to the text material include the following:
- **Comprehensive cases:** *All the comprehensive cases are new and current*. The selection of cases has been drawn from a broad array of geographical settings: China, Germany, India, the Middle East, Finland, France, Japan, Switzerland, the United States, as well as "global" cases. The cases place the student in the decision-making role of the manager regarding issues of strategy, culture, HRM, social responsibility, technology, and politics in the global arena. **Examples are Nokia's Business Interests versus German Pressures; MTV Networks: The Arabian Challenge; Google's Country Experiences; eBay in Japan: Stategic and Cultural Missteps; The Chrysler-Fiat Alliance; Ratan Tata—Leading The Tata Group into the 21st Century — leadership and strategy.**
- **Chapter-Opening Profiles: We have added nine New Profiles,** keeping some favorites. These give practical and current illustrations of the chapter topics, such as "Economic Crisis Spreads Through Financial Globalization."
- **Comparative Management in Focus sections** provide in-depth comparative application of chapter topics in a broad range of specific countries or regions with **new or updated sections** such as **"China's Economy Just Keeps Chugging," "Profiles in Culture: Japan, Germany, Latin America, and South Korea," "Strategic Planning for the EU Market (updated)," "Joint Ventures in the Russian Federation (updated)," "Comparative IHRM Practices," "Communicating with Arabs," "Motivation in Mexico (revised)."**
- **Management Focus Boxes: Five new focus boxes, others updated,** giving management and company examples around the world to highlight the chapter topics, such as **"Intel Brings Changes to Vietnam's Economy and Culture," "India's IT Industry Brings Cultural Changes," "Cultural Misunderstanding: The Danone-Wahaha Joint venture in China," "Mexico's Cemex Reverses Course to Respond to Global Downturn,"** and **"The Role of Women in International Management."**
- **Chapter-Ending Cases: Six *New* cases; three favorites updated.** Examples are "Indian BPOs Waking Up to the Philippines Opportunity," "Australia and New Zealand: Doing

Business with Indonesia," "YouTube LLC: Going Global by Acting Local," "Acer Restructures for Global Growth," "Kelly's Assignment in Japan."
- **Experiential Exercises** at the end of each chapter, challenging students on topics such as ethics in decision making, cross-cultural negotiations, and strategic planning.
- **Integrative Term Project** outlined at the end of the text and providing a vehicle for research and application of the course content.
- **Integrative Case: New case—"The International Committee of the Red Cross: Managing Across Cultures." This case provides the students with the challenge to integrate the topics in the book, such as Strategy, Structure, IHRM, Communication, Cross-Cultural Management, and political issues, in a Not-for-Profit organization.**
- **Internet Study Guide and** chapter quizzes are available on the text's Web site. These quizzes ask a variety of multiple choice, true/false, and essay questions which provide student's with immediate feedback. Go to http://www.prenhall.com/deresky.

SUPPLEMENTS PACKAGE

Instructor's Manual: The Instructor's Manual has been completely revised. For each chapter, the Instructor's Manual provides a comprehensive lecture outline with references to slides in the PowerPoint package, chapter discussion questions and answers, as well as additional Teaching Resources, a list of related Web sites, and additional Experiential Exercises for selected chapters.

Test Item File: The Test Item File consists of multiple choice questions, discussion questions, and comprehensive essay questions. Each question is followed by a page reference, a difficulty rating of easy, moderate, or difficult, and a classification of either application or recall to help you build a well-balanced test.

Instructor's Resource Center: Using the Instructor's Resource Center, you will find the following faculty supplements:

PowerPoints: A fully revised, comprehensive package of slides, which outline each chapter and include exhibits from the text. The PowerPoint package is designed to aid the educator and supplement in-class lectures.

TestGen software: Containing all of the questions in the printed Test Item File, TestGen is a comprehensive suite of tools for testing and assessment.

Instructor's Manual

Test Item File

Custom Videos on DVD: This DVD, drawn from Prentice Hall's custom video series, features experts discussing a wide range of issues in the global marketplace. Topics include:

The Debate on Globalization	Entering Global Markets: Lands' End and Yahoo!
Global Business & Ethics	Global Human Resource Management
Impact of Culture-Latin America	KPMG-Global HRM
Entering Chinese Markets	

Companion Web site

The companion Web site for this text, located at http://www.pearsonhighered.com/deresky, contains valuable resources for both students and professors, including an interactive student study guide.

ACKNOWLEDGMENTS

The author would like to acknowledge, with thanks, the individuals who made this text possible. For the seventh edition, these people include Bruce Rosenthal who updated the Instructor's Manual and Internet Study Guide, Mohamad Sepehri who updated the PowerPoints, and Emily Yelverton who updated the Test Item File, as well as the following reviewers:

Charles M. Byles, Virginia Commonwealth University
JoAnn Flynn, Georgia College & State University
Gwen Moore, University of Missouri – St. Louis
John O. Okpara, Bloomsburg University of Pennsylvania
Kathleen M. Premo, St. Bonaventure University

—Helen Deresky

The Global Manager's Environment

PART

1

Assessing the Environment

Political, Economic, Legal, Technological

OBJECTIVES:

1. To understand the global business environment and how it affects the strategic and operational decisions which managers must make.

2. To critically assess the developments, advantages and disadvantages of globalization.

3. To review the role of technology in international business.

4. To develop an appreciation for the ways in which political, economic, legal and technological factors and changes impact the opportunities that companies face.

5. To discuss the complexities of the international manager's job.

Opening Profile: Economic Crisis Spreads Through Financial Globalization

A perilous global crisis of confidence has revealed both the scale and the limitations of globalization.[1]

The 2009 World Economic Forum in Davos, Switzerland, announced its theme—"Shaping the Post-Crisis World." What crisis? What caused the crisis? Some of the developments **as they occurred** are discussed below, and the effects will no doubt be continuing as you read this book. Discuss updates in your class and how the effects are impacting international business.

In September 2008, fears of a global recession fed a stock market panic as worries about toxic assets (highly leveraged securities mainly linked to risky mortgages taken out in the United States) spread from the financial sector to the credit markets and then to the broader economy.[2]

The American export—the subprime mortgage mess—caused the global economy to hit the brakes. The problem is that Finance has become one of the most international of industries, with banks from around the world doing business across numerous countries. However, regulation of that industry is still only national or local. Because fear gripped depositors around the world concerned that their deposits and savings will disappear, and fear led banks worldwide to cease lending to one another, the entire credit system shut down. Lending to even creditworthy companies dried up in Europe in 2008, causing the International Institute for Labor in Geneva to state:

The financial crisis is hitting the world of work. . .

The financial crisis which developed over the past year and erupted last August represents one of the most significant threats to the world economy in modern history. The credit crunch and collapse of stock markets are starting to affect firms' investment decisions as well as workers' incomes and jobs. Several major developed economies have practically entered into recession and unemployment is on the rise. Economic growth in emerging economies and developing countries has slowed down, in some cases significantly.

INTERNATIONAL INSTITUTE FOR LABOR.[3]

The United States Treasury Secretary, Henry Paulson, proposed a $700 billion bailout plan for banks, which (then) President Bush signed on October 3, 2008, the beginning of the most expensive government bailout in history, and there was an unprecedented coordination of central banks on three continents to cut interest rates. However, these moves seemed only to generate more fear, and did little to free up credit lines either between banks or to their customers. Stock markets around the world continued their massive losses—estimated at $6.5 trillion on October 6 and 7, 2008. Iceland came to the brink of bankruptcy because several banks whose assets were greater than the country's economy were experiencing problems.

The failure of banks and other financial institutions prompted governments to attempt to intervene. In the United States, the giant mortgage companies Fannie Mae and Freddie Mac were nationalized, Lehman Brothers and Washington Mutual companies were allowed to fail, but then the government later decided to bail out AIG, the huge global insurer, for fear of the global repercussions. A global problem called for a global solution. However, coordinating policies for Europe's many countries, for example, presents many difficulties. Some of the government rescue actions taken around the world were widely reported, and examples are summarized below as they developed in late 2008 and early 2009.

The International Monetary Fund said it was ready to lend to countries hit by the credit crunch, using an emergency funding mechanism first used in the 1990s Asian financial crisis.

CHINA: China joined the interest rate offensive, cutting rates by 0.27 percentage points.

SOUTH KOREA, HONG KONG, TAIWAN: The central banks of South Korea, Hong Kong, and Taiwan joined the growing number of countries to cut their interest rates.

AUSTRIA and GREECE officially announced a guarantee for all personal bank savings.

BELGIUM and DENMARK's governments agreed to guarantee bank deposits.

ICELAND: With the country on the brink of bankruptcy, Iceland's parliament passed emergency legislation giving the government wide-ranging powers to dictate banks' operations. Negotiations were under way with Russia for a big loan to support the country's banking system. Moscow has offered more than $5 billion in emergency loans.

IRELAND: Ireland was the first government to come to the rescue of its citizens' savings, promising on 30 September to guarantee all deposits, bonds, and debts in its six main banks for two years. The move initially prompted consternation among some European partners, but several countries have since followed suit.

ARAB STATES: Share prices dropped precipitously, amid fears of weakness in Dubai's property boom and exposure to global markets.

INDIA: The central bank moved to inject 600bn rupees ($12.2bn) into the money markets after sharp falls in Mumbai's stock exchange and the plunge of the rupee to an all-time low.[4]

These moves made it clear that the global ripple effect of Wall Street's woes had debunked the theory of "decoupling," the notion that the rest of the world was robust enough to ride out a U.S. domestic crisis. While attempts to stabilize the global financial system seemed to stagnate, Britain's Prime Minister Gordon Brown announced a plan to recapitalize its major banks and try to find a broader international solution. The U.S. then followed on October 14, 2008 with a similar plan to buy $250 billion of non-voting preferred stock in major banks and financial institutions—thus also partially nationalizing the U.S. banking system. At that juncture, it became clear that Europe—led by Britain—was leading the way with a financial bailout plan that set the pace for Washington. However, by the end of 2008, it became clear that "the world's dramatic financial rescue efforts are both unprecedented in scope and creativity—and wholly inadequate."[5]

In spite of the huge amounts of money that governments around the world are spending to attempt to stanch the bleeding, there seems little to prevent the world economy from major downturn, according to the International Monetary Fund. Some encouraging news to combat the global slowdown came as China announced a huge economic stimulus plan on November 9, 2008, aimed at bolstering its weakening economy. The Chinese government topped the world in its rescue package saying it would spend an estimated $586 billion over the next two years—roughly 14 percent of its gross domestic product each year—to construct new railways, subways, and airports. China's banks, at least, remained relatively unscathed.

Not to be outdone in the fight, The United States Federal Reserve and the Treasury announced $800 billion in new lending programs, sending a message that they would print as much money as needed to revive the nation's crippled banking system. That commitment amounted to about $7.8 trillion in direct and indirect financial obligations—equal to about half the size of the nation's entire economy and far greater than the $700 billion that Congress authorized for the Treasury's financial rescue plan.

European countries then mounted a joint approach; the EU commission announced a 200 billion euro rescue plan among the 27 member states. The EU Commissioner urged that all attempts be made to bolster the sagging growth and confidence in the region.

However, at least as of early 2009, although it seemed that the various measures had staved off financial collapse, the world awaited the stimulus that governments were spending billions of their taxpayers' money to gain. Meanwhile, credit was still tight and confidence was low; companies around the world were retrenching, shuttering plants and offices, and laying off thousands of workers. Protectionism and nationalism were increasing, further hampering trade, and the World Bank announced that the global economy is likely to shrink by one or two percent in 2009.

In February 2009, President Obama signed a $787 billion stimulus package (3 percent of GDP). However, while the goal of much of the package was to create jobs in the U.S., concern about "Buy American" clauses, such as for the steel industry, led to cries of protectionism that aroused fears of retaliation in trade wars.

Increasing awareness of the causes and effects of the financial crisis led many to conclude, as posed in the *New York Times*, that:

> *This crisis has shown the Achilles' heel of a globalized financial system to be a lack of high-quality, and consistent, regulation to prevent overconfident bankers from taking irresponsible risks. A year and a half ago, when it appeared to be a subprime mortgage issue for the United States, most countries thought they could glide past it. But it turned out that everyone in that globalized system was vulnerable to the collapse that began at the center.*

> WWW.NYTIMES.COM,
> *February 8, 2009.*

In addition, the irony seemed to be that the rapid growth in open economies, as a result of globalization, was coming back to bite them; whereas those with more restricted financial systems appeared more able to weather the storm. Iceland is broke; India was one of the few to expect continuing economic growth.[6]

Another unfortunate result, as noted at the global economic conference in Davos, Switzerland, in February 2009, was the warning that the global recession could sharply reduce lending across borders. Investment of private capital to emerging markets in 2009 was expected to be 82% lower than it was in

2007. British Prime Minister Gordon Brown said in an interview, "It's the first stage of a financial protectionism that will lead eventually to the kind of trade protectionism that we've seen in the past."[7]

Time will tell the long-term consequences around the world, but clearly executives and their companies have been caught in the grip of a storm that will likely revolutionize business.

> *The deep freeze of capital markets, the implosion of financial groups and the resulting rise in governments' sway over the private sector has called into question some of the foundations of Anglo-Saxon capitalism.*[8]

In an effort to develop consensus about how to revive a paralyzed global economy, the leaders of the world's largest economies met at the Group of 20 (G20) meeting in London on April 2, 2009. They agreed to bail out developing countries, stimulate world trade, and regulate financial firms more stringently. Leaders of those countries committed to $1.1 trillion in new funds to be available to the International Monetary Fund with the goal of a revival in trade, which was expected to contract in 2009 for the first time in 30 years. But differences of opinion between Continental Europe and the United States over whether to act now or wait to see whether existing spending measures took effect resulted in what many considered a shortfall of measures needed to stimulate the world economy. Prime Minister Gordon Brown of Britain concluded the conference saying:

> *This is the day the world came together to fight against the global recession. Our message today is clear and certain: we believe that global problems require global solutions.*[9]

As evidenced in the opening profile, managers in the twenty-first century are being challenged to operate in an increasingly complex, interdependent, and dynamic global environment. In a globalized economy, developments such as those described in the opening profile can have repercussions around the world almost instantaneously. Clearly, those involved in international and global business have to adjust their strategies and management styles to those kinds of global developments as well as to those regions of the world in which they want to operate, whether directly or through some form of alliance.

Typical challenges that managers must face involve politics, cultural differences, global competition, terrorism, and technology. In addition, the opportunities and risks of the global marketplace increasingly bring with them the societal obligations of operating in a global community. An example is the dilemma faced by Western drug manufacturers of how to fulfill their responsibilities to stockholders, acquire capital for research, and protect their patents while also being good global citizens by responding to the cry for free or low-cost drugs for AIDS in poor countries. Managers in those companies are struggling to find ways to balance their social responsibilities, their images, and their competitive strategies.

To compete aggressively, firms must make considerable investments overseas—not only capital investment but also investment in well-trained managers with the skills essential to working effectively in a multicultural environment. In any foreign environment, managers need to handle a set of dynamic and fast-changing variables, including the all-pervasive variable of culture that affects every facet of daily management. Added to that "behavioral software" are the challenges of the burgeoning use of technological software and the borderless Internet, which are rapidly changing the dynamics of competition and operations.

International management, then, is the process of developing strategies, designing and operating systems, and working with people around the world to ensure sustained competitive advantage. Those management functions are shaped by the prevailing conditions and ongoing developments in the world, as outlined in the following sections.

THE GLOBAL BUSINESS ENVIRONMENT

Following is a summary of some of the global situations and trends that managers need to monitor and incorporate in their strategic and operational planning.

Globalization

> *The World Is Flat*
>
> THOMAS FRIEDMAN[10]

The forces and effects of globalization seem to be inescapably evident in our daily lives:

> *An estimated 2 billion people witness Live Earth, a series of concerts held in 11 locations around the world to raise environmental awareness. Chinese manufacturers decorate toys with paint containing lead, and children around the world have to give up their Batmans and Barbie dolls. Mortgage lenders in the United States face a liquidity crunch, and global stock markets go berserk.*[11]

Business competitiveness has now evolved to a level of sophistication commonly called **globalization**—global competition characterized by networks of international linkages that bind countries, institutions, and people in an interdependent global economy. Economic integration results from the lessening of trade barriers and the increased flow of goods and services, capital, labor, and technology around the world. The invisible hand of global competition is being propelled by the phenomenon of an increasingly borderless world, by technological advancements, and by the rise of developing economies such as China and India—a process that Thomas Friedman refers to as "leveling the playing field" among countries—or the "flattening of the world."[12]

Whereas the general concept of globalization has been that business expanded from developed to emerging economies, now it is just as likely to refer to business flowing from and among developing economies. Sirkin et al. use the term "globality" stating that business these days is all about "competing with everyone from everywhere for everything."[13] On a more strategic level, Ghemawat argues, rather, that the business world is in a state of "semi-globalization," and will remain so for decades to come. He bases this conviction on his analysis that "most types of economic activity that can be conducted either within or across borders are still quite localized by country."[14]

Globality and Emerging Markets

It is clear, however, that globalization—in the broader sense—has led to the narrowing of differences in regional output growth rates as economic activity increased, driven largely by increases led by China, India, and Russia. In spite of the recent slowdown, world trade continues to grow – it has grown by 133 percent in the last 15 years and is over $54 trillion. Importantly, global trade is increasingly including the developing nations. Exhibit 1-1 shows the results from research by the A.T. Kearney Company of the Foreign Direct Investment (FDI) intentions and preferences of the leaders of top companies in 17 industry sectors spanning six continents. The exhibit shows the top 25 countries in which those executives have confidence for their investment opportunities. Their results show that China and India continue to rank at the top of the FDI Confidence Index and that six of the top 10 countries are emerging markets.[15] This phenomenon, says Fareed Zakaria, is something much broader than the much-ballyhooed rise of China or even Asia. Rather, he says:

> *It is the rise of the rest—the rest of the world.*
>
> FAREED ZAKARIA, THE POST-AMERICAN
WORLD, 2008.[16]

"The rest," he says, include countries such as Brazil, Mexico, South Korea, Taiwan, India, China, and Russia. He states that, as traditional industries in the United States continue to decline, "the rest" are picking up those opportunities. Even so, the United States remains dominant in many "new age" industries such as nanotechnology and biotechnology, and is ranked as the globe's most competitive economy by the World Economic Forum. It is clear, also, that as emerging markets continue to grow their countries' economies, they will provide growth markets for the products and services of developed economies.

Evidence of the growing number of companies from emerging markets can be seen in the Fortune 500 rankings of the world's biggest firms. It now stands at 62, mostly from the so-called BRIC economies of Brazil, Russia, India and China, up from 31 in 2003.[17] Further evidence that "globalization" is no longer just another word for "Americanisation," is the increase in the number of emerging-market companies acquiring established large businesses and brands from the so-called "developed" countries. For example, in 2008 Budweiser, America's favourite beer, was bought by a Belgian-Brazilian conglomerate, and "several of America's leading financial institutions avoided bankruptcy only by going cap in hand to the

EXHIBIT 1-1   2007 Foreign Direct Investment Confidence Index Top 25 Targets for FDI

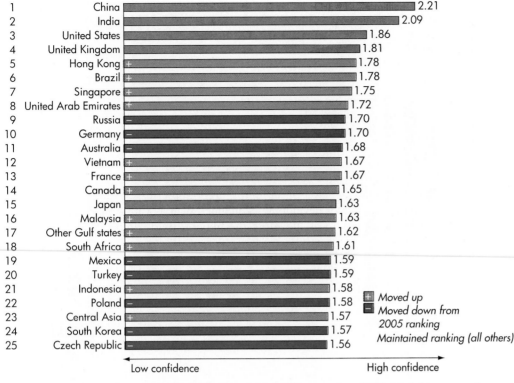

1	China	2.21
2	India	2.09
3	United States	1.86
4	United Kingdom	1.81
5	Hong Kong	1.78
6	Brazil	1.78
7	Singapore	1.75
8	United Arab Emirates	1.72
9	Russia	1.70
10	Germany	1.70
11	Australia	1.68
12	Vietnam	1.67
13	France	1.67
14	Canada	1.65
15	Japan	1.63
16	Malaysia	1.63
17	Other Gulf states	1.62
18	South Africa	1.61
19	Mexico	1.59
20	Turkey	1.59
21	Indonesia	1.58
22	Poland	1.58
23	Central Asia	1.57
24	South Korea	1.57
25	Czech Republic	1.56

+ Moved up
− Moved down from 2005 ranking
Maintained ranking (all others)

Low confidence   High confidence

Source: A. T. Kearney, September 12, 2008. Copyright A.T. Kearney, Inc., 2007. All rights reserved. Reprinted with permission.

The main types of FDI are acquisition of a subsidiary or production facility, joint ventures, licensing, investing in new facilities on expansion of facilities.

sovereign-wealth funds (state-owned investment funds) of various Arab kingdoms and the Chinese government."[18] Clearly companies in emerging markets are providing many opportunities for investment and alliances around the world, as well as establishing themselves as competitors to reckon with.

However, there are important aspects of globalization other than economic factors, though these aspects are intertwined. Exhibit 1-2 shows the top 20 countries as measured by four comprehensive factors— economic integration, technological connectivity, personal contact, and political engagement; the details for those categories are given below the chart. As you can see, although the United States leads the world in technology, it falls behind a number of countries on the other three factors.

As we consider the many facets of globalization and how they intertwine, we observe how economic power and shifting opinions and ideals about politics and religion, for example, result in an increasing backlash against globalization and a rekindling of nationalism. Globalization has been propelled by capitalism and open markets, most notably by Western companies. Now,

> . . . economic power is shifting fast to the emerging nations of the south. China and India are replacing the U.S. as the engines of world economic growth.
>
> FINANCIAL TIMES,
> *March 3, 2006.*[19]

The rising nationalist tendencies are evident as emerging and developing nations— wielding their economic power in attempted takeovers and inroads around the world—encounter protectionism. There is hostility to takeovers such as the Indian company Mittal Steel's bid for Europe's largest steel company, Arcelor. At times Europe seems to be closing its borders; and even the United States reacted to an attempted takeover of the British P&O by Dubai Ports World early in 2006. In particular, as the demand on energy resources burgeons with heightened industrial activity in China, we see increased protectionism of those resources around the world as Russia, Venezuela, and Bolivia have privatized their energy resources.

EXHIBIT 1-2 Measuring Globalization

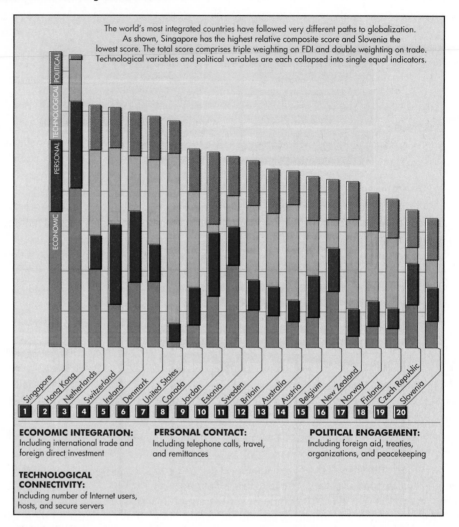

The world's most integrated countries have followed very different paths to globalization. As shown, Singapore has the highest relative composite score and Slovenia the lowest score. The total score comprises triple weighting on FDI and double weighting on trade. Technological variables and political variables are each collapsed into single equal indicators.

Countries (ranked 1–20): Singapore, Hong Kong, Netherlands, Switzerland, Ireland, Denmark, United States, Canada, Jordan, Estonia, Sweden, Britain, Australia, Austria, Belgium, New Zealand, Norway, Finland, Czech Republic, Slovenia

ECONOMIC INTEGRATION: Including international trade and foreign direct investment

PERSONAL CONTACT: Including telephone calls, travel, and remittances

POLITICAL ENGAGEMENT: Including foreign aid, treaties, organizations, and peacekeeping

TECHNOLOGICAL CONNECTIVITY: Including number of Internet users, hosts, and secure servers

Source: Global Retail Development Index, Copyright A. T. Kearney, 2008. All rights reserved. Reprinted with permission.

Recently, there has been increasing backlash against globalization coming from those who feel that it benefits advanced industrial countries at the expense of many other countries and people within them who are not sharing in those benefits. Joseph Stiglitz, for example, argues that such an economic system has been pressed upon many developing countries at the expense of their sovereignty, their well-being, and their environment. Critics point to the growing numbers of people around the world living in poverty.[20] Recently, globalization has also become increasingly unpopular with many in the United States as growth in emerging markets has raised prices for energy and commodities, as their jobs are being lost overseas, driving down wages, and as the weak dollar makes companies in the United States vulnerable to foreign buyers.[21]

While the debate about the effects of globalization continues, it is clear that economic globalization will be advanced by corporations looking to maximize their profits with global efficiencies, by politicians and leaders wishing to advance their countries' economies, and by technological and transportation advances which make their production and supply networks more efficient. However, pressure by parties against those trends, as well as the resurgence in nationalism and protectionism, may serve to pull back those advances to a more regional scope in some areas, or bilateral pacts. This was made clear by the breakdown in the Doha round of talks; unfortunately,

> *In pursuit of the perfect—an international trade deal agreed upon by some 150 countries with vastly different goals—negotiators wound up with nothing. The way forward is likely to be via bilateral and regional agreements. A global deal, if one can be reached, may be a package of smaller agreements between subsets of the full body.*[22]

In addition, while competition to provide the best and cheapest products to consumers exerts pressure on corporations to maximize efficiencies around the world, there is also increasing pressure and publicity for them to consider the social responsibility of their activities (discussed further in Chapter 2).

Effects of Institutions on Global Trade[23]

Two major groups of institutions (supranational and national) play a differing role in globalization. Supranational institutions such as the World Trade Organization (WTO) and the International Labor Organization (ILO) promote the convergence of how international activities should be conducted. For example, the WTO promotes the lowering of tariffs and a common set of trade rules among its member countries. Similarly, the ILO promotes common standards of how workers should be treated. While many supranational institutions frequently promote rules or laws favorable to foreign firms (e.g., requiring intellectual property rights protections in China), others have been criticized for infringing on national sovereignty (e.g., challenges to certain environmental laws in the United States).

National institutions, in contrast, play a role in creating favorable conditions for domestic firms and may make it more difficult for foreign firms to compete in those countries. For example, the stringent drug testing rules required by the U.S. Food and Drug Administration (FDA) and the anti-dumping rules enforced by the U.S. Department of Commerce's International Trade Administration act as entry barriers for foreign firms (see Chapter 6 for a more detailed discussion of these).

Some supranational institutions represent the interests of a smaller group of countries. For example, the European Commission acts in the interest of the 27 EU members as a whole rather than the interest of individual member countries. The European Commission is the executive arm of the EU and is responsible for implementing the decisions of the European Parliament and the European Council. Of relevance to international business, the European Commission speaks for the EU at the World Trade Organization, and is responsible for negotiation trade agreements on behalf of the EU.[24]

Effects of Globalization on Corporations

In returning to our discussion at the corporate level, we can see that almost all firms around the world are affected to some extent by globalization. Firms from any country now compete with your firm both at home and abroad, and your domestic competitors are competing on price by outsourcing or offshoring resources and services anywhere in the world. Often it is difficult to tell which competing products or services are of domestic or foreign origin. While Ford, for example, is pushing its Mustang with the slogan "buy American," only about 65 percent of the car content comes from the United States or Canada—the rest is purchased abroad. In contrast, Japan's Toyota Sienna model is far more American, with 90 percent local components being assembled in Indiana.[25] This didn't happen overnight. Toyota has been investing in North America for 20 years in plants, suppliers, and dealerships, as well as design, testing, and research centers. Toyota became the largest auto-manufacturer in the world in sales in 2009. In fact, on June 1, 2009, General Motors (GM) filed for Chapter 11 bankruptcy, pushed into a temporary partial nationalization by the U.S. government in order to save the company in a drastically downsized form.[26]

Clearly, competition is borderless, with most global companies producing and selling more of their global brands and services abroad than domestically. Avon, for example, estimates it employs 5 million sales representatives globally, and believes a large share of future revenues will come from China, where it hired an additional 399,000 sales representatives in 2006.[27] Nestlé has 50 percent of its sales outside of its home market, Coca-Cola has 80 percent, and Procter & Gamble has 65 percent. The Tata Group, a conglomerate originating in India, has operations in 85 countries and has made a number of acquisitions of large firms around the world.

Investment by global companies around the world means that this aspect of globalization benefits developing economies—through the transfer of financial, technological, and managerial resources, as well as through the development of local allies that later become self-sufficient and have other operations. Global companies are becoming less tied to specific locations, and their operations and allies are spread around the world as they source and coordinate resources and activities in the most suitable areas, and as technology facilitates faster and more flexible interactions and greater efficiencies.

It is essential, therefore, for managers to look beyond their domestic market. If they do not, they will be even further behind the majority of managers who have already recognized that they must have a global vision for their firms, beginning with preparing themselves with the skills and tools of managing in a global environment. Companies that desire to remain globally competitive and to expand their operations to other countries will have to develop a cadre of top management with experience operating abroad and an understanding of what it takes to do business in other countries and to work with people of other cultures. Many large firms around the world are getting to the stage of evolution known as the stateless multinational, where work is sourced wherever it is most efficient; the result of this stage of development is that

> *for business leaders, building a firm that is seamlessly integrated across time zones and cultures presents daunting obstacles. Rather than huddling together in a headquarters building in Armonk or Millbank, senior managers will increasingly be spread around the world, which will require them to learn some new tricks.*[28]
>
> THE ECONOMIST,
> *September 20, 2008.*

Small and medium-sized companies (SMEs) are also affected by, and in turn affect, globalization. They play a vital role in contributing to their national economies—through employment, new job creation, development of new products and services, and international operations, typically exporting. The vast majority (about 98 percent) of businesses in developed economies are small and medium-sized enterprises (SMEs), which are typically referred to as those companies having fewer than 500 employees. Small businesses are rapidly discovering foreign markets. Although many small businesses are affected by globalism only to the extent that they face competing products from abroad, an increasing number of entrepreneurs are being approached by potential offshore customers, thanks to the burgeoning number of trade shows, federal and state export initiatives, and the growing use of Web sites, with the ease of making contact and placing orders online.[29]

There has never been a better time for SMEs to go global; the Internet is as valid a tool for small companies to find customers and suppliers around the world as it is for large companies. By using the Internet, email, and web-conferencing, small companies can inexpensively contact customers and set up their global businesses. One example of a very small global business (two people) is that of Gayle Warwick Fine Linen—a multinational player based in London. Its high-end, handmade bed and table linens are woven in Europe, embroidered in Vietnam, and sold in Britain and the United States. Sales are soaring, and its full-time staff recently doubled—to two: Gayle Warwick and the assistant she recently hired. As she expanded, Ms. Warwick hired a French freight forwarder, SDV International Logistics, to handle her far-flung business by shipping unfinished and finished fabrics within Europe and to Vietnam, then delivering the embroidered linens to London and the United States. (Freight forwarders can also manage payments, a potential godsend for small exporters dealing with partners scattered around the globe.)[30]

Regional Trading Blocs

> *The dominance of the United States is already over. What is emerging is a world economy of blocs represented by the North American Free Trade Agreement (NAFTA), the EU, and the Association of Southeast Asian Nations (ASEAN). There's no one center in this world economy.*
>
> (The late) PETER DRUCKER[31]

Much of today's world trade takes place within three regional free-trade blocs (Western Europe, Asia, and the Americas) grouped around the three dominant currencies (the euro, the yen, and the dollar). These trade blocs are continually expanding their borders to include neighboring countries, either directly or with separate agreements.

MAP 1.1 **EU Member States and Candidate Countries**

THE EUROPEAN UNION   The European Union (EU) now comprises a 27-nation unified market of approximately 500 million people, as shown in the map (Map 1-1). This "borderless" market now includes ten Central and Eastern Europe (CEE) countries—the Czech Republic, Estonia, Hungary, Latvia, Lithuania, Poland, the Slovak Republic, and Slovenia—as well as Malta and Cyprus. They joined the EU in May 2004, having met the EU accession requirements, including privatizing state-run businesses, improving the infrastructure, and revamping their finance and banking systems.[32] Bulgaria and Romania joined in January 2007. Turkey, Croatia, and the Republic of Macedonia are official candidates but must meet the requirements before 2015.

Since the euro became a legally tradable currency, Europe's business environment has been transformed. The vast majority of legislative measures have been adopted to create an internal market with free movement of goods and people among the EU countries. The elimination of internal tariffs and customs, as well as financial and commercial barriers, has not eliminated national pride. Although most people in Europe are thought of simply as Europeans, they still think of themselves first as British, French, Danish, Italian, etc., and are wary of giving too much power to centralized institutions or of giving up their national culture. The continuing enlargement of the EU to include many less prosperous countries has also promoted divisions among the "older" members.[33]

Global managers face two major tasks. One is strategic (dealt with more fully in Chapter 6): How firms outside of Europe can deal with the implications of the EU and of what some have called a "Fortress Europe"—that is, a market giving preference to insiders. The other task is cultural: How to deal effectively with multiple sets of national cultures, traditions, and customs within Europe, such as differing attitudes about how much time should be spent on work versus leisure activities.

ASIA

It would be difficult to overstate the power of the fundamental drivers of Asian growth. First, Asian economies have been enjo ing a remarkable period of productivit catch-up, adopting modern technologies, industrial practices, and wa s of organi ing in some cases leapfrogging Western competitors.[34]

HARVARD BUSINESS REVIEW,
Jul /August 2009.

Manufacturing accounted for approximately 30 percent of GDP in Asia's emerging markets in 2009, thus helping to fuel the demand for materials and supplies from the developed world and lending hope for a quick global economic recovery.[35] Japan and the Four Tigers—Singapore, Hong Kong, Taiwan, and South Korea, each of which has abundant natural resources and labor—have provided most of the capital and expertise for Asia's developing countries. Now the focus is on China's role in driving closer integration in the region through its rapidly growing exports. Japan continues to negotiate trade agreements with its neighbors; China is negotiating with the entire thirteen-member Association of Southeast Asian Nations (ASEAN), while ASEAN is negotiating for earlier development of its own free trade area, Asean Free Trade Area (AFTA).

> *The Chinese market offers big opportunities for foreign investment, but you must learn to tolerate ambiguity and find a godfather to look after your political connections.*
>
> FINANCIAL TIMES[36]

China has enjoyed success as an export powerhouse, a status built on its strengths of low costs and a constant flow of capital. Its growth phenomenon is further discussed in the accompanying feature "Comparative Management in Focus—China's Economy Keeps on Chugging."

India: While China is known as the world's factory, India is becoming known as the world's services supplier, providing highly skilled and educated workers to foreign companies. India is the world's leader for outsourced back-office services, and increasingly for high-tech services, with outsourcing firms like Infosys becoming global giants themselves. India is the fastest-growing free market democracy, yet its biggest hindrance to growth, in particular for the manufacturing sector, remains its poor infrastructure, with both local and foreign companies experiencing traffic gridlocks and power outages. Nevertheless, with growth around 8.5 percent in recent years, second only to China, optimism abounds about the country's prospects.

Trade liberalization started in 1991; India's Foreign Direct Investment (FDI) rules are more open, and the refining sector is now open to outside investors. While there is talk of reduced tariffs, there is serious political concern for protecting India's small to medium size enterprises, comprising 35% of exports. But with a middle class growing at 100 million people per year, improvements in customs processes, and 30% annual growth in tax revenues, trade is looking steady.[42]

After the Indian economy began opening up to the outside world, there has been a surge based on strong industry and agriculture and rising Indian and foreign investment. The expanding middle class of almost 300 million is fuelling demand-led growth. Increasing deregulation is allowing whole sectors to be competitive. Here too there is considerable diversity in markets, incomes and economies; there are fifteen major languages and over 1,600 dialects.

A common comparison between China and India goes that China's economy grows because of its government, while India's economy grows in spite of it. However, with its one billion people, many are still mired in poverty, with per capita GDP below $1,000, although the poverty rate is half that of twenty years ago. While India's large upcoming youth bulge, compared with China, will bring a wave of workers for the economy, it also brings many more mouths to feed. However, in many areas the economic transformation is startling, with growth fed by firms like the Tata Group—a global conglomerate producing everything from cars and steel to software and consulting systems. In August, 2008, India joined a free-trade agreement with the ten fast-growing countries in the Association of South-East Asian Nations (ASEAN)—making it clear that a regional deal was preferable to a compromise to protect its farmers by saying "no" to the multilateral trading system in the Doha trade talks.[43]

In **South Asia,** an agreement was signed to form the South Asia Association of Regional Cooperation (SAARC), a free trade pact among seven South Asian nations: Bangladesh, Bhutan, India, the Maldives, Nepal, Pakistan, and Sri Lanka, effective January 1, 2006. The agreement will lower tariffs to 25 percent within three to five years and eliminate them within seven years. The member nations comprise 1.5 billion people, with an estimated one-third of them living in poverty. Trade in South Asia is estimated at $14 billion, though the majority of that trade will be

COMPARATIVE MANAGEMENT IN FOCUS

China's Economy Keeps on Chugging

China's gross domestic product (GDP) growth rate—over 9 percent a year for thirty years—has been the fastest in the world.[37] Its economy has doubled every eight years for thirty years and the income of its people has increased sevenfold. Even in 2009, with most of the world in a global recession, China's economy quickly snapped back, growing at 8 percent by mid-year, because of the aggressive approach to the slowdown by committing $586 billion—9 percent of GDP—to infrastructure projects, and because its banking system remained relatively unscathed compared with others around the world. Indeed, China surpassed Germany in 2009 as the world's largest exporter.[38] Continuing its aggressive long-term approach, China stepped up to the plate in early 2009 to take advantage of the economic downturn by going on a major shopping spree, investing in energy and other natural resources that could give it an economic advantage it has never had before. Examples were lending the Brazilian oil giant Petrobras $10 billion in exchange for a long-term commitment to send oil to China; and similar deals with Russia and Venezuela, bringing Beijing's total oil investments for February 2009 alone to $41 billion; as well as deals such as a $19.5 billion investment in Rio Tinto, an Australian mining company. Such moves put China in an advantageous position of increased access to oil and other commodities at a better price than it would likely be as the world pulls out of the recession. In fact, PetroChina passed Exxon Mobil as the world's most valuable company in May 2009.[39]

However, faced with a possible global recession and weakening demand for Chinese exports, there was concern in China and the rest of the world that the Chinese government would not be able to prevent the financial crisis from derailing the country's economic miracle; continued Chinese growth is vital to the global economy as the United States and Europe face severe downturns. The United States, for example, had imported $321 billion worth of goods in 2007, but that demand reduced substantially because of the recession in the U.S., and also because of reduced imports of some tainted products such as toys. The precipitous decline of the housing industry in the United States, for example, which sources 70 percent of its furniture from China, indicates the interdependence of the two economies. However, as mentioned earlier, as of mid-2009, China's resurgence promised to provide leadership for the world's economic rebound, in particular as the Chinese government provided incentives to its people so as to stoke a consumer-driven economy. Indeed,

MAP 1.2   China

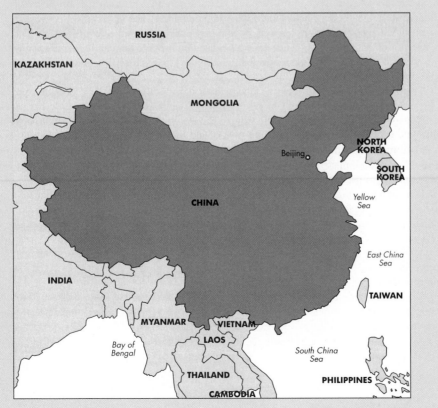

China has become a battleground for companies wanting a piece of the action in this rapidly growing and opening economy. In fact, over 400 of the Fortune 500 Global companies are operating there. China's rapid rise—and the burgeoning opportunities for foreign businesses—is partly attributable to its membership in the World Trade Organization (WTO) and its actions for structural reforms and opening of many of its industries to foreign investment. China is now a market-driven economy—driven by competition, capital and entrepreneurship.

What accounts for China's rapid rise? China's recent exports in a single day have been more than it exported in all of 1978. With its 1.3 billion people, China benefits greatly from its large and rapidly growing foreign and domestic market size, which provides significant economies of scale. The World Economic Forum assessment of China is that its "macroeconomic stability is a source of competitive advantage, with the government budget moving into surplus, and manageable debt levels, although rising inflation has become an area of concern. Innovation is becoming another competitive advantage, with rising company spending on R&D coupled with strong university-industry research collaboration, and an increasing rate of patenting." Indeed, China has the world's largest foreign-exchange reserves—three times the holdings of the entire EU, for example. As of September 2009, China had accumulated $2 trillion in foreign reserves, mostly in Treasury bonds and other dollar-denominated assets.[40]

China's vast population of low-wage workers and massive consumer market potential has attracted offshoring of manufacturing from companies around the world. In fact there are 49,000 U.S. companies alone operating in China. It is estimated that China has over 160 cities with populations of over 1 million:

> *One town manufactures most of the eyeglass frames in the world, while the town next door produces most of the portable cigarette lighters in the world, and the next one is doing most of the computer screens for Dell, and another is specializing in mobile phones.*
>
> THOMAS FRIEDMAN, 2005.[41]

It is this low-cost manufacturing base that contributes greatly to its exports and growth—as a major factor in China's uniqueness—according to Fareed Zakaria in his book "The Post American World"—making it the world's largest manufacturer, second-largest consumer, largest saver, and probably the second-largest military spender. China has the world's largest shipped goods port capacity. For these reasons China would seem well positioned to expand globally as long as global demand for its products and manufacturing continues. In addition, with its substantial foreign exchange reserves from trade surpluses and heavy foreign investment in China, it could acquire discounted stakes in Western banks and industrial companies. The government is aware that it must stoke consumer spending among its own people in order to stave off unemployment. There are still over 500 million people living on less than $2 a day, and average per capita income is under $2,000. The Boston Consulting Group estimates that, in 2009, some sixty million households are considered middle class.

There are considerable differences among the country's regions, making for quite varied markets. The great diversity is indicated by China's eight major languages, several dialects, and several other minority languages. Mandarin is the main language in the north; Cantonese in the south, in particular in Hong Kong. Each language reflects its own history and culture, and therefore markets and economies. Generally speaking, it is clear that China is aggressively opening its doors. The fact remains, however, that, in virtually all industrial sectors, state firms play a significant or dominant role. Sixteen State-owned enterprises make up about half of GDP.

In addition, central, regional, and local political influences create unpredictability for businesses, as do the arbitrary legal systems, suspect data, and underdeveloped infrastructure. However, in addition to foreign investment, China continues to enjoy significant inflows of money from the ethnic Chinese outside of China, often called the "Bamboo Network" or the "Chinese Commonwealth" network. Using their contacts (*guanxi*) and their familiarity with the culture, language and how to navigate layers of government, Chinese business people around the world—though primarily in Asia—invest large amounts in China.

One of the many challenges for international managers is how to negotiate with the Chinese business people and government representatives. This is the subject of the Comparative Management section in Chapter 5.

between India and Pakistan, the two largest countries in the region.[44] Officials in those countries hope to follow the success of the other Asian regional bloc, the ASEAN.

Australia—while not regarded as part of Southeast Asia, but of the region called Oceania that includes also New Zealand and neighboring islands in the Pacific Ocean—did sign an ASEAN friendship treaty with Southeast Asia. Australia is one of the richest countries in the world, and over 50 percent of her exports go to East Asia, with more transported through the region to markets around the world.

THE AMERICAS

Mexico's exports have exploded under NAFTA, quintupling to $292 billion in 2008, but Mexico is still exporting people too, almost half a million each year, seeking opportunities in the United States that they do not have at home.[45]

NAFTA: The goal of the North American Free Trade Agreement (NAFTA) between the United States, Canada, and Mexico was to bring faster growth, more jobs, better working conditions, and a cleaner environment for all as a result of increased exports and trade. This trading bloc—"one America"—has 421 million consumers. Now, many years since the 1993 agreement, the debate continues about the extent to which those goals have been accomplished. That perspective varies, of course, among the three NAFTA countries and also varies according to how it has affected individual business firms and employees in various parts of those countries. The Canada-United States trade is the largest bilateral flow between two countries. In addition, the vast majority—around 84 percent—of both Canadian and Mexican exports goes to the United States. From Mexico's perspective, the country's exports have exploded under NAFTA, quintupling to $292 billion in 2008, but Mexico is still exporting people too, almost half a million each year, seeking opportunities in the United States that they do not have at home, in particular because MNCs displaced farming. However, Mexico's dependence on the United States for its exports—NAFTA's greatest success—has become a liability, as Mexico feels the full brunt of declining consumption in the United States. The auto industry, for example, which has flourished under NAFTA, ground to a virtual standstill early 2009. Mexican auto exports fell more than 50 percent in the first two months of 2009 compared with 2008, and production dropped almost 45 percent. In addition, since NAFTA attracted so many multinationals, which, in turn sourced parts from its own suppliers, Mexico's domestic industries were severely curtailed. Overall, many feel that attracting MNCs was short-sighted for an overall strategy—in particular because their low wages have perpetuated poverty and therefore also low purchasing power, thus weakening the economy. "Economic growth has averaged about 3 percent a year since NAFTA took effect, far below what is needed to create jobs for the million young people who enter the work force each year and the millions more who barely scrape by."[46]

However, some changes for Mexico in those years are not debatable, whether or not they all are attributable to the NAFTA. Mexican trade policy is among the most open in the world, and Mexico has become an important exporting and importing power. While the Mexican economic cycles are very dependent on American economic behavior, she has signed 12 trade agreements with 43 nations, putting 90 percent of its trade under free trade regulations; the latest agreement was made with Japan in 2005.[47]

The trade agreements have resulted in an increase in GDP from $403 billion in 1993 to $893.4 billion in 2007, with exports of $213.4 billion.[48] Mexico's 3.3 percent GDP growth in 2007 also included an increase in remittances by migrants—those contributions made by Mexicans living abroad both legally and illegally, mostly in the United States, to their families at home in Mexico; they comprised $18 billion in 2005, up from $2.4 billion in 1994.[49] Recent competition from China for offshored jobs from foreign firms has put downward pressure on opportunities for Mexico, as manufacturing facilities and some service facilities migrate from Mexico to China in a race for the lowest cost operations.[50]

CAFTA: Modeled after the NAFTA agreement, the goal of the U.S.-Central America Free Trade Agreement (**CAFTA**) was to promote trade liberalization between the United States and five Central American countries: Costa Rica, El Salvador, Guatemala, Honduras, and Nicaragua. In 2004, the Dominican Republic joined the negotiations, and the agreement was renamed DR-CAFTA. The treaty must be approved by the U.S. Congress and by National

Assemblies in the Central American countries before it becomes law. CAFTA is considered to be a stepping-stone to the larger Free Trade Area of the Americas (FTAA) that would encompass 34 economies, but which has met with considerable resistance.[51]

MERCOSUR is the fourth largest trading bloc after the EU, NAFTA and ASEAN. Established in 1991, it comprises the original parties—Brazil, Argentina, Paraguay, and Uruguay; Venezuela is an applicant country awaiting ratification. This regional trading bloc comprises 250 million people and accounts for 75 percent of South America's GDP.

Other Regions in the World

Sweeping political, economic, and social changes around the world present new challenges to global managers. The worldwide move away from communism, together with the trend toward privatization, has had an enormous influence on the world economy. Economic freedom is a critical factor in the relative wealth of nations.

One of the most striking changes today is that almost all nations have suddenly begun to develop decentralized, free market systems in order to manage a global economy of intense competition, the complexity of high-tech industrialization, and an awakening hunger for freedom.

The Russian Federation Foreign investment in Russia, as well as its consumers' climbing confidence and affluence, bode well for the economy. In the first quarter of 2009, for example, FDI into the Russian economy was about $8.4 billion.[52] However, corruption and government interference persist:

> *The writing has been on the wall for years. The Kremlin won't stop until it has recouped control of all the energy assets that were sold off at bargain prices when the Iron Curtain fell—and it will use any means necessary to achieve that goal.*

> INTERNATIONAL HERALD TRIBUNE,
> *March 20, 2008.*[53]

Until recently, Russia has been regarded as more politically stable. New land, legal and labor codes, as well as the now-convertible ruble have encouraged foreign firms to take advantage of opportunities in that immense area, in particular the vast natural resources and the well-educated population of 145 million. Moscow, in particular, is teeming with new construction sites, high-end cars, and new restaurants. Growth has been steady, but the real GDP growth for Russia is considered to be controlled by the so-called business "oligarchs"—a small group of businesspeople with political influence who capitalized on the privatization of Russia's economy and who limit competitive opportunities for small businesses. However, foreign investors became very wary after the break up of the Yukos oil group, including jailing its head Mikhail Khodorkovsky with an eight-year sentence; this made foreign investors reluctant to propose new deals that would require political approval. About two dozen Russian companies have come under the control of the Kremlin in the last few years, including newspapers and banks.[54] As an example, in September 2008, British Petroleum had to make deep concessions to its Russian partner in its TNK-BP oil joint venture in order to avoid a forced sale of its assets there to a state company. BP had to agree to dismiss the American chief executive of its joint venture and give up some board seats to its Russian partners.[55]

The Middle East. The United Arab Emirates is the most competitive economy in the Arab world among the countries at the third and most advanced stage of development according to The Arab World Competitiveness Report 2007 by the World Economic Forum. It is followed by Qatar and Kuwait. Among countries at the second stage of development, Tunisia and Oman are the best performing Arab economies while Egypt is the regional best performer in the third group of countries. The Forum predicted there will be prosperity with challenges for the Middle East:

> *Oil and gas revenues provide unique investment opportunities, but the region's greatest challenges are likely to be in managing expectations, lowering trade and investment barriers and educating the next generation to handle the wealth that is now being produced. Education is the biggest challenge.*[56]

Developing Economies are characterized by change that has come about more slowly as they struggle with low gross national product (GNP) and low per capita income, as well as the burdens of large, relatively unskilled populations and high international debt. Their economic situation and the often-unacceptable level of government intervention discourage the foreign investment they need. Many countries in Central and South America, the Middle East, and Africa desperately hope to attract foreign investment to stimulate economic growth.

The African Union (AU): The AU comprises the 53 African countries and was formed from the original Organization of African Unity (OAU) primarily to deal with political issues. However, that union is not able to provide a vehicle for integration of trade and economic growth because of the many major problems in the region. Unfortunately, Africa has been virtually ignored by most of the world's investors, although it receives increasing investment from companies in South Africa, which has the region's biggest economy.

South Africa: The South African economy has been growing continuously since 1998, amid a more stable political environment since the defeat of apartheid. It is the longest economic upswing in the country's history, although, according to Statistics South Africa, GDP had slowed near the end of 2008 to +0.2 percent. In addition, unemployment was 23.2 percent of the population of 48.7 million (as of January, 2009).[57] The rapid growth of consumer demand, along with increasing tourism and foreign business investment, has made the country's outlook very positive. Foreign investment is encouraged through the Strategic Industrial Project, which provides approved companies with substantial tax reductions as well as other incentives. These incentives, along with more political stability, encouraged the return of most of the foreign companies which had left during the apartheid era. In addition, companies in South Africa no doubt realize that they have a competitive edge on the African continent that they do not have in more developed parts of the world.[58]

For firms willing to take the economic and political risks, developing economies offer considerable potential for international business. Assessing the risk-return trade-offs and keeping up with political developments in these developing countries are two of the many demands on international managers. Among proactive managers taking advantage of such opportunities are those at Intel—a corporation that epitomizes the ways in which "globalization" is affecting less-developed countries (LDCs) and developing economies such as Vietnam, as discussed in the accompanying Management Focus.

MANAGEMENT FOCUS

Intel Brings Changes to Vietnam's Economy and Culture[59]

The United States opened trade relations with Vietnam in 2000, opening the way for that country's expansion. Although Vietnam is a communist country, its rapid growth can be attributed to its entrepreneurial traditions and those aspects of globalization that attract corporations such as Intel to take advantage of new markets and lower costs of production. While the debate continues about whether globalization brings overall positive or negative effects to less developed countries, the inevitable march of trade and investment has led Daniel Altman to believe that "the more relevant question today is whether these multinational relationships can be managed in a way that benefits both guests and hosts." Intel's success in this regard started with the awareness of the tight control of the Vietnamese government in all aspects of society and on foreign companies wishing to do business there.

After painstaking and secret negotiations with Vietnamese government officials who were unused to market economics, Intel's general manager, Rick Howath, decided to build its biggest semiconductor manufacturing plant ever along the Hanoi Highway in Vietnam, a nation of 85 million with limited higher education opportunities. This is Intel Corporation's seventh assembly site of its global network. (Other sites include Penang and Kulim, Malaysia; Cavite, Philippines; Chengdu and Shanghai, China; and San Jose, Costa Rica.) Planning to hire 4,000 workers by 2010 to produce chips for the company's extensive global supply chain, Intel has demonstrated how multinationals which are industry leaders can change the economic and cultural dynamics in a developing country by the decision to locate a plant there. However, this was no light decision. Intel's company strategic decision-makers spent years investigating and evaluating the benefits and constraints of locating there and considerable effort in working with the government in Hanoi. The company's investigations were relentless, evaluating school curricula, traffic congestion, the poor infrastructure, and the size of the average adult in order to tailor the factory to them. Their main concern was finding enough qualified engineers.

In the end, the Vietnamese government's desire to attract multinationals, along with the country's proximity to China and its young, low-cost workforce, convinced Intel to invest $1 billion there for its 115-acre construction site in the new Saigon Hi-Tech Park. The company called the project A-9. (Nine is regarded as a lucky number in Vietnam.) However, this was not until the government-owned Saigon Hi-Tech Park signed a pact with Intel to fight against corruption and improper business conduct. This was the first time a state agency had made such a pact and also a first for Intel, who was concerned about Vietnam's reputation as one of the world's most corrupt countries.

Changes resulting from Intel's investment in Vietnam are already evident. The Vietnamese government is giving Intel's managers unprecedented access to high-ranking officials, and other global giants are showing interest in investing there. The plant will create a higher-end manufacturing base beyond garment assembly lines and create desperately needed professional jobs for its youth. Intel is also bringing its culture to Vietnam. Executives work alongside the workers, with no big offices for the bosses—contrary to Vietnam's hierarchical culture. It also sponsors team-building exercises like karaoke Fridays. Intel's company buses shuttle workers to the plant, passing low-slung shacks, which house so many Vietnamese.

In all, the Vietnamese view the new plant in Ho Chi Minh City with patriotic pride and hope for further economic emergence. For its part, Intel's success is largely attributable to cultivating government officials and to understanding the government's goals and work towards them. These include the desire to increase the use of personal computers and the Internet, and also to get a reputation for Vietnam to export high-tech items. Focusing on local traditions and working with the government's Communist youth group, Intel developed a program under the brand Thanh Giong, a Vietnamese hero, with the goal of beating back the enemy of illiteracy.

Information Technology

Of all the developments propelling global business today, the one that is transforming the international manager's agenda more than any is the rapid advance in information technology (IT). The speed and accuracy of information transmission are changing the nature of the global manager's job by making geographic barriers less relevant. Indeed, the necessity of being able to access IT is being recognized by managers and families around the world, who are giving priority to being "plugged in" over other lifestyle accoutrements.

Information can no longer be totally controlled by governments; political, economic, market, and competitive information is available almost instantaneously to anyone around the world, permitting informed and accurate decision-making. Even cultural barriers are being lowered gradually by the role of information in educating societies about one another. Indeed, as consumers around the world become more aware, through various media, of how people in other countries live, their tastes and preferences begin to converge.

The explosive growth of information technology is both a cause and an effect of globalism. The information revolution is boosting productivity around the world. Denmark is the most networked economy in the world, followed by Sweden and Switzerland, according to the 2008 edition of the *Global Information Technology Report*. Among the top ten, the Republic of Korea (9) and, to a lesser extent, the United States (4) post the most notable improvements.[60]

In addition, use of the Internet is propelling electronic commerce around the world (as discussed later in this chapter). Companies around the world are linked electronically to their employees, customers, distributors, suppliers, and alliance partners in many countries. Technology, in all its forms, gets dispersed around the world by **multinational enterprises (MNEs)** and their alliance partners in many countries. However, some of the information intended for electronic transmission is currently subject to export controls by an EU directive intended to protect private information about its citizens. So, perhaps IT is not yet "borderless" but rather is subject to the same norms, preferences, and regulations as "human" cross-border interactions.

The Globalization of Human Capital

The high cost of fuel is going to radically transform the way people look at the geography of their manufacturing.

BUSINESS WEEK,
June 30, 2008.[61]

Firms around the world have been offshoring manufacturing jobs to low-cost countries for decades—that is, they close down all or part of a factory, say, in Detroit and open it back up in

China or Mexico. An increasing number of firms have been producing or assembling parts of their products in many countries and then integrating them into their global supply chains. Although, with the greatly higher cost of fuel recently, greatly increasing shipping rates, some firms were fearful that their cost advantage of producing abroad was being lost. But shipping costs do not affect non-manufacturing jobs, and more and more firms are outsourcing white-collar jobs to India, China, Mexico, and the Philippines: customer support, medical analysis, technical work, computer programming, form filling and claims processing—all these jobs can now move around the globe in the same way that farming and factory jobs could a century ago.[62] We have all experienced talking to someone in India when we call the airlines or a technology support service; now increasingly sophisticated jobs are being outsourced, leaving many people in developed economies to worry about job retention. For example, as of May 2009, General Electric has about 14,500 employees in India, I.B.M. more than 74,000, and Citigroup more than 10,000.[63]

Forrester Research predicted that 3.3 million (U.S.) jobs would be lost in service-sector outsourcing around the world by 2015, and added that "the information technology industry will lead the initial overseas exodus."[64] A programmer in India, for example—well educated, skilled, and English-speaking—earns about $20,000 a year, compared to $80,000 in the United States. In Bangalore, India, MNCs such as Intel, Dell, IBM, Yahoo!, and AOL employ workers in chip design, software, call centers, and tax processing.[65] Dell has four call centers in India, where the bulk of its 10,000 employees work, as well as software development and product testing centers. The annual salary for a call-center agent in India is $2,667, compared to $29,000 in the United States. Moreover, while most call centers serve their own domestic markets, 73 percent of India's call centers serve foreign markets.[66] Overall, the Indian ITES sector (IT-enabled services) has 700,000 people worldwide and comprises 35 percent of the Business Process Outsourcing market (BPO).[67] India's software services exports are expected to reach $60 billion by 2010. However, two recent trends in the globalization of IT jobs are changing this scene. One is that large Indian IT outsourcing companies such as Infosys technologies Ltd. and the Tata Group are hiring their staff in the United States. The other is that the growth in such jobs in India and elsewhere is being threatened by the economic downturn resulting from the financial crisis, which started in the fall of 2008.

> *India's seemingly unstoppable outsourcing industry is grappling with the woes of the financial firms that make up as much as half of revenues for some players. "How this plays out, who knows?" says Pramod Bhasin, CEO of Genpact, the world's largest business process outsourcing company. Although he's optimistic, he says: "The ability to predict has gone away.*
>
> BUSINESS WEEK,
> *October 13, 2008.*[68]

However, Infosys CEO Kris Gopalakrishnan was cautiously optimistic in late 2008 that Infosys and other top Indian tech services firms will fare reasonably well in the downturn, saying that

> *Companies look for ways to cut costs during a recession, and, in spite of wage inflation among the Indian services outfits, work done there still carries a price advantage. In fact, the 8.4 percent drop in value of the rupee versus the dollar last quarter means Indian labor is become MORE competitive, not less.*[69]
>
> BUSINESS WEEK ASIA,
> *October 10, 2008.*

In China—long the world's low-cost manufacturing hub—jobs are on the upswing for back-office support for financial services and for telecom and retail companies in Asia. Such employees communicate to people in Hong Kong and Taiwan in local languages.[70] While backlash from some firms' clients has resulted in them repatriating high-end jobs, white-collar job migration is still on the rise for firms around the world, bringing with it a new phase in economic globalization and competition. For global firms, winning the 'war for talent' is one of the most pressing issues, especially as hot labor markets in emerging markets are causing extremely high turnover rates.[71]

EXHIBIT 1-3   An Open Systems Model

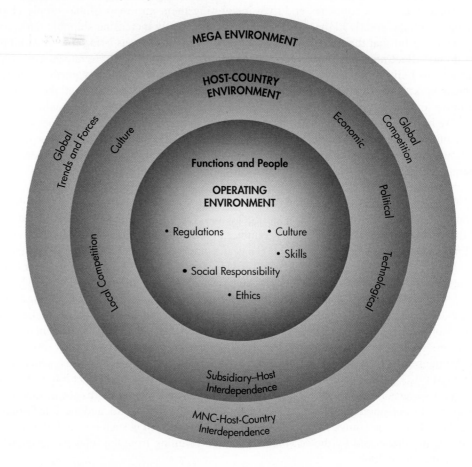

The Global Manager's Role

Whatever your level of involvement, it is important to understand the global business environment and its influence on the manager's role. This complex role demands a contingency approach to dynamic environments, each of which has its own unique requirements. Within the larger context of global trends and competition, the rules of the game for the global manager are set by each country (see Exhibit 1-3): its political and economic agenda, its technological status and level of development, its regulatory environment, its comparative and competitive advantages, and its cultural norms. The astute manager will analyze the new environment, anticipate how it may affect the future of the company, and then develop appropriate strategies and operating styles.

THE POLITICAL AND ECONOMIC ENVIRONMENT

Proactive globally-oriented firms maintain an up-to-date profile of the political and economic environment of the countries in which they maintain operations (or have plans for future investment). Surveys of top executives around the world show that **Sustainability**—economic, political, social, and environmental—has become a significant worldwide issue. Executives who recognize that fact are leading their companies to develop new policies and to invest in sustainability projects with the purpose of benefiting the environment as well as profitability.[72] Among the strategic and operational risks reported by global companies are government regulation, country financial risks and currency risk and political and social disturbances. These concerns and other risks, as reported by those companies, are shown in Exhibit 1-4.

An important aspect of the political environment is the phenomenon of ethnicity—a driving force behind political instability around the world. In fact, many uprisings and conflicts that are thought to be political in nature are actually expressions of differences among ethnic groupings. Often, religious disputes lie at the heart of those differences. Uprisings based on religion operate either in conjunction with ethnic differences (as probably was the case in the former Yugoslavia) or as separate from them (as in Northern Ireland). Many terrorist activities

EXHIBIT 1-4 Greatest Risks affecting FDI Decisions, As Reported by Global Companies

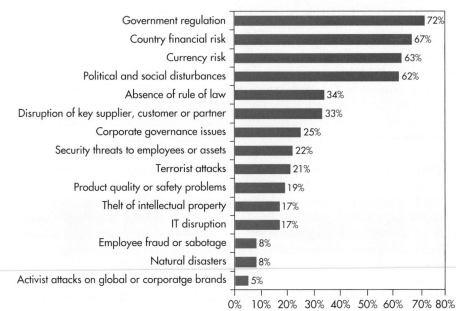

are also based on religious differences, as in the Middle East. Managers must understand the ethnic and religious composition of the host country in order to anticipate problems of general instability, as well as those of an operational nature, such as effects on the workforce, on production and access to raw materials, and on the market. For example, consider the following:

> *In Pakistan one must understand the differences between Punjabi and Sindi. In Malaysia it is essential to recognize the special economic relationship between Chinese and Malay. In the Philippines it is important to understand the significant and lead financial role played by the Filipino-Chinese.*[73]

Political Risk

As shown in the example below, firms operating in some countries are exposed to political risks that can drastically affect them with little warning:

> *Venezuela will take control of cement plants and offices belonging to Mexico's Cemex as of midnight Monday night (August 18, 2008) after failing to reach an agreement in nationalization talks, the government said. The expropriation is part of a drive by the socialist president, Hugo Chávez, to place key industries under state control.*[74]

> WWW.BUSINESSWEEK.COM,
> *August 19, 2008.*

In another example, Bolivian President Evo Morales' move to nationalize the national gas industry followed that in Venezuela, where Mr. Chavez, in a move against Big Oil, forced major oil companies to accept a minority stake in fields that they had owned, also giving more money for higher taxes and royalties.[75]

The managers of a global firm need to investigate the political risks to which they expose their company in certain countries—and the implications of those risks for the economic success of the firm. **Political risks** are any governmental action or politically motivated event that could adversely affect the long-run profitability or value of a firm. The Middle East, as we have seen, has traditionally been an unstable area where political risk heavily influences business decisions.

Nationalization in unstable areas, multinational corporations weigh the risks of nationalization or expropriation, as in Bolivia and Venezuela in the examples previously cited. **Nationalization** refers to the forced sale of an MNC's assets to local buyers, with some compensation to the firm, perhaps leaving a minority ownership with the MNC. As the fallout from the financial meltdown spread around the world in 2009, government moves to take stakes in ailing industries was verging on partial or full nationalization—though for the most part not forced. Japan, for example, was taking the cue from the United States in taking majority stakes in major banks, while in Russia, The Kremlin was exploiting the economic crisis to establish more control over industries such as energy that it has long coveted.[76]

In Europe, nationalist impulses gathered storm in 2009, with many politicians arguing—as in the United States—that if the government is going to bail out banks, then taxpayers should get some ownership and some say in how they operate. For instance, few banks expanded more rapidly in Germany over the last decade than Royal Bank of Scotland. "The British financier muscled onto Continental turf with attractive financing packages for German manufacturers. Today, Royal Bank is majority-owned by the British government after losses in 2008 from £7 billion to £8 billion, or $9.2 billion to $10.5 billion."[77]

Expropriation occurs when a local government seizes and provides inadequate compensation for the foreign-owned assets of an MNC; when no compensation is provided, it is confiscation. In countries that have a proven history of stability and consistency, the political risk to a multinational corporation is relatively low. The risk of expropriation is highest in countries that experience continuous political upheaval, violence, and change, as evidenced by actions such as that by Hugo Chavez in his continuing drive to place key industries under state control, as shown in the previous quote when he took control of Mexico's Cemex cement plants in Venezuela.

Although political risk is typically higher in emerging markets, it is also evident in developed economies. Dubai Ports World found this when its bid in 2006 to manage six American ports for the British owner, P&O, met with such opposition in the U.S. Congress that it withdrew its bid. The Chinese National Offshore Oil Company (CNOOC) ran into similar opposition when it tried unsuccessfully to buy Unocal, the American oil company.

An event that affects all foreign firms doing business in a country or region is called a **macropolitical risk event.** In the Middle East, Iraq's invasion of Kuwait in 1990 abruptly halted all international business with and within both of those countries and caught businesses wholly unprepared.

In many regions, **terrorism** poses a severe and random political risk to company personnel and assets and can, obviously, interrupt the conduct of business. According to Micklous, terrorism is "the use, or threat of use, of anxiety-inducing . . . violence for ideological or political purposes."[78] The increasing incidence of terrorism around the world concerns MNCs. In particular, the kidnapping of business executives has become quite common.

An event that affects one industry or company or only a few companies is called a **micropolitical risk event.** Such events have become more common than macropolitical risk events. Such micro action is often called "creeping expropriation," indicating a government's gradual and subtle action against foreign firms. This is a situation when you haven't been expropriated, but it takes ten times longer to do anything. Typically, such continuing problems with an investment present more difficulty for foreign firms than do major events that are insurable by political-risk insurers. The following list describes seven typical political risk events common today (and possible in the future):

1. Expropriation of corporate assets without prompt and adequate compensation
2. Forced sale of equity to host-country nationals, usually at or below depreciated book value
3. Discriminatory treatment against foreign firms in the application of regulations or laws
4. Barriers to **repatriation** of funds (profits or equity)
5. Loss of technology or other intellectual property (such as patents, trademarks, or trade names)
6. Interference in managerial decision making
7. Dishonesty by government officials, including canceling or altering contractual agreements, extortion demands, and so forth.[79]

Political Risk Assessment

International companies must conduct some form of political risk assessment to manage their exposure to risk and to minimize financial losses. Typically, local managers in each country assess potentially destabilizing issues and evaluate their future impact on their company, making suggestions for dealing with possible problems. Corporate advisers then establish guidelines for each local manager to follow in handling these problems. Dow Chemical has a program in which it uses line managers trained in political and economic analysis, as well as executives in foreign subsidiaries, to provide risk analyses of each country.

Risk assessment by multinational corporations usually takes two forms. One uses experts or consultants familiar with the country or region under consideration. Such consultants, advisers, and committees usually monitor important trends that may portend political change, such as the development of opposition or destabilizing political parties. They then assess the likelihood of political change and develop several plausible scenarios to describe possible future political conditions.

A second and increasingly common means of political risk assessment used by MNCs is the development of internal staff and in-house capabilities. This type of assessment may be accomplished by having staff assigned to foreign subsidiaries, by having affiliates monitor local political activities, or by hiring people with expertise in the political and economic conditions in regions critical to the firm's operations. Frequently, all means are used. The focus must be on monitoring political issues before they become headlines; the ability to minimize the negative effects on the firm—or to be the first to take advantage of opportunities—is greatly reduced once a major media source, such as CNN, has put out the news.

No matter how sophisticated the methods of political risk assessment become, nothing can replace timely information from people on the front line. In other words, sophisticated techniques and consultations are useful as an addition to, but not as a substitute for, the line managers in foreign subsidiaries, many of whom are host-country nationals. These managers represent the most important resource for current information on the political environment, and how it might affect their firm, because they are uniquely situated at the meeting point of the firm and the host country. Prudent MNCs, however, weigh the subjectivity of these managers' assessments and also realize that similar events will have different effects from one country to another.

In addition to assessing the political risk facing a firm, alert managers also examine the specific types of impact that such risks may have on the company. For an autonomous international subsidiary, most of the impact from political risks (nationalization, terrorism) will be at the level of the ownership and control of the firm because its acquisition by the host country would provide the state with a fully operational business. For global firms, the primary risks are likely to be from restrictions (on imports, exports, currency, and so forth), with the impact at the level of the firm's transfers (or exchanges) of money, products, or component parts.

Managing Political Risk

After assessing the potential political risk of investing or maintaining current operations in a country, managers face perplexing decisions on how to manage that risk. On one level, they can decide to suspend their firm's dealings with a certain country at a given point—either by the avoidance of investment or by the withdrawal of current investment (by selling or abandoning plants and assets). On another level, if they decide that the risk is relatively low in a particular country or that a high-risk environment is worth the potential returns, they may choose to start (or maintain) operations there and to accommodate that risk through adaptation to the political regulatory environment. That adaptation can take many forms, each designed to respond to the concerns of a particular local area. Some means of adaptation suggested by Taoka and Beeman are as follows:

1. **Equity sharing** includes the initiation of joint ventures with nationals (individuals or those in firms, labor unions, or government) to reduce political risks.
2. **Participative management** requires that the firm actively involve nationals, including those in labor organizations or government, in the management of the subsidiary.
3. **Localization of the operation** includes the modification of the subsidiary's name, management style, and so forth, to suit local tastes. Localization seeks to transform the subsidiary from a foreign firm to a national firm.
4. **Development assistance** includes the firm's active involvement in infrastructure development (foreign-exchange generation, local sourcing of materials or parts, management training, technology transfer, securing external debt, and so forth).[80]

In addition to avoidance and adaptation, two other means of risk reduction available to managers are dependency and hedging. Some means that managers might use to maintain *dependency*—keeping the subsidiary and the host nation dependent on the parent corporation—are as follows:

1. **Input control** means that the firm maintains control over key inputs, such as raw materials, components, technology, and know-how.

2. Market control requires that the firm keep control of the means of distribution (for instance, by only manufacturing components for the parent firm or legally blocking sales outside the host country).
3. Position control involves keeping certain key subsidiary management positions in the hands of expatriate or home-office managers.
4. Staged contribution strategies mean that the firm plans to increase, in each successive year, the subsidiary's contributions to the host nation (in the form of tax revenues, jobs, infrastructure development, hard-currency generation, and so forth). For this strategy to be most effective, the firm must inform the host nation of these projected contributions as an incentive.[81]

Finally, even if the company cannot diminish or change political risks, it can minimize the losses associated with these events by hedging. Some means of **hedging** are as follows:

1. Political risk insurance is offered by most industrialized countries. In the United States, the Overseas Private Investment Corporation (OPIC) provides coverage for new investments in projects in friendly, less developed countries. Insurance minimizes losses arising from specific risks—such as the inability to repatriate profits, expropriation, nationalization, or confiscation—and from damage as a result of war, terrorism, and so forth.[82] The Foreign Credit Insurance Association (FCIA) also covers political risks caused by war, revolution, currency inconvertibility, and the cancellation of import or export licenses. However, political risk insurance covers only the loss of a firm's assets, not the loss of revenue resulting from expropriation.[83]
2. Local debt financing (money borrowed in the host country), where available, helps a firm hedge against being forced out of operation without adequate compensation. In such instances, the firm withholds debt repayment in lieu of sufficient compensation for its business losses.

Multinational corporations also manage political risk through their global strategic choices. Many large companies diversify their operations both by investing in many countries and by operating through joint ventures with a local firm or government or through local licensees. By involving local people, companies, and agencies, firms minimize the risk of negative outcomes due to political events. (See Chapters 6 and 7 for further discussion of these and other global strategies.)

Managing Terrorism Risk

No longer is the risk of terrorism for global businesses focused only on certain areas such as South America or the Middle East. That risk now has to be considered in countries such as the United States, which had previously been regarded as safe. Eighty countries lost citizens in the World Trade Center attack on September 11, 2001. Many companies from Asia and Europe had office branches in the towers of the World Trade Center; most of those offices, along with the employees from those countries, were destroyed in the attack. Thousands of lives and billions of dollars were lost, not only by those immediately affected by the attack but also by countless small and large businesses impacted by the ripple effect; global airlines and financial markets were devastated.

As incidents of terrorism accelerate around the world, many companies are increasingly aware of the need to manage the risk of terrorism. In high-risk countries, both IBM and Exxon try to develop a benevolent image through charitable contributions to the local community. They also try to maintain low profiles and minimize publicity in the host countries by using, for example, discreet corporate signs at company sites.[84]

Some companies have put together teams to monitor the patterns of terrorism around the world. Kidnappings are common in Latin America (as a means of raising money for political activities). In the Middle East, airplane hijackings, kidnapping of foreigners, and blackmail (for the release of political prisoners) are common. In Western Europe, terrorists typically aim bombs at U.S.-owned banks and computer companies. Almost all MNCs have stepped up their security measures abroad, hiring consultants in counterterrorism (to train employees to cope with the threat of terrorism) and advising their employees to avoid U.S. airlines when flying overseas. For many firms, however, the opportunities outweigh the threats, even in high-risk areas.

Economic Risk

Closely connected to a country's political stability is its economic environment—and the relative risk that it may pose to foreign companies. A country's level of economic development generally determines its economic stability and, therefore, its relative risk to a foreign firm. Most industrialized nations pose little risk of economic instability; less developed nations pose more risk. However, going into 2009, the global economic risks started by the financial woes in the United States threatened all.

A country's ability or intention to meet its financial obligations determines its economic risk. The economic risk incurred by a foreign corporation usually falls into one of two main categories. Its subsidiary (or other investment) in a specific country may become unprofitable if (1) the government abruptly changes its domestic monetary or fiscal policies or (2) the government decides to modify its foreign-investment policies. The latter situation would threaten the company's ability to repatriate its earnings and would create a financial or interest-rate risk. Furthermore, the risk of exchange-rate volatility results in currency translation exposure to the firm when the balance sheet of the entire corporation is consolidated, and may cause a negative cash flow from the foreign subsidiary. Currency translation exposure occurs when the value of one country's currency changes relative to that of another. For a U.S. company operating in Mexico, the recent peso devaluation meant that the company's assets in that country were worth less when translated into dollars on the financial statements, but the firm's liabilities in Mexico were also less.

When exchange-rate changes are radical, repercussions are felt around the world. For example, when the Russian ruble was devalued in 1998, it was unfortunate for the Russian people because their money bought much less and for Russian firms because they did not have enough buying power to purchase products from overseas, which meant that the sales of foreign companies declined. On the other hand, foreign companies suddenly had more purchasing power in Russia to outsource raw materials, labor, and so on.

Because every MNC operating overseas exposes itself to some level of economic risk, often affecting its everyday operational profitability, managers constantly reassess the level of risk their companies may face in any specific country or region of the world. Four methods of analyzing economic risk, or a country's creditworthiness, are recommended by John Mathis, a professor of international economics who has also served as senior financial policy analyst for the World Bank. These methods are (1) the quantitative approach, (2) the qualitative approach, (3) a combination of both of these approaches, and (4) the checklist approach.

The **quantitative approach,** says Mathis, "attempts to measure statistically a country's ability to honor its debt obligation."[85] This measure is arrived at by assigning different weights to economic variables in order to produce a composite index used to monitor the country's creditworthiness over time and to make comparisons with other countries. A drawback of this approach is that it does not take into account different stages of development among the countries it compares.

The **qualitative approach** evaluates a country's economic risk by assessing the competence of its leaders and analyzing the types of policies they are likely to implement. This approach entails a subjective assessment by the researcher in the process of interviewing those leaders and projecting the future direction of the economy.

The **checklist approach** relies on a few easily measurable and timely criteria believed to reflect or indicate changes in the creditworthiness of the country. Researchers develop various vulnerability indicators that categorize countries in terms of their ability to withstand economic volatility.

Most corporations recognize that no single approach can provide a comprehensive economic risk profile of a country. Therefore, they try to use a combination of approaches.

THE LEGAL ENVIRONMENT

The prudent global manager consults with legal services, both locally and at headquarters, to comply with host-country regulations and to maintain cooperative long-term relationships in the local area. If the manager waits until a problem arises, little legal recourse may be available outside of local interpretation and enforcement. Indeed, this has been the experience of many foreign managers in China, where financial and legal systems remain limited in spite of attempts to show the world a capitalist face. Managers there often simply ignore their debts to foreign companies as they did under the old socialist system. The lesson for many foreign companies in China is that they are losing millions because Beijing often does not stand behind the commitments of its state-owned enterprises. David Ji, a Chinese-American electronics entrepreneur, experienced this painful lesson:

> *A year after the Chinese police apprehended him in his hotel room during a business trip, Mr. Ji remains in China as a pawn—his colleagues say a hostage—in a commercial dispute that pits Changhong, China's largest television manufacturer, against Apex Digital, Mr. Ji's electronics trading company based in Los Angeles.*
>
> NEW YORK TIMES,
> *November 1, 2005.*[86]

Changhong claimed that Apex owed it $470 million, but Mr. Ji claimed the amount is less than $150 million. Mr. Ji, after two months in custody, had no recourse under China's judicial system, which fiercely protects its powerful companies like Changhong. There is heavy pressure from foreign companies for Beijing to embrace global legal norms with the same determination that it has pursued foreign trade.[87]

Although no guarantee is possible, the risk of massive losses may be minimized, among other ways, by making sure you get approval from related government offices (national, provincial, and local), seeing that you are not going to run amok of long-term government goals, and getting loan guarantees from the headquarters of one of Beijing's main banks. Some of the contributing factors in cases like Mr. Ji's are often the personal connections—*guanxi*—involved and the fact that some courts offer their services to the business community for profit. In addition, many judges get their jobs through nepotism rather than by virtue of a law degree.

Although the regulatory environment for international managers consists of the many local laws and the court systems in those countries in which they operate, certain other legal issues are covered by international law, which governs relationships between sovereign countries, the basic units in the world political system. One such agreement, which regulates international business by spelling out the rights and obligations of the seller and the buyer, is the United Nations Convention on Contracts for the International Sale of Goods (CISG). This applies to contracts for the sale of goods between countries that have adopted the convention.

Generally speaking, the manager of the foreign subsidiary or foreign operating division will comply with the host country's legal system. Such systems, derived from common law, civil law, or Muslim law, are a reflection of the country's culture, religion, and traditions. Under **common law,** used in the United States and 26 other countries of English origin or influence, past court decisions act as precedents to the interpretation of the law and to common custom. **Civil law** is based on a comprehensive set of laws organized into a code. Interpretation of these laws is based on reference to codes and statutes. About 70 countries, predominantly in Europe (e.g., France and Germany), are ruled by civil law, as is Japan. In Islamic countries, such as Saudi Arabia, the dominant legal system is **Islamic law;** based on religious beliefs, it dominates all aspects of life. Islamic law is followed in approximately 27 countries and combines, in varying degrees, civil, common, and indigenous law.

Contract Law

A **contract** is an agreement by the parties concerned to establish a set of rules to govern a business transaction. Contract law plays a major role in international business transactions because of the complexities arising from the differences in the legal systems of participating countries and because the host government in many developing and communist countries is often a third party in the contract. Both common law and civil law countries enforce contracts, although their means of resolving disputes differ. Under civil law, it is assumed that a contract reflects promises that will be enforced without specifying the details in the contract; under common law, the details of promises must be written into the contract to be enforced. Astute international managers recognize that they will have to draft contracts in legal contexts different from their own, and they prepare themselves accordingly by consulting with experts in international law before going overseas.

In some countries, "The risk is, you could have a contract torn up or changed. We're just going to have to adjust to that in the West," says Robert Broadfoot, who heads the Political &

Economic Risk Consultancy in Hong Kong. He says that Western companies think they can avoid political risk by spelling out every detail in a contract, but "in Asia, there is no shortcut for managing the relationship."[88] In other words, the contract is in the relationship, not on the paper, and the way to ensure the reliability of the agreement is to nurture the relationship.

Even a deal that has been implemented for some time may start to get watered down at a time when you cannot do anything about it. A Japanese-led consortium experienced this problem after it built an expressway in Bangkok. The Thai government later lowered the toll that it had agreed could be charged for use of the road. This is a subtle form of expropriation, since a company cannot simply pack up a road and leave.[89] Neglect regarding contract law may leave a firm burdened with an agent who does not perform the expected functions, or a firm may be faced with laws that prevent management from laying off employees (often the case in Belgium, the Netherlands, Germany, Sweden, and elsewhere).

Other Regulatory Issues

Differences in laws and regulations from country to country are numerous and complex. These and other issues in the regulatory environment that concern multinational firms are briefly discussed here.

Countries often impose protectionist policies, such as tariffs, quotas, and other trade restrictions, to give preference to their own products and industries. The Japanese have come under much criticism for protectionism, which they use to limit imports of foreign goods while they continue exporting consumer goods (e.g., cars and electronics) on a large scale. The U.S. auto industry continues to ask the U.S. government for protection from Japanese car imports. Calls to "Buy American," however, are thwarted by the difficulty of identifying cars that are truly U.S.-made; the intricate web of car-manufacturing alliances between Japanese and American companies often makes it difficult to distinguish the maker.

A country's tax system influences the attractiveness of investing in that country and affects the relative level of profitability for an MNC. Foreign tax credits, holidays, exemptions, depreciation allowances, and taxation of corporate profits are additional considerations the foreign investor must examine before acting. Many countries have signed tax treaties (or conventions) that define such terms as "income," "source," and "residency" and spell out what constitutes taxable activities.

The level of government involvement in the economic and regulatory environment varies a great deal among countries and has a varying impact on management practices. In Canada, the government has a significant involvement in the economy. It has a powerful role in many industries, including transportation, petrochemicals, fishing, steel, textiles, and building materials—forming partly owned or wholly owned enterprises. Wholly owned businesses are called Crown Corporations (Petro Canada, Ontario Hydro, Saskatchewan Telecommunications, and so forth), many of which are as large as major private companies. The government's role in the Canadian economy, then, is one of both control and competition. Government policies, subsidies, and regulations directly affect the manager's planning process, as do other major factors in the Canadian legal environment, such as the high proportion of unionized workers (30 percent). In Quebec, the law requiring official bilingualism imposes considerable operating constraints and expenses. For a foreign subsidiary, this regulation forces managers to speak both French and English and to incur the costs of language training for employees, translators, the administration of bilingual paperwork, and so on.

THE TECHNOLOGICAL ENVIRONMENT

The effects of technology around the world are pervasive—both in business and in private lives. In many parts of the world, whole generations of technological development are being skipped over. For example, many people will go straight to a digital phone without ever having had their houses wired under the analog system. In Entasopia, Kenya, its 4,000 inhabitants have no bank, no post office, and scant infrastructure of any kind. Yet it was there that three young engineers, with financial backing from Google, installed a small satellite dish powered by a solar panel, to hook up a handful of computers in the community center to the rest of the world. Google is paying the monthly fees for bandwith connection. Locals can now send information instantly instead of having to physically travel to deliver it.[90]

Advances in information technology are bringing about increased productivity—for employees, for companies, and for countries. As noted by Thomas Friedman, technology, as well as other factors that are opening up borders—"the opening of the Berlin Wall, Netscape, work flow, outsourcing, offshoring, open-sourcing, insourcing, supply-chaining, in-forming"—have converged to create a more level playing field. The result of this convergence was

> *The creation of a global, Web-enabled playing field that allows for multiple forms of collaboration—the sharing of knowledge and work—in real time, without regard to geography, distance, or, in the near future, even language.*
>
> THOMAS FRIEDMAN,
> *The World Is Flat, 2005.*[91]

Now that we are in a global information society, it is clear that corporations must incorporate into their strategic planning and their everyday operations the accelerating macro-environmental phenomenon of technoglobalism—in which the rapid developments in information and communication technologies (ICTs) are propelling globalization and vice versa. Investment-led globalization is leading to global production networks, which results in global diffusion of technology to link parts of the value-added chain in different countries. That chain may comprise parts of the same firm, or it may comprise suppliers and customers, or technology-partnering alliances among two or more firms. Either way, technological developments are facilitating, indeed necessitating, the network firm structure that allows flexibility and rapid response to local needs.

Clearly, the effects of technology on global trade and business transactions cannot be ignored; in addition, the Internet is propelling electronic commerce around the world. The ease of use and pervasiveness of the Internet raise difficult questions about ownership of intellectual property, consumer protection, residence location, taxation, and other issues.

New technology specific to a firm's products represents a key competitive advantage to firms and challenges international businesses to manage the transfer and diffusion of proprietary technology, with its attendant risks. Whether it is a product, a process, or a management technology, an MNC's major concern is the **appropriability of technology**—that is, the ability of the innovating firm to profit from its own technology by protecting it from competitors.

An MNC can enjoy many technological benefits from its global operations. Advances resulting from cooperative research and development (R&D) can be transferred among affiliates around the world, and specialized management knowledge can be integrated and shared. However, the risks of technology transfer and pirating are considerable and costly. Although firms face few restrictions on the creation and dissemination of technology in developed countries, less developed countries often impose restrictions on licensing agreements, royalties, and so forth, as well as on patent protection.

In most countries, governments use their laws to some extent to control the flow of technology. These controls may be in place for reasons of national security. Other countries, LDCs in particular, use their investment laws to acquire needed technology (usually labor-intensive technology to create jobs), increase exports, use local technology, and train local people.

The most common methods of protecting proprietary technology are the use of patents, trademarks, trade names, copyrights, and trade secrets. Various international conventions afford some protection in participating countries; more than 80 countries adhere to the International Convention for the Protection of Industrial Property, often referred to as the Paris Union, for the protection of patents. However, restrictions and differences in the rules in some countries not signatory to the Paris Union, as well as industrial espionage, pose continuing problems for firms trying to protect their technology.

One risk to a firm's intellectual property is the inappropriate use of the technology by joint-venture partners, franchisees, licensees, and employees (especially those who move to other companies). Some countries rigorously enforce employee secrecy agreements.

Another major consideration for global managers is the need to evaluate the appropriateness of technology for the local environment—especially in less developed countries. Studying the possible cultural consequences of the transfer of technology, managers must assess whether the local people are ready and willing to change their values, expectations, and behaviors on the job to use new technological methods, whether applied to production, research, marketing, finance, or some other aspect of business. Often, a decision regarding the level of technology transfer is dominated by the host government's regulations or requirements. In some instances, the host country may require that foreign investors import only their most modern machinery and methods so that the local area may benefit from new technology. In other cases, the host country may insist that foreign companies use only labor-intensive processes, which can help to reduce high unemployment in an area.

When the choice is left to international managers, experts in economic development recommend that managers make informed choices about appropriate technology. The choice of technology may be capital intensive, labor intensive, or intermediate, but the key is that it should suit the level of development in the area and the needs and expectations of the people who will use it.

Global E-Business

Without doubt, the Internet has had a considerable impact on how companies buy and sell goods around the world—mostly raw materials and services going to manufacturers. Internet-based electronic trading and data exchange are changing the way companies do business, while breaking down global barriers of time, space, logistics, and culture. However, the Internet is not totally open; governments still make sure that their laws are obeyed in cyberspace. This was evidenced when France forced Yahoo! to stop displaying Nazi trinkets for sale where French people could view them.[92] The reality is that

> *Different nations, and different peoples, may want a different kind of Internet—one whose language, content and norms conform more closely to their own.*
>
> FINANCIAL TIMES,
> *May 17, 2006.*[93]

There is no doubt, however, that the Internet has introduced a new level of global competition by providing efficiencies through reducing numbers of suppliers and slashing administration costs throughout the value chain. **E-business** is "the integration of systems, processes, organizations, value chains, and entire markets using Internet-based and related technologies and concepts."[94] **E-commerce** refers directly to the marketing and sales process via the Internet. Firms use e-business to help build new relationships between businesses and customers.[95] The Internet and e-business provide a number of uses and advantages in global business, including the following:

1. Convenience in conducting business worldwide; facilitating communication across borders contributes to the shift toward globalization and a global market.
2. An electronic meeting and trading place, which adds efficiency in conducting business sales.
3. A corporate Intranet service, merging internal and external information for enterprises worldwide.
4. Power to consumers as they gain access to limitless options and price differentials.
5. A link and efficiency in distribution.[96]

Although most early attention was on e-commerce, experts now believe the real opportunities are in business-to-business (**B2B**) transactions. In addition, while the scope, complexity, and sheer speed of the B2B phenomenon, including e-marketplaces, have global executives scrambling to assess the impact and their own competitive roles, estimates for growth in the e-business marketplace may have been overzealous because of the global economic slowdown and its resultant dampening of corporate IT spending. While we hear mostly about large companies embracing B2B, it is noteworthy that a large proportion of current and projected B2B use is by small and medium-sized firms, for three common purposes: supply chain, procurement, and distribution channel.

A successful Internet strategy—especially on a global scale—is, of course, not easy to create. Potential problems abound, as experienced by the European and U.S. companies surveyed by Forrester Research. Such problems include internal obstacles and politics, difficulties in regional coordination and in balancing global versus local e-commerce, and cultural differences. Such a large-scale change in organizing business clearly calls for absolute commitment from the top, empowered employees with a willingness to experiment, and good internal communications.[97] Barriers to the adoption and progression of e-business around the world include lack of readiness of partners in the value chain, such as suppliers. If companies want to have an effective marketplace, they usually must invest in increasing their trading partners' readiness and their customers' capabilities. Other barriers are cultural. In Europe, for example, "Europe's e-commerce excursion has been hindered by a laundry list of cultural and regulatory obstacles, like widely varying tax systems, language hurdles, and currency issues."[98]

In other areas of the world, barriers to creating global e-businesses include differences in physical, information, and payment infrastructure systems. In such countries, innovation is required to use local systems for implementing a Web strategy. In Japan, for example, very few transactions are conducted using credit cards. Typically, bank transfers and COD are used to pay for purchases. Also, many Japanese use convenience stores, such as 7-Eleven Japan, to pay for their online purchases by choosing that option online.[99]

For these reasons, B2B e-business is likely to expand globally faster than **B2C** (business-to-consumer) transactions. In addition, consumer e-commerce depends on each country's level of access to computers and the Internet, as well as the relative efficiency of home delivery. Clearly, companies who want to go global through e-commerce must localize to globalize, which means much more than just presenting online content in local languages.

> *Localizing . . . also means recognizing and conforming to the nuances, subtleties and tastes of multiple local cultures, as well as supporting transactions based on each country's currency, local connection speeds, payment preferences, laws, taxes and tariffs.*[100]

In spite of various problems, use of the Internet to facilitate and improve global competitiveness continues to be explored and discovered. In the public sector in Europe, for example, the European Commission advertises tender invitations online in order to transform the way public sector contracts are awarded, using the Internet to build a truly single market.

It is clear that e-business is not only a new Web site on the Internet but also a source of significant strategic advantage. Hoping to capture this strategic advantage, the European Airbus venture—a public and private sector combination—joined a global aerospace B2B exchange for aircraft parts. The exchange illustrates two major trends in global competition: (1) those of cooperative global alliances, even among competitors, to achieve synergies and (2) the use of technology to enable those connections and synergies.

CONCLUSION

A skillful global manager cannot develop a suitable strategic plan or consider an investment abroad without first assessing the environment—political, economic, legal, and technological—in which the company will operate. This assessment should result not so much in a comparison of countries as in a comparison of (1) the relative risk and (2) the projected return on investments among these countries. Similarly, for ongoing operations, both the subsidiary manager and headquarters management must continually monitor the environment for potentially unsettling events or undesirable changes that may require the redirection of certain subsidiaries or the entire company. Some of the critical factors affecting the global manager's environment (and therefore requiring monitoring) are listed in Exhibit 1-5.

Environmental risk, as discussed in this chapter, has become the new frontier in global business. The skills of companies and the measures taken to manage their exposure to environmental risk on a world scale will soon largely replace their ability to develop, produce, and market global brands as the key element in global competitive advantage.

The pervasive role of culture in international management will be discussed fully in Part II, with a focus on how the managerial functions and the daily operations of a firm are also affected by a subtle, but powerful, environmental factor in the host country—that of societal culture.

Chapter 2 presents some more subtle, but critical, factors in the global environment—those of social responsibility and ethical behavior. We will consider a variety of questions: What is the role of the firm in the future of other societies and their people? What stakeholders must managers consider in their strategic and operational decisions in other countries? How do the expectations of firm behavior vary around the world, and should those expectations influence the international manager's decisions? What role does long-term global economic interdependence play in the firm's actions in other countries?

EXHIBIT 1-5 The Environment of the Global Manager

Political Environment	Economic Environment
• Form of government	• Economic system
• Political stability	• State of development
• Foreign policy	• Economic stability
• State companies	• GNP
• Role of military	• International financial standing
• Level of terrorism	• Monetary/fiscal policies
• Restrictions on imports/exports	• Foreign investment
Regulatory Environment	**Technological Environment**
• Legal system	• Level of technology
• Prevailing international laws	• Availability of local technical skills
• Protectionist laws	• Technical requirements of country
• Tax laws	• Appropriability
• Role of contracts	• Transfer of technology
• Protection for proprietary property	• Infrastructure
• Environmental protection	

Cultural Environment (see Part II)

Summary of Key Points

1. Competing in the twenty-first century requires firms to invest in the increasingly refined managerial skills needed to perform effectively in a multicultural environment. Managers need a global orientation to meet the challenges of world markets and rapid, fundamental changes in a world of increasing economic interdependence.

2. Global management is the process of developing strategies, designing and operating systems, and working with people around the world to ensure sustained competitive advantage.

3. One major direction in world trade is the rise of rapidly developing economies, such as China, India, Brazil, and Russia (often called the BRIC countries).

4. Drastic worldwide changes present dynamic challenges to global managers, including the political and economic trend toward the privatization of businesses, rapid advances in information technology, and the management of offshore human capital. In 2009, global economic woes were causing a resurgence of protectionism and nationalism around the world.

5. Global managers must be aware of political risks around the world that can adversely affect the long-run profitability or value of a firm. International managers must evaluate various means to either avoid or minimize the effects of political risk.

6. The risk of terrorist activity represents an increasing risk around the world. Managers have to decide how to incorporate that risk factor in their strategic and operational plans.

7. Economic risk refers to a country's ability to meet its financial obligations. The risk is that the government may change its economic policies, thereby making a foreign company unprofitable or unable to repatriate its foreign earnings.

8. The regulatory environment comprises the many different laws and courts of those nations in which a company operates. Most legal systems derive from the common law, civil law, or Islamic law.

9. Use of the Internet in e-commerce—in particular, in business-to-business (B2B) transactions—and for intracompany efficiencies is rapidly becoming an important factor in global competitiveness.

10. The appropriability of technology is the ability of the innovating firm to protect its technology from competitors and to obtain economic benefits from that technology. Risks to the appropriability of technology include technology transfer and pirating and legal restrictions on the protection of proprietary technology. Intellectual property can be protected through patents, trademarks, trade names, copyrights, and trade secrets.

Discussion Questions

1. Poll your classmates about their attitudes towards "globalization." What are the trends and opinions around the world that underlie those attitudes?

2. Describe the recent effects of financial globalization on the world economy. What actions have governments taken to offset negative effects? Are they working?

3. How has the economic downturn impacted trends in protectionism and nationalization?

4. Discuss examples of recent macropolitical risk events and the effect they have or might have on a foreign subsidiary. What are micropolitical risk events? Give some examples and explain how they affect international business.

5. What means can managers use to assess political risk? What do you think is the relative effectiveness of these different methods? At the time you are reading this, what countries or areas do you feel have political risk sufficient to discourage you from doing business there?

6. Can political risk be "managed"? If so, what methods can be used to manage such risk, and how effective are they? Discuss the lengths to which you would go to manage political risk relative to the kinds of returns you would expect to gain.

7. Explain what is meant by the economic risk of a nation. Use a specific country as an example. Can economic risk in this country be anticipated? How? How does economic instability affect other nations?

8. Discuss the importance of contracts in international management. What steps must a manager take to ensure a valid and enforceable contract?

9. Discuss the effects of various forms of technology on international business. What role does the Internet play? Where is all this leading? Explain the meaning of the "appropriability of technology." What role does this play in international competitiveness? How can managers protect the proprietary technology of their firms?

10. Discuss the risk of terrorism. What means can managers use to reduce the risk or the effects of terrorism? Where in the world, and from what likely sources, would you anticipate terrorism?

Application Exercises

1. Do some further research on the technological environment. What are the recent developments affecting businesses and propelling globalization? What problems have arisen regarding use of the Internet for global business transactions, and how are they being resolved?

2. Consider recent events and the prevailing political and economic conditions in the Russian Federation. As a manager who has been considering investment there, how do you assess the political and economic risks at this time? What should be your company's response to this environment?

Experiential Exercise

In groups of three, represent a consulting firm. You have been hired by a diversified multinational corporation to advise on the political and economic environment in different countries. The company wants to open one or two manufacturing facilities in Asia. Choose a specific type of company and two specific countries in Asia and present them to the class, including the types of risks that would be involved and what steps the firm could take to manage those risks.

Internet Resources

Visit the Deresky Companion Website at www.pearsonhighered.com/deresky for this chapter's Internet resources.

CASE STUDY

Indian BPOs—Waking Up to the Philippines Opportunity?

Since the mid-1990s, Business Process Outsourcing (BPO) firms have been one of the largest job creators in India, redefining pay scales and the work environment for many young Indians. The sector witnessed a flurry of activity in 2004–05, with many multinational companies (MNCs) and Indian companies increasing operations and therefore their hiring numbers. A number of mergers and acquisitions within the sector also signified maturity and consolidation for the industry. The number of captive and third party service providers added up to about 400 companies in the Indian BPO sector. According to industry experts, an educated, young and English speaking population and the cheaper bandwidth were the key factors behind this growth.

In addition to India, outsourcing companies were looking at Singapore, China, the Philippines, and Malaysia as outsourcing destinations. In the mid-2000s the Philippines emerged as a promising outsourcing destination for the western world. Indian companies too started establishing operations in the country. By 2008, companies such as Sitel, Genpact, and Citibank had already set up offices there, and were even shifting local talent from India to fill up senior and middle level management positions in the Philippines.

In 2008, the BPO industry had been in India for about a decade. In these ten years, it had shown tremendous growth and was no longer limited to being an activity of global MNCs. Leading Indian information technology (IT) software and service organizations had also contributed to the growth of the BPO industry in India.

Indian companies offered a bouquet of outsourced services like customer care, medical transcription, medical billing, payroll management, and tax processing. On the strength of this growth, the government identified the information technology enabled services (ITES)/BPO sector as a key contributor to economic growth, and offered them benefits like tax holidays, previously enjoyed by the software industry. In 1999, after the deregulation of the telecom industry, national long distance and international connectivity also became open to competition.

India's success as an outsourcing destination was attributed to these reasons—an abundant, skilled, and English speaking manpower; high-end telecom and infrastructure; strong quality orientation within the industry; India's location on the map which allowed it to leverage on time zone differences; a positive policy environment that encouraged investment in the industry; and an attractive and friendly tax structure. NASSCOM[1] surveys showed that Indian companies were more focused on maintaining quality and performance standards. For overseas companies, outsourcing to India offered significant improvements in quality and productivity on crucial parameters such as number of correct transactions, number of total transactions, total satisfaction factor, number of transactions/hour, and the average speed of answers. Indian companies adhered to metrics much better than the peers in some other countries.

The Indian ITES/BPO industry also recorded a growth rate of over 50 percent in the year 2002–03.[2] All these were viewed by experts as an indication of the success and the growth that the industry would enjoy in the future. According to research firm IDC India, India's exports of ITES/BPO services in 2005 were estimated at Rs. 311.91 billion. This was expected to grow at a compound annual growth rate of 26 percent through 2010 to Rs. 1101.75 billion by 2010.[3]

Despite the growth story and promises of a rosy future, industry experts felt that the Indian BPO industry was losing its sheen. There were many reasons for this, the strength of the rupee and the weakening dollar being among the main ones. With the US economy slowing down and market forecasts also being glum, the industry was beginning to feel the heat. Quite simply, with the dollar weakening, the rupees per dollar received went down, affecting the profitability of all international players. To add to their woes, the Indian government was unwilling to extend the STPI (Software Technology Park of India) tax holiday for BPO units beyond 2009. The estimate was that the effective tax rate would be 20 percent once the exemption was removed, as opposed to about 7 percent[4] (approximately) with the tax holiday, and this would put BPO margins under tremendous pressure. The growing infrastructure and transportation costs were also putting more pressure on the margins. The Indian industry faced issues like poor infrastructure, high spending on transporting people, and above all, no incentive of low taxes.

In contrast, countries like the Philippines had world class infrastructure and ten-year tax breaks, and were culturally a better fit owing to 50 years of colonial influence. They had a young, educated workforce, and a history of close ties with the US. Their culture was much more Americanized. The wage structure also was higher than that in India, but the affinity to Western culture and the conversational American-style English that Philippine BPOs offered mattered more to most Western companies. The good basic infrastructure, good language skills, and lower taxation rates were ultimately what made companies favour the Philippines vis-à-vis India. According to research firm IDC, Philippines' capital Manila has already emerged as the #2 among outsourcing destinations in the Asia-Pacific, behind Bangalore.[5]

The statement of Pramod Bhasin, CEO of Genpact, sums up the feeling of major BPO operators in India: "The amount of additional costs I have to bear to do business in India is massive. In The Philippines I don't have to spend a dime on transporting employees—a luxury I can't afford in India. The government there spends $100 million exclusively to train people specific to BPOs' requirements and we get a ten-year tax break. I won't say we can completely shift operations somewhere else in the near future, but it is a definite Plan B."[6]

---

[1] NASSCOM (acronym for National Association of Software and Service Companies) is the premier trade body and the chamber of commerce of the IT industry in India.
[2] www.outsource2india.com
[3] "India's ITeS-BPO Industry Ready to Face New Challenges; Skilled Manpower, Processes and Enabling Technology 'on tap' to Fuel Future Growth Prospects, says IDC," www.idcindia.com, October 12, 2006.
[4] T. R. Vivek, "Indian BPO Industry in for Tough Times Ahead," *The Economic Times*, April 4, 2008.
[5] "Indians Write the BPO Script in Philippines," http://economictimes.indiatimes.com, July 22, 2008.
[6] T. R. Vivek, "Indian BPO Industry in for Tough Times Ahead," *The Economic Times*, April 4, 2008.

Additional Readings and References

1. "India's ITeS-BPO Industry Ready to Face New Challenges; Skilled Manpower, Processes and Enabling Technology 'on tap' to Fuel Future Growth Prospects, Says IDC," www.idcindia.com, October 12, 2006.
2. "A Brief History of BPO in the Philippines," http://manilamuse.typepad.com, June 4, 2007.
3. TR Vivek, "Indian BPO Industry in for Tough Times Ahead," *Economic Times*, April 4, 2008.
4. "Indians Write the BPO Script in Philippines," http:/economictimes.indiatimes.com, July 22, 2008.
5. Paul Ancheta, "Manila Calling," www.PaulAncheta.com (Retreived on July 24, 2008)
6. www.en.wikipedia.org
7. www.outsource@india.com/why_india/articles/outsourcing_history.asp (Retreived on July 24, 2008)

Author Information: This case was written by **Barkha Modi** under the direction of **Debapratim Purkayastha**, ICMR. It was compiled from published sources, and is intended to be used as a basis for class discussion rather than to illustrate either effective or ineffective handling of a management situation.

Case Questions

1. How has the global economic downturn, discussed in the opening profile and throughout this chapter, impacted jobs outsourcing in the BPO industry?
2. Referring to this chapter and this case, discuss the general trends in the globalization of human capital.
3. What are the effects of the Indian government policies on the Indian BPO industry and on MNC decisions regarding locations for outsourcing jobs?
4. How does this case highlight the threats and opportunities facing global companies in developing their strategies?

Managing Interdependence

Social Responsibility and Ethics

OBJECTIVES:

1. To appreciate the complexities involved in the corporation's obligations toward its various constituencies around the world.

2. To understand the changing perceptions and demands of corporations doing business in other countries, in particular the responsibilities toward human rights.

3. To acknowledge the strategic role that CSR and codes of ethics must play in global management.

4. To provide guidance to managers to maintain ethical behavior amid the varying standards and practices around the world.

5. To recognize that companies must provide benefits to the host country in which they operate in order to maintain cooperation.

6. To discuss the need for corporations to consider Sustainability in their long-term plans in order to manage environmental impacts on host locations.

7. To identify the challenges involved in human rights issues when operating in China.

Opening Profile: Primark's Moral Maze: Embroidered T-Shirt—Price: £4. Cost: Misery . . . . . . or Survival?[1]

For Primark, the U.K. clothing retailer owned by Associated British Foods, there are few clear answers to the moral maze faced by retailers in the developed world which are reliant on suppliers in less developed economies. Primark announced in June 2008 that it had fired three suppliers in India after it was found that they had subcontracted work to home workers who used child labor; company executives protested that the factories had engaged in systematic deception and that regular audits had not exposed the breaches. Primark's executives were alerted about child labor being used by its garment suppliers in southern India after an expose by the BBC's *Panorama* program. One of the three factories the documentary exposed as subcontracting to child laborers had been supplying Primark for 12 years.

Primark's response to the expose increased as various stakeholders communicated their positions. The initial reaction was to fire the offending suppliers. However, that brought criticism that such action was insufficient and also only served to punish those workers who spoke up about their working conditions. When consumers protested, the company withdrew the clothes from sale and offered refunds. The company said it would appoint an organization in southern India to check on the suppliers. However, according to the Ethical Trade Initiative, an organization set up by retailers, NGOs, and trade unions of which Primark is a member, audits are essential, but not foolproof; while all companies have problems in supply chains, the key is what they do about them. Later Primark said that the company is setting up a charity to improve the lives of children in its suppliers' locations.

Consumers, too, come under fire for expecting that they can pay £4 for an embroidered t-shirt without realizing that something in the supply chain has got to give. According to Richard Welford, Chairman of CSR Asia, anyone with any experience of supply chains in Asia knows that regular audits will uncover breaches. However many suppliers are determined to keep their breaches from being discovered. Instead, companies need to get suppliers to recognize that adhering to sound employment practices is in their own interests and to help suppliers develop policies and practices for a long-term relationship. Simply to cut the contracts of factories that indirectly employ children has the potential to make a bad situation worse. Parents in less-developed economies cannot chose between sending their children to school or work—their choice is only whether they work or go hungry.

While little over a decade ago a company's responsibility was almost exclusively profit, now corporate social responsibility (CSR) has come to the forefront. "Transparency" has become the watchword, and the issue of sweatshops must be carefully evaluated and controlled by manufacturers such as Primark or The Gap. Primark's case is a warning to other corporations because it reveals how much scrutiny is being applied to all levels of an organization's operations. The lesson is that CSR is now a vital part of corporate culture and strategy, and in fact can become an organization's license to keep operating.

Global interdependence is a compelling factor in the global business environment, creating demands on international managers to take a positive stance on issues of social responsibility and ethical behavior, economic development in host countries, and ecological protection around the world.

Managers today are usually quite sensitive to issues of social responsibility and ethical behavior because of pressures from the public, from interest groups, from legal and governmental concerns, and from media coverage, as illustrated in the opening profile. In August 2003, for example, the United Nations published draft guidelines for the responsibilities of transnational corporations and called for companies to be subject to monitoring, verification, and censure. Though many companies agree with the guidelines, they resist the notion that corporate responsibility should be regulated and question where to draw the line between socially responsible behavior and the concerns of the corporation's other stakeholders.[2] In the domestic arena, managers are faced with numerous ethical complexities. In the international arena, such concerns are compounded by the larger numbers of stakeholders involved, including customers, communities, allies, and owners in various countries.

This chapter's discussion focuses separately on issues of social responsibility and ethical behavior, though considerable overlap can be observed. The difference between the two is a matter of scope and degree. Whereas ethics deals with decisions and interactions on an individual level, decisions about social responsibility are broader in scope, tend to be made at a higher level, affect more people, and reflect a general stance taken by a company or a number of decision makers.

THE SOCIAL RESPONSIBILITY OF MNCs

Multinational corporations (MNCs) and multinational enterprises (MNEs) have been, and—to a lesser extent—continue to be, at the center of debate regarding **corporate social responsibility (CSR)**, particularly the benefits versus harm wrought by their operations around the world, especially in less developed countries. The criticisms of MNCs have been lessened in recent years by the decreasing economic differences among countries, by the emergence of less developed countries' (LDCs) multinationals, and by the greater emphasis on social responsibility by MNCs.

Issues of social responsibility continue to center on the poverty and lack of equal opportunity around the world, the environment, consumer concerns, and employee safety and welfare. Many argue that, since MNCs operate in a global context, they should use their capital, skills, and power to play proactive roles in handling worldwide social and economic problems and that, at the least, they should be concerned with host-country welfare. Others argue that MNCs already have a positive impact on developing economies by providing managerial training, investment capital, and new technology, as well as by creating jobs and improving infrastructure. Certainly, multinational corporations constitute a powerful presence in the world economy and often have a greater capacity than local governments to induce change. The sales, debts, and resources of some of the largest multinationals exceed the gross national product, the public and private debt, and the resources, respectively, of some nations.

The concept of **international social responsibility** includes the expectation that MNCs concern themselves with the social and economic effects of their decisions. The issue is how far that concern should go and what level of planning and control that concern should take. Such dilemmas are common for MNC managers. Del Monte managers, for example, realize that growing pineapples in the rich coastal lands of Kenya brings mixed results there. Although badly needed foreign-exchange earnings are generated for Kenya, poor Kenyans living in the region experience adverse effects because less land is available for subsistence agriculture to support them.

Opinions on the level of social responsibility that a domestic firm should demonstrate range from one extreme—the only responsibility of a business is to make a profit, within the confines of the law, in order to produce goods and services and serve its shareholders' interests[3]—to another extreme—companies should anticipate and try to solve problems in society. Between these extremes are varying positions described as socially reactive, in which companies respond to some degree of currently prevailing social expectations, to the environmental and social costs of their actions, as illustrated in the opening profile on the Primark Company.

The stance toward social responsibility that a firm should take in its international operations, however, is much more complex—ranging perhaps from assuming some responsibility for economic development in a subsidiary's host country to taking an active role in identifying and solving world problems. The increased complexity regarding the social responsibility and ethical behavior of firms across borders is brought about by the additional stakeholders in the firm's activities through operating overseas. As illustrated in Exhibit 2-1, managers are faced with not only considering stakeholders in the host country but also with weighing their rights against the rights of their domestic stakeholders. Most managerial decisions will have a trade-off of the rights of these stakeholders—at least in the short term. For example, a decision to discontinue using children in Pakistan to sew soccer balls means the company will pay more for adult employees and will, therefore, reduce the profitability to its owners. That same decision—while taking a stand for human rights according to the social and ethical expectations in the home country and bowing to consumers' demands—may mean that those children and their families go hungry or are forced into worse working situations. Another decision to keep jobs at home to satisfy local employees and unions will mean higher prices for consumers and less profit for stakeholders. In addition, if competitors take their jobs to cheaper overseas factories, a company may go out of business, which will mean no jobs at all for the domestic employees and a loss for the owners. In spite of conflicting agendas, there is some consensus about what CSR means at a basic level—that "corporate activity should be motivated in part by a concern for the welfare of some non-owners, and by an underlying commitment to basic principles such as integrity, fairness and respect for persons."[4]

In addition, it is clear that there are long-term competitive benefits deriving from CSR, much of which results from the goodwill, attractiveness, and loyalty of the various stakeholders connected with the company. These may be in the local area, such as government, suppliers, employees, brand reputation, etc., or far-flung such as consumers. Manuela Weber suggests a CSR impact model can be derived that reflects the main clusters of CSR business benefits as shown in Exhibit 2-2.

EXHIBIT 2-1 MNC Stakeholders

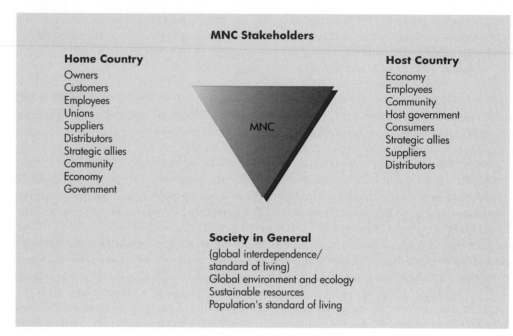

EXHIBIT 2-2 CSR Impact Model

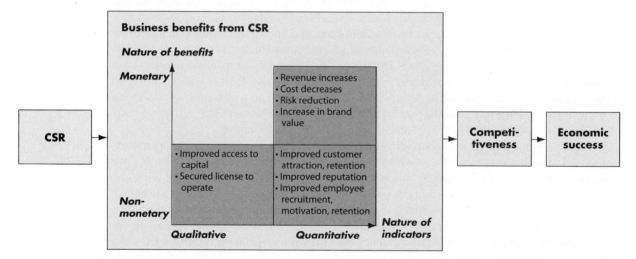

Source: Reprinted from Manuela Weber, "The Business Case for Corporate Social Responsibility: A Company-Level Measurement Approach for CSR," *European Management Journal* 26, no. 4 (2008): 247–61. Copyright 2008, with permission from Elsevier.

CSR: Global Consensus or Regional Variation?

With the growing awareness of the world's socioeconomic interdependence, global organizations are beginning to recognize the need to reach a consensus on what should constitute moral and ethical behavior. Some think that such a consensus is emerging because of the development of a **global corporate culture**—an integration of the business environments in which firms currently operate. This integration results from the gradual dissolution of traditional boundaries and from the many intricate interconnections among MNCs, internationally linked securities markets, and communication networks. Nevertheless, there are commonly acknowledged regional variations in how companies respond to corporate social responsibility (CSR):

> *The U.S. and Europe adopt strikingly different positions that can be traced largely to history and culture. In the U.S., CSR is weighted more towards "doing business right" by following basic business obligations; . . . in Europe, CSR is weighted more*

towards serving—or at least not conflicting with—broader social aims, such as envi-
ronmental sustainability.

THE FINANCIAL TIMES,
June 3, 2005.[5]

While making good faith efforts to implement CSR, companies operating abroad face confusion about the cross-cultural dilemmas it creates, especially how to behave in host countries, which have their own differing expectations and agendas. Recommendations about how to deal with such dilemmas include:

- Engaging stakeholders (and sometimes nongovernmental organizations, or NGOs) in a dialogue.
- Establishing principles and procedures for addressing difficult issues such as labor standards for suppliers, environmental reporting, and human rights.
- Adjusting reward systems to reflect the company's commitment to CSR.[6]

Although it is very difficult to implement a generalized code of morality and ethics in individual countries, such guidelines do provide a basis of judgment regarding specific situations. Bowie uses the term **moral universalism** to address the need for a moral standard that is accepted by all cultures.[7] Although, in practice, it seems unlikely that a universal code of ethics will ever be a reality, Bowie says that this approach to doing business across cultures is far preferable to other approaches, such as ethnocentrism or ethical relativism. With an **ethnocentric approach,** a company applies the morality used in its home country—regardless of the host country's system of ethics.

A company subscribing to **ethical relativism,** on the other hand, simply adopts the local moral code of whatever country in which it is operating. With this approach, companies run into value conflicts, such as continuing to do business in China despite home-country objections to China's continued violation of human rights. In addition, public pressure in the home country often forces the MNC to act in accordance with ethnocentric value systems anyway. In one instance, public outcry in the United States and most of the world resulted in major companies (IBM, General Motors, Coca-Cola, and Eastman Kodak) either selling or discontinuing their operations in South Africa during the 1980s to protest that country's apartheid policies. More recently, the Food and Drug Administration (FDA) has been pressuring U.S. manufacturers of silicone-filled breast implants (prohibited in the United States for cosmetic surgery because of health hazards) to adopt a voluntary moratorium on exports. While Dow Corning has ceased its foreign sales—citing its responsibility to apply the same standards internationally as it does domestically—other major manufacturers continue to export the implants, often from their factories in other countries.

The difficulty, even in adopting a stance of moral universalism, is in deciding where to draw the line. Individual managers must at some point decide, based on their own morality, when they feel a situation is simply not right and to withdraw their involvement.

One fact is inescapable, however, and that is that, in a globalized market economy, CSR is part of modern business.

MNC Responsibility Toward Human Rights

With almost all tech products now made by contract manufacturers in low-wage
nations where sweatshops are common, . . . Hewlett Packard, Dell, IBM, Intel, and
twelve other tech companies decided to unite to create the Electronic Industry Code
of Conduct (EICC)

BUSINESS WEEK,
June 19, 2006.[8]

Whereas many situations regarding the morality of the MNC's presence or activities in a country are quite clear, other situations are not, especially when dealing with human rights. So loud has been the cry about products coming from so-called sweatshops around the world that former President Bill Clinton established an Anti-Sweatshop Code of Conduct, which includes a ban on forced labor, abuse, and discrimination, and it requires companies to provide a healthy and safe work environment and to pay at least the prevailing local minimum wage, among other requirements. A group has been named to monitor compliance; enforcement is difficult, of course, but publicity helps. The Department of Labor publishes the names of companies that comply with the code, including Nike, Reebok, Liz Claiborne, Wal-Mart, and Phillips-Van Heusen.[9] Nike's efforts to address its problems include publishing its entire list of contract manufacturers on the Internet in order to gain transparency. The company admits that it is difficult to keep track of what goes on at its 800 plus contracted factories around the world.[10] (See the case at the end of this chapter for a review of Nike's approach to human rights in its factories.)

What constitutes "human rights" is clouded by the perceptions and priorities of people in different countries. While the United States often takes the lead in the charge against what it considers human rights violations around the world, other countries point to the homelessness and high crime statistics in the United States. Often the discussion of human rights centers around Asia because many of the products in the West are imported from Asia by Western companies using manufacturing facilities located there. It is commonly held in the West that the best chance to gain some ground on human rights issues is for large MNCs and governments around the world to take a unified stance; many global players now question the morality of trading for goods that have been produced by forced labor or child labor. Although laws in the United States ban prison imports, shady deals between the manufacturers and companies acting as intermediaries make it difficult to determine the origin of many products—and make it easy for companies wanting access to cheap products or materials to ignore the law. However, under pressure from their labor unions (and perhaps their consciences), a number of large image-conscious companies, such as Reebok and Levi Strauss, have established corporate codes of conduct for their buyers, suppliers, and contractors and have instituted strict procedures for auditing their imports. In addition, some companies are uniting with others in their industry to form their own code for responsible action. One of these is the Electronic Industry Code of Conduct (EICC), which comprises Hewlett-Packard, Dell, IBM, Intel, and 12 other tech companies who have agreed on the following policies:

- The EICC bans forced and child labor and excessive overtime.
- The EICC requires contract manufacturers to follow some basic environmental requirements.
- The EICC requires each company to audit its overseas suppliers to ensure compliance, following a common factory inspection system for all members.[11]

CODES OF CONDUCT

A considerable number of organizations have developed their own codes of conduct; some have gone further to group together with others around the world to establish standards to improve the quality of life for workers around the world. Companies such as Avon, Sainsbury Plc., Toys "R" Us, and Otto Versand have joined with the Council on Economic Priorities (CEP) to establish SA8000 (Social Accountability 8000, on the lines of the manufacturing quality standard ISO9000). Their proposed global labor standards would be monitored by outside organizations to certify whether plants are meeting those standards, among which are the following:

- Do not use child or forced labor.
- Provide a safe working environment.
- Respect workers' rights to unionize.
- Do not regularly require more than 48-hour work weeks.
- Pay wages sufficient to meet workers' basic needs.[12]

In addition, four **international codes of conduct** provide some consistent guidelines for multinational enterprises (MNEs). These codes were developed by the International Chamber of Commerce, the Organization for Economic Cooperation and Development, the International Labor Organization, and the United Nations Commission on Transnational Corporations. Getz has integrated these four codes and organized their common underlying principles, thereby establishing MNE behavior toward governments, publics, and people, as shown in Exhibit 2-3 (the originating institutions are in parentheses). Getz concludes, "As international organizations and institutions (including MNEs themselves) continue to refine the codes, the underlying moral issues will be better identified, and appropriate MNE behavior will be more readily apparent."[13] The examples shown in Exhibit 2-3 are excerpted from the codes and show how companies can provide a cooperative, long-term relationship with the local people and governments where they operate.

COMPARATIVE MANAGEMENT IN FOCUS

Doing Business in China—The Human Rights Challenge

Beijing promised to lift Internet censorship for foreign reporters covering the Olympic Games in 2008, but continued to block sites it considered sensitive. . . . "Mission accomplished, from the leaders' point of view," says Minky Worden, media director for Human Rights Watch.[14]

BUSINESS WEEK,
August 22, 2008.

Even as the global economic downturn slowed China's high-speed economic train in 2009, its growth engine continues to drive the global economy, propelled by China's $586 billion economic stimulus plan. However, many of its people and their basic rights remain largely behind. As discussed in Chapter 1, China retains a strong appeal, in particular for manufacturers, with its cheap labor rates and an expanding market of over one billion people. It is now the world's third biggest manufacturer after the United States and Japan, with that part of its economy having quadrupled in size since 1990—a rate ten times faster than for the whole of global industry.[15] Growth in higher skilled jobs and in services is now well under way. However, there is a swelling tide among MNCs about the pitfalls of operating in China—among them the uncertain legal climate; the difficulty of protecting intellectual property there; the repression of free speech; and the difficulty of monitoring, let alone correcting, human rights violations in factories. As discussed in detail in this chapter's ending case, Nike found rampant violations of workers' rights in many of its factories throughout Asia, including making workers work 60 hours a week, forcing overtime, and ignoring laws on minimum wages and child labor.[16] MNCs like Nike face considerable pressure in their home markets to address human rights in China and elsewhere. Consumers boycott their products, and trade unions in the United States, for example, complain that repression of workers' rights has enabled Chinese companies to push down labor costs, causing considerable loss of manufacturing jobs at home.[17]

MAP 2.1   China

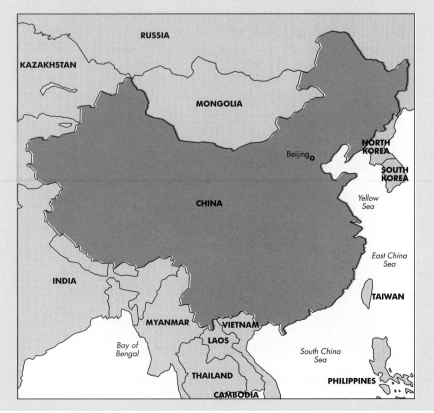

In 2006, the crackdown over what President Hu Jintao's government called "propaganda" escalated with reporters being jailed, editorial staffs fired, and publications closed.[18] The PRC Communist Party "exerts near complete control over China's 358 television stations and 2,119 newspapers, according to the nonprofit group Freedom House."[19] In 2005, China ranked 159th out of 167 countries in a survey of press freedom, according to Reporters Without Borders, the Paris-based international rights group.[20]

> *. . . a vast security network and compliant multinationals keep the mainland's Net under Beijing's thumb.*
>
> BUSINESS WEEK,
> *January 23, 2006.*[21]

Freedom of information took a particularly hard hit with the news that Google had agreed to China's demands to apply censors' blacklists to its search engine there. In spite of Google's founding principle "Don't be evil," their business interests apparently clashed with their principles, leading many to conclude that Google is putting its own freedoms at risk in China; however, that is also occurring with Microsoft and Yahoo! in China.[22]

While Internet and technology executives were called to Capitol Hill in February 2006 to defend their companies' practices in China, it was clear that the future of American corporations and foreign policy interests would prevail.[23] Rather, the debate continues over how Internet companies can engage more effectively with Beijing on human rights issues. But, in a blow to the industry, in July 2006, Amnesty International accused Yahoo! Microsoft, and Google of overlooking their human rights obligations in order to tap into China's dynamic online market, stating that "all three companies have in different ways facilitated or participated in the practice of government censorship in China."[24]

Shoe factory of an unnamed company in China, where women work very long hours. If they finish their lunch early, they may rest at their posts until the lunch time is over.

Source: (c) Michael Wolf 2003

EXHIBIT 2-3 International Codes of Conduct for MNEs

MNE and Host Governments

Economic and developmental policies

- MNEs should consult with governmental authorities and national employers' and workers' organizations to ensure that their investments conform to the economic and social development policies of the host country. (ICC; OECD; ILO; UN/CTC)
- MNEs should not adversely disturb the balance-of-payments or currency exchange rates of the countries in which they operate. They should try, in consultation with the government, to resolve balance-of-payments and exchange rate difficulties when possible. (ICC; OECD; UN/CTC)
- MNEs should cooperate with governmental policies regarding local equity participation. (ICC; UN/CTC)
- MNEs should not dominate the capital markets of the countries in which they operate. (ICC; UN/CTC)
- MNEs should provide the information necessary for correctly assessing taxes to be paid to host government authorities. (ICC; OECD)
- MNEs should not engage in transfer pricing policies that modify the tax base on which their entities are assessed. (OECD; UN/CTC)
- MNEs should give preference to local sources for components and raw materials if prices and quality are competitive. (ICC; ILO)
- MNEs should reinvest some profits in the countries in which they operate. (ICC)

Laws and regulations

- MNEs are subject to the laws, regulations, and jurisdiction of the countries in which they operate. (ICC; OECD; UN/CTC)
- MNEs should respect the right of every country to exercise control over its natural resources, and to regulate the activities of entities operating within its territory. (ICC; OECD; UN/CTC)
- MNEs should use appropriate international dispute settlement mechanisms, including arbitration, to resolve conflicts with the governments of the countries in which they operate. (ICC, OECD)
- MNEs should resolve disputes arising from expropriation by host governments under the domestic law of the host country. (UN/CTC)

Political involvement

- MNEs should refrain from improper or illegal involvement in local political activities. (OECD; UN/CTC)
- MNEs should not pay bribes or render improper benefits to any public servant. (OECD; UN/CTC)
- MNEs should not interfere in intergovernmental relations. (UN/CTC)

MNEs and the Public

Technology transfer

- MNEs should cooperate with governmental authorities in assessing the impact of transfers of technology to developing countries and should enhance the technological capacities of developing countries. (OECD; UN/CTC)
- MNEs should develop and adapt technologies to the needs and characteristics of the countries in which they operate. (ICC; OECD; ILO)
- MNEs should conduct research and development activities in developing countries, using local resources and personnel to the greatest extent possible. (ICC; UN/CTC)

Environmental protection

- MNEs should respect the laws and regulations concerning environmental protection of the countries in which they operate. (OECD; UN/CTC)
- MNEs should cooperate with host governments and with international organizations in the development of national and international environmental protection standards. (ICC; UN/CTC)
- MNEs should supply to appropriate host governmental authorities information concerning the environmental impact of the products and processes of their entities. (ICC; UN/CTC)

MNEs and Persons

Consumer protection

- MNEs should respect the laws and regulations of the countries in which they operate with regard to consumer protection. (OECD; UN/CTC)
- MNEs should preserve the safety and health of consumers by disclosure of appropriate information, proper labeling, and accurate advertising. (UN/CTC)

Employment practices (exerpts)

- MNEs should cooperate with host governments' efforts to create employment opportunities in particular localities. (ICC)
- MNEs should try to increase employment opportunities and standards in the countries in which they operate. (ILO)
- MNEs should give advance notice of plant closures and mitigate the resultant adverse effects. (ICC; OECD; ILO)
- MNEs should provide standards of employment equal to or better than those of comparable employers in the countries in which they operate. (ICC; OECD; ILO)
- MNEs should pay, at minimum, basic living wages. (ILO)

EXHIBIT 2-3 *(Continued)*

- MNEs should maintain the highest standards of safety and health, and should provide adequate information about work-related health hazards. (ILO)

Human rights

- MNEs should respect human rights and fundamental freedoms in the countries in which they operate. (UN/CTC)

- MNEs should not discriminate on the basis of race, color, sex, religion, language, social, national and ethnic origin, or political or other opinion. (UN/CTC)
- MNEs should respect the social and cultural objectives, values, and traditions of the countries in which they operate. (UN/CTC)

International agency sources:

OECD: The Organization for Economic Cooperation and Development Guidelines for Multinational Enterprises

ILO: The International Labor Office Tripartite Declarations of Principles Concerning Multinational Enterprises and Social Policy

ICC: The International Chamber of Commerce Guidelines for International Investment

UN/CTC: The United Nations Universal Declaration of Human Rights

The UN Code of Conduct on Transnational Corps.

ETHICS IN GLOBAL MANAGEMENT

National, as well as corporate, cultures need to be taken into account if multinationals are to enforce their codes across different regions.

FINANCIAL TIMES,
March 7, 2005.[25]

Globalization has multiplied the ethical problems facing organizations. However, business ethics have not yet been globalized. Attitudes toward ethics are rooted in culture and business practices. Swee Hoon Ang found, for example, that while East Asians tended to be less ethical than their expatriate counterparts from the United States and Britain, it was because they considered deception as amoral and acceptable if it has a positive effect on larger issues such as the company, the extended family, or the state.[26] For an MNC, it is difficult to reconcile consistent and acceptable behavior around the world with home-country standards. One question, in fact, is whether it should be reconciled. It seems that, while the United States has been the driving force to legislate moral business conduct overseas, perhaps more scrutiny should have been applied to those global MNCs headquartered in the United States, such as Enron and WorldCom, that so greatly defrauded their investors, employees, and all who had business with them.

The term **international business ethics** refers to the business conduct or morals of MNCs in their relationships with individuals and entities. Such behavior is based largely on the cultural value system and the generally accepted ways of doing business in each country or society, as we have discussed throughout this book. Those norms, in turn, are based on broadly accepted guidelines from religion, philosophy, professional organizations, and the legal system. The complexity of the combination of various national and cultural factors in a particular host environment that combine to determine ethical or unethical societal norms is illustrated in Exhibit 2-4. The authors, Robertson and Crittenden, note,

Varying legal and cultural constraints across borders have made integrating an ethical component into international strategic decisions quite challenging.[27]

Should managers of MNC subsidiaries, then, base their ethical standards on those of the host country or those of the home country—or can the two be reconciled? What is the moral responsibility of expatriates regarding ethical behavior, and how do these issues affect business objectives? How do expatriates simultaneously balance their responsibility to various stakeholders—to owners, creditors, consumers, employees, suppliers, governments, and societies? The often conflicting objectives of host and home governments and societies also must be balanced.

EXHIBIT 2-4   A Moral Philosophy of Cross-cultural Societal Ethics

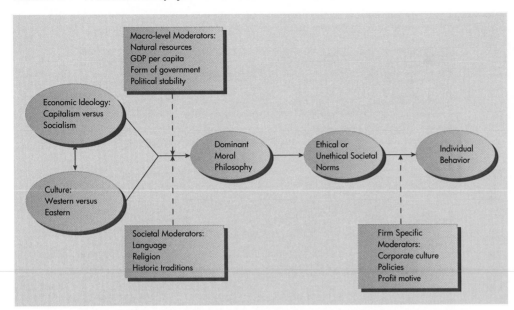

Source: C. J. Robertson and W. F. Crittenden, "Mapping Moral Philisophies: Strategic Implications for Multinational Firms," *Strategic Management Journal* 24: 385–92 (2003) © John Wiley & Sons, Inc. Reproduced with permission.

The approach to these dilemmas varies among MNCs from different countries. While the American approach is to treat everyone the same by making moral judgments based on general rules, managers in Japan and Europe tend to make such decisions based on shared values, social ties, and their perceptions of their obligations. According to many U.S. executives, there is little difference in ethical practices among the United States, Canada, and Northern Europe. According to Bruce Smart, former U.S. Undersecretary of Commerce for International Trade, the highest ethical standards seem to be practiced by the Canadians, British, Australians, and Germans. As he says, "a kind of noblesse oblige still exists among the business classes in those countries"—compared with the prevailing attitude among many U.S. managers that condones "making it" whatever way one can.[28] Another who experienced few problems with ethical practices in Europe is Donald Petersen, former CEO of Ford Motor Company. However, he warns us about underdeveloped countries, in particular those under a dictatorship where bribery is a generally accepted practice.[29]

Petersen's experience has been borne out by research by Transparency International, a German nongovernmental organization (NGO) that fights corruption. It draws on data from fourteen different polls and surveys from twelve independent institutions around the world to rank 180 countries, based on results from 63,199 respondents. The organization's year 2007 Global Corruption Barometer (selections are shown in Exhibit 2-5) shows the results of research into the extent that business and other sectors of their society are affected by corruption, as perceived by businesspeople, academics, and risk analysts in 69 countries. A primary focus of the research was the relative prevalence of bribery in various spheres of people's lives, including political and business practices.

Overall, the data show that those countries in Western Europe, Canada, and Australia, were the least corrupt, closely followed by Hong Kong and Japan; the United States scored 7.2 for example, compared with 9.4 for Denmark. South Africa and South Korea both ranked 5.1. Brazil, China, India, and Mexico scored 3.5; other countries such as Vietnam, and African countries scored far lower.[30]

The biggest single problem for MNCs in their attempt to define a corporate-wide ethical posture is the great variation of ethical standards around the world. Many practices that are considered unethical or even illegal in some countries are accepted ways of doing business in others. More recently, this dilemma has taken on new forms because of the varied understandings of the ethical use of technology around the world, as illustrated by the electronic data privacy laws in Europe. The EU Directive on Data Protection guarantees European citizens absolute control over data concerning them. A U.S. company wanting personal information must get permission from that person and explain what the information will be used for; the company must also guarantee that the information won't be used for anything else without the person's consent.

EXHIBIT 2-5 2007 Corruption Perceptions Index—Selected Ranks

The score relates to perceptions of the degree of corruption as seen by business people and country analysts, and ranges between 10 (highly clean) and 0 (highly corrupt).

Rank	Country	Score
1	Denmark	9.4
1	Finland	9.4
1	New Zealand	9.4
4	Sweden	9.3
4	Singapore	9.3
9	Canada	8.7
11	Australia	8.6
12	United Kingdom	8.4
14	Hong Kong	8.3
16	Germany	7.8
17	Japan	7.5
19	France	7.3
20	USA	7.2
21	Belgium	7.1
22	Chile	7.0
30	Israel	6.1
34	Taiwan	5.7
34	United Arab Emirates	5.7
41	Czech Republic	5.2
41	Italy	5.2
43	South Africa	5.1
43	South Korea	5.1
56	Greece	4.6
61	Poland	4.2
64	Turkey	4.1
72	Brazil	3.5
72	China	3.5
72	India	3.5
72	Mexico	3.5
79	Saudi Arabia	3.4
79	Serbia	3.4
84	Thailand	3.3
105	Argentina	2.9
105	Bolivia	2.9
123	Vietnam	2.6
131	Philippines	2.5
143	Indonesia	2.3
147	Nigeria	2.2

Source: Selected data from the TI Corruption perceptions Index, 2007, www.transparencyinternational.org, January 10, 2009.

Bribery

There are few other areas where a single employee can, with one instance of misjudgment, create huge embarrassment [for the company].

FINANCIAL TIMES[31]

The computer is on the dock, it's raining, and you have to pay $100 [bribe] to get it picked up.

WILLIAM C. NORRIS,

Control Data Corporation

MNCs are often caught between being placed at a disadvantage by refusing to go along with a country's accepted practices, such as bribery, or being subject to criticism at home for using "unethical" tactics to get the job done. Large companies that have refused to participate have led the way in taking a moral stand because of their visibility, their potential impact on the local economy, and, after all, their ability to afford such a stance. Whereas the upper limits of ethical standards for international activities are set by the individual standards of certain leading companies—or, more realistically, by the moral values of their top managers—it is more difficult to set the lower limits of those standards; that limit gets set by whether the laws are actually enforced in that location.

The bribery of officials is prohibited by law in all countries, but it still goes on as an accepted practice; often, it is the only way to get anything done. In such cases, the MNC managers have to decide which standard of behavior they will follow. What about the $100 bribe to get the computer off the rainy dock? William Norris says he told his managers to pay the $100 because to refuse would be taking things too far. Generally, Control Data did not yield to such pressure, though it said sales were lost as a result.[32]

A specific ethical issue for managers in the international arena is that of **questionable payments.** These are business payments that raise significant questions of appropriate moral behavior either in the host nation or in other nations. Such questions arise out of differences in laws, customs, and ethics in various countries, whether the payments in question are political payments, extortion, bribes, sales commissions, or "grease money"—payments to expedite routine transactions. Other common types of payments are made to speed the clearance of goods at ports of entry and to obtain required certifications. They are called different names in different countries: tokens of appreciation, *la mordida* (the bite, in Mexico), *bastarella* ("little envelope" in Italy), *pot-de-vin* (jug of wine in France). For the sake of simplicity, all these different types of questionable payments are categorized in this text as some form of bribery. In Mexico, for example, companies make monthly payments to the mail carriers or their mail gets "lost."

Most managers perceive bribery as "endemic in business and government in parts of Africa and south and east Asia. Corruption and bribery are considered to be part of the culture and environment of certain markets, and will not simply go away."[33] In some parts of Latin America, for example, customs officers are paid poorly and so are encouraged to take bribes to supplement their incomes. However, developed countries are not immune to bribery—as demonstrated in 2002 when several members of the International Olympic Committee were expelled for accepting bribes during Salt Lake City's campaign to host the 2002 Winter Olympics.

The dilemma for Americans operating abroad is how much to adhere to their own ethical standards in the face of foreign customs or how much to follow local ways to be competitive. Certainly, in some societies, gift giving is common to bind social and familial ties, and such gifts incur obligation. Nevertheless, a bribe is different from a gift or other reciprocation, and those involved know that by whether it has a covert nature. According to Noonan:

> *Bribery is universally shameful. There is not a country in the world that does not treat bribery as criminal on its books . . . . In no country do bribetakers speak publicly of their bribes, nor do bribegivers announce the bribes they pay. No newspaper lists them. No one advertises that he can arrange a bribe. No one is honored precisely because he is a big briber or bribee. No one writes an autobiography in which he recalls the bribes he has taken or paid . . . . Not merely the criminal law—for the transaction could have happened long ago and prosecution be barred by time—but an innate fear of being considered disgusting restrains briber and bribee from parading their exchange. Significantly, it is often the Westerner with ethnocentric prejudice who supposes that a modern Asian or African society does not regard the act of bribery as shameful in the way Westerners regard it.*[34]

However, Americans must be able to distinguish between harmless practices and actual bribery, between genuine relationships and those used as a cover-up. To help them distinguish, the **Foreign Corrupt Practices Act** (FCPA) of 1977 was established, which prohibits U.S. companies from making illegal payments, other gifts, or political contributions to foreign government officials for the purposes of influencing them in business transactions. The goal was to stop MNCs from contributing to corruption in foreign government and to upgrade the image of the United States and its companies operating overseas. The penalties include severe fines and sometimes imprisonment. Many managers feel the law has given them a more even playing field, and so they have been more willing to do business in certain countries where it seemed impossible to do business without bribery and kickbacks.

Since then, in 1997 the Organisation for Economic Co-operation and Development Convention on Bribery was signed by 36 countries in an attempt to combat corruption.[35] However, evidential problems continue to hinder prosecution. Unless there is a complaint or whistle-blowing, there are few avenues for regulators to ferret out incidents in bribery in corporations. Unfortunately, bribery continues, mostly on a small scale, where it often goes undetected. In any event, it is prudent (and hopefully honorable) for companies to set in place processes to minimize the risk of prosecution, including:

- Having a global compliance system which shows that employees have understood, and signed off on, the legal obligations regarding bribery and corruption in the countries where they do business.
- Making employees aware of the penalties and ramifications for lone actions, such as criminal sanctions.
- Having a system in place to investigate any foreign agents and overseas partners who will be negotiating contracts.
- Keeping an effective whistle-blowing system in place.[36]

As far as the actions that individual managers take when doing business overseas, if we agree that accepting or giving a bribe is always wrong, then our decisions as managers, salespersons, and so on are always clear, no matter where we are.

However, many businesspeople believe that it is just part of the cost of doing business in many countries to pay small bribes to get people simply to do their jobs and they are willing to engage in bribery as an everyday part of meeting their business objectives. Frequently corporate officials, in fact, avoid any moral issue by simply "turning a blind eye" to what goes on in subsidiaries. Some companies avoid these issues by hiring a local agent who takes care of the paperwork and pays all the so-called fees in return for a salary or consultant's fee. However, while the FCPA does allow "grease" payments to facilitate business in a foreign country, if those payments are lawful there, other payments prohibited by the FCPA remain subject to prosecution even if the company says it did not know that its agents or subsidiaries were making such payments—the so-called "reason to know" provision.

Critics of the FCPA contend that the law represents an ethnocentric attempt to impose U.S. standards on the rest of the world and puts U.S. firms at a competitive disadvantage. In any event, many feel that business activities that cannot stand scrutiny are clearly unethical, corrupt, and, in the long run, corrupting. Bribery fails three important tests of ethical corporate actions: (1) Is it legal? (2) Does it work (in the long run)? (3) Can it be talked about?[37]

Many MNCs have decided to confront concerns about ethical behavior and social responsibility by developing worldwide practices that represent the company's posture. Among those policies are the following:

- Develop worldwide codes of ethics.
- Build ethical policies into strategy development.
- Plan regular assessment of the company's ethical posture.
- If ethical problems cannot be resolved, withdraw from that market.

As an example, General Electric (GE) decided to take a hard line on corruption, electing to "level up, not down," and withdrawing from Nigeria and Russia when corruption was especially rife.[38] In fact, according to GE's Mr. Rice:

The firm's hard line on corruption is actually helping it win business in many developing countries. Increasingly they understand that corruption is a barrier to improving the standard of living of the poorest people and they want to do business more and more with an ethical firm.[39]

THE ECONOMIST,
September 20, 2008.

Making the Right Decision

How is a manager operating abroad to know what is the "right" decision when faced with questionable or unfamiliar circumstances of doing business? The first line of defense is to consult the laws of both the home and the host countries—such as the FCPA. If any of those laws would be violated, then you, the manager, must look to some other way to complete the business transaction, or withdraw altogether.

Second, you could consult the International Codes of Conduct for MNEs (see Exhibit 2-2). These are broad and cover various areas of social responsibility and ethical behavior; even so, many issues are subject to interpretation.

If legal consultation does not provide you with a clear answer about what to do, you should consult the company's code of ethics (if there is one). You, as the manager, should realize that you are not alone in making these kinds of decisions. It is also the responsibility of the company to provide guidelines for the actions and decisions made by its employees. In addition, you are not the first, and certainly not the last, to be faced with this kind of situation—which also sets up a collective experience in the company about what kinds of decisions your colleagues typically make in various circumstances. Those norms or expectations (assuming they are honorable) can supplement the code of ethics or substitute for the lack of a formal code. If your intended action runs contrary to the norms or the formal code, discontinue that plan.

If you are still unsure of what to do, you have the right and the obligation to consult your superiors. Unfortunately, often the situation is not that clear-cut, or your boss will tell you to "use your own judgment." Sometimes your superiors in the home office just want you to complete the transaction to the benefit of the company and don't want to be involved in what you have to do to consummate the deal.

If your dilemma continues, you must fall back upon your own moral code of ethics. One way to consider the dilemma is to ask yourself what the rights of the various stakeholders involved are (see Exhibit 2-1), and how you should weigh those rights. First, does the proposed action (rigged contract bid, bribe, etc.) harm anyone? What are the likely consequences of your decision in both the short run and long run? Who would benefit from your contemplated action? What are the benefits to some versus potential harm to others? In the case of a rigged contract bid through bribery, for example, people are put at a disadvantage, especially over the long term, with a pattern of this behavior. This is because, if competition is unfair, not only are your competitors harmed by losing the bid, but also the consumers of the products or services are harmed because they will pay more to attain them than they would under an efficient market system.

In the end, you have to follow your own conscience and decide where to draw the line in the sand in order to operate with integrity—otherwise the line moves further and further away with each transgression. In addition, what can start with a small bribe or cover-up here—a matter of personal ethics—can, over time, and in the aggregate of many people covering up, result in a situation of a truly negligent, and perhaps criminal, stance toward social responsibility to society, like that revealed by investigations of the tobacco industry in the United States. Indeed, executives are increasingly being held personally and criminally accountable for their decisions; this is true even for people operating on the board of directors of a company. Criminal charges were brought against 15 executives of WorldCom in 2003, for example, and the noose was thrown around the world after the Enron convictions in 2006 as international banks such as Citigroup and JP Morgan Chase were charged with taking part in sham deals to disguise Enron's financial problems.

Richard Rhodes, CEO of Rhodes Architectural Stone, Inc., is one executive who has drawn a line in the sand for himself and his company, and who holds himself and his employees accountable to a high moral standard when it comes to issues of bribery and human rights. He explains how they deal with difficult situations abroad in the accompanying Management Focus, "CEO Speaks Out: Ethics Abroad—Business Fundamentals, Value Judgments."

MANAGEMENT FOCUS

CEO Speaks Out: Ethics Abroad—Business Fundamentals, Value Judgments

You've just finished negotiating the deal, and it's time for a celebration, drinks and dinner all around, and you go to bed only to wake up the next morning to learn that the other side wants to start all over again.

Or, you try to buy something—say a collection of antique vessels for resale for decorative uses—and you're told that the artifacts are yours but only for a price. You wonder, should I agree to pay a bribe just this once?

So it goes sometimes when it comes to the business of doing business abroad, which has been the case for my company, Rhodes Architectural Stone, Inc., ever since its launch (under another name) in 1998. Ours is the business of buying artifacts slated for demolition in areas of the world, such as Africa, China, India, and Indonesia, and, in turn, selling to discriminating clients in the United States.

If there is one thing we've learned, it is that the ethical landscape is different in the third world. In the United States—notwithstanding the recent spate of corporate scandals that have set a woefully new low for ethical business behavior—the fact remains that standards do exist against which improprieties can be measured.

Not so in some other countries. The tenets that underlie our U.S. business language—that your word is your bond, that transparency is expected in joint ventures and contractual engagements, that each party walks away from the table getting as well as giving something—are not always understood in all parts of the world.

This inherent conflict between first- and third-world business standards has meant that our journey as a design-driven firm has been at times extremely difficult. A core value of the company, which we call "value in the round," meaning that value must be created for all parties in the deal, has involved familiarizing ourselves with an alien environment in order to establish business fundamentals. Needing to respect cultural differences must be carefully investigated and evaluated while all the time taking care not to cross the line to engage in practices we abhor.

Business Black and White

In short, in the world of grays that characterizes business dealings in countries in which ethics are at best rudimentary by U.S. standards, and at worst nonexistent, we've taken the position that we must establish a black and white.

Let me explain. Take the word "transparency," for example, which in the United States involves a baseline understanding of capitalism, allowing that each party is able to get something in a negotiation without necessarily having cheated another. With that common understanding, negotiators don't need to resort to taking money out of the game—bribing, to be precise—because all of the money is in the game.

Nor is there a need to have to renegotiate a deal that has already been agreed upon because of a belief that the deal that was struck couldn't be good—or why would the parties have agreed to it?

In countries whose business laws are nascent, if they exist at all, and whose thinking has been shaped by philosophies vastly different from our own, our first challenge is to take what I call the "entry-level" business players, who disproportionately populate the developing countries in which we do business, and bring them up to speed in the business fundamentals of the United States.

In the all-too-common instance of being asked that a deal be renegotiated, we see it as our duty to teach the fundamentals that underlie the business practices of the West, such as your word is your bond, and that, while it's all right to take as much time as you need to negotiate a deal, once you've agreed, you stand by it.

In the wake of a request to go back to the table after the celebratory dinner, for example, I begin by outlining what it's going to take for them to do business with us. We put it down in writing, even though I've learned that such documents are unenforceable. And, if they ask again to renegotiate, we walk.

In short, in a world in which business fundamentals are shades of gray, we've determined a black-and-white process that is our blueprint for doing business.

Moral Black and White

Back to the bribes: Simply put, we don't do them. In the case of our wanting to buy the collection of antique vessels, for example, we walked when told we would have to make such a payment. The good news in that case was that we were actually invited back a year later to make the purchase on our terms.

The matter of bribes, however, is more than just shall we or shall we not. It goes to the heart of the other issue underlying doing business in the third world, and that is the need for a way to respect cultural differences without crossing the line to engage in practices that are inappropriate or immoral by Western standards.

Looked at this way, Rhodes Architectural Stone not only draws the line at paying bribes, but also at child labor and the mistreatment of women. The matter of child labor will serve to illustrate the dilemma. Imagine an American entrepreneur, traveling in the bitter cold in the remote country-side dressed in a Gore-Tex® parka, Thinsulate socks, and the most comfortable and technologically advanced clothing money can buy. We arrive and state that we will not buy anything fabricated or procured with child labor. Now contrast that with the local reality of the labor of the entire family required to put bread on the table and a roof over one's head.

If my children were starving, I suppose I would do the same. In fact, our own forbearers in the United States did employ children in factories well into the twentieth century, and because of that, we don't have to do it any more.

Into this moral gray area, we've established another black and white: namely, that we cannot and will not do business with entities that engage in the practice of child labor, but we will not go the next step and preach. In other words, we will not tell them they are wrong.

Surely, we bring a powerful lever when it comes to backing up this moral stance. Unlike foreign companies that go into native countries to sell products to people who can't afford to buy them, we are there to buy what they have to sell. We bring the twin carrots of hard currency and jobs.

That advantage notwithstanding, the decision to establish a moral black and white wasn't easy. It's one thing to come to that imperative in the matter of formulating business standards where none exist, for that involves the neutral task of teaching. It's quite another to tread into territory in which the actions are criminal or immoral by Western standards and, yet, understandable within the context of the foreign culture.

The decision to do so, therefore, is actually a process, one of thought and reflection and, in the final analysis, leadership.

Putting it all Together

In coming to the imperatives that Rhodes Architectural Stone has determined for its business dealings overseas, I was fortunate to have the counsel of a member of our board, a former Whirlpool executive, who had extensive business experience throughout the world.

This individual taught me that when dealing with the grays that characterize the business landscape in the third world, it is necessary to establish a black and white, both for the way you will conduct business and account for your moral imperatives. And, if the reality differs considerably when you are actually at the table, it is necessary to be strong enough to walk away.

In sum, you must ask yourself questions such as: Who am I? How do I feel about this or that action? Can I sleep at night if I so engage in this or that behavior?

In the milieu of grays that characterizes the world beyond our oceans, be strong enough to formulate your black and whites, which, in turn, will become your guiding principles.

MANAGING INTERDEPENDENCE

Because multinational firms (or other organizations, such as the Red Cross) represent global interdependency, their managers at all levels must recognize that what they do, in the aggregate, has long-term implications for the socioeconomic interdependence of nations. Simply to describe ethical issues as part of the general environment does not address the fact that managers must control their activities at all levels—from simple, daily business transactions involving local workers, intermediaries, or consumers, to global concerns of ecological responsibility—for the future benefit of all concerned. Whatever the situation, the powerful long-term effects of MNC and MNE action (or inaction) should be planned for and controlled—not haphazardly considered part of the side effects of business. The profitability of individual companies depends on a cooperative and constructive attitude toward global interdependence.

Foreign Subsidiaries in the United States

Much of the preceding discussion has related to U.S. subsidiaries around the world. However, to globally highlight the growing interdependence and changing balance of business power, foreign subsidiaries in the United States should also be considered. Since much criticism about a lack of responsibility has been directed toward MNCs with headquarters in the United States, we must think of these criticisms from an outsider's perspective. The number of foreign subsidiaries in the United States has grown and continues to grow dramatically; **foreign direct investment (FDI)** in the United States by other countries is, in many cases, far more than U.S. investment outward. Americans are thus becoming more sensitive to what they perceive as a lack of control over their own country's business.

Things look very different from the perspective of Americans employed at a subsidiary of an overseas MNC. Interdependence takes on a new meaning when people "over there" are calling the shots regarding strategy, expectations, products, and personnel. Often, Americans' resentment about different ways of doing business by "foreign" companies in the United States inhibits cooperation, which gave rise to the companies' presence in the first place.

Today, managers from all countries must learn new ways, and most MNCs are trying to adapt. In Japan, corporate social responsibility has traditionally meant that companies take care of their employees, whereas in the United States the public and private sectors are expected to share the responsibility for the community. Part of the explanation for this difference is that U.S. corporations get tax deductions for corporate philanthropy, whereas Japanese firms do not; nor are Japanese managers familiar with community needs. For these and other reasons, Japanese subsidiaries in the United States have not been active in U.S. philanthropy.

Managing Subsidiary–Host-Country Interdependence

When **managing interdependence,** international managers must go beyond general issues of social responsibility and deal with the specific concerns of the MNC subsidiary–host-country relationship. Outdated MNC attitudes that focus only on profitability and autonomy are short-sighted and usually result in only short-term realization of those goals. MNCs must learn to accommodate the needs of other organizations and countries:

> *Interdependence rather than independence, and cooperation rather than confrontation are at the heart of that accommodation . . . the journey from independence to interdependence managed badly leads to dependence, and that is an unacceptable destination.*[40]

Most of the past criticism levied at MNCs has focused on their activities in LDCs. Their real or perceived lack of responsibility centers on the transfer in of inappropriate technology, causing unemployment, and the transfer out of scarce financial and other resources, reducing the capital available for internal development. In their defense, MNCs help LDCs by contributing new technology and managerial skills, improving the infrastructure, creating jobs, and bringing in investment capital from other countries by exporting products. The infusion of outside capital provides foreign-exchange earnings that can be used for further development. The host government's attitude is often referred to as a love–hate relationship: It wants the economic growth that MNCs can provide, but it does not want the incursions on national sovereignty or the technological dependence that may result. Most criticisms of MNC subsidiary activities, whether in less developed or more developed countries, are along the following lines:

1. MNCs locally raise their needed capital, contributing to a rise in interest rates in host countries.
2. The majority (sometimes even 100 percent) of the stock of most subsidiaries is owned by the parent company. Consequently, host-country people do not have much control over the operations of corporations within their borders.
3. MNCs usually reserve the key managerial and technical positions for expatriates. As a result, they do not contribute to the development of host-country personnel.
4. MNCs do not adapt their technology to the conditions that exist in host countries.
5. MNCs concentrate their research and development activities at home, restricting the transfer of modern technology and know-how to host countries.
6. MNCs give rise to the demand for luxury goods in host countries at the expense of essential consumer goods.

7. MNCs start their foreign operations by purchasing existing firms rather than by developing new productive facilities in host countries.

8. MNCs dominate major industrial sectors, thus contributing to inflation, by stimulating demand for scarce resources and earning excessively high profits and fees.

9. MNCs are not accountable to their host nations but only respond to home-country governments; they are not concerned with host-country plans for development.[41]

Specific MNCs have been charged with tax evasion, union busting, and interference in host-country politics. Of course, MNCs have both positive and negative effects on different economies. For every complaint about MNC activities (whether about capital markets, technology transfer, or employment practices), we can identify potential benefits (see Exhibit 2-6).

Numerous conflicts arise between MNC companies or subsidiaries and host countries, including conflicting goals (both economic and noneconomic) and conflicting concerns, such as the security of proprietary technology, patents, or information. Overall, the resulting trade-offs create an interdependent relationship between the subsidiary and the host government, based on relative bargaining power. The power of MNCs is based on their large-scale, worldwide economies, their strategic flexibility, and their control over technology and production location. The bargaining chips of the host governments include their control of raw materials and market access and their ability to set the rules regarding the role of private enterprise, the operation of state-owned firms, and the specific regulations regarding taxes, permissions, and so forth.

MNCs run the risk of their assets becoming hostage to host control, which may take the form of nationalism, protectionism, or governmentalism. Under **nationalism,** for example, public opinion is rallied in favor of national goals and against foreign influences. Under **protectionism,** the host institutes a partial or complete closing of borders to withstand competitive foreign products, using tariff and nontariff barriers, such as those used by Japan. Under **governmentalism,** the government uses its policy-setting role to favor national interests, rather

EXHIBIT 2-6   Potential Benefits and Costs to Host Countries of MNC Operations There[42]

Benefits	Costs
Capital Market Effects	
• Broader access to outside capital	• Risk sharing
• Economic growth	• Increased competition for local scarce capital
• Foreign-exchange earnings	• Increased interest rates as supply of local
• Import substitution effects allow governments to save foreign exchange for priority projects	capital decreases
	• Capital service effects of balance of payments
Technology and Production Effects	
• Access to new technology and R&D developments	• Technology is not always appropriate
• Employee training in new technology	• Plants are often for assembly only and can be dismantled
• Infrastructure development and support	• Government infrastructure investment is higher than expected benefits
• Export diversification	• Increased pollution
• Introduction of new management techniques	
Employment Effects	
• Direct creation of new jobs	• Limited skill development and creation
• Introduction of more humane employment standards	• Competition for scarce skills
• Opportunities for indigenous management development	• Low percentage of managerial jobs for local people
• Income multiplier effects on local community business	• Employment instability because of ability to move production operations freely to other countries

Source: Adapted from R. H. Mason and R. S. Spich, *Management: An International Perspective*, (202) (Homewood, IL: Irwin, 1987).

than relying on market forces, as illustrated by the actions of governments around the world to support their banking systems in 2008 and 2009.[43]

The intricacies of the relationship and the relative power of an MNC subsidiary and a host-country government are situation specific. Clearly, such a relationship should be managed for mutual benefit; a long-term, constructive relationship based on the MNC's socially responsive stance should result in progressive strategic success for the MNC and economic progress for the host country. The effective management of subsidiary–host-country interdependence must have a long-term perspective. Although temporary strategies to reduce interdependence via controls on the transnational flows by firms (for example, transfer-pricing tactics) or by governments (such as new residency requirements for skilled workers) are often successful in the short run, they result in inefficiencies that must be absorbed by one or both parties, with negative long-term results. In setting up and maintaining subsidiaries, managers are wise to consider the long-term trade-offs between strategic plans and operational management. By finding out for themselves the pressing local concerns and understanding the sources of past conflicts, they can learn from mistakes and recognize the consequences of the failure to manage problems. Furthermore, managers should implement policies that reflect corporate social responsibility regarding local economic issues, employee welfare, or natural resources. At the least, the failure to effectively manage interdependence results in constraints on strategy. In the worst case, it results in disastrous consequences for the local area, for the subsidiary, and for the global reputation of the company.

The interdependent nature of developing economies and the MNCs operating there is of particular concern when discussing social responsibility because of the tentative and fragile nature of the economic progression in those countries. MNCs must set a high moral standard and lay the groundwork for future economic development. At the minimum, they should ensure that their actions will do no harm. Some recommendations for MNCs operating in and doing business with developing countries are as follows:

1. Do no intentional harm. This includes respect for the integrity of the ecosystem and consumer safety.
2. Produce more good than harm for the host country.
3. Contribute by their activity to the host country's development.
4. Respect the human rights of their employees.
5. To the extent that local culture does not violate ethical norms, respect the local culture and work with and not against it.
6. Pay their fair share of taxes.
7. Cooperate with the local government in developing and enforcing just background (infrastructure) institutions (i.e., laws, governmental regulations, unions, and consumer groups, which serve as a means of social control).[44]

Managing Environmental Interdependence and Sustainability

International managers can no longer afford to ignore the impact of their activities on the environment. The demand for corporations to consider **sustainability** in their CSR plans comes from various stakeholders around the world. A generally accepted definition of **sustainable development** for business enterprises is that of . . .

> *adopting business strategies and activities that meet the needs of the enterprise and its stakeholders today, while protecting, sustaining and enhancing the human and natural resources that will be needed in the future.*[45]

JOURNAL OF SOCIO-ECONOMICS,
June 2008.

Existing literature generally agrees on three dimensions of sustainability: (1) economic, (2) social, and (3) environmental. A sustainable business has to take into account "the interests of future generations, biodiversity, animal protection, human rights, life cycle impacts, and principles like equity, accountability, transparency, openness, education and learning, and local action and scale."[46]

The dilemma for corporations is that they are faced with trying to meet two often contradictory requirements: (1) selling at low prices and (2) being environmentally and socially conscious. However, competitive pressures limit the company's ability to raise prices in order to cover the cost of socially responsible policies. This is obviously contradictory to the well-being of societies.[47]

The Coca-Cola Company in India, for example, is struggling to accommodate the rising concerns and protests from local farmers about the company's depletion of water resources. As reported on the PBS *Newshour*,[48] farmers are particularly angry in Kala Dera, in the drought-stricken state of Rajasthan. The Coca-Cola factory is one of 49 across India. The company has invested over $1 billion dollars building a market for its products in this country. The plant used about 900,000 liters of water in 2007, about a third of it for the soft drinks, the rest to clean bottles and machinery. It is drawn from wells at the plant but also from aquifers Coca-Cola shares with neighboring farmers. The water is virtually free to all users. The farmers say their problems began after the Coca-Cola factory arrived in 1999. According to the farmers:

> *Before, the water level was descending by about one foot per year. Now it's 10 feet every year. We have a 3.5-horsepower motor. We cannot cope. They (Coca-Cola) have a 50-horsepower pump.*

> PBS Newshour with Jim Lehrer,
> *November 17, 2008.*

Coca-Cola agreed to an independent third-party assessment of some of its operations in India, which confirmed that the Rajasthan plant is contributing to a worsening water situation. It recommended that the company bring water in from outside the area or shut the factory down. Coca-Cola rejected that recommendation. For his part, Coca-Cola's India head, Atul Singh, says it would be irresponsible to leave, saying that "walking away is the easiest thing we can do. That's not going to help that community build sustainability."[49] So Coca-Cola, while insisting its impact on the water supply was minimal, said it would stay and help. The company has agreed to subsidize one-third of the cost of water-efficient drip irrigation systems for 15 neighboring farmers. The government pays most of the rest; growers themselves must chip in 10 percent. Coca-Cola has also set up concrete collection systems for rainwater. The farmers remain skeptical. They also are critical of the government locally for attracting Coca-Cola to a water-scarce region and nationally for ignoring water policy in a rush to attract industry and foreign investment.[50]

This example makes clear to global managers that effectively managing environmental interdependence and sustainability includes considering ecological interdependence as well as the economic and social implications of MNC activities. There is an ever-increasing awareness of, and a mounting concern worldwide about, the effects of global industrialization on the natural environment. Government regulations and powerful interest groups are demanding ecological responsibility regarding the use of scarce natural resources and production processes that threaten permanent damage to the planet. MNCs have to deal with each country's different policies and techniques for environmental and health protection. Such variations in approach reflect different levels of industrialization, living standards, government–business relations, philosophies of collective intervention, patterns of industrial competition, and degrees of sophistication in public policy.

In recent years, the export of hazardous wastes from developed countries to less developed ones has increased considerably. E-waste—from electronic components, computers, and cell phones, for example, all of which are full of hazardous materials—has become a major problem for developing economies, producing sickness and deaths to their handlers there; this continues in spite of laws against such dumping by U.S. companies and others. Another instance was the dumping of over 8,000 drums of waste, including drums filled with polychlorinated biphenyl (PCB), a highly toxic compound, in Koko, Nigeria.[51] While not all dumping is illegal, the large international trade in hazardous wastes (as a result of the increasing barriers to domestic disposal) raises disturbing questions regarding social responsibility. Although the importer of waste must take some blame, it is the exporter who shoulders the ultimate responsibility for both generation and disposal. Often, companies choose to dispose of hazardous waste in less developed countries to take advantage of weaker regulations and lower costs. Until we have strict international regulation of trade in hazardous wastes, companies should take it upon themselves to monitor their activities, as Singh and Lakhan demand:

> *To export these wastes to countries which do not benefit from waste-generating industrial processes or whose citizens do not have lifestyles that generate such wastes is unethical. It is especially unjust to send hazardous wastes to lesser-developed countries which lack the technology to minimize the deleterious effects of these substances.*[52]

The exporting of pesticides poses a similar problem, with the United States and Germany being the main culprits. The United States exports about 200 million pounds of pesticides each year that are prohibited, restricted, or not registered for use in the United States. One MNC, Monsanto Chemical Corporation, for example, sells DDT to many foreign importers, even though its use in the United States has been essentially banned. Apart from the lack of social responsibility toward the people and the environment in the countries that import DDT, this action is also irresponsible to U.S. citizens because many of their fruits and meat products are imported from those countries.

These are only two of the environmental problems facing countries and large corporations today. According to Graedel and Allenby, the path to truly sustainable development is for corporations to broaden their concept of industrial ecology:

> *The concept [of industrial ecology] requires that an industrial system be viewed not in isolation from its surrounding systems, but in concert with them. It is a systems view in which one seeks to optimize the total materials cycle from virgin material, to finished material, to component, to product, to obsolete product, and to ultimate disposal.*[53]

Essentially, this perspective supports the idea that environmental citizenship is necessary for a firm's survival as well as responsible social performance.

It is clear, then, that MNCs must take the lead in dealing with ecological interdependence by integrating goals of sustainability into strategic planning. Along with an investment appraisal, a project feasibility study, and operational plans, such planning should include an environmental impact assessment. At the least, MNC managers must deal with the increasing scarcity of natural resources in the next few decades by (1) looking for alternative raw materials, (2) developing new methods of recycling or disposing of used materials, and (3) expanding the use of by-products.[54]

Multinational corporations already have had a tremendous impact on foreign countries, and this impact will continue to grow and bring about long-lasting changes. Even now, U.S. MNCs alone account for about 10 percent of the world's gross national product (GNP). Because of interdependence at both the local and global level, it is not only moral but also in the best interest of MNCs to establish a single clear posture toward social and ethical responsibilities worldwide and to ensure that it is implemented. In a real sense, foreign firms enter as guests in host countries and must respect the local laws, policies, traditions, and culture as well as those countries' economic and developmental needs.

CONCLUSION

When research findings and anecdotal evidence indicate differential attitudes toward ethical behavior and social responsibility across cultures, MNCs must take certain steps. For example, they must be careful when placing a foreign manager in a country whose values are incongruent with his or her own because this could lead to conflicts with local managers, governmental bodies, customers, and suppliers. As discussed earlier, expatriates should be oriented to the legal and ethical ramifications of questionable foreign payments, the differences in environmental regulations, and the local expectations of personal integrity. They should also be supported as they attempt to integrate host-country behaviors with the expectations of the company's headquarters.

Social responsibility, ethical behavior, and interdependence are important concerns to be built into management control—not as afterthoughts but as part of the ongoing process of planning and controlling international operations for the long-term benefit of all.

Part II focuses on the pervasive and powerful influence of culture in the host-country environment in which the international manager operates. Chapter 3 examines the nature of culture—what are its various dimensions and roots? How does culture affect the behavior and expectations of employees, and what are the implications for how managers operating in other countries should behave?

Summary of Key Points

1. The concept of international social responsibility (known in business circles as CSR—corporate social responsibility) includes the expectation that MNCs should be concerned about the social and economic effects of their decisions on activities in other countries, and should build appropriate provisions into their strategic plans to deal with those potential effects.

2. Moral universalism refers to the need for a moral standard that is accepted around the world; however, varying cultural attitudes and business practices make this goal

unattainable at this time. A number of groups of corporations within industries have collaborated on sets of policies for CSR both for their companies and those in their supply chains. Such collaborations help to raise the standard in host countries and to level the playing field for managers within those industries.

3. Concerns about MNC social responsibility revolve around issues of human rights in other countries.. Many organizations develop codes of conduct that specifically deal with human rights in their operations around the world.

4. International business ethics refers to the conduct of MNCs in their relationships to all individuals and entities with whom they come into contact. Ethical behavior is judged and based largely on the cultural value system and the generally accepted ways of doing business in each country or society. MNC managers must decide whether to base their ethical standards on those of the host country or those of the home country and whether these different standards can be reconciled.

5. MNCs must balance their responsibility to various stakeholders, such as owners, creditors, consumers, employees, suppliers, governments, and societies. Firms with a long-term perspective recognize the need to consider all of their stakeholders in their business plans.

6. Managers operating abroad are often faced with differing attitudes towards bribery or other payments that raise significant questions about appropriate moral behavior in either the host nation or other nations, and yet frequently are demanded to conduct business. The Foreign Corrupt Practices Act prohibits most questionable payments by U.S. companies doing business in other countries.

7. Managers must control their activities relative to interdependent relationships at all levels—from simple, daily business transactions involving local workers, intermediaries, or consumers to global concerns of ecological responsibility. Issues of "sustainability" have come to the forefront as firms consider their long-term relationships with host countries.

8. The failure to effectively manage interdependence will result in constraints on strategy, in the least, or in disastrous consequences for the local area, the subsidiary, and the global reputation of the company.

9. Managing environmental interdependence includes the need to consider ecological interdependence as well as the economic and social implications of MNC activities.

10. The MNC–host-country relationship is generally a love–hate relationship from the host country's viewpoint in that it wants the economic growth that the MNC can provide but does not want the dependency and other problems that result.

Discussion Questions

1. Discuss the concept of CSR. What role does it play in the relationship between a company and its host country?
2. Discuss the criticisms that have been leveled against MNCs in the past regarding their activities in less developed countries. What counterarguments are there to those criticisms?
3. What does moral universalism mean? Discuss your perspective on this concept. Do you think the goal of moral universalism is possible? Is it advisable?
4. What do you think should be the role of MNCs toward human rights issues in other countries? What are the major human rights concerns at this time? What ideas do you have for dealing with these problems? What is the role of corporate codes of conduct in dealing with these concerns?
5. What is meant by international business ethics? Should the local culture affect ethical practices? What are the implications of local norms for ethical decisions by MNC managers?
6. As a manager in a foreign subsidiary, how can you reconcile local expectations of questionable payments with the Foreign Corrupt Practices Act? What is your stance on the problem of "payoffs?" How does the degree of law enforcement in a particular country affect ethical behavior in business?
7. Explain what is meant by managing interdependence in the global business arena. Discuss the love–hate relationship between MNCs and host countries.
8. What do you think are the responsibilities of MNCs toward the global environment? Give some examples of MNC activities that run counter to the concepts of ecological interdependence and sustainability.
9. Discuss the ethical issues that have developed regarding the use of IT in cross-border transactions. What new conflicts have developed since the printing of this book? What solutions can you suggest?

Application Exercise

1. Do some research to determine the codes of conduct of two MNCs. Compare the issues that they cover and share your findings with the class. After several students have presented their findings, prepare a chart showing the commonalities and differences of content in the codes presented. How do you account for the differences?

Experiential Exercise

Consider the ethical dilemmas in the following situation and decide what you would do. Then meet in small groups of students and come to a group consensus. Discuss your decisions with the class.

I am CEO of an international trading company in Turkey. One state-owned manufacturing company (Company A) in one of the Middle East countries opened a tender for 15,000 tons PVC granule K value

70. Company A makes all its purchases through tenders. For seven years in that market, my company has never been able to do any business with Company A (though we have sold many bulk materials to other state-owned companies in that market). One of our new managers had a connection with the purchasing manager of Company A, who promised to supply us with all of our competitors' bids if we pay him a 2 percent commission on all of our sales to his company. Our area manager accepted this arrangement. He got the competing bids, made our offer, and we got the tender. I learned of this situation when reviewing our income and expenses chart, which showed the 2 percent commission.

What shall I do, given the following: (1) If I refuse to accept the business without any legitimate reasons (presently there are none) my company will be blacklisted in that country—where we get about 20 percent of our gross yearly profit. (2) If I accept the business and do not pay the 2 percent commission, the purchasing manager will make much trouble for us when he receives our shipment. I am sure that he will not release our 5 percent bank guarantee letter about the quality and quantity of the material. (3) If I accept the business and pay the 2 percent commission, it will go against everything I have achieved in the 30 years of my career.

You have three ethical problems here: First, your company has won a rigged bid. Second, you must pay the person who rigged it or he will make life miserable for you. Third, you have to decide what to do with the area manager who accepted this arrangement.

SOURCE: J. Delaney and D. Sockell, "Ethics in the Trenches," *Across the Board* (October 1990): 17.

Internet Resources

Visit the Deresky Companion Website at www.pearsonhighered.com/deresky for this chapter's Internet resources.

CASE STUDY

Nike's CSR Challenge

IN 2005 NIKE returned to reporting on its social and environmental practices after a couple of years of silence due to legal concerns. The sports and clothing company is very important to countries such as Vietnam, where it is the largest private-sector employer with more than 50,000 workers producing shoes through subcontractors.[1] Nike's new report makes sobering reading, as it describes widespread problems in Asian factories. The company said it audited hundreds of factories in 2003 and 2004 and found cases of abusive treatment in more than a quarter of its South Asian plants. For example, between 25% and 50% of the factories in the region restrict access to toilets and drinking water during the workday. The same percentage of factories deny workers at least one day off in seven. In more than half of Nike's factories employees work more than 60 hours per week. In up to 25%, workers refusing overtime were punished. Wages were below the legal minimum at up to 25% of factories.[2]

For the first time in a major corporate report the details of all the factories were published. The report was significant for this transparency and being so candid about the problems that workers for Nike still face, and therefore the challenges that remain for the management. The NGOs working on these issues know that Nike is not alone in facing such problems. Indeed, they realise that the company has invested more in improving conditions than many of its competitors. Studies of voluntary corporate attempts at improving labor standards in global supply chains have suggested that they are delivering widespread improvements, and instead new approaches are needed that engage governments, NGOs, and local businesses.[3]

This realization has led to a new strategy from Nike. In May Nike's Vice President of Corporate Responsibility, Hannah Jones, told delegates at the Ethical Trading Initiative (ETI) conference that, whereas the company had previously been looking into how to solve problems for themselves, now they are exploring how to create systemic change in the industry. She explained that "premium brands are in a lonely leadership position" because "consumers are not rewarding us" for investments in improved social performance in supply chains. Like other companies, they have realized that the responsibility of one is to work towards the accountability of all. Consequently, one of Nike's new corporate citizenship goals is "to effect positive, systemic change in working conditions within the footwear, apparel and equipment industries." This involves the company engaging labor ministries, civil society and competitors around the world to try to raise the bar so that all companies have to attain better standards of social and environmental performance. One example is its involvement in the Multi-Fibre Agreement (MFA) Forum to help countries, unions and others plan for the consequences of the end of the MFA.

This new strategy is beyond what many consultants, media commentators and academics currently understand. By claiming to be an advance in thinking, an article in *The Economist* in May, by the worldwide managing director of McKinsey & Company, illustrated the limits of current consulting advice. It suggested that seeking good societal relations should be seen as both good for society and good for profitability. "Profits should not be seen as an end in themselves," suggested Ian Davis, "but rather as a signal from society that their company is succeeding in its mission of providing something people want."[4] However, those who have experience working in this field for some years, including Nike realise that, however we may wish to talk about the compatibility of profits with people and planet, the current societal frameworks for business are not making this a reality. The implication is that we have to make this so by changing those frameworks.

The key strategic shift for Nike's management is that they no longer regard the company as a closed system. Instead, they understand its future depends on the way customers, suppliers, investors, regulators and others relate to it. Their challenge is to reshape the signals being given out by those groups to itself and its competitors, so that the company can operate in a sustainable and just way, which is also financially viable.

Nike's experience is pertinent to other companies, whose voluntary efforts are failing to address the root causes of the problems associated with their industry. Unilever, for example, was criticised by ActionAid for profiting from worsening conditions for workers on plantations.[5] Falling prices have led to plantations laying off workers and wages going unpaid—a trend that has seen a consequent increase in attacks against owners and managers. Applying a systems view to the situation would suggest that Unilever reconsider how it influences the global political economy that is driving down prices for tea.

The challenge is not only one of strategy but also leadership. Traditionally, analysts and educators on corporate leadership have assumed that it involves leading people towards the goal of their employer, the company. In May an article on leadership in Conference Board Canada's *Organizational Performance Review* quoted the thoughts of leaders from World War II and the Korean War.[6] This reflects what Mark Gerzon describes as a focus on "leadership within borders", when what the world needs is "leaders beyond borders."[7] This means people who can see across borders created by others, such as the borders of their job, and reach across such borders to engage others in dialogue and action to address systemic problems. We could call this "transcending leadership," which was alluded to by James McGregor Burns, in his path-breaking book *Leadership*.[8] It is a form of leadership that transcends the boundaries of one's professional role and the limits of one's own situation to engage people on collective goals. It is a form of leadership that transcends a limited conception of self, as the individual leader identifies with ever-greater wholes. It is a form of leadership that transcends the need for a single leader, by helping people to transcend their limited states of consciousness and concern and inspire them to lead.

Perhaps the best modern example of transcending leadership is Gandhi, who aroused and elevated the hopes and demands of millions of Indians and whose life and personality were enhanced in the process. It is an irony of our times that this anti-imperialist who chose to spin his own cloth could be an inspiration for the future direction of executives in large companies sourcing clothes from factories across Asia. Gandhi called on us to understand our connectedness to "all that lives", and identify with ever-greater wholes. There is a lesson here for Nike and others. The apparel sector is an open system, and so wider issues of trade flows, governance, media, financial markets and politics impact on the potential of the sector, and thus Nike, to become sustainable and just. Without changes to the financial markets, Nike may find its efforts are in vain.

References

1. www.csr-asia.com/index.php?p=1925
2. www.csr-asia.com/index.php?p=1855
3. BSR and PWC, "Public Sector Support for the Implementation of Corporate Social Responsibility (CSR) in Global Supply Chains: Conclusions From Practical Experience" (2004); bsr.org/Meta/BSR_worldbankscm.pdf.
4. Ian Davis, "The Biggest Contract," *The Economist*, 26 May 2005.
5. www.mallenbaker.net/csr/nl/82.html

6. Jeffrey Gandz, "Leadership Character and Competencies," Organizational Performance Review, Spring/ Summer 2005 (Conference Board Canada).

7. M. Gerzon, Leaders beyond Borders (2004); www.mediatorsfoundation.org.

8. J. M. Burns, *Leadership* (New York: Harper & Row, 1978).

Source: **"Nike Says Time to Team Up,"** *The Journal of Corporate Citizenship*, **Autumn 2005, i19 p. 10(3).** By Jem Bendell. Auckland University of Technology, Director, Lifeworth. COPYRIGHT 2005 Greenleaf Publishing, reprinted with permission.

Case Questions

1. In referring to the opening profile and the closing case for this chapter, discuss the challenges regarding corporate social responsibility that companies in the apparel industry face in its supply chains around the world?

2. Discuss the meaning and implications of the statement by a Nike representative that "consumers are not rewarding us for investments in improved social performance in supply chains."

3. What does it mean to have an industry open-systems approach to social responsibility? What parties are involved? Who are the stakeholders?

4. What is meant by "leadership beyond borders"?

5. Is it possible to have "a compatibility of profits with people and planet"? Whose responsibility is it to achieve that state?

PART I: Comprehensive Cases

ICMR
Center for
Management Research

CASE 1 THE BRIBERY SCANDAL AT SIEMENS AG

"Based on our investigation so far, we have reason to suspect that Siemens ran 'black accounts' . . . that allowed it to open new markets through secret payments to potential and existing business partners."[1]

–JEANETTE BALMER,
A spokeswoman for the office of the Swiss federal prosecutor, in 2006.

"Many people within Siemens knew about the method of payment. Getting a contract isn't easy."[2]

–HORST VIGENER,
Former Siemens employee convicted in a bribery case, in 2007.

"What hopefully will come out of the Siemens affair . . . is that senior business leaders, when they see what happens to Siemens in terms of fines and the lost reputation of individuals like von Pierer or Kleinfeld, is that they will say 'OK, we need to start taking this seriously'."[3]

–JERMYN BROOKS,
Director of private sector programs at Transparency International, in 2007.

Introduction

In December 2008, the Munich, Germany-based Siemens AG agreed to pay fines to the tune of €1 billion towards settlement of corruption charges that had hit the company since 2006. This included a record US$800 million fine imposed by the U.S. authorities and another €395 million imposed by German authorities. This €1 billion was in addition to the billions of euro that it paid in fines, back taxes, and late interest charges by 2007.[4] Peter Loescher (Loescher), who joined as the CEO of Siemens in 2007 following the major bribery scandal that broke out in the company, said, "We regret what happened in the past. But we have learned from it and taken appropriate measures. Siemens is now a stronger company."[5]

On May 14, 2007, a German court convicted two former managers of Siemens AG for diverting the company's money to bribe employees of Enel SpA,[6] an Italian energy company.[7] Both the former managers admitted that they had bribed employees at Enel who had demanded money in return for contracts. They also said that they had not done anything wrong as they did it for the benefit of the company and not for any personal gain. Moreover, they said there was no other way to win contracts in several countries abroad where bribing for contracts was a common practice.

Earlier, in late 2006, another scandal had surfaced in the telecommunications division of Siemens involving slush funds[8] created to bribe foreign officials to secure contracts abroad. In still another case, Siemens was accused by IG Metall,[9] a dominant labor union in Germany, of having tried to bribe a small union called AUB to gain support for its policies. Siemens was also being probed in several other countries like Italy, Switzerland, Greece, and the US for possible misconduct. Analysts said that the bribery scandals at Siemens reflected the ethical costs of intense competition in global markets. Companies were resorting to underhand payments to win contracts. In several developing countries it was common practice to take money from companies in return for contracts, it was said. The companies themselves considered it as a business cost.

In the light of the number of scandals that rocked Siemens in a short span of time, questions were raised as to how the top management had failed to notice such a deep network of embezzlement involving huge amounts of money. The crisis ultimately led to the exit of the chairman of Siemens' supervisory board,

Author Information:
This case was written by **Bharath Krishna**, under the direction of **Rajiv Fernando**, ICMR (Updated by **Debapratim Purkayastha** in March 2009). It was compiled from published sources, and is intended to be used as a basis for class discussion rather than to illustrate either effective or ineffective handling of a management situation.

[1] Michael Pohl, "Siemens Investigation Yields 5 Arrests," www.boston.com, November 16, 2006.
[2] "Former Siemens Managers Admit to Paying Bribes for Contracts," www.dw-world.de, March 13, 2007.
[3] Associated Press, "Questions Linger after Bribery Scandal Claims Pair of Siemens Executives," www.iht.com, May 03, 2007.
[4] Heide B. Malhotra, "Siemens Looks for New Beginning after Bribery Scandals," http://en.epochtimes.com, March 27, 2008.
[5] "Siemens Bribery Fines Top 1 Billion Euros," www.dw-world.de, December 15, 2008.

[6] Enel SpA (Enel) was Italy's largest power company. Enel produced and sold electricity mostly in Europe, North, and Latin America. Enel was one of the largest distributors and vendors of natural gas in Italy, with a 12% market share. The company's revenues stood at 38.5 billion euros for the year 2006. (Source: www.enel.it).
[7] "Former Siemens Managers Convicted of Paying Bribes," www.dw-world.de, May 14, 2007.
[8] A slush fund is an auxiliary monetary account or a reserve fund. The term is commonly used in the context of corrupt dealings (such as bribery or graft) by governments, large corporations or other bodies and individuals.
[9] IG Metall is one of the dominant metalworkers' unions in Germany. It has nearly 2.4 million members in Germany. IG Metall represents both blue-collar and white-collar workers. (Source: www.wikipedia.org).

Heinrich von Pierer and its then-CEO, Klaus Kleinfeld. Though they were not directly implicated in the scandals, the new board chairman said that the leadership change had been made to give the company a clean break from the past.

Critics felt that Kleinfeld should not have been replaced, since he had been instrumental in bringing back Siemens into profit. Kleinfeld had often been dubbed "the Jack Welch of Germany," and his exit raised questions about the role of supervisory boards in the management of German companies. According to the Co-determination law or *Mitbestimmung* in Germany (Refer to Exhibit I for a note on Germany's Co-determination law or *Mitbestimmung*), every company had to have a two-tier system of management, in which the supervisory board consisting of labor representatives oversaw the management board. This system often led to collusion between management and labor representatives, and some critics felt it needed a thorough overhauling.

Background Note

Siemens was initially started as Telegraphen-Bauanstalt von Siemens & Halske in 1847 by Werner von Siemens (Werner) and a mechanical engineer, Johann Georg Halske. In 1853, the company won its first international contract to build a telegraph network that stretched around 10,000 kilometers and provide maintenance services for it, in Russia. In 1855, Werner set up subsidiaries in Russia and Britain to serve the growing opportunities for the company outside Germany and entrusted their responsibility to his brothers. In 1865, the British subsidiary was renamed Siemens Brothers.

In 1866, Werner discovered the dynamo-electric principle and got the necessary patents in Germany and Britain to enable the company to cash in on the invention. In the late 1870s, power engineering began to develop rapidly in Germany with the advent of electric railways, electric street lighting, electric elevators, electric tramways, etc. In order to prepare the company to meet these growing business opportunities, Siemens & Halske concentrated on retaining qualified and reliable employees. The company shared its profits with its employees through stock options. A pension fund was created for the benefit of employees and their families. The company introduced the concept of fixed working hours per day. It also started focusing on training its employees for specific jobs and career progression.

Siemens & Halske was successful in setting up foreign branches in all the key markets during the 1870s. Werner retired from active management of the company in 1890 and was succeeded by his sons who looked after the management of the company together with Werner's brother. The company progressed strongly especially in the area of rail transport. In Budapest, it built Europe's first underground rail line, opened in 1896. In 1903,

EXHIBIT I   A Note on the Co-Determination Law or *Mitbestimmung*

In Europe, participation of workers in management decision making was an established idea that gained momentum after World War II. The idea evolved into laws in several European countries. On similar lines, the Co-determination law or *Mitbestimmung* (a German word literally meaning "a voice in") was enacted in Germany in 1976 to provide a greater role for employees in the management of companies.[10] The law advocated a two-tier system of management (i.e., a supervisory board above the management board in every registered company). The supervisory board normally consisted of 20 non-executive directors, and was meant to oversee the management board in the two-tier system. The law required the representation of employees on the supervisory board. Any company with more than 2,000 employees was required to reserve half the seats of its supervisory board for labor representatives.[11]

This system was praised across the world in the initial years for the stability it brought to German companies. Those who supported the law said that it created a consensus-driven culture in corporate Germany that helped the country recover strongly from the devastating effects of the two world wars and hyperinflation to emerge as an economic power. Even critics who faulted the law on the grounds that it led to corruption and bribery agreed that the two levels helped demarcate and define corporate responsibilities more clearly than the single company board. However, in the opinion of many experts, the law had become irrelevant and needed a thorough overhauling. With managements needing to get the supervisory boards' approval for their new plans and strategies, they often simply bribed labor representatives to get their way. Therefore, rather than representing labor fairly, the labor representatives just lined their own pockets. Nowhere else in Europe was the labor and management hand in glove like this, and the Co-determination law was seen as the cause.

Compiled from various sources.

[10]Benjamin Weinthal, "Where Is the German Trade Union Movement and Where Is It Going?" http://mrzine.monthlyreview.org, February 21, 2007.
[11]Richard Milne, "Germany's Two-Tier Governance System Comes under Fire," http://us.ft.com, May 08, 2007.

Siemens & Halske acquired Elektrizitats-Aktiengesellschaft vorm Schuckert & Co. and merged it with its own power engineering unit to form Siemens-Schuckertwerke GmbH, which oversaw all areas of electrical engineering.

By 1914, Siemens & Halske was one of the largest companies of Germany with a workforce of 82,000 employees. However, World War I had a devastating impact on the company's businesses. It lost most of its foreign assets and its patent rights were expropriated. The company was forced to reorganize its manufacturing operations and foreign businesses. Carl von Siemens, one of Werner's sons, undertook several initiatives to reorganize all the businesses of Siemens & Halske in such a way that individual areas of business were assigned to specialized subsidiaries and related companies, while maintaining a consistent corporate identity across the subsidiaries.

Again in 1945, Germany's political, military, and economic collapse during the World War II led to the closure of many plants of Siemens & Halske in Germany. By the time the war came to an end, the greater part of the company's buildings and industrial installations had been destroyed and the company had suffered huge losses. Siemens & Halske started reconstructing its businesses in 1946 after the war was over, with manufacturing programs focusing on public services and utilities like rail network, postal service, power generation, etc. Due the political uncertainty prevailing in Berlin, Siemens & Halske relocated its headquarters to Munich in 1949.

Though the company recovered its domestic business fast, businesses outside Germany took a long time to recover. In 1966, Siemens & Halske, Siemens-Schuckertwerke AG and Siemens-Reiniger-Werke AG merged to form Siemens AG; this was prompted by the growing convergence of the power engineering and communications engineering sectors. The move helped to build a stronger position for Siemens in the global market in later years. In 1969, the entire company's business was reorganized into 6 operating groups, and this structure remained in place until 1990, when Siemens was comprehensively reorganized again. The primary objective of the new round of restructuring was to divide the company's large business units into smaller entities that would be better equipped to operate successfully in an increasingly complex global market.

In 1990, the largest European company in the computer industry, Siemens-Nixdorf Informationssysteme AG (SNI), was created. In 1998, Siemens acquired Westinghouse's fossil power plant activities in the U.S. so as to boost its earnings in the power generation sector through increased business volume and extensive synergy benefits. In an effort to build a stronger position in the US, the world's largest market for electrical and electronic products, Siemens obtained a listing on the New York Stock Exchange in 2001. In 2006, Siemens purchased Bayer Diagnostics which was added to its Medical Solutions Diagnostics division officially on January 1, 2007. In April 2007, the Fixed Networks, Mobile Networks and Carrier Services divisions of Siemens merged with Nokia's Network Business Group in a 50:50 joint venture, creating a fixed and mobile network company called Nokia Siemens Networks.

Before 2008, the operations of Siemens could be divided into six major business areas namely Information and Communications, Automation and Control, Power, Transportation, Medical, Lighting. In addition, the company also had a presence in the areas of Financing and Real Estate. As of early 2009, as part of changes brought about in January 1, 2008, the company was divided into three sectors and 15 divisions (Refer to Exhibit IIa and Exhibit IIb for more information on various business activities of Siemens). Siemens was one of the largest electrical engineering companies in the world, with operations in nearly 190 countries and 400,000 employees around the world, as of early 2009.[12] During the fiscal year 2008 (ended on September 30), the revenues of the company stood at €77.34 billion.[13] (Refer to Exhibit III for more details on the financials of Siemens).

EXHIBIT II(A)   Major Business Activities of Siemens (before 2008)

#	Business Area	Sub-area
1	Information and Communications	-
2	Automation and Control	Automation and Devices
		Industrial Solutions and Services
		Siemens Building Technologies
3	Power	Power generation
		Power Transmission and Distribution
4	Transportation	Transportation Systems
		Siemens VDO Automotive
5	Medical Solutions	-
6	Lighting	-
7	Financing and Real Estate	Siemens Financial Services
		Siemens Real Estate

Source: www.siemens.com.

[12] www.siemens.com.
[13] www.hoovers.com.

EXHIBIT II(B) Major Business Activities of Siemens (As of 2009)

#	Sectors	Divisions
1.	Industry	Industry Automation
		Motion Control
		Business Technologies
		Osram
		Industry Solutions
		Mobility
2.	Energy	Fossil Power Generation
		Renewable Energy
		Oil & Gas
		Service Rotating Equipment
		Power Transmission
		Power Distribution
3.	Healthcare	Imaging & IT
		Workflow & Solutions
		Diagnostics

Source: www.siemens.com.

EXHIBIT III Income Statement of Siemens: 2004–08

(All figures in billions of Euro except per share amounts)

	September 2008	September 2007	September 2006	September 2005	September 2004
Revenue	77.33	78.89	87.33	75.44	75.17
Cost of Goods Sold	56.28	74.86	63.82	53.5	53.52
Gross Profit	21.04	4.04	23.51	21.94	21.64
Gross Profit Margin (%)	27.2	5.1	26.9	29.1	28.8
SG&A Expense	15.34	−4.63	17.28	15.42	15.44
Depreciation & Amortization	3.21	3.75	3.01	3.42	3.34
Operating Income	2.49	4.91	3.22	3.09	2.86
Operating Margin (%)	3.2	6.2	3.7	4.1	3.8
Nonoperating Income	0.96	−1.67	1.19	1.12	1.37
Nonoperating Expenses	0.83	–	.04	0.03	–
Income Before Taxes	2.87	3.25	4.37	4.18	4.23
Income Taxes	1.02	0.96	1.08	0.97	0.66
Net Income After Taxes	1.86	2.29	3.29	10.52	9.08
Continuing Operations	1.86	2.06	3.09	3.20	3.57
Discontinued Operations	4.03	0.35	−0.05	−0.81	–
Total Operations	5.89	2.42	3.03	2.24	3.4
Total Net Income	5.89	2.42	3.03	2.24	3.4
Net Profit Margin (%)	7.6	3.1	3.5	3	4.5
Diluted EPS from Total Net Income (€)	–	2.68	3.26	2.42	–
Dividends per Share	1.27	1.03	1.02	1.06	0.88

Source: www.hoovers.com.

A Series of Scandals Rocks Siemens

Slush funds to win contracts abroad

On November 15, 2006, around 30 offices and private homes related to Siemens and its employees were raided by some 200 police officers, tax inspectors and prosecutors in Munich, and other cities of Germany, to probe suspicions of bribery, embezzlement of company funds and tax evasion.[14] Five Siemens employees were taken into custody in connection with the case. Swiss prosecutors were also involved in the raids, as part of their independent investigations launched in 2005, against three people connected to Siemens.[15] Siemens acknowledged that certain company employees were engaged in fraud and the damage to the company because of this fraud could be around €10–30 million.[16] As the probe continued, the scandal deepened and the estimate of the total cash used in suspect payments increased to €200 million from €10–30 million, and finally the figure touched €420 million.[17]

The €420 million of illegal payments dated back to 1999 and were made over a period of about seven years. Siemens said that it was working with the investigators to trace whether there was a valid business purpose and to ascertain the exact recipients of the payments. Apart from damaging the reputation of the company, the fraud also impacted the financials of Siemens. The company announced on December 11, 2006 that because of the fraud it was burdened with additional income tax charges of €168 million since 1999 from when the payments were suspected to be made. As a result, in the financial results it released in November 2006, Siemens was forced to restate the net profit of the company for the 2006 fiscal year, which ended on September 30, 2006, down to €3.033 billion from €3.106 billion.[18]

In connection with this case a former board executive of Siemens, Thomas Ganswindt, who was allegedly aware of some of the suspect transactions, was also arrested. According to some reports, the suspicious payments were shown to be made to external consultants for Siemens, whereas they were actually made to secure contracts in the fixed line telecommunications business in various international markets. Bribes were suspected to have been paid to purchasing officials in Italy, Puerto Rico, Greece, the U.S., and several other countries. However the exact routing of the embezzled money remained to be traced through the investigation process. The bribery scandal raised concerns for the company under the legislations of several other countries like the US, Italy, Greece, etc. For example, the late Sani Abacha, the former Nigerian leader, and some of his intermediaries were suspected to be involved in contracts for the security

system for the 2004 Olympic Games in Athens, Greece. An investigation into this was launched in Greece.[19] In the U.S., the U.S. Securities and Exchange Commission[20] (SEC) and the U.S. Department of Justice[21] (DOJ) had launched an investigation to find out whether Siemens breached any American laws, in April 2007.[22]

Analysts felt that Siemens ought to have woken up to the suspicious nature of the transactions earlier, as there were several early warning signs that everything was not above board. For instance, the bank accounts of some Siemens employees in Liechtenstein[23] were seized in 2004 on suspicion that they were used for fraudulent payments.[24] In August 2005, it came to the company's notice that some bank accounts in Geneva, Switzerland, held by a former Siemens employee, had been seized. In June 2006, the company also became aware of the existence of an escrow account[25] in Switzerland held by one of its employees. In July 2006, Siemens requested the trustee of the account to provide documentation of the account and to transfer the funds to the company.[26] The €420 million bribery scandal itself came to light through an anonymous complaint to the company and requests for judicial assistance from Switzerland and Italy because of suspected fraud in Siemens' units there. Given this background, Siemens could have mitigated the damage to its reputation internationally by taking proactive measures to set things straight.

Siemens charged for bribing employee representatives

On February 14, 2007, authorities in Nuremberg, Germany, raided several Siemens offices following allegations that the company was involved in bribing employee representatives to secure their support for its policies.[27] Wilhelm Schelsky, chairman of a small German labor union, AUB, was taken into custody for interrogation earlier in connection with the case. Prosecutors were examining whether the money Schelsky received for consulting duties as claimed by the company might

[14] "Siemens' Munich Offices Raided by Police, Prosecutors," www.iht.com, November 15, 2006.

[15] Michael Pohl, "Siemens Investigation Yields 5 Arrests," www.boston.com, November 16, 2006.

[16] "Siemens' Munich Offices Raided by Police, Prosecutors," www.iht.com, November 15, 2006.

[17] Chris Mellor, "Siemens Slush Fund Scandal Deepens," www.techworld.com, December 13, 2006.

[18] "Siemens Slush-Fund Scandal Deepens, Former Exec in Custody," www.dw-world.de, December 13, 2006.

[19] "Siemens Crisis Deepens as Corruption Scandal Widens," www.neurope.eu, December 16, 2006.

[20] The US Securities and Exchange Commission (SEC) is a regulatory body with a mandate to protect investors, maintain fair, orderly, and efficient markets, and facilitate capital formation. (Source: www.sec.gov).

[21] The US Department of Justice (DOJ) enforces the law and defends the interests of USA according to the law. It ensures public safety against foreign and domestic threats, helps to prevent and control crime and seeks punishment for those guilty of unlawful behavior. (Source: www.usdoj.gov).

[22] "SEC launches full-scale probe into Siemens," http://business.timesonline.co.uk, April 26, 2007.

[23] Liechtenstein (The Principality of Liechtenstein) is a tiny, landlocked country situated between Switzerland and Austria. Much of its wealth is based on its status as a low tax haven. (Source: http://news.bbc.co.uk/2/hi/europe/country_profiles/1066002.stm).

[24] Chris Mellor, "Siemens Slush Fund Scandal Deepens," www.techworld.com, December 13, 2006.

[25] Escrow account is a separate account into which the borrower makes monthly payments for obligations such as taxes, insurance, etc. The funds are held by the lender who pays out the amount as they become due.

[26] Chris Mellor, "Siemens Slush Fund Scandal Deepens," www.techworld.com, December 13, 2006.

[27] Carter Dougherty, "Bribery Trial Deepens Siemens Woes," www.iht.com, March 13, 2007.

have been aimed at persuading members of AUB to support Siemens policies. However Schelsky denied any wrongdoing and said he had not breached any German law. His lawyer, Jurgen Lubojanski said, "He disputes the notion that he was supposed to create a tame and lame union for Siemens. More I cannot say."[28]

The case was brought up by IG Metall, the dominant labor union which held nearly half of the board seats in Siemens. IG Metall accused Siemens of bribing labor representatives to try to influence them. In its case, it accused Siemens of showing favoritism to AUB. It alleged that Siemens had illegally financed AUB, a small union which had one seat in Siemens board, hoping to elevate AUB as a counterweight to IG Metall. "We have the suspicion and indications that AUB was financed by Siemens in order to build it up into a sort of counter union to IG Metall," said Jurgen Peters, chief of IG Metall.[29] IG Metall expressed its suspicions that AUB had received money for not bargaining strongly on the pay rates and other benefits that are negotiated for industrial workers. IG Metall said that AUB was not a proper labor union as it was unusually friendly with the management, something which was not in the best interests of the labor. There was also a general perception in Germany that AUB was soft on employers when compared to IG Metall.

In March 2007, a member of Siemens' central management board, Johannes Feldmayer, who oversaw the company's information technology services division, was taken into custody for interrogation over his alleged involvement in this case.[30] It was the first time an acting management board member had been arrested in a corruption scandal at Siemens. In the same case, the role of Siemens' former finance chief, Karl-Hermann Baumann (Baumann), was also investigated. Both Feldmayer and Baumann were charged with giving €15–20 million in bogus consultancy fees to Schelsky.[31]

Former Siemens managers convicted of bribing foreign officials

On May 14, 2007, a German court convicted two former managers of Siemens, Andreas Kley and Horst Vigener, for embezzling the company funds to bribe employees of an Italian energy company, Enel.[32] Though they were not accused of corruption intended for personal enrichment, both the former employees admitted to having paid €6 million of Siemens funds to managers of Enel in order to win orders for gas turbines between 1999 and 2002.[33] The bribes were meant to secure gas turbine contracts valued at

€450 million for Siemens. The payments were allegedly made to executives in Dubai, Abu Dhabi, and Monaco[34] through a web of bank accounts in Switzerland and Liechtenstein. Kley, a former finance head of the Siemens power plant unit, received a two-year suspended sentence, and Vigener, a consultant engineer, received a nine-month suspended sentence in the case. The court also ordered Siemens to pay €38 million for benefiting from the deal secured through bribing.[35]

Both the former managers of Siemens said that the payments were made to two Enel managers who demanded money in the bidding process. They defended themselves arguing that they had done it for the benefit of the company, to enable Siemens to establish itself in the power generation equipment market of Italy. "The alternative would have been to turn down the project, which would have denied Siemens not only that business but also a foot in the door in the Italian market," Kley said during the court proceedings.[36]

The employees also argued that the payments did not harm Siemens or break any German law at that time. The German law under which they were prosecuted prohibited bribery of public officials abroad, but Enel was a private entity during the time they transacted with it, the employees said. However the charges on the former employees sustained as the Italian state owned a controlling 68% stake in Enel when the bribes were paid. Also in 2002, another law was passed in Germany, which prohibited bribing any employee whether at a public or a private company.[37] Siemens officially stated that it would appeal against the fine in the Enel case. In a statement, the company said, "We maintain that the court's order to forfeit the profits from two orders placed by Enel with Siemens' power generation division for the supply of power plant equipment in 2000 and 2001 is illegal. The court's decision has no basis in law or in fact."[38]

Probes in Other Countries

Siemens was also being probed in several other countries like Italy, Switzerland, Greece, and the US for possible misconduct. The company and its units in Venezuela, Argentina, and Bangladesh were also being probed.[39] It also faced allegations that it had channeled millions of euros to people in countries like Nigeria, Russia, and Libya to obtain infrastructure contracts.[40] In late 2007, the Nigerian authorities initiated a probe

---

[28] Carter Dougherty, "Bribery Trial Deepens Siemens Woes," www.iht.com, March 13, 2007.

[29] "German Trade Union Sues Siemens over Bribe Allegations," www.dw-world.de, April 02, 2007.

[30] "Siemens Board Member Johannes Feldmayer Arrested for Paying off Labor Organization," www.cio.com, March 29, 2007.

[31] "German Trade Union Sues Siemens over Bribe Allegations," www.dw-world.de, April 02, 2007.

[32] "Former Siemens Managers Convicted of Paying Bribes," www.dw-world.de, May 14, 2007.

[33] "Siemens Fined $51 Mn in Bribery Case," http://economictimes.indiatimes.com, May 15, 2007.

[34] The Principality of Monaco is the second-smallest independent state in the world, located between the Mediterranean Sea and France. It is an attractive tourist destination owing to its climate and the beauty of its setting. It is also a tax haven for the wealthy due to its advantageous tax regime. (Source: http://news.bbc.co.uk).

[35] G. Thomas Sims, "2 Former Siemens Officials Convicted for Bribery," www.nytimes.com, May 15, 2007.

[36] Carter Dougherty, "Bribery Trial Deepens Siemens Woes," www.iht.com, March 13, 2007.

[37] Karin Matussek, Simon Thiel, "Ex-Siemens Managers Convicted of Bribing Enel Units," www.bloomberg.com, May 14, 2007.

[38] "Former Siemens Managers Convicted of Paying Bribes," www.dw-world.de, May 14, 2007.

[39] Cary O'Reilly and Karin Matussek, "Siemens Agrees to Pay $1.6 Billion," www.washingtonpost.com, December 16, 2008.

[40] "Inside the Siemens Bribery Scandal," www.newser.com, December 28, 2007.

into allegations that some former ministers had taken bribes from Siemens and subsequently cancelled a contract awarded to the company.[41]

Repercussions of the Scandals

The series of bribery allegations came in the aftermath of Siemens' sale of its loss-making mobile handset unit in 2005, to a Taiwanese company, BenQ. Here too, Siemens did not cover itself in glory as it was seen as having got rid of the unit because it could not easily lay off its employees. With BenQ eventually filing for insolvency, the ex-Siemens workers lost their jobs, and some people felt that Siemens ought to have foreseen this and been more responsible towards its long-time employees. Siemens was urged to take on the responsibility of compensating the workers, and it was forced to delay its planned hefty pay hikes for its top management and compensate the employees who lost jobs.

Even Siemens felt that it could take some time for the company to regain its reputation internationally and come out of the legal battles it was facing in several countries. "Siemens currently cannot exclude the possibility that criminal or civil sanctions may be brought against the company itself or against certain of its employees in connection with possible violations of law. The Company's operating activities may also be negatively affected due to imposed penalties, compensatory damages or due to the exclusion from public procurement contracts," the Siemens board said.[42]

Following the wave of scandals at Siemens, the supervisory board head, von Pierer, and CEO, Kleinfeld had to resign. While von Pierer quit as board chairman in April 2007, Kleinfeld would leave the company by June 2007.[43] Though the bribery scandals came to light during Kleinfeld's time, most of the payments were made when von Pierer was the CEO of the company. Kleinfeld took over as the CEO of Siemens in 2005 from von Pierer, who held the job from 1992 till 2005. Both of them were not directly implicated in the bribery scandals, but they were widely criticized for failing to trace the embezzlement of large company funds and payments made over several years.

Siemens announced in April 2007 that Loescher would take over as CEO in July 2007. Loescher was president of the Global Human Health unit of Merck & Co., Inc.[44] and was responsible for its worldwide sales and marketing. It was for the first time in Siemens that a CEO was being appointed from outside the company. Siemens said that it wanted to infuse new leadership in view of the several scandals that had rocked the company. The head of Siemens' supervisory board, Gerhard Cromme said of Loescher, "His upright character, his global

background, his outstanding international reputation and his wide-ranging experience in business development and strategy, the financial markets and technology-related issues were the key factors in our decision."[45] He added, "I am convinced that Mr. Loescher has what it takes to steer Siemens through its current difficulties and into a better future."[46]

However, some analysts felt that Loescher might face some resistance as he was considered an outsider in the German corporate circles as well as in Siemens. His immediate challenge would be to work towards being accepted by everyone in Siemens. "The question is how quickly Loescher can learn the ropes of Siemens as it's a very complex and huge company in the middle of a major restructuring and tarnished by a corruption affair," said Morgan Stanley analyst Ben Uglow.[47]

The exit of Kleinfeld met with mixed reactions. Some were admiring of him as Kleinfeld had managed a major restructuring at Siemens in just two years. The stock price of the company rose by 26% during his two year tenure[48] (Refer to Exhibit IV for the stock price movement of Siemens). He pushed Siemens' employees to make decisions faster and focus as much on customers as on technology. He sold off the unprofitable mobile phone production to BenQ, and fostered a joint venture between Siemens and Nokia to merge their mobile and fixed-line phone network equipment businesses to create one of the world's biggest network firms. He had also spent US$8.6 billion in 2006 on acquisitions in growing areas such as medical diagnostics and wind power.[49] But Kleinfield's aggressive style of management was disliked by older conservatives in the company. Some analysts speculated that Kleinfeld's working style could have been an additional reason for his ouster from the job.

In addition to loss of image, the scandal also hit Siemens hard financially. By the end of 2007, the company had to pay US$1.7 billion in fines (including a US$314 million fine imposed by the Munich public prosecutors), US$2 billion in back taxes for illegal deductions, and US$44 million in late interest charges.[50] Subsequently in December 2008, the company agreed to pay a record US$800 million fine in the US and another €395 million in Germany as it pleaded guilty to corruption charges.[51]

Initiatives at Siemens

After the bribery scandals were unearthed at Siemens, the company started many initiatives to strengthen its corporate governance and compliance controls. A law firm Debevoise &

[41] "Nigeria Suspends Siemens Dealings," http://news.bbc.co.uk, December 6, 2007.

[42] Chris Mellor, "Siemens Slush Fund Scandal Deepens," www.techworld.com, December 13, 2006.

[43] Simon Thiel, "Siemens Names Merck & Co.'s Peter Loescher New Chief," www.bloomberg.com, May 20, 2007.

[44] Merck & Co., Inc. (Merck) is one of the top pharmaceutical companies in the world. It was founded in 1891. Merck discovers, develops, manufactures and markets vaccines and medicines. (Source: www.merck.com).

[45] "Siemens Names First Outsider as CEO," www.politicalgateway.com, May 21, 2007.

[46] "Siemens Names First Outsider as CEO," www.politicalgateway.com, May 21, 2007.

[47] Simon Thiel, "Siemens Names Merck & Co.'s Peter Loescher New Chief," www.bloomberg.com, May 20, 2007.

[48] Jack Ewing, "Siemens' Culture Clash," www.businessweek.com, January 18, 2007.

[49] Jack Ewing, "Siemens' Culture Clash," www.businessweek.com, January 18, 2007.

[50] Heide B. Malhotra, "Siemens Looks for New Beginning after Bribery Scandals," http://en.epochtimes.com, March 27, 2008.

[51] "Siemens Bribery Fines Top 1 Billion Euros," www.dw-world.de, December 15, 2008.

EXHIBIT IV   Stock Price Movement of Siemens

Source: www.bigcarts.com.

Plimpton LLP[52] was appointed to conduct an independent and comprehensive investigation into the company's compliance and control system, with the help of the independent auditor for Siemens, KPMG.[5354] Debevoise & Plimpton worked with companies in the area of internal corporate investigations and supported them in managing investigations by authorities. Siemens also appointed Michael Hershman, co-founder of Transparency International[55] (TI), as its compliance adviser. TI had earlier threatened to terminate Siemens' membership in light of the fraud allegations. Siemens set up an internal Compliance Task Force, led by Corporate Executive Committee member Jurgen Radomski. An external legal expert was appointed as the head of the Siemens Compliance Office.

Siemens claimed that responsible corporate governance had always formed the basis of all its decision-making and monitoring processes. As stated by the CFO of Siemens, Joe Kaeser "Clearly structured and practiced corporate governance has always had a priority at Siemens. It stands for a responsible and value creating management and control of the company. Efficient cooperation between Executive Board and Supervisory Board,

respect for shareholder interests, transparency and responsibility are key aspects of good Corporate Governance for us."[56] Accordingly, Siemens business practices worldwide were guided by a compliance program with internal guidelines and international guidelines. The compliance program outlined guidelines for conducting business and a large number of other rules and regulations for their implementation and monitoring. The internal guidelines emphasized on integrity in all dealings with business partners, employees, shareholders and the general public. They included the recommendations of several national and international organizations for Siemens to conduct itself as a true global company. There was also an "Anti-public-corruption compliance" notice issued by the Corporate Compliance Office of Siemens on May 02, 2007, which covered business conduct guidelines in dealing with government officials (Refer to Exhibit V for a note on Siemens' Anti-public-corruption compliance).

Kleinfeld hoped that the investigations would lead to total exposure of the wrong practices existing in the company and that proper measures would be taken to eliminate the same. "Siemens tolerates absolutely no illegal or irregular conduct by employees—and I really mean zero tolerance. We are employing the knowledge and experience of external and independent experts to track down specific cases of misconduct and gaps in Siemens' regulations, structures and processes and to make our compliance system absolutely watertight," Kleinfeld said.[57]

After Loescher joined Siemens, he took forward the various initiatives to promote compliance with a "zero tolerance policy" that covered everyone from grassroots level to the top level management. He initiated measures to change

---

[52] Debevoise & Plimpton LLP was a sophisticated legal services firm, committed to a comprehensive, modern practice of law spanning the Americas, Europe and Asia. It had a cross border focus due to its international approach to the practice of law. (www.debevoise.com).

[53] KPMG was a global network of professional firms providing Audit, Tax, and Advisory services. It operated in 148 countries and had more than 113,000 professionals working in member firms around the world. (Source: www.kpmg.org).

[54] "Siemens Slush-Fund Scandal Deepens, Former Exec in Custody," www.dw-world.de, December 13, 2006.

[55] Transparency International (TI) is an international non-governmental organization dealing with issues related to corruption, including political corruption. It releases an annual Corruptions Perceptions Index, a comparative listing of corruption worldwide. TI is organized as a group of some 100 national chapters, with an international secretariat in Berlin, Germany. It was founded in Germany in 1993. (Source: www.wikipedia.org).

[56] www.siemens.com.

[57] Chris Mellor, "Siemens Slush Fund Scandal Deepens," www.techworld.com, December 13, 2006.

EXHIBIT V   A Note on Siemens' Anti-Public-Corruption Compliance

Siemens has laid down business conduct guidelines for its employees in dealing with government officials in a document on "Anti-public corruption compliance". The main aspects of the document are:

1. **Policy:** It is the policy of Siemens not to offer government officials money or anything of value to obtain an improper advantage. It is also the policy of the company to keep accurate records that fairly reflect all transactions.

2. **Scope:** The policy applies to all the company employees globally, and to all the company's agents, consultants and third parties.

3. **Background:** Apart from Germany, several countries have laws prohibiting the bribery of government officials. Apart from cash payments, providing gifts, travel or entertainment may also be unlawful depending on the circumstances. Persons found guilty of bribery may face imprisonment and fines. It is the responsibility of employees to exercise common sense in all dealings as it is not possible to document each and every possible situation. When in doubt, employees should consult their compliance officers.

4. **Practices:** A government official could be the employee of a state-owned enterprise, local police officer, judge, prosecutor, court clerk, mayoral candidate, customs official, military personnel, etc. The prohibition encompasses not only cash but also gifts and gratuities of any kind; inappropriate travel, meals or entertainment; contributions to charity specified by the government official; offers of employment to the relatives of the government official.

5. **Reporting:** If any company employee is suspected of engaging in conduct inconsistent with company policy on anti-corruption, it may be reported to the concerned supervisors or compliance officers or the Siemens Ombudsman may be contacted.

Adapted from www.siemens.com.

the company's culture and standards. "What we need is a cultural revolution . . . It is a job that will take several years,"[58] said Loescher. By March 2008, Siemens charged 500 employees with compliance violations, out of which 150 were dismissed, 310 were reprimanded, and various kinds of benefits were withdrawn from the rest.[59]

Questions Relating to Ethics in Corporate Germany

Around the same time as the Siemens cases came out, unethical practices surfaced in other German companies including Volkswagen AG, Deutsche Telekom AG, Deutsche Bahn AG, and Deutsche Post AG. At Volkswagen, a senior executive was fined €576,000 and received a suspended prison sentence in January 2007 for bribing labor representatives with money, foreign trips and prostitutes.[60] Since several of the corruption scandals involved the bribing of labor representatives on the boards of German companies, some analysts felt that the Co-determination law or Mitbestimmung in Germany was flawed.

According to the Co-determination law, the supervisory board of a company had to have 20 members, of whom 10 were to be labor representatives. This led to a suspicious alliance be-

tween the management and the labor representatives, which could never set a stage for proper discussions during the board meetings. The presence of workers on boards sometimes forced a situation wherein the main issues were discussed and agreed on even before the meetings. Manuel Theisen, a professor at the University of Munich, opined that when heads of a company's worker councils sat on the supervisory boards, they could control the management decisions even before the board meetings happened as they were very much insiders in the company.

The law was also criticized because it did not allow non-German directors of multinational German companies to be members of the supervisory board. In companies like Siemens and Volkswagen, a large part of their business came from outside Germany but non-Germans who could bring in a wider dimension on the board could not play a part.

Experts also pointed out that the two-tier system gave rise to an environment of mistrust and a conflict of interests between the executives and the supervisory board. For instance, in the case of Siemens, Kleinfeld was ousted by the overpowerful supervisory board despite his good performance and not being directly implicated in the bribery scandal. Many felt that the bribery scandals were used to get rid of Kleinfeld, who was not received well by the conservative old generation at Siemens. Because of his aggressive style of management, Kleinfeld's working style was often described as an American style of management by the German media. However, Siemens' supervisory board defended the decision saying that it was an effort to give a new beginning to the company. Analysts and

[58] "Inside Bribery Probe of Siemens," www.australianit.news.com, January 3, 2008.
[59] Heide B. Malhotra, "Siemens Looks for New Beginning after Bribery Scandals," http://en.epochtimes.com, March 27, 2008.
[60] "German Parliamentarian Resigns over Role in VW Scandal," www.dw-world.de, May 30, 2007.

many top executives called for an urgent need to have a re-look into the functioning of Co-determination law in Germany. "Management boards have changed quite a bit. But supervisory boards are an unreformed area," said Hans Hirt, head of European corporate governance, supporting the idea of reforming the Co-determination law.[61]

Analysts also pointed out to companies increasingly exploring ways to escape compliance with Co-determination law. Some companies got themselves incorporated outside Germany or changed their legal structure so as not to be within the purview of the law. For example, under the Societas Europae (SE) legal structure, which was created by the European Union in 2004, companies were allowed to shrink their supervisory board members to 12 and include foreign workers. Companies like Allianz SE[62] and BASF AG[63] opted for this route and many more were likely to join them.[64] Among the companies that shifted their base outside Germany was Air Berlin[65] which became a British Plc. when it was listed on the London Stock Exchange in 2006. Commenting on the move, its chief executive, Joachim Hunold, said, "[Co-determination law] is no longer competitive internationally. There are always cases in which companies always must compromise, as was the case with Volkswagen."[66]

Analysts attributed the suspicious relationship between the management and labor representatives in Germany to Co-determination law. Among the other members of the European Union, only Austria and Luxembourg had such laws with mandatory one-third representation and many had no such requirements at all. With widespread resentment over the law and its effectiveness, the Confederation of German Employers' Associations, the group that lobbied on the behalf of companies, announced that it would take up the issue of modifying the Co-determination law to suit to the present day business environment. "We will continue our fight to make Germany more competitive," said Thomas Prinz, a member of the group's legal department.[67] In view of the string of bribery scandals in several companies, the German government was reported to be planning to curb corporate corruption by modifying laws that had loopholes allowing companies to write off bribes as expenses.

Outlook

Analysts opined that on account of increasing competition, companies were resorting to illegal payments to win international contracts especially in some emerging economies where the practice was common. Siemens along with many other companies was found guilty of paying bribes to secure contracts abroad. That the company officials had resorted to bribing was not in question, but the remaining questions were even more worrying—how deep were the scandals rooted in the company and to what extent was the board aware of the fraud. As Manuel Theisen, a professor of business and tax law at Ludwig-Maximilians-Universitat in Munich said, "This individual case is of significance because it shows clearly that a system of bribery was installed. The rest is now just a question of numbers and dimension. This [unearthing the system of bribery] is certainly an important milestone."[68] There was also mounting pressure on Siemens to explain how all these cases of bribery—both within Germany and externally—went unchecked by the top management for so many years.

However, Siemens continued to officially maintain that individual employees were responsible for illicit payments that were made without the approval of the top management. Siemens acknowledged that its internal controls were insufficient and that it would take sufficient steps to become a model of corporate governance and transparency. The company hired outside legal experts and auditing firms to revamp its internal accounting and control systems. Analysts opined that because of the vast size of the company, with its businesses spread across several areas and countries, establishing strict norms of corporate governance and transparency would be a great challenge for Siemens. Also the growth of the company might slow down at least in the short run owing to the bribery scandals resulting in investigations into its business practices, a leadership change, and a dent in its image.

The bribery scandals aside, Kleinfeld left an illustrious legacy for the new CEO. The main challenge for Loscher would be to bring the company out of the cloud of the bribery scandals, sustain the growth momentum set by Kleinfeld and above all gain the confidence of labor and management within Siemens, where outsiders were not easily accepted.

[61] Richard Milne, "Germany's Two-Tier Governance System Comes under Fire," http://us.ft.com, May 08, 2007.

[62] Allianz SE, (formerly Allianz AG) was one of the largest financial service provider headquartered in Munich, Germany. Its core and focus was s on the insurance business. Allianz SE was the biggest insurance company in Germany and one of the largest in the world. Allianz AG converted to Allianz SE in 2006. (Source: www.wikipedia.org).

[63] BASF was a German chemical company and one of the largest chemical companies in the world. The BASF Group comprised more than 160 subsidiaries and joint ventures and operated in more than 150 production sites in Europe, Asia, North America, South America and Africa. BASF had customers in over 200 countries and supplied products to a wide variety of industries. It had businesses in the areas like Chemicals, Plastics, Performance Products, Agricultural Products & Nutrition and Oil & Gas. (Source: www.wikipedia.org). The company will be officially BASF SE officially from the beginning of 2008. (Source: http://corporate.basf.com).

[64] Richard Milne, "Germany's Two-Tier Governance System Comes under Fire," http://us.ft.com, May 08, 2007.

[65] Air Berlin is Germany's second largest airline after Lufthansa. It is based in Berlin, Germany, and operates extensive low-cost services.

[66] G. Thomas Sims, "Germany Rethinks Board Structure after Corruption Scandals," http://www.iht.com, April 05, 2007.

[67] G. Thomas Sims, "Germany Rethinks Board Structure after Corruption Scandals," http://www.iht.com, April 05, 2007.

[68] G. Thomas Sims, "2 Former Siemens Officials Convicted for Bribery," www.nytimes.com, May 15, 2007.

Questions for Discussion

1. In your opinion, is 'bribing' unethical and illegal or just a cost of doing business? Discuss this in the light of Siemens' bribery scandal. What options do companies have to win business contracts without bribing, especially in foreign countries?

2. Was the board right in not extending Kleinfeld's term, especially in view of his overall performance as a CEO? What is likely to be the impact of his departure on the company? Was Siemens really at fault or was it just unfortunate to have got caught given the perception that many companies have to resort to bribing to win contracts?

References and Suggested Readings:

1. "Siemens Proves Prudence Is a Virtue," www.businessweek.com, November 11, 2002.
2. "All Eyes on the Corner Office," www.businessweek.com, March 01, 2004.
3. "Siemens' New Boss," www.businessweek.com, January 24, 2005.
4. "The Real Scandal at Volkswagen," www.businessweek.com, July 18, 2005.
5. "Corporate Scandals Plague Top German Firms," www.msnbc.msn.com, August 08, 2005.
6. "Siemens the Fall Guy in BenQ Insolvency Scandal," www.dw-world.de, October 02, 2006.
7. "Police Raid Siemens Offices over Fraud Allegations," www.fiercewireless.com, November 15, 2006.
8. "Siemens Sets up Anti-Corruption Task Force," http://today.reuters.com, November 23, 2006.
9. "German Business Image Tarnished by Wave of Corruption Cases," www.dw-world.de, November 27, 2006.
10. "Siemens Forced to Battle Internal Corruption," www.spiegel.de, November 28, 2006.
11. Benjamin Dierks, "Corruption Probe Reaches Ever Higher at Siemens," http://business.guardian.co.uk, December 13, 2006.
12. Chris Mellor, "Siemens Slush Fund Scandal Deepens," www.itworld.com, December 13, 2006.
13. "Former Siemens Exec Arrested in Bribery Probe," http://news.com.com, December 13, 2006.
14. Colleen Taylor, "In Siemens Scandal Fallout, Nokia Hesitates on Merger Plans," www.edn.com, December 15, 2006.
15. Richard Milne, "Siemens Bribery Scandal Raises Further Questions," www.ft.com, December 21, 2006.
16. Stephen Taub, "Ex-Siemens CFO Questioned in Probe," www.cfo.com, January 15, 2007.
17. Simon Thiel, "Siemens Investors Grill Management on Bribery Charges," www.iht.com, January 25, 2007.
18. "Siemens Chief Promises Full Explanation of Bribery Scandal," www.dw-world.de, January 25, 2007.
19. "Vote Call by Siemens Shareholders," http://news.bbc.co.uk, January 25, 2007.
20. Michael Woodhead, "Focus: Dirty Rotten Business," http://business.timesonline.co.uk, January 28, 2007.
21. "Future Nokia Siemens Networks Takes Shape with Unveiling of Portfolio Plan," www.siemens.com, February 12, 2007.
22. Benjamin Weinthal, "Where Is the German Trade Union Movement and Where Is It Going?" http://mrzine.monthlyreview.org, February 21, 2007.
23. Carter Dougherty, "Bribery Trial Deepens Siemens Woes," www.iht.com, March 13, 2007.
24. "Siemens Execs Admit Bribery Was Common," www.businessweek.com, March 14, 2007.
25. "Siemens Board Member Detained in Bribery Probe," www.dw-world.de, March 27, 2007.
26. G. Thomas Sims, "Siemens Scandal Threatens to Ensnare Leadership," www.iht.com, April 01, 2007.
27. "German Trade Union Sues Siemens over Bribe Allegations," www.dw-world.de, April 02, 2007.
28. G. Thomas Sims, "Germany Rethinks Board Structure after Corruption Scandals," http://www.iht.com, April 05, 2007.
29. "Siemens Shares Jump as Chairman Quits," http://business.timesonline.co.uk, April 20, 2007.
30. John Blau, "Siemens CEO Could Be Next to Go," www.infoworld.com, April 24, 2007.
31. "Siemens Post-Kleinfeld," www.ft.com, April 26, 2007.
32. "Siemens CEO Undermined by Board," www.spiegel.de, April 26, 2007.
33. Thomas Sims, "Siemens Struggles to Regain Equilibrium," www.nytimes.com, April 27, 2007.
34. "Germany: The Siemens Syndrome," http://globaltechforum.eiu.com, April 27, 2007.
35. Narayan Bhat, "Kleinfeld's Resignation Leaves Power Vacuum," www.tmcnet.com, April 30, 2007.
36. Stefanie Marsh, "Sleazy Business," www.timesonline.co.uk, May 02, 2007.
37. William Boston, "Siemens Goes Mega," www.time.com, May 03, 2007.
38. Richard Milne, "Germany's Two-Tier Governance System Comes under Fire," http://us.ft.com, May 08, 2007.
39. Dearbail Jordan, "Siemens Ordered to Pay for Bribery Gains," http://business.timesonline.co.uk, May 14, 2007.
40. "Siemens to Pay €38mn to Settle Bribery Case," www.newratings.com, May 14, 2007.
41. "German Court Convicts Former Siemens Officials," www.cnbc.com, May 14, 2007.
42. David Rising, "Munich-Based Siemens Names New CEO," http://biz.yahoo.com, May 20, 2007.
43. Jack Ewing, "Siemens Taps Merck Exec as New CEO," www.businessweek.com, May 20, 2007.
44. Nicola Leske, "Siemens Names Peter Loescher as New CEO," www.reuters.com, May 20, 2007.
45. "Siemens Hopes Outsiders Will Rebuild Morale," www.ft.com, May 20, 2007.
46. Simon Morgan, "Siemens' New CEO Could Face Uphill Struggle," www.industryweek.com, May 21, 2007.
47. "Siemens Makes a Clean Break from Scandal at the Top," www.dw-world.de, May 21, 2007.

48. "Siemens Names First Outsider as CEO," www.themoneytimes.com, May 22, 2007.

49. "Siemens at The Crossroads," www.e-health-insider.com, May 22, 2007.

50. "German Parliamentarian Resigns over Role in VW Scandal," www.dw-world.de, May 30, 2007.

51. "Nigeria Suspends Siemens Dealings," http://news.bbc.co.uk, December 6, 2007.

52. "Siemens Organizes Operations in Three Sectors with Total of 15 Divisions," www.w1.siemens.com, November 28, 2007.

53. "Inside the Siemens Bribery Scandal," www.newser.com, December 28, 2007.

54. "Inside Bribery Probe of Siemens," www.australianit.news.com, January 3, 2008.

55. Heide B. Malhotra, "Siemens Looks for New Beginning after Bribery Scandals," http://en.epochtimes.com, March 27, 2008.

56. "Siemens Bribery Fines Top 1 Billion Euros," www.dw-world.de, December 15, 2008.

57. Cary O'Reilly and Karin Matussek, "Siemens Agrees to Pay $1.6 Billion," www.washingtonpost.com, December 16, 2008.

58. www.hoovers.com.

59. www.siemens.com.

CASE 2 MICROSOFT'S PARTNERSHIP WITH UNHCR—Pro Bono Publico?

Using Microsoft's core business competencies and expertise enhances UNHCR's technological capacity, bringing the benefit of technology solutions closer to refugee communities and at the same time providing support for UNHCR's general mandate - awareness raising and advocacy for refugees.

JOOSTEN FRAUKE,
Associate External Relations Officer for Private Sector Fundraising and Public Affairs Service at UNHCR

The system handles a broad range of demographic information – the number of men, women, and children – the age of people, the mortality rate, where people come from and what their protection needs are," he said. "It's recorded their medical status and details on food and nutrition. It's a scorecard of sorts, that helps you plan and make sure you have the right material and help available to provide refugees with the services they need. *Patrick De Smedt, Former Chairman of Microsoft Europe, Middle East and Africa.*

Kosovo, 1999

It was in 1999, at the time of the Kosovo crisis. For days people across the world had been watching the events unfold, following desperate Kosovars fleeing the Serbs bundled with as many belongings as possible leaving their home behind. Microsoft employees were watching the news together during lunchtime. However, this time a particularly strong shared feeling of

Case study

Reference no 708-035-[1]

This case was written by Nina Marie Nicolas and Dr Gabriele Suder, CERAM Business School. It is intended to be used as the basis for class discussion rather than to illustrate either effective or ineffective handling of a management situation. The case was written with the support of a Philip Law Scholarship awarded by ecch. The case was made possible by the co-operation of Olivier Pierre Delarue, UNHCR and Elena Bonfiglioli, Microsoft.

[1] The authors would like to thank J.P. Courtois, President, Microsoft International, E. Bonfiglioli, Director, Microsoft EMEA Corporate Citizenship, Olivier Delarue, Head of Corporate and Foundation Partnership Unit at UNHCR, J. Frauke, Associate External Relations Officer for Private Sector Fundraising and Public Affairs Service at UNHCR , Uli Holtz, Microsoft EMEA, Human Resources Director, and the many other sources of support and information at Microsoft Corp. and at UNHCR that made this case study possible.

empathy arose for those affected by the conflict, which in turn led to a sincere desire to reach out to the many distressed people that filled the TV screen and take action. How could they make a difference to this terrible humanitarian disaster?

Meanwhile, Jean-Philippe Courtois, then CEO of Microsoft Europe, Middle East and Africa, also followed the crisis closely. He began to consider how a company such as Microsoft could contribute to improve these situations by using its particular skills and expertise instead of resorting to regular charity or the typical philanthropy.

At the time philanthropy was widespread among companies, foundations and institutions particularly in the United States. Corporate social responsibility, however, was still an unfamiliar term. In Europe one could find a social awareness as well as random examples of equivalents to corporate citizenship, which has since evolved and increased in visibility, expertise and practice throughout the corporate, NGO and political world.

Corporate Social Responsibility or Corporate Citizenship— as the latter is commonly defined in Microsoft—was not explicitly stated as corporate strategy or as a set of activities within the company before 1999. However, a team of Community Affairs professionals were in charge of handling Microsoft´s various social investment and philanthropic activities.

Given the urgency of the situation, a small team of employees was formed to handle societal initiatives and community contributions like this one. Employees were brought in from the Community Affairs team, the business development team, as well as a business manager working for Jean Philippe Courtois. They assessed the different strategies for action in order to aid the victims of the Kosovo crisis through leveraging the company's expertise, its talents and the personal motivation of its employees.

The Microsoft team asked how the company could be actively useful for the UNHCR. Upon analysis of refugees' needs, it was found that, beyond the most basic ones, the people in the region were left without homes and identity papers. As a result they were completely unprotected.

UNHCR suggested that Microsoft could help resolve these problems, by providing technology software and hardware with which a refugees' registration system could be created and through collaboration with NGOs, with UNHCR and organisations that were taking care of the many displaced victims.

This was the beginning of what was to become an important partnership for both UNHCR and Microsoft. One of the Microsoft Executives, who had followed this initiative from the very first lunch, had the opportunity to visit one of the refugee camps in Albania during the planning process:

It was probably the most horrific thing I had ever seen. There were probably 5000 people in this camp.

FRANK SCHOTT,
Microsoft EMEA

Other Microsoft volunteers had similar experiences. Women, children and men were crammed together in small tents. By talking to the refugees directly the Microsoft volunteers were able to experience first hand how these were people just like them selves, people with homes and jobs who suddenly were forced to leave everything behind. Their home was no longer theirs and fleeing from the Serbs they had not only lost their possessions but also part of their identity.

It's very hard to go to a refugee camp and leave without thinking, "We've got to do something Frank Schott[2]

Given clear objectives and fuelled by a strong motivation to bring about change, Microsoft employees initiated a project that would become wide cross-sector collaboration and provide the foundation for the future partnership. The employees were also encouraged by their success, to bring in other technological companies with complementary expertise. And so they did. Microsoft decided to go into partnership with Compaq as well as other technology companies and together the taskforce went on to provide assistance and consultancy to the UNHCR. The UNHCR chief technology officer at the time was working side by side with the taskforce to achieve the best result. Loyal to its field of competence, Microsoft donated cash, software, technology assistance, and volunteers' working hours.

The first phase of the UNHCR partnership which lasted two years (1999–2001) was driven by the urgency of a deep humanitarian crisis. However, as things stabilized, the establishing of a more formal understanding of the evolving partnership was needed. In Kosovo the involved companies worked pro bono to establish the refugee registration scheme called Project Profile—which by then had become the real solution to UNHCR's very first problem analysis. The second phase started in 2003–04 when UNHCR wanted to expand the pilot version of Project Profile into a mainstreamed solution. At that point Microsoft Consulting Services (MCS) helped draft the

specifications of the technology solution for UNHCR. Having assisted pro bono to the development of the specs, MCS decided not to bid for the UNHCR tender to develop the software solution. The bid was awarded to a local company based in Geneva called ELCA.[3] Microsoft partnered with ELCA to help implement the mainstream version of Project Profile, it assisted UNHCR in the overall project management pro-bono and provided pro bono time from employees to help roll out the technology in various refugee camps.[4]

In December 2003, the partnership was renewed and framed in a Memorandum of Understanding co-signed by Jean Philippe Courtois and the UNHCR High Commissioner at the time, Ruud Lubbers. The Letter of Understanding (LoU) set in writing the important framework of the partnership. Below is an extraction of the LoU detailing the major elements of the co-operation:

. . . Whereas the co-operation consists of three major elements outlined herewith:

1. *leadership and support in the establishment of Community Technology Learning Centres for mutually selected refugee populations within the scope of enhancing UNHCR's contribution to personal development, education and protection activities;*
2. *provision of technical expertise for UNHCR Project PROFILE;*
3. *opportunities for raising awareness of UNHCR's mission and activities among the general public and aimed toward increasing the support of individuals for UNHCR"*[5]

Since 2003 Microsoft has constantly increased its engagement to what is known throughout the company today as Corporate Citizenship.

Thus the question arises as to why a company, this particular company, would engage into activities of citizenship and community work? Is doing good for doing well a necessity for market leaders?

Microsoft Corporation

Known around the globe and used by the vast majority of the computerized world, Microsoft Corporation is a software technology company that was founded by Paul Allen and Bill Gates in 1975. More than 30 years later the company earns revenues of $44.28 billion and employs 71,553 people. As a world leader in its field, the company faces competitive challenges on many levels, in the software, internet and the home entertainment domain. On the legislative level, Microsoft faces anti-trust cases and engages into intellectual property, websecurity and webdomain protection cases. At the time of the Kosovo crisis in 1999, the share value of Microsoft peaked, but soon dropped

---

[2] "Office Angels," *Financial Times Weekend,* December 31, 2004.

[3] UNHCR (2006), "UNHCR and Microsoft Partnership", Toyota Meeting, UNHCR's Corporate Partnership Programme, Belgium
[4] "Office Angels," *Financial Times Weekend,* December 31, 2004.
[5] Letter of Understanding between Microsoft Corporation EMEA and United Nations High Commissioner for Refugees, pp. 1, December, 2003

severely, and Microsoft's external image was suffering. There was an increasingly obvious missing link between engineering potential and consumers' demands which paired with high excess reserves of cash and lack of investment opportunities can be seen as key reasons to the fall in share value.[6] At the time, Microsoft being a market leader was easily related to and yet also thought of as an impersonal giant swallowing its competitors, expressed in the allegations of monopoly powers in the US at the time.

The power of computing enables people to pursue their passions and realize their potential, no matter who they are. Through global citizenship efforts and local partnerships, one of the ways we are helping to strengthen communities is to extend the benefits of technology to the people that can benefit most."

BILL GATES.

Microsoft Chairman and Chief Software Architect, about Microsoft global citizenship efforts.[7]

Microsoft's Global Citizenship Activities

The time period in which Microsoft's Corporate Citizenship initiatives were born also corresponds with the launch period of the Melinda & Bill Gates Foundation, which is positioned well outside of the company sphere. A new awareness of the stakeholder model also developed during this period. Was the company only to be responsive to shareholder expectations for profits, as Friedman prominently argued, or did it need to take other actors into account, such as the community around it, employees, civil society, governments, customers and partners? Is it possible to sustain longer term business success and even shareholder value in today's marketplace without a proper management of stakeholders' expectations?

Is it feasible to marry the two in a complementary manner; to satisfy those vital shareholder expectations and to engage into activities going further than the development, production, marketing and distribution of a product or service?

The World Business Council for Sustainable Development action team created the CSR definition stating that "Corporate Social Responsibility is the sustainable commitment by business to contribute to development and to the well-being and the improvement of the quality of life of employees, their families and the community at large."[8] Critical events in the corporate world, amongst those, Shell Brent Spa (1995), the Nike child labour case (1995), and the Asian Financial Crisis (1997) rose awareness of the fact that time and space were shrinking rapidly for international business and citizens: globalization had started

to leave its marks. The Seattle protests at WTO meeting were a wake up call for the multilateral organizations and led to the creation of the UN Global Compact. At the same time in Europe, the Heads of State, and Government appealed "companies for a new sense of corporate responsibility." For the first time ever, CSR was clearly written in the core recommendations of an EU policy document, the Lisbon Strategy setting targets and objectives towards 2010 and reinforcing Europe's twin objectives of competitiveness and inclusion.

Very soon the world was forced to realize the effects of 9/11/2001 which meant finance and business had globalized as well as risks. This called for yet further development and understanding of corporations' role in society and in the larger community. Terrorism had started to attack the very foundations of international values and exchanges: the major corporations' economic foundations and system. The link between poverty, lack of education, wealth polarization and terrorism started to take new and clearer shapes than ever before.

In the same time period, the progressive development of partnerships, ISO and Social Accountability norms and the Triple Bottom Line concept (1998) had started to influence a generation of business leaders. It became increasingly clear that good citizenship would need to be closely connected to the corporate mission and not be an "add-on." At the very same time, Microsoft went through a revision of its own corporate mission and values. It was at that point that the firm's global citizenship activities were to be based on the global corporate mission: "to enable people and businesses throughout the world to realize their full potential."[9]

The Corporate Citizenship team of Microsoft was staring to take shape in 2003 within the Corporate Affairs team and in collaboration with various other teams, from Communications to Public sector and other parts of the business. The terms corporate citizenship and corporate social responsibility became synonyms. The company refers to its corporate citizenship initiatives as its "Global Citizenship" activities. It was to be defined and to be given a content and a body of practice that would reach across shareholders and stakeholders, through specific projects and initiatives with business and societal relevance.

The Chief Executive Officer (CEO) of Microsoft Europe, Middle-East and Africa, Jean- Philippe Courtois, had been a major player in the creation of this vision. His efforts were to engage Microsoft as a responsible leader, servicing the public good through partnerships with customers, governments, local communities and other stakeholders in order to provide economic and social growth.

In short the following three areas of responsibility can summarize this. First of all, this means to practice responsible business, throughout all processes and with all stakeholders. Secondly it involves addressing the challenges and opportunities that lie in the broad societal impact of the rapidly evolving software technology sector. This means in particular addressing security, privacy, and online child safety issues

[6] Suder / Payte, "Microsoft—A Case in Cross Company Transformation" *Thunderbird International Business Review* 48 no. 4 (July-August 2006): 555–69.
[7] Citizenship Report 2005, pp.4 Bill Gates, Microsoft Chairman and Chief Software Architect, WWW.microsofT.com/mscorP/ciTiZenshiP
[8] Regelbrugge (1999), "Promoting Corporate Citizenship—Opportunities for Business and Civil Society Engagement," CIVICUS World Alliance for Citizen Participation, 32.

[9] http://www.microsoft.com/about/corporatecitizenship/citizenship/about/mission.mspx, 12.08.06

through investments in collaborative agreements to enhance a safe computing experience for all. Finally, it involves making sure that the benefits of the knowledge economy involve everyone and be spread across the world.

Looking at its various areas of responsibility, Microsoft chooses to specify ambitious targets for success. In the knowledge economy area, it commits to broaden technology skills and reach a quarter billion people world-wide, underserved by technology by 2010. This target applies to Europe with the bold goal to help provide technology opportunities, content, IT skills training to 20 million people through the creation of the European Alliance on Skills for Employability and the investments of the Unlimited Potential Community Technology Skills Program. When the mission refers to help people realize their potential, and when we look at the most disadvantaged, it is clear why Microsoft saw the opportunity to make social investments relating to education and training. In this framework they decided to educate refugees and give them life opportunities. Training and education, humanitarian relief support and responsible capacity building can be seen as long-term business investments and enabling the most underserved to benefit from technology and realize their full potential. Aligning global citizenship to its core business, the social investments made by Microsoft were based on the core expertise, competences and resources of the company.[10]

Building upon the company focus on the provision of education and technology skills training to the most disadvantaged, Microsoft top management decided that the partnership with UNHCR would be a strategic part of its corporate citizenship, and compatible with the knowledge economy programs. The Unlimited Potential Community Technology Centres were used to drive forward the provision of training for refugees as the UNHCR partnership became a grantee of the Unlimited Potential program launched in 2003. At the same time, the refugees' registration kit called project Profile became a core part of the emergency response program: the first practical example of how to combine Microsoft's citizenship efforts with its core competencies as a technology and innovation developer. It was conceived to give refugees an identity card providing access to health care and education as well as the possibility to be reunited with family members. In the follow-up, an extension of this work led to numerous employees volunteering and sent to remote places in Africa to work with UNHCR.[11]

Today Jean-Philippe Courtois reflects upon the lessons learned from the corporate citizenship developments within the company; what these developments have meant for the company, its employees, the community and Microsoft's partners, all cooperating in this effort to work out synergies. Has the partnership with UNHCR been the most efficient to undertake as a strategy? What has each organisation gained from the partnership and what ethical assumptions have each partner been making when agreeing to cooperate? While it is possible to argue that Microsoft's motives are strictly pro-bono and humanitarian, the cynic could perceive the possibility of commercially-beneficial publicity being gained, offsetting some negative and widely held perceptions of a dominant company.

Conversely, one could argue that UNHCR's decision to take advantage of Microsoft's support to further its important humanitarian aims were responsible whilst others may be less sympathetic, arguing for example that all UN agencies properly receive non-partisan governmental support for what they do, and shouldn't risk the possible "taint" of commercial sponsorship in any form, particularly if that might encourage governments to reduce their commitments to it, or citizens that then feel that their consumer perceptions influence their opinion on UNHCR projects.

The United Nations High Commissioner for Refugees

United Nations High Commissioner for Refugees (UNHCR) is headquartered in Geneva, Switzerland and was established in 1950 by UN General Assembly after several earlier international institutions had been established to provide protection for refugees. It was first called the League of Nations (UN) and launched with the appointment of the Norwegian scientist and explorer Fridtjof Nansen as its first High Commissioner in 1921. In 1999, at the time when UNHCR entered into partnership with Microsoft the High Commissioner post was held by Sadako Ogata, followed by António Guterres 2005–09. Originally UNHCR was given a three year mandate, under the Geneva Convention of 1951 by the United Nations, to help settle the refugees of the Second World War, though due to the continuous new conflicts and therefore also refugees, it was changed in 2003 giving a mandate lasting until the refugee problem is solved. Overall UNHCR has helped an estimated 50 million people, earning two Nobel Peace Prizes. There are 6,540 people working for UNHCR in 116 countries[12] helping 20.8 million people.[13]

The UNHCR mandate based on the 1951 Geneva Refugee Convention and the 1967 Protocol involves coordinating international efforts to protect and aid refugees. The aim of UNHCR is to shield and help the 8.4 million refugees bring their lives back to a normal situation. A refugee is defined according to Geneva Convention 1951 § 1 A2 as: "people who are outside their countries because of a well-founded fear of persecution based on their race, religion, nationality, political opinion or membership in a particular social group, and who cannot or do not want to return home."[14] The mandate also covers assistance to asylum seekers. Basic help provided by UNHCR consists mainly of shelter, food, water, sanitation and medical care. UNHCR also provides help for approximately 6.6 million internally displaced people: These are people who have fled their homes, but not crossed any country borders. Because this group is not covered by their mandate, the international community is working to help this group in a more appropriate and complete

---

[10] E. Bonfiglioli, Director of Corporate Citizenship, Microsoft EMEA, interviewed 07.07.06
[11] http://www.microsoft.com/about/corporatecitizenship/citizenship/knowledge/emergencyresponse.mspx, 29.07.06

[12] http://www.unhcr.org/cgi-bin/texis/vtx/basics, 28.07.06
[13] UNHCR (2006) "2005 Global Refugee Trends," Field Information and Coordinated Support Section, Division of Operational Services, UNHCR Geneva, http://unhcr.org/statistics
[14] Wilkinson for UNHCR (2001), "The Wall Behind Which Refugees Can Shelter," *Refugees* 2, no. 123, Italy

way.[15] In addition UNHCR looks after 2.4 million stateless people, 1.6 million returnees and 773,000 asylum seekers. The remaining 960,000 are refugees of other concerns.[16]

Funding Partners

UN subsidises a little less than two percent of the UNHCR regular budget for administrative costs. The total UNHCR budget is of $1 billion annually (2004 figures).

In terms of funding, UNHCR is hence mainly dependent on donations made by countries, institutions, corporations and individuals. (For more information about direct contributions and annual budgets visit the www.unhcr.org.) Cooperative partnering institutions include; World Food Program, World Health Organisation, UN Development Program, International Committee of the Red Cross and the International Federation of the Red Cross and the Red Crescent among others. These partnerships, therefore, are essential for the achievement of the goals of UNHCR.[17]

UNHCR's partnership with Microsoft is one of the strategic corporate partnerships, which UNHCR had agreed to engage into at various levels of depth. Other main partners are Armani Group, Fuji Optical, Marionnaud, Nestlé, Nike, Schneider Electric, Merck & Co. Inc, PricewaterhouseCoopers, Manpower, and Statoil.

In their partnership with UNHCR, corporations agree to the UNHCR Corporate Code of Conduct, meaning that the corporations involved have to abide to the code both in principle and in practice: The intentions are that a code of conduct will lead to enduring and transparent relationships. UNHCR enters into partnership with the goal of fulfilling its mandate, not for personal financial gains. This is explicitly described to corporate partners. Further UNHCR seeks to engage with corporations that are socially responsible and which do not engage in irresponsible operations as described in the three criteria for responsible operations set forward by UNHCR:

1. Manufacture or sale of weapons or components
2. Child labour
3. Operations in countries subject to UN sanctions

Under these criteria, UNHCR is free to choose not to engage with any partner which has a public image reflecting the above mentioned three criteria. It is the responsibility of the corporation to inform of their previous and present business activities. In this, the partnership between Microsoft and UNHCR was an obvious choice for both parties.

The criteria also demand an engagement to operate with transparency and that all partnership information should be available to the public. UNHCR maintains its right to the sole decision power over its operations and the partnership should not compromise the integrity of UNHCR or its partner. This is also why the agency does not grant exclusivity to any corporation in

terms of partners, use, preference of promotion of any products and services. Finally, it was to be considered that the use of the UNHCR logo is allowed only when predetermined in writing for a particular activity and only during the time of the contract. For other uses specific authorisation had to be granted from the UNHCR agency.

Choosing UNHCR

During the past decades we have seen an increase in the number of companies, non-governmental organisations, institutions and foundations as well as intergovernmental organisations, which work for the public good. The competition for resources has become fierce and as a result business will have to choose with whom to collaborate.

UNHCR claims that it is in their own interest for business to invest in the work of UNHCR and refugees. The reason is that due to crisis and war, markets experience a negative impact; instability and insecurity, while businesses prosper in communities that are viably stable and safe. This includes the work of UNHCR.

UNHCR offers the framework of a global institution, with experience and expertise in its field operating across the world, as well as a being a proud winner of the NOBEL Peace Prize, twice. One of the most important factors is that 90% of donations are directly used for the target market. It makes a difference, indeed, to numerous institutions and NGOs that have been criticised for using a high percentage of donations for administrative costs. Finally also, it made a difference that UNHCR works with capacity building and durable solutions in their work to protect the refugees, which appeared of importance to the business side of Microsoft in its decision process.

Common Ground

After the first phase of the emergency response project, during the Kosovo crisis, the partnership was to be based on a common ground in order to develop and survive; with goals and objectives laid down in the Letter of Understanding. At the base lie the objectives to improve the livelihoods of refugees, through technology support and transfer of know-how used to raise the awareness and advocacy on Refugees' needs and potential. Microsoft's support with employee involvement, education and IT skills training was key to demonstrate the "human face of technology." The partnership was therefore to be based on commitment and core competences as well as trust and public relations.

For Microsoft and UNHCR these aspects were essential. For Microsoft it involved a substantial amount of resources, both in kind and cash to invest in humanitarian response and community building projects; and in principle, without a direct or immediate return on investment. For UNHCR the essentials lie in the fact that it is an intergovernmental organization—and a non-partisan organisation. A failure to keep the partnership would lead to loss of specific expertise and opportunities for developing pro bono innovation, direct cash grants and in kind support for training of UNHCR refugees. This again, would have a direct impact on refugees' livelihoods. For Microsoft a failure could lead to loss of reputational capital as well as employee pride and morale.

---

[15] http://www.unhcr.org/cgi-bin/texis/vtx/basics ,entered 28.07.06
[16] http://www.unhcr.org/cgi-bin/texis/vtx/events?id=3e7f46e04 09.08.06
[17] UNHCR (2005), "UNHCR's Mid-Year Financial Report for 2005," found on http://www.unhcr.org , entered 20.07.06

Upon the decision to work together, UNHCR and Microsoft engaged into a durable relationship that stimulated the enlargement and institutionalization of the firm's corporate citizenship staff.

Amongst these growth stimuli, the recruitment of several professionals in the area of Corporate Citizenship, Community Affairs and strategic partnerships were essential to structure global citizenship. As a vital part of this Elena Bonfiglioli, Director of Corporate Citizenship at Microsoft EMEA, was brought in to apply the most efficient contemporary strategies in the field. Mrs Bonfiglioli previously worked at CSR Europe— the European Business Network on Corporate Social Responsibility (www.csreurope.org) where she had worked with several companies on CSR programs and strategies. Amongst numerous initiatives she has also worked with the creation of the European Academy of Business in Society (EABIS).

Outcomes: The case of Project PROFILE

At the time, in 1999 Microsoft employed about 31,575 persons and had a net revenue of $19.75 billion an equivalent of 29% growth. Seven years later, in 2006 these numbers had accumulated heavily. Microsoft employed 71,172 persons and earned net revenues of $44.28 billion. Microsoft began with a dream of a PC on every desk and in every home. Thirty years ago that seemed impossible. Today, for the more than one billion people, life has changed profoundly: information is more readily available; connections are more easily made; commerce is achieved quicker; and success is closer than ever.

Initiated by Microsoft's employees, the Project PROFILE is an example of the technology innovation and skills-for-humanity initiatives of the company. The Project Profile registration system, the "Refugee Field Kit" is a self-contained transportable registration system which includes basic refugee bio-data and a digital photo of each refugee. The kit produces an ID card and a signature is taken from the refugee. The card also contains a two-dimensional bar-code which includes the coded refugee bio-data. The system keeps track of refugees, but also helps UNHCR identify their needs. During the Kosovo crisis, Microsoft donated 100 "registration kits" to UNHCR and the project was rolled out in over a dozen countries worldwide. Subsequently the kit has been adapted and upgraded to cope with other situations. The field kit was developed as a card-producing solution which does not include identification elements, except for the photo and the signature. These ID cards are primarily used for quick identification and as a protection document. The production of this type of card can be done by relatively inexpensive off-the-shelf computer equipment. The standardized system has proved very useful for UNHCR and it has had a major impact on refugees. The ID cards provide refugees with protection from forcible recruitment, arbitrary arrests and detention. It also ensures basic rights, family reunification and identification of special needs.[18]

John Bankuwiha, Burundian refugee in the UNHCR Refugee Camp, Lukole "B" Camp expressed the vital importance

of the registration kit and why the refugees prize the registration system:

By confusion I had registered for voluntary repatriation to Burundi. Realizing my mistake I ran over to the registration centre. Showing my ration card I hoped that they could find my name in the system. To my great relief my picture came up on the screen and the UNHCR staff could verify my status and my right to food. Once we are registered, we refugees are sure that our records in the computer will not be tampered with. This way our rights as refugees are protected and we can get all the assistance we are entitled to in the camps and once we return to our home country.

JOHN BANKUWIHA,
Burundian refugee, Tanzania.[19]

Innovating upon success: Unlimited Potential and the Community Technology Skills Program (CTSP)

The Unlimited Potential Community Technology Skills Program (CTSP) is part of a community initiative aimed to bring computer skills and training to the most disadvantaged, in this case to refugees and asylum seekers. It is part of Microsoft's Unlimited Potential initiative (UP) designed to help five billion people realize new opportunities, learn, connect, create and improve life by using the power of software. By partnering with governments, NGOs, educators and academics Microsoft aims to take an innovative approach to enabling new ways of social and economic empowerment for the underserved populations of the world.

The first centre to train refugees was created in St. Petersburg, Russia in collaboration with UNHCR and Red Cross. Computer literacy is becoming increasingly important in everyday-life. The aim is to help refugees live a normal life after repatriation, pursuing higher education and employment.

The UNHCR and Red Cross do vital work and make a real difference to the lives of millions of people in need. The St. Petersburg Learning Centre marks another significant milestone in our long-term partnership with UNHCR, and the start of an exciting new partnership with the Red Cross. Our employees have a genuine passion and commitment for putting information technology to work to overcome big challenges and we are proud and honoured to support them and our partners, here in St. Petersburg and around the world.

JEAN-PHILIPPE
Courtois at the opening ceremony April 15, 2004.[20]

The Centre provides refugees as well as the local community with sources of learning, distance education and Internet access and external sources of support for entrepreneurial projects. A new centre was developed in Tanzania, and was launched in September 2006.[21]

---

[18] Frauke Joosten Associate External Relations Officer for Private Sector Fundraising and Public Affairs Service at UNHCR, written interview 24.08.06

[19] "Microsoft and UNHCR team up to better protect refugees," 10.04.05 http://www.unhcr.org/cgi-bin/texis/vtx/partners?id=3d8f1be44

[20] "Hi-tech hope for refugees in Russia, thanks to UNHCR, Red Cross and Microsoft initiative", St. Petersburg, Russia 15.04.04 http://www.unhcr.org/cgi- bin/texis/vtx/partners/opendoc.htm?tbl=PARTNERS&page=home&id=40e2c66b4

[21] Frauke Joosten, UNHCR, 24.08.06

The St. Petersburg centre is equipped with personal computers, a server, software and community staff trained by Microsoft employees to deliver an IT curriculum designed to provide students at the Centre with basic and advanced IT skills, as well as provide support for self-study and other community-building activities.

This is a unique and important initiative. As the world's first such community learning centre for refugees, it is a defining moment on the road to a truly inclusive information society, and in our five-year partnership with Microsoft. Working with committed, passionate and innovative people from the business community is enabling UNHCR to really solve problems and provide modern, lasting solutions.

DENNIS BLAIR,
UNHCR Deputy Representative in the Russian Federation, at the opening ceremony.[22]

The UNHCR Council of Business Leaders

As the years progressed, UNHCR started to realize the potential of its various corporate partners. Some of the partner companies also pressed UNHCR to bring forces together and facilitate exchange and synergies amongst its various partners.

In January 2005, stimulated by discussions with Microsoft and Nike, UNHCR spear- headed the creation of the UNHCR Council of Business Leaders. It was launched in Davos, by the UNHCR High Commissioner together with executives from Microsoft, Nike, Manpower, Merck and PwC. The Council aims to create more solid avenues for leveraging the value from various business partnerships. The Council seeks to provide organizational support to UNHCR, capacity building on UNHCR activities like branding and PR, and also to provide the structure for an end-to-end approach to companies' investments for the refugees cause.

Its structure and organisation is so that corporate partners can mobilize the expertise of their executives, assess opportunities for direct or joint funding to UNHCR, and/or donate other resources such as tools, equipment and/ or volunteers. Companies are also encouraged to use their external media and communication tools to reach customers and partners to promote the image and cause of UNHCR. Internally the use of companies' network consisting of suppliers and employees is important as well to raise funds for UNHCR.

Entering into a partnership with UNHCR was an important choice at the time. It was the first time the company entered in a partnership with a UN Agency trying to find joint solutions for a common cause. The company learnt over time to mobilize all its assets: cash and software donations through the Community affairs team, the time, competencies and expertise of its volunteers to deliver real technology innovation through Microsoft Consulting Services, the management skills of its executives and its online marketing strategy through MSN.

Over time, the relationship started to be managed jointly by Corporate Affairs and the Global Strategic Accounts (GSA) team, which now manages other UN partnerships.

Working with UNHCR was a great opportunity to see how the company's core business intelligence could make a real difference to society in very unexpected ways. It is an example of what Porter today calls the "INSIDE OUT" and "OUTSIDE IN" model of CSR.

ELENA BONFIGLIOLI,
Director of Corporate Citizenship at Microsoft.[23]

Commitment and Core Competences

UNHCR and Microsoft categorised their efforts and projects around core commitments, which appears to allow for

EXHIBIT I Common grounds, Microsoft and UNHCR[24]

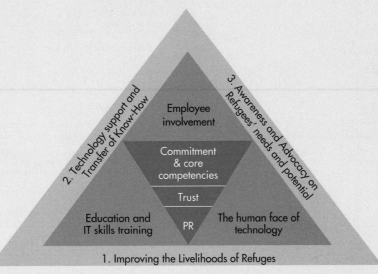

[22] "Hi-tech hope for refugees in Russia, thanks to UNHCR, Red Cross and Microsoft initiative" 15.04.04

[23] *Harvard Business Review*, December 2006.
[24]UNHCR Council of Business Leaders, "Partnering for Impact," 2006.

complementary action while being exclusive in nature. Microsoft's expertise and technology support has been used to create the projects and initiative commonly based on the functional needs of UNHCR and the competitive advantage of Microsoft. Subsequently this involves IT capacity building and application development.

Jean-Philippe Courtois remembers that employee volunteering had always played a very important role in the partnership, for both partners. Those Microsoft employees participating in the volunteering program were very passionate about helping fellow humans. In turn Microsoft excelled in citizenship practices, employee benefits, research and development and accessibility work.

On the other hand, during an internal study conducted for the company, PricewaterhouseCoopers found, in 2004, that there was little awareness and understanding of the company's citizenship initiative among Microsoft employees. As Microsoft began to structure its work more thoroughly, the challenge was to implement citizenship programs consistently in all of the worldwide subsidiaries and countries while being locally relevant and efficient. It was essential for Microsoft to put sufficient focus on key performance indicators, to develop appropriate metrics, and external reporting. There is still a lot yet to be done within and beyond the specific UNHCR partnership

Microsoft had enabled UNHCR to use advanced and complex systems making their work more efficient.

Using Microsoft's core business competencies and expertise enhances UNHCR's technological capacity, bringing the benefit of technology solutions closer to refugee communities and at the same time providing support for

UNHCR's general mandate - awareness raising and advocacy for refugees.

JOOSTEN FRAUKE,
Associate External Relations Officer for Private Sector Fundraising and Public Affairs Service at UNHCR.

Technology systems have been placed or improved at UNHCR headquarters, for UNHCR field offices and onsite in refugee camps, serving, again, both parties in the partnerships and the community involved.

In order to help refugees more directly, Microsoft moved rapidly into training grants through its global community investment program, Unlimited Potential. But also, the investment mentioned above, in Calks in St. Petersburg and Tanzania, bring efforts to improve the refugees' livelihood through access to education and opportunities.

But another very important aspect of the partnership became the public relations (PR) and branding exposure of UNHCR to promote the awareness of the UNHCR cause and brand amongst the general public. The budget of UNHCR still relies heavily on donors, and it does not always stretch to cover all expenditures. Especially within the business community, it is important to leverage the exposure and the brand of UNHCR. This is done by public relations and/or third party advertorials focusing on raising the awareness of refugees.

Evolution and Progress

Transitional Phase 2002–03

Despite the ambitious and enthusiastic beginnings with the Kosovo crisis, the partnership underwent a flex point, as organizational transition took place in 2002 and 2003 both in

EXHIBIT II Evolution of Partnership[25]

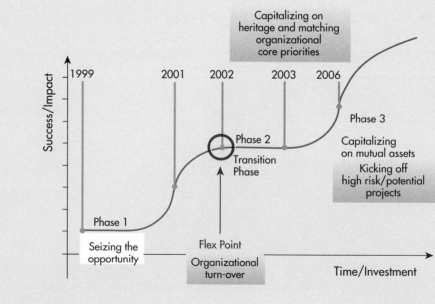

[25]UNHCR (2006), "Toyota Meeting" UNHCR's Corporate Partnership Programme, Bruxelles, January 19, 2006.

UNHCR and in Microsoft. The partnership managers in both organizations moved on to new challenges and the partnership, still in its piloting phase, was left with no direct owner. People managing the partnership changed. As a result the progress in the partnership slowed down in the short run.

Consolidation Phase 2003–05

In the aftermath of the transition period at Microsoft and in UNHCR, the years 2003 and 2004 brought a consolidation phase and new spirit. In December 2003 a formalization of the partnership took place as a three year contract was signed. The technology solution created for the Kosovo crisis was now further developed and rolled out to different refugee camps in Europe, Middle East and Africa (EMEA) region. Some improvements were now adopted to make the registration kit more adaptable, flexible and interoperable, in particular to language differences. However the system proved to be efficient and UNHCR decided to adopt it in all its operations.

The Project PROFILE was rolled out in the summer months of 2004 in various camps and Microsoft employees were encouraged to volunteer. The President of Microsoft EMEA at the time, Michel Lacombe, e-mailed employees across the region, seeking volunteers. Out of the 5000 contacted, over 400 employees were ready to contribute with their competences and time. Those who, for whatever reason, could not participate were supportive and proud of the initiative:

> *This is a fantastic initiative! I really felt proud of Microsoft when I read your email. Running a profitable business is big, delivering innovative products that change the way people work and behave is bigger, but doing all this and still without ignoring countries hit by war or other catastrophes is huge."*
>
> *Microsoft employee to CEO Jean-Philippe Courtois*[26]

In less than two weeks 250 employees responded, of which 12 were selected as technology experts in the fields of server systems, database and access management, and sent to various refugee camps for periods of 2–3 weeks.[27] The first pilot project to bring IT skills training opportunities to refugees was initiated in April 2004. The Community Technology Centre in Russia, St. Petersburg, proved successful and was, in 2006, undergoing an assessment period to determine the outcomes of the project at the same time of the launch of a centre in Tanzania.

Expansion and the Future of a Global Leader: How to Adapt to the Diversity of Stakeholders?

Yet, Jean-Philippe Courtois reflected, more needs to be done . . . with the partnership expanding in time and size, the creation of a team with credible resources was essential in order to achieve the objectives laid down in the framework.

---

[26] UNHCR (2006), "UNHCR and Microsoft Partnership," Toyota Meeting, UNHCR's Corporate Partnership Programme, Belgium
[27] Bonfiglioli, E., Director of Corporate Citizenship, Microsoft EmEA, interviewed 07.07.06

Top-management and world leaders gathered at the World Economic Forum in Davos in 2005 and created the Council of Business Leaders.

An expansion in the partnership took place. A briefing analyzed for UNHCR to note what and where further possibilities lay. Based on the core competencies of the member companies, this Council of Business Leaders, under the management of Bill Gates, Chief Architect of Microsoft, Angelina Jolie, goodwill ambassador, UNHCR, and Wendy Chamberlin, Deputy High Commission, UNHCR was established. The recognition of the communication resources and the network available to Microsoft and other partners, was used to promote the cause of UNHCR, which was turned into a major campaign; ninemillion.org.

Nonetheless, Microsoft reached a point of re-assessment of several projects. While global citizenship had become an integral part of the company, it was urgent to define if this field was to be expanded and how.

Both Project Profile and the building of the centre in St. Petersburg served as milestones to evaluate the effectiveness, capacity and impact of Microsoft's support. The creation of the Council was a milestone as it brought together a distinct partnership approach and it also led to the support of MSN to help raise awareness on the UNHCR brand which was crystallized in the www.ninemillion.org fundraising campaign with Nike and Right to play on the World refugee Day on June 20, 2006

As of now, would the company be able to explore the most efficient and effective strategies, initiatives, innovations and markets? Would it not benefit from the recruitment of managers of yet other fields, from private and public sectors, bringing fresh thinking from external minds into a company that came to the market lead three decades ago?

It was stated, and can be read on www.microsoft.com that: *"At Microsoft, we believe that constructive stakeholder engagement improves our business decision-making processes and helps us anticipate and address the changing expectations of society. We understand that our reputation outside the company is a direct reflection of how we demonstrate our corporate values. Engagement with customers, partners, shareholders, NGOs, governments, and other stakeholders will be essential in helping us identify and manage key issues that will test how successfully we live our values."*

Case Questions:

1. Is "partnership" the answer and can the company leverage all its assets to contribute pro bono publico?
2. Is Microsoft creating the right partnerships to complement its market opening and opportunity raising?
3. Was that lunchtime initiative, in 1999 during the Kosovo crisis, a sign for this vast multinational to serve the challenges of diversity internally and externally?
4. Was it an accident that Microsoft's corporate citizenship initiatives were formed at the very same time as the company's share value fell and anti-trust cases multiplied? Can a company explain its corporate citizenship activities as investments in the future?

CASE 3 NOKIA: BUSINESS INTERESTS VS GERMAN PRESSURES

*We did not get our message through early enough. Considering that the
reaction was so strong, something could have been done better.*[1]

–OLLI-PEKKA KALLASVUO,
Nokia President and CEO

The world's largest cellphone maker, Finland-based Nokia, in January 2008 announced that it would be closing its plant in Bochum in the German western state of North Rhine-Westphalia. The plant, which makes mobile phones would be closed by the middle of the year and production moved to a new plant in Romania—the latest entrant to the European Union (EU).[2] The move was being made to secure Nokia's long-term competitiveness.

The announcement sparked a wave of grief and indignation in the western German city. The next day, there were hundreds of employees demonstrating outside the Bochum plant in protest against the closure. Adding fuel to fire was Nokia's announcement of an annual global profit of €7.2 billion in 2007.[3] There were anti-Nokia and anti-Finnish sentiments with many consumers turning their backs on Nokia products. Politicians, trade unions and even some business leaders were among the protestors. Nokia was accused of behaving irresponsibly for closing down a profitable factory. Its move was labelled "caravan capitalism" and the company called a "subsidy locust" equating it to unwelcome profit-hungry foreign investors.

Nokia and the Mobile Handset Industry

Nokia produced four out of every 10 mobile phones sold worldwide and was well ahead of its competitors.[4] In 2007, its profits increased by 67% over the previous year. Nokia had stayed ahead of competition—on the strength of its brand, supply chain efficiency, a dominant position in emerging markets, understanding consumer needs and providing phones ranging from less than $50 to advanced devices featuring satellite

navigation and email. Nokia based its strategy on maintaining a large market share and economies of scale, which both accompany and support such a share.

For long, the mobile handset industry enjoyed healthy margins but since 2001, faced tremendous cost pressure, leading to weak profitability of many players and ongoing consolidation. Even though the markets resurged in 2004, growth was predicted to slow down from 2008. As demand in the developed markets of US and Europe saturated, handset makers turned to high-growth markets of the Middle East, Southeast Asia, Africa, China and India. According to Frost and Sullivan, a global business research and consulting firm, the Eastern European mobile communications market in 2006 had a penetration rate of 88% and was expected to reach 100% penetration before 2011.[5] For the emerging economies and developing nation markets, cheaper models were in demand. The companies provided low-cost handsets and for this, they reduced their Average Selling Prices (ASPs) with the international mobile phone prices falling by 35% in recent years.[6] In the price-conscious emerging markets, the basic phones were sold below $50 and there was a growing market for $25 and even $10 phones. For Nokia, China was the biggest market followed by India and Germany (Exhibit I).

As a result of rising cost levels, declining prices and high competition; low-cost manufacturing had become a necessity.

EXHIBIT I **Nokia: 10 Major Markets, Net Sales (€million)**

	2005	2006	2007	2008
China	3,403	4,913	5,898	5916
India	2,022	2,713	3,684	3719
Germany	1,982	2,060	2,641	2294
UK	2,405	2,425	2,574	2382
US	2,743	2,815	2,124	1907
Russia	1,410	1,518	2,012	2083
Spain	923	1,139	1,830	–
Italy	1,160	1,394	1,792	–
Indonesia	727	1,069	1,754	2046
Brazil	614	1,044	1,257	–

Source: Compiled by the author from "Markets", http://www.nokia.com/A4126480, February 2008 and "Form 20-F 2008", http://nokia.com/NOKIA_COM_1/ About_Nokia/Financials/form20-f_08.pdf

This case was written by Shanul Jain, under the direction of Rajendar Singh Rathore, Icfai Business School Case Development Centre. It is intended to be used as the basis for class discussion rather than to illustrate either effective or ineffective handling of a management situation. This case was compiled from published sources.

© 2009, Icfai Business School Case Development Centre

[1] "Nokia CEO Kallasvuo: 'No lifetime jobs in open competitive market'", http://www.hs.fi/english/article/Nokia+CEO+Kallasvuo+No+lifetime+jobs+in+open+competitive+market/1135233531655
[2] Romania joined the EU in January 2007 along with Bulgaria, taking the EU count to 27 members. Romania had the second lowest GDP in Europe.
[3] "Nokia, we want our money back", http://www.businessweek.com/globalbiz/content/mar2008/gb20080311_833979.htm, March 11th 2008
[4] "German politicians return cellphones amid Nokia boycott calls", http://www.dw-world.de/dw/article/0,2144,3076534,00.html, January 18th 2008

[5] Conti Pablo Juan, "Drive for the East", http://www2.theiet.org/OnComms/sector/magazine.cfm?issueID=276&articleID=062D42B5-CE1F-C7EF-720B14AE507F78B9, 2008
[6] Williamson Hugh, "Nokia to rethink communication policy", http://us.ft.com/ftgateway/superpage.ft?news_id=fto051320081558153914&page=2, May 13th 2008

EXHIBIT II   Europe's Low-cost Backyard

Monthly minimum wage, 2003, €

Croatia
Hungary
Poland
Czech Republic
Turkey*
Slovakia
Romania
Shanghai**
Bulgaria

* Gross wages in industry   **2004

Monthly minimum wage, as of January 1st 2008, €

- Croatia – 330
- Hungary – 271
- Poland – 312
- Czech Republic – 301
- Turkey – 302.61*
- Slovakia – 240
- Romania – 138
- Shanghai – 69
- Bulgaria – 112

* As of January 1st 2007

Compiled by the author from "Transformed", http://www.economist.com/surveys/displaystory.cfm?story_id=E1_QTDDVGQ, June 23rd 2005 and "Statutory minimum wages", http://www.databasece.com/en/statutory-minimum-wages

On the trend, Santosh Kumar, an analyst at Frost and Sullivan remarked, "This is encouraging the continuing migration of manufacturing processes in the electronics industry to low-cost Asian countries and, lately, to Eastern Europe."[7] Labour costs in the Central and Eastern European (CEE) countries were much lower than in the Western European nations (Exhibit II). Criteria for the inclusion of the CEE nations to the EU included stability of institutions, democratic governments, respect for human rights, a functioning market economy, the capacity to cope with market forces and competition within the EU and commitment to the aims of the European economic and monetary union. Apart from low wages, investors were lured there by high productivity and simple taxes. Multinationals built operations there and set new standards for—wages, training, workplace safety and technology transfer creating a "meritocracy in which hard work, ethical behaviour and a desire to learn" were properly valued. However, it was estimated that even these countries could lose their competitive advantage as wage costs were rising and labour force shrinking with people emigrating to the richer Western European nations like Britain and Germany.

Nokia's plant in Romania—its 11th around the world—was a part of a programme to shift production to low-cost locations. In Europe, Nokia had manufacturing units in Finland, Germany and Hungary principally supplying Europe, the Middle East and Africa. There was a plant in Britain, which manufactured Vertu—Nokia's line of luxury phones. Most of Nokia's cellphone production was in low-cost countries. A plant each in Brazil and Mexico supplied to the North and South American markets and two plants in China and one each in India and South Korea, supplied to China and the Asia-Pacific market. Even though there were a number of low-cost production sites, the majority of the workforce was in Finland (Exhibits III(a) and III(b)) followed by Germany. In Germany, apart from a production facility, Nokia also had a sales and marketing unit in Düsseldorf and a devices R&D team in Ulm.

However, Nokia had admitted that labour costs even in a high-cost country such as Germany made up significantly less than 5% of the total product costs.[8]

EXHIBIT IIIA   Nokia: 10 Major Countries, Personnel, December 31st 2007

	2007	2006	2005
Finland	23,015	23,894	23,485
Germany	13,926	3,887	3,610
China	12,856	7,191	5,860
India	11,491	6,494	1,609
Brazil	8,527	1,960	2,184
Hungary	6,601	4,947	4,186
US	5,269	5,127	5,883
Mexico	3,056	2,764	1,901
UK	2,618	2,317	1,956
Italy	2,129	493	–

Source: "Personnel", http://www.nokia.com/A4126479, February 2008

EXHIBIT IIIB   Number of Employees at Nokia: Region-wise (2008)

Finland	23,478
Other European countries	37,714
Middle•East & Africa	5,032
China	14,099
Asia•Pacific	20,359
North America	8,427
Latin America	12,614
Nokia Group	**121,723**

Source: "Form 20-F 2008", http://nokia.com/NOKIA_COM_1/About_Nokia/Financials/form20-f_08.pdf, page 116

---

[7] "Drive for the East", op.cit.

[8] "Commentary: Nokia's relocation plans stir globalisation debate", http://eetimes.eu/showArticle.jhtml?articleID=205907701, January 22nd 2008

German Competitiveness

Germany, the world's third largest economy after the US and Japan, was the largest contributor to EU funds. Its socialist market concept allowed the economy to be governed by market forces while the state's role was to support poor people and correct market imperfections. The conviction was that the economy and society were interdependent and that companies were responsible not only to shareholders but to other stakeholders, including employees and local communities. Non-business institutions—like the unions and government—had a say in the business and management. Employers and unions were known as "Soziale Partner" or "social partners." Labour was considered a full participant in economic and social life. Most companies had to participate in collective bargaining—nationally, regionally or both, depending on the industry.

Worker's representation at the workplace was through the agency of the works council (Betriebsrat), which was formally independent of unions. The principle of co-determination meant that unions and employees had a say in company policy as well as shared responsibility for the firm. Information and consultation about restructuring processes—particularly those including the closure of a whole site—were central tasks of the works councils and they usually worked to discourage changes such as relocations and the entry of new firms.

Germany's workforce was highly skilled, well educated, very productive and among the world's highest wage and benefits earners. According to *The Economist*, in 2004, workers in Germany earned an average of $26 an hour, compared with $21 in America and $17 in France and Britain.[9] It also had some of the strictest labour laws, especially those related to hiring and firing practices (Exhibit IV). Ironically, these same labour laws resulted in a low reemployment rate of 40% as compared to 70% in the US of workers who lost their jobs as a result of offshoring of operations.

After reunification in 1990, Germany stumbled from its position as the economic powerhouse of Europe. Unemployment levels rose as a result of many German businesses considering relocating abroad. The high labour costs, the lesser work hours and also the highest basic corporate tax rate in western Europe made firms choose relocating. The co-determination principle also made the works council too powerful.

However, in the past 4–5 years, Germany had worked to become more business-friendly with lower corporate taxes, flexible workers and less bureaucracy. Since 2001, Germany's unit labour costs had fallen by around 20% relative to Italy's and Spain's.[10] However, the 2007–08 Global Competitiveness Report of the World Economic Forum showed that wages in Germany were higher than justified by competitiveness with the situation only deteriorating (Exhibit V).

The fall of the iron curtain within Europe and the transition of state socialist societies opened up new markets for Western European companies. Since the mid-1990s, these companies as well as global players from other world regions increasingly used the emerging options in CEE. In 2004, German firms sent roughly 60% of their offshore work to Eastern Europe. Between 2001 and 2006, almost 188,000 jobs moved from Germany to Eastern Europe.

In the first quarter of 2008, according to a European Restructuring Monitoring report, there were 268 cases of restructuring in the EU, involving 65,319 job losses with Germany and the UK accounting for over a half of all announced job losses.[11] The greatest restructuring was in the post and telecommunications sector, added to by Nokia's decision to relocate its factory to Romania.

EXHIBIT IV   **The Strictness of Regulations Governing Employment Protection in OECD (Organisation for Economic Cooperation and Development) Countries**

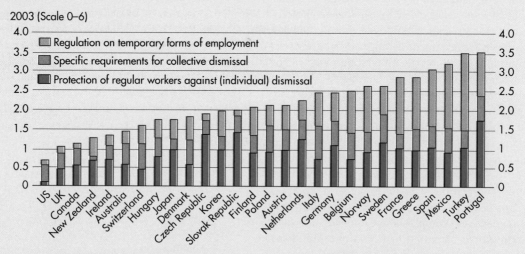

2003 (Scale 0–6)

Legend:
- Regulation on temporary forms of employment
- Specific requirements for collective dismissal
- Protection of regular workers against (individual) dismissal

Countries (left to right): US, UK, Canada, New Zealand, Ireland, Australia, Switzerland, Hungary, Japan, Denmark, Czech Republic, Korea, Slovak Republic, Finland, Poland, Austria, Netherlands, Italy, Germany, Belgium, Norway, Sweden, France, Greece, Spain, Mexico, Turkey, Portugal

Source: "Eastern Influx: Automotive manufacturing in Central and Eastern Europe", http://www.pwc.com/extweb/pwcpublications.nsf/docid/5272B7569A7EAE4F85257279006605B3/$File/EasternInfluxPart3Final.pdf, August 2007

[9] "How to pep up Germany's economy", http://www.economist.com/finance/displaystory.cfm?story_id=E1_NGQSPDG, May 6th 2004

[10] "Back above the bar again", http://www.economist.com/finance/displaystory.cfm?story_id=9469031, July 12th 2007

[11] "European Restructuring Monitor Quarterly", http://www.eurofound.europa.eu/emcc/erm/templates/displaydoc.php?docID=46, 2008

EXHIBIT V   Wages vs Competitiveness

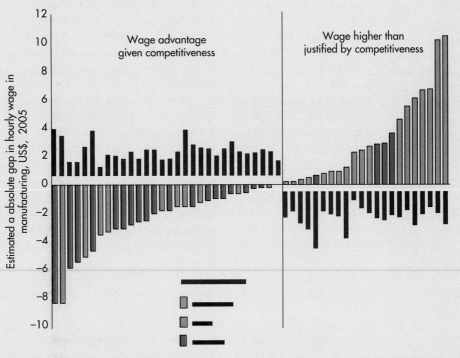

Source: "The Global Competitiveness Report 2007–2008", http://www.gcr.weforum.org/, October 31st 2007

Nokia's Decision to Close its German Plant and the Resulting Backlash

Nokia was the last major cellphone manufacturer in Germany and was often praised for this, as other companies had offshored production long ago. The telecommunications industry was not faring well. Over 3,000 people had lost their jobs when BenQ Mobile declared bankruptcy in 2006. Motorola too had announced that it would dismantle its factory in Flensburg in northern Germany. The BenQ closure saw a series of unsuccessful protests and demonstrations and the BenQ works council agreed to set up a holding company to find replacement jobs, but one year down the line, more than half the people were still unemployed.

In recent years, Siemens, Volkswagen and Opel, the General Motors subsidiary had closed their plants in Germany. Added to the list now was Nokia. The Nokia move, for some analysts, did not come as a surprise. Jari Honko, an analyst with the Finnish bank eQ, said, "In the long term I consider this a smart move. In the short term, we don't know yet about the costs. Generally, Germany is an expensive country to ramp down a plant or lay off staff. This is likely to be an expensive move in the short term."[12] The spectre of protests that followed the earlier closures was repeated on Nokia's move too.

Germany's biggest union, IG Metall, called Nokia's plans 'inhuman' and 'socially unacceptable'. It also said that steps needed to be taken to keep companies from abandoning

Germany. Berthold Huber, union head, said, "In Germany it is much too easy for companies to close factories and leave people unemployed. These companies do enormous damage to society, and they need to be held responsible for it."[13]

Nokia had announced its plan to set up a plant in the Cluj-Napoca county of Romania in 2007. The plant would be built with an investment of €60 million and employ 500 people in the first phase, reaching a count of 3,500 by the end of 2009. Since the new production facility would be built from scratch, it would gradually allow a tight integration of suppliers and partners who would locate their operations there and thus overall productivity would improve. Nokia would be increasing its production capacity for supplying phones to Europe, the Middle East and Africa.

As the plant in Romania would become functional, the plant in Germany would be closed. According to Nokia, the Bochum plant, opened in 1987, even with additional investments for its renewal would not be globally competitive. Nokia chairman, Olli-Pekka Kallasvuo said, "Unfortunately, the costs of labour, including non-wage labour costs, in Germany are not competitive enough for the mass-production of Nokia products." He pointed out that the Bochum plant was responsible for 6% of the company's global mobile phone manufacturing and even for 23% of all personnel costs within its production unit.[14] The production process would be in Romania and other functions moved to Hungary and Finland.

In Romania, the average monthly salaries at €219 ($318) would be about one-tenth of the average wage of workers in

[12] "Nokia to cut up to 2,300 staff", http://www.reuters.com/article/rbssTech MediaTelecomNews/idUSL153076420080115?sp=true, January 15th 2008

[13] "German politicians return cellphones amid Nokia boycott calls", op.cit.
[14] "Nokia, we want our money back", op.cit.

Bochum.[15] The plant closure would result in 2,300 job losses and an estimated 2,000 jobs at suppliers and temporary employment agencies would also be affected. The Bochum region, once a booming steel-and-coal industry centre, was already reeling under an unemployment rate of 10.5%—significantly higher than the German average.[16]

Following Nokia's announcement, there were demonstrations and calls for boycott of Nokia phones. The decision was also condemned because the Bochum plant had never operated at a loss. In 2007, the plant had made a €134 million operating profit, corresponding to a profit of €90,000 per production worker.[17] A labour specialist at IW, a business-friendly think-tank, said, Nokia's announcement came completely unexpectedly, with "no clear explanation of why such a profitable company needed to close a productive factory."[18]

Ulrike Kleinebrahm, local head of IG Metall and member of the supervisory board of Nokia GmbH (Germany) said, "That is a catastrophe for Bochum. The news hit us like a bomb. We cannot understand why Nokia closes down this site despite having earned so much money here. The union will take action against Nokia's decision."[19]

The term 'Nokia' in German parlance became synonymous with seemingly uncaring companies reaping globalisation's benefits at the expense of employees and local communities. With elections imminent in several German states, politicians too joined the protests. There were many who sent their Nokia handset back to the vendor. Nokia was criticised for not making any attempts to reduce expenses to maintain production in Germany. German Economics Minister Michael Glos said this would taint Nokia's reputation, "When a very large and globally recognised company, which lives from its brand and image, makes this kind of decision, it would be well advised to look at the consequences." Guenter Verheugen, EU commissioner for Enterprise and Industry and a German pointed to "serious management failures", saying that "Nokia's behaviour is the product of a new religion which idolises shareholder value(. . .)That is the wrong path."[20]

Nokia was also accused of ingratitude and of misusing German state subsidies. The company had accepted €88 million in subsidies in the past and guaranteed 2,856 jobs in Bochum, but there were only 2,300 people working in the plant. Nokia countered by saying that it had not only fulfilled but also exceeded the terms of the agreement, by employing more than 3,200 workers on average from 2001 onwards. Even though the deadline for the job guarantee expired in September 2006, Christa Toben, North Rhine-Westphalia's State Minister for Economy, announced to check whether Nokia should pay back €17 million in subsidies.

Nokia officials agreed that in Romania and Hungary, the local governments granted higher subsidies for establishing activities than Germany did and the firm could have indirectly received subsidies in Romania in the form of financial help, for example, for building roads to the factory. The left-leaning newspaper *Süddeutsche Zeitung* wrote, "People can and will examine whether Nokia has a legal obligation to repay its subsidies. But it seems at first sight that they will not need to, assuming that the deadlines agreed (for guaranteeing jobs) had already passed. . . . Nevertheless, Nokia would be well advised to make a gesture of good will. The amount involved is €88 million, a relatively modest sum for the global company, and something of much higher value is at stake, namely its good reputation."[21]

German leaders suspected that the Romanian government had lured Nokia with the help of subsidies from the European Regional Development Fund. The EU while refuting these charges said that it may offer funding to Nokia workers set to lose their jobs. Commission President, José Manuel Barroso, said, "I can understand the shock of the people in Bochum. It is precisely because we know how difficult transformation is that we mobilise our social and globalisation funds so that member states do not have to absorb these changes on their own."[22]

People were taken aback by the abrupt nature of Nokia's decision given the company's customer-friendly image and description of itself as "very human" on its website.[23] There were arguments that Nokia did not take the usual approach to a plant closure in Germany. Companies, before announcing a closure, usually explained in public that there were problems and the company needed to make big cuts. After this, the workforce, trade unions and local politicians were involved in considering possible solutions. The blow would be softened even if the closure was inevitable. "Even if this still happens, this process adds to the legitimacy of the company's decision. It can say (that) it exhausted all options", observed professor Volker Wittke of Göttingen university.[24] He further added that it was surprising that Nokia, being a global player and having roots in Scandinavia with its moderate labour relations traditions, "didn't know about acting this way in Germany"[25]

Nokia, while refusing to enter discussions with German authorities about keeping the plant in operation, stated that it would adopt the same strategy if such a situation arose again. The company knew of the option of involving the various parties in discussions and had considered it before announcing the closure, but had finally rejected it as it did not fit with Nokia's way of doing business. Juha Äkräs (Äkräs), Nokia's senior vice president for human resources, said, "Our core values as a company are to face the reality of tough decisions and be honest about them with our employees. We are a values-driven, responsible company that does not play internal politics (with employees)."[26]

[15] Ibid.
[16] "Commentary: Nokia's relocation plans stir globalisation debate", op.cit.
[17] Sokoll Lean and Kreickenbaum Martin, "Europe: Nokia unions side with management", http://www.wsws.org/articles/2008/feb2008/noki-f05.shtml, February 5th 2008
[18] Williamson Hugh, "Crossed lines between Finland and Germany", http://us.ft.com/ftgateway/superpage.ft?news_id=fto051320081745313940, May 13th 2008
[19] "Nokia to cut up to 2,300 staff", op.cit.
[20] "Germany's Nokia workers may receive EU help", http://www.euractiv.com/en/socialeurope/germany-nokia-workers-may-receive-eu-help/article-169749, January 21st 2008

[21] Smith Gordon David, "Germany Rages at Nokia Plant closure", http://www.businessweek.com/globalbiz/content/jan2008/gb20080117_788133.htm?campaign_id=rss_daily, January 17th 2008
[22] "Germany's Nokia workers may receive EU help", op.cit.
[23] Williamson Hugh, "Nokia accused of 'caravan capitalism'", http://www.business-standard.com/ft/storypage_ft.php?&autono=311214, January 21st 2008
[24] "Crossed lines between Finland and Germany", op.cit.
[25] Ibid.
[26] "Crossed lines between Finland and Germany", op.cit.

Others in the Nokia management echoed the same sentiment with Arja Suominen, Nokia's senior vice president of communications, adding that the German approach may "lengthen the pain. False hopes do not necessarily make the situation better. You can only announce bad news once."[27]

Äkräs, while admitting that Nokia after the announcement failed to explain clearly why the closure was necessary, rejected the charge that Nokia should have adapted to German practices. He said, "We are not used to having discussions in public before such a decision is made. It's a cultural issue; we don't normally do it like that in Finland."[28] The company had to think about its global operations and international staff – and not just Germany – and "has to be consistent, he said."

Case Questions

1. What are the trends in the mobile handset industry? What is Nokia's strategy and how has globalisation changed its way of operation?

2. Was the German backlash against Nokia justified? How can nations make themselves more competitive?

3. What, if any, were the flaws in Nokia's approach to announcing and handling its plant closure? What can the company do now for damage control?

[27] Ibid.

[28] Ibid

The Cultural Context of Global Management

Understanding the Role of Culture

OBJECTIVES:

1. To understand how culture affects all aspects of international management.

2. To be able to distinguish the major dimensions which define cultural differences among societies or groups.

3. To emphasize the need for international managers to have cultural intelligence in order to interact successfully in host countries.

4. To recognize the critical value differences which frequently affect job behaviors.

5. To be able to develop a working "cultural profile" typical of many people within a certain society, as an aid to expected attitudes toward work, negotiations, etc.

6. To understand the interaction between culture and the use of the internet.

Opening Profile: Adjusting Business to Saudi Arabian Culture

For most outsiders, Saudi Arabia is a land of contrasts and paradoxes. (Map 3-1 shows its location.) It has supermodern cities, but its strict Islamic religious convictions and ancient social customs, on which its laws and customs depend, often clash with modern economic and technical realities. Saudi Arabians sometimes employ latitude in legal formation and enforcement to ease these clashes and sometimes accommodate different behaviors from foreigners. Nevertheless, many foreigners misunderstand Saudi laws and customs or find them contrary to their own value systems. Foreign companies have had mixed success in Saudi Arabia, due in large part to how well they understood and adapted imaginatively to Saudi customs.

Companies from countries with strict separation between state and religion or where few people actively engage in religion find Saudi Arabia's pervasiveness of religion daunting. Religious decrees have sometimes made companies rescind activities. For example, an importer halted sales of the children's game Pokémon because the game might encourage the un-Islamic practice of gambling, and a franchisor was forced to remove the face under the crown in Starbucks' logo because Saudi authorities felt the public display of a woman's face was religiously immoral. However, most companies know the requirements in advance. For instance, Coty Beauty omits models' faces on point-of-purchase displays that it depicts in other countries. Companies know that they must remove the heads and hands from mannequins and must not display them scantily clad. Companies, such as McDonald's, dim their lights, close their doors, and stop attending to customers during the five times per day that men are called to pray. Companies also adjust voluntarily to gain the good will of customers—for example, by converting revenue-generating space to prayer areas. (Saudi Arabian Airlines does this in the rear of its planes, and the U.K.'s Harvey Nichols does this in its department store.) During the holy period of Ramadan, people are less active during the day because they fast, so many stores shift some operating hours to the evenings when people prefer to shop.

In 2000, Saudi Arabia ratified an international agreement designed to eliminate the discrimination of women; however, its prescribed behaviors for women appear paradoxical to outsiders. On the one hand, women now outnumber men in Saudi Arabian universities and own about 20 percent of all Saudi businesses. (There are separate male and female universities, and female-owned businesses can sell only to women.) Women also comprise a large portion of Saudi teachers and doctors. On the other hand, women account for only about 7 percent of the workforce. They cannot have private law or architectural firms, nor can they be engineers. They are not permitted to drive, because this may lead to evil behavior. They must wear *abayas* (robes) and cover their hair completely when in public. They cannot work alongside men except in the medical profession, and they cannot sell directly to male customers. If they are employed where men work, they must have separate work entrances and be separated from males by partitions. They must be accompanied by an adult male relative when dealing with male clerks.

MAP 3-1 Saudi Arabia comprises most of the Arabian peninsula. All of the countries bordering Saudi Arabia are Arab countries (meaning that the first language is Arabic), and all are predominately Islamic.

The female prescriptions have implications for business operations. For example, the Saudi American Bank established branches for and staffed only by women. Pizza Hut installed two dining rooms—one for single men and one for families. (Women do not eat there without their families.) Both Harvey Nichols and Saks Fifth Avenue have created women-only floors in their department stores. On lower levels, there is mixed shopping, all male salespeople (even for products like cosmetics and bras), and no changing rooms or places to try cosmetics. On upper floors, women can check their *abayas* and shop in jeans, spandex, or whatever. The stores have also created drivers' lounges for their chauffeurs. A downside is that male store managers can visit upper floors only when the stores are closed, which limits their observations of situations that might improve service and performance. Similarly, market research companies cannot rely on discussions with family-focused groups to determine marketing needs. Because men do much more of the household purchasing, companies target them more in their marketing than in other countries.

Why do high-end department stores and famous designers operate in Saudi Arabia where women cover themselves in *abayas* and men typically wear *thobes* (long robes)? Simply, the many very rich people in Saudi Arabia are said to keep Paris couture alive. Even though Saudi Arabia prohibits fashion magazines and movies, this clientele knows what is in fashion. (The government also prohibits satellite dishes, but some estimates say that two-thirds of Saudi homes have them.) Women buy items from designers' collections, which they wear abroad or in Saudi Arabia only in front of their husbands and other women. Underneath their *abayas*, they often wear very expensive jewelry, makeup, and clothing. Wealthy men also want the latest high-end fashions when traveling abroad.

Another paradox is that about 60 percent of the Saudi private workforce is foreign, even though the unemployment rate is about 30 percent. Changing economic conditions are at least partially responsible for this situation. In the early 1980s, Saudi oil revenues caused per capita income to jump to about $28,000, but this plummeted below $7,000 by the early 2000s. When incomes were high, Saudis brought in foreigners to do most of the work. At the same time, the government liberally supported university training, including study abroad. Saudis developed a mentality of expecting foreigners to do all the work, or at least some of the work, for them. The New Zealand head of National Biscuits & Confectionery said that Saudis now want only to be supervisors and complain if they have to work at the same level as people from Nepal, Bangladesh, and India. Although the government has taken steps to replace foreign workers with Saudis, prevailing work attitudes impede this transition. For example, the acceptance by a Saudi of a bellboy job at the Hyatt Regency hotel in Jidda was so unusual that Saudi newspapers put his picture on their front pages.

Saudi Arabian legal sanctions seem harsh to many outsiders. Religious patrols may hit women if they show any hair in public. The government carries out beheadings and hand-severances in public and expects passers-by to observe the punishments, some of which are for crimes that would not be offenses in other countries. For example, the government publicly beheaded three men in early 2002 for being homosexuals. However, there are inconsistencies. For example, religious patrols are more relaxed about women's dress codes in some Red Sea resorts, and they are more lenient toward the visiting female executives of MNEs than toward Saudi women. Whereas they don't allow Saudi women to be flight attendants on Saudi Arabian Airlines because they would have to work alongside men, they permit women from other Arab countries to do so. Further, in foreign investment compounds where almost everyone is a foreigner, these religious patrols make exceptions to most of the strict religious prescriptions.

Interesting situations concern the charging of interest and the purchase of accident insurance, both of which are disallowed under strict Islamic interpretations of the Koran. In the case of interest, the Saudi government gives interest-free loans for mortgages. This worked well when Saudi Arabia was awash with oil money, but borrowers must now wait about 10 years for a loan. In the case of accident insurance (by strict Islamic doctrine, there are no accidents, only preordained acts of God), the government eliminated prohibitions because businesses needed the insurance.

Personal interactions between cultures are tricky, and those between Saudis and non-Saudis are no exception. For example, Parris-Rogers International (PRI), a British publishing house, sent two salesmen to Saudi Arabia and paid them on a commission basis. They expected that by moving aggressively, the two men could make the same number of calls as they could in the United Kingdom. They were used to working eight-hour days, to having the undivided attention of potential clients, and to restricting conversation to the business transaction. To them, time was money. However, they found that appointments seldom began at the scheduled time and most often took place at cafés where the Saudis would engage in what the salesmen considered idle chitchat. Whether in a café or in the office, drinking coffee or tea and talking to acquaintances seemed to take precedence over business matters. The salesmen began showing so much irritation at "irrelevant" conversations, delays, and interruptions from friends that they caused irrevocable damage to the company's objectives. The Saudi counterparts considered them rude and impatient.

Whereas businesspersons from many countries invite counterparts to social gatherings at their homes to honor them and use personal relationships to cement business arrangements, Saudis view the home as private and even consider questions about their families as rude and an invasion of privacy. In contrast, Saudi businessmen seldom regard business discussions as private; they thus welcome friends to sit in. The opposite is true in many countries.

In spite of contrasts and paradoxes, foreign companies find ways to be highly successful in Saudi Arabia. In some cases, legal barriers to some products, such as alcoholic beverages and pork products, have created boons for other products, such as soft drinks and turkey ham. In addition, some companies have developed specific practices in response to Saudi conditions and have later benefited from them in their home countries. For example, companies, such as Fuji and Kodak, created technology for while-you-wait photo development for Saudi Arabia because customers wanted to retrieve photos without anyone else seeing them. They transferred this technology to the United States several years later.

Source: John D. Daniels, Lee H. Radebaugh, and Daniel P. Sullivan, *International Business: Environments and Operations*, 10th ed. © 2004. Reprinted by permission of Pearson Education, Inc., Upper Saddle River, NJ.

This chapter's opening profile describes how an understanding of the local culture and business environment can give managers an advantage in competitive industries. Foreign companies—no matter how big—can ignore those aspects to their peril. Such differences in culture and the way of life in other countries necessitate that managers develop international expertise to manage on a contingency basis according to the host-country environment. Powerful, interdependent factors in that environment—political, economic, legal, technological, and cultural—influence management strategy, functions, and processes.

A critical skill for managing people and processes in other countries is **cultural savvy**—that is, a working knowledge of the cultural variables affecting management decisions. (More recently, that skill has become known as cultural intelligence, or cultural quotient (CQ)). Managers have often seriously underestimated the significance of cultural factors. According to numerous accounts, many blunders made in international operations can be attributed to a lack of cultural sensitivity.[1] Examples abound. Scott Russell, senior vice president for human resources at Cendant Mobility in Danbury, Connecticut, recounts the following:

> *An American company in Japan charged its Japanese HR manager with reducing the workforce. The Japanese manager studied the issue but couldn't find a solution within cultural Japanese parameters; so when he came back to the Americans, he reduced the workforce by resigning—which was not what they wanted.*[2]

Cultural sensitivity, or **cultural empathy,** is an awareness and an honest caring about another individual's culture. Such sensitivity requires the ability to understand the perspective of those living in other (and very different) societies and the willingness to put oneself in another's shoes.

International managers can benefit greatly from understanding the nature, dimensions, and variables of a specific culture and how these affect work and organizational processes. This cultural awareness enables them to develop appropriate policies and determine how to plan, organize, lead, and control in a specific international setting. Such a process of adaptation to the environment is necessary to successfully implement strategy. It also leads to effective interaction in a workforce of increasing cultural diversity, in both the United States and other countries.

Company reports and management studies make it clear that a lack of cultural sensitivity costs businesses money and opportunities. One study of U.S. multinational corporations found that poor intercultural communication skills still constitute a major management problem. Managers' knowledge of other cultures lags far behind their understanding of other organizational processes.[3] In a synthesis of the research on cross-cultural training, Black and Mendenhall found that up to 40 percent of expatriate managers leave their assignments early because of poor performance or poor adjustment to the local environment. About half of those who remain are considered only marginally effective. Furthermore, they found that cross-cultural differences are the cause of failed negotiations and interactions, resulting in losses to U.S. firms of over $2 billion a year for failed expatriate assignments alone.[4]

Other evidence indicates, however, that cross-cultural training is effective in developing skills and enhancing adjustment and performance. In spite of such evidence, U.S. firms do little to take advantage of such important research and to incorporate it into their ongoing training programs, whose purpose is ostensibly to prepare managers before sending them overseas.

Too often, the importance of such training in developing cultural sensitivity is realized much too late.

This chapter provides a conceptual framework with which companies and managers can assess relevant cultural variables and develop cultural profiles of various countries. This framework is then used to consider the probable effects of cultural differences on an organization and their implications for management. To do this, the powerful environmental factor of cultural context is examined. The nature of culture and its variables and dimensions are first explored, and then specific differences in cultural values and their implications for the on-the-job behavior of individuals and groups are considered. Cultural variables, in general, are discussed in this chapter. The impact of culture on specific management functions and processes is discussed in later chapters as appropriate.

CULTURE AND ITS EFFECTS ON ORGANIZATIONS

Societal Culture

As generally understood, the **culture** of a society comprises the shared values, understandings, assumptions, and goals that are learned from earlier generations, imposed by present members of a society, and passed on to succeeding generations. This shared outlook results, in large part, in common attitudes, codes of conduct, and expectations that subconsciously guide and control certain norms of behavior.[5] One is born into, not with, a given culture, and gradually internalizes its subtle effects through the socialization process. Culture results in a basis for living grounded in shared communication, standards, codes of conduct, and expectations.[6] Over time, cultures evolve as societies adapt to transitions in their external and internal environments and relationships. A manager assigned to a foreign subsidiary, for example, must expect to find large and small differences in the behavior of individuals and groups within that organization. As depicted in Exhibit 3-1, these differences result from the societal, or sociocultural, variables of the culture, such as religion and language, in addition to prevailing national variables, such as economic, legal, and political factors. National and sociocultural variables, thus, provide the context for the development and perpetuation of cultural variables. These cultural variables, in turn, determine basic attitudes toward work, time, materialism, individualism, and change. Such attitudes affect an individual's motivation and expectations regarding work and group relations, and they ultimately affect the outcomes that can be expected from that individual.

EXHIBIT 3-1 Environmental Variables Affecting Management Functions

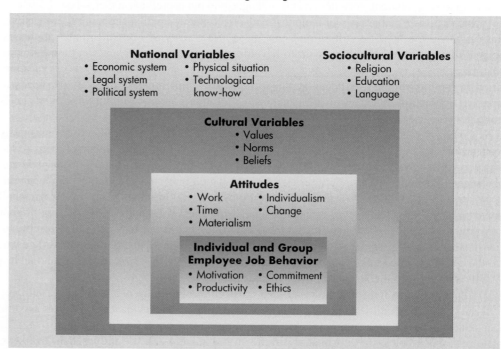

Organizational Culture

Compared to societal culture, which is often widely held within a region or nation, **organizational culture** varies a great deal from one organization, company, institution, or group to another. Organizational culture represents those expectations, norms, and goals held in common by members of that group. For a business example, consider the oft-quoted comparison between IBM, considered traditionally to be very formal, hierarchical, and rules-bound, and with its employees usually in suits, and Apple Computer, whose organizational culture is very organic, or "loose" and informal, with its employees typically wearing casual clothes and interacting informally.

A policy change made by KLM (Royal Dutch Airlines), with which the organizational culture responded to national cultural values and accepted practices, illustrated the way these sets of variables can interact, and how societal culture can influence organizational culture. The culture of social responsiveness in the Netherlands was incorporated into business policy when the airline revised its travel-benefits policy for families of employees. For some time, many KLM stewards had protested the rule that only immediate family members were eligible for low fares on KLM flights. They found it discriminatory that even just-married heterosexual spouses received the benefit, whereas long-term homosexual partners were not eligible. Upon reconsideration, KLM responded that any couple who formally registered as living together, which is a normal legal practice in the Netherlands, would be eligible for the low fares. However, a year had to elapse between partners before a new partner could be registered. By changing its policy, KLM put the emphasis on committed relationships rather than on marital status or sexual preference.

McDonald's provides another example, with its 58 restaurants in Russia. The company's experience with setting up businesses there since the first restaurant opened in Moscow demonstrates the combined effects of national and cultural variables on work. In Russia, local employees require lengthy training to serve up "Bolshoi Maks" in the "McDonald's way." Unfortunately, many Russians are still not familiar with working under the capitalist system; they have been victims of the inertia brought about by the old system of central planning for so long that productivity remains low.

Culture's Effects on Management

Which organizational processes—technical and otherwise—are most affected by cultural differences, and how, is the subject of ongoing cross-cultural management research and debate.[7] Some argue that the effects of culture are more evident at the individual level of personal behavior than at the organizational level, as a result of convergence. **Convergence** describes the phenomenon of the shifting of individual management styles to become more similar to one another. The convergence argument is based on the belief that the demands of industrialization, worldwide coordination, and competition tend to factor out differences in organizational-level processes, such as choice of technology and structure. In a study of Japanese and Korean firms, Lee, Roehl, and Choe found that globalization and firm size were sources of convergence of management styles.[8] These factors are discussed in more detail later in this chapter.

The effects of culture on specific management functions are particularly noticeable when we attempt to impose our own values and systems on another society. Exhibit 3-2 gives some examples of the values typical of U.S. culture, compares some common perspectives held by people in other countries, and shows which management functions might be affected, clearly implying the need for the differential management of organizational processes. For example, American managers plan activities, schedule them, and judge their timely completion based on the belief that people influence and control the future, rather than assuming that events will occur only at the will of Allah, as managers in an Islamic nation might believe.

Many people in the world understand and relate to others only in terms of their own culture. This unconscious reference point of one's own cultural values is called a **self-reference criterion**. The result of such an attitude is illustrated in the following story:

> *Once upon a time there was a great flood, and involved in this flood were two creatures, a monkey and a fish. The monkey, being agile and experienced, was lucky enough to scramble up a tree and escape the raging waters. As he looked down from his safe perch, he saw the poor fish struggling against the swift current. With the very best of intentions, he reached down and lifted the fish from the water. The result was inevitable.*[9]

EXHIBIT 3-2   U.S. Values and Possible Alternatives

Aspects of U.S. Culture*	Alternative Aspect	Examples of Management Function Affected
The individual can influence the future (where there is a will there is a way).	Life follows a preordained course, and human action is determined by the will of God.	Planning and scheduling
The individual can change and improve the environment.	People are intended to adjust to the physical environment rather than to alter it.	Organizational environment, morale, and productivity
An individual should be realistic in his or her aspirations.	Ideals are to be pursued regardless of what is "reasonable."	Goal setting and career development
We must work hard to accomplish our objectives (Puritan ethic).	Hard work is not the only prerequisite for success; wisdom, luck, and time are also required.	Motivation and reward system
Commitments should be honored (people will do what they say they will do).	A commitment may be superseded by a conflicting request, or an agreement may only signify intention and have little or no relationship to the capacity for performance.	Negotiating and bargaining
One should effectively use one's time (time is money that can be saved or wasted).	Schedules are important, but only in relation to other priorities.	Long- and short-range planning
A primary obligation of an employee is to the organization.	The individual employee has a primary obligation to his or her family and friends.	Loyalty, commitment, and motivation
The employer or employee can terminate the relationship.	Employment is for a lifetime.	Motivation and commitment to the company
The best-qualified people should be recruiting selection, given the positions available.	Family, friendship, and other considerations should determine employment practices.	Employment, promotions, and reward

*Aspect here refers to a belief, value, attitude, or assumption that is a part of a culture in that it is shared by a large number of people in that culture.

Source: Excerpted from *Managing Cultural Differences* by Philip R. Harris and Robert T. Moran, 5th ed. Copyright © 2000 by Gulf Publishing Company, Houston, TX. Used with permission. All rights reserved.

The monkey assumed that its frame of reference applied to the fish and acted accordingly. Thus, international managers from all countries must understand and adjust to unfamiliar social and commercial practices—especially the practices of that mysterious and unique nation, the United States. Japanese workers at a U.S. manufacturing plant learned to put courtesy aside and interrupt conversations with Americans when there were problems. Europeans, however, are often confused by Americans' apparent informality, which then backfires when the Europeans do not get work done as the Americans expect.

As a first step toward cultural sensitivity, international managers should understand their own cultures. This awareness helps to guard against adopting either a parochial or an ethnocentric attitude. **Parochialism** occurs, for example, when a Frenchman expects those from or in another country to automatically fall into patterns of behavior common in France. **Ethnocentrism** describes the attitude of those who operate from the assumption that their ways of doing things are best—no matter where or under what conditions they are applied. Companies both large and small have demonstrated this lack of cultural sensitivity in countless subtle (and not so subtle) ways, with varying disastrous effects.

Procter & Gamble (P&G) was one such company. In an early Japanese television commercial for Camay soap, a Japanese woman is bathing when her husband walks into the bathroom. She starts telling him about her new beauty soap. Her husband, stroking her shoulder, hints that he has more on his mind than suds. The commercial, which had been popular in Europe, was a disaster in Japan. For the man to intrude on his wife "was considered bad manners," says Edwin L. Artzt, P&G's vice chairman and international chief. "And the Japanese didn't think it was very funny." P&G has learned from its mistakes and now generates about half of its revenue from foreign sales.[10]

After studying his or her own culture, the manager's next step toward establishing effective cross-cultural relations is to develop cultural sensitivity. Managers not only must be aware of cultural variables and their effects on behavior in the workplace, but also must appreciate cultural diversity and understand how to build constructive working relationships anywhere in the world. The following sections explore cultural variables and dimensions. Later chapters suggest specific ways in which managers can address these variables and dimensions to help build constructive relationships.

Given the great variety of cultures and subcultures around the world, how can a student of cross-cultural management, or a manager wishing to be culturally savvy, develop an understanding of the specific nature of a certain people? With such an understanding, how can a manager anticipate the probable effects of an unfamiliar culture within an organizational setting and thereby manage human resources productively and control outcomes?

One approach is to develop a cultural profile for each country or region with which the company does or is considering doing business. Developing a cultural profile requires some familiarity with the cultural variables universal to most cultures. From these universal variables, managers can identify the specific differences found in each country or people—and hence anticipate their implications for the workplace.

Managers should never assume that they can successfully transplant American, or Japanese, or any other country's styles, practices, expectations, and processes. Instead, they should practice a basic tenet of good management—contingency management. Contingency management requires managers to adapt to the local environment and people and to manage accordingly. That adaptation can be complex because the manager may confront differences not only in culture, but also in business practices.

Influences on National Culture

Managers should recognize, of course, that generalizations in cultural profiles will produce only an approximation, or stereotype, of national character. Many countries comprise diverse **subcultures** whose constituents conform only in varying degrees to the national character. In Canada, distinct subcultures include anglophones and francophones (English-speaking and French-speaking people) and indigenous Canadians.

Above all, good managers treat people as individuals, and they consciously avoid any form of **stereotyping.** However, a cultural profile is a good starting point to help managers develop some tentative expectations—some cultural context—as a backdrop to managing in a specific international setting. It is useful, then, to look at what cultural variables have been studied and what implications can be drawn from the results.

Before we can understand the culture of a society, we need to recognize that there are subsystems in a society which are a function of where people live; these subsystems influence, and are influenced by, people's cultural values and dimensions and so affect their behaviors, both on and off the job. Harris and Moran identified eight categories that form the subsystems in any society.[11] This systems approach to understanding cultural and national variables—and their effects on work behavior—is consistent with the model shown in Exhibit 3-1 that shows those categories as a broad set of influences on societal culture. Those categories are: the *kinship* system of relationships among families; the *education system*; the *economic and political systems*; the associations which make up formal and informal groups; the *health system*; attitudes toward *recreation* and leisure; and—perhaps most importantly—*religion*. Religion underlies both moral and economic norms and influences everyday business transactions and on-the-job behaviors.

CULTURAL VALUE DIMENSIONS

Cultural variables result from unique sets of shared values among different groups of people. Most of the variations between cultures stem from underlying value systems, which cause people to behave differently under similar circumstances. **Values** are a society's ideas about what is good or bad, right or wrong—such as the widespread belief that stealing is immoral and unfair. Values determine how individuals will probably respond in any given circumstance. As a powerful component of a society's culture, values are communicated through the eight subsystems just described and are passed from generation to generation. Interaction and pressure among these subsystems (or more recently from foreign cultures) may provide the impetus for slow change. The dissolution of the Soviet Union and the formation of the Commonwealth of Independent States is an example of extreme political change resulting from internal economic pressures and external encouragement to change.

Project GLOBE Cultural Dimensions

Recent research results on cultural dimensions have been made available by the GLOBE (Global Leadership and Organizational Behavior Effectiveness) Project team. The team comprises 170 researchers who have collected data over seven years on cultural values and practices and leadership attributes from 18,000 managers in 62 countries. Those managers were from a wide variety of industries and sizes of organizations from every corner of the globe. The team identified nine cultural dimensions that distinguish one society from another and have important managerial implications: assertiveness, future orientation, performance orientation, humane orientation, gender differentiation, uncertainty avoidance, power distance, institutional collectivism versus individualism, and in-group collectivism. Only the first four are discussed here; this avoids confusion for readers since the other five dimensions are similar to those researched by Hofstede, which are presented in the next section. (Other research results from the GLOBE Project are presented in subsequent chapters where applicable, such as in the Leadership section in Chapter 11.) The descriptions are as follows and selected results are shown in Exhibit 3-3.[12]

EXHIBIT 3-3   Selected Cultural Dimensions Rankings from the GLOBE Research Project

Country Rankings on Assertiveness

Least Assertive Countries in GLOBE		Medium Assertive Countries in GLOBE		Most Assertive Countries in GLOBE	
Sweden	3.38	Egypt	3.91	Spain	4.42
New Zealand	3.42	Ireland	3.92	United States	4.55
Switzerland	3.47	Philippines	4.01	Greece	4.58
Japan	3.59	Ecuador	4.09	Austria	4.62
Kuwait	3.63	France	4.13	Germany (Former East)	4.73

Country Rankings on Performance Orientation

Least Performance-Oriented Countries in GLOBE		Medium Performance-Oriented Countries in GLOBE		Most Performance-Oriented Countries in GLOBE	
Russia	2.88	Sweden	3.72	United States	4.49
Argentina	3.08	Israel	3.85	Taiwan	4.56
Greece	3.20	Spain	4.01	New Zealand	4.72
Venezuela	3.32	England	4.08	Hong Kong	4.80
Italy	3.58	Japan	4.22	Singapore	4.90

Country Rankings on Future Orientation

Least Future-Oriented Countries in GLOBE		Medium Future-Oriented Countries in GLOBE		Most Future-Oriented Countries in GLOBE	
Russia	2.88	Slovenia	3.59	Denmark	4.44
Argentina	3.08	Egypt	3.86	Canada (English-speaking)	4.44
Poland	3.11	Ireland	3.98	Netherlands	4.61
Italy	3.25	Australia	4.09	Switzerland	4.73
Kuwait	3.26	India	4.10	Singapore	5.07

Country Rankings on Humane Orientation

Least Humane-Oriented Countries in GLOBE		Medium Humane-Oriented Countries in GLOBE		Most Humane-Oriented Countries in GLOBE	
Germany (Former West)	3.18	Hong Kong	3.90	Indonesia	4.69
Spain	3.32	Sweden	4.10	Egypt	4.73
France	3.40	Taiwan	4.11	Malaysia	4.87
Singapore	3.49	United States	4.17	Ireland	4.96
Brazil	3.66	New Zealand	4.32	Philippines	5.12

Source: Adapted from Mansour Javidan and Robert J. House, "Cultural Acumen for the Global Manager: Lessons from Project GLOBE," *Organizational Dynamics* (Spring 2001): 289–305, with permission from Elsevier.

Assertiveness   This dimension refers to how much people in a society are expected to be tough, confrontational, and competitive versus modest and tender. Austria and Germany, for example, are highly assertive societies that value competition and have a "can-do" attitude. This compares with Sweden and Japan, less assertive societies, which tend to prefer warm and co-operative relations and harmony. The GLOBE team concluded that those countries have sympathy for the weak and emphasize loyalty and solidarity.

Future Orientation   This dimension refers to the level of importance a society attaches to future-oriented behaviors such as planning and investing in the future. Switzerland and Singapore, high on this dimension, are inclined to save for the future and have a longer time horizon for decisions. This perspective compares with societies such as Russia and Argentina, which tend to plan more in the shorter term and place more emphasis on instant gratification.

Performance Orientation   This dimension measures the importance of performance improvement and excellence in society and refers to whether or not people are encouraged to strive for continued improvement. Singapore, Hong Kong, and the United States score high on this dimension; typically, this means that people tend to take initiative and have a sense of urgency and the confidence to get things done. Countries like Russia and Italy have low scores on this dimension; they hold other priorities ahead of performance, such as tradition, loyalty, family, and background, and they associate competition with defeat.

Humane Orientation   This dimension measures the extent to which a society encourages and rewards people for being fair, altruistic, generous, caring, and kind. Highest on this dimension are the Philippines, Ireland, Malaysia, and Egypt, indicating a focus on sympathy and support for the weak. In those societies paternalism and patronage are important, and people are usually friendly and tolerant and value harmony. This compares with Spain, France, and the former West Germany, which scored low on this dimension; people in these countries give more importance to power and material possessions, as well as self-enhancement.

Clearly, research results such as these are helpful to managers seeking to be successful in cross-cultural interactions. Anticipating cultural similarities and differences allows managers to develop the behaviors and skills necessary to act and decide in a manner appropriate to the local societal norms and expectations.

Cultural Clusters

Gupta et al., from the GLOBE research team, also analyzed their data on the nine cultural dimensions to determine where similarities cluster geographically. Their results support the existence of ten cultural clusters: South Asia, Anglo, Arab, Germanic Europe, Latin Europe, Eastern Europe, Confucian Asia, Latin America, Sub-Sahara Africa, and Nordic Europe. They point out the usefulness to managers of these clusters:

> *Multinational corporations may find it less risky and more profitable to expand into more similar cultures rather than those which are drastically different.*[13]

These clusters are shown in Exhibit 3-4. To compare two of their cluster findings, for example, Gupta et al. describe the Germanic cluster as masculine, assertive, individualistic, and result-oriented. This compares with the Latin American cluster, which they characterize as practicing high power distance, low performance orientation, uncertainty avoidance, and collective:

> *Latin American societies tend to enact life as it comes, taking its unpredictability as a fact of life, and not overly worrying about results.*[14]

Hofstede's Value Dimensions

Earlier research resulted in a pathbreaking framework for understanding how basic values underlie organizational behavior; this framework was developed by Hofstede, based on his research on over 116,000 people in 50 countries. He proposed four value dimensions: power distance, uncertainty avoidance, individualism, and masculinity.[15] We should be cautious when interpreting these results, however, because his research findings are based on a sample drawn from one

EXHIBIT 3-4 Geographic Culture Clusters

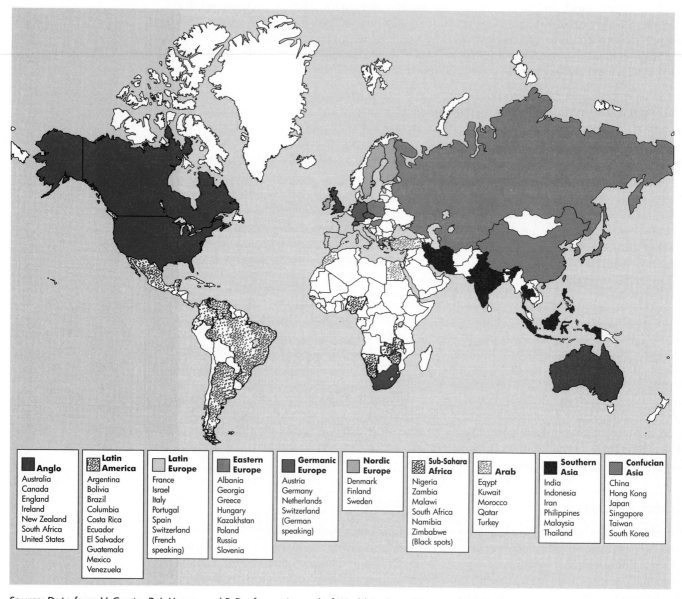

Anglo	**Latin America**	**Latin Europe**	**Eastern Europe**	**Germanic Europe**	**Nordic Europe**	**Sub-Sahara Africa**	**Arab**	**Southern Asia**	**Confucian Asia**
Australia	Argentina	France	Albania	Austria	Denmark	Nigeria	Eqypt	India	China
Canada	Bolivia	Israel	Georgia	Germany	Finland	Zambia	Kuwait	Indonesia	Hong Kong
England	Brazil	Italy	Greece	Netherlands	Sweden	Malawi	Morocco	Iran	Japan
Ireland	Columbia	Portugal	Hungary	Switzerland		South Africa	Qatar	Philippines	Singapore
New Zealand	Costa Rica	Spain	Kazakhstan	(German		Namibia	Turkey	Malaysia	Taiwan
South Africa	Ecuador	Switzerland	Poland	speaking)		Zimbabwe		Thailand	South Korea
United States	El Salvador	(French	Russia			(Black spots)			
	Guatemala	speaking)	Slovenia						
	Mexico								
	Venezuela								

Source: Data from V. Gupta, P. J. Hanes, and P. Dorfman, *Journal of World Business* 37, no. 1 (2002): 13.

multinational firm, IBM, and because he does not account for within-country differences in multicultural countries. Although we introduce these value dimensions here to aid in the understanding of different cultures, their relevance and application to management functions will be discussed in later chapters.

The first of these value dimensions, **power distance,** is the level of acceptance by a society of the unequal distribution of power in institutions. In the workplace, inequalities in power are normal, as evidenced in hierarchical boss–subordinate relationships. However, the extent to which subordinates accept unequal power is societally determined. In countries in which people display high power distance (such as Malaysia, the Philippines, and Mexico), employees acknowledge the boss's authority simply by respecting that individual's formal position in the hierarchy, and they seldom bypass the chain of command. This respectful response results, predictably, in a centralized structure and autocratic leadership. In countries where people display low power distance (such as Austria, Denmark, and Israel), superiors and subordinates are apt to regard one another as equal in power, resulting in more harmony and cooperation. Clearly, an autocratic management style is not likely to be well received in low power distance countries.

The second value dimension, **uncertainty avoidance,** refers to the extent to which people in a society feel threatened by ambiguous situations. Countries with a high level of uncertainty

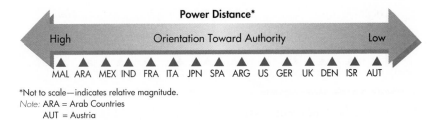

*Not to scale—indicates relative magnitude.
Note: ARA = Arab Countries
AUT = Austria

Source: Based on G. Hofstede, "National Cultures in Four Dimensions,"
International Studies of Management and Organization (Spring-Summer 1983).

avoidance (such as Japan, Portugal, and Greece) tend to have strict laws and procedures to which their people adhere closely, and a strong sense of nationalism prevails. In a business context, this value results in formal rules and procedures designed to provide more security and greater career stability. Managers have a propensity for low-risk decisions, employees exhibit little aggressiveness, and lifetime employment is common. In countries with lower levels of uncertainty avoidance (such as Denmark, Great Britain, and, to a lesser extent, the United States), nationalism is less pronounced, and protests and other such activities are tolerated. As a consequence, company activities are less structured and less formal, some managers take more risks, and high job mobility is common.

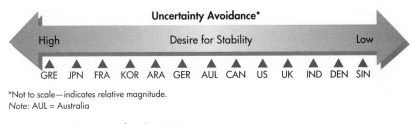

*Not to scale—indicates relative magnitude.
Note: AUL = Australia

Source: Based on G. Hofstede, 1983.

The third of Hofstede's value dimensions, **individualism,** refers to the tendency of people to look after themselves and their immediate families only and to neglect the needs of society. In countries that prize individualism (such as the United States, Great Britain, and Australia) democracy, individual initiative, and achievement are highly valued; the relationship of the individual to organizations is one of independence on an emotional level, if not on an economic level.

In countries such as Pakistan and Panama, where low individualism prevails—that is, where **collectivism** predominates—one finds tight social frameworks, emotional dependence on belonging to "the organization," and a strong belief in group decisions. People from a collectivist country, like Japan, believe in the will of the group rather than that of the individual, and their pervasive collectivism exerts control over individual members through social pressure and the fear of humiliation. The society valorizes harmony and saving face, whereas individualistic cultures generally emphasize self-respect, autonomy, and independence. Hiring and promotion practices in collectivist societies are based on paternalism rather than achievement or personal capabilities, which are valued in individualistic societies. Other management practices (such as the use of quality circles in Japanese factories) reflect the emphasis on group decision-making processes in collectivist societies.

Hofstede's findings indicate that most countries scoring high on individualism have both a higher gross national product and a freer political system than those countries scoring low on individualism—that is, there is a strong relationship among individualism, wealth, and a political system with balanced power. Other studies have found that the output of individuals working in a group setting differs between individualistic and collectivist societies. In the United States, a highly individualistic culture, social loafing is common—that is, people tend to perform less when working as part of a group than when working alone.[16] In a comparative study of the United States and the People's Republic of China (a highly collectivist society), Earley found that the Chinese did not exhibit as much social loafing as the Americans.[17] This result can be attributed to Chinese cultural values, which subordinate personal interests to the greater goal of helping the group succeed.

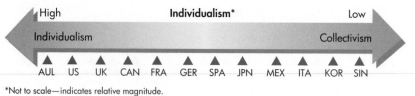

*Not to scale—indicates relative magnitude.

Source: Based on G. Hofstede, 1983.

The fourth value dimension, **masculinity,** refers to the degree of traditionally "masculine" values—assertiveness, materialism, and a lack of concern for others—that prevail in a society. In comparison, femininity emphasizes "feminine" values—a concern for others, for relationships, and for the quality of life. In highly masculine societies (Japan and Austria, for example), women are generally expected to stay home and raise a family. In organizations, one finds considerable job stress, and organizational interests generally encroach on employees' private lives. In countries with low masculinity (such as Switzerland and New Zealand), one finds less conflict and job stress, more women in high-level jobs, and a reduced need for assertiveness. The United States lies somewhat in the middle, according to Hofstede's research. American women typically are encouraged to work, and families often are able to get some support for child care (through day-care centers and maternity leaves).

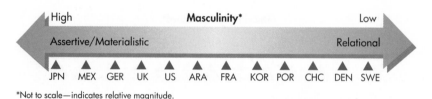

*Not to scale—indicates relative magnitude.

Source: Based on G. Hofstede, 1983.

The four cultural value dimensions proposed by Hofstede do not operate in isolation; rather, they are interdependent and interactive—and thus complex—in their effects on work attitudes and behaviors. For example, in a 2000 study of small to medium-sized firms in Australia, Finland, Greece, Indonesia, Mexico, Norway, and Sweden, based on Hofstede's dimensions, Steensma, Marino, and Weaver found that "entrepreneurs from societies that are masculine and individualistic have a lower appreciation for cooperative strategies as compared to entrepreneurs from societies that are feminine and collectivist. Masculine cultures view cooperation in general as a sign of weakness and individualistic societies place a high value on independence and control."[18] In addition, they found that high levels of uncertainty avoidance prompted more cooperation, such as developing alliances to share risk.

Long-term/Short-term Orientation   Later research in 23 countries, using a survey developed by Bond and colleagues called the Chinese Value Survey, led Hofstede to develop a fifth dimension called the Confucian work dynamism, which he labeled a long-term/short-term dimension. He defined long-term orientation as "the extent to which a culture programs its members to accept delayed gratification of their material, social, and emotional needs."[19] In other words, managers in most Asian countries are more future-oriented and so stride toward long-term goals;

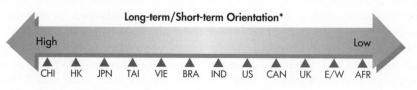

*Not to scale—indicates relative magnitude.

Source: Based on G. Hofstede, 2001.

they value investment in the future and are prepared to sacrifice short-term profits. Those countries such as Great Britain, Canada, and the United States place a higher value on short-term results and profitability, and evaluate their employees accordingly.

Trompenaars's Value Dimensions

Fons Trompenaars also researched value dimensions; his work was spread over a ten-year period, with 15,000 managers from 28 countries representing 47 national cultures. Some of those dimensions, such as individualism, people's attitude toward time, and relative inner-versus outer-directedness, are similar to those discussed elsewhere in this chapter and others, and so are not presented here; other selected findings from Trompenaars's research that affect daily business activities are explained next, along with the placement of some of the countries along those dimensions, in approximate relative order.[20] If we view the placement of these countries along a range from personal to societal, based on each dimension, some interesting patterns emerge.[21] One can see that the same countries tend to be at similar positions on all dimensions, with the exception of the emotional orientation.

Looking at Trompenaars's dimension of **universalism versus particularism,** we find that the universalistic approach applies rules and systems objectively, without consideration for individual circumstances, whereas the particularistic approach—more common in Asia and in Spain, for example—puts the first obligation on relationships and is more subjective. Trompenaars found, for example, that people in particularistic societies are more likely to pass on insider information to a friend than those in universalistic societies.

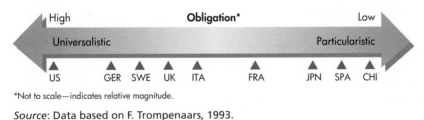

*Not to scale—indicates relative magnitude.

Source: Data based on F. Trompenaars, 1993.

In the **neutral versus affective** dimension, the focus is on the emotional orientation of relationships. The Italians, Mexicans, and Chinese, for example, would openly express emotions even in a business situation, whereas the British and Japanese would consider such displays unprofessional; they, in turn would be regarded as "hard to 'read'."

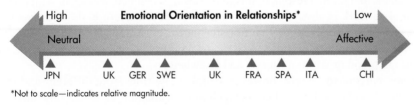

*Not to scale—indicates relative magnitude.

Source: Data based on F. Trompenaars, 1993.

As far as involvement in relationships goes, people tend to be either **specific or diffuse** (or somewhere along that dimension). Managers in specific-oriented cultures—the United States, United Kingdom, France—separate work and personal issues and relationships; they compartmentalize their work and private lives, and they are more open and direct. In diffuse-oriented cultures—Sweden, China—work spills over into personal relationships and vice versa.

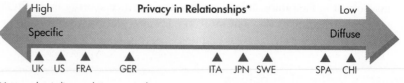

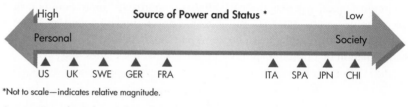

*Not to scale—indicates relative magnitude.

Source: Data based on F. Trompenaars, 1993.

In the **achievement versus ascription** dimension, the question that arises is "What is the source of power and status in society?" In an achievement society, the source of status and influence is based on individual achievement—how well one performs the job and what level of education and experience one has to offer. Therefore, women, minorities, and young people usually have equal opportunity to attain position based on their achievements. In an ascription-oriented society, people ascribe status on the basis of class, age, gender, and so on; one is more likely to be born into a position of influence. Hiring in Indonesia, for example, is more likely to be based on who you are than is the case in Germany or Australia.

*Not to scale—indicates relative magnitude.

Source: Data based on F. Trompenaars, 1993.

It is clear, then, that a lot of what goes on at work can be explained by differences in people's innate value systems, as described by Hofstede, Trompenaars, and the GLOBE researchers. Awareness of such differences and how they influence work behavior can be very useful to you as a future international manager.

Critical Operational Value Differences

After studying various research results about cultural variables, it helps to identify some specific culturally based variables that cause frequent problems for Americans in international management. Important variables are those involving conflicting orientations toward time, change, material factors, and individualism. We try to understand these operational value differences because they strongly influence a person's attitudes and probable response to work situations.

Time   Americans often experience much conflict and frustration because of differences in the concept of time around the world—that is, differences in temporal values. To Americans, time is a valuable and limited resource; it is to be saved, scheduled, and spent with precision, lest we waste it. The clock is always running—time is money. Therefore, deadlines and schedules have to be met. When others are not on time for meetings, Americans may feel insulted; when meetings digress from their purpose, Americans tend to become impatient. Similar attitudes toward time are found in Western Europe and elsewhere.

In many parts of the world, however, people view time from different and longer perspectives, often based on religious beliefs (such as reincarnation, in which time does not end at death), on a belief in destiny, or on pervasive social attitudes. In Latin America, for example, a common attitude toward time is *mañana,* a word that literally means "tomorrow." A Latin American person using this word, however, usually means an indefinite time in the near future. Similarly, the word *bukra* in Arabic can mean "tomorrow" or "some time in the future." While Americans usually regard a deadline as a firm commitment, Arabs often regard a deadline imposed on them as an insult. They feel that important things take a long time and therefore cannot be rushed. To ask an Arab to rush something, then, is to imply that you have not given him an important task or that he would not treat that task with respect. International managers have to be careful not to offend people—or lose contracts or employee cooperation—because they misunderstand the local language of time.

Change   Based largely on long-standing religious beliefs, values regarding the acceptance of change and the pace of change can vary immensely among cultures. Western people generally believe that an individual can exert some control over the future and can manipulate events, particularly in a business context—that is, individuals feel they have some internal control. In many non-Western societies, however, control is considered external; people generally believe in destiny or the will of their God, and therefore adopt a passive attitude or even feel hostility toward those introducing the "evil" of change. In societies that place great importance on tradition (such as Japan), one small area of change may threaten an entire way of life. However, the younger generations are becoming more exposed to change through globalization, technology, and media exposure. International firms are agents of change throughout the world. Some changes are more popular than others; for example, McDonald's hamburgers are apparently one change the Japanese are willing to accept.

Material Factors   In large part, Americans consume resources at a far greater rate than most of the rest of the world. Their attitude toward nature—that it is there to be used for their benefit—differs from the attitudes of Indians and Koreans, for example, whose worship of nature is part of their religious beliefs. Whereas Americans often value physical goods and status symbols, many non-Westerners find these things unimportant; they value the aesthetic and the spiritual realm. Such differences in attitude have implications for management functions, such as motivation and reward systems, because the proverbial carrot must be appropriate to the employee's value system.

Individualism   In general, Americans tend to work and conduct their private lives independently, valuing individual achievement, accomplishments, promotions, and wealth above any group goals. In many other countries, individualism is not valued (as discussed previously in the context of Hofstede's work). In China, for example, much more of a "we" consciousness prevails, and the group is the basic building block of social life and work. For the Chinese, conformity and cooperation take precedence over individual achievement, and the emphasis is on the strength of the family or community—the predominant attitude being, "We all rise or fall together."

International managers often face conflicts in the workplace as a result of differences in these four basic values of time, change, materialism, and individualism. If these operational value differences and their likely consequences are anticipated, managers can adjust expectations, communications, work organization, schedules, incentive systems, and so forth to provide for more constructive outcomes for the company and its employees. Some of these operational differences are shown in Exhibit 3-5, using Japan and Mexico as examples. Note in particular the factors of time, individualism, change (fatalism), and materialism (attitudes toward work) expressed in the exhibit.

EXHIBIT 3-5   Fundamental Differences Between Japanese and Mexican Culture that Affect Business Organizations[22]

Dimension	Japanese Culture	Mexican Culture
Hierarchical nature	Rigid in rank and most communication; blurred in authority and responsibility	Rigid in all aspects
Individualism vs. collectivism	Highly collective culture; loyalty to work group dominates; group harmony very important	Collective relative to family group; don't transfer loyalty to work group; individualistic outside family
Attitudes toward work	Work is sacred duty; acquiring skills, working hard, thriftiness, patience, and perseverance are virtues	Work is means to support self and family; leisure more important than work
Time orientation	Balanced perspective; future oriented; monochronic in dealings with outside world	Present oriented; time is imprecise; time commitments become desirable objectives
Approach to problem solving	Holistic, reliance on intuition, pragmatic, consensus important	Reliance on intuition and emotion, individual approach
Fatalism	Fatalism leads to preparation	Fatalism makes planning, disciplined routine unnatural
View of human nature	Intrinsically good	Mixture of good and evil

THE INTERNET AND CULTURE

Koreans are an impatient people, and we like technology. So everyone wants the fastest Internet connection.

HWANG KYU-JUNE[23]

We would be remiss if we did not acknowledge the contemporary phenomenon of the increasingly pervasive use of the Internet in society, for it seems to be encroaching on many of the social variables discussed earlier—in particular associations, education, and the economy. In South Korea, for example, where information technology makes up about 30 percent of the gross domestic product (GDP), there is an obsession for anything digital. Over 70 percent of homes are connected to a high-speed Internet service. That compares with 50 percent in Canada—the next highest user—and 23 percent in the United States.[24] This phenomenon seems to be changing the lives of many Koreans. Teenagers, used to hanging out at the mall, now do so at the country's 20,000 personal computer (PC) parlors to watch movies, check email, and surf the Net for as little as US$1. Korean housewives are on a waiting list for ADSL lines when the $35 billion high-speed government telecommunications project is completed. By then 95 percent of Korean households will have Internet access.[25]

At the same time that the Internet is affecting culture, culture is also affecting how the Internet is used. One of the pervasive ways that culture is determining how the Internet may be used in various countries is through the local attitude to **information privacy**—the right to control information about oneself—as observed in the following quote:

You Americans just don't seem to care about privacy, do you?

SWEDISH EXECUTIVE[26]

While Americans collect data about consumers' backgrounds and what they buy, often trading that information with other internal or external contacts, the Swedes, for example, are astounded that this is done, especially without governmental oversight.[27] The Swedes are required to register all databases of personal information with the Data Inspection Board (DIB), their federal regulatory agency for privacy, and to get permission from that board before that data can be used. Indeed, the Swedish system is typical of most countries in Europe in their societal approaches to privacy.[28] One example of a blocked data transfer occurred when Sweden would not allow U.S. airlines to transmit passenger information, such as wheelchair need and meal preferences, to the United States.[29]

Generally in Europe, each person must be informed, and given the chance to object, if the information about that person is going to be used for direct marketing purposes or released to another party. That data cannot be used for secondary purposes if the consumer objects.

In Italy, data cannot be sent outside—even to other EU countries—without the explicit consent of the data subject

In Spain, all direct mail has to include the name and address of the data owner so that the data subject is able to exercise his rights of access, correction, and removal.[30]

The manner in which Europe views information privacy has its roots in culture and history, leading to a different value set regarding privacy. The preservation of privacy is considered a human right, perhaps partially as a result of an internalized fear about how personal records were used in war times in Europe. In addition, research by Smith on the relationship between level of concern about privacy and Hofstede's cultural dimensions revealed that high levels of uncertainty avoidance were associated with the European approach to privacy, whereas higher levels of individualism, masculinity, and power distance were associated with the U.S. approach.[31]

It seems, then, that societal culture and the resultant effects on business models can render the assumptions about the "global" nature of information technology incorrect. U.S. businesspeople, brought up on a strong diet of the market economy, need to realize that they will often need to "localize" their use of IT to different value sets about its use. This advice applies in particular to the many e-commerce companies doing business overseas. With 75 percent of the world's Internet market living outside the United States, multinational e-businesses are learning the hard way that their Web sites must reflect local markets, customs, languages, and currencies to be successful in foreign markets. Different legal systems, financial structures, tastes, and experiences necessitate attention to every detail to achieve global appeal. In other words, e-businesses must localize to globalize, which means much more than translating online content to local languages. Lycos Europe, for example, based its privacy policies upon German law since it is the most stringent.

One problem area often beyond the control of e-business is the costs of connecting to the Internet for people in other countries. In Asia, for example, such costs are considerably higher than in the United States. Other practical problems in Asia, as well as in Germany, the Netherlands, and Sweden, include the method of payment, which in most of these places still involves cash or letters of credit and written receipts. Dell tackled this problem by offering debit payments from consumers' checking accounts. Some companies have learned the hard way that they need to do their homework before launching sites aimed at overseas consumers. Dell, for example, committed a faux pas when it launched an e-commerce site in Japan with black borders on the site; black is considered negative in the Japanese culture, so many consumers took one look and didn't want anything else to do with it. Dell executives learned that the complexity of language translation into Japanese was only one area in which they needed to localize.

As much as cultural and societal factors can affect the use of the internet for business, it is also clear that IT can have dramatic changes on culture and society, as illustrated by the accompanying Management Focus about the changes occurring as a result of India's burgeoning IT industry.

MANAGEMENT FOCUS

India's IT Industry Brings Cultural Changes[32]

Many longtime residents of Bangalore, India, seem locked in a cultural struggle with Infosys Technologies (INFY), Wipro Technologies (WIT), and others in the software industry, even though they have made Bangalore famous and increased its wealth. They complain that Bangalore used to be one of India's most pleasant cities. But with the addition of 500,000 IT workers living alongside nearly 7 million other residents, the city has become very crowded and expensive. The locals ask:

> Does the city belong to the IT industry, with all its riches? Or does it belong to those who arrived first, whose children must now work for outsiders who don't speak the local language, Kannada?[33]

Apart from the early curfew on nightlife, the old-timers contend, in a city where few locals can afford cars, the government is spending too much of the city's resources on building wider roads to speed tech workers around. In its defense, the software industry claims that it has benefited everyone by improving the city and bringing new wealth and services such as a new subway system. Although the global credit crunch has slowed its growth, over the past decade the tech sector has created tens of thousands of jobs, not only in the software and back-office support industries, but also for all the people who support those companies. While most of India's IT companies still get at least half of their revenue from the United States alone, now they are finding more business domestically. As a result the digital divide between urban and rural areas is narrowing and helping support industries to grow in a domestic economy expanding 9 percent a year—this all thanks to India's IT talent.

It is these kinds of opportunities, amid the benefits of increasing economic openness in India, that have attracted Anand Giridharad, and others whose families had earlier emigrated to the United States, to return to India. The idea of returning to India is spreading virally in émigré

A Typical Call Center in India for Business Process Outsourcing (BPO) for Foreign Companies.

Source: Getty Images Inc.

homes as the U.S. economy declines and the job market tightens. This phenomenon led Anand to ask:

> If our parents left India and trudged westward for us, if they manufactured from scratch a new life there for us, if they slogged, saved, sacrificed to make our lives lighter than theirs, then what does it mean when we choose to migrate to the place they forsook?[34]

He noted that his father, in the 1970s, felt frustrated in companies that awarded roles based on age, not achievement, and that doctors and engineers were revered and others neglected and mistreated. Since then, India has liberalized, privatized, globalized with the economy growing rapidly, bringing with it much optimism for its people. At the same time, America has declined and many jobs have moved to India, particularly in IT and back-office services.

In a sign of the times, India offered an Overseas Citizen of India card in 2006, offering foreign citizens of Indian origin visa-free entry for life and making it easier to work in the country. By July 2008 more than 280,000 émigrés had signed up, including 120,000 from the United States.

Those émigrés are now re-learning those many aspects of Indian culture that remain, for example the formalities and hierarchies left from British rule; that making friends entails befriending the whole family; and the very relaxed attitude toward time. Those second-generation returnees to their motherland are now mixing western and Indian cultures:

> They have built boutiques that fuse Indian fabrics with Western cuts, founded companies that train a generation to work in Western companies, become dealmakers in investment firms that speak equally to Wall Street and Dalal Street, mixed albums that combine throbbing tabla with Western melodies.[35]

Much of the traditional cultural underpinnings remain, of course. Narayana Murthy, founder and now chairman of the board of Infosys, the Indian IT giant, was asked recently to comment on what explains the success of great Indian businesses such as Infosys, Wipro, and the Tata group. Mr. Murthy said that there are some culturally specific qualities, but also some universal ones, that lie behind the achievements. He commented that, of course honesty, decency, integrity and a strong work ethic all matter. But these are not unique to India. Rather, he said:

> *It is the concept of the family which perhaps sets India apart. Family bonds are strong and intense in India. People inevitably bring that ethos to work with them.*[36]

Of course, much of India has not been directly touched by the IT industry, and so in those areas the Indian culture remains untouched by the IT industry and globalization. Management is often paternalist and autocratic, based on formal authority and charisma, with decision making mostly centralized, an emphasis on rules and a low propensity for risk. Nepotism prevails in job hiring and placement, and for the most part:

> *Relationship orientation seems to be a more important characteristic of effective leaders in India than performance or task orientation.*[37]

DEVELOPING CULTURAL PROFILES

Managers can gather considerable information on cultural variables from current research, personal observation, and discussions with people. From these sources, managers can develop cultural profiles of various countries—composite pictures of working environments, people's attitudes, and norms of behavior. As we have previously discussed, these profiles are often highly generalized; many subcultures, of course, may exist within a country. However, managers can use these profiles to anticipate drastic differences in the level of motivation, communication, ethics, loyalty, and individual and group productivity that may be encountered in a given country. More such homework may have helped Wal-Mart's expansion efforts into Germany and South Korea, from which it withdrew in 2006. Wal-Mart's executives simply did not do enough research about the culture and shopping habits of people there; for example:

> *In Germany, Wal-Mart stopped requiring sales clerks to smile at customers—a practice that some male shoppers interpreted as flirting—and scrapped the morning Wal-Mart chant by staff members. "People found these things strange; Germans just don't behave that way," said Hans-Martin Poschmann, the secretary of the Verdi union, which represents 5,000 Wal-Mart employees here.*
>
> NEW YORK TIMES,
> *July 31, 2006*[38]

It is relatively simple for Americans to pull together a descriptive profile of U.S. culture, even though regional and individual differences exist, because Americans know themselves and because researchers have thoroughly studied U.S. culture. The results of one such study by Harris and Moran are shown in Exhibit 3-6, which provides a basis of comparison with other cultures and, thus, suggests the likely differences in workplace behaviors.

It is not so easy, however, to pull together descriptive cultural profiles of peoples in other countries unless one has lived there and been intricately involved with those people. Still, managers can make a start by using what comparative research and literature are available. The following Comparative Management in Focus provides brief, generalized country profiles based on a synthesis of research, primarily from Hofstede[39] and England,[40] as well as numerous other sources.[41] These profiles illustrate how to synthesize information and gain a sense of the character of a society—from which implications may be drawn about how to manage more effectively in that society. More extensive implications and applications related to managerial functions are drawn in later chapters.

EXHIBIT 3-6   Americans at a Glance

1. *Goal and achievement oriented*—Americans think they can accomplish just about anything, given enough time, money, and technology.

2. *Highly organized and institutionally minded*—Americans prefer a society that is institutionally strong, secure, and tidy or well kept.

3. *Freedom-loving and self-reliant*—Americans fought a revolution and subsequent wars to preserve their concept of democracy, so they resent too much control or interference, especially by government or external forces. They believe in an ideal that all persons are created equal; though they sometimes fail to fully live that ideal, they strive through law to promote equal opportunity and to confront their own racism or prejudice.

   They also idealize the self-made person who rises form poverty and adversity, and think they can influence and create their own futures. Control of one's destiny is popularly expressed as "doing your own thing." Americans think, for the most part, that with determination and initiative, one can achieve whatever one sets out to do and thus, fulfill one's individual human potential.

4. *Work-oriented and efficient*—Americans possess a strong work ethic, though they are learning in the present generation to constructively enjoy leisure time. They are conscious of time and efficient in doing things. They tinker with gadgets and technological systems, always searching for easier, better, more efficient ways to accomplish tasks.

5. *Friendly and informal*—Americans reject the traditional privileges of royalty and class but defer to those with affluence and power. Although informal in greeting and dress, they are a noncontact culture (e.g., usually avoid embracing in public) and maintain a certain physical/psychological distance with others (e.g., about 2 feet).

6. *Competitive and aggressive*—Americans in play or business generally are so oriented because of their drives to achieve and succeed. This is partially traced to their heritage of having to overcome a wilderness and hostile elements in their environment.

7. *Values in transition*—Traditional American values of family loyalty, respect and care of the aged, marriage and the nuclear family, patriotism, material acquisition, forthrightness, and the like are undergoing profound reevaluation as people search for new meanings.

8. *Generosity*—Although Americans seemingly emphasize material values, they are a sharing people, as has been demonstrated in the Marshall Plan, foreign aid programs, refugee assistance, and their willingness at home and abroad to espouse a good cause and to help neighbors in need. They tend to be altruistic and some would say naive as a people.

Source: From *Managing Cultural Differences* by Philip R. Harris and Robert T. Moran, 5th ed. Copyright © 2000 by Gulf Publishing Company, Houston, TX. Used with permission. All rights reserved.

Recent evidence points to some convergence with Western business culture resulting from Japan's economic contraction and subsequent bankruptcies. Focus on the group, life-time employment, and a pension has given way to a more competitive business environment with job security no longer guaranteed and an emphasis on performance-based pay. This has led Japan's "salarymen" to recognize the need for personal responsibility on the job and in their lives. Although only a few years ago emphasis was on the group, Japan's long economic slump seems to have caused some cultural restructuring of the individual. Corporate Japan is changing from a culture of consensus and groupthink to one touting the need for an "era of personal responsibility" as a solution to revitalize its competitive position in the global marketplace.[42]

> *To tell you the truth, it's hard to think for yourself, says Mr. Kuzuoka . . . [but, if you don't] . . . in this age of cutthroat competition, you'll just end up drowning.*[43]

COMPARATIVE MANAGEMENT IN FOCUS
Profiles in Culture—Japan, Germany, Latin America, and South Korea

Japan

The traditional Japanese business characteristics of politeness and deference have left companies without the thrusting culture needed to succeed internationally.

FINANCIAL TIMES,
October 10, 2005[44]

With intense global competition many Japanese companies are recognizing the need for more assertiveness and clarity in their business culture in order to expand abroad. As a result, many Japanese employees are recognizing the need to manage their own careers as companies move away from lifetime employment to be more competitive. Only a handful of large businesses, such as Toyota, Komatsu, and Canon, have managed to become indisputable global leaders by maintaining relationships and a foundation for their operations around the world.[45] For the majority of Japanese, the underlying cultural values still predominate—for now anyway.

Much of Japanese culture—and the basis of working relationships—can be explained by the principle of *wa*, "peace and harmony." This principle, embedded in the value the Japanese attribute to *amae* ("indulgent love"), probably originated in the Shinto religion, which focuses on spiritual and physical harmony. *Amae* results in *shinyo*, which refers to the mutual confidence, faith, and honor necessary for successful business relationships. Japan ranks high on pragmatism, masculinity, and uncertainty avoidance, and fairly high on power distance. At the same time, much importance is attached to loyalty, empathy, and the guidance of subordinates. The result is a mix of authoritarianism

MAP 3-2 Japan and South Korea

and humanism in the workplace, similar to a family system. These cultural roots are evident in a homogeneous managerial value system, with strong middle management, strong working relationships, strong seniority systems that stress rank, and an emphasis on looking after employees. The principle of *wa* carries forth into the work group—the building block of Japanese business. The Japanese strongly identify and thus seek to cooperate with their work groups. The emphasis is on participative management, consensus problem solving, and decision making with a patient, long-term perspective. Open expression and conflict are discouraged, and it is of paramount importance to avoid the shame of not fulfilling one's duty. These elements of work culture result in a devotion to work, collective responsibility, and a high degree of employee productivity.

Professor Nonaka, a specialist in how companies tap the collective intelligence of their workers discusses a similar Japanese concept of *ba*: an interaction among colleagues on the job that leads to knowledge-sharing. He says that

> Ba *can occur in a work group, a project team, an ad hoc meeting, a virtual e-mail list, or at the frontline point of contact with customers. It serves as a petri dish in which shared insights are cultivated and grown. Companies can foster ba by designing processes that encourage people to think together.*[46]

The message is clear that, in Japan, companies that give their employees freedom to interact informally are likely to benefit from new ideas and collaboration.

If we extend this cultural profile to its implications for specific behaviors in the workplace, we can draw a comparison with common American behaviors. Most of those behaviors seem to be opposite to those of their counterparts; it is no wonder that many misunderstandings and conflicts in the workplace arise between Americans and Japanese (see Exhibit 3-7). For example, a majority of the

EXHIBIT 3-7   The American–Japanese Cultural Divide

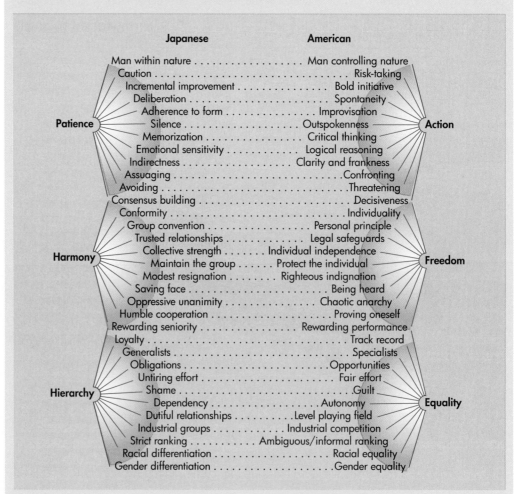

Source: R. G. Linowes, "The Japanese Manager's Traumatic Entry into the United States: Understanding the American–Japanese Cultural Divide," *The Academy of Management Executive* 7, no. 4 (1993): 24.

attitudes and behaviors of many Japanese stems from a high level of collectivism, compared with a high level of individualism common to Americans. This contrast is highlighted in the center of Exhibit 3-7—"Maintain the group"—compared with "Protect the individual." In addition, the strict social order of the Japanese permeates the workplace in adherence to organizational hierarchy and seniority and in loyalty to the firm. This contrasts markedly with the typical American responses to organizational relationships and duties based on equality. In addition, the often blunt, outspoken American businessperson offends the indirectness and sensitivity of the Japanese for whom the virtue of patience is paramount, causing the silence and avoidance that so frustrates Americans. As a result, Japanese businesspeople tend to think of American organizations as having no spiritual quality and little employee loyalty, and of Americans as assertive, frank, and egotistic. Their American counterparts, in turn, respond with the impression that Japanese businesspeople have little experience and are secretive, arrogant, and cautious.[47]

GERMANY   The reunited Germany is somewhat culturally diverse inasmuch as the country borders several nations. Generally, Germans rank quite high on Hofstede's dimension of individualism, although their behaviors seem less individualistic than those of Americans. They score fairly high on uncertainty avoidance and masculinity and have a relatively small need for power distance. These cultural norms show up in the Germans' preference for being around familiar people and situations; they are also reflected in their propensity to do a detailed evaluation of business deals before committing themselves.

Christianity underlies much of German culture—more than 96 percent of Germans are Catholics or Protestants. This may be why Germans tend to like rule and order in their lives, and why there is a clear public expectation of acceptable and the unacceptable ways to act. Public signs everywhere in Germany dictate what is allowed or *verboten* (forbidden). Germans are very strict with their use of time, whether for business or pleasure, frowning on inefficiency or on tardiness.

In business, Germans tend to be assertive, but they downplay aggression. Decisions are typically centralized, although hierarchical processes sometimes give way to consensus decision making. However, strict departmentalization is present in organizations, with centralized and final authority at the departmental manager level. Employees do not question the authority of their managers. German companies typically have a vertical hierarchical structure with detailed planning and standardized rules and procedures; the emphasis is on order and control to avoid risk.

> *In the business setting, Germans look for security, well-defined work procedures, rules, established approaches, and clearly defined individual assignments. In short, the German business environment is highly structured. "Ordnung" (order) is the backbone of company life.*[48]

What the Germans call *Ordnung* (the usual translation is "order," but it is a much broader concept) is the unwritten road map of how to live one's life. "A group of Germans lined up on an empty street corner, even in the middle of the night, waiting for a light to change before crossing, is one of the favorite first impressions taken away by visiting Americans, who are usually jaywalking past as they observe it."[49] For self-reliant Americans, the German adherence to precise rules and regulations is impressive but often stifling.

Hall and Hall describe the German preference for closed doors and private space as evidence of the affinity for compartmentalization in organizations and in their own lives. They also prefer more physical space around them in conversation than do most other Europeans, and they seek privacy so as not to be overheard. German law prohibits loud noises in public areas on weekend afternoons. Germans are conservative, valuing privacy, politeness, and formality; they usually use last names and titles for all except those close to them. Business interactions are specifically task-focused, not for relationship-building.

Most Germans prefer to focus on one task or issue at a time, that task taking precedence over other demands; strict schedules are important, as is punctuality, both showing respect for all concerned. Overall, Germany is what Walker et al call a "doing-oriented" culture—that is, a task and achievement orientation of "work first, pleasure second."[50] Such cultures include Switzerland, Germany, Austria, the Netherlands, and the Scandinavian countries. (This compares with "being-oriented" cultures—such as those of Belgium, France Greece, Ireland, and most Latin American countries—where the general predisposition is more towards "work to live," rather than "live to work." Priority is given to affiliation and personal qualities in "being-oriented" cultures.)

In negotiations, Germans want detailed information before and during discussions, which can become lengthy. They give factors such as voice and speech control much weight. However, since Germany is a low-context society, communication is explicit, and Americans find negotiations easy to understand.[51] On the other hand, Germans communicating with businesspeople from a high-context culture such as those in Japan will be perceived as abrupt, insensitive, and indifferent. Whereas most

Asians, for example, will be implicit and indirect, always aware of the need to "save face" for everyone concerned, most Germans are very direct and straightforward; tact and diplomacy takes second place to voicing their opinions.

LATIN AMERICA   Latin America is not one homogenous area, of course; rather, it comprises many diverse, independent nations (most commonly referred to as those territories in the Americas where the Spanish or Portuguese languages prevail: Mexico, most of Central and South America, plus Cuba, the Dominican Republic, and Puerto Rico in the Caribbean). Business people are most likely to go to the rapidly developing economies of Chile and Brazil, and, of course, to Mexico. (Portuguese is the language in Brazil.) Christianity—predominantly Roman Catholicism—prevails throughout Latin America. (The reader is referred to www.wikipedia.org for further information on demographics, geography, economies, lifestyles, etc.)

While we acknowledge the many cultural differences, for our purposes here we can draw upon the similarities of culture and business practices as a starting point in developing a helpful profile. Some of these generalities are discussed here.

Using Hofstede's dimensions, we can generalize that most people are high on Power Distance and Uncertainty Avoidance, fairly high on Masculinity, low on Individualism, and tend to have a comparatively short-term orientation towards plans.

Latin Americans are typically "being-oriented"—with a primary focus on relationships and enjoying life in the present—as compared with the "doing-oriented" German (and mostly Western) culture discussed earlier. For Latin Americans, work lives and private lives are much more closely integrated than that of Westerners and so they emphasize enjoying life and have a more relaxed attitude towards work; because of that, Westerners often stereotype them as "lazy," rather than realizing that it is simply a different attitude to the role of work in life. Connected with that attitude is the tendency to be rather fatalistic—that is that events will be determined by God—rather than a feeling of their own control or responsibility for the future.

Most people in those countries have a fluid orientation towards time and tend to be multi-focused, as discussed earlier in this chapter. Planning, negotiations, and scheduling take place in a more relaxed and loose time framework; those processes take second place to building a trusting relationship and reaching a satisfactory agreement.[52] Communication is based on their high-context culture (this concept is discussed further in Chapter 4). This means that communication tends to be indirect and implicit, based largely on non-verbal interactions and the expectation that the listener draws inference from understanding the people and the circumstances, without the need to be blunt or critical. Westerners need to take time, to be subtle and tactful, and to be incremental at discussing business to avoid being viewed as being pushy and so cutting off the relationship. Maintaining harmony and saving face is very important, as is the need to avoid embarrassing the other people involved. Managers must avoid any public criticism of employees and any reprimand should be by way of suggestion.

Communication is also very expressive and demonstrative; courtesy, formality, and good manners are respected and lead to very complimentary and hospitable expressions to guests. They tend to stand closer and touch more often than most Westerners, exuding the warmth and hospitality that is typical in the region.

Hierarchy prevails in all areas of life, from family to institutions such as government and the workplace. Each level and relationship is expected to show deference, honor, and respect to the next person or level. Status is conveyed by one's position and title and the formality of dress and etiquette. Traditional managers have the respect of their position and are typically autocratic and paternal. Loyalty is to the superior as a person. Employees expect to be assigned tasks with little participation involved, although younger managers who have been educated in Europe or the United States are starting to delegate. However, while most Latin Americans can show some flexibility in structure, Chile is probably the most order-oriented country; managers there are very high on uncertainty and try hard to minimize risk and strictly adhere to social and business norms.[53]

Relationships have priority whether family, friends, or business contacts. Loyalty among family and friends leads to obligations, and, often, nepotism, which can lead to varying levels of quality in the work performance and less initiative than a Western business person might expect. Business is conducted through social contacts and referrals—that is, success depends not on what you know as much as whom you know. Latin Americans do business with people with whom they develop a trusting relationship, so it behooves business people, as in much of the world, to take time to develop a friendly, trusting relationship before getting down to business.

Western managers need to develop a warm attitude towards employees and business contacts and cultivate a sense of family at work; they should communicate individually with employees and colleagues and develop a trusting relationship.

Further discussion about the Mexican culture in particular is in the Comparative Management in Focus section in Chapter 11.

SOUTH KOREA Koreans rank high on collectivism and pragmatism, fairly low on masculinity, moderate on power distance, and quite high on uncertainty avoidance. Although greatly influenced by U.S. culture, Koreans are still very much bound to the traditional Confucian teachings of spiritualism and collectivism. Korea and its people have undergone great changes, but the respect for family, authority, formality, class, and rank remain strong. Koreans are demonstrative, friendly, quite aggressive and hard-working, and very hospitable. For the most part, they do not subscribe to participative management. Family and personal relationships are important, and connections are vital for business introductions and transactions. Business is based on honor and trust; most contracts are oral. Although achievement and competence are important to Koreans, the priority of guarding both parties' social and professional reputations is a driving force in relationships. Thus, praise predominates, and honest criticism is rare.

Further insight into the differences between U.S. and Korean culture can be derived from the following excerpted letter from Professor Jin K. Kim in Plattsburgh, New York, to his high school friend, MK, in South Korea, who just returned from a visit to the United States. MK, whom Dr. Kim had not seen for 20 years, planned to emigrate to the United States, and Dr. Kim wanted to help ward off his friend's culture shock by telling him about U.S. culture from a Korean perspective.

Dear MK,

I sincerely hope the last leg of your trip home from the five-week fact-finding visit to the United States was pleasant and informative. Although I may not have expressed my sense of exhilaration about your visit through the meager lodging accommodations and "barbaric" foods we provided, it was sheer joy to spend four weeks with you and Kyung-Ok. (Please refrain from hitting the ceiling. My use of your charming wife's name, rather than the usual Korean expression "your wife" or "your house person," is not an indication of my amorous intentions toward her as any red-blooded Korean man would suspect. Since you are planning to immigrate to this country soon, I thought you might as well begin to get used to the idea of your wife exerting her individuality. Better yet, I thought you should be warned that the moment the plane touches U.S. soil, you will lose your status as the center of your familial universe.) At any rate, please be assured that during your stay here my heart was filled with memories of our three years together in high school when we were young in Pusan.

During your visit, you called me, on several occasions, an American. What prompted you to invoke such a reference is beyond my comprehension. Was it my rusty Korean expressions? Was it my calculating mind? Was it my pitifully subservient (at least when viewed through your cultural lens) role that I was playing in my family life? Or, was it my familiarity with some facets of the cultural landscape? This may sound bewildering to you, but it is absolutely true that through all the years I have lived in this country, I never truly felt like an American. Sure, on the surface, our family followed closely many ritualistic routines of the American culture: shopping malls, dining out, PTA, Little League, picnics, camping trips, credit card shopping sprees, hot dogs, and so on. But mentally I remained stubbornly in the periphery. Naturally, then, my subjective cultural attitudes stayed staunchly Korean. Never did the inner layers of my Korean psyche yield to the invading American cultural vagaries, I thought. So, when you labeled me an American for the first time, I felt a twinge of guilt.

Several years ago, an old Korean friend of mine, who settled in the United States about the same time I did, paid a visit to Korea for the first time in some fifteen years. When he went to see his best high school friend, who was now married and had two sons, his friend's wife made a bed for him and her husband in the master bedroom, declaring that she would spend the night with the children. It was not necessarily the sexual connotation of the episode that made my friend blush; he was greatly embarrassed by the circumstance in which he imposed himself to the extent that the couple's privacy had to be violated. For his high school friend and his wife, it was clearly their age-old friendship to which the couple's privacy had to yield. MK, you might empathize rather easily with this Korean couple's state of mind, but it would be a gross mistake even to imagine there may be occasions in your adopted culture when a gesture of friendship breaks the barrier of privacy. Zealously guarding their privacy above all, Americans are marvelously adept at drawing the line where friendship—that elusive "we" feeling—stops and privacy begins. . . .

Indeed, one of the hardest tasks you will face as an "alien" is how to find that delicate balance between your individuality (for example, privacy) and your collective identity (for example, friendship or membership in social groups).

Privacy is not the only issue that stems from this individuality—collectivity continuum. Honesty in interpersonal relationships is another point that may keep you puzzled. Americans are almost brutally honest and frank about issues that belong to public domains; they are not afraid of discussing an embarrassing topic in most graphic details as long as the topic is a matter of public concern. Equally frank and honest gestures are adopted when they discuss their own personal lives once the presumed benefits from such gestures are determined to outweigh the risks involved. Accordingly, it is not uncommon to encounter friends who volunteer personally embarrassing and even shameful information lest you find it out from other sources. Are Americans equally straightforward and forthcoming in laying out heartfelt personal criticisms directed at their friends? Not likely. Their otherwise acute sense of honesty becomes significantly muted when they face the unpleasant task of being negative toward their personal friends. The fear of an emotion-draining confrontation and the virtue of being polite force them to put on a facade or mask.

The perfectly accepted social behavior of telling "white lies" is a good example. The social and personal virtues of accepting such lies are grounded in the belief that the potential damage that can be inflicted by directly telling a friend the hurtful truth far outweighs the potential benefit that the friend could gain from it. Instead of telling a hurtful truth directly, Americans use various indirect communication channels to which their friend is likely to be tuned. In other words, they publicize the information in the form of gossip or behind-the-back recriminations until it is transformed into a sort of collective criticism against the target individual. Thus objectified and collectivized, the "truth" ultimately reaches the target individual with a minimal cost of social discomfort on the part of the teller. There is nothing vile or insidious about this communication tactic, since it is deeply rooted in the concern for sustaining social pleasantry for both parties.

This innocuous practice, however, is bound to be perceived as an act of outrageous dishonesty by a person deeply immersed in the Korean culture. In the Korean cultural context, a trusted personal relationship precludes such publicizing prior to direct," criticism to the individual concerned, no matter what the cost in social and personal unpleasantry. Indeed, as you are well aware, MK, such direct reproach and even recrimination in Korea is in most cases appreciated as a sign of one's utmost love and concern for the target individual. Stressful and emotionally draining as it is, such a frank expression of criticism is done out of "we" feeling. Straight-talking friends did not want me to repeat undesirable acts in front of others, as it would either damage "our reputation" or go against the common interest of "our collective identity." In Korea, the focus is on the self-discipline that forms a basis for the integrity of "our group." In America, on the other hand, the focus is on the feelings of two individuals. From the potential teller's viewpoint, the primary concern is how to maintain social politeness, whereas from the target person's viewpoint, the primary concern is how to maintain self-esteem. Indeed, these two diametrically opposed frames of reference—self-discipline and self-esteem—make one culture collective and the other individualistic.

MK, the last facet of the individualism-collectivism continuum likely to cause a great amount of cognitive dissonance in the process of your assimilation to American life is the extent to which you have to assert your individuality to other people. You probably have no difficulty remembering our high school principal, K. W. Park, for whom we had a respect–contempt complex. He used to lecture, almost daily at morning assemblies, on the virtue of being modest. As he preached it, it was a form of the Confucian virtue of self-denial. Our existence or presence among other people, he told us, should not be overly felt through communicated messages (regardless of whether they are done with a tongue or pen). . . . One's existence, we were told, should be noticed by others in the form of our acts and conduct. One is obligated to provide opportunities for others to experience one's existence through what he or she does. Self-initiated effort for public recognition or self-aggrandizement was the most shameful conduct for a person of virtue.

This idea is interesting and noble as a philosophical posture, but when it is practiced in America, it will not get you anywhere in most circumstances. The lack of self-assertion is translated directly into timidity and lack of self-confidence. This is a culture where you must exert your individuality to the extent that it would make our high school principal turn in his grave out of shame and disgust. Blame the size of the territory or the population of this country. You may even blame the fast-paced cadence of life or the social mobility that moves people around at a dizzying speed. Whatever the specific reason might be,

Americans are not waiting to experience you or your behaviors as they exist. They want a "documented" version of you that is eloquently summarized, decorated, and certified. What they are looking for is not your raw, unprocessed being with rich texture; rather, it is a slickly processed self, neatly packaged, and, most important, conveniently delivered to them. Self-advertising is encouraged almost to the point of pretentiousness.

The curious journey toward the American end of the individualism–collectivism continuum will be inevitable, I assure you. The real question is whether it will be in your generation, your children's, or their children's. Whenever it happens, it will be a bittersweet revenge for me, since only then will you realize how it feels to be called an American by your best high school chum.

Source: Excerpted from a letter by Dr. Jin K. Kim, State University of New York—Plattsburgh. Copyright © 2001 by Dr. Jin K. Kim. Used with permission of Dr. Kim.

CULTURE AND MANAGEMENT STYLES AROUND THE WORLD

As an international manager, once you have researched the culture of a country in which you may be going to work or with which to do business, and after you have developed a cultural profile, it is useful then to apply that information to develop an understanding of the expected management styles and ways of doing business that predominate in that region, or with that type of business setting. Two examples follow: Saudi Arabia and Chinese Small Family Businesses.

Saudi Arabia

Understanding how business is conducted in the modern Middle East requires an understanding of the Arab culture, since the Arab peoples are the majority there and most of them are Muslim. As discussed in the opening profile, the Arab culture is intertwined with the pervasive influence of Islam. Even though not all Middle Easterners are Arab, Arab culture and management style predominate in the Arabian Gulf region. Shared culture, religion, and language underlie behavioral similarities throughout the Arab world. Islam permeates Saudi life—Allah is always present, controls everything, and is frequently referred to in conversation. Employees may spend more than two hours a day in prayer as part of the life pattern that intertwines work with religion, politics, and social life.

Arab history and culture are based on tribalism, with its norms of reciprocity of favors, support, obligation, and identity passed on to the family unit, which is the primary structural model. Family life is based on closer personal ties than in the West. Arabs value personal relationships, honor, and saving face for all concerned; these values take precedence over the work at hand or verbal accuracy. "Outsiders" must realize that establishing a trusting relationship and respect for Arab social norms has to precede any attempts at business discussions. Honor, pride, and dignity are at the core of "shame" societies, such as the Arabs. As such, shame and honor provide the basis for social control and motivation. Circumstances dictate what is right or wrong and what constitutes acceptable behavior.

Arabs avoid open admission of error at all costs because weakness (*muruwwa*) is a failure to be manly. It is sometimes difficult for westerners to get at the truth because of the Arab need to avoid showing weakness; instead, Arabs present a desired or idealized situation. Shame is also brought on someone who declines to fulfill a request or a favor; therefore, a business arrangement is left open if something has yet to be completed.

The communication style of Middle Eastern societies is high context (that is, implicit and indirect), and their use of time is polychronic: Many activities can be taking place at the same time, with constant interruptions commonplace. The imposition of deadlines is considered rude, and business schedules take a backseat to the perspective that events will occur "sometime" when Allah wills (*bukra insha Allah*). Arabs give primary importance to hospitality; they are cordial to business associates and lavish in their entertainment, constantly offering strong black coffee (which you should not refuse) and banquets before considering business transactions. Westerners must realize the importance of personal contacts and networking, socializing and building close relationships and trust, practicing patience regarding schedules, and doing

EXHIBIT 3-8 Behavior that Will Likely Cause Offense in Saudi Arabia

- Bringing up business subjects until you get to know your host, or you will be considered rude.
- Commenting on a man's wife or female children over 12 years of age.
- Raising colloquial questions that may be common in your country but possibly misunderstood in Saudi Arabia as an invasion of privacy.
- Using disparaging or swear words and off-color or obscene attempts at humor.
- Engaging in conversations about religion, politics, or Israel.
- Bringing gifts of alcohol or using alcohol, which is prohibited in Saudi Arabia.
- Requesting favors from those in authority or esteem, for it is considered impolite for Arabs to say no.
- Shaking hands too firmly or pumping—gentle or limp handshakes are preferred.
- Pointing your finger at someone or showing the soles of your feet when seated.

Source: P. R. Harris and R. T. Moran, *Managing Cultural Differences*, 5th ed. (Houston: Gulf Publishing, 2000).

business in person. Exhibit 3-8 gives some selected actions and nonverbal behaviors that may offend Arabs. The relationship between cultural values and norms in Saudi Arabia and managerial behaviors is illustrated in Exhibit 3-9.

EXHIBIT 3-9 The Relationship Between Culture and Managerial Behaviors in Saudi Arabia

Cultural Values	Managerial Behaviors
Tribal and family loyalty	Work group loyalty
	Paternal sociability
	Stable employment and a sense of belonging
	A pleasant workplace
	Careful selection of employees
	Nepotism
Arabic language	Business as an intellectual activity
	Access to employees and peers
	Management by walking around
	Conversation as recreation
Close and warm friendships	A person rather than task and money orientation
	Theory Y management
	Avoidance of judgment
Islam	Sensitivity to Islamic virtues
	Observance of the Qur'an and Sharia
	Work as personal or spiritual growth
	Consultative management
	A full and fair hearing
	Adherence to norms
Honor and shame	Clear guidelines and conflict avoidance
	Positive reinforcement
	Training and defined job duties
	Private correction of mistakes
	Avoidance of competition
An idealized self	Centralized decision making
	Assumption of responsibility appropriate to position
	Empathy and respect for the self-image of others
Polychronic use of time	Right- and left-brain facility
	A bias for action
	Patience and flexibility
Independence	Sensitivity to control
	Interest in the individual
Male domination	Separation of sexes
	Open work life; closed family life

Source: R. R. Harris and R. T. Moran, *Managing Cultural Differences* 5th ed. (Houston: Gulf Publishing, 2000).

Chinese Small Family Businesses

The predominance of small businesses in China and the region highlights the need for managers from around the world to gain an understanding of how such businesses operate. Many small businesses—most of which are family or extended-family businesses—become part of the value chain (suppliers, buyers, retailers, etc.) within industries in which "foreign" firms may compete.

Some specifics of Chinese management style and practices in particular are presented here as they apply to small businesses. (Further discussion of the Chinese culture continues in Chapter 5 in the context of negotiation.) It is important to note that no matter the size of a company, but especially in small businesses, it is the all-pervasive presence and use of *guanxi* that provides the little red engine of business transactions in China. *Guanxi* means "connections"—the network of relationships the Chinese cultivate through friendship and affection; it entails the exchange of favors and gifts to provide an obligation to reciprocate favors. Those who share a *guanxi* network share an unwritten code.[54] The philosophy and structure of Chinese businesses comprise paternalism, mutual obligation, responsibility, hierarchy, familialism, personalism, and connections. Autocratic leadership is the norm, with the owner using his or her power—but with a caring about other people that may predominate over efficiency.

According to Lee, the major differences between Chinese management styles and those of their Western counterparts are human-centeredness, family-centeredness, centralization of power, and small size.[55] Their human-centered management style puts people ahead of a business relationship and focuses on friendship, loyalty, and trustworthiness.[56] The family is extremely important in Chinese culture, and any small business tends to be run like a family.

Globalization has resulted in the ethnic Chinese businesses (in China or other Asian countries) to adapt to more competitive management styles. They are moving away from the traditional centralized power structure in Chinese organizations which comprised the boss and a few family members at the top and the employees at the bottom, with no ranking among the workers. In fact, many are no longer managed by family members. Frequently, the managers are those sons and daughters who have studied and worked overseas before returning to the family company; or even foreign expatriates. Examples of Chinese capitalism responding to change and working to globalize through growth are Eu Yan Sang Holdings Ltd., the Hiap Moh Printing businesses, and the Pacific International Line.[57]

As Chinese firms in many modern regions in the Pacific Rim seek to modernize and compete locally and globally, a tug of war has begun between the old and the new: the traditional Chinese management practices and the increasingly "imported" Western management styles. As discussed by Lee, this struggle is encapsulated in the different management perspectives of the old and young generations. A two-generational study of Chinese managers by Ralston et al. also found generational shifts in work values in China. They concluded that the new generation manager is more individualistic, more independent, and takes more risks in the pursuit of profits. However, they also found the new generation holding on to their Confucian values, concluding that the new generation may be viewed as "crossverging their Eastern and Western influences, while on the road of modernization."[58]

CONCLUSION

This chapter has explored various cultural values and how managers can understand them with the help of cultural profiles. The following chapters focus on application of this cultural knowledge to management in an international environment (or, alternatively in a domestic multicultural environment)—especially as relevant to cross-cultural communication (Chapter 4), negotiation and decision making (Chapter 5), and motivating and leading (Chapter 11). Culture and communication are essentially synonymous; what happens when people from different cultures communicate, and how can international managers understand the underlying process and adapt their styles and expectations accordingly? For the answers, read the next chapter.

Summary of Key Points

1. The culture of a society comprises the shared values, understandings, assumptions, and goals that are passed down through generations and imposed by members of the society. These unique sets of cultural and national differences strongly influence the attitudes and expectations and therefore the on-the-job behavior of individuals and groups.

2. Managers must develop cultural sensitivity to anticipate and accommodate behavioral differences in various societies. As part of that sensitivity, they must avoid parochialism—an attitude that assumes one's own management techniques are best in any situation or location and that other people should follow one's patterns of behavior.

3. From his research in 50 countries, Hofstede proposes four underlying value dimensions that help to identify and describe the cultural profile of a country and affect organizational processes: power distance, uncertainty avoidance, individualism, and masculinity.

4. Through his research, Fons Trompenaars confirmed some similar dimensions, and found other unique dimensions: obligation, emotional orientation, privacy, and source of power and status.

5. The GLOBE project team of 170 researchers in 62 countries concluded the presence of a number of other dimensions, and ranked countries on those dimensions, including assertiveness, performance orientation, future orientation, and humane orientation. Gupta et al. from that team found geographical clusters on nine of the GLOBE project cultural dimensions.

6. On-the-job conflicts in international management frequently arise out of conflicting values and orientations regarding time, change, material factors, and individualism.

7. Managers can use research results and personal observations to develop a character sketch, or cultural profile, of a country. This profile can help managers anticipate how to motivate people and coordinate work processes in a particular international context.

Discussion Questions

1. What is meant by the culture of a society, and why is it important that international managers understand it? Do you notice cultural differences among your classmates? How do those differences affect the class environment? How do they affect your group projects?

2. Describe the four dimensions of culture proposed by Hofstede. What are the managerial implications of these dimensions? Compare the findings with those of Trompenaars and the GLOBE project team.

3. Discuss the types of operational conflicts that could occur in an international context because of different attitudes toward time,

change, material factors, and individualism. Give examples relative to specific countries.

4. Discuss how the internet and culture interact. Which most affects the other, and how? Give some examples.

5. Discuss collectivism as it applies to the Japanese workplace. What managerial functions does it affect?

6. Discuss the role of Islam in cross-cultural relations and business operations.

Application Exercises

1. Develop a cultural profile for one of the countries in the following list. Form small groups of students and compare your findings in class with those of another group preparing a profile for another country. Be sure to compare specific findings regarding religion, kinship, recreation, and other subsystems. What are the prevailing attitudes toward time, change, material factors, and individualism?

    Any African country
    People's Republic of China
    Saudi Arabia
    Mexico
    France
    India

2. In small groups of students, research Hofstede's findings regarding the four dimensions of power distance, uncertainty avoidance, masculinity, and individualism for one of the following countries in comparison to the United States. (Your instructor can assign the countries to avoid duplication.) Present your findings to the class. Assume you are a U.S. manager of a subsidiary in the foreign country and explain how differences on these dimensions are likely to affect your management tasks. What suggestions do you have for dealing with these differences in the workplace?

    Brazil
    Italy
    People's Republic of China
    Russia

Experiential Exercises

1. A large Baltimore manufacturer of cabinet hardware had been working for months to locate a suitable distributor for its products in Europe. Finally invited to present a demonstration to a reputable distributing company in Frankfurt, it sent one of its most

promising young executives, Fred Wagner, to make the presentation. Fred not only spoke fluent German but also felt a special interest in this assignment because his paternal grandparents had immigrated to the United States from the Frankfurt area during the

1920s. When Fred arrived at the conference room where he would be making his presentation, he shook hands firmly, greeted everyone with a friendly *guten tag,* and even remembered to bow the head slightly as is the German custom. Fred, an effective speaker and past president of the Baltimore Toastmasters Club, prefaced his presentation with a few humorous anecdotes to set a relaxed and receptive atmosphere. However, he felt that his presentation was not well received by the company executives. In fact, his instincts were correct, for the German company chose not to distribute Fred's hardware products.

What went wrong?

2. Bill Nugent, an international real estate developer from Dallas, had made a 2:30 P.M. appointment with Mr. Abdullah, a high-ranking government official in Riyadh, Saudi Arabia. From the beginning things did not go well for Bill. First, he was kept waiting until nearly 3:45 P.M. before he was ushered into Mr. Abdullah's office. When he finally did get in, several other men were also in the room. Even though Bill felt that he wanted to get down to business with Mr. Abdullah, he was reluctant to get too specific because he considered much of what they needed to discuss sensitive and private. To add to Bill's sense of frustration, Mr. Abdullah seemed more interested in engaging in meaningless small talk than in dealing with the substantive issues concerning their business.

How might you help Bill deal with his frustration?

3. Tom Forrest, an up-and-coming executive for a U.S. electronics company, was sent to Japan to work out the details of a joint venture with a Japanese electronics firm. During the first several weeks, Tom felt that the negotiations were proceeding better than he had expected. He found that he had very cordial working relationships with the team of Japanese executives, and in fact, they had agreed on the major policies and strategies governing the new joint venture. During the third week of negotiations, Tom was present at a meeting held to review their progress. The meeting was chaired by the president of the Japanese firm, Mr. Hayakawa, a man in his mid-forties, who had recently taken over the presidency from his 82-year-old grandfather. The new president, who had been involved in most of the negotiations during the preceding weeks, seemed to Tom to be one of the strongest advocates of the plan that had been developed to date. Hayakawa's grandfather, the recently retired president, also was present at the meeting. After the plans had been discussed in some detail, the octogenarian past president proceeded to give a long soliloquy about how some of the features of this plan violated the traditional practices on which the company had been founded. Much to Tom's amazement, Mr. Hayakawa did nothing to explain or defend the policies and strategies that they had taken weeks to develop. Feeling extremely frustrated, Tom then gave a fairly strong argued defense of the plan. To Tom's further amazement, no one else in the meeting spoke up in defense of the plan. The tension in the air was quite heavy, and the meeting adjourned shortly thereafter. Within days the Japanese firm completely terminated the negotiations on the joint venture.

How could you help Tom better understand this bewildering situation?

Source: Gary P. Ferraro, *The Cultural Dimensions of International Business,* 2nd ed. (Upper Saddle River, NJ: Prentice Hall, 1994).

Internet Resources

Visit the Deresky Companion Website at www.pearsonhighered.com/deresky for this chapter's Internet resources.

CASE STUDY

Australia and New Zealand: Doing business with Indonesia

There are thousands of Australians, both individually and as members of organizations, who share trade and education with Indonesia and provide support—as do New Zealanders. Yet, though geographically part of Asia, citizens of Australia and New Zealand are members of cultures very different from any other in Asia.

As increasingly they seek to trade in Asia, so also do they need to learn to manage such differences; and doing business in Indonesia is a good example. Travelling time by air from Perth, Western Australia, is slightly less than four hours, yet the cultural distance is immeasurable.

In January 2007 the Jakarta Post reported GDP growth had risen to over 5%. Consumer consumption drives the economy but exports are thriving and therein lies opportunities for Australia and New Zealand.

Indonesia is a country of more than 17,000 islands and the world's largest Muslim nation. In her lecture, Dr Joan Hardjono[59] of Monash University, discussed the historical and geographic contexts of modern Indonesia. She spoke of the many clusters of islands worldwide that have come together as nation states—for example, the Philippines and some island groups in the Pacific—but described the Indonesian archipelago as in a class of its own.

It is unique in terms of extent and diversity. For example, Java and Bali have fertile volcanic soils, while elsewhere the land is rich in mineral resources such as oil, natural gas and coal. Climatic conditions vary from island to island. Some regions experience annual heavy rains and floods, while others suffer regularly from droughts that often lead to famines.

With a population of more than 230 million people, Indonesia is the fourth most populous country in the world but there is a great imbalance in population distribution within the archipelago. Settlement has always been greatest on the island of Java, and today about 60% of the Indonesian population lives there.

National ties are strong, as revealed by the great response from within Indonesia to the recent natural disasters in Aceh and Nias. Unfortunately, there are still very obvious socio-economic disparities in all regions of the country. At the top of the social structure are wealthy elites, below them an increasingly demanding middle class, and at the bottom an impoverished majority.

As Indonesia has become more integrated with ASEAN, North Asian trading partners have become more important: but well-to-do Indonesians now travel the world. Globalization has been the buzzword of international business for many years. International markets have split up into unified trade zones; individual marketplaces, particularly in the developing countries, are exposed to transnational pressures.

Some Asian countries are pulling back from perceived threats of international contagion, but Indonesia continues to open up its markets to world enterprise. However Australians and New Zealanders cannot expect to do business with Indonesians just because they are neighbours. They have to learn the moves.

Business opportunities in Indonesia include agribusiness, the automotive industry, business and financial services, construction and infrastructure, information and communication technology, e-commerce, education and training; environmental products and services, food and beverages, fresh produce, health and medical provisions, mining and mineral services, oil and petroleum drilling, transport and storage, science and technology.

Taking advantage of these opportunities requires skilful negotiation. One of the biggest challenges of working in a foreign country is learning how to operate in a different cultural setting. International managers tell endless stories of cross-cultural breakdowns, missed appointments, problems over differences in management style, lost orders or down time on production lines, labour problems between foreign management and local staff and many other examples of miscommunication. Many could have been avoided or at least mitigated had the expatriate managers and their local counterparts been better prepared for differences in work patterns.

Some cross cultural behaviour such as patience and courtesy is no more than good manners, it applies to all interpersonal communication: but in Indonesia, as in the rest of Asia, there is more need to develop a long-term relationship to produce a profit than there is in Australia or New Zealand. Relationships rely on shared expectations—for example, about how first contacts should be made, how appointments should be set and kept, how deals should be closed, how time should be managed (including the Indonesian concept of 'jam karet', or 'rubber time,' that infuriates punctuality-conscious Westerners).

Sensible but inexperienced international managers seek information that more seasoned veterans can provide. They might be colleagues, business associates, friends, or paid consultants, but in any case most people are eager to give advice. On the other hand, even managers with a highly developed global outlook may have too generalist a viewpoint on international business. They may overlook the need for a local perspective in each host country.

Indonesia is one of those countries in which a foreign manager's home office priorities of task over relationship, of corporate rather than human priorities, may not be the most effective ways to achieve productivity and effectiveness. Indonesian managers usually place more value on harmony, understanding, and mutual respect. It may be sometimes that this emphasis outweighs the importance of job performance and productivity.

On the other hand there are a number of concerns for Indonesian managers working with their Western counterparts. For example, they believe Westerners should make an effort to adjust to the culture, taboos, and language of their Indonesian colleagues. Foreign managers should avoid bad language that might set a bad example for the workers. They should give instructions slowly and clearly in Standard English and should ask for paraphrase to ensure understanding. They should be willing to consider individual cases and cultural needs (e.g., prayer times or other religious obligations, time off for cemetery visits before Ramadan, weddings, funerals).

On the other hand, Indonesian managers should be willing to make many adjustments to working in an international company. Important areas where Western management techniques are most successful include strategic planning and timetable deadlines, efficiency and punctuality, handling conflict and taking responsibility.

Sensitivity to the needs of employees is a management area that is seldom stressed in most Western business cultures where efficiency, productivity, and effectiveness take priority. For example, when somebody loses their self-control through anger, distress, or confusion, Javanese will usually advise the need to 'eling' (in translation, not to allow oneself to be overwhelmed by feelings and mixed-up thoughts but to regain self-control). Self-control is of high value to Javanese, maybe of the highest. This value is not unique to Indonesia. It is shared by the indigenous peoples of South Asia, the Himalayan Range and Central Asia, East Asia, South-east Asia, Africa; Oceania, the Caribbean and South America; and Northern America and the Arctic: hence a common cultural emphasis on the art of making and wearing masks to represent hidden emotions. Regardless of the cultures they come from, masks convey the essential emotions.[60]

Thus situations can arise in business contexts where hiding true feelings and keeping up appearances may take precedence over solving a problem.

Maintaining the harmony of the office by giving the outward appearance that there is nothing wrong is a fairly common situation in traditional Indonesian offices. Bad news may not be communicated to the boss and situations that seem insurmountable to an employee may simply be ignored.[61] Since this behaviour is not generally accepted to be part of Western culture—though certainly it exists there—Western managers need to spend more time observing and listening to their Indonesian employees than they would back home.

Another reason why such attentiveness is important is that Indonesian business relationships are paternal or maternal. Workers expect their supervisors to look after their interests rather as parents do for their children; and their supervisors understand and accept this responsibility. Furthermore, the tension involved in being the bearer of bad news to one's boss is felt very keenly by Indonesian employees, and this needs to be taken into account by supervisors and managers. The English language injunction is "Don't shoot the messenger" but some Indonesian workers seem to expect a firing squad when they have to report failure. Therefore, Western managers should make clear that they want and expect subordinates to come to them with questions or problems and that the response will be non-judgmental and self-controlled. Faces should be without masks; they should not portray negative emotions of anger, confrontation, or aggression. Managers in Indonesia are expected always be polite and to keep smiling, no matter how angry they may be inside.

Nevertheless, cross-cultural sensitivity works—or should work—both ways. Foreign managers should understand Indonesian culture and business customs, and Indonesian managers should be given clearly to understand what foreign managers will expect from them.

Case Questions

1. Using this case and the cultural dimensions explored in this chapter, discuss some of the ways in which citizens of Australia and New Zealand are members of cultures very different from any other in Asia.
2. In what respects is the Indonesian archipelago unique in Asia?
3. What characteristics of Indonesian workplaces are referred to in this profile?
4. How does the population appear to be socially stratified?
5. What are some business opportunities in Indonesia for foreign direct investment?

Sources:

Joan Hardjono, 05/08/2005, Herb Feith Lecture, "Can Indonesia Hold?" Centre of Southeast Asian Studies and Faculty of Arts, Monash University, in association with ABC Radio Australia and the Melbourne Institute of Asian Languages & Societies, University of Melbourne: http://www.abc.net.au/ra/news/ infocus/s1429967.htm;

Javanese mystical movements, January 2007, http://www.xs4all.nl/~wichm/javmys1.html

Phil King, December 2006, "Facing disaster: The 27 May earthquake shook a kingdom, not just a city," Inside Indonesia: http://www.insideindonesia.org/

Rupa-Pratirupa - Man & Mask 20th Feb.1998 - 12th Apr.1998, Matighar, IGNCA, http://ignca.nic.in/ ex_0032.htm.

Stephen Schwartz, January 2007, "Maintain momentum to overcome challenges" in Jakarta Post: http://www.thejakartapost.com/Outlook2006/eco11b.asp

Patrick Underwood, 23/11/2006, "Asia Update", Meat & Livestock Australia Limited (MLA) http://www.mla.com.au/; Inside indonesia, http://www.insideindonesia.org/edit80/p11-12mahony.html

Western Australia Dept of Industry and resources: export and trade, http://www.doir.wa.gov.au/exportandtrade/F3130D5AECA54ACF8ABBBBA831766203.asp

George B. Whitfield, 2006, Executive Orientation Services of Jakarta (EOS) www.indo.net.id/EOS/.

World Bank, http://0-siteresources.worldbank.org.library.vu.edu.au/INTINDONESIA/Resources/htm

Source: Adapted from Helen Deresky and Elizabeth Christopher, "Australia and New Zealand as part of Asia: Doing Business with Indonesia," *International Management: Managing across borders and Cultures,* Pearson Education Australia, 2008.

Communicating Across Cultures

OBJECTIVES:

1. To recognize the cultural variables in the communication process and what factors can cause "noise" in that process.

2. To develop an awareness of differences in non-verbal behaviors, context, and attitudes and how they affect cross-cultural communication.

3. To understand the complexities of Western-Arab communications.

4. To be aware of the impact of IT on cross-border communications.

5. To learn how to successfully manage cross-cultural business communications.

Opening Profile: Google's Internet Communications Clash with European Culture[1]

Google has been expanding into European markets for five years and now has a headquarters in Dublin, large offices in Zurich and London, and smaller centers in countries like Denmark, Russia and Poland. However, Google is now getting caught in a cultural web of privacy laws that threaten its growth and the positive image it has cultivated.

The latest clash is over Google's plan to introduce "Street View," a mapping service that provides a vivid, 360-degree, ground-level photographic panorama from any address. However, data protection officials in Switzerland are pressing Google to cancel those plans, since "Street View" would violate strict Swiss privacy laws that prohibit the unauthorized use of personal images or property. In Germany, where Street View is also not available, simply taking photographs for the service violates privacy laws. At the same time, the EU Article 29 Data Protection Working Group, which is a collaboration among all the information and data protection watchdogs within the European Union, is also contesting Google's practices. The EU Justice Commissioner, Franco Frattini, was backing the investigation. Google, the world's largest search engine, provoked a debate about internet privacy in May 2008, when it announced it would institute changes to its policies on holding personal information about its customers. The policy change related to Google's server logs (the information a browser sends back to Google when somebody visits a site). At present, the search engine retains a log of every search indefinitely, including information—such as the unique computer address, browser type and language—which could be traced back to a particular computer. The policy change was to reduce how long that information was retained to 18–24 months.

Peter Schaar, chair of Article 29, who is also Germany's federal commissioner for freedom of information, developed a report on the relationship between search-engine business models and European privacy laws. The draft report concluded that IP addresses are personal information because they can help identify a person. Europeans fiercely protect their privacy and trust that the government enforces it in law. Mr. Schaar has challenged Peter Fleischer of Google's global privacy law team to explain why such a long storage period was chosen and to give a legal justification for the storage of server logs in general. Google's response so far, from founders Sergei Brin and Larry Page, was to identify others as the bigger threat to internet users' privacy. They stated that information posted on social networking sites, such as photographs of young people at drunken parties, are a greater privacy concern. They defended the value of users' information for refining search results, and blamed the way some companies have used that information for privacy problems in the industry. The outcome of this cross-cultural internet communication clash remains to be seen. One thing that is clear is that the European Union (EU) has fired a warning shot across the bows of the search-engine companies.

Cultural communications are deeper and more complex than spoken or written messages. The essence of effective cross-cultural communication has more to do with releasing the right responses than with sending the "right" messages.

HALL AND HALL[2]

Multi-local online strategy . . . is about meeting global business objectives by tuning in to the cultural dynamics of their local markets.

"THINK GLOBALLY, INTERACT LOCALLY,"
New Media Age[3]

As the opening profile suggests, communication is a critical factor in the cross-cultural management issues discussed in this book, particularly those of an interpersonal nature, involving motivation, leadership, group interactions, and negotiation. Culture is conveyed and perpetuated through communication in one form or another. Culture and communication are so intricately intertwined that they are, essentially, synonymous.[4] By understanding this relationship, managers can move toward constructive intercultural management.

Communication, whether in the form of writing, talking, listening, or via the Internet, is an inherent part of a manager's role and takes up the majority of a manager's time on the job. Studies by Mintzberg demonstrate the importance of oral communication; he found that most managers spend between 50 and 90 percent of their time talking to people.[5] The ability of a manager to effectively communicate across cultural boundaries will largely determine the success of international business transactions or the output of a culturally diverse workforce. It is useful, then, to break down the elements involved in the communication process, both to understand the cross-cultural issues at stake and to maximize the process.

THE COMMUNICATION PROCESS

The term **communication** describes the process of sharing meaning by transmitting messages through media such as words, behavior, or material artifacts. Managers communicate to co-ordinate activities, to disseminate information, to motivate people, and to negotiate future plans. It is of vital importance, then, for a receiver to interpret the meaning of a particular communication in the way the sender intended. Unfortunately, the communication process (see Exhibit 4-1) involves stages during which meaning can be distorted. Anything that serves to undermine the communication of the intended meaning is typically referred to as **noise.**

The primary cause of noise stems from the fact that the sender and the receiver each exist in a unique, private world thought of as her or his life space. The context of that private world, largely based on culture, experience, relations, values, and so forth, determines the interpretation of meaning in communication. People filter, or selectively understand, messages consistent with their own expectations and perceptions of reality and their values and norms of behavior. The more dissimilar the cultures of those involved, the more the likelihood of misinterpretation. In this way, as Samovar, Porter, and Jain state, cultural factors pervade the communication process:

> *Culture not only dictates who talks with whom, about what, and how the communication proceeds, it also helps to determine how people encode messages, the meanings they have for messages, and the conditions and circumstances under which various messages may or may not be sent, noticed, or interpreted. In fact, our entire repertory of communicative behaviors is dependent largely on the culture in which we have been raised. Culture, consequently, is the foundation of communication. And, when cultures vary, communication practices also vary.*[6]

Communication, therefore, is a complex process of linking up or sharing the perceptual fields of sender and receiver; the perceptive sender builds a bridge to the life space of the receiver.[7] After the receiver interprets the message and draws a conclusion about what the sender meant, he or she will, in most cases, encode and send back a response, making communication a circular process.

The communication process is rapidly changing, however, as a result of technological developments, therefore propelling global business forward at a phenomenal growth rate. These changes are discussed later in this chapter.

Cultural Noise in the Communication Process

> *In Japanese there are several words for "I" and several words for "you" but their use depends on the relationship between the speaker and the other person. In short, there is no "I" by itself; the "I" depends on the relationship.*[8]

EXHIBIT 4-1   The Communication Process

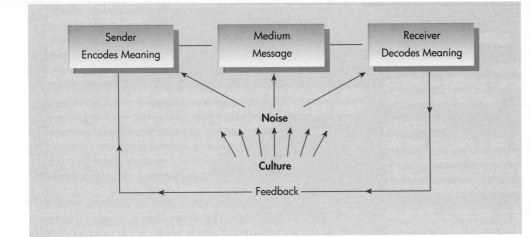

Because the focus in this text is on effective cross-cultural communication, it is important to understand what cultural variables cause noise in the communication process. This knowledge of **cultural noise**—the cultural variables that undermine the communications of intended meaning—will enable us to take steps to minimize that noise and so to improve communication.

When a member of one culture sends a message to a member of another culture, **intercultural communication** takes place. The message contains the meaning intended by the encoder. When it reaches the receiver, however, it undergoes a transformation in which the influence of the decoder's culture becomes part of the meaning.[9] Exhibit 4-2 provides an example of intercultural communication in which the meaning got all mixed up. Note how the attribution of behavior differs for each participant. **Attribution** is the process in which people look for an explanation of another person's behavior. When they realize that they do not understand another, they tend, say Hall and Hall, to blame their confusion on the other's "stupidity, deceit, or craziness."[10]

In the situation depicted in Exhibit 4-2, the Greek employee becomes frustrated and resigns after experiencing communication problems with his American boss. How could this outcome have been avoided? We do not have much information about the people or the context of the situation, but we can look at some of the variables that might have been involved and use them as a basis for analysis.

EXHIBIT 4-2   Cultural Noise in International Communication[11]

Behavior		Attribution	
American:	"How long will it take you to finish this report?"	*American:*	I asked him to participate.
		Greek:	His behavior makes no sense. He is the boss. Why doesn't he tell me?
Greek:	"I don't know. How long should it take?"	*American:*	He refuses to take responsibility.
		Greek:	I asked him for an order.
American:	"You are in the best position to analyze time requirements."	*American:*	I press him to take responsibility for his actions.
		Greek:	What nonsense: I'd better give him an answer.
Greek:	"10 days."	*American:*	He lacks the ability to estimate time; this time estimate is totally inadequate.
American:	"Take 15. Is it agreed? You will do it in 15 days?"	*American:*	I offer a contract.
		Greek:	These are my orders: 15 days.

In fact, the report needed 30 days of regular work. So the Greek worked day and night, but at the end of the 15th day, he still needed to do one more day's work.

American:	"Where is the report?"	*American:*	I am making sure he fulfills his contract.
		Greek:	He is asking for the report.
Greek:	"It will be ready tomorrow."	(Both attribute that it is not ready.)	
American:	"But we agreed it would be ready today."	*American:*	I must teach him to fulfill a contract.
		Greek:	The stupid, incompetent boss! Not only did he give me the wrong orders, but he doesn't even appreciate that I did a 30-day job in 16 days.
The Greek hands in his resignation.			The American is surprised.
		Greek:	I can't work for such a man.

THE CULTURE–COMMUNICATION LINK

The following sections examine underlying elements of culture that affect communication. The degree to which one is able to effectively communicate largely depends on how similar the other person's cultural expectations are to our own. However, cultural gaps can be overcome by prior learning and understanding of those variables and how to adjust to them.

Trust in Communication

The key ingredient in a successful alliance is trust.

JAMES R. HOUGHTON,
Former Chairman, Corning, Inc.[12]

Effective communication, and therefore collaboration in alliances across national boundaries, depends on the informal understandings among the parties that are based on the trust that has developed between them. However, the meaning of trust and how it is developed and communicated vary across societies. In China and Japan, for example, business transactions are based on networks of long-standing relationships based on trust rather than on the formal contracts and arm's-length relationships typical of the United States. When there is trust between parties, implicit understanding arises within communications. This understanding has numerous benefits in business, including encouraging communicators to overlook cultural differences and minimize problems. It allows communicators to adjust to unforeseen circumstances with less conflict than would be the case with formal contracts, and it facilitates open communication in exchanging ideas and information.[13] From his research on trust in global collaboration, John Child suggests the following guidelines for cultivating trust:

- Create a clear and calculated basis for mutual benefit. There must be realistic commitments and good intentions to honor them.
- Improve predictability: Strive to resolve conflicts and keep communication open.
- Develop mutual bonding through regular socializing and friendly contact.[14]

What can managers anticipate with regard to the level of trust in communications with people in other countries? If trust is based on how trustworthy we consider a person to be, then it must vary according to that society's expectations about whether that culture supports the norms and values that predispose people to behave credibly and benevolently. Are there differences across societies in those expectations of trust? Research by the World Values Study Group of 90,000 people in 45 societies provides some insight on cultural values regarding predisposition to trust. When we examine the percentage of respondents in each society who responded that "most people can be trusted," we can see that the Nordic countries and China had the highest predisposition to trust, followed by Canada, the United States, and Britain, while Brazil, Turkey, Romania, Slovenia, and Latvia had the lowest level of trust in people.[15]

The GLOBE Project

Results from the GLOBE research on culture, discussed in Chapter 3, provide some insight into culturally appropriate communication styles and expectations for the manager to use abroad. GLOBE researchers Javidan and House make the following observations:[16] For people in societies that ranked high on performance orientation—for example, the United States—presenting objective information in a direct and explicit way is an important and expected manner of communication; this compares with people in Russia or Greece—which ranked low on performance orientation—for whom hard facts and figures are not readily available or taken seriously. In those cases, a more indirect approach is preferred. People from countries ranking low on assertiveness, such as Sweden, also recoil from explicitness; their preference is for much two-way discourse and friendly relationships.

People ranking high on the "humane" dimension, such as those from Ireland and the Philippines, make avoiding conflict a priority and tend to communicate with the goal of being supportive of people rather than of achieving objective end results. This compares to people from France and Spain whose agenda is achievement of goals.

The foregoing provides examples of how to draw implications for appropriate communication styles from the research findings on cultural differences across societies. Astute global managers have learned that culture and communication are inextricably linked and that they should prepare themselves accordingly. Most will also suggest that you carefully watch and listen to how your hosts are communicating and to follow their lead.

Cultural Variables in the Communication Process

On a different level, it is also useful to be aware of cultural variables that can affect the communication process by influencing a person's perceptions; some of these variables have been identified by Samovar and Porter and discussed by Harris and Moran, and others.[17] These variables are as follows: attitudes, social organization, thought patterns, roles, language (spoken or written), nonverbal communication (including kinesic behavior, proxemics, paralanguage, and object language), and time. Although these variables are discussed separately in this text, their effects are interdependent and inseparable—or, as Hecht, Andersen, and Ribeau put it, "Encoders and decoders process nonverbal cues as a conceptual, multichanneled gestalt."[18]

Attitudes   We all know that our attitudes underlie the way we behave and communicate and the way we interpret messages from others. Ethnocentric attitudes are a particular source of noise in cross-cultural communication. In the incident described in Exhibit 4-2, both the American and the Greek are clearly attempting to interpret and convey meaning based on their own experiences of that kind of transaction. The American is probably guilty of stereotyping the Greek employee by quickly jumping to the conclusion that he is unwilling to take responsibility for the task and the scheduling.

This problem, **stereotyping,** occurs when a person assumes that every member of a society or subculture has the same characteristics or traits. Stereotyping is a common cause of misunderstanding in intercultural communication. It is an arbitrary, lazy, and often destructive way to find out about people. Astute managers are aware of the dangers of cultural stereotyping and deal with each person as an individual with whom they may form a unique relationship.

Social Organization   Our perceptions can be influenced by differences in values, approach, or priorities relative to the kind of social organizations to which we belong. These organizations may be based on one's nation, tribe, or religious sect, or they may consist of the members of a certain profession. Examples of such organizations include the Academy of Management or the United Auto Workers (UAW).[19]

Thought Patterns   The logical progression of reasoning varies widely around the world and greatly affects the communication process. Managers cannot assume that others use the same reasoning processes, as illustrated by the experience of a Canadian expatriate in Thailand:

> While in Thailand a Canadian expatriate's car was hit by a Thai motorist who had crossed over the double line while passing another vehicle. After failing to establish that the fault lay with the Thai driver, the Canadian flagged down a policeman. After several minutes of seemingly futile discussion, the Canadian pointed out the double line in the middle of the road and asked the policeman directly, "What do these lines signify?" The policeman replied, "They indicate the center of the road and are there so I can establish just how far the accident is from that point." The Canadian was silent. It had never occurred to him that the double line might not mean "no passing allowed.[20]

In the Exhibit 4-2 scenario, perhaps the American did not realize that the Greek employee had a different rationale for his time estimate for the job. Because the Greek was not used to having to estimate schedules, he just took a guess, which he felt he had been forced to do.

Roles   Societies differ considerably in their perceptions of a manager's role. Much of the difference is attributable to their perceptions of who should make the decisions and who has responsibility for what. In the Exhibit 4-2 example, the American assumes that his role as manager is to delegate responsibility, to foster autonomy, and to practice participative management. He prescribes the role of the employee without any consideration of whether the employee will understand that role. The Greek's frame of reference leads him to think that the manager is the boss and should give the order about when to have the job completed. He interprets the

American's behavior as breaking that frame of reference, and therefore he feels that the boss is "stupid and incompetent" for giving him the wrong order and for not recognizing and appreciating his accomplishment. The manager should have considered what behaviors Greek workers would expect of him and then either should have played that role or discussed the situation carefully, in a training mode.

Language   Spoken or written language, of course, is a frequent cause of miscommunication, stemming from a person's inability to speak the local language, a poor or too-literal translation, a speaker's failure to explain idioms, or a person missing the meaning conveyed through body language or certain symbols. Even among countries that share the same language, problems can arise from the subtleties and nuances inherent in the use of the language, as noted by George Bernard Shaw: "Britain and America are two nations separated by a common language." This problem can exist even within the same country among subcultures or subgroups.[21]

Many international executives tell stories about lost business deals or lost sales because of communication blunders:

> *When Pepsi Cola's slogan "Come Alive with Pepsi" was introduced in Germany, the company learned that the literal German translation of "come alive" is "come out of the grave."*
>
> *A U.S. airline found a lack of demand for its "rendezvous lounges" on its Boeing 747s. They later learned that "rendezvous" in Portuguese refers to a room that is rented for prostitution.*[22]

More than just conveying objective information, language also conveys cultural and social understandings from one generation to the next. Examples of how language reflects what is important in a society include the 6,000 different Arabic words used to describe camels and their parts and the 50 or more classifications of snow used by the Inuit, the Eskimo people of Canada.

Inasmuch as language conveys culture, technology, and priorities, it also serves to separate and perpetuate subcultures. In India, 14 official and many unofficial languages are used, and over 800 languages are spoken on the African continent.

Because of increasing workforce diversity around the world, the international business manager will have to deal with a medley of languages. For example, assembly-line workers at the Ford plant in Cologne, Germany, speak Turkish and Spanish as well as German. In Malaysia, Indonesia, and Thailand, many of the buyers and traders are Chinese. Not all Arabs speak Arabic; in Tunisia and Lebanon, for example, French is the language of commerce.

In North Africa—Morocco, Tunisia, Algeria, Libya, Egypt—people are used to doing business with Europe and the United States. People in Morocco, Algeria, and Tunisia, with their history of French rule, are familiar with the business practices in Europe—they speak French and use the metric system, for example. Egypt has a similar history with the British and so its citizens commonly speak English as their second language. Egypt also has a close political relationship and business ties with the United States.[23]

International managers need either a good command of the local language or competent interpreters. The task of accurate translation to bridge cultural gaps is fraught with difficulties, as Joe Romano, a partner of High Ground, an emerging technology-marketing company in Boston, found out on a business trip to Taiwan, how close a one-syllable slip of the tongue can come to torpedoing a deal. He noted that one is supposed to say 'au-ban,' meaning 'Hello, No.1. Boss.' But instead he said 'Lau-ban ya,' which means 'Hello, wife of the boss." Essentially Mr. Romano called him a woman in front of twenty senior Taiwanese executives, who all laughed; but the boss was very embarrassed, because men in Asia have a very macho attitude.[24]

Even the direct translation of specific words does not guarantee the congruence of their meaning, as with the word "yes" used by Asians, which usually means only that they have heard you, and, often, that they are too polite to disagree. The Chinese, for example, through years of political control, have built into their communication culture a cautionary stance to avoid persecution by professing agreement with whatever opinion was held by the person questioning them.[25]

Sometimes even a direct statement can be misinterpreted instead as an indirect expression, as when a German businessman said to his Algerian counterpart, "My wife would love something like that beautiful necklace your wife was wearing last night. It was beautiful." The next day the Algerian gave him a box with the necklace in it as a gift to his wife. The Algerian had interpreted the compliment as an indirect way of expressing a wish to possess a similar necklace. The German was embarrassed, but had to accept the necklace. He realize he needed to be careful how he expressed such things in the future—such as asking where that kind of jewelry is sold.[26]

Politeness and a desire to say only what the listener wants to hear creates noise in the communication process in much of the world. Often, even a clear translation does not help a person to understand what is meant because the encoding process has obscured the true message. With the poetic Arab language—replete with exaggeration, elaboration, and repetition—meaning is attributed more to how something is said rather than what is said.

Businesspeople need to consider another dimension of communication style that can cause noise whether in verbal or non-verbal language—that of *instrumental versus expressive communicators.* Expressive communicators—such as those from Russia, Hungary, Poland—are those who make their communications personal by showing their emotions openly or using emotional appeals to persuade others. This compares with instrumental communicators—whom we find as one moves west and north, such as in the Czech Republic, Slovenia; emphasis is on the content of the communication, not personal expressions.[27]

For the American supervisor and Greek employee cited in Exhibit 4-2, it is highly likely that the American could have picked up some cues from the employee's body language, which probably implied problems with the interpretation of meaning. How might body language have created noise in this case?

Nonverbal Communication   Behavior that communicates without words (although it often is accompanied by words) is called **nonverbal communication.** People will usually believe what they see over what they hear—hence the expression, "A picture is worth a thousand words." Studies show that these subtle messages account for between 65 and 93 percent of interpreted communication.[28] Even minor variations in body language, speech rhythms, and punctuality, for example, often cause mistrust and misperception of the situation among cross-national parties.[29] The media for such nonverbal communication can be categorized into four types: (1) kinesic behavior, (2) proxemics, (3) paralanguage, and (4) object language.

The term **kinesic behavior** refers to communication through body movements— posture, gestures, facial expressions, and eye contact. Although such actions may be universal, often their meaning is not. Because kinesic systems of meaning are culturally specific and learned, they cannot be generalized across cultures. Most people in the West would not correctly interpret many Chinese facial expressions; sticking out the tongue expresses surprise, a widening of the eyes shows anger, and scratching the ears and cheeks indicates happiness.[30] Research has shown for some time, however, that most people worldwide can recognize displays of the basic emotions of anger, disgust, fear, happiness, sadness, surprise, and contempt.[31]

Visitors to other countries must be careful about their gestures and how they might be interpreted. In the United States, for example, a common gesture is that for "O.K."—making a circle with the index finger and the thumb. That is an obscene gesture to the Brazilians, Greeks and Turks. On the other hand people in Japan may point with their middle finger, considered an obscene gesture to others. To Arabs, showing the soles of one's feet is an insult; recall the reporter who threw his shoe at President Bush in late 2008 during his visit to Iraq. This was, to Arabs, the ultimate insult.

Many businesspeople and visitors react negatively to what they feel are inappropriate facial expressions, without understanding the cultural meaning behind them. In his studies of cross-cultural negotiations, Graham observed that the Japanese feel uncomfortable when faced with the Americans' eye-to-eye posture. They are taught since childhood to bow their heads out of humility, whereas the automatic response of Americans is "look at me when I'm talking to you!"[32]

Subtle differences in eye behavior (called *oculesics*) can throw off a communication badly if they are not understood. Eye behavior includes differences not only in eye contact but also in the use of eyes to convey other messages, whether or not that involves mutual gaze. Edward T. Hall, author of the classic *The Silent Language*, explains the differences in eye contact between the British and the Americans. During speech, Americans will look straight at you, but the British keep your attention by looking away. The British will look at you when they have finished speaking, which signals that it is your turn to talk. The implicit rationale for this is that you can't interrupt people when they are not looking at you.[33]

It is helpful for U.S. managers to be aware of the many cultural expectations regarding posture and how they may be interpreted. In Europe or Asia, a relaxed posture in business meetings may be taken as bad manners or the result of poor upbringing. In Korea, you are expected to sit upright, with feet squarely on the floor, and to speak slowly, showing a blending of body and spirit.

Managers can also familiarize themselves with the many different interpretations of hand and finger signals around the world, some of which may represent obscene gestures. Of course, we cannot expect to change all of our ingrained, natural kinesic behavior, but we can be aware of what it means to others. We also can learn to understand the kinesic behavior of others and the role it plays in their society, as well as how it can affect business transactions. Misunderstanding the meanings of body movements—or an ethnocentric attitude toward the "proper" behavior—can have negative repercussions.

Proxemics deals with the influence of proximity and space on communication—both personal space and office space or layout. Americans expect office layout to provide private space for each person, and usually a larger and more private space as one goes up the hierarchy. In much of Asia, the custom is open office space, with people at all levels working and talking in close proximity to one another. Space communicates power in both Germany and the United States, evidenced by the desire for a corner office or one on the top floor. The importance of French officials, however, is made clear by a position in the middle of subordinates, communicating that they have a central position in an information network, where they can stay informed and in control.[34]

Do you ever feel vaguely uncomfortable and start moving backward slowly when someone is speaking to you? This is because that person is invading your "bubble"—your personal space. Personal space is culturally patterned, and foreign spatial cues are a common source of misinterpretation. When someone seems aloof or pushy, it often means that she or he is operating under subtly different spatial rules.

Hall and Hall suggest that cultural differences affect the programming of the senses and that space, perceived by all the senses, is regarded as a form of territory to be protected.[35] South Americans, Southern and Eastern Europeans, Indonesians, and Arabs are **high-contact cultures,** preferring to stand close, touch a great deal, and experience a "close" sensory involvement. Latin Americans, for example, have a highly physical greeting such as putting their arms around a colleague's back and grabbing him by the arm. On the other hand, North Americans, Asians, and Northern Europeans are **low-contact cultures** and prefer much less sensory involvement, standing farther apart and touching far less. They have a "distant" style of body language. In France, a relationship-oriented culture, good friends greet members of the opposite sex with a peck on each cheek; a handshake is a way to make a personal connection.

Interestingly, high-contact cultures are mostly located in warmer climates, and low-contact cultures in cooler climates. Americans are relatively nontouching, automatically standing at a distance so that an outstretched arm will touch the other person's ear. Standing any closer than that is regarded as invading intimate space. However, Americans and Canadians certainly expect a warm handshake and maybe a pat on the back from closer friends, though not the very warm double handshake of the Spaniards (clasping the forearm with the left hand). The Japanese, considerably less **haptic (touching),** do not shake hands; an initial greeting between a Japanese and a Spanish businessperson would be uncomfortable for both parties if they were untrained in cultural haptics. The Japanese bow to one another—the depth of the bow revealing their relative social standing.

When considering high- and low-contact cultures, we can trace a correlation between Hofstede's cultural variables of individualism and collectivism and the types of kinesic and proxemic behaviors people display. Generally, people from individualistic cultures are more remote and distant, whereas those from collectivist cultures are interdependent: They tend to work, play, live, and sleep in close proximity.[36]

The term **paralanguage** refers to how something is said rather than the content—the rate of speech, the tone and inflection of voice, other noises, laughing, or yawning. The culturally aware manager learns how to interpret subtle differences in paralanguage, including silence. Silence is a powerful communicator. It may be a way of saying no, of being offended, or of waiting for more information to make a decision. There is considerable variation in the use of silence in meetings. While Americans get uncomfortable after 10 or 15 seconds of silence, Chinese prefer to think the situation over for 30 seconds before speaking. The typical scenario between Americans and Chinese, then, is that the American gets impatient, says something to break the silence, and offends the Chinese by interrupting his or her chain of thought and comfort level with the subject.[37] Graham, a researcher on international negotiations, taped a bargaining session held at Toyota's U.S. headquarters in California. The U.S. executive had made a proposal to open a new production facility in Brazil and was waiting for a response from the three Japanese executives, who sat with lowered eyes and hands folded on the table. After about 30 seconds—an eternity to Americans, accustomed to a conversational response time of a few tenths of a second—the American blurted out that they were getting nowhere—and the meeting ended in a stalemate. More sensitivity to cultural differences in communication might have led him to wait longer or perhaps to prompt some further response through another polite question.[38]

The term **object language, or material culture,** refers to how we communicate through material artifacts, whether architecture, office design and furniture, clothing, cars, or cosmetics. Material culture communicates what people hold as important. In the United States, for example, someone wishing to convey his important status and wealth would show guests his penthouse office or expensive car. In Japan, a businessman presents his business card to a new contact and expects the receiver to study it and appreciate his position. In Mexico, a visiting international executive or salesperson is advised to take time out, before negotiating business, to show appreciation for the surrounding architecture, which is prized by Mexicans. The importance of family to people in Spain and much of Latin America, would be conveyed by family photographs around the office and therefore an expectation that the visitor would enquire about the family.

Time   Another variable that communicates culture is the way people regard and use time (see also Chapter 3). To Brazilians, relative punctuality communicates the level of importance of those involved. To Middle Easterners, time is something controlled by the will of Allah.

To initiate effective cross-cultural business interactions, managers should know the difference between *monochronic time systems* and *polychronic time systems* and how they affect communications. Hall and Hall explain that in **monochronic cultures** (Switzerland, Germany, and the United States), time is experienced in a linear way, with a past, a present, and a future, and time is treated as something to be spent, saved, made up, or wasted. Classified and compartmentalized, time serves to order life. This attitude is a learned part of Western culture, probably starting with the Industrial Revolution. Monochronic people, found in individualistic cultures, generally concentrate on one thing at a time, adhere to time commitments, and are accustomed to short-term relationships.

In contrast, **polychronic cultures** tolerate many things occurring simultaneously and emphasize involvement with people. Two Latin friends, for example, will put an important conversation ahead of being on time for a business meeting, thus communicating the priority of relationships over material systems. Polychronic people—Latin Americans, Arabs, and those from other collectivist cultures—may focus on several things at once, be highly distractible, and change plans often.[39]

The relationship between time and space also affects communication. Polychronic people, for example, are likely to hold open meetings, moving around and conducting transactions with one party and then another, rather than compartmentalizing meeting topics, as do monochronic people.

The nuances and distinctions regarding cultural differences in nonverbal communication are endless. The various forms are listed in Exhibit 4-3; wise intercultural managers will take careful account of the role that such differences might play.

What aspects of nonverbal communication might have created noise in the interactions between the American supervisor and the Greek employee in Exhibit 4-2? Undoubtedly, some cues could have been picked up from the kinesic behavior of each person. It was the responsibility of the manager, in particular, to notice any indications from the Greek that could have prompted him to change his communication pattern or assumptions. Face-to-face communication permits the sender of the message to get immediate feedback, verbal and nonverbal, and thus to have some idea as to how that message is being received and whether additional information is needed. What aspects of the Greek employee's kinesic behavior or paralanguage might have been evident to a more culturally sensitive manager? Did both parties' sense of time affect the communication process?

EXHIBIT 4-3 Forms of Nonverbal Communication

- Facial expressions
- Body posture
- Gestures with hands, arms, head, etc.
- Interpersonal distance (proxemics)
- Touching, body contact
- Eye contact
- Clothing, cosmetics, hairstyles, jewelry
- Paralanguage (voice pitch and inflections, rate of speech, and silence)
- Color symbolism
- Attitude toward time and the use of time in business and social interactions
- Food symbolism and social use of meals

Context

> *East Asians live in relatively complex social networks with prescribed role relations; attention to context is, therefore, important for their effective functioning. In contrast, westerners live in less constraining social worlds that stress independence and allow them to pay less attention to context.*
>
> RICHARD E. NISBETT,
> *September 2005*[40]

A major differentiating factor that is a primary cause of noise in the communication process is that of context—which actually incorporates many of the variables discussed earlier. The **context** in which the communication takes place affects the meaning and interpretation of the interaction. Cultures are known to be high- or low-context cultures, with a relative range in between.[41] In **high-context cultures** (Asia, the Middle East, Africa, and the Mediterranean), feelings and thoughts are not explicitly expressed; instead, one has to read between the lines and interpret meaning from one's general understanding. Two such high-context cultures are those of South Korea and Arab cultures. In such cultures, key information is embedded in the context rather than made explicit. People make assumptions about what the message means through their knowledge of the person or the surroundings. In these cultures, most communication takes place within a context of extensive information networks resulting from close personal relationships. See the following Management Focus for further explanation of the Asian communication style.

In **low-context cultures** (Germany, Switzerland, Scandinavia, and North America), where personal and business relationships are more compartmentalized, communication media have to be more explicit. Feelings and thoughts are expressed in words, and information is more readily available. Westerners focus more on the individual, and therefore tend to view events as the result of specific agents, while easterners view events in a broader and longer-term context.[42]

In cross-cultural communication between high- and low-context people, a lack of understanding may preclude reaching a solution, and conflict may arise. Germans, for example, will expect considerable detailed information before making a business decision, whereas Arabs will base their decisions more on knowledge of the people involved—the information is present, but it is implicit. People in low-context cultures, such as those in Germany, Switzerland Austria, and the United States, convey their thoughts and plans in a direct, straightforward communication style, saying something like "we have to make a decision on this today." People in high-context cultures, such as in Asia, and, to a lesser extent, in England, convey their thoughts in a more indirect, implicit manner; this means that someone from Germany needs to have more patience and tact and be willing to listen for clues—verbal and nonverbal—as to their colleagues' wishes.

People in high-context cultures expect others to understand unarticulated moods, subtle gestures, and environmental clues that people from low-context cultures simply do not process. Misinterpretation and misunderstanding often result.[43] People from high-context cultures

MANAGEMENT FOCUS

Oriental Poker Face: Eastern Deception or Western Inscrutability?

Among many English expressions that are likely to offend those of us whose ancestry may be traced to the Far East, two stand out quite menacingly for me: "Oriental poker face" and "idiotic Asian smile." The former refers to the supposedly inscrutable nature of a facial expression that apparently reflects no particular state of mind, while the latter pokes fun at a face fixed with a perpetually friendly smile. Westerners' perplexity, when faced with either, arises from the impression that these two diametrically opposed masquerading strategies prevent them from extracting useful information—at least the type of information that at least they could process with a reasonable measure of confidence—about the feelings of the person before them. An Asian face that projects no signs of emotion, then, seems to most Westerners nothing but a facade. It does not matter whether that face wears an unsightly scowl or a shining ray; a facial expression they cannot interpret poses a genuine threat.

Compassionate and sympathetic to their perplexity as I may be, I am also insulted by the Western insensitivity to the significant roles that subtle signs play in Asian cultures. Every culture has its unique modus operandi for communication. Western culture, for example, apparently emphasizes the importance of direct communication. Not only are the communicators taught to look directly at each other when they convey a message, but they also are encouraged to come right to the point of the message. Making bold statements or asking frank questions in a less than diplomatic manner (i.e., "That was really a very stupid thing to do!" or "Are you interested in me?") is rarely construed as rude or indiscreet. Even embarrassingly blunt questions such as "President Clinton, did you have sexual intercourse with Monica Lewinsky?" are tolerated most of the time. Asians, on the other hand, find this direct communicative communication style quite unnerving. In many social interactions, they avoid direct eye contact. They "see" each other without necessarily looking directly at each other, and they gather information about inner states of mind without asking even the most discreet or understated questions. Many times they talk around the main topic, and, yet, they succeed remarkably well in understanding one another's position. (At least they believe they have developed a reasonably clear understanding.)

To a great extent, Asian communication is listening-centered; the ability to listen (and a special talent for detecting various communicative cues) is treated as equally important as, if not more important than, the ability to speak. This contrasts clearly with the American style of communication that puts the utmost emphasis on verbal expression; the speaker carries most of the burden for ensuring that everyone understands his or her message. An Asian listener, however, is prone to blame himself or herself for failing to reach a comprehensive understanding from the few words and gestures performed by the speaker. With this heavier burden placed on the listener, an Asian speaker does not feel obliged to send clearly discernible message cues (at least not nearly so much as he or she is obliged to do in American cultural contexts). Not obligated to express themselves without interruption, Asians use silence as a tool in communication. Silence, by most Western conventions, represents discontinuity of communication and creates a feeling of discomfort and anxiety. In the Orient, however, silence is not only comfortably tolerated but is considered a desirable form of expression. Far from being a sign of displeasure or animosity, it serves as an integral part of the communication process, used for reflecting on messages previously exchanged and for carefully crafting thoughts before uttering them.

It is not outlandish at all, then, for Asians to view Americans as unnecessarily talkative and lacking in the ability to listen. For the Asian, it is the American who projects a mask of confidence by being overly expressive both verbally and nonverbally. Since the American style of communication places less emphasis on the act of listening than on speaking, Asians suspect that their American counterparts fail to pick up subtle and astute communicative signs in conversation. To one with a cultural outlook untrained in reading those signs, an inscrutable face represents no more than a menacing or amusing mask.

Source: Dr. Jin Kim, State University of New York–Plattsburgh. Copyright © 2003 by Dr. Jin Kim. Used with permission of Dr. Kim.

EXHIBIT 4-4 Cultural Context and Its Effects on Communication[45]

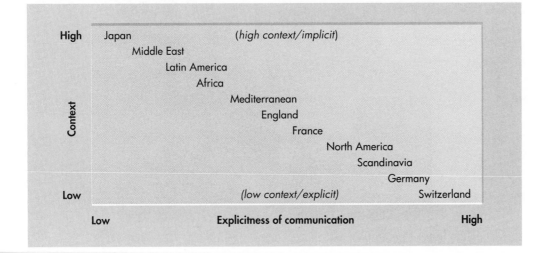

perceive those from low-context cultures as too talkative, too obvious, and redundant. Those from low-context cultures perceive high-context people as nondisclosing, sneaky, and mysterious. Research indicates, for example, that Americans find talkative people more attractive, whereas Koreans, high-context people, perceive less verbal people as more attractive. Finding the right balance between low- and high-context communications can be tricky, as Hall and Hall point out: "Too much information leads people to feel they are being talked down to; too little information can mystify them or make them feel left out."[44] Exhibit 4-4 shows the relative level of context in various countries.

The importance of understanding the role of context and nonverbal language to avoid misinterpretation is illustrated in the Comparative Management in Focus: Communicating with Arabs.

COMPARATIVE MANAGEMENT IN FOCUS
Communicating with Arabs

In the Middle East, the meaning of a communication is implicit and interwoven, and consequently much harder for Americans, accustomed to explicit and specific meanings, to understand.

Arabs are warm, emotional, and quick to explode: "sounding off" is regarded as a safety valve. In fact, the Arabic language aptly communicates the Arabic culture, one of emotional extremes. The language contains the means for overexpression, many adjectives, words that allow for exaggeration, and metaphors to emphasize a position. What is said is often not as important as *how* it is said. Eloquence and flowery speech are admired for their own sake, regardless of the content. Loud speech is used for dramatic effect.

At the core of Middle Eastern culture are friendship, honor, religion, and traditional hospitality. Family, friends, and connections are very important on all levels in the Middle East and will take precedence over business transactions. Arabs do business with people, not companies, and they make commitments to people, not contracts. A phone call to the right person can help to get around seemingly insurmountable obstacles. An Arab expects loyalty from friends, and it is understood that giving and receiving favors is an inherent part of the relationship; no one says no to a request for a favor. A lack of follow-through is assumed to be beyond the friend's control.[46]

Because hospitality is a way of life and highly symbolic, a visitor must be careful not to reject it by declining refreshment or rushing into business discussions. Part of that hospitality is the elaborate system of greetings and the long period of getting acquainted, perhaps taking up the entire first meeting. While the handshake may seem limp, the rest of the greeting is not. Kissing on the cheeks is common among men, as is hand-holding between male friends. However, any public display of intimacy between men and women is strictly forbidden by the Arab social code.

Women play little or no role in business or entertainment; the Middle East is a male-dominated society, and it is impolite to inquire about women. Other nonverbal taboos include showing the soles of one's feet and using the left (unclean) hand to eat or pass something. In discussions, slouching in a seat or leaning against a wall communicates a lack of respect.

Westerner Meeting with Arab Businessmen.

Source: Getty Images/Digital Vision

The Arab society also values honor. Harris and Moran explain: "Honor, social prestige, and a secure place in society are brought about when conformity is achieved. When one fails to conform, this is considered to be damning and leads to a degree of shame."[47] Shame results not just from doing something wrong but from having others find out about that wrongdoing. Establishing a climate of honesty and trust is part of the sense of honor. Therefore, considerable tact is needed to avoid conveying any concern or doubt. Arabs tend to be quite introverted until a mutual trust is built, which takes a long time.[48]

In their nonverbal communication, most Arab countries are high-contact cultures. Arabs stand and sit closer and touch people of the same sex more than Westerners. They do not have the same concept of "public" and "private" space, or as Hall puts it, "Not only is the sheer noise level much higher, but the piercing look of the eyes, the touch of the hands, and the mutual bathing in the warm moist breath during conversation represent stepped-up sensory inputs to a level which many Europeans find unbearably intense. On the other hand, the distance preferred by North Americans may leave an Arab suspicious of intentions because of the lack of olfactory contact."[49]

The Muslim expression *Bukra insha Allah*—"Tomorrow if Allah wills"—explains much about the Arab culture and its approach to business transactions. A cultural clash typically occurs when an American tries to give an Arab a deadline. "I am going to Damascus tomorrow morning and will have to have my car tonight," is a sure way to get the mechanic to stop work," explains Hall, "because to give another person a deadline in this part of the world is to be rude, pushy, and demanding."[50] In such instances, the attitude toward time communicates as loudly as words.

In verbal interactions, managers must be aware of different patterns of Arab thought and communication. Compared to the direct, linear fashion of American communication, Arabs tend to meander: They start with social talk, discuss business for a while, loop round to social and general issues, then back to business, and so on.[51] American impatience and insistence on sticking to the subject will "cut off their loops," triggering confusion and dysfunction. Instead, westerners should accept that there will be considerable time spent on "small talk" and socializing, with frequent interruptions, before getting down to business.

Exhibit 4-5 illustrates some of the sources of noise that are likely to interfere in the communication process between Americans and Arabs.

For people doing business in the Middle East, the following are some useful guidelines for effective communication:

- Be patient. Recognize the Arab attitude toward time and hospitality—take time to develop friendship and trust, for these are prerequisites for any social or business transactions.
- Recognize that people and relationships matter more to Arabs than the job, company, or contract—conduct business personally, not by correspondence or telephone.
- Avoid expressing doubts or criticism when others are present—recognize the importance of honor and dignity to Arabs.
- Adapt to the norms of body language, flowery speech, and circuitous verbal patterns in the Middle East, and don't be impatient to "get to the point."
- Expect many interruptions in meetings, delays in schedules, and changes in plans.[52]

EXHIBIT 4-5 **Miscommunication Between Americans and Arabs Caused by Cross-cultural Noise**

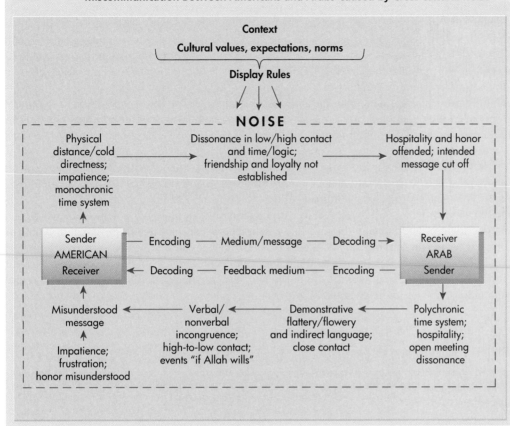

Communication Channels

In addition to the variables related to the sender and receiver of a message, the variables linked to the channel itself and the context of the message must be taken into consideration. These variables include fast or slow messages and information flows, as well as different types of media.

Information Systems Communication in organizations varies according to where and how it originates, the channels, and the speed at which it flows, whether it is formal or informal, and so forth. The type of organizational structure, the staffing policies, and the leadership style will affect the nature of an organization's information system.

As an international manager, it is useful to know where and how information originates and the speed at which it flows, both internally and externally. In centralized organizational structures, as in South America, most information originates from top managers. Workers take less responsibility to keep managers informed than in a typical company in the United States, where delegation results in information flowing from the staff to the managers. In a decision-making system in which many people are involved, such as the **ringi system** of consensus decision making in Japan, the expatriate needs to understand that there is a systematic pattern for information flow.

Context also affects information flow. In high-context cultures (such as in the Middle East), information spreads rapidly and freely because of the constant close contact and the implicit ties among people and organizations. Information flow is often informal. In low-context cultures (such as Germany or the United States), information is controlled and focused, and thus it does not flow so freely.[53] Compartmentalized roles and office layouts stifle information channels; information sources tend to be more formal.

It is crucial for an expatriate manager to find out how to tap into a firm's informal sources of information. In Japan, employees usually have a drink together on the way home from work, and this becomes an essential source of information. However, such communication networks are based on long-term relationships in Japan (and in other high-context cultures). The same information may not be readily available to "outsiders." A considerable barrier in Japan separates strangers from familiar friends, a situation that discourages communication.

Americans are more open and talk freely about almost anything, whereas Japanese will disclose little about their inner thoughts or private issues. Americans are willing to have a wide "public self," disclosing their inner reactions verbally and physically. In contrast, the Japanese prefer to keep their responses largely to their "private self." The Japanese expose only a small portion of their thoughts; they reduce, according to Barnlund, "the unpredictability and emotional intensity of personal encounters."[54] Cultural clashes between the public and private selves in intercultural communication between Americans and Japanese result when each party forces its cultural norms of communication on the other. In the American style, the American's cultural norms of explicit communication impose on the Japanese by invading the person's private self. The Japanese style of implicit communication causes a negative reaction from the American because of what is perceived as too much formality and ambiguity, which wastes time.[55]

Cultural variables in information systems and context underlie the many differences in communication style between Japanese and Americans. Exhibit 4-6 shows some specific differences. The Japanese *ningensei* ("human beingness") style of communication refers to the preference for humanity, reciprocity, a receiver orientation, and an underlying distrust of words and analytic logic.[56] The Japanese believe that true intentions are not readily revealed in words or contracts but are, in fact, masked by them. In contrast to the typical American's verbal agility and explicitness, Japanese behaviors and communications are directed to defend and give face for everyone concerned; to do so, they avoid public disagreements at all costs. In cross-cultural negotiations, this last point is essential.

EXHIBIT 4-6 Difference Between Japanese and American Communication Styles

Japanese Ningensei Style of Communication	U.S. Adversarial Style of Communication
1. Indirect verbal and nonverbal communication	1. More direct verbal and nonverbal communication
2. Relationship communication	2. More task communication
3. Discourages confrontational strategies	3. Confrontational strategies more acceptable
4. Strategically ambiguous communication	4. Prefers more to-the-point communication
5. Delayed feedback	5. More immediate feedback
6. Patient, longer-term negotiators	6. Shorter-term negotiators
7. Uses fewer words	7. Favors verbosity
8. Distrustful of skillful verbal communicators	8. Exalts verbal eloquence
9. Group orientation	9. More individualistic orientation
10. Cautious, tentative	10. More assertive, self-assured
11. Complementary communicators	11. More publicly critical communication
12. Softer, heart like logic	12. Harder, analytic logic preferred
13. Sympathetic, empathetic, complex use of pathos	13. Favors logos, reason
14. Expresses and decodes complex relational strategies and nuances	14. Expresses and decodes complex logos, cognitive nuances
15. Avoids decision making in public	15. Frequent decision making in public
16. Makes decisions in private venues, away from public eye	16. Frequent decision in public at negotiating tables
17. Decisions via *ringi* and *nemawashi* (complete consensus process)	17. Decisions by majority rule and public compromise is more commonplace
18. Uses go-betweens for decision making	18. More extensive use of direct person-to-person, player-to-player interaction for decisions
19. Understatement and hesitation in verbal and nonverbal communication	19. May publicly speak in superlatives, exaggerations, nonverbal projection

EXHIBIT 4-6 *(Continued)*

20. Uses qualifiers, tentativeness, humility as communicator	20. Favors fewer qualifiers, more ego-centered
21. Receiver/listening-centered	21. More speaker- and message-centered
22. Inferred meanings, looks beyond words to nuances, nonverbal communication	22. More face-value meaning, more denotative
23. Shy, reserved communicators	23. More publicly self-assertive
24. Distaste for purely business transactions	24. Prefers to "get down to business" or "nitty gritty"
25. Mixes business and social communication	25. Tends to keep business negotiating more separated from social communication
26. Utilizes *matomari* or "hints" for achieving group adjustment and saving face in negotiating	26. More directly verbalizes management's preference at negotiating tables
27. Practices *haragei* or "belly logic" and communication	27. Practices more linear, discursive, analytical logic; greater reverence for cognitive than for affective

Source: Reprinted from A. Goldman, "The Centrality of 'Ningensei' to Japanese Negotiating and Interpersonal Relationships: Implications for U.S. Japanese Communication," *International Journal of Intercultural Relations* 18, no. 1 (1994), with permission from Elsevier.

The speed with which we try to use information systems is another key variable that needs attention to avoid misinterpretation and conflict. Americans expect to give and receive information very quickly and clearly, moving through details and stages in a linear fashion to the conclusion. They usually use various media for fast messages—letters or emails giving all the facts and plans up front, faxes, and familiar relationships. In contrast, the French use the slower message channels of deep relationships, culture, and sometimes mediators to exchange information. A French written communication will be tentative, with subsequent letters slowly building up to a new proposal. The French preference for written communication, even for informal interactions, echoes the formality of their relationships—and results in a slowing down of message transmission that often seems unnecessary to Americans. Jean-Louis Reynal, a plant manager at Citröen, explains that "it wouldn't be too much of an exaggeration to say that, until they are written, until they are entrusted to the blackboard, the notepad, or the flip chart, ideas have no reality for the French manager. You could even say that writing is an indispensable aid to 'being' for us."[57]

In short, it behooves Americans to realize that, because most of the world exchanges information through slower message media, it is wise to schedule more time for transactions, develop patience, and learn to get at needed information in more subtle ways—after building rapport and taking time to observe the local system for exchanging information.

We have seen that cross-cultural misinterpretation can result from noise in the actual transmission of the message—the choice or speed of media. Interpreting the meaning of a message can thus be as much a function of the transmission channel (or medium) as it is of examining the message itself.

INFORMATION TECHNOLOGY: GOING GLOBAL AND ACTING LOCAL

All information is local; IT systems can connect every corner of the globe, but IT managers are learning they have to pay attention to regional differences.

COMPUTERWORLD[58]

Deploying B2B e-commerce technology [globally] . . . becomes exponentially more difficult because systems must address concerns not germane to domestic networks, such as language translation, currency conversion and even cultural differences.

INTERNETWEEK[59]

Using the Internet as a global medium for communication has enabled companies of all sizes to quickly develop a presence in many markets around the world—and, in fact, has enabled them to "go global." However, their global reach cannot alone translate into global business. Those companies are learning that they have to adapt their e-commerce and their enterprise resource planning (ERP) applications to regional idiosyncrasies beyond translation or content management issues; even asking for a name or an email address can incur resistance in many countries where people do not like to give out personal information.[60] While communication over the Internet is clearly not as personal as face-to-face cross-cultural communication, those transactions must still be regionalized and personalized to adjust to differences in language, culture, local laws, and business models, as well as differences in the level of development in the local telecommunications infrastructure. Yet, if the Internet is a global medium for communication, why do so many U.S. companies treat the Web as a U.S.-centric phenomenon? Giving preference to some geographic regions, languages, and cultures is "a short-sighted business decision that will result in diminished brand equity, market share, profits and global leadership."[61] With an annual predicted growth rate of 70 percent in non–English-language sites and usage, this soon puts English-language sites in the minority.[62]

It seems essential, then, that a global online strategy must also be multilocal. The impersonal nature of the Web must somehow be adapted to local cultures to establish relationships and create customer loyalty. Effective technological communication requires even more cultural sensitivity than face-to-face communication because of the inability to assess reactions and get feedback, or even to retain contact in many cases. It is still people, after all, who respond to and interact with other people through the medium of the Internet, and those people interpret and respond according to their own languages and cultures, as well as their local business practices and expectations. In Europe, for example, significant differences in business cultures and e-business technology have slowed e-business progress there. However, some companies are making progress in pan-European integration services, such as *leEurope*, which aims to cross language, currency, and cultural barriers. Specifically, *leEurope* is building a set of services "to help companies tie their back-end e-business systems together across European boundaries through aseries of mergers involving regional e-business integrators in more than a dozen countries."[63]

MANAGING CROSS-CULTURAL COMMUNICATION

Steps toward effective intercultural communication include the development of cultural sensitivity, careful encoding, selective transmission, careful decoding, and appropriate follow-up actions.

Developing Cultural Sensitivity

When acting as a sender, a manager must make it a point to know the receiver and to encode the message in a form that will most likely be understood as intended. On the manager's part, this requires an awareness of his or her own cultural baggage and how it affects the communication process. In other words, what kinds of behaviors does the message imply, and how will they be perceived by the receiver? The way to anticipate the most likely meaning that the receiver will attach to the message is to internalize honest cultural empathy with that person. What is the cultural background—the societal, economic, and organizational context—in which this communication is taking place? What are this person's expectations regarding the situation, what are the two parties' relative positions, and what might develop from this communication? What kinds of transactions and behaviors is this person used to? Cultural sensitivity (discussed in Chapter 3) is really just a matter of understanding the other person, the context, and how the person will respond to the context. Americans, unfortunately, have a rather negative reputation overseas of not being culturally sensitive. One not-for-profit group, called Business for Diplomatic Action, has the following advice for Americans when doing business abroad, in its attempts to counteract the stereotypical American traits such as boastfulness, loudness, and speed:

- **Read a map:** Familiarize yourself with the local geography to avoid making insulting mistakes.
- **Dress up:** In some countries, casual dress is a sign of disrespect
- **Talk small:** Talking about wealth, power, or status—corporate or personal—can create resentment.
- **No slang:** Even casual profanity is unacceptable.

- **Slow down:** Americans talk fast, eat fast, move fast, live fast. Many cultures do not.
- **Listen as much as you talk:** Ask people you're visiting about themselves and their way of life.
- **Speak lower and slower:** A loud voice is often perceived as bragging.
- **Religious restraint:** In many countries, religion is not a subject for public discussion.
- **Political restraint:** Steer clear of this subject. If someone is attacking U.S. politicians or policies, agree to disagree.[64]

Careful Encoding

In translating his or her intended meaning into symbols for cross-cultural communication, the sender must use words, pictures, or gestures that are appropriate to the receiver's frame of reference. Of course, language training is invaluable, but senders should also avoid idioms and regional sayings (such as "Go fly a kite" or "Foot the bill") in a translation, or even in English when speaking to a non-American who knows little English.

Literal translation, then, is a limited answer to language differences. Even for people in English-speaking countries, words may have different meanings. Ways to avoid problems are to speak slowly and clearly, avoid long sentences and colloquial expressions, and explain things in several different ways and through several media, if possible. However, even though English is in common use around the world for business transactions, the manager's efforts to speak the local language will greatly improve the climate. Sometimes people from other cultures resent the assumption by English-speaking executives that everyone else will speak English.

Language translation is only part of the encoding process; the message also is expressed in nonverbal language. In the encoding process, the sender must ensure congruence between the nonverbal and the verbal message. In encoding a message, therefore, it is useful to be as objective as possible and not to rely on personal interpretations. To further clarify their messages, managers can hand out written summaries of verbal presentations and use visual aids, such as graphs or pictures. A good general guide is to move slowly, wait, and take cues from the receivers.

Selective Transmission

The type of medium chosen for the message depends on the nature of the message, its level of importance, the context and expectations of the receiver, the timing involved, and the need for personal interaction, among other factors. Typical media include email, letters or memos, reports, meetings, telephone calls, teleconferences, videoconferences, or face-to-face conversations. The secret is to find out how communication is transmitted in the local organization—how much is downward versus upward or vertical versus horizontal, how the grapevine works, and so on. In addition, the cultural variables discussed earlier need to be considered: whether the receiver is from a high- or low-context culture, whether he or she is used to explicit or implicit communication, and what speed and routing of messages will be most effective.

For the most part, it is best to use face-to-face interaction for relationship building or for other important transactions, particularly in intercultural communications, because of the lack of familiarity between parties. Personal interactions give the manager the opportunity to get immediate verbal and visual feedback and to make rapid adjustments in the communication process.

International dealings are often long-distance, of course, limiting the opportunity for face-to-face communication. However, personal rapport can be established or enhanced through telephone calls or videoconferencing and through trusted contacts. Modern electronic media can be used to break down communication barriers by reducing waiting periods for information, clarifying issues, and allowing instant consultation. Global telecommunications and computer networks are changing the face of cross-cultural communication through the faster dissemination of information within the receiving organization. Ford Europe uses videoconferencing for engineers in Britain and Germany to consult about quality problems. Through the video monitors, they examine one another's engineering diagrams and usually find a solution that gets the factory moving again in a short time.

Careful Decoding of Feedback

Timely and effective feedback channels can also be set up to assess a firm's general communication about the progression of its business and its general management principles. The best means for getting accurate feedback is through face-to-face interaction because this allows the manager to hear, see, and immediately sense how a message is being interpreted. When visual feedback on important issues is not possible or appropriate, it is a good idea to use several means of attaining feedback, in particular, employing third parties.

Decoding is the process of translating the received symbols into the interpreted message. The main causes of incongruence are (1) the receiver misinterprets the message, (2) the receiver encodes his or her return message incorrectly, or (3) the sender misinterprets the feedback. Two-way communication is thus essential for important issues so that successive efforts can be made until an understanding has been achieved. Asking other colleagues to help interpret what is going on is often a good way to break a cycle of miscommunication.

Perhaps the most important means for avoiding miscommunication is to practice careful decoding by improving one's listening and observation skills. A good listener practices projective listening, or empathetic listening—listening without interruption or evaluation to the full message of the speaker, attempting to recognize the feelings behind the words and nonverbal cues, and understanding the speaker's perspective.

At the multinational corporation (MNC) level, avenues of communication and feedback among parent companies and subsidiaries can be kept open through telephone calls, regular meetings and visits, reports, and plans, all of which facilitate cooperation, performance control, and the smooth running of the company. Communication among far-flung operations can be best managed by setting up feedback systems and liaison people. The headquarters people should maintain considerable flexibility in cooperating with local managers and allowing them to deal with the local context as they see fit.

Follow-up Actions

Managers communicate through both action and inaction. Therefore, to keep open the lines of communication, feedback, and trust, managers must follow through with action on what has been discussed and then agreed upon—typically a contract, which is probably the most important formal business communication. Unfortunately, the issue of contract follow-through is a particularly sensitive one across cultures because of the different interpretations regarding what constitutes a contract (perhaps a handshake, perhaps a full legal document) and what actions should result. Trust, future communications, and future business are based on such interpretations, and it is up to managers to understand them and to follow through on them.

The management of cross-cultural communication depends largely on a manager's personal abilities and behavior. Those behaviors that researchers indicate to be most important to intercultural communication effectiveness (ICE) are listed here, as reviewed by Ruben:

1. Respect (conveyed through eye contact, body posture, voice tone, and pitch)
2. Interaction posture (the ability to respond to others in a descriptive, nonevaluative, and nonjudgmental way)
3. Orientation to knowledge (recognizing that one's knowledge, perception, and beliefs are valid only for oneself and not for everyone else)
4. Empathy
5. Interaction management
6. Tolerance for ambiguity
7. Other-oriented role behavior (one's capacity to be flexible and to adopt different roles for the sake of greater group cohesion and group communication)[65]

Whether at home or abroad, certain personal capabilities facilitate effective intercultural communication; these abilities can help the expatriate to adapt to the host country and enable productive working relations to develop in the long term. Researchers have established a relationship between personality traits and behaviors and the ability to adapt to the host-country's cultural environment.[66] What is seldom pointed out, however, is that communication is the mediating factor between those behaviors and the relative level of adaptation the expatriate achieves. The communication process facilitates cross-cultural adaptation, and, through this process, expatriates learn the dominant communication patterns of the host society. Therefore, we can link those personality factors shown by research to ease adaptation with those necessary for effective intercultural communication.

Kim has consolidated the research findings of these characteristics into two categories: (1) **openness**—traits such as open-mindedness, tolerance for ambiguity, and extrovertedness; and (2) **resilience**—traits such as having an internal locus of control, persistence, a tolerance of ambiguity, and resourcefulness.[67] These personality factors, along with the expatriate's cultural and racial identity and the level of preparedness for change, comprise that person's potential for adaptation. The level of preparedness can be improved by the manager before his or her assignment by gathering information about the host country's verbal and nonverbal communication patterns and norms of behavior. Kim explains that the major variables that affect the level of communication competence achieved between the host and the expatriate are the adaptive predisposition of the expatriate and the conditions of receptivity and conformity to pressure in the host environment. These factors affect the process of personal and social communication, and, ultimately, the adaptation outcome. Explains Kim, "Three aspects of strangers' adaptive change—increased functional fitness, psychological health, and intercultural identity—have been identified as direct consequences of prolonged communication-adaptation experiences in the host society."[68] Chapter 10 explores areas where the firm has responsibility to improve the employee/managerial ability to adapt.

In identifying personal and behavioral specifics that facilitate ICE, however, we cannot lose sight of the whole picture. We must remember the basic principle of contingency management, which is that managers operate in a system of many interacting variables in a dynamic context. Studies show that situational factors—such as the physical environment, time constraints, degree of structure, feelings of boredom or overwork, and anonymity—are strong influences on intercultural communication competence.[69]

It is this interdependence of many variables that makes it difficult for intercultural researchers to isolate and identify factors for success. Although managers try to understand and control up front as many factors as possible that will lead to management effectiveness, often they only find out what works from the results of their decisions.

CONCLUSION

Effective intercultural communication is a vital skill for international managers and domestic managers of multicultural workforces. Because miscommunication is much more likely to occur among people from different countries or racial backgrounds than among those from similar backgrounds, it is important to be alert to how culture is reflected in communication—in particular through the development of cultural sensitivity and an awareness of potential sources of cultural noise in the communication process. A successful international manager is thus attuned to these variables and is flexible enough to adjust his or her communication style to best address the intended receivers—that is, to do it "their way."

Cultural variables and the manner in which culture is communicated underlie the processes of negotiation and decision making. How do people around the world negotiate: What are their expectations and their approach to negotiations? What is the importance of understanding negotiation and decision-making processes in other countries? Chapter 5 addresses these questions and makes suggestions for the international manager to handle these important tasks.

Summary of Key Points

1. Communication is an inherent part of a manager's role, taking up the majority of the manager's time on the job. Effective intercultural communication largely determines the success of international transactions or the output of a culturally diverse workforce.

2. Culture is the foundation of communication, and communication transmits culture. Cultural variables that can affect the communication process by influencing a person's perceptions include attitudes, social organizations, thought patterns, roles, language, nonverbal language, and time.

3. Language conveys cultural understandings and social norms from one generation to the next. Body language, or nonverbal communication, is behavior that communicates without words. It accounts for 65 to 93 percent of interpreted communication.

4. Types of nonverbal communication around the world are kinesic behavior, proxemics, paralanguage, and object language.

5. Effective cross-cultural communication must take account of whether the receiver is from a country with a monochronic or a polychronic time system.

6. Variables related to channels of communication include high- and low-context cultures, fast or slow messages and information flows, and various types of media.

7. In high-context cultures, feelings and messages are implicit and must be accessed through an understanding of the person and the system. In low-context cultures, feelings and thoughts are expressed, and information is more readily available.

8. The effective management of intercultural communication necessitates the development of cultural sensitivity, careful encoding, selective transmission, careful decoding, and follow-up actions.

9. Certain personal abilities and behaviors facilitate adaptation to the host country through skilled intercultural communication.

10. Communication via the Internet must still be localized to adjust to differences in language, culture, local laws, and business models.

Discussion Questions

1. How does culture affect the process of attribution in communication? Can you relate this to some experiences you have had with your classmates?

2. What is stereotyping? Give some examples. How might people stereotype you? How does a sociotype differ from a stereotype?

3. What is the relationship between language and culture? How is it that people from different countries who speak the same language may still miscommunicate?

4. Give some examples of cultural differences in the interpretation of body language. What is the role of such nonverbal communication in business relationships?

5. Explain the differences between monochronic and polychronic time systems. Use some examples to illustrate their differences and the role of time in intercultural communication.

6. Explain the differences between high- and low-context cultures, giving some examples. What are the differential effects on the communication process?

7. Discuss the role of information systems in a company, how and why they vary from country to country, and the effects of these variations.

Application Exercises

1. Form groups in your class—multicultural groups, if possible. Have each person make notes about his or her perceptions of (1) Mexican-Americans, (2) Native Americans, (3) African-Americans, and (4) Americans of European descent. Discuss your notes and draw conclusions about common stereotypes. Discuss any differences and why stereotyping occurs.

2. Invite some foreign students to your class. Ask them to bring photographs, slides, and so forth of people and events in their native countries. Have them explain the meanings of various nonverbal cues, such as gestures, dress, voice inflections, architecture, and events. Discuss with them any differences between their explanations and the attributions you assigned to those cues.

3. Interview a faculty member or a businessperson who has worked abroad. Ask him or her to identify factors that facilitated or inhibited adaptation to the host environment. Ask whether more preparation could have eased the transition and what, if anything, that person would do differently before another trip.

Experiential Exercise: Script for Juan Perillo and Jean Moore

Scene I: February 15, San Juan, Puerto Rico

JUAN: Welcome back to Puerto Rico, Jean. It is good to have you here in San Juan again. I hope that your trip from Dayton was a smooth one.

JEAN: Thank you, Juan. It's nice to be back here where the sun shines. Fred sends his regards and also asked me to tell you how important it is that we work out a firm production schedule for the next three months. But first, how is your family? All doing well, I hope.

JUAN: My wife is doing very well, but my daughter, Marianna, broke her arm and has to have surgery to repair the bone. We are very worried about that because the surgeon says she may have to have several operations. It is very difficult to think about my poor little daughter in the operating room. She was out playing with some other children when it happened. You know how roughly children sometimes play with each other. It's really amazing that they don't have more injuries. Why, just last week, my son . . .

JEAN: Of course I'm very sorry to hear about little Marianna, but I'm sure everything will go well with the surgery. Now, shall we start work on the production schedule?

JUAN: Oh, yes, of course, we must get started on the production schedule.

JEAN: Fred and I thought that June 1 would be a good cutoff date for the first phase of the schedule. And we also thought that 100 A-type computers would be a reasonable goal for that phase. We know that you have some new assemblers whom you are training, and that you've had some problems getting parts from your suppliers in the past few months. But we're sure you have all those problems worked out by now and that you are back to full production capability. So, what do you think? Is 100 A-type computers produced by June 1 a reasonable goal for your people?

JUAN: (hesitates a few seconds before replying): You want us to produce 100 of the newly designed A-type computers by June 1? Will we also be producing our usual number of Z-type computers, too?

JEAN: Oh, yes. Your regular production schedule would remain the same as it's always been. The only difference is that you would be producing the new A-type computers, too. I mean, after all, you have a lot of new employees, and you have all the new manufacturing and assembling equipment that we have in Dayton. So, you're as ready to make the new product as we are.

JUAN: Yes, that's true. We have the new equipment, and we've just hired a lot of new assemblers who will be working on the A-type computer. I guess there's no reason we can't meet the production schedule you and Fred have come up with.

JEAN: Great, great. I'll tell Fred you agree with our decision and will meet the goal of 100 A-type computers by June 1. He'll be delighted to know that you can deliver what he was hoping for. And, of course, Juan, that means that you'll be doing just as well as the Dayton plant.

Scene II: May 1, San Juan, Puerto Rico

JEAN: Hello, Juan. How are things here in Puerto Rico? I'm glad to have the chance to come back and see how things are going.

JUAN: Welcome, Jean. It's good to have you here. How is your family?

JEAN: Oh, they're fine, just fine. You know, Juan, Fred is really excited about that big order we just got from the Defense Department for 50 A-type computers. They want them by June 10, so we will ship them directly to Washington from San Juan as the computers come off

your assembly line. Looks like it's a good thing we set your production goal at 100 A-type computers by June 1, isn't it?

JUAN: Um, yes, that was certainly a good idea.

JEAN: So, tell me, have you had any problems with the new model? How are your new assemblers working out? Do you have any suggestions for changes in the manufacturing specs? How is the new quality control program working with this model? We're always looking for ways to improve, you know, and we appreciate any ideas you can give us.

JUAN: Well, Jean, there is one thing . . .

JEAN: Yes? What is that?

JUAN: Well, Jean, we have had a few problems with the new assemblers. Three of them have had serious illnesses in their families and have had to take off several days at a time to nurse a sick child or elderly parent. And another one was involved in a car accident and was in the hospital for several days. And you remember my daughter's surgery? Well, her arm didn't mend properly, and we had to take her to Houston for additional consultations and therapy. But, of course, you and Fred knew about that.

JEAN: Yes, we were aware that you had had some personnel problems and that you and your wife had had to go to Houston with Marianna. But what does that have to do with the 50 A-type computers for the Defense Department?

JUAN: Well, Jean, because of all these problems, we have had a few delays in the production schedule. Nothing serious, but we are a little bit behind our schedule.

JEAN: How far behind is "a little bit"? What are you trying to tell me, Juan? Will you have 50 more A-type computers by June 1 to ship to Washington to fill the Defense Department order?

JUAN: Well, I certainly hope we will have that number ready to ship. You know how difficult it can be to predict a precise number for manufacturing, Jean. You probably have many of these same problems in the Dayton plant, don't you?

Source: L. Catlin and T. White, *International Business: Cultural Sourcebook and Case Studies* (Cincinnati, Ohio: South-Western, 1994), used with permission.

Exercise Questions

1. Drawing from this chapter, explain in detail what went wrong for Jean in Puerto Rico. Could this have been avoided? What should she have done differently?

2. Replay the role of Jean and Juan during their conversation, establishing a more constructive communication and management style than Jean did previously.

Internet Resources

Visit the Deresky Companion Website at www.pearsonhighered.com/deresky for this chapter's Internet resources.

CASE STUDY

Elizabeth Visits GPC's French Subsidiary

Elizabeth Moreno is looking out the window from her business-class seat somewhere over the Indian Ocean on Thai Air en route to Paris's Orly International Airport from the Philippines, where she has just spent a week of meetings and problem solving in a pharmaceutical subsidiary of the Global Pharmaceutical Company (GPC).

GPC has the lion's share of the worldwide market in ethical pharmaceutical products. Ethical drugs are those that can be purchased only through a physician's prescription. In the United States, GPC has research and manufacturing sites in New York, New Jersey, Pennsylvania, and Michigan. The company also has subsidiaries in Canada, Puerto Rico, Australia, the Philippines, Brazil, England, and France. GPC has its administrative headquarters in Pennsylvania.

Because of the geographically dispersed locations of its subsidiaries, GPC's top scientists and key managers log thousands of jet miles a year visiting various offices and plants. Its top specialists and executives regularly engage in multisite real-time video and telephone conferences, and they also use electronic mail, faxes, modems, and traditional mail to keep in touch with key personnel.

Despite these technological advances, face-to-face meetings and on-site consultations are used widely. In the case of the French subsidiary, nothing can take the place of face-to-face consultations. The French manager is suspicious of figures in the balance sheet, of the telephone, of his subordinates, of what he reads in the newspaper, and of what Americans tell him in confidence. In contrast, the American trusts all these. This is the reason GPC regularly sends its scientists and executives to France.

Elizabeth Moreno is one of the key specialists within GPC. Her expertise in chemical processing is widely known not only within her company but also in the pharmaceutical industry worldwide. She has been working at GPC for more than twelve years since finishing her advanced degree in chemistry from a university in the Midwest. While working for GPC, she has been given more and more responsibilities leading to her current position as vice president of chemical development and processing.

From a hectic visit in the Philippines, her next assignment is to visit the French subsidiary plant for one week to study a problem with shelf-life testing of one of its newest anti-allergy capsules. It seems that the product's active ingredient is degrading sooner than the expiration date. During her stay, she will conduct training for chemists in state-of-the-art techniques for testing and for training local managers in product statistical quality control. These techniques are now currently used in other GPC locations.

To prepare for her foreign assignments, Elizabeth attended a standard three-hour course given by her company's human resource management department on dealing with cross-cultural issues. Moreover, she recalls reading from a book on French management about the impersonal nature of French business relations. This was so much in contrast with what she just has experienced during her visit to the Philippine subsidiary. The French tend to regard authority as residing in the role and not in the person. It is by the power of the position that a French manager gets things done. With this knowledge, she knows that her expertise and her position as vice president will see her through the technical aspects of the meetings that are lined up for the few days she will be in Paris.

French managers view their work as an intellectual challenge that requires application of individual brainpower. What matters to them is the opportunity to show one's ability to grasp complex issues, analyze problems, manipulate ideas, and evaluate solutions.

There are a few challenges for Elizabeth on this assignment. She is not fluent in French. Her only exposure to France and the language was a two-week vacation with her husband in Paris a couple of years ago. However, in her highly technical field, the universal language is English. Thus, she believes she will not have much difficulty communicating with the French management to get her assignment successfully completed.

Americans place high value on training and education. In the United States, the field of management has principles that are generally applicable and can be taught and learned. In contrast, the French place more emphasis on the person who can adapt to any situation by virtue of his intellectual quality. Expertise and intellectual ability are inherent in the individual and cannot be acquired simply through training or education.

It appears that Elizabeth will be encountering very different ways of doing business in France. While she thought about the challenges ahead, her plane landed at Orly International Airport. She whisked through customs and immigration without any delays. No limousine was waiting for her curbside at the arrival. Instead she took the train to downtown Paris and checked into an apartment hotel that was reserved for her in advance of her arrival.

After a week in Paris, she is expected back in her home office to prepare reports to GPC management about her foreign assignments.

Case Questions

1. Drawing from your understanding of verbal and nonverbal communication patterns from this chapter, explain what Elizabeth Moreno can do to establish her position in front of French managers. How can she get them to help her accomplish her assignment in five days?
2. What should Elizabeth know about high-context versus low-context cultures in Europe? How can this knowledge help her be successful there?
3. What should Elizabeth include in her report, and what should be the manner in which it is communicated, so that future executives and scientists avoid communications pitfalls?
4. How can technical language differ from everyday language in corporate communications? Explain.

Source: This case was prepared by Edwin J. Portugal, MBA, Ph.D., who teaches multinational management at State University of New York–Potsdam. It is intended to be used as a basis for discussion on the complexity of multicultural management and not to illustrate effective versus ineffective management styles. Copyright © 2004 by Edwin J. Portugal.

Cross-cultural Negotiation and Decision Making

OBJECTIVES:

1. To learn how to prepare for cross-cultural business negotiations.

2. To recognize the need to build trusting relationships as a prerequisite for successful negotiations and long-term commitments.

3. To be aware of the role of culturally-based behavioral differences, values and agendas of the negotiating parties.

4. To learn the complexities of negotiating with the Chinese.

5. To appreciate the variables in the decision-making process and understand the influence of culture on decision making.

6. To become familiar with the Japanese decision-making process and how it is influenced by their cultural norms.

Opening Profile: BP's Troubled Joint Venture in Russia[1]

Country-specific restrictions and problems in cross-cultural negotiations and decision making styles are major contributing factors in the demise of international JVs. In global business, disputes between states and MNCs are common and often take the form of restrictions and interference on the part of host governments, resulting in regulatory hurdles and resource nationalism. One such case took place between 2007 and 2009 when British Petroleum (BP) was asked to renegotiate and surrender its control and ownership of oil and gas fields in Russia. BP formed a $6.7 billion joint venture (JV) called TNK-BP in August 2003 with pomp and circumstance. In the Western world, the JV received extensive media coverage because of its future viability and long-term foreign direct investment (FDI) prospects in Russia. Interestingly, the JV was majority-controlled by the British company.

At the time of signing, the JV was hailed as a major project since it brought tangible FDI to Russia. In the post-Soviet Union era, Russia was facing financial difficulties and desperately needed the Western FDI to seek stable economic conditions. BP's FDI was seen as a viable solution in Russia. TNK-BP's Russian partners included Alfa Group, Access and Renova (AAR). Robert Dudley, TNK-BP President commented in 2003: "I believe the structure we have developed for TNK-BP through an exhaustive and co-operative integration process has created a very strong foundation for the future success of TNK-BP" (*TNK-BP*, 2009, p. 1).

Many politicians, including then-Russian President Vladimir Putin and former British Prime Minister Tony Blair, hailed the JV as a major milestone in the relations between Russia and the UK. In 1997, BP had entered into Russia when it acquired a 10 percent stake in a Russian oil company Sidanco for $500 million. In 2006–07, global oil prices started to rise, bringing significant revenues to the Russian government and its economic prowess. During the same period, BP started to witness state interference in the TNK-BP project that came in the forms of ownership disputes and raids by the FSB (Russian Secret Service) on the offices of BP. Because of these frequent altercations with Russian authorities, TNK-BP ended up losing its control in the Kovykta gas field to Gazprom, a state-controlled gas company.

In early 2008, state interventions and investigations took the forms of visa hassles encountered by 148 foreign staff of BP, tax evasions, and environmental-related investigations of TNK-BP's oil fields. Other allegations surfaced regarding labor and employment-related inquiries that pressured BP to hire more Russian staff. TNK-BP was asked to relieve Dudley of his daily duties but BP refused to comply. In 2008, the situation became so acute that the British Foreign and Commonwealth Office got involved in negotiations to help seek an acceptable solution. In June 2008, Peter Mendelson, the European Union's Trade Commissioner accused TNK-BP's Russian shareholders of their "menacing behavior" (Timesonline, 2008, p. 2). In July 2008, BP filed a $365 million law suit against its Russian shareholders in London. Dudley was forced to leave Russia in July 2008 and started working from an undisclosed location. Later Tony Hayward, CEO of BP arranged a meeting with the AAR shareholder Mikhail Fridman in Prague. In September 2008, BP ended up signing a memorandum of understanding with the JV's Russian partners that led to Dudley's resignation from the JV.

As of April 2009, TNK-BP continued to struggle with its board's appointments and selection of a CEO. The governance structure of the JV has been stabilized but relationship-building and cooperation between BP and its Russian partners is far from healthy. Since the TNK-BP JV became so much embroiled in Russian politics, resource nationalism, and partners' cross-cultural misunderstandings, it is useful to note the following lessons for similar future ventures:

1. Restrictions and interference on the part of host governments are common in those countries where resource nationalism is prevalent and the rule of law is weak (Buchanan and Anwar, 2009).
2. Multinational corporations often become victims of JV-related disputes and operational hassles.
3. Shareholder disputes are common in international JVs and often culminate from cross-cultural misunderstandings, decision making styles, weak relationships, and governance issues which could have been better resolved in the negotiation phases.
4. By not speaking the Russian language, Dudley was separated from the mainstream Russian corporate culture.
5. There is a risk in doing business in the former socialist countries. This was evidenced by the statement "Boardroom brawl roils BP's Russia venture." which appeared in the *Wall Street Journal* (June 12, 2008, p. A1) The *Financial Times* (June 5, 2008, p. 9) equally corroborated and observed: "Russian roulette: How BP is falling out with its parents at TNK." Looking at the TNK-BP JV, we witness a multitude of cultural and political hurdles that MNCs face when negotiating and doing business with other corporate cultures and regulatory authorities.

** Written exclusively for this book by Syed Tariq Anwar, West Texas A&M University. Copyright © 2009 by Syed Tariq Anwar. Used with permission.

As illustrated in the opening profile, global managers negotiate with parties in other countries to make specific plans for strategies (exporting, joint ventures, acquisitions, etc.) and for continuing operations. While the complexities of cross-cultural negotiations among firms around the world present challenge enough, managers such as those for BP may also be faced with negotiating with government-owned companies. Google's negotiations with the Chinese government, as another example, ended in a compromise that to enter the Chinese market the company had to obey China's censorship laws and agree to purge its search results of any websites disapproved of by the Chinese government.[2]

Managers must prepare for strategic negotiations. Next the operational details must be negotiated—the staffing of key positions, the sourcing of raw materials or component parts, and the repatriating of profits, to name a few. As globalism burgeons, the ability to conduct successful cross-cultural negotiations cannot be overemphasized. Failure to negotiate productively will result in lost potential alliances and lost business at worst, and confusion and delays at best.

During the process of negotiation—whether before, during, or after negotiating sessions—all kinds of decisions are made, both explicitly and implicitly. A consideration of cross-cultural negotiations must therefore include the various decision-making processes that occur around the world. Negotiations cannot be conducted without decisions being made.

This chapter examines the processes of negotiation and decision making as they apply to international and domestic cross-cultural contexts. The objective is a better understanding of successful management.

NEGOTIATION

Implementing strategy depends on management's ability to negotiate productively—a skill widely considered one of the most important in international business. In the global arena, cultural differences produce great difficulties in the negotiation process. Ignorance of native bargaining rituals, more than any other single factor, accounts for unimpressive sales efforts.[3] Important differences in the negotiation process from country to country include (1) the amount and type of preparation for a negotiation, (2) the relative emphasis on tasks versus interpersonal relationships, (3) the reliance on general principles rather than specific issues, and (4) the number of people present and the extent of their influence.[4] In every instance, managers must familiarize themselves with the cultural background and underlying motivations of the negotiators—and the tactics and procedures they use—to control the process, make progress, and therefore maximize company goals.

The term **negotiation** describes the process of discussion by which two or more parties aim to reach a mutually acceptable agreement. For long-term positive relations, the goal should be to set up a win-win situation—that is, to bring about a settlement beneficial to all parties concerned. This process, difficult enough when it takes place among people of similar backgrounds, is even more complex in international negotiations because of differences in cultural values, lifestyles, expectations, verbal and nonverbal language, approaches to formal procedures, and problem-solving techniques. The complexity is heightened when negotiating across borders because of the greater number of stakeholders involved. These stakeholders are illustrated in Exhibit 5-1. In preparing for negotiations, it is critical to avoid projective cognitive similarity—that is, the

EXHIBIT 5-1 **Stakeholders in Cross-cultural Negotiations**

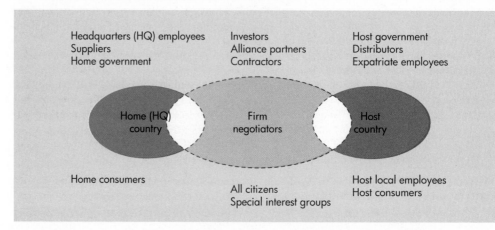

assumption that others perceive, judge, think, and reason in the same way when, in fact, they do not because of differential cultural and practical influences. Instead, astute negotiators empathetically enter into the private world or cultural space of their counterparts, while willingly sharing their own view of the situation.[5]

THE NEGOTIATION PROCESS

The negotiation process comprises five stages, the ordering of which may vary according to the cultural norms; for most people, relationship building is part of a continuous process in any event: (1) preparation, (2) relationship building, (3) the exchange of task-related information, (4) persuasion, and (5) concessions and agreement.[6] Of course, in reality these are seldom distinct stages but rather tend to overlap; negotiators may also temporarily revert to an earlier stage. With that in mind, it is useful to break down the negotiation process into stages to discuss the issues relevant to each stage and what international managers might expect, so that they might more successfully manage this process. These stages are shown in Exhibit 5-2 and discussed in the following sections.

Stage One: Preparation

The importance of careful preparation for cross-cultural negotiations cannot be overstated. To the extent that time permits, a distinct advantage can be gained if negotiators familiarize themselves with the entire context and background of their counterparts (no matter where the meetings will take place) in addition to the specific subjects to be negotiated. Because most negotiation problems are caused by differences in culture, language, and environment, hours or days of tactical preparation for negotiation can be wasted if these factors are not carefully considered.[7]

To understand cultural differences in negotiating styles, managers first must understand their own styles and then determine how they differ from the norm in other countries. They can do this by comparing profiles of those perceived to be successful negotiators in different countries. Such profiles reflect the value system, attitudes, and expected behaviors inherent in a given society. Other sections of this chapter describe and compare negotiating styles around the world.

VARIABLES IN THE NEGOTIATING PROCESS   Adept negotiators conduct research to develop a profile of their counterparts so that they know, in most situations, what to expect, how to prepare, and how to react. Exhibit 5-3 shows 12 variables to consider when preparing to negotiate. These variables can, to a great degree, help managers understand the deep-rooted cultural and national motivations and traditional processes underlying negotiations with people from other countries.

EXHIBIT 5-2   The Negotiation Process

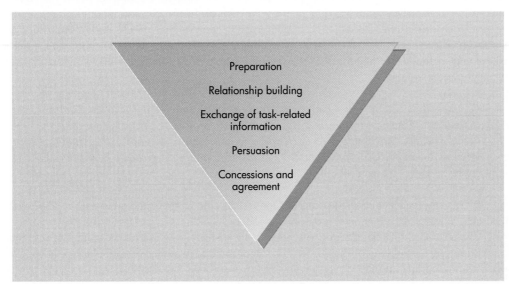

EXHIBIT 5-3   **Variables in the Negotiation Process**[8]

1. *Basic conception of negotiation process:* Is it a competitive process or a problem-solving approach?
2. *Negotiator selection criteria:* Is selection based on experience, status, expertise, personal attributes, or some other characteristic?
3. *Significance of type of issues:* Is it specific, such as price, or is the focus on relationships or the format of talks?
4. *Concern with protocol:* What is the importance of procedures, social behaviors, and so forth in the negotiation process?
5. *Complexity of communicative context:* What degree of reliance is placed on nonverbal cues to interpret information?
6. *Nature of persuasive arguments:* How do the parties attempt to influence each other? Do they rely on rational arguments, on accepted tradition, or on emotion?
7. *Role of individuals' aspirations:* Are motivations based on individual, company, or community goals?
8. *Bases of trust:* Is trust based on past experience, intuition, or rules?
9. *Risk-taking propensity:* How much do the parties try to avoid uncertainty in trading information or making a contract?
10. *Value of time:* What is each party's attitude toward time? How fast should negotiations proceed, and what degree of flexibility is there?
11. *Decision-making system:* How does each team reach decisions—by individual determination, by majority opinion, or by group consensus?
12. *Form of satisfactory agreement:* Is agreement based on trust (perhaps just a handshake), the credibility of the parties, commitment, or a legally binding contract?

After developing thoughtful profiles of the other party or parties, managers can plan for the actual negotiation meetings, at the same time remaining open to realizing that specific people may not fit the assumed cultural prototype. Prior to the meetings, they should find out as much as possible about (1) the kinds of demands that might be made, (2) the composition of the "opposing" team, and (3) the relative authority that the members possess. After this, the managers can gear their negotiation strategy specifically to the other side's firm, allocate roles to different team members, decide on concessions, and prepare an alternative action plan in case a negotiated solution cannot be found.[9]

Following the preparation and planning stage, which is usually done at the home office, the core of the actual negotiation takes place on-site in the foreign location (or at the manager's home office if the other team has decided to travel there). In some cases, a compromise on the location for negotiations can signal a cooperative strategy, which Weiss calls "Improvise an Approach: Effect Symphony"—a strategy available to negotiators familiar with each other's culture and willing to put negotiation on an equal footing. Weiss gives the following example of this negotiation strategy:

> *For their negotiations over construction of the tunnel under the English Channel, British and French representatives agreed to partition talks and alternate the site between Paris and London. At each site, the negotiators were to use established, local ways, including the language . . . thus punctuating approaches by time and space.*[10]

In this way, each side was put into the context and the script of the other culture about half the time.

The next stage of negotiation—often given short shrift by Westerners—is that of relationship building. In most parts of the world, this stage usually has already taken place or is concurrent with other preparations.

Stage Two: Relationship Building

Relationship building is the process of getting to know one's contacts in a host country and building mutual trust before embarking on business discussions and transactions. This process is regarded with much more significance in most parts of the world than it is in the United States. U.S. negotiators are, generally speaking, objective about the specific matter at hand and usually want to waste no time in getting down to business and making progress. This approach, well understood in the United States, can be disastrous if the foreign negotiators want to take enough time to build trust and respect as a basis for negotiating contracts. In such cases, American efficiency interferes with the patient development of a mutually trusting relationship—the very cornerstone of an Asian business agreement.[11]

In many countries, such as Mexico and China, personal commitments to individuals, rather than the legal system, form the basis for the enforcement of contracts. Effective negotiators allow plenty of time in their schedules for such relationship building with bargaining partners. This process usually takes the form of social events, tours, and ceremonies, along with much **nontask sounding**—general, polite conversation and informal communication before meetings—while all parties get to know one another. In such cultures, one patiently waits for the other party to start actual business negotiations, aware that relationship building is, in fact, the first phase of negotiations.[12] It is usually recommended that managers new to such scenarios use an intermediary—someone who already has the trust and respect of the foreign managers and who therefore acts as a "relationship bridge." Middle Easterners, in particular, prefer to negotiate through a trusted intermediary, and for them as well, initial meetings are only for the purpose of getting acquainted. Arabs do business with the person, not the company, and therefore mutual trust must be established.

In their best seller on negotiation, *Getting to Yes,* Fisher and Ury point out the dangers of not preparing well for negotiations:

> *In Persian, the word "compromise" does not have the English meaning of a midway solution which both sides can accept, but only the negative meaning of surrendering one's principles. Also, "mediator" means "meddler," someone who is barging in uninvited. In 1980, United Nations Secretary-General Kurt Waldheim flew to Iran to deal with the hostage situation. National Iranian radio and television broadcast in Persian a comment he was said to have made upon his arrival in Tehran: "I have come as a mediator to work out a compromise." Less than an hour later, his car was being stoned by angry Iranians.[13]*

As a bridge to the more formal stages of negotiations, such relationship building is followed by posturing—that is, general discussion that sets the tone for the meetings. This phase should result in a spirit of cooperation. To help ensure this result, negotiators must use words like "respect" and "mutual benefit" rather than language that would suggest arrogance, superiority, or urgency.

Stage Three: Exchanging Task-Related Information

In the next stage—exchanging task-related information—each side typically makes a presentation and states its position; a question-and-answer session usually ensues, and alternatives are discussed. From an American perspective, this represents a straightforward, objective, efficient, and understandable stage. However, negotiators from other countries continue to take a more indirect approach at this stage. Mexican negotiators are usually suspicious and indirect, presenting little substantive material and more lengthy, evasive conversation. French negotiators enjoy debate and conflict and will often interrupt presentations to argue about an issue even if it has little relevance to the topic being presented. The Chinese also ask many questions of their counterparts, and delve specifically and repeatedly into the details at hand; conversely, Chinese presentations contain only vague and ambiguous material. For instance, after about 20 Boeing officials spent six weeks presenting masses of literature and technical demonstrations to the Chinese, the Chinese said, "Thank you for your introduction."[14]

The Russians also enter negotiations well prepared and well versed in the specific details of the matter being presented. To answer their (or any other side's) questions, it is generally a good idea to bring along someone with expertise to answer any grueling technical inquiries. Russians also put a lot of emphasis on protocol and expect to deal only with top executives.

Adler suggests that negotiators should focus not only on presenting their situation and needs but also on showing an understanding of their opponents' viewpoint. Focusing on the entire situation confronting each party encourages the negotiators to assess a wider range of alternatives for resolution, rather than limiting themselves to their preconceived, static positions. She suggests that to be most effective, negotiators should prepare for meetings by practicing role reversal.[15]

Stage Four: Persuasion

In the next phase of negotiations—persuasion—the hard bargaining starts. Typically, both parties try to persuade the other to accept more of their position and to give up some of their own. Often, some persuasion has already taken place beforehand in social settings and through mutual contacts. In the Far East, details are likely to be worked out ahead of time through the backdoor approach (*houmani*). For the most part, however, the majority of the persuasion takes place over one or more negotiating sessions. International managers usually find that this process of bargaining and making concessions is fraught with difficulties because of the different uses and interpretations of verbal and nonverbal behaviors. Although variations in such behaviors influence every stage of the negotiation process, they can play a particularly powerful role in persuasion, especially if they are not anticipated.

Studies of negotiating behavior have revealed the use of certain tactics, which skilled negotiators recognize and use, such as promises, threats, and so on. Other, less savory tactics are sometimes used in international negotiations. Often called "dirty tricks," these tactics, according to Fisher and Ury, include efforts to mislead "opponents" deliberately.[16] Some negotiators may give wrong or distorted factual information or use the excuse of ambiguous authority—giving conflicting impressions about who in their party has the power to make a commitment. In the midst of hard bargaining, the prudent international manager will follow up on possibly misleading information before taking action based on trust.

Other rough tactics are designed to put opposing negotiators in a stressful situation physically or psychologically so that their giving in is more likely. These include uncomfortable room temperatures, too-bright lighting, rudeness, interruptions, and other irritations. International negotiators must keep in mind, however, that what might seem like dirty tricks to Americans is simply the way other cultures conduct negotiations. In some South American countries, for example, it is common to start negotiations with misleading or false information.

The most subtle behaviors in the negotiation process, and often the most difficult to deal with, are usually the nonverbal messages—the use of voice intonation, facial and body expressions, eye contact, dress, and the timing of the discussions. Nonverbal behaviors, discussed in previous chapters, are ingrained aspects of culture used by people in their daily lives; they are not specifically changed for the purposes of negotiation. Among those behaviors impacting negotiations is the direct communication style, such as with Germans, compared with the indirect style, such as with Japanese. Clearly, also, the individualism-collectivism cultural dimension is one which greatly guides negotiation because of the relative motivation of personal self-interest in individualistic societies, such as the United States; this compares with the group-interest in Asian cultures, so that negotiators will likely give more importance to their social obligations and the needs of the group.[17]

Although persuasion has been discussed as if it were always a distinct stage, it is really the primary purpose underlying all stages of the negotiation process. In particular, persuasion is an integral part of the process of making concessions and arriving at an agreement.

Stage Five: Concessions and Agreement

In the last stage of negotiation—concessions and agreement—tactics vary greatly across cultures. Well-prepared negotiators are aware of various concession strategies and have decided ahead of time what their own concession strategy will be. Familiar with the typical initial positions that various parties are likely to take, they know that Russians and Chinese generally open their bargaining with extreme positions, asking for more than they hope to gain, whereas Swedes usually start with what they are prepared to accept.

Research in the United States indicates that better end results are attained by starting with extreme positions. With this approach, the process of reaching an agreement involves careful timing of the disclosure information and of concessions. Most people who have studied negotiations believe that negotiators should disclose only the information that is necessary at a given point and that they should try to obtain information piece by piece to gradually get the whole picture without giving away their goals or concession strategy. These guidelines will not always work in intercultural negotiations because the American process of addressing issues one at a time, in a linear fashion, is not common in other countries or cultures. Negotiators in the Far East, for example, approach issues in a holistic manner, deciding on the whole deal at the end, rather than making incremental concessions.

Again, at the final stage of agreement and contract, local practices determine how these agreements will be honored. Whereas Americans take contracts very seriously, Russians often renege on their contracts. The Japanese, on the other hand, consider a formal contract to be somewhat of an insult and a waste of time and money in legal costs, since they prefer to operate on the basis of understanding and social trust.[18] More attention to this and all the negotiation phases might have led to better results in the French-Chinese joint venture discussed in the management focus.

MANAGEMENT FOCUS

Cultural Misunderstanding—The Danone-Wahaha Joint Venture in China[19]

Many cross-border joint ventures encounter problems because the partners' differences in management styles, corporate control, and cross-cultural issues do not get recognized and resolved during the negotiation phase, and so continue to fester during the operations phase. One such JV is the Sino-French collaboration that was formed by Groupe Danone (hereafter Danone), and Hangzhou Wahaha Group Co. (hereafter WHH). Danone is one of the largest food conglomerates from France. Wahaha is China's largest beverage company that was started in 1987 and was controlled by the government of Hangzhou's Shangcheng District. From its inception, Zong Qinghou ran the operations of WHH. When the company converted itself into a private entity, Qinghou took the role of a minority shareholder.

The Danone-WHH joint venture was established in March 1996 and took the trademark name of Wahaha because of its strong brand visibility in the Chinese market. In emerging markets, Danone grew by creating a multitude of profitable JVs in India, Pakistan, Vietnam, Columbia, and other countries. On the other hand, WHH achieved its market expansion and corporate growth in China by turning itself into a national brand and highly successful food and beverage company. The Danone-Wahaha JV dealt with the areas of food and beverages and grew at a respectable rate. For Danone, this was a good strategy to enter into China. For WHH, the JV helped the company to make a linkage with a well known global brand.

Negotiations resulted in the following salient features of the JV:

1. Ownership of the JV included foreign partners (51 percent), WHH (39 percent), and employees (10 percent).
2. The JV encompassed five entities: Hangzhou Wahaha Baili Foods, Hangzhou Wahaha Health Foods, Hangzhou Wahaha Foods Co., Hangzhou Wahaha Beverages Co., and Hangzhou Wahaha Quick Frozen Foods. Danone and Peregine collectively invested $70 million in the five entities of the JV.
3. As agreed by Danone, the day-to-day operations of the JV resided with Qinghou.

As the JV's business operations expanded in China, activities of Danone and WHH also became intertwined and complex leading to differences in opinion, corporate control, and management styles. Between 1996 and 2006, the following changes took place in the structure and operations of the Danone-WHH JV:

1. Because of consumer demand and market growth, the JV's operations in China witnessed the emergence of 37 business entities. Danone attempted to buy out Qinghou but the negotiations were unsuccessful.
2. Public rows erupted between the two companies when they kept on blaming each other for breach of contract. Danone blamed Qinghou for going outside of the contract and profiting from 80 unauthorized businesses. This included misusing the Danone brand and its distribution system in China.

3. The dispute between Danone and Qinghou became even more personal when Danone filed a law suit against Qinghou's wife and daughter in a Los Angeles court regarding their business interests and unauthorized JV-related dealings outside of China.

4. Danone filed for arbitration proceedings in Stockholm in May 2007.

5. During the dispute, Danone also filed legal claims against ten business entities that were believed to be controlled by WHH in Samoa and the British Virgin Island.

6. The Danone-WHH case became so much embroiled that Chinese and French governments asked the companies to negotiate an "amicable" resolution.

From this highly publicized dispute between Danone and WHH, we learn the following lessons:

1. Cross-cultural misunderstandings and unfamiliarity with the JV partners were at the heart of this dispute. Qinghou's entrepreneurial style and WHH's consistent growth in China could have been one of the causes of this dispute since Danone management was alienated in the process.

2. Both partners used media and public relations campaigns in China and Western markets to justify their arguments, instead of having open negotiations.

3. In any JV, relationship-building and exchange of project-related information is critical in the post-negotiation phase that is based on concessions and agreement.

4. It seems that Danone and WHH lacked open communication in their day-to-day management of the JV. Also important was the area of trust that happened to be missing in the partners' dealings.

5. According to *China Economic Review*, Chinese companies often become an extension of their founders' personal goals regarding day-to-day business operations. Most Chinese businesses do not see a major difference between 51/49 ownership and enforcement of rights. Foreign partners must make sure that their designated managers and staff members are included in the day-to-day management of the JV. In international markets, JV-related contracts can be abused and could lead to cross-cultural misunderstands and operational disruptions.

6. Finally, in JVs, relationship-building takes time and a good amount of interaction is needed between the partners. In the case of Danone-WHH JV, partner conflict, face-saving problems, blame-game, and accusations could have been avoided had the two companies communicated openly during the negotiation phase and afterwards. Also it seems that Danone and WHH did not understand their low-context and high-context cultures and management styles that eventually led to this conflict.

** Written exclusively for this book by Syed Tariq Anwar, West Texas A&M University. Copyright © 2009 by Syed Tariq Anwar. Used with permission.

UNDERSTANDING NEGOTIATION STYLES

Global managers can benefit from studying differences in negotiating behaviors (and the underlying reasons for them), which can help them recognize what is happening in the negotiating process. Exhibit 5-4 shows some examples of differences among North American, Japanese, and Latin American styles. Brazilians, for example, generally have a spontaneous, passionate, and dynamic style. They are very talkative and particularly use the word "no" extensively—more than 40 times per half-hour compared with 4.7 times for Americans, and only 1.9 times for the Japanese. They also differ markedly from Americans and the Japanese by their use of extensive physical contact.[20]

The Japanese are typically skillful negotiators. They have spent a great deal more time and effort studying U.S. culture and business practices than Americans have spent studying Japanese practices. A typical example of this contrast was apparent when Charlene Barshefsky—a tough American international lawyer who had never visited Japan before—was sent there as a trade negotiator and had little knowledge of its counterparts. But Mr. Okamatsu, like most Japanese negotiators, was very familiar with America. He had lived with his family in New York for three years and had spent many years handling bilateral trade disputes between the two countries. The different styles of the two negotiators were apparent in the negotiations. Ms. Barshefsky wanted specific import goals. Mr. Okamatsu wanted to talk more about the causes of trade problems rather than set specific targets, which he called the "cooperative

EXHIBIT 5-4   Comparison of Negotiation Styles—Japanese, North American, and Latin American[22]

Japanese	North American	Latin American
Emotional sensitivity highly valued	Emotional sensitivity not highly valued	Emotional sensitivity Valued
Hiding of emotions	Dealing straightforwardly or Impersonally	Emotionally passionate
Subtle power plays; conciliation	Litigation not so much as conciliation	Great power plays; use of weakness
Loyalty to employer; employer takes care of employees	Lack of commitment to employer; breaking of ties by either if necessary	Loyalty to employer (who is often family)
Face-saving crucial; decisions often on basis of saving someone from embarrassment	Decisions made on a cost-benefit basis; face-saving does not always matter	Face-saving crucial in decision making to preserve honor, dignity
Decision makers openly influenced by special interests	Decision makers influenced by special interests but often not considered ethical	Execution of special interests of decision expected, condoned
Not argumentative; quiet when Right	Argumentative when right or wrong, but impersonal	Argumentative when right or wrong; passionate
What is down in writing must be accurate, valid	Great importance given to documentation as evidential proof	Impatient with documentation as obstacle to understanding general principles
Step-by-step approach to decision making	Methodically organized decision making	Impulsive, spontaneous decision making
Good of group is the ultimate aim	Profit motive or good of individual is the ultimate aim	What is good for group is good for the individual
Cultivate a good emotional social setting for decision making; get to know decision makers	Decision making impersonal; avoid involvements, conflict of interest	Personalism necessary for good decision making

approach." Ms. Barshefsky snapped that the approach was nonsense and "would analyze the past to death, with no link to future change."[21]

Such differences in philosophy and style between the two countries reflect ten years of anger and feelings of betrayal in trade negotiations. John Graham, a California professor who has studied international negotiating styles, says that the differences between United States and Japanese styles are well illustrated by their respective proverbs: the Americans believe that "The squeaking wheel gets the grease," and the Japanese say that "The pheasant would not be shot but for its cry."[23] The Japanese are calm, quiet, patient negotiators; they are accustomed to long, detailed negotiating sessions. Whereas Americans often plunge straight to the matter at hand, the Japanese instead prefer to develop long-term, personal relationships. The Japanese want to get to know those on the other side and will spend some time in nontask sounding.

In negotiations, the Japanese culture of politeness and hiding of emotions can be disconcerting to Americans when they are unable to make straightforward eye contact or when the Japanese maintain smiling faces in serious situations. It is important that Americans understand what is polite and what is offensive to the Japanese—and vice versa. Americans must avoid anything that resembles boasting because the Japanese value humility, and physical contact or touching of any sort must be avoided.[24] Consistent with the culture-based value of maintaining harmony, the Japanese are likely to be evasive or even leave the room rather than give a direct negative answer.[25] Fundamental to Japanese culture is a concern for the welfare of the group; anything that affects one member or part of society affects the others. Thus, the Japanese view decisions carefully in light of long-term consequences; they use objective, analytic thought patterns; and they take time for reflection.[26]

Further insight into negotiating styles around the world can be gained by comparing the North American, Arab, and Russian styles. Basic cultural values often shed light on the way information is presented, whether and how concessions will be made, and the general nature and duration of the relationship.For North Americans, negotiations are businesslike; their factual appeals are based on what they believe is objective information, presented with the assumption that it is understood by the other side on a logical basis. Arabs use affective appeals based on emotions and subjective feelings. Russians employ axiomatic appeals—that is, their appeals are based on the ideals generally accepted in their society. The Russians are tough negotiators; they stall for time until they unnerve Western negotiators by continuously delaying and haggling. Much of this approach is based on the Russians' different attitude toward time. Because Russians traditionally do not subscribe to the Western belief that "time is money," they are more patient, more determined, and more dogged negotiators. They try to keep smiles and other expressions of emotion to a minimum to present a calm exterior.[27]

In contrast to the Russians, Arabs are more interested in long-term relationships and are, therefore, more likely to make concessions. Compared with Westerners, Arabs have a casual approach to deadlines, and frequently the negotiators lack the authority to finalize a deal.[28]

Successful Negotiators Around the World

Following are selected profiles of what it takes to be a successful negotiator, as perceived by people in their home countries. These are profiles of American, Indian, Arab, Swedish, and Italian negotiators, according to Pierre Casse, and give some insight into what to expect from different negotiators and what they expect from others.[29]

AMERICAN NEGOTIATORS   According to Casse, a successful American negotiator acts as follows:

1. Knows when to compromise
2. Takes a firm stand at the beginning of the negotiation
3. Refuses to make concessions beforehand
4. Keeps his or her cards close to his or her chest
5. Accepts compromises only when the negotiation is deadlocked
6. Sets up the general principles and delegates the detail work to associates
7. Keeps a maximum of options open before negotiation
8. Operates in good faith
9. Respects the "opponents"
10. States his or her position as clearly as possible
11. Knows when he or she wishes a negotiation to move on
12. Is fully briefed about the negotiated issues
13. Has a good sense of timing and is consistent
14. Makes the other party reveal his or her position while keeping his or her own position hidden as long as possible
15. Lets the other negotiator come forward first and looks for the best deal

INDIAN NEGOTIATORS   Indians, says Casse, often follow Gandhi's approach to negotiation, which Gandhi called *satyagraha,* "firmness in a good cause." This approach combines strength with the love of truth. The successful Indian negotiator thus acts as follows:

1. Looks for and says the truth
2. Is not afraid of speaking up and has no fears
3. Exercises self-control ("The weapons of the *satyagraha* are within him.")
4. Seeks solutions that will please all the parties involved ("*Satyagraha* aims to exalt both sides.")
5. Respects the other party ("The opponent must be weaned from error by patience and sympathy. Weaned, not crushed; converted, not annihilated.")
6. Neither uses violence nor insults

7. Is ready to change his or her mind and differ with himself or herself at the risk of being seen as inconsistent and unpredictable
8. Puts things into perspective and switches easily from the small picture to the big one
9. Is humble and trusts the opponent
10. Is able to withdraw, use silence, and learn from within
11. Relies on himself or herself, his or her own resources and strengths
12. Appeals to the other party's spiritual identity ("To communicate, the West moves or talks. The East sits, contemplates, suffers.")
13. Is tenacious, patient, and persistent
14. Learns from the opponent and avoids the use of secrets
15. Goes beyond logical reasoning and trusts his or her instinct as well as faith

ARAB NEGOTIATORS   Many Arab negotiators, following Islamic tradition, use mediators to settle disputes. A successful Arab mediator acts in the following way:

1. Protects all the parties' honor, self-respect, and dignity
2. Avoids direct confrontations between opponents
3. Is respected and trusted by all
4. Does not put the parties involved in a situation where they have to show weakness or admit defeat
5. Has the necessary prestige to be listened to
6. Is creative enough to come up with honorable solutions for all parties
7. Is impartial and can understand the positions of the various parties without leaning toward one or the other
8. Is able to resist any kind of pressure that the opponents could try to exercise on him
9. Uses references to people who are highly respected by the opponents to persuade them to change their minds on some issues ("Do it for the sake of your father.")
10. Can keep secrets and in so doing gains the confidence of the negotiating parties
11. Controls his temper and emotions (or loses it when and where necessary)
12. Can use conferences as mediating devices
13. Knows that the opponents will have problems in carrying out the decisions made during the negotiation
14. Is able to cope with the Arab disregard for time
15. Understands the impact of Islam on the opponents who believe that they possess the truth, follow the Right Path, and are going to "win" because their cause is just

SWEDISH NEGOTIATORS   Swedish negotiators, according to Casse, are:

1. Very quiet and thoughtful
2. Punctual (concerned with time)
3. Extremely polite
4. Straightforward (they get straight down to business)
5. Eager to be productive and efficient
6. Heavy going
7. Down to earth and overcautious
8. Rather flexible
9. Able to and quite good at holding emotions and feelings
10. Slow at reacting to new (unexpected) proposals
11. Informal and familiar
12. Conceited
13. Perfectionist
14. Afraid of confrontations
15. Very private

ITALIAN NEGOTIATORS   Italians, says Casse, value a negotiator who acts as follows:

1. Has a sense of drama (acting is a main part of the culture)
2. Does not hide his or her emotions (which are partly sincere and partly feigned)

3. Reads facial expressions and gestures very well
4. Has a feeling for history
5. Does not trust anybody
6. Is concerned about the *bella figura*—the "good impression"—he or she can create among those who watch his or her behavior
7. Believes in the individual's initiatives, not so much in teamwork
8. Is good at being obliging and simpatico at all times
9. Is always on the *qui vive*—the "lookout"
10. Never embraces definite opinions
11. Is able to come up with new ways to immobilize and eventually destroy his or her opponents
12. Handles confrontations of power with subtlety and tact
13. Has a flair for intrigue
14. Knows how to use flattery
15. Can involve other negotiators in complex combinations

COMPARING PROFILES   Comparing such profiles is useful. Indian negotiators, for example, are humble, patient, respectful of the other parties, and very willing to compromise, compared with Americans, who are firmer about taking stands. An important difference between Arab negotiators and those from most other countries is that the negotiators are mediators, not the parties themselves; hence, direct confrontation is made impossible. Successful Swedish negotiators are conservative and careful, dealing with factual and detailed information. This profile contrasts with Italian negotiators, who are expressive and exuberant but less straightforward than their Swedish counterparts.

MANAGING NEGOTIATION

Skillful global managers must assess many factors when managing negotiations. They must understand the position of the other parties in regard to their goals—whether national or corporate—and whether these goals are represented by principles or specific details. They should have the ability to recognize the relative importance attached to completing the task versus developing interpersonal relationships. Managers also must know the composition of the teams involved, the power allotted to the members, and the extent of the teams' preparation. In addition, they must grasp the significance of personal trust in the relationship. As stated earlier, the culture of the parties involved affects their negotiating styles and behavior and thus the overall process of negotiation. However, whatever the culture, research by Tse, Francis, and Walls has found person-related conflicts to "invite negative, more relation-oriented (versus information-oriented) responses," leading them to conclude that "The software of negotiation—that is, the nature and the appearance of the relationship between the people pursuing common goals—needs to be carefully addressed in the negotiation process.[30]

This is particularly true when representatives of individual-focused cultures (such as the Americans) and group-focused cultures (such as the Chinese) are on opposite sides of the table. Many of these culture-based differences in negotiations came to light in Husted's study on Mexican negotiators' perceptions of the reasons for the failure of their negotiations with U.S. teams.[31] The Mexican managers' interpretations were affected by their high-context culture, with the characteristics of an indirect approach, patience in discussing ideas, and maintenance of dignity. Instead, the low-context Americans conveyed an impatient, cold, blunt communicative style. To maintain the outward dignity of their Mexican counterparts, Americans must approach negotiations with Mexicans with patience and tolerance and refrain from attacking ideas because these attacks may be taken personally. The relationships among the factors of cross-cultural negotiation discussed in this chapter are illustrated in Exhibit 5-5.

The successful management of intercultural negotiations requires that a manager go beyond a generalized understanding of the issues and variables involved. She or he must (1) gain specific knowledge of the parties in the upcoming meeting, (2) prepare accordingly to adjust to and control the situation, and (3) be innovative.[32]

Research has shown that a problem-solving approach is essential to successful cross-cultural negotiations, whether abroad or in the home office, although the approach works

EXHIBIT 5-5 Cross-cultural Negotiation Variables

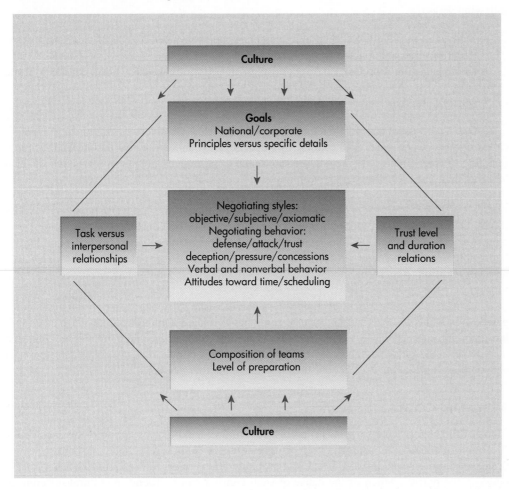

differently in various countries.[33] This problem-solving approach requires that a negotiator treat everyone with respect, avoid making anyone feel uncomfortable, and not criticize or blame the other parties in a personal way that may make someone feel shame—that is, lose face.

Research by the Huthwaite Research Group reveals how successful negotiators, compared to average negotiators, manage the planning process and their face-to-face behavior. The group found that during the planning process, successful negotiators consider a wider range of options and pay greater attention to areas of common ground. Skillful negotiators also tend to make twice as many comments regarding long-term issues and are more likely to set upper and lower limits regarding specific points. In their face-to-face behavior, skillful negotiators make fewer irritating comments—such as "We're making you a generous offer," make counterproposals less frequently, and use fewer reasons to back up arguments. In addition, skilled negotiators practice active listening—asking questions, clarifying their understanding of the issues, and summarizing the issues.[34]

Using the Internet to Support Negotiations

Modern technology can provide support for the negotiating process, though it can't take the place of the essential face-to-face ingredient in many instances. A growing component for electronic commerce is the development of applications to support the negotiation of contracts and resolution of disputes. As Web applications develop, they may provide support for various phases and dimensions, such as "Multiple- issue, multiple- party business transactions of a buy–sell nature; international dispute resolution (business disputes, political disputes); and internal company negotiations and communications, among others."[35]

Negotiation support systems (NSS) can provide support for the negotiation process in the following ways:

- Increasing the likelihood that an agreement is reached when a zone of agreement exists (solutions that both parties would accept)
- Decreasing the direct and indirect costs of negotiations, such as costs caused by time delays (strikes, violence), and attorneys' fees, among others
- Maximizing the chances for optimal outcomes[36]

One Web-based support system, developed at Carleton University in Ottawa, Canada—called INSPIRE—provides applications for preparing and conducting negotiations and for renegotiating options after a settlement. Users can specify preferences and assess offers; the site also has graphical displays of the negotiation process.[37]

E-NEGOTIATIONS The advantages of electronic communications are well known: speed, less travel, the ability to lay out much objective information to be considered by the other party over time. The disadvantages, however, might kill a deal before it gets off the ground by not being able to build trust and interpersonal relationships over time before getting down to business. In addition, non-verbal nuances are lost, although videoconferencing is a compromise for that purpose.

Rosette et al. noted that "opening offers may be especially aggressive in e-mail as compared to face-to-face negotiations because computer-mediated communications, such as e-mail, loosen inhibitions and cause negotiators to become more competitive and more risk seeking. The increase in competitive and risky behavior occurs because e-mail does not communicate social context cues in the same way as does the presence of another person."[38]

Managing Conflict Resolution

Much of the negotiation process is fraught with conflict—explicit or implicit—and such conflict can often lead to a standoff, or a lose–lose situation. This is regrettable, not only because of the situation at hand, but also because it probably will shut off future opportunities for deals between the parties. Much of the cause of such conflict can be found in cultural differences between the parties—in their expectations, in their behaviors, and particularly in their communication styles—as illustrated in the Comparative Management in Focus, Negotiating with the Chinese.

COMPARATIVE MANAGEMENT IN FOCUS
Negotiating with the Chinese

The Chinese way of making decisions begins with socialization and initiation of personal guanxi rather than business discussion. The focus is not market research, statistical analysis, facts, PowerPoint presentations, or to-the-point business discussion. My focus must be on fostering guanxi.

SUNNY ZHOU,
*General Manager of Kunming Lida Wood
and Bamboo Products*[39]

When Westerners initiate business negotiations with representatives from the People's Republic of China, cultural barriers confront both sides. However, we should recognize that there are regional cultural differences which may affect negotiations, as detailed in Table 1, as well as regional economic differences. In addition, as concluded in research by Tung et al., there are considerable generational differences, in particular with those younger people who have been educated in the west and are more familiar with western ways and languages, whereas the older generation holds to more traditional culture and negotiation strategies.[40]

MAP 5.1   China

TABLE 1   Generalized Characteristics Associated with Chinese from Beijing, Shanghai, Guangzhou/Shenzhen and Select Cities in Western China

Beijing (capital city, center of political power in the country)	*Shanghai* (commercial center)
• Politically-oriented—everyone talks about politics • Bureaucratic—given the prevalence of state-owned enterprises (SOEs) in Beijing and surrounding areas, people tend to be more bureaucratic • Emphasis on integrity—people place more emphasis on trust and honesty in business dealings • Highly educated—many of the bureaucrats are highly educated • More relationship-focused • More fluid perception of time • Face comparatively more important • More holistic in approaching issues • Focus on general principles • More diversified cultural life • More direct and straightforward	• Business savvy—they are known for their business acumen • Bottom-line oriented • Focus on details—they perform due diligence before meetings and because of this, some people find it difficult to transact business with Shanghainese because they tend to argue over trivial matters • Confident and arrogant—because Shanghai has been an important economic center and is the trendsetter in fashion, Shanghainese tend to look down upon people from other cities, referring to them as "villagers" • Materialistic—Shanghainese are more concerned with brand names and one-upmanship • More tactical, i.e., calculating • Greater admiration of the West • More younger people who have attained high positions • Obsessed with career progression

Guangzhou/Shenzhen (southern city close to Hong Kong)	Western China (cities like Chongqing and Chengdu)
• Hard working and highly efficient—in the 1980s, Guangzhou/Shenzhen was recognized for its efficiency in building one entire floor of a skyscraper in three days	• People's mentality more like Beijing, Shanghai, and Guangzhou/Shenzhen 5–6 years ago
• Larger concentration of mass-assembly manufacturing	• More conservative
• Entrepreneurial—many prefer to start up their own businesses as opposed to working for established corporations	• More clannish
	• More traditional
	• Particularistic—emphasize knowing your counterpart first before doing business
• Pride in cuisine and more exotic cuisine	• Socializing (eating, drinking, and smoking) is very important
• Greater deviation from the norm	
• Less concerned about politics	• Greater emphasis on personal relations, i.e., rely on people more than laws or negotiations
• Identify more closely with Hong Kong	
• More concerned with work-life balance issues	• Less experience with international business
• Superstitious—because many businesspeople there are entrepreneurs, they tend to be more superstitious	• More laid back
	• More hardy
	• More emotional
• More informal in protocol and clothing	• In general, westerners find it more difficult to negotiate/do business here
• More risk taking	

Source: Rosalie L. Tung, Verner Worm, and Tony Fang, "Sino-Western Business Negotiations Revisited—30 Years after China's Open Door Policy," *Organizational Dynamics* 37, no 1, January 2008, 60–74; reprinted with permission from Elsevier.

For the most part, however, negotiation process used by the chinese is mystifying to most Westerners. For instance, the chinese put much greate emphasis than Americans and Europeans on respect and friendship, on saving face, and on group goals. Long-term goals are more important to the Chinese than the specific current objectives typical of Western negotiators. Even though market forces now have more influence in China, political and economic agendas are still expected to be considered in negotiations. Research by Xinping Shi of 198 managers in Beijing, 185 in Shanghai, and 189 in Guangzhou shows that prevailing economic conditions, political pervasiveness, and "constituent shadow" (the influence that constituents, such as political and state agencies, have on the negotiating parties in China) are key practical factors that, added to cultural factors, make up the context affecting Chinese negotiations. These antecedent factors, when filtered through the specific negotiator's profile, result in various behaviors, processes, and outcomes from those negotiations. Moreover, little difference in those influence factors was found among the different regions in China. Exhibit 5-6 shows these environmental factors and the relationships among the factors involved in Western–Chinese business negotiation.

Businesspeople report two major areas of conflict in negotiating with the Chinese: (1) The amount of detail the Chinese want about product characteristics, and (2) their apparent insincerity about reaching an agreement. In addition, Chinese negotiators frequently have little authority, frustrating Americans who do have the authority and are ready to conclude a deal.[41] This situation arises because many Chinese companies report to the government trade corporations, which are involved in the negotiations and often have a representative on the team. Often,

EXHIBIT 5-6   Influences on Western–Chinese Business Negotiations

Source: Xinping Shi, "Antecedent Factors of International Business Negotiations in the China Context," *Management International Review*, no. 2 (April 2001): 182.

the goals of Chinese negotiators remain primarily within the framework of state planning and political ideals. Although China is becoming more profit-oriented, most deals are still negotiated within the confines of the state budget allocation for that project rather than on the basis of a project's profitability or value. It is crucial, then, to find out which officials—national, provincial, local—have the power to make, and keep, a deal. According to James Broering of Arthur Andersen, who does much business in China, "companies have negotiated with government people for months, only to discover that they were dealing with the wrong people."[42]

Research shows that for the Chinese, the negotiation process is greatly affected by three cultural norms: their ingrained politeness and emotional restraint, their emphasis on social obligations, and their belief in the interconnection of work, family, and friendship. Because of the Chinese preference for emotional restraint and saving face, aggressive or emotional attempts at persuasion in negotiation are likely to fail. Instead, the Chinese tendency to avoid open conflict will more likely result in negative strategies such as discontinuing or withdrawing from negotiation.[43] The concept of face is at the heart of this kind of response—it is essential for foreigners to recognize the role that face behavior plays in negotiations. There are two components of face—*lien* and *mien-tzu*. *Lien* refers to a person's moral character; it is the most important thing defining that person, and without it one cannot function in society. It can only be earned by fulfilling obligations to others. *Mien-tzu* refers to one's reputation or prestige, earned through accomplishments or through bureaucratic or political power.[44] Giving others one's time, gifts, or praise enhances one's own face. In negotiations, it is vital that you do not make it obvious that you have "won" because that means that the other party has "lost" and will lose face. One must, therefore, make token concessions and other attempts to show that respect must be demonstrated, and modesty and control must be maintained; otherwise anyone who feels he or she has "lost face" will not want to deal with you again. The Chinese will later ignore any dealings or incidents that caused them to lose face, maintaining the expected polite behavior out of social consciousness and concern for others. When encountering an embarrassing situation, they will typically smile or laugh in an attempt to save face, responses that are confusing to Western negotiators.[45]

Research by Kam-hon Lee et al. explored sources of tension felt by Chinese and Americans during negotiations. For the Americans, sources of tension and lack of trust were attributed to what they referred to as Chinese misrepresentations, and to the Chinese not following what the Americans considered normative negotiation procedures. Generally, the Americans felt that the Chinese team was not being truthful with them and were not giving straight answers. From the perspective of the Chinese, tension on the part of the Americans damaged the interpersonal relationships between the parties, which are so important to the Chinese; this resulted in the Chinese not trusting the Americans and having negative expectations about the Americans' cooperativeness in the future. Further, Lee et al. found that intransigence was the most frequent cause of tension in both the Chinese and the American parties.[46]

The emphasis on social obligations underlies the strong orientation of the Chinese toward collective goals. Therefore, appeals to individual members of the Chinese negotiating team, rather than appeals to benefit the group as a whole, will probably backfire. The Confucian emphasis on the kinship system and the hierarchy of work, family, and friends explains the Chinese preference for doing business with familiar, trusted people and trusted companies. "Foreign" negotiators, then, should focus on establishing long-term, trusting relationships, even at the expense of some immediate returns.

Deeply ingrained in the Chinese culture is the importance of harmony for the smooth functioning of society. Harmony is based primarily on personal relationships, trust, and ritual. After the Chinese establish a cordial relationship with foreign negotiators, they use this relationship as a basis for the give-and-take of business discussions. This implicit cultural norm is commonly known as *guanxi*, which refers to the intricate, pervasive network of personal relations that every Chinese carefully cultivates. It is the primary means of getting ahead, in the absence of a proper commercial legal system.[47] In other words, *guanxi* establishes obligations to exchange favors in future business activities.[48] Even within the Chinese bureaucracy, *guanxi* prevails over legal interpretations. Although networking is important anywhere to do business, the difference in China is that "*guanxi* networks are not just commercial, but also social, involving the exchange both of favor and affection."[49] Firms that have special *guanxi* connections and give preferential treatment to one another are known as members of a *guanxihu* network.[50] Sunny Zhou, general manager of Kumming Lida Wood and Bamboo

Products, states that when he shops for lumber, "The lumber price varies drastically, depending on whether one has strong *guanxi* with the local administrators."[51] However, research by Fang, et al indicates some transition to a more business environment, where *guanxi* is still important, but not always decisive, and quotes a Chinese business woman as follows:

> *For example, I started my industrial systems business in Shanghai and Wuhan ten years ago. At that time, if you knew people in the government and had a good guanxi with them you would get your projects irrespective of your nengli (professional ability). Today, nengli becomes more and more important. Without nengli and benshi (professional skills), even your best government guanxi contacts would not let you win the bidding. If he did, he would risk losing his own job.*[52]

FANG ET AL,
International Business Review, 17, April, 2008.

Western managers should thus anticipate extended preliminary visiting (relationship building), in which the Chinese expect to learn more about them and their trustworthiness. The Chinese also use this opportunity to convey their deeply held principles. They attach considerable importance to mutual benefit.[53] The Chinese expect Western firms to sacrifice corporate goals and above-average profits to Chinese national goals and principles, such as meaningful friendship, Chinese national development, and the growth and enhancement of the Chinese people. Misunderstandings occur when Americans show polite acceptance of these general principles without understanding their significance—because they do not have any obvious relationship to American corporate goals, such as profit. Nor do such principles seem relevant to practical decisions on plant locations, employee practices, or sourcing.[54]

Americans often experience two negotiation stages with the Chinese: the technical and the commercial. During the long technical stage, the Chinese want to hammer out every detail of the proposed product specifications and technology. If there are two teams of negotiators, it may be several days before the commercial team is actually called in to deal with aspects of production, marketing, pricing, and so forth. However, the commercial team should sit in on the first stage to become familiar with the Chinese negotiating style.[55] The Chinese negotiating team is usually about twice as large as the Western team; about a third of the time is spent discussing technical specifications, and another third on price negotiations, with the rest devoted to general negotiations and posturing.[56]

The Chinese are among the toughest negotiators in the world. American managers must anticipate various tactics, such as their delaying techniques and their avoidance of direct, specific answers: Both ploys are used to exploit the known impatience of Americans. The Chinese frequently try to put pressure on Americans by "shaming" them, thereby implying that the Americans are trying to renege on the friendship—the basis of the implicit contract. Whereas Westerners come to negotiations with specific and segmented goals and find it easy to compromise, the Chinese are reluctant to negotiate details. They find it difficult to compromise and trade because they have entered negotiations with a broader vision of achieving development goals for China, and they are offended when Westerners don't internalize those goals.[57] Under these circumstances, the Chinese will adopt a rigid posture, and no agreement or contract is final until the negotiated activities have actually been completed.

Successful negotiations with the Chinese depends on many factors. Research by Fang et al. found the top success factors to be sincerity on behalf of the Western team, their team's preparation, technical expertise, patience, knowledge of PC business practices, and good personal relationships.[58] Generally speaking, patience, respect, and experience are necessary prerequisites for anyone negotiating in China. For the best outcomes, older, more experienced people are more acceptable to the Chinese in cross-cultural negotiations. The Chinese want to deal with the top executive of an American company, under the assumption that the highest officer has attained that position by establishing close personal relationships and trust with colleagues and others outside the organization. Western delegation practices are unfamiliar to them, and they are reluctant to come to an agreement without the presence of the Chinese foreign negotiator.[59] From the Western perspective, confusing jurisdictions of government ministries hamper decisions in negotiations.[60] Americans tend to send specific technical personnel with experience in the task at hand; therefore, they have to take care in selecting the most suitable negotiators. In addition, visiting negotiating teams should realize that the Chinese are probably negotiating with other foreign teams, often at the same time, and will use that setup to play one company's offer against the others. On an interpersonal level, Western negotiators must also realize that, while a handshake is polite, physical contact is not acceptable in Chinese social behavior, nor are personal discussion topics such as one's family. However, it is customary to give and take small gifts as tokens of friendship. Pye offers the following additional tips to foreigners conducting business with the Chinese:[61]

- Practice patience
- Accept prolonged periods of stalemate
- Refrain from exaggerated expectations and discount Chinese rhetoric about future prospects
- Expect the Chinese to try to manipulate by shaming
- Resist the temptation to believe that difficulties may have been caused by one's own mistakes
- Try to understand Chinese cultural traits, but realize that a foreigner cannot practice them better than the Chinese

In conclusion, it is evident that China's rapidly changing business environment is evident in more professionalism in the negotiation process. At the same time, research by Fang et al. shows that "one should not underestimate the impact of culture on Chinese business negotiations. Western companies that seek to succeed in China need to demonstrate sincerity and commitment in conducting business in order to gain the Chinese partner's trust as this appears to be the ultimate predictor for success of business relations in China."[62]

As discussed in Chapter 4, much of the difference in communication styles is attributable to whether you belong to a high-context or low-context culture (or somewhere in between, as shown in Exhibit 4-4). In low-context cultures such as that in the United States, conflict is handled directly and explicitly. It is also regarded as separate from the person negotiating—that is, the negotiators draw a distinction between the people involved and the information or opinions they represent. They also tend to negotiate on the basis of factual information and logical analysis. That approach to conflict is called **instrumental-oriented conflict.**[63] In high-context cultures, such as in the Middle East, the approach to conflict is called **expressive-oriented conflict**—that is, the situation is handled indirectly and implicitly, without clear delineation of the situation by the person handling it. Such negotiators do not want to get in a confrontational situation because it is regarded as insulting and would cause a loss of "face," so they tend to use evasion and avoidance if they cannot reach agreement through emotional appeals. Their avoidance and inaction conflict with the expectations of the low-context negotiators who are looking to move ahead with the business at hand and arrive at a solution.

The differences between high- and low-context cultures that often lead to conflict situations are summarized in Exhibit 5-7. Most of these variables were discussed previously in this chapter or in Chapter 4. They overlap because the subjects, culture, and communication are inseparable and because negotiation differences and conflict situations arise from variables in culture and communication.

The point here is, how can a manager from France, Japan, or Brazil, for example, manage conflict situations? The solution, as discussed previously, lies mainly in one's ability to know and understand the people and the situation to be faced. Managers must be prepared by developing an understanding of the cultural contexts in which they will be operating. What are the expectations of the persons with whom they will be negotiating? What kinds of communication styles and negotiating tactics should they expect, and how will they differ from their own? It is important to bear in mind one's own expectations and negotiating style, as well as to be aware of the other parties' expectations. Managers ought to consider in advance what it will take to arrive at a win-win solution. Often it helps to use the services of a host-country adviser or mediator, who may be able to help with early diffusion of a conflict situation.

DECISION MAKING

Negotiation actually represents the outcome of a series of small and large decisions. The decisions include those made by each party before actual negotiations start—for example, in determining the position of the company and what fallback proposals it may suggest or accept.

EXHIBIT 5-7   Sources of Conflict Between Low-Context and High-Context Cultures[64]

Key Questions	Low-Context Conflict	High-Context Conflict
Why	Analytic, linear logic; instrumental oriented; dichotomy between conflict and conflict parties	Synthetic, spiral logic; expressive oriented; integration of conflict and conflict parties
When	Individualistic oriented; low collective normative expectations; violations of individual expectations create conflict potentials	Group oriented; high collective normative expectations; violations of collective expectations create conflict potentials
What	Revealment; direct, confrontational attitude; action and solution oriented	Concealment; indirect nonconfrontational attitude; "face" and relationship oriented
How	Explicit communication codes; line-logic style: rational-factual rhetoric; open, direct strategies	Implicit communication codes; point-logic style: intuitive-effective rhetoric; ambiguous, indirect strategies

The decisions also include incremental decisions, made during the negotiation process, on how to react and proceed, when to concede, and on what to agree or disagree. Negotiation can thus be seen as a series of explicit and implicit decisions, and the subjects of negotiation and decision making become interdependent.

For instance, sometimes just the way a decision is made during the negotiation process can have a profound influence on the outcome, as this example shows:

> *In his first loan negotiation, a banker new to Japan met with seven top Japanese bankers who were seeking a substantial amount of money. After hearing their presentation, the American agreed on the spot. The seven Japanese then conferred among themselves and told the American they would get back to him in a couple of days regarding whether they would accept his offer or not. The American banker learned a lesson he never forgot.*[65]

The Japanese bankers expected the American to negotiate, to take time to think it over, and to consult with colleagues before giving the final decision. His immediate decision made them suspicious, so they decided to reconsider the deal.

There is no doubt that the speed and manner of decision making affect the negotiation process. In addition, how well negotiated agreements are implemented is affected by the speed and manner of decision making. In that regard, it is clear that the effective use of technology is playing an important role, especially when dealing with complex cross-border agreements in which the hundreds of decision makers involved are separated by time and space.

The role of decision making in management, however, goes far beyond the finite occasions of negotiations. It is part of the manager's daily routine—from operational-level, programmed decisions requiring minimal time and effort to those nonprogrammed decisions of far broader scope and importance, such as the decision to enter into a joint venture in a foreign country.

The Influence of Culture on Decision Making

It is crucial for international managers to understand the influence of culture on decision-making styles and processes. Culture affects decision making both through the broader context of the nation's institutional culture, which produces collective patterns of decision making, and through culturally based value systems that affect each individual decision maker's perception or interpretation of a situation.[66]

The extent to which decision making is influenced by culture varies among countries. For example, Hitt, Tyler, and Park have found a "more culturally homogenizing influence on the Korean executives' cognitive models" than on those of U.S. executives, whose individualistic tendencies lead to different decision patterns.[67] The ways that culture influences an executive's decisions can be studied by looking at the variables involved in each stage of the rational decision-making process. These stages are (1) defining the problem, (2) gathering and analyzing relevant data, (3) considering alternative solutions, (4) deciding on the best solution, and (5) implementing the decision.

One of the major cultural variables affecting decision making is whether a people tend to assume an objective approach or a subjective approach. Whereas the Western approach is based on rationality (managers interpret a situation and consider alternative solutions based on objective information), this approach is not common throughout the world. Latin Americans, among others, are more subjective, basing decisions on emotions.

Another cultural variable that greatly influences the decision-making process is the risk tolerance of those making the decision. Research shows that people from Belgium, Germany, and Austria have a considerably lower tolerance for risk than people from Japan or the Netherlands—whereas American managers have the highest tolerance for risk.[68]

In addition, an often-overlooked but important variable in the decision-making process is the manager's perception of the locus of control over outcomes—whether that locus is internal or external. Some managers feel they can plan on certain outcomes because they are in control of events that will direct the future in the desired way. In contrast, other managers believe that such decisions are of no value because they have little control over the future—which lies in the hands of outside forces, such as fate, God, or nature. American managers believe strongly in self-determination and perceive problem situations as something they can control and should change. However, managers in many other countries, Indonesia and Malaysia among them, are resigned to problem situations and do not feel that they can change them. Obviously, these different value systems will result in a great difference in the stages of consideration of alternative actions and choice of a solution, often because certain situations may or may not be viewed as problems in the first place.

Yet another variable that affects the consideration of alternative solutions is how managers feel about staying with familiar solutions or trying new ones. Many managers, particularly those in Europe, value decisions based on past experiences and tend to emphasize quality. Americans, on the other hand, are more future oriented and look toward new ideas to get them there.

Approaches to Decision Making

In addition to affecting different stages of the decision-making process, value systems influence the overall approach of decision makers from various cultures. The relative level of utilitarianism versus moral idealism in any society affects its overall approach to problems. Generally speaking, utilitarianism strongly guides behavior in the Western world. Research has shown that Canadian executives are more influenced by a short-term, cost–benefit approach to decision making than their Hong Kong counterparts.

Another important variable in companies' overall approach to decision making is that of autocratic versus participative leadership. In other words, who has the authority to make what kinds of decisions? A society's orientation—whether it is individualistic or collectivist (see Chapter 3)—influences the level at which decisions are made. In many countries with hierarchical cultures—Germany, Turkey, and India, among others—authorization for action has to be passed upward through echelons of management before final decisions can be made. Most employees in these countries simply expect the autocrat—the boss—to do most of the decision making and will not be comfortable otherwise. Even in China, which is a highly collectivist society, employees expect autocratic leadership because their value system presupposes the superior to be automatically the most wise. In comparison, decision-making authority in Sweden is very decentralized. Americans talk a lot about the advisability of such participative leadership, but in practice they are probably near the middle between autocratic and participative management styles.

Arab managers have long traditions of consultative decision making, supported by the Qur'an and the sayings of Muhammed. However, such consultation occurs more on a

EXHIBIT 5-8 Cultural Variables in the Decision-Making Process

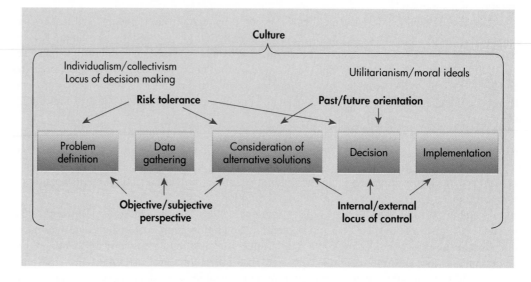

person-to-person basis than during group meetings and thus diffuses potential opposition.[69] Although business in the Middle East tends to be transacted in a highly personalized manner, the final decisions are made by the top leaders, who feel that they must impose their will for the company to be successful. In comparison, in cultures that emphasize collective harmony, such as Japan, participatory or group decision making predominates, and consensus is important. The best-known example is the bottom-up (rather than top-down) decision-making process used in most Japanese companies, described in more detail in the following Comparative Management in Focus section.

One final area of frequent incongruence concerns the relative speed of decision making. A country's culture affects how fast or slow decisions tend to be made. The relative speed may be closely associated with the level of delegation, as just discussed—but not always. The pace at which decisions are made can be very disconcerting for outsiders. North Americans and Europeans pride themselves on being decisive; managers in the Middle East, with a different sense of temporal urgency, associate the importance of the matter at hand with the length of time needed to make a decision. Without knowing this cultural attitude, a hasty American would insult an Egyptian; a quick decision, to the Egyptian, would reflect a low regard for the relationship and the deal.

Exhibit 5-8 illustrates, in summary form, how all the variables just discussed can affect the steps in the decision-making process.

COMPARATIVE MANAGEMENT IN FOCUS

Decision Making in Japanese Companies

Japanese companies are involved in joint ventures throughout the world, especially with U.S. companies. The GM-Toyota joint venture agreement process, for example, was the result of more than two years of negotiation and decision making, and in similar alliances, Americans and Japanese are involved in decision making at all levels on a daily basis. The Japanese decision-making process differs greatly not only from the U.S. process but from that of many other countries—especially at the higher levels of their organizations.

An understanding of the Japanese decision-making process—and indeed of many Japanese management practices—requires an understanding of Japanese national culture. Much of the Japanese culture, and therefore the basis of Japanese working relationships, can be explained by the principle of *wa*, meaning "peace and harmony." This principle is one aspect of the value the Japanese attribute to *amae*, meaning "indulgent love," a concept probably originating in the Shinto religion, which focuses on spiritual and physical harmony. *Amae* results in *shinyo*, which refers to the mutual confidence, faith, and honor required for successful business relationships. The principle of *wa* influences the work group, the basic building block of Japanese work and management. The Japanese strongly identify with their work groups, where the emphasis is on cooperation, participative management, consensus problem solving, and decision making based on a patient, long-term perspective. Open expression of conflict is discouraged, and it is of utmost importance to avoid embarrassment or shame—to lose face—as a result of not fulfilling one's obligations. These elements of work culture generally result in a devotion to work, a collective responsibility for decisions and actions, and a high degree of employee productivity. It is this culture of collectivism and shared responsibility that underlies the Japanese *ringi* system of decision making.

In the *ringi* system, the process works from the bottom up. Americans are used to a centralized system, where major decisions are made by upper-level managers in a top-down approach typical of individualistic societies. The Japanese process, however, is dispersed throughout the organization, relying on group consensus.

The *ringi* process is one of gaining approval on a proposal by circulating documents to those concerned throughout the company. It usually comprises four steps: proposal, circulation, approval, and record.[70] Usually the person who originates the written proposal, which is called a *ringi-sho,* has already worked for some time to gain informal consensus and support for the proposal within the section and then from the department head.[71] The next step is to attain a general consensus in the company from those who would be involved in implementation. To this end, department meetings are held, and if necessary expert opinion is sought. If more information is needed, the proposal goes back to the originator, who finds and adds the required data. In this way, much time and effort—and the input of many people—go into the proposal before it becomes formal.[72]

Up to this point, the process has been an informal one to gain consensus; it is called the *nemawashi* process. Then the more formal authorization procedure begins, called the *ringi* process. The *ringi-sho* is passed up through successive layers of management for approval—the approval made official by seals. In the end, many such seals of approval are gathered, thereby ensuring collective agreement and responsibility and giving the proposal a greater chance of final approval by the president. The whole process is depicted in Exhibit 5-9.

EXHIBIT 5-9   Decision-Making Procedure in Japanese Companies

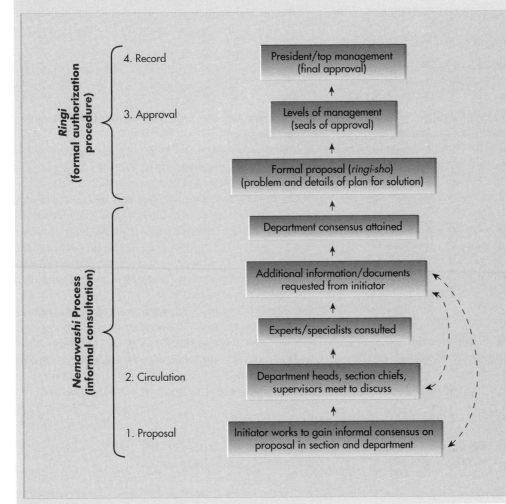

The *ringi* system is cumbersome and very time-consuming prior to the implementation stage, although implementation is facilitated because of the widespread awareness of and support for the proposal already gained throughout the organization. However, its slow progress is problematic when decisions are time-sensitive. This process is the opposite of the Americans' top-down decisions, which are made quite rapidly and without consultation, but which then take time to implement because unforeseen practical or support problems often arise.

Another interesting comparison is often made regarding the planning horizon (aimed at short- or long-term goals) in decision making between the American and Japanese systems. The Japanese spend considerable time in the early stages of the process defining the issue, considering what the issue is all about, and determining whether there is an actual need for a decision. They are more likely than Americans to consider an issue in relation to the overall goals and strategy of the company. In this manner, they prudently look at the "big picture" and consider alternative solutions, instead of rushing into quick decisions for immediate solutions, as Americans tend to do.[73]

Of course, in a rapidly changing environment, quick decisions are often necessary—to respond to competitors' actions, a political uprising, and so forth—and it is in such contexts that the *ringi* system sometimes falls short because of its slow response rate. The system is, in fact, designed to manage continuity and to avoid uncertainty, which is considered a threat to group cohesiveness.[74]

CONCLUSION

It is clear that competitive positioning and long-term successful operations in a global market require a working knowledge of the decision-making and negotiating processes of managers from different countries. These processes are complex and often interdependent. Although managers may make decisions that do not involve negotiating, they cannot negotiate without making decisions, however small, or they would not be negotiating. In addition, managers must understand the behavioral aspects of these processes to work effectively with people in other countries or with a culturally diverse workforce in their own countries.

With an understanding of the environment and cultural context of international management as background, we move next in Part III to planning and implementing strategy for international and global operations.

Summary of Key Points

1. The ability to negotiate successfully is one of the most important in international business. Managers must prepare for certain cultural variables that influence negotiations, including the relative emphasis on task versus interpersonal relationships, the use of general principles versus specific details, the number of people present, and the extent of their influence.

2. The negotiation process typically progresses through the stages of preparation, relationship building, exchange of task-related information, persuasion, and concessions and agreement. The process of building trusting relationships is a prerequisite to doing business in many parts of the world.

3. Culturally based differences in verbal and nonverbal negotiation behavior influence the negotiation process at every stage. Such tactics and actions include promises, threats, initial concessions, silent periods, interruptions, facial gazing, and touching; some parties resort to various dirty tricks.

4. The effective management of negotiation requires an understanding of the perspectives, values, and agendas of other parties and the use of a problem-solving approach.

5. Decision making is an important part of the negotiation process, as well as an integral part of a manager's daily routine. Culture affects the decision-making process both through a society's institutions and through individuals' risk tolerance, their objective versus subjective perspectives, their perceptions of the locus of control, and their past versus future orientations.

6. The Internet is used increasingly to support the negotiation of contracts and resolution of disputes. Web sites that provide open auctions take away the personal aspects of negotiations, though those aspects are still essential in many instances.

Discussion Questions

1. Discuss the stages in the negotiation process and how culturally-based value systems influence these stages. Specifically, address the following:
   - Explain the role and relative importance of relationship-building in different countries.
   - Discuss the various styles and tactics that can be involved in exchanging task-related information.
   - Describe differences in culturally-based styles of persuasion.
   - Discuss the kinds of concession strategies a negotiator might anticipate in various countries.

2. Discuss the relative use of nonverbal behaviors, such as silent periods, interruptions, facial gazing, and touching, by people from various cultural backgrounds. How does this behavior affect the negotiation process in a cross-cultural context?

3. Describe what you would expect in negotiations with the Chinese and how you would handle various situations.

4. What are some of the differences in risk tolerance around the world? What is the role of risk propensity in the decision-making process?

5. Explain how objective versus subjective perspectives influences the decision-making process. What role do you think this variable has played in all the negotiations conducted and decisions made by Iraq and the United Nations?

6. Explain differences in culturally-based value systems relative to the amount of control a person feels he or she has over future outcomes. How does this belief influence the decision-making process?

Experiential Exercises

EXERCISE 1: MULTICULTURAL NEGOTIATIONS

Goal

To experience, identify, and appreciate the problems associated with negotiating with people of other cultures.

Instructions (Note: Your Professor will give out additional intruction sheets)

1. Eight student volunteers will participate in the role play. Four represent a Japanese automobile manufacturer, and four represent a U.S. team that has come to sell microchips and other components to the Japanese company. The remainder of the class will observe the negotiations.

2. The eight volunteers will divide into the two groups and then separate into different rooms, if possible. At that point, they will be given instruction sheets. Neither team can have access to the other's instructions. After dividing the roles, the teams should meet for 10 to 15 minutes to develop their negotiation strategies based on their instructions.

3. While the teams are preparing, the room will be set up using a rectangular table with four seats on each side. The Japanese side will have three chairs at the table with one chair set up behind the three. The American side of the table will have four chairs side by side.

4. Following these preparations, the Japanese team will be brought in, so they may greet the Americans when they arrive. At this point, the Americans will be brought in and the role play begins. Time for the negotiations should be 20 to 30 minutes. The rest of the class will act as observers and will be expected to provide feedback during the discussion phase.

5. When the negotiations are completed, the student participants from both sides and the observers will complete their feedback questionnaires. Class discussion of the feedback questions will follow.

Feedback Questions for the Japanese Team

1. What was your biggest frustration during the negotiations?
2. What would you say the goal of the American team was?
3. What role (e.g., decider, influencer, etc.) did each member of the American team play?
   Mr. Jones
   Mr./Ms. Smith
   Mr./Ms. Nelson
   Mr./Ms. Frost
4. How would you rate the success of each of the American team members in identifying your team's needs and appealing to them?
   Mr./Ms. Jones, Vice President and Team Leader
   Mr./Ms. Smith, Manufacturing Engineer
   Mr./Ms. Nelson, Marketing Analyst
   Mr./Ms. Frost, Account Executive
5. What strategy should the American team have taken?

Feedback Questions for the American Team

1. What was your biggest frustration during the negotiations?
2. What would you say the goal of the Japanese team was?

3. How would you rate the success of each of the American team members?
   Mr. Jones, Vice President and Team Leader
   Mr./Ms. Smith, Manufacturing Engineer
   Mr./Ms. Nelson, Marketing Analyst
   Mr./Ms. Frost, Account Executive
4. What would you say the goal of the American team was?
5. What role (e.g., decider, influencer, etc.) did each member of the Japanese team play?
   Mr. Ozaka
   Mr. Nishimuro
   Mr. Sheno
   Mr. Kawazaka
6. What strategy should the American team have taken?

Feedback Questions for the Observers

1. What was your biggest frustration during the negotiations?
2. What would you say the goal of the Japanese team was?
3. How would you rate the success of each of the American team members?
   Mr./Ms. Jones, Vice President and Team Leader
   Mr./Ms. Smith, Manufacturing Engineer
   Mr./Ms. Nelson, Marketing Analyst
   Mr./Ms. Frost, Account Executive
4. What would you say the goal of the American team was?
5. What role (e.g., decider, influencer, etc.) did each member of the Japanese team play?
   Mr. Ozaka
   Mr. Nishimuro
   Mr. Sheno
   Mr. Kawazaka
6. What strategy should the American team have taken?

EXERCISE 2: JAPANESE DECISION MAKING

Time: Two class meetings
Goal

To allow students to experience the process and results of solving a problem or initiating a project using the Japanese decision processes of *nemawashi* and *ringi*.

Preparation

Review Chapters 4 and 5 and the Comparative Management in Focus: Decision Making in Japanese Companies.
Note: Instructions for this exercise will be given by your Professor, from the Instructor's Manual.

Source: E. A. Diodati, in C. Harvey and M.J. Allard, *Understanding Diversity* (New York: HarperCollins Publishers, 1995). Used with permission.

Internet Resources

Visit the Deresky Companion Website at www.pearsonhighered.com/
deresky for this chapter's Internet resources.

CASE STUDY

The Alcatel-Lucent Merger—What went wrong?

*It did not take long after the merger for things to start going wrong for Alcatel-Lucent
CEO Patricia Russo, who opted to leave the vendor last month after admitting she could
no longer work with fellow board resignee chairman Serge Tchuruk.*

MicroScope,
August 11–17, 2008.[1]

It seems that this deal was not meant to happen. The original merger negotiations between
Alcatel of France, the communications equipment maker based in Paris, and Lucent
Technologies, the U.S. telecommunications giant, took place in 2001. However, the finely
detailed deal collapsed on May 29, 2001, after the two companies could not agree on how much
control the French company would have. Lucent's executives apparently wanted the deal as a
"merger of equals," rather than a takeover by Alcatel.[2]

The failed deal was regarded as a severe blow to Lucent's image. Industry watchers questioned how Lucent would be able to survive this most recent blow. Although it was not clear
which company initiated the negotiations, it was reported that Lucent ended them after much of
the senior management detected that the proposed deal would not be a merger of equals.[3]

In 2006, however, renewed negotiations took place, resulting in the transatlantic relationship
being consummated. Shareholders in France approved the merger of the telecommunications equipment makers Alcatel and Lucent on September 7, 2006. However, Alcatel investors still had
concerns about the leadership and financial health of their new American partner. Alcatel's chief
executive, Serge Tchuruk, tried to reassure the 1,500 shareholders gathered in Paris to back the
merger, saying the company—to be called Alcatel-Lucent—is "truly global and has no equivalent
today and won't in the future."[4] Mr. Tchuruk had agreed in April 2006 to pay 10.6 billion euro
($13.5 billion then) for Lucent, in a deal to create the world's biggest telephone equipment maker,
although industry watchers considered the bid as financially inadequate for Alcatel investors. The
stock swap was valued at one Alcatel American depository share for every five Lucent shares.
Tchuruk said the combined company would realize 1.4 billion euro ($1.8 billion) in cost savings
over the following three years, in part by cutting 9,000 jobs, about 10 percent of the combined
workforce.[5] He noted that Alcatel-Lucent's revenue would be spread almost equally across Europe,
the United States and Asia, offering greater long-term stability. Alcatel does most of its business in
Europe, while Lucent does the majority of its business in the United States. Lucent Shareholders
also endorsed the deal.

"We are another step closer to creating the first truly global communications solutions
provider with the broadest wireless, wireline and services portfolio in the industry," said the chief
executive of Lucent, Patricia F. Russo, who was to retain that role in the combined company.

At that time, the company had combined sales of $25 billion.[6] Amid concerns about the
potential for cross-cultural conflicts, Tchuruk said that, while cultural issues could arise, "everything
is under way to make sure this human factor is dealt with," he said, adding that Alcatel already operated as an international company with a wide mix of nationalities; English is the official language of
the company.[7] Other industry commentators cast Alcatel-Lucent as "a Franco-American telecoms
behemoth that many regard as a giant transatlantic experiment in multinational diversity."[8]

After the shareholders of both companies endorsed the deal, regulatory hurdles were
cleared in both the EU and the U.S.[9]

An Alcatel-Lucent merger provided the combined company a strong position in several
categories of equipment sold to the major telecommunications carrier: wireless telecommunications

equipment, wireline equipment, wireless infrastructure, Internet routers, equipment for carrying calls over the Internet, etc.[10]

However, success was illusive. Overall, it seemed that "the difficulties of integrating a French company with an American one dominated during Russo's tenure, with analysts suggesting the corporate culture of Lucent clashed with Alcatel's French business model. One source close to the company saw little evidence of cooperation between the two factions from the outside."[11] In July 2008, the Alcatel-Lucent CEO Patricia Russo resigned, citing the inability to get along with Serge Tchuruk, her fellow board member; subsequently he too resigned. Much of the resentment came from Alcatel management because the overall leadership had been handed to the target company, Lucent, an unusual decision; in addition, it became clear that it was a poor decision to appoint leaders based on their nationality rather than skills. Other factors seemed to be against Ms. Russo, however, as she struggled to bring together the vastly different cultures of the two companies amid a tough business climate. As the first woman to run a company listed on the CAC 40, she had to make her way in the clubby, male-dominated world where French business and politics overlap.[12]

In addition, the combined, but still rather weak companies, faced low-cost competition from new Chinese rivals and were struggling in a business that Internet technology was changing beyond recognition. Worse, demand has been weakening across the industry. A *Barron's* article in August 2008 noted that "while it might have been helpful if outgoing CEO Patricia Russo had spoken French, that's not why she and Chairman Serge Tchuruk failed to make a go of the 2006 merger of Alcatel and Lucent Technologies. They were pushed into each other's arms out of desperation as the industry began a painful, necessary consolidation. . . . the telephone-equipment business is brutal and likely to see more attrition. The marriage didn't avert six straight quarterly losses."[13]

The series of quarterly losses ($7 billion loss since the merger) led to a bombardment of negative comment as Alcatel-Lucent initiated restructuring and cut around 16,500 jobs.[14]

In September the new chiefs were announced—a French chairman, who lives in America, and a Dutch chief executive, who will be based in Paris. Both Philippe Camus and Ben Verwaayen were considered to have the personality and experience that could iron out the beleaguered telecoms group's problems. Mr. Verwaayen accepted the new job only when he found he could get along with Mr. Camus, who had already agreed to be chairman. "We share the same sense of humour," he says. "You need to have complete understanding at the top of the house."[15] "We must deliver on the merger," Ben Verwaayen, the former head of BT, who was appointed to succeed Patricia F. Russo as chief executive, said at a meeting with journalists. Acknowledging that there remained "a divided Alcatel-Lucent," Mr. Verwaayen said, "We need to move quickly to become an integrated company."[16] Mr. Verwaayen speaks fluent French and English. Alcatel-Lucent operates in 130 countries, and like many global enterprises, its language of business is English. He was quoted in *The Economist* as saying that he "sees his job as removing barriers within the company and unleashing its talents." But perhaps his biggest advantage in rescuing a failed Franco-American merger is that he is neither French nor American.[17]

References

1. Alex Scroxton, *Microscope*, August 11–17, 2008, 7.
2. A. Sorkin and S. Romero, "Alcatel and Lucent Call Off Negotiations Toward a Merger," *New York Times*, May 30, 2001; S. Shiesel, "Pride and Practicalities Loom Behind Failed Lucent 'Merger'," *New York Times*, May 31, 2001.
3. L. H. LaBarba, "Let's Call the Whole Thing Off," *Telephony* 240, no. 23, June 4, 2001, 14–16.
4. J. Kanter, "Shareholders in Paris Approve Merger of Alcatel and Lucent," *New York Times*, September 6, 2006.
5. Ibid.
6. Ibid.
7. Ibid.
8. I. Austen and V. Bajaj, "A Continental Shift," *New York Times*, March 25, 2006.
9. "EU Clears Proposed Alcatel-Lucent Merger," *Wall Street Journal*, July 25, 2006.
10. Data from Austen and Bajaj.

11. Scroxton, 2008.
12. David Jolly, "New Alcatel-Lucent Leaders Vow to Persist on Integration," *New York Times*, Sep 3, 2008.
13. Mark Veverka. "Chiefs, not Problems, leave Alcatel-Lucent," *Barron's*, Aug 11, 2008, 16.
14. Scroxton, 2008.
15. Anonymous, "Bring down the Barriers: Alcatel-Lucent," *The Economist*, September 6, 2008
16. *Jolly*, 2008.
17. *The Economist*, 2008.

Case Questions

1. Referring to the case and this chapter, discuss what conditions and negotiation factors pushed forth the merger in 2006 that were not present in 2001.
2. Research the status of the merged company at the time of your reading of this case. What has happened in the industry since the merger, and how is the company faring?
3. Evaluate the comment that the merger is "a giant transatlantic experiment in multicultural diversity." What evidence is there that the company has run into cross-cultural problems since the merger took place in 2006?
4. How much of the decline do you attribute to leadership problems, as opposed to industry factors?
5. What, if any, factors should have been negotiated differently?

ICMR
Center for
Management Research

CASE 4   MTV NETWORKS: THE ARABIAN CHALLENGE

"[. . .] MTV has a penchant for airing controversial material and making a mockery of convention. And of course, it's an American brand . . . The challenge, therefore, is transforming a notoriously risqué channel into a Middle Eastern-friendly platform for music and creativity without stripping MTV of its edge. It isn't without some irony that a channel known for angering religious, political, and conservative communities is operating in and catering to a region renowned for reacting (and sometimes overreacting) negatively to controversial content."[1]

DANA EL BALTAJI,
Special Projects Manager, Trends magazine in Dubai, in 2008.

"In many ways (MTV Arabia) is the epitome of our localization strategy. It's a different audience (in the Middle East) but this is what we do – we reflect culture and we respect culture. The programming mix on this one is going to be a little more local than normal."[2]

WILLIAM H. ROEDY,
Vice Chairman for MTV Networks and President MTVI Network International, in 2007.

A Litmus Test for MTV's Localization Strategy

MTV Networks (MTVN) launched MTV Arabia on November 17, 2007, in partnership with Arabian Television Network[3] (ATN) as part of its global expansion strategy. According to analysts, MTV's presence in the Middle East would provide the region with an international music brand, which till then, did not have an international music brand though it had clusters of local music channels. On its part, the region promised to offer tremendous growth opportunities to MTVN.

Analysts felt that MTV Arabia was MTVN's most ambitious and challenging venture. The Middle East offered huge growth potential to MTVN given its huge youth populace. However, according to analysts, MTV's success in the Middle East was contingent upon a tactical balancing between deliv-

ery of international quality music and the culturally sensitive environment prevalent in the region. Some analysts felt that the channel was well equipped to achieve this considering MTVN's extensive experience in the global market and its ability to provide localized content without diluting what MTV stood for.

To ensure that its programs won over the hearts of the Arabs and adhered to the local taste and culture without diluting MTV's global brand, MTV Arabia designed a much localized Arabic version of its international music and reality shows. In this connection, Patrick Samaha (Samaha), General Manager of MTV Arabia, said, "We've created programs that are an Arabic version of MTV programs. It is the first time that programs like this will really reflect the youth culture here, but we've been mindful all the way about respecting the local culture."[4]

According to the company, the launch of MTV Arabia was also expected to act as a culturally unifying force by propelling Arabic Music to the global forefront and vice versa. While launching MTV Arabia, William H. Roedy, Vice Chairman for MTV Networks and President of MTVI, said, "Tonight's [November 16, 2007] MTV Arabia launch show celebrates one of the most important landmarks in MTV's 25-year history. MTV Arabia will reach the largest potential audience of any MTV channel outside the United States. MTV is proud to celebrate the voice of the Arab youth and through our global network we can showcase what this rich and diverse culture is all about to new audiences around the world."[5]

Author Information:
This case was written by **Debapratim Purkayastha**, ICMR. It was compiled from published sources, and is intended to be used as a basis for class discussion rather than to illustrate either effective or ineffective handling of a management situation.

[1] Dana El Baltaji, "I Want My MTV," www.arabmediasociety.com, May 11, 2008.
[2] Lynne Roberts, "MTV Set for Middle East Launch," www.arabianbusiness. com, October 17, 2007.
[3] Arabian Television Network (ATN) is a Dubai, United Arab Emirates based broadcast media company, part of the Arab Media Group's Arabian Broadcasting Network (ABN). ABN is a part of the Arab Media Group (AMG). As of 2007, AMG was the largest media group in the UAE, with approximately 1,500 employees. It was an unit of TECOM Investments that was controlled by Dubai's ruler.

[4] Jolanta Chudy, "MTV's Arab Net Thinking Locally," www.hollywoodreporter. com, November 6, 2007.
[5] "Akon and Ludacris Dazzle the Desert in their Middle East Debuts to Celebrate the Launch of MTV Arabia," www.dubaicityguide.com, November 16, 2007.

Background Note

MTV (short for Music Television), which pioneered the concept of a cable music channel, was launched on August 1, 1981, and marked the commencement of the cable TV revolution. It was promoted by Warner Amex Satellite Entertainment Company, a joint venture between Warner Communications and American Express. In 1984, the company was renamed MTV Networks (MTVN) with its operations confined to the US.

At the time of its launch, the MTV channel primarily catered to those in the 12 to 24 age group, airing heavy-metal and rap music. However, over the years, it also launched many sister channels such as VH-1 (short for video hits one) which was formed in 1985 to play light popular music; Rhythm and Blues (R&B, for jazz, country music, and classics targeted at the 18 to 35 age group; and Nickelodeon,[6] which was launched in 1977 keeping children as its target segment. While these sister channels of MTVN continued playing different varieties of music, the core channel MTV began to diversify in 1990.

Besides playing music, it also started airing non-music, reality shows. *The Real World* and *MTV Fear* were some of the popular reality shows aired. Animated cartoon series were also introduced, the most popular of them being *Beavis and Butthead.*

In 1986, MTVN was acquired by Viacom Inc. (Refer to Exhibit I for a note on Viacom). Thereafter, in 1987, MTVN launched its first overseas channel in Europe and this marked the beginning of MTV's global expansion. The international arm of MTVN was known as MTVI. In addition to MTV, MTVI managed a bouquet of channels like VH-1 and Nickelodeon.

By the mid-1990s MTVI realized that to become a successful brand globally, it had to adapt to local conditions. Hence it adopted a strategy of "Think Globally, Act Locally." Thereafter, MTVI became the first international TV network to offer channels like MTV Australia, MTV Asia, MTV India, MTV China, MTV Germany, etc. in local languages with localized content.[7] To penetrate any new market, MTVI initially tied

EXHIBIT I   A Note on Viacom Inc.

Viacom was established as a public company in 1971. In 1985, it acquired a 65 percent stake in MTV Networks, which included MTV, VH-1, and Nickelodeon, and purchased the remaining interest in 1986. In 1991, Viacom completed its purchase of MTV Europe by acquiring a 50 percent stake from British Telecommunications and other parties. In 1994, the Viacom Entertainment Group was formed through a merger with Paramount Communications Inc. In 2000, CBS Corporation, a major media network in the US, merged with Viacom, as a result of which TNN (re-named as Spike TV in 2003) and CMT (Country Music Television) joined the MTV Networks. The BET (Black Entertainment Television) channel was acquired by Viacom in 2001. In the early 2000s, Viacom launched many channels worldwide under MTV Networks and BET.

In 2005, Viacom Corporation split into Viacom Inc. and CBS Corporation. In 2006, Viacom Inc. was one of the world's leading media companies operating in the Cable and Satellite Television Networks (C&S) and film production divisions.

VIACOM INC. BRANDS*
Cable Networks & Digital Media

• MTV Networks (Comedy Central, CMT, LOGO, MTV, MTV 2, MTV U, MTV Networks Digital Suite, **MTV International**, MTV Networks online, Nickelodeon, Nick @ Nite, The N, Noggin, Spike, TV Land, VH-1)

• BET Networks presents the best in Black media and entertainment featuring traditional and digital platforms. Brands including BET, BET J, BET Gospel, BET Hip Hop, BET.com, BET Mobile, BET Event Productions, and BET International deliver relevant and insightful content to consumers of Black culture in more than 84 million households.

Entertainment (Film & Music Publishing)
• Paramount Pictures
• Paramount Home Entertainment
• DreamWorks SKG
• Famous Music

* The list is not exhaustive
Source: www.viacom.com

---

[6] Nickelodeon's primarily caters to children in age group 7–11, but along with this it also airs weekend programmes in TEENick catering to children in age group 12–17 and also weekday morning programs aimed at chidren in age group 2–6 and a late-night segment known as Nick at nite aimed at general audiences.

---

[7] Dirk Smillie, "Tuning in First Global TV Generation," *The Christian Science Monitor*, June 4, 1997.

up with a local music channel and in course of time, it acquired the local company in that region. For instance, in the early 2000s, MTVI entered the Australian market by setting up a joint venture between Austereo (a national commercial radio network in the country) and MTVN. Later on, it acquired Austereo to become MTV Australia.

Initially, some analysts were doubtful as to how far MTVN's global expansion would be successful, given the latent and overt anti-American sentiments in various parts of the world. However, the channel did not face too many difficulties. Commenting on this, Roedy said, "We've had very little resistance once we explain that we're not in the business of exporting American culture."[8] According to some analysts, Roedy was instrumental in taking MTVI across many countries worldwide. To gain an entry into difficult markets such as China, Israel, and Cuba, Roedy even met the political leaders of those countries to explain the network's initiatives to them.

Overall, despite the initial hiccups, the channel's global expansion strategy proved successful. Thus, by following a policy of having a global presence with a local outlook, by mid-2006, MTVI catered to an audience of more than 1 billion and expanded its presence in 179 countries across Europe, Asia, Latin America, and Australia.[9] It operated more than 130 channels in over 25 languages and it comprised MTV Networks Europe (MTVN Europe), MTV Networks Asia-Pacific (MTVN Asia-Pacific), and MTV Networks Latin America (MTVN Latin America). In addition to this, it operated some broadband services and more than 130 websites.[10]

According to analysts, a noteworthy reason behind MTV's global success was that the channel adopted a decentralized structure and gave commercial and creative autonomy to the local staff. This policy of minimal interference in local operations led to innovation and rapid expansion. Commenting on this, Roedy said, "Something we decided early on was to not export just one product for the world but to generate a very different experience for our brands depending on the local cultures."[11]

MTV's impressive growth globally contributed significantly to the revenues of its holding company Viacom over the years and it also became Viacom's core network. As of end 2007, MTVI had more than 140 channels around the world catering to a potential 1.5 billion viewers globally.[12] In the U.S. alone, it reached 87.6 million homes.[13] Its Emerging Markets group was the network's fastest growing business segment.[14] For the year

---

EXHIBIT II Selected Financials of Viacom

(US$, million)	2008	2007	2006
Revenues	14,625	13,423	11,361
Operating Income	2,523	2,936	2,767
Net Earnings	1,251	1,838	1,592
From Media Networks			
Revenue	8,756	8,101	7,241
Operating Income	2,729	3,048	2,904

Adapted from http://www.viacom.com/news/News_Docs/78157ACL.PDF

---

ending 2008, Viacom's total revenues (including cable network and entertainment divisions) were US$14,625 million. Out of this, the revenue from Media Network channels (which includes MTVN) was US$8,756 million (Refer to Exhibit II for selected financials of Viacom).

Preparing for the Launch

With the growing popularity of MTV, there was a mushrooming of many similar channels across the world. Though the Arab media was late in adopting this concept, some European and US channels had started offering such programs in this region, analysts pointed out. In the mid-1990s, some Arab music channels too entered the fray. Some of these channels were influenced by MTV. By the mid-2000s, there were a number of Arab music channels (Refer to Exhibit III for a note on major music channel in Saudi Arabia). These channels relied heavily on Arab artists but also aired international numbers by entering into agreements with production houses and other TV networks. MTV was available in the region through a special deal with Showtime Arabia.[15] As part of the deal, Showtime aired Nickelodeon and MTV in English with Arabic subtitles.[16] The channel catered to the middle and upper classes, who had been exposed to the West and had an interest in Western entertainment. Analysts felt that MTV was popular with a section of the audience in the region who were waiting eagerly for its launch there.

The first announcement that MTVI was preparing to launch MTV Arabia came in August 2006. During MTV's 25th anniversary of its first US channel, the company said that it was on the lookout for local partners in the Middle East and would provide the audience in the region content that would be very different from that offered by popular Arab music channels. Dean Possenniskie, Vice President and General Manager for Emerging Markets, MTVI, said, "[MTV is] very interested in the [Arab satellite channel] market and realizes how important it is . . . Hopefully [we] will be in the market in the next 24 months . . . it all depends on finding the right

---

[8] Kerry Capell, Catherine Belton, Tom Lowry, Manjeet Kripalani, Brian Bremner, and Dexter Roberts, "MTV's World," *BusinessWeek*, February 18, 2002.

[9] www.viacom.com/cable.jhtml.

[10] MTVI operated more than 130 websites of its international channels while MTVN, totally, operated more than 150 websites, which included online representations of channels broadcast in the US.

[11] Brad Nemer, "How MTV Channels Innovation," *BusinessWeek*, November 6, 2006.

[12] Tamara Walid, "Finally Got My MTV," www.arabianbusiness.com, November 22, 2007.

[13] "MTV to Launch Music TV Channels in Three Baltic States," www.eubusiness.com, March 6, 2006.

[14] "Arab Media Group and MTV Networks International to Launch Nickelodeon Arabia in 2008," www.media.ameinfo.com, October 20, 2007.

[15] Showtime Arabia is one of the leading subscription-based television networks in the Middle East. It is partly owned by Viacom.

[16] Zeid Nasser, "Showtime Braces for Impact of Free-to-air MTV Arabia & Arabic Nickelodeon," http://mediame.com, October 16, 2007.

EXHIBIT III   Music and Entertainment Channels in Saudi Arabia

As of early 2008, there are 370 Arabic satellite TV networks broadcasting in the Middle East. This is an increase of 270 percent since 2004.[17] Among these, 56 belong to private companies, 54 are music channels, and 38 are state owned. Most of these are headquartered in United Arab Emirates (22 percent), Saudi Arabia (15 percent), and Egypt (11 percent). In Saudi Arabia alone, there are more than 200 free-to-air satcasters and 50 music channels in the region. Some of the important music and entertainment channels are:

Mazzika, which offers a variety of music and light entertainment programs.

Melody Hits, which is a music channel airing Arabic and international music videos.

MBC, headquartered in Dubai, which is a pan-Arab news and entertainment television channel. MBC 2 is a non-stop premium movie channel. MBC 3 is a children's channel and it broadcasts famous animated kids' shows, including exclusive translated titles and live action and animated feature films. It also airs family shows and family movies for younger audiences as well as the adult audience. MBC 4 broadcasts specifically American programs.

Nojoom, which is a music channel airing Arabic and international music videos.

Rotana TV network, which broadcasts Arabic music and films. It has six channels under its wings—Mousica, Rotana Clip, Rotana Tarab, Rotana Khalijiyya, Rotana Cinema, and Rotana Zaman. The channels are dedicated to Arabic pop music, Arabic classical music, interactive games, Gulf music, cinema, featuring the biggest and latest blockbuster releases, and old classical movies.

Saudi Arabian TV, which features live coverage of Ramadan, Hajj, and Eid prayers. It also shows popular movies and news programs.

Shada channel—a part of the Al Majd Group—which is a channel totally devoted to Islamic songs (Anasheed).

Wanasah TV channel, which broadcasts music videos and some variety programs. All its programs are in Arabic.

Panorama FM, which is a music radio channel in Arabic.

Radio Rotana FM, which broadcasts customized programs and the latest Arabic hits fifteen days ahead of any of its competitors due to an exclusive deal with Rotana Music.

Radio Fann FM, which broadcasts a mix of the latest Arabic, English, and International music hits, along with hourly news broadcasts and various customized programs.

Al-Ikhbariya channel, which broadcasts news and current affairs.

* The list is not exhaustive

Compiled from various sources.

local partners."[18] By the end of the year, it was announced that MTVI would launch the channel in the region in partnership with Arabian Television Network (ATN), which was a part of the Arabian Broadcasting Network (ABN).[19]

MTVI's venturing into the Middle East was a result of the combined efforts of innovative and enthusiastic personalities such as Roedy, Bhavneet Singh,[20] Senior Vice President and Managing Director of MTVNI Emerging Markets group, and Abdullatif Al Sayegh, CEO and Chairman of ABN.

Analysts felt that it would have been very difficult for a western company like MTVI to venture into the highly regulated and complex business arena of the Middle East on its own. In this regard, Singh said, "A market such as the Middle East, however, also brings a level of complexity in the way business is done and regulatory challenges which mean it takes a western media company a long time to get its head around it."[21] Hence, it entered the Middle East by tying up with a local partner, the Arab Media Group (AMG), an established player in the Arab media industry with eight radio stations and three daily newspapers. The channel MTV Arabia was formed as a result of a licensing arrangement between MTV and AMG. MTV would earn an estimated US$10 million annually in licensing fees from AMG for 10 years.[22]

[17]"Arab Satellite TV channels Rapidly Expanding," www.xrdarabia.org, November 14, 2007.

[18] Faisal Abbas, "MTV Eyes Middle East Market," www.asharq-e.com, August 8, 2006.

[19] "Arabian Television Network Partners with MTV to Launch MTV Arabiya," http://mediame.com, December 27, 2006.

[20] On April 23, 2007, Bhavneet Singh was promoted to Senior Vice President and Managing Director of MTVNI's Emerging Markets group.

[21] Andrew Edgecliffe-Johnson, "MTV Tunes in to a Local Audience," www.us.ft.com, October 26, 2007.

[22] Sarah Raper Larenaudie, "MTV's Arab Prizefight," www.time.com, November 2, 2007.

On the other hand, an alliance with MTV was a winning deal for AMG too as it could access the former's world class resources to enhance its visibility in the Arab media as well as across the globe. "We found it very good to start our TV business with MTV Arabia because it's a great name to start with. Great team, great people; they provided us with a lot of resources. We believe that MTV is the beginning of a new era in television in this part of the world,"[23] said Sayegh.

However, the tie-up with a local partner was not enough to guarantee the success of MTV's launch in the Middle East given the conflict between the hip-hop explicit music culture portrayed by MTV and the conservative social culture prevalent in the Middle East. Hence, before launching the channel, Samaha conducted an extensive survey of the region to understand what people wanted. The survey team targeted people in the 18–24 age group and travelled around the region to schools and universities canvassing opinions. They also spoke to the elderly and figures of authority to assure them that they were there to entertain people within the limits of Arab traditions and had no intention of showing disrespect to the local culture. On this Samaha commented, "We also spoke to the governments, leaders, and parents and said, 'Don't worry, it will be nice,' so they know what's going on,"[24] said Samaha.

Accordingly, MTV Arabia's programming team decided to air MTVN's globally successful music shows but with a local flavor that would suit the Arab mindset and this laid the foundation for a planned launch of MTV in Arabia. The launch team comprised a mix of Saudis, Palestinians, Emiratis, Iraqis, and Lebanese.[25] "MTV first launched in 1981 when cable television was in its infancy. Since then we've grown into the world's largest TV network by becoming part of the fabric of youth culture, and by respecting audience diversity and different cultures. We're delighted to be launching MTV Arabiya and looking forward to working with our partners to provide the best youth programming,"[26] said Singh.

MTV commissioned ad agencies TBWA\Raad and Fortune Promoseven to handle the launch of the Channel in the Middle East.[27] "We're targeting normal Arabs. We're not targeting educated, private school people. Those are Arab society's niche. They are not more than 10 percent of the population. We are trying to appeal to the masses,"[28] said Samer Al Marzouqi, channel manager, MTV Arabia.

MTV Enters the Middle East

MTV Arabia was considered by experts as the biggest launch in MTVI's history in terms of potential audience at launch.[29] An exclusive, star-studded preview event marked the launch of MTV in the Middle East. The launch featured performances by eminent stars such as Akon, Ludacris, and Karl Wolf along with local hip hop group Desert Heat. The channel was formally launched on November 17, 2007, as a 24-hour, free-to-air television channel, having a target audience in Saudi Arabia, Egypt, United Arab Emirates, Lebanon, Bahrain, Jordan, Kuwait, Oman, Qatar, Yemen, Palestine, and Syria. MTVa.com, an Arabic and English language website, complemented the channel and provided users with a wide range of online community and interactive elements.

In line with its mixed-content strategy, MTV Arabia was to showcase 60 percent international music and 40 percent Arabic music, along with the local version of the channel's popular international non-music shows. About 45 percent of MTV Arabia's content was to be produced locally, with the rest translated. In this regard, Roedy commented, "The key is that the packaging, attitude, and obviously the language, should reflect the country. There is already great music there."[30] The channel's programming was to have a mix of music videos, music-based programming, general lifestyle and animated programs, reality shows, comedy and dramatic series, news specials, interviews, and documentaries. Besides international MTV shows, MTV Arabia was also to design new shows in Arabic to cater to pan-Arab youth audiences.

The company also said that the channel could act as a cultural unifying force in a region known for its political tensions. "The launch of MTV's 60th channel is a chance to correct misconceptions of the region . . . This part of the world has been associated with stresses and tensions . . . the one thing music can do is act as a unifying cultural force across regions,"[31] Roedy said.

Rationale Behind the Venture

Favorable demographics had been one of the key rationales behind MTV's commercial launch in the Middle East. About 65 percent of the Arab population consisted of youth under the age of 25, and the launch of MTV Arabia would provide MTV an opportunity to cater to a 190 million audience.[32] Further, though the Arab market was crowded with more than 50 channels, none of them provided a global platform to export the musical talent of the local youth. In this regard, Sayegh said, "Through our network, we now have more platforms to talk to our youth and in ways that have never been done before in the Middle East." Since young people "represent 65% of the population in the Middle East, it's time they were heard . . . Understanding the next generation is a key priority."[33] MTV being an international brand, had global reach and this became its key selling proposition for gaining critical mass in the Arab music world. Singh commented,

[23] Tamara Walid, "Finally Got my MTV," www.arabianbusiness.com, November 22, 2007.

[24] Matt Pomroy, "The Revolution Will be Televised," www.arabianbusiness.com, November 15, 2007.

[25] Sarah Raper Larenaudie, "MTV's Arab Prizefight," www.time.com, November 2, 2007.

[26] "Arabian Television Network Partners with MTV to Launch MTV Arabia," www.mediame.com, December 27, 2006.

[27] Iain Akerman, "MTV Hires Two Agencies for Launch of MTV Arabiya," www.brandrepublic.com, May 23, 2007.

[28] Dana El Baltaji, "I Want My MTV," www.arabmediasociety.com, May 2008.

[29] Irene Lew, "MTVNI Ups Singh," www.worldscreen.com, April 30, 2008.

[30] Lynne Roberts, "MTV Set for Middle East Launch," www.arabianbusiness.com, October 17, 2007.

[31] Simeon Kerr and Peter Aspden, "MTV Arabia Beams 'Bling' to Gulf," www.ft.com, November 17, 2007.

[32] "MTV Arabia to launch November 17," www.mediame.com, October 28, 2007.

[33] Ali Jaafar, "MTV Arabia Announces Lineup," www.variety.com, October 28, 2007.

"The fact that there has been no real youth platform, no real brand out there for the kids, makes us [feel] there is an opportunity for us."[34]

Moreover, the Middle East had the potential to offer MTV not only lucrative ad revenues but also numerous media like mobiles and the Internet to reach its end consumers. Singh said, "There are 37 million mobile subscribers in the wider Middle East, which is phenomenal and the average revenue per user is comparable to Western Europe. We believe that's where the future is—the ability to watch content wherever and however you want. We want to provide Middle East youth with the opportunity to watch MTV on mobile, on broadband, and on television. We're in discussions with mobile operators in the UAE, Kuwait, and Egypt, to look at how to distribute MTV content. There's been a huge amount of interest in that."[35] Products such as MTV Overdrive in which the user could download the video at broadband speed, and MTV Flux in which the online users could create their own TV channel were expected to help in luring the various Internet service providers in the region to MTV and to become major sources of its revenue.

The existence of various communication media with mass reach was expected to act as a catalyst in augmenting the channel's penetration rate in the Arabic region. In times to come if the channel validated its success in the Middle East, it would become a major revenue contributor to the MTV group.

Key Challenges and Success Strategy

MTV was known for airing sexually explicit and provocative programmes. In other words, it carried with it an image of open Western culture. This explicit Western culture projected by MTV went contrary to the socially conservative culture of the Middle East and could be a key bottleneck to the channel's acceptance in the Arab region, according to analysts. "As a brand, one would think that MTV is the ultimate example of what the religious, conservative cultures of the Middle East would most revile about Western pop culture,"[36] according to leading brand portal brandchannel.com. Adapting content to suit local tastes too could prove challenging because of many different countries comprising the region. What was acceptable in Dubai may not be acceptable in other parts of Saudi Arabia; what was acceptable in Egypt may not be acceptable in Jeddah (in Saudi Arabia). Analysts felt that the company also had to maintain what it stood for and too much localization could dilute its brand. And to complicate matters, there were strong anti-American sentiments prevalent among a large section of the population. Issues such as the US invasion of Iraq and its support to arch enemy Isreal had left many Arabs angry.

However the channel seemed well prepared to overcome such impediments to its growth plans in the Arab market. Though MTV Arabia would air its popular international programs, the network said that music videos and reality shows like "HIP Hop Na" and "Pimp my Ride" would be appropriately edited to ensure their alignment with the cultural ethos prevailing in the Middle East. Commenting on this, Sayegh said, "when we come to people's homes, we want to earn their respect."[37] He explained that there would be "culturally sensitive editors going through content of the programming."[38] In short, the channel expected to respect the local culture without diluting its brand. The channel aimed to prove that despite being a global brand, it would be a channel for the Arabs and made by Arabs—by people just like them.

Analysts said that MTVN's entry into the Middle East, which already had more than 50 local music channels operating, would be marked by stiff competition. In other words, unlike its past forays into India and Europe, MTV would not be entering a virgin music industry when it came to the Middle East. If on the one hand, the existence of a youth population was a business opportunity for MTVN, the same favorable demographic factor had also led to the explosion of dozens of local music channels which had a better understanding of the local audience's taste and could pose a formidable threat to MTVN's growth in the Middle East.

Also channels such as Rotana and Melody, which had already created a niche for themselves in the region, could pose a big competitive threat to MTVN. These channels had been functioning taking into account the tastes of the youth and had been able to attract a huge chunk of their target segment by offering creative concepts like games that allowed viewers to be part of the action from home along with interesting programs, music videos, and various artist albums and concerts. Moreover, some popular Arab music stars had already signed exclusive deals with some local channels. The challenge for MTV would be to not only find the right content but also ways to connect and captivate the Arabian youth, who were habituated to log on to any number of sites and enjoy music channel and videos according to their whims and fancies.

However, MTV Arabia was confident of scoring over its competitors and posting an impressive growth in the years to come. To overcome competition, the channel planned to project itself as unique and different from the existing lot. It proposed to establish itself as a platform wherefrom the Arab youth could voice their local concerns as well as advertise their music talent. For instance, MTV Arabia's flagship show "HIP Hop Na" would audition the best local hip-hop acts in seven different Middle Eastern cities. Thereafter, the winner from each city would get a chance to record a track for a compilation CD produced by Fred Wrecks.[39]

In a nutshell, MTV Arabia would not only provide entertainment but would also leverage on its global reach to advertise the musical talent of Arab youths. In this connection, Samaha said, "We are not only a music channel, we are an

[34] Von Andrew Edgecliffe Johnson, "MTV Tunes in to a Local Audience," www.ftd.de, October 26, 2007.

[35] "MTV Arabia to be Launched Soon," www.oceancreep.com, October 8, 2007.

[36] "Will the MTV Brand Change the Middle East?" www.brandchannel.com, December 3, 2007.

[37] "MTV Aims to Win over Middle East," www.cnn.com, November 19, 2007.

[38] "MTV Aims to Win over Middle East," www.cnn.com, November 19, 2007.

[39] Fred Wrecks is a Palestinian-born hip-hop producer who has worked under some of the eminent record label such as Dogghouse Records, Virgin Records, etc. He has also worked with many distinguished rap stars like 50 Cent and Snoop Dogg.

entertainment channel where young Arabs will get a voice."[40] He added, "MTV Arabia is a fresh take on MTV the brand, made by Arabs for Arab youth, and is dedicated to their self-expression. We've done extensive research to listen to our audiences, and MTV Arabia will be the first free-to-air channel to celebrate young people and their lives and talents from across this dynamic, vibrant region. We'll also offer audiences a window to the world of global youth culture, bringing top international entertainment to the region and showcasing the Arab region in the context of what's happening around the world. Through MTV's global network, we'll also be able to export Arabic music and culture to the international stage."[41]

Also, the programming line-up would feature more local content (Refer to Exhibit IV for a note on local production program to be aired on MTV Arabia) in comparison to other localized MTV ventures. There would be a localized version of popular shows such as "MADE" (al Helm) and "Boiling Point" (Akher Takka), which would constitute 40 percent of the content to be aired on MTV Arabia.

The company also said it did not expect anti-American sentiments to affect its chances in the region. MTV said that it expected to win over the target segment with content relevant to them. Moreover, it said that its research before the launch had shown that the majority of respondents thought that MTV was a European or Indian brand.[42]

The Road Ahead

MTVN catered to a huge market segment of nearly 2 billion people worldwide and was expected to provide a global platform for Arabic music and culture. It had influenced young people all over the world and given them a voice and it would try to do the same in the Middle East. An Arabic category was already added in MTV Europe Music Awards 2007, giving Arabic music the much needed global platform.

The MTV-AMG combine would not only provide entertainment to the region but would also take up social issues and try to contribute to Arab society, according to the network. In this regard, Sayegh commented, "We are going to encourage education and look for solutions to problems such as unemployment. These are all causes on our agenda."[43]

MTVN, along with AMG, planned to expand its operations in the Middle East. It had already announced the launch of Nickelodeon Arabia in 2008. It would be the first free-to-air channel for children in Arabic. Roedy commented, "Adding the voices of Arab children to our worldwide Nickelodeon family is a significant milestone in our history, and advances our ambitious strategy to build a portfolio of integrated kids businesses across the region. The Middle East is a dynamic, thriving market with vast growth opportunities, and we look forward to launching even more MTVNI brands and businesses through our successful partnership

EXHIBIT IV　Local Productions to be Aired on MTV Arabia

The flagship local show :

Hip Hop Na, a twelve-episode series which follows auditions to uncover the best local hip hop acts in four different Middle Eastern cities

Music Related Shows:

Waslati, viewers with webcams become VJs and introduce three of their favorite videos.

Baqbeeq is a music trivia show with a twist, where interesting and hilarious bits of trivia pop up through the most popular videos in the world.

Introducing Block goes behind the scenes in the music industry, with exclusive interviews and performances by the biggest international and Arab stars.

Other Programs:

Al Helm, based on MTV's *MADE* format, follows the journey of aspiring teenagers looking to fulfill their dreams with the help of an MTV Arabia-supplied "coach."

Al Hara tours the Middle East's street scene, and features previously unknown artists displaying innovative talent in skills like beat-boxing, break-dancing, or magic acts. The show is based on MTV's international program format, *Barrio 19*.

In *Akher Takka*, based on MTV's hit format, *Boiling Point*, actors antagonize stressed-out "victims" who can win a cash prize if they manage to keep their cool in extremely annoying situations.

Compiled from various sources.

[40] "MTV Looks to Conquer Middle East Market," www.aol.in, November 18, 2007.
[41] "MTV Arabia to Launch November 17," www.middleeastevents.com, October 27, 2007.
[42] Adam Sherwin, "MTV Arabia to Feature Regional Talent and Tone Down Network's Risque Content," www.business.timesonline.co.uk, November 16, 2007.
[43] Simeon Kerr and Peter Aspden, "MTV Arabia Beams 'Bling' to Gulf," www.ft.com, November 17, 2007.

with AMG."[44] Singh added, "The launch of Nickelodeon Arabia is a part of our wider, ongoing multi-platform strategy encompassing consumer products, digital media, hotels and theme parks, which we hope will establish Nickelodeon as the premier destination for kids in the region."[45]

Thus far, MTVN's model of entering a market in partnership with a local partner and following a localization strategy had worked well for the company. Analysts felt that only time would tell whether the company would succeed in the Middle East. But Singh had a rather philosophical take on what success meant. To him, the venture would be a success when people in the smallest cities of the Middle East came up to him and professed their love for MTV. "After all, it's not about how many eyeballs you reach, it's about how many people relate to you," he said.[46]

Case Questions

1. Experts felt that one of the biggest challenges faced by MTV while launching MTV Arabia was the prevalent culture in the Arab world. Discuss the Arab culture. How is it expected to pose a challenge to MTV?

2. Critically analyze MTV's strategy in the Middle East. Comment on its entry strategy and also its strategy of providing mixed content to the market. Do you think MTV will be able to succeed in this market?

References and Suggested Readings:

1. Dirk Smillie, "Tuning in First Global TV Generation," *The Christian Science Monitor*, June 4, 1997.
2. Kerry Capell, Catherine Belton, Tom Lowry, Manjeet Kripalani, Brian Bremner, and Dexter Roberts, "MTV's World," *BusinessWeek*, February 18, 2002.
3. "MTV to Launch Music TV Channels in Three Baltic States," www.eubusiness.com, March 6, 2006.
4. Faisal Abbas, "Q&A with Showtime Arabia's CEO Peter Einstein," www.asharq-e.com, June 29, 2006.
5. Faisal Abbas, "MTV Eyes Middle East Market," www.asharq-e.com, August 8, 2006.
6. Brad Nemer, "How MTV Channels Innovation," *BusinessWeek*, November 6, 2006.
7. "Arabian Television Network Partners with MTV to Launch MTV Arabiya," www.mediame.com, December 27, 2006.
8. Michael Learmonth, "MTV Maps Mideast Move," www.variety.com, December 27, 2006.
9. Iain Akerman, "MTV Hires Two Agencies for Launch of MTV Arabiya," www.brandrepublic.com, May 23, 2007.
10. Salman Dossari, "A Talk With MTV Vice Chairman Bill Roedy," www.asharq-e.com, July 23, 2007.
11. Ali Jaafar, "MTV Arabia Ready to Rock Middle East," www.variety.com, September 25, 2007.
12. "MTV Arabia to be Launched Soon," www.oceancreep.com, October 8, 2007.
13. Kerry Capell, "The Arab World Wants Its MTV," www.businessweek.com, October 11, 2007.
14. Lynne Roberts, "MTV Set for Middle East launch," www.arabianbusiness.com, October 17, 2007.
15. Stuart Kemp, "MTV, Arab Media to Launch Nickelodeon Arabia," www.hollywoodreporter.com, October 17, 2007.
16. Andrew Edgecliffe Johnson, "MTV Targets Muslim Countries as it Tunes in to Local Audiences," www.theaustralian.news.com, October 18, 2007.
17. "Arab Media Group and MTV Networks International to Launch Nickelodeon Arabia in 2008," www.ameinfo.com, October 20, 2007.
18. Von Andrew Edgecliffe Johnson, "MTV Tunes in to a Local Audience," www.ftd.de, October 26, 2007,
19. "MTV Arabia to Launch November 17," www.middleeastevents.com, October 27, 2007.
20. Ali Jaafar, "MTV Arabia Announces Lineup," www.variety.com, October 28, 2007.
21. "MTV Arabia to Launch November 17," www.mediame.com, October 28, 2007.
22. Irene Lew, "MTV Arabia to Launch in November," www.worldscreen.com, October 29, 2007.
23. Sarah Raper Larenaudie, "MTV's Arab Prizefight," www.time.com, November 2, 2007.
24. Jolanta Chudy, "MTV's Arab Net Thinking Locally," www.hollywoodreporter.com, November 6, 2007.
25. Matt Pomroy, "The Revolution Will be Televised," www.arabianbusiness.com, November 15, 2007.
26. "Akon and Ludacris Dazzle The Desert in their Middle East Debuts to Celebrate the Launch of MTV Arabia," www.dubaicityguide.com, November 16, 2007.
27. Adam Sherwin, "MTV Arabia to Feature Regional Talent and Tone Down Network's Risque Content," www.timesonline.co.uk, November 16, 2007.
28. Simeon Kerr and Peter Aspden, "MTV Arabia Beams 'Bling' to Gulf," www.ft.com, November 17, 2007.
29. "MTV Launches New Arabic Service," www.news.bbc.co.uk, November 18, 2007.
30. "MTV Looks to Conquer Middle East Market," www.aol.in, November 18, 2007.
31. ""MTV Arabia": Will It Work?" www.scopical.com, November 19, 2007.
32. "MTV Aims to Win over Middle East," www.cnn.com, November 19, 2007.

---

[44] "Arab Media Group and MTV Networks International to Launch Nickelodeon Arabia in 2008," www.ameinfo.com, October 20, 2007.
[45] Stuart Kemp, "MTV, Arab Media to Launch Nickelodeon Arabia," www.hollywoodreporter.com, October 17, 2007.
[46] Tamara Walid, "Finally Got My MTV," www.arabianbusiness.com, November 22, 2007.

33. "Muslim Hip-hop Turban Wrote, That's Good," www.reuters. donga.com, November 19, 2007.

34. Barbara Surk, "MTV for Young Arab is Less Naughty," www. cincinnati.com, November 21, 2007.

35. Barbara Surk, "MTV Launches Arab Music Video Channel," www.theeagle.com, November 22, 2007.

36. Tamara Walid, "Finally Got My MTV," www.arabianbusiness. com, November 22, 2007.

37. "Will the MTV Brand Change the Middle East?" www. brandchannel.com, December 2, 2007.

38. Irene Lew, "MTVNI Ups Singh," www.worldscreen.com, April 30, 2008.

39. Dana El Baltaji, "I Want My MTV," www.arabmediasociety.com, May 11, 2008.

40. www.topfive.com

41. www.en.wikipedia.org

42. www.mtva.com

43. www.viacom.com

CASE 5   GOOGLE'S COUNTRY EXPERIENCES: FRANCE, GERMANY, JAPAN

"We must take up the global challenge of the American giants Yahoo! and Google." "Culture is not merchandise and cannot be left to blind market forces." "We must staunchly defend the world's cultural diversity against the looming threat of uniformity."[1]

–JACQUES CHIRAC,
French President

"Search engine users aren't terribly loyal, so a better or more targeted technology could make headway."[2]

– CHARLENE LI,
*Analyst at Forrester Research Inc., a technology
and market research company*

"It would be interesting to see if we're about to have a trade war emerge in the search space over government backing, similar to the arguments that are made about government support given to aircraft makers Airbus in Europe and Boeing in the US."[3]

– DANNY SULLIVAN,
*Editor, Search Engine Watch, a site providing
analysis of the search engine industry*

Google Inc.—founded in September 1998 by Stanford graduates Sergey Brin and Larry Page—by June 2000, became the world's largest search engine with its introduction of a billion-page index.[4] Web search was increasingly used as a way to find products and services. In August 2007 alone, there were more than 61 billion individual searches worldwide. Google, based in the US, became widely popular because it could provide simple, fast and relevant search results. It used PageRank technology to display results by not only looking for keywords inside web pages, but also gauging the importance of a search result based on the number and popularity of other sites that linked to the page. The search results were algorithmically determined, with no hand-editing of the results. Over the years, Google perfected its technology to display results that were more accurate and relevant. Google did not follow the practice of paid inclusion, i.e., one could not buy their way into the search results. Paid results were shown outside regular search results.

Google's business was split between advertising on its website and selling its technology to other sites. Its business model (Exhibit I) of AdWords allowed companies to purchase keywords for advertising purposes. An Internet user searching on that keyword would get the organic (unsponsored) results as well as the advertisements (sponsored links).

Google's advertising revenues rose steadily and stood at $21.1 billion in 2008 (Exhibit II).

A key component in Google's strategy was to expand its reach into new international markets. By 2000, Google users could search for content in 10 different languages. Google's new search index released in 2000 included a large collection of international websites signifying Google's plans to expand into new international markets. Google saw its revenues going up, more from its international forays (Exhibit III).

By 2007, Internet users could use the Google search interface in almost 120 languages and it was available in almost 160 local domains.[5] For a query, originating outside the US, the location of the surfer would be determined and google.com would automatically assume the local domain. Messages in the local language and custom-tailored results for that location were shown. For instance, if a user in the UK made a Google search, the results would be served up by google.co.uk.

As the Internet grew bigger, Google got better. It launched its IPO in 2004, with an offer price of $85 that rose to $670 by November 2007, giving it a market capitalisation of $211.70 billion.[6] In a survey released by comScore Inc., a global Internet information provider, Google sites ranked as the top worldwide search property in August 2007 with 37.1 billion searches.[7] Apart from search, Google expanded its portfolio by introducing an array of new software and added services. It sought ways to import offline media, such as books and television shows, into its search engine. Through 2001 to July 2007,

---

This case was written by Shanul Jain, under the direction of R. Muthukumar, Icfai Business School Case Development Centre. It is intended to be used as the basis for class discussion rather than to illustrate either effective or ineffective handling of a management situation. This case was compiled from published sources.

[1] "Attack of the Eurogoogle", http://www.economist.com/research/articles BySubject/displaystory.cfm?subjectid= 10009611&story_id=E1_VVSTQJG, March 19th 2006

[2] Regan Keith, "Japanese Government May start Rival Search Engine", http://www.ecommercetimes.com/story/AUhp9eKd2SP8AX/Japanese-Government-May-Start-Rival-Search- Engine.xhtml, December 20th 2005

[3] Ibid.

[4] "Google Milestones", http://www.google.com/corporate/history.html

[5] "Language Tools", http://www.google.com/language_tools?hl=EN, 2007

[6] "61 billion searches conducted worldwide in August", http://www.comscore .com/press/release.asp?press=1802, October 10th 2007

[7] "Google Inc.", http://finance.google.com/finance?q=GOOG

EXHIBIT I How Google Earns its Revenues

> Google's original business model was licensing its search engine services to other websites. In the first quarter of 2000, it introduced its first advertising programme— premium sponsorships. Through its direct sales force, it offered advertisers the ability to place text-based ads on its websites targeted to the user's search queries. Advertisers paid based on the number of times their ads were displayed on search results pages. It launched AdWords in the fourth quarter of 2000 that enabled advertisers to place targeted text-based ads on Google's sites. Here advertisers paid on a Cost-Per-Click basis—only when a user clicked on one of its ads. In the first quarter of 2002, Google released its AdSense service that distributed relevant ads from advertisers, for display with search results on the Google Network members' sites, which was a large group of websites and other products such as e-mail programs and blogs, who had partnered with Google to display AdWords ads.

Compiled by the author

EXHIBIT II Select Google Financials ($ million)

Year	Revenues	Net Income	Advertising Revenues	Spend on R&D
2008	21,795.5	4,226.8	21,128.5	2,793.2
2007	16,593.9	4,203.7	16,412.6	2,119.9
2006	10,604.9	3,077.4	10,492.6	1,228.6
2005	6,138.6	1,465.4	6,065.0	599.5
2004	3,189.2	399.1	3,143.3	395.2
2003	1,465.9	105.6	1,420.7	229.6
2002	439.5	99.7	410.9	40.5
2001	86.4	7.0	Not Available	16.5

Compiled by the author from "Financial Tables", http://investor.google.com/fin_data.html

EXHIBIT III Google Quarterly Revenues ($ billion)

Year	Q1	IR*	Q2	IR	Q3	IR	Q4	IR
2008	5.18	51%	5.36	52%	5.54	51%	5.70	50%
2007	3.66	47%	3.87	48%	4.23	48%	4.82	48%
2006	2.25	42%	2.46	42%	2.69	44%	3.21	44%
2005	1.26	39%	1.38	39%	1.58	39%	1.92	38%
2004	N/A	N/A	N/A	N/A	0.8058	N/A	1.032	N/A

*IR: International Revenues, i.e., the % of revenues from outside the US
N/A: Not Available
Compiled by the author from "Financial Tables", http://investor.google.com/fin_data.html

the company made about 44 acquisitions, including the video sharing service YouTube and online advertising company DoubleClick.[8] Google's rapid rise and its dominance in search and other web areas, prompted concerns in a number of countries. The nature of Google's services and its AdWords programme saw Google defending itself in a number of lawsuits against it for copyright infringement.

Action against Google was sparked by fear of US dominance over the local cultures, to the kind of information that Google provided. There were demands that Google censor its search results according to government regulations. Google, for instance, in France and Germany, removed links to pro-Nazi, anti-semitic and other controversial sites. Its AdWords model attracted a number of lawsuits. More and more companies sought control over their brand names and trademarked search in paid terms.

Google France

Europe was a surging market for Internet advertising and Google's multi-language search service, started in 2000, included the French and German versions. The same year, Google launched a webpage with a French domain name—

---

[8] "Google acquisitions by year, 2001–2007", http://mashable.com/2007/07/03/google-acquisitions/, July 3rd 2007

google.fr. Given its rapid growth in the country, it opened its sales office in 2002 to facilitate a direct point of contact to the French businesses and incorporate targeting by language, by country, and by keyword in its advertising programmes. Google soon became the dominant search engine in France and offered services in regional French dialects like Breton, Basque and Corsican.

However, Europe's patchwork of languages and cultures was seen as an advantage by companies, seeking to break into the search market to compete with Google, by entertaining demand for locally focused search. Nate Elliott, an analyst for JupiterResearch, remarked, "Europe's diversity can play toward exploiting niches."[9] Aiming for this niche were search engines like Paris-based Exalead and international media groups like Oslo-based Schibsted, that saw Google as the prime competitor in the media industry. To challenge Google, the French and German governments reacted with plans to develop their country-specific search engines.

To many French companies, Google's business model of displaying sponsored links amounted to trademark counterfeiting. Numerous advertisers sued Google and the French courts ruled mostly in favour of copyright holders. The court ruling called into question the legality of the search system. It stated that Google should "find the means to block advertisements by third parties who have no right to these trademarks."[10] Google paid €75,000 in damages and costs to Luteciel and Viaticum, two French travel companies. Louis Vuitton, French luxury goods maker, too filed a suit for trademark infringement, saying that handbag producers could pay to ensure that their ads would pop up when someone googled for Louis Vuitton. A court ruling ordered Google to cease the practice and pay fines. In another ruling, Google was ordered to stop linking ads to the trademarks of European resort chain Le Meridien Hotels and Resorts. Even the French news service, Agence France-Presse (AFP) alleged that Google had stolen its copyrighted material by including it on the Google News website. Similar lawsuits against Google in US had either been dismissed or gone in Google's favour. Google spokeswoman Myriam Boublil said, "French law is just very protective of trademarks."[11]

There was further uproar when Google announced its plans to digitise books and documents, from a handful of US and British university libraries. Google would spend between $150 million and $200 million over a decade to digitise collections of Harvard, Stanford, the University of Michigan, the New York Public Library and Oxford University. This caused alarm, as it was felt that the initiative—rather than democratising knowledge—would further strengthen US power to set a global cultural agenda. Of the Google-Print (renamed Google Book Search) project, the French chief librarian Jean-Noël Jeanneney said, "The libraries that are taking part in this enterprise are of course themselves generously open to the civilisations and works of other countries, but still, their criteria for selection

will be profoundly marked by the Anglo-Saxon outlook."[12] In response, in March 2005, the French president Jacques Chirac announced that the country would start its own digital-book project. The culture minister, Renaud Donnedieu de Vabres and Jeanneney were asked to digitise French texts. Even Google's criterion to rank results was condemned. "I do not believe that the only key to access our culture should be the automatic ranking by popularity, which has been behind Google's success,"[13] stated de Vabres. Jeanneney believed that Europe should not only convert its books into digital files, but should also control the page rankings of responses to searches, "European ranking should reflect a European vision of history and culture."[14] The question was how to manage the digitised knowledge? For this, Europe could either have its own search engine or reach an agreement with Google or other Internet search providers.

In April 2005, President Chirac and the German chancellor Gerhard Schröder endorsed a plan to build a Franco-German multimedia search engine—*Quaero*, meaning, "I seek" in Latin. The project was a public-private consortium including among others Thomson and France Telecom in France, Siemens and Deutsche Telekom in Germany— with the government as the main financier and developer of the search engine. The Agency for Industrial Innovation (AII) was created in Paris to oversee the project. AII got an initial endowment of €1.7 billion ($2 billion), to be spent on *Quaero* and other centrally directed high-tech initiatives. Out of this, €250 million ($294 million) would go for *Quaero*.

Quaero would be superior to existing search engine technology. Search engines displayed results by matching the user's keywords with the text, image, audio and video files. *Quaero* would enable keywords search in the usual way, but would also allow users to query using pictures and sounds. The process was 'image mining', where the software would recognise shapes and colours and then retrieve still images and video clips quite similar to the query image. Researchers at the University of Karlsruhe, Germany would develop voice recognition and translation technology. The software would find audio files, automatically transcribe and translate them into a number of European languages. In short, it would offer multimedia search features. Marie-Vincente Pasdeloup of Thomson remarked, "It's beyond Google."[15]

The European Union however had to rule whether the money earmarked for the project amounted to unfair subsidy— something stringently forbidden by European law. Observers stated *Quaero*'s main aims as being cultural and political, rather than commercial. Alexander Waibel, a member of *Quaero*'s steering committee, said, "Europe wants to secure access that does not have to be channelled through American technology."[16]

[9] Crampton Thomas, "European search engines take on Google", http://www.iht.com/articles/2006/12/17/business/search.php, December 17th 2006

[10] "Handbag maker Vuitton sues Google", http://edition.cnn.com/2003/TECH/biztech/10/24/france.google.ap/, October 24th 2003

[11] Lamb Scott, "What does France have against Google?", http://journalism.nyu.edu/portfolio/bestof/2005/001617.html

[12] "Why Google Scares Jacques Chirac", http://www.expatica.com/actual/article.asp?subchannel_id=58&story_id=18407, March 2005

[13] "Google à la française", http://www.economist.com/research/articles By Subject/displaystory.cfm?subjectid=10009611&story_id=E1_PRTJTGJ, March 31st 2005

[14] Riding Alan, "Entr'acte: A French call to arms over Google challenge", http://www.iht.com/articles/2005/03/30/news/entracte.php, March 31st 2005

[15] "Attack of the Eurogoogle", op.cit.

[16] Ibid.

Hal Varian, an Internet economics specialist at the University of California at Berkley, opined that the European desire for "search parity" was understandable and that "it was not so long ago that the US was paranoid about Japanese super-computer initiatives for pretty much the same reason: control of a critical piece of infrastructure."[17]

The *Quaero* alliance included companies like Exalead, for search technology; France Telecom, for communications; Jouve, for scanning and other digital publishing expertise and Thompson, for information technology. Alongside, there would be German counterparts including Deutsche Telekom and the publishing giant, Bertelsmann. The French side would look at the image search research and Germany at the voice clip and sound media searches and the subsequent translation into text and other languages.

Google Germany

In 2000, Google launched the google.de domain. In Germany, Google's free e-mail (Gmail) came under the court scanner. Daniel Giersch, a German-born venture capitalist, insisted that Google had infringed on his trademark registration of Gmail, the name by which his electronic postal delivery service went. He remarked, "Google's behaviour is very threatening, very aggressive and very unfaithful, and to me, it's very evil."[18] Google lost the courtroom battle and was asked to remove all 'Gmail' references from its German service and cease handing out gmail.com aliases to users within the geographic area. Google stopped the use of Gmail in Germany and instead adopted google mail.

In 2006, Angela Merkel took over from Schröder as the new German chancellor. Under the new government, the Germans did not officially commit to the *Quaero* project. In January 2007, Germany pulled out to set up its alternative development project—*Theseus*—named after a legendary Greek hero who found his way out of a labyrinth inhabited by a monster. Hendrik Luchtmeier, a spokesman for Germany's Economics Ministry, said, "We will still see cooperation, but in another form, such as work groups. The consortium between the German and French governments is over."[19]

This decision underscored the difficulty of cross-border projects, mostly because of the personal differences between project managers. Some argued that the Germans were fed up with the French need to develop a Google killer. Francois Bourdoncle, a French participant in the project, remarked, "The truth is that the German and French projects were only remotely connected. We wanted to develop multimedia search and the Germans wanted to develop text search. Part of the problem is talk of a European challenge to Google exaggerated expectations."[20]

The European Union gave Germany the go-ahead to spend €120 million ($167 million) on *Theseus*. An additional

€90 million would be chipped in, by the companies and institutes involved in the research. There were in all 22 partner organisations, companies and universities—including SAP, Siemens and Deutsche Thompson. The German Economic Minister Michael Glos opined, "With Theseus we want to improve Germany and Europe's ability to compete and reach a top position in IT and communication technology."[21]

Google Japan

Along with Europe, the Asia-Pacific was another important region on Google's global expansion list and it built additional search services for Asian character-based languages like Japanese, Korean and Chinese. Google's Japanese subsidiary, established in 2002, was its fourth business venture outside the US. Considering the significance of overseas markets to its revenues, Google opened an R&D centre in Tokyo in 2004, the third such one outside the US. It was meant to blend Japan's advanced technology in broadband and mobile phone services, into Google's corporate activities.

In 2005, Japan's Ministry of Economy, Trade and Industry organised a study group consisting of about 20 Japanese electronics companies and universities. The group was to consider the merits of creating a search tool specifically for the Japanese users. Fumihiro Kajikawa, a Ministry Official, said, "The group will look into issues including whether Japan will start its own search engine."[22] The government would spend up to $885 million on the plan. The search engine technology would be developed to compete with search companies like AJ Japan, Google Japan, Yahoo Japan and others. The trigger for a Japanese project came from concerns that the country's pre-eminence in consumer electronics had faded and value in the technology industry was moving away from hardware. There were fears that the country's manufacturers were falling behind in innovation. The government wanted a Japan-centric search engine that would likely wrest back some of the domestic market share and advertising revenue that the large search firms were getting.

In 2007, Japan launched its project to counter Google's and Yahoo!'s dominance of searching. The state-led project comprised 10 partnerships, each tasked with a specific next-generation search function. The country hoped to use its strength in developing devices such as mobile phones and car navigation systems, to create proprietary search and information retrieval functions. As a part of the initiative in '2008 information Grand Voyage Project'[23]

'Laddering search service' was included. Toshihide Yahiro, director of the information service industry division at the Ministry of Trade, said, "The key to Japan's competitiveness has been our core technology but we need to create a new value-added service that is personalised."[24]

[17] Ross E. Philip, "Loser: What's the Latin for 'Delusional'?", http://sepctrum.ieee.org/print/4842
[18] Broache Anne, "Behind Google's German courtroom battle", http://news.zdnet.com/2100-9588_22-6115056.html, September 14th 2006
[19] Spongenberg Helena, "Germany Quits Quaero Web Search Project", http://www.businessweek.com/globalbiz/content/jan2007/gb20070104_427008.htm?chan=search, January 4th 2007
[20] Ibid.
[21] "Germany to fund rival to Google search engine", http://www.dw-world.de/dw/article/0,2144,2698176,00.html, July 20th 2007
[22] Wearden Graeme, "Japan may create its own search engine", http://www.sakshay.in/news/technologynews4.html, December 21st 2005
[23] It enables users to find what they are looking for on the web through dialogues with a computer. It was jointly developed by OKi Electric Industry Co. and Recruit Co., Ltd.
[24] Sanchanta Mariko and Waters Richard, "Japan to fight Google search dominance", http://www.ft.com/cms/s/0/b3046d5c-5b1d-11dc-8c32-0000779fd2ac.html, September 4th 2007

Google: Understanding the Competition

All these countries stressed on search not only because it was crucial, but also they were wary of US dominance in information business. Google on its part focused on strengthening its R&D efforts in Europe. In January 2007, it opened another R&D centre in Poland. It also worked to bolster its presence in Japan. It considered the possibility of partnering with Japan's largest mobile carrier, NTT DoCoMo, to provide search and e-mail services to mobile handsets. Google's market share in 2007 reached 85.8% and 88.5% of the French and German markets (Exhibit IV); whereas the government search engines are yet to be rolled out. Can these search engines, backed by the national governments, overhaul Google? Will Google's country experiences question the exportability of its business model?

Google, as it expands to emerging economies in the Asia-Pacific, has to tackle competition from the local search engines. China, with one of the highest and fastest growing Internet population, is an attractive and important market for all search companies, but there, Google has a tough contender in the local search engine, Baidu. China's cultural differences could also question Google's ability to serve overseas markets. In its international growth, Google is in the unenviable position of deciding who poses a bigger threat to its dominance—the international search companies as Yahoo! and Microsoft, the local search engines as Baidu or the unfinished government-backed country search engines.

EXHIBIT IV   Search Engine Market Share (%): July 2007 and July 2008

Year		US	France	Germany	Japan
2008	Google	61.9	–	79.8	39.0[**]
	Yahoo!	20.5	–	0.9	51.2[**]
2007	Google	55.2	85.8	88.5[*]	35.0
	Yahoo!	23.5	3.8	3.4[*]	47.4

[*] German Market Share figures are for August 2007 and [**] Japanese Market Share figures are for September 2008

Compiled by the author from comScore Inc. press releases

Assignment Questions

1. How does a search engine work and make money? What is the exportability of a search engine's technology and business model?
2. Why did many governments appear threatened by Google? How did they counter this threat? Discuss each country separately

3. Is the threat, from the government-sponsored search engines, real or imagined? What can Google do to secure its dominance in those countries? What can Google learn from those experiences to guide its entry strategy for other countries?

Formulating and Implementing Strategy for International and Global Operations

Formulating Strategy

Outline

OBJECTIVES

1. To understand why companies engage in international business.

2. To learn the steps in global strategic planning and the models available to direct the analysis and decision-making involved.

3. To appreciate the techniques of environmental assessment, internal and competitive analysis, and how those results can be used to judge the relative opportunities and threats to be considered in international strategic plans.

4. To profile the types of strategies available to international managers – both on a global level and on the level of specific entry strategies for different markets.

5. To gain insight into the issues managers face when strategic planning for the EU market.

Opening Profile: Global Companies Take Advantage of Opportunities in South Africa

Global companies with a presence in South Africa all cite numerous advantages for setting up shop in the country, from low labor costs to excellent infrastructure—and a base to export products internationally. Jim Myers, president of the American Chamber of Commerce in South Africa, says that nearly 50% of the chamber's members are Fortune 500 companies, and that over 90% operate beyond South Africa's borders into southern Africa, sub-Saharan Africa and across the continent. "The sophisticated business environment of South Africa provides a powerful strategic export and manufacturing platform for achieving global competitive advantage, cost reductions and new market access," says Myers.[1]

Businesses are taking advantage of opportunities because of the legal protection of property, labor productivity, low tax rates, reasonable regulation, a low level of corruption and good access to credit, which were seen as factors contributing to the country's investment climate. Threats include the low level of skills and education of workers, labor regulation, exchange rate instability, and crime. Nevertheless, the business environment is favorable.

Following are some examples of the many global companies taking advantage of the opportunities and incentives in South Africa.[2] In addition, The 2010 Fifa World Cup was expected to present huge opportunities for businesses, especially emerging entrepreneurs, in South Africa's tourism industry.

Acer Africa

In 1995, Acer Africa acquired ownership of a locally based company they had been working with to distribute peripherals and printers since 1980.

A leading international PC manufacturer and vendor, Acer recognised the wealth of opportunities in South Africa as local IT companies rapidly came abreast of world standards following the country's first democratic elections in 1994.

For Acer, South Africa's modern banking and telephone systems and exceptional water and power rates made the country a sound business location.

Acer Africa was established as a base to export to the Southern African Development Community (SADC), Angola and the islands along the Indian Ocean.

"South Africa is the only port of entry to Africa, the only place that one would be able to succeed . . . " —*Peter Ibbotson (Acer Africa)*

Alcatel

"Alcatel has built its worldwide reputation on its production. Investing with local partners [electronics group Altech and black empowerment company Rethabile] in South Africa has meant that we have

MAP 6-1 South Africa has a population of 43.1 million and consists of 1,221,037 sq km.

MAP 6-2   Africa

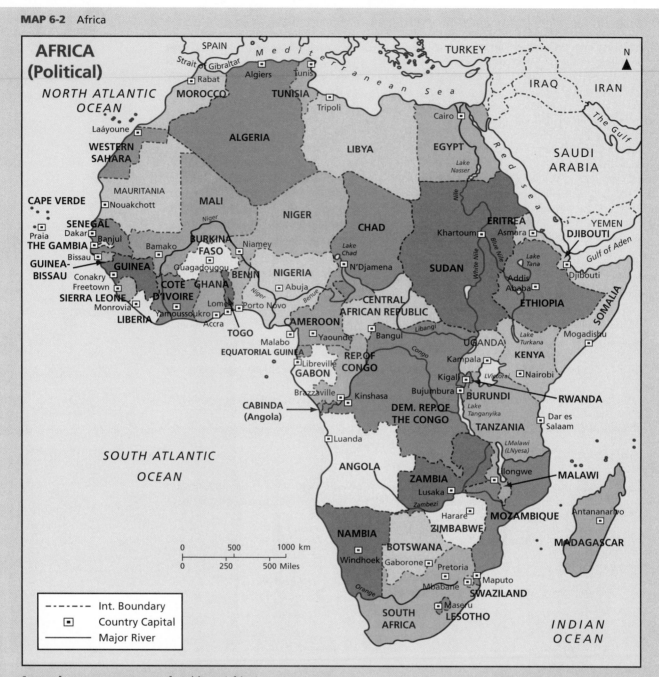

Source for maps: www.mapsofworld.com/africa/

demanded a high standard of technology and capability, and believe that in many respects South Africa compares very favourably with the most advanced countries in the world." —*Bernard Vaslin, executive vice president, Alcatel*

General Electric

"The re-entry of General Electric (USA) to the South and southern African market has been exciting and has well exceeded our operating plan expectations.

"South Africa's excellent infrastructure, together with first-class financial, legal and commercial systems, makes this country a natural location to pursue the significant opportunities of South and southern Africa.

"The friendly business environment ensures that we can run our business efficiently, and we look forward to successful and profitable operations in southern Africa that meet our global goals and create wealth for the GE shareholder." —*GE South Africa president Michael C Hendry*

Source: www.southafrica.info, accessed February 15, 2009, used with permission.

As the opening profile on South Africa illustrates, companies continue to look for opportunities around the world in search of profitable new markets, outsourcing facilities, acquisitions, and alliances—and this search is increasingly directed at emerging markets. Foreign Direct Investment (FDI) from OECD countries jumped 50% in 2007—a record U.S.$1.82 trillion, but have fallen sharply since as a result of the global economic slowdown.[3]

Indeed, as of this book going to press, companies across the board were retrenching rather than expanding in order to conserve cash flow in the economic slowdown. *Business Week* reported in February 2009, that "Companies are swinging hard—chopping jobs, slashing spending, and reducing inventory . . . as they head into 2009 in all-out retrenchment mode."[4] In fact, on April 27, 2009, under government pressure to downsize in order to justify government aid, General Motors (GM) announced that it would eliminate another 21,000 factory jobs, close 13 plants, cut its vast network of 6,500 dealers almost in half, and shutter its Pontiac division. As a result of the downsizing, GM expects to have only 38,000 union workers and 34 factories left in the United States, compared with 395,000 workers in more than 150 plants at its peak employment in 1970.[5] Thus, while much of the focus in this chapter is on "going international" and expansion abroad, we need to keep in mind that retrenchment is also a very real strategy, especially in difficult economic times such as this. And, for GM, the unwilling strategy now includes partial nationalization. The result of GM's retrenchment has a global impact; the company is closing factories abroad, and its many foreign parts suppliers will be drastically affected, if not put out of business.

However, the overall increases in FDI in the last few years do not tell the whole story as far as global competition is concerned. After the Boston Consulting Group identified 100 emerging-market companies that they felt have the potential to reach the top rank of global corporations in their industries, *Business Week* challenged that:

> *Multinationals from China, India, Brazil, Russia, and even Egypt are coming on strong. They're hungry—and want your customers. They're changing the global game.*[6]

Management consultant Ram Charan advises that we are now truly in a global game, one that he calls a "seismic change" to the competitive landscape brought about by globalization and the Internet. This first wave of emerging-nation players, he says, are taking advantage of three forces spurred on by the Internet—mobility of talent, mobility of capital, and mobility of knowledge. The strategies of companies such as America Movil of Mexico, China Mobile, Petrobras of Brazil, and Mahindra and Mahindra of India (which is penetrating Deere's market on its own U.S. turf) are to use their bases in their emerging markets—from which they have had to eke out meager profits—as "springboards to build global empires."[7] Add these new challengers to the already hyper-competitive arena of global players, and it is clear that managers need to pay close and constant attention to strategic planning. *Business Week* gives an example of two global companies:

> *Which company is more "American"—Mumbai-based Tata Consultancy Services (TCS), or Armonk (New York)-based IBM? Evaluate the two based on where they make their sales, and the answer is surprising. TCS, India's largest tech-services company, collected 51 percent of its revenues in North America the first quarter of 2008, while 65 percent of IBM's were overseas.*
>
> BUSINESS WEEK,
> *April 23, 2008.*[8]

As it will be explained in this chapter, however, corporate strategies must change in response to shifting global economic conditions and other environmental and competitive factors. With the recession deepening in the U.S. and Europe, TCS must consider how it will respond, but it is strengthened by its geographic diversification. IBM, meanwhile, now making about half its revenues in its services business, in particular in emerging markets, has diversified with a two-track approach. The company is helping clients in the U.S. to cut costs, and in emerging markets, it helps customers develop their technology infrastructure.[9] These are examples of corporate strategies that are being developed to respond to or anticipate current global trends, as noted by Beinhocker et al. of McKinsey & Company and discussed in various chapters throughout this book. They note that:

> *Companies' strategic behavior should be tied closely to ten important trends: strains on natural resources, a damper on globalization, the loss of trust in business, the growing role of government, investment in quantitative decision tools, shifting patterns of global consumption, the economic rise of Asia, industry structure upheaval, technological innovation, and price instability.*[10]

HARVARD BUSINESS REVIEW,
July/August, 2009.

Because international opportunities are far more complex than those in domestic markets, managers must plan carefully—that is, strategically—to benefit from them. Many experienced managers are wary about expanding into politically risky areas or those countries where they find government practices to be prohibitive. This wariness was noted by the OED in June 2006, when they warned for the first time "that investment and growth were threatened by 'knee-jerk' reactions against takeovers, based on national security concerns and a sense that not all countries and their companies played by the same rules."[11]

The process by which a firm's managers evaluate the future prospects of the firm and decide on appropriate strategies to achieve long-term objectives is called **strategic planning.** The basic means by which the company competes—its choice of business or businesses in which to operate and the ways in which it differentiates itself from its competitors—is its **strategy.** Almost all successful companies engage in long-range strategic planning, and those with a global orientation position themselves to take full advantage of worldwide trends and opportunities. Multinational corporations (MNCs), in particular, report that strategic planning is essential to contend with increasing global competition and to coordinate their far-flung operations.

In reality, however, that rational strategic planning is often tempered, or changed at some point, by a more incremental, sometimes messy, process of strategic decision making by some managers. When a new CEO is hired, for example, he or she will often call for a radical change in strategy. That is why new leaders are carefully chosen, on the basis of what they are expected to do. So, although the rational strategic planning process is presented in this text because it is usually the ideal, inclusive method of determining long-term plans, managers must remember that people are making decisions, and their own personal judgments, experiences, and motivations will shape the ultimate strategic direction.

REASONS FOR GOING INTERNATIONAL

Companies of all sizes "go international" for different reasons, some reactive (or defensive) and some proactive (or aggressive). The threat of their own decreased competitiveness is the overriding reason many large companies adopt an aggressive global strategy. To remain competitive, these companies want to move fast to build strong positions in key world markets with products tailored to the common needs of customers in Europe, Latin America, and Asia. Building on their past success, companies such as IBM and Digital Equipment are plowing profits back into operations overseas. Europe is now attracting much new investment capital because of both the European Union (EU) and the opening of extensive new markets in Eastern Europe. Indeed, AOL Europe was launched as a counterpoint to AOL's declining business in the United States. The company lobbied hard to establish rules guaranteeing AOL Europe equal access to telecommunications networks.[12]

Reactive Reasons

GLOBALIZATION OF COMPETITORS   One of the most common reactive reasons that prompt a company to go overseas is global competition. If left unchallenged, competitors who already have overseas operations or investments may get so entrenched in foreign markets that it becomes difficult for other companies to enter at a later time. In addition, the lower costs and market power available to these competitors operating globally may also give them an advantage domestically. Nor is this global perspective limited to industries with tangible products. Following the global expansion of banking, insurance, credit cards, and other financial services, financial exchanges have been going global by buying or forming partnerships with exchanges in other countries, their strategies facilitated by advances in technology.[13]

Strategic moves by competing global giants prompt countermoves by other firms in the industry in order to solidify and expand their global presence. Such was the case after the Pfizer takeover of Wyeth in January 2009; Pfizer, the world's biggest drug maker bid $68 billion for Wyeth. Subsequently, Roche, the Swiss pharmaceutical company, paid $46.8 billion to acquire the biotechnology company Genentech, in which it already owned a majority stake. Not to be outdone, Merck, the American pharmaceutical giant, announced in March 2009 that it will pay $41 billion to acquire its rival Schering-Plough—the combined company to keep the Merck name. Clearly, Merck will benefit from the worldwide reach of Schering-Plough, which generates about 70 percent of its sales outside of the United States, including more than $2 billion in a year from emerging markets. Mr. Clark, Merck's CEO, stated that

> *We are creating a strong, global health care leader built for sustainable growth and success. The combined company will benefit from a formidable research and development pipeline, a significantly broader portfolio of medicines and an expanded presence in key international markets, particularly in high-growth emerging markets.*[14]

> www.nytimes.com
> *March 10, 2009*

TRADE BARRIERS   Although trade barriers have been lessened in recent years as a result of trade agreements, which have led to increased exports, some countries' restrictive trade barriers do provide another reactive reason that companies often switch from exporting to overseas manufacturing. Barriers such as tariffs, quotas, buy-local policies, and other restrictive trade practices can make exports to foreign markets too expensive and too impractical to be competitive. Many firms, for example, want to gain a foothold in Europe—to be regarded as insiders—to counteract trade barriers and restrictions on non-European Union (EU) firms (discussed further in the Comparative Management in Focus: Strategic Planning for the EU Market in this chapter). In part, this fear of "Fortress Europe" is caused by actions such as the EU's block exemption for the franchise industry. This exemption prohibits a franchisor (such as McDonald's) from contracting with a single company (such as Coca-Cola) to supply all its franchisees, as it does in the United States.

REGULATIONS AND RESTRICTIONS   Similarly, regulations and restrictions by a firm's home government may become so expensive that companies will seek out less restrictive foreign operating environments. Avoiding such regulations prompted U.S. pharmaceutical maker SmithKline and Britain's Beecham to merge. Both thereby guaranteed that they would avoid licensing and regulatory hassles in their largest markets: Western Europe and the United States. The merged company is now an insider in both Europe and America.

CUSTOMER DEMANDS   Operations in foreign countries frequently start as a response to customer demands or as a solution to logistical problems. Certain foreign customers, for example, may demand that their supplying company operate in their local region so that they have better control over their supplies, forcing the supplier to comply or lose the business. McDonald's is one company that asks its domestic suppliers to follow it to foreign ventures. Meat supplier OSI Industries does just that, with joint ventures in 17 countries, such as Bavaria, so that it can work with local companies making McDonald's hamburgers.

Proactive Reasons

> *Many more companies are using their bases in the developing world as springboards to build global empires, such as Mexican cement giant Cemex, Indian drugmaker Ranbaxy, and Russia's Lukoil, which has hundreds of gas stations in New Jersey and Pennsylvania.*[15]

ECONOMIES OF SCALE   Careful, long-term strategic planning encourages firms to go international for proactive reasons. One pressing reason for many large firms to expand overseas is to seek economies of scale—that is, to achieve world-scale volume to make the fullest use of modern capital-intensive manufacturing equipment and to amortize staggering research and development costs when facing brief product life cycles.[16] The high costs of research and development, such as in the pharmaceutical industry (for example Merck and Pfizer), along with the cost of keeping up with new technologies, can often be recouped only through global sales.

GROWTH OPPORTUNITIES

> *. . . at the time (1989) it was prescient, giving FedEx a ten-year jump on rivals . . . but we saw the puck and skated toward it.*
>
> MICHAEL DUCKER,
> *VP International, FedEx Express Unit, April 3, 2006.*[17]

As illustrated by the above comment, companies in mature markets in developed countries experience a growth imperative to look for new opportunities in emerging markets. In this example, FedEx founder and CEO Frederick W. Smith was farsighted in predicting that Asia would become an economic juggernaut and purchased Tiger International Inc. for $895 million in 1989. Tiger was a struggling cargo hauler; however, it had the assets that Smith wanted—flying rights into major Asian airports and managers with local knowledge. This brave move rewarded FedEx with 39 percent of the China-to-U.S. air express market. Continuing to seek aggressive growth opportunities in the region, FedEx moved its hub to Guangzhou, China, with a $150 million investment, in 2008.[18]

When expansion opportunities become limited at home, firms such as McDonald's are often driven to seek expansion through new international markets. Indeed, in spite of global economic problems (or perhaps because of them), McDonald's Corp. announced plans for a significant investment of $2.1 billion for about roughly 1,000 new locations in 2010—240 of which will be in Europe, 165 in the United States, and 600 in Asia—as the company continues to globalize its business.[19] Currently, nearly two-thirds of all sales are generated outside the United States.

As with McDonalds, a mature product or service with restricted growth in its domestic market often has "new life" in another country, where it will be at an earlier stage of its life cycle. Avon Products, for example, has seen a decline in its U.S. market since its traditional sales and marketing strategy of "Avon Calling" (house-to-house sales) now meets with empty houses, due to the spiraling number of women who work outside the home. To make up for this loss, Avon pushed overseas to 26 emerging markets, such as Mexico, Poland, China, India, South Africa, and Vietnam (bringing its total to 100 countries in which it operates overseas). In Brazil, for instance, Josina Reis Teixeira carries her sample kit to the wooden shacks in the tiny village of Registro, just outside of São Paulo. In some markets, Avon adapted to cultural influences, such as in China, where consumers are suspicious of door-to-door salespeople. There, Avon set up showrooms (beauty boutiques) in its branch offices in major cities so that women can consult cosmeticians and sample products. Subsequently, the company's patience paid off when it was awarded a direct selling license in China in June 2006, and began recruiting over 399,000 direct sales agents.[20]

In addition, new markets abroad provide a place to invest surplus profits as well as employ underutilized resources in management, technology, and machinery. When entirely new markets open up, such as in Eastern Europe, both experienced firms and those new to international competition usually rush to take advantage of awaiting opportunities. Such was the case with the proactive stance that Unisys took in preparing for and jumping on the newly opened market opportunity in Vietnam.

Cemex, the Mexican cement giant, has been one company aggressively taking advantage of growth opportunities through acquisitions. After learning his family's business from the bottom up for eighteen years, Lorenzo Zambrano became CEO and started his gutsy expansion into world markets. His strategy has been to acquire foreign companies, allow time to integrate them into Cemex and pay off the debt, and then look for the next acquisition. In 2009, however, environmental factors forced strategic changes, as discussed in the accompanying Management Focus.

RESOURCE ACCESS AND COST SAVINGS   Resource access and cost savings entice many companies to operate from overseas bases. The availability of raw materials and other resources offers both greater control over inputs and lower transportation costs. Lower labor costs (for production, service, and technical personnel), another major consideration, lead to lower unit costs and have proved a vital ingredient to competitiveness for many companies.

MANAGEMENT FOCUS

Mexico's Cemex Reverses Course to Respond to Global Downturn[21]

> *Lorenzo Zambrano is a poster boy for globalization, a swashbuckling executive who turned a sleepy local cement maker into Mexico's first true multinational, with holdings on five continents.*[22]
>
> *The turnabout underscores a hard lesson of the financial crisis: For all the promise globalization holds for aggressive companies and executives, it carries hidden risks that can slam both operations and reputations.*[23]

The Mexican cement giant Cemex is based in Monterrey and operates in more than 50 countries. The company continued its global expansion when it made an unsolicited bid of $12.8 billion for the Rinker Group of Australia, a group with considerable U.S. interests. The Rinker group accepted a revised $14.25 billion acquisition by Cemex in 2007. The deal created one of the world's largest construction materials companies, and looked sure to strengthen Cemex's leading position in the American housing market, particularly in Sun Belt states like Florida and Arizona. Eighty percent of Rinker's sales come from the United States.

Cemex's acquisition of the Rinker Group was the largest ever by a Mexican company. Over the last 15 years, Cemex's chairman, Lorenzo Zambrano, had transformed his company into a multinational company with operations on five continents and $21 billion in revenue.

The global cement and construction materials industry has been slowly consolidating as giants like Lafarge of France, Holcim of Switzerland, and Cemex have sought to grow through acquisitions.

After taking over 23 years ago at a business co-founded by his grandfather, Mr. Zambrano pushed into country after country with daring acquisitions. Mr. Zambrano, a graduate of Stanford Business School, has been aggressive in expanding its global presence by taking on billions in debt to expand first in Spain, then in Latin America and the United States. Zambrano's acquisitions in Europe helped the company learn about efficiencies in managing inventory and dealing with clients in other countries.

Cemex became the world's largest producer of ready-mix concrete in 2005 when it bought RMC of Britain for $5.8 billion, giving it a strong presence in Europe. Zambrano also invested heavily in high technology, allowing managers at its Monterrey headquarters in northern Mexico to track global operations.

In 2009, however, the global economic downturn led to declining construction demand, notably in the United States, UK, and Spain. The construction industry stalled for residential and commercial projects, while the prospect for infrastructure spending awaited government spending to prime the economy in those countries.

With rising costs for crucial raw materials such as coal, heavy oil and gas, the focus for Cemex in 2009 changed from expansion and acquisitions to cost-cutting and retrenchment. The company announced it would cut costs and jobs in its attempt to absorb the effects of the U.S. housing crisis and global market volatility. Added to its reduced sales, the company also suffered because of the weakness of the peso, which had fallen by more than 30 per cent against the dollar since July 2008.

Confounding the problems for Cemex—as with many victims of the financial crisis— the company was not able to refinance a significant portion of its debt (estimated at between $16 billion to $20 billion). Emerging market companies across the board were falling prey to the perception of a higher risk in refinancing debt. In a rapid reversal of fortune, the company known for relentless expansion was forced into selling assets, negotiating with creditors, and cutting its work force and spending. However, the tightened credit market also reduced the price Cemex could get for selling its assets in Spain, Hungary, and Austria.

It is unfortunate that the ill-timed takeover of the Rinker group, along with the global financial crisis, has so negatively affected not only the Cemex company, but also the reputation of Mr. Zambrano He had become corporate Mexico's informal ambassador to the world. Cemex gave other Latin American businesspeople the confidence to expand abroad. Mr. Zambrano was a philanthropist and arts patron, and raised millions of dollars for a prominent university, El Instituto Tecnologico de Monterrey, from which he has an engineering degree. However, strategists may challenge whether Mr. Zambrano had sufficiently considered potential global threats which could cause such a rapid downturn in the company.

What is your opinion? Was the situation a result of a rare confluence of negative events, or was Mr. Zambrano insufficiently apprised and cautious about the risks in continuing expansion and debt burdens?

Sometimes just the prospect of shifting production overseas improves competitiveness at home. When Xerox Corporation started moving copier-rebuilding operations to Mexico, the union agreed to needed changes in work style and productivity to keep the jobs at home. Lower operational costs in other areas—power, transportation, and financing—frequently prove attractive.

INCENTIVES   Governments in countries such as Poland seeking new infusions of capital, technology, and know-how willingly provide incentives—tax exemptions, tax holidays, subsidies, loans, and the use of property. Because they both decrease risk and increase profits, these incentives are attractive to foreign companies. Russia, for example, has a number of special economic zones, both for industrial production and for technical research, offering various tax concessions such as exemption from property and land taxes for the first five years, as well as customs privileges.[24]

In February 2009, for example, companies were rushing to conclude M&A deals in Brazil while a tax break which allows companies to deduct 34 percent of the premium paid in an acquisition is still guaranteed, amid fears that it would be rescinded. This kind of tax incentive is rare, so it attracts considerable interest from foreign investors. Coupled with the recent devaluation of the Brazilian real, which made acquisitions cheaper for foreign bidders, tax deductions are currently one of the great attractions for acquisition deals in Brazil.[25]

One study surveyed 103 experienced managers concerning the relative attractiveness of various incentives for expansion into the Caribbean region (primarily Mexico, Venezuela, Colombia, Dominican Republic, and Guatemala). The results indicate the opinion of those managers about which incentives are most important; however, the most desirable mix would depend on the nature of the particular company and its operations. The first two issues reflect managers' concerns about limiting foreign exchange risk, where restrictions often change overnight and limit the ability of the firm to repatriate profits. Other concerns are those of political instability and the possibility of expropriation, and those of tax concessions.[26] Nor are those incentives limited to emerging economies. The state of Alabama in the United States has spent hundreds of millions to attract the Honda, Hyundai, and Toyota plants.[27]

STRATEGIC FORMULATION PROCESS

Typically, the strategic formulation process is necessary both at the headquarters of the corporation and at each of the subsidiaries. Most organizations operate on planning cycles of five or more years, with intermediate reviews.

The global strategic formulation process, as part of overall corporate strategic management, parallels the process followed in domestic companies. However, the variables, and therefore the process itself, are far more complex because of the greater difficulty in gaining accurate and timely information, the diversity of geographic locations, and the differences in political, legal, cultural, market, and financial processes. These factors introduce a greater level of risk in strategic decisions. However, for firms that have not yet engaged in international operations (as well as for those that do), an ongoing strategic planning process with a global orientation identifies potential opportunities for (1) appropriate market expansion, (2) increased profitability, and (3) new ventures by which the firm can exploit its strategic advantages. Even in the absence of immediate opportunities, monitoring the global environment for trends and competition is important for domestic planning.

The strategic formulation process is part of the strategic management process in which most firms engage, either formally or informally. The planning modes range from a proactive, long-range format to a reactive, more seat-of-the-pants method, whereby the day-by-day decisions of key managers, in particular owner-managers, accumulate to what can be discerned retroactively as the new strategic direction.[28] The stages in the strategic management process are shown in Exhibit 6-1. In reality, these stages seldom follow such a linear format. Rather, the process is continuous and intertwined, with data and results from earlier stages providing information for the next stage.

The first phase of the strategic management process—the *planning phase*—starts with the company establishing (or clarifying) its mission and its overall objectives. The next two steps comprise an assessment of the external environment that the firm faces in the future and an analysis of the firm's relative capabilities to deal successfully with that environment. Strategic alternatives are then considered, and plans are made based on the strategic choice. These five steps constitute the planning phase, which will be further explained in this chapter.

The second part of the strategic management process is the *implementation phase*. Successful implementation requires the establishment of the structure, systems, and processes

EXHIBIT 6-1 The Strategic Management Process

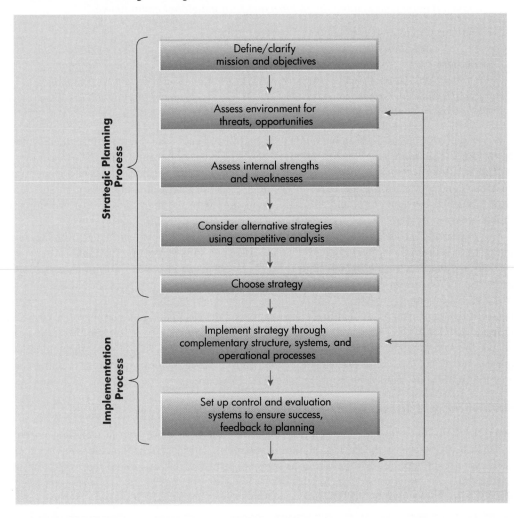

suitable to make the strategy work. These variables, as well as functional-level strategies, are explored in detail in the remaining chapters on organizing, leading, and staffing. At this point, however, it is important to note that the strategic planning process by itself does not change the posture of the firm until the plans are implemented. In addition, feedback from the interim and long-term results of such implementation, along with continuous environmental monitoring, flows directly back into the planning process.

STEPS IN DEVELOPING INTERNATIONAL AND GLOBAL STRATEGIES

In the planning phase of strategic management—strategic formulation—managers need to carefully evaluate dynamic factors, as described in the stages that follow. However, as discussed earlier, managers seldom consecutively move through these phases; rather, changing events and variables prompt them to combine and reconsider their evaluations on an ongoing basis.

Mission and Objectives

The *mission* of an organization is its overall *raison d'être* or the function it performs in society. This mission charts the direction of the company and provides a basis for strategic decision making. It also conveys the cultural values that are important to the company, as contrasted in the following two mission statements:

> **Sanyo** (A Japanese company)
> *Corporate philosophy: to make products and services indispensable for people all over the world, offering a more enjoyable life. Digital technology and core*

competence (the source of our competitiveness) generate joy, excitement, and impact, a more comfortable life in harmony with the global environment.[29]

Siemens (A German company)

Success depends on success of our customers. We provide experience and solutions so they can achieve their objectives fast and effectively. We turn our people's imagination and best practices in successful technologies and products. This makes us a premium investment for our shareholders. Our ideas, technologies and activities help create a better world.[30]

While both mission statements indicate a focus on customers, Sanyo offers them a more enjoyable life, is more relationship-oriented, and emphasizes harmony and the environment, indicating a long-term focus, factors typical of Japanese culture. Siemens offers efficiency to its customers and a premium return to its shareholders; this mission statement is explicit and decisive, typical of German communication; this compares with the more descriptive and implicit statement given by Sanyo.[31]

A company's overall *objectives* flow from its mission, and both guide the formulation of international corporate strategy. Because we are focusing on issues of international strategy, we will assume that one of the overall objectives of the corporation is some form of international operation (or expansion). The objectives of the firm's international affiliates should also be part of the global corporate objectives. A firm's global objectives usually fall into the areas of marketing, profitability, finance, production, and research and development, among others, as shown in Exhibit 6-2. Goals for market volume and for profitability are usually set higher for international than for domestic operations because of the greater risk involved. In addition, financial objectives on the global level must take into account differing tax regulations in various countries and how to minimize overall losses from exchange rate fluctuations.

Environmental Assessment

After clarifying the corporate mission and objectives, the first major step in weighing international strategic options is the **environmental assessment.** This assessment includes environmental scanning and continuous monitoring to keep abreast of variables around the world that are

EXHIBIT 6-2 Global Corporate Objectives

Marketing
Total company market share—worldwide, regional, national
Annual percentage sales growth
Annual percentage market share growth
Coordination of regional markets for economies of scale

Production
Relative foreign versus domestic production volume
Economies of scale through global production integration
Quality and cost control
Introduction of cost-efficient production methods

Finance
Effective financing of overseas subsidiaries or allies
Taxation—globally minimizing tax burden
Optimum capital structure
Foreign-exchange management

Profitability
Long-term profit growth
Return on investment, equity, and assets
Annual rate of profit growth

Research and Development
Develop new products with global patents
Develop proprietary production technologies
Worldwide research and development labs

pertinent to the firm and that have the potential to shape its future by posing new opportunities (or threats). Firms must adapt to their environment to survive. The focus of strategic planning is how to adapt.

The process of gathering information and forecasting relevant trends, competitive actions, and circumstances that will affect operations in geographic areas of potential interest is called **environmental scanning.** This activity should be conducted on three levels—global, regional, and national (discussed in detail later in this chapter). Scanning should focus on the future interests of the firm and should cover the following major variables (as discussed by Phatak[32] and others):

- *Political instability.* This variable represents a volatile and uncontrollable risk to the multinational corporation, as illustrated by the upheaval in the Middle East in recent years. MNCs must carefully assess such risk because it may result in a loss of profitability or even ownership.
- *Currency instability.* This variable represents another risk; inflation and fluctuations in the exchange rates of currencies can dramatically affect profitability when operating overseas. For example, both foreign and local firms got a painful reminder of this risk when the Mexican peso declined by about 30 percent against the U.S. dollar in 2008.
- *Nationalism.* This variable, representing the home government's goals for independence and economic improvement, often influences foreign companies. The home government may impose restrictive policies—import controls, equity requirements, local content requirements, limitations on the repatriation of profits, and so forth. Japan, for example, protects its home markets with these kinds of restrictive policies. Other forms of nationalism may be exerted through the following: (1) pressure from national governments—exemplified by the United States putting pressure on Japan to curtail unfair competition; (2) lax patent and trademark protection laws, such as those in China in recent years, which erode a firm's proprietary technology through insufficient protection; and (3) the suitability of infrastructure, such as roads and telecommunications.
- *International competition.* Conducting a global competitor analysis is perhaps the most important task in environmental assessment and strategy formulation. The first step in analyzing the competition is to assess the relevant industry structures as they influence the competitive arena in the particular country (or region) being considered. For example, will the infrastructure support new companies in that industry? Is there room for additional competition? What is the relative supply and demand for the proposed product or service? The ultimate profit potential in the industry in that location will be determined by these kinds of factors.[33]
- *Environmental Scanning.* Managers must also specifically assess their current competitors—global and local—for the proposed market. They must ask some important questions: What are our competitors' positions, their goals and strategies, and their strengths and weaknesses, relative to those of our firm? What are the likely competitor reactions to our strategic moves?

The firm can also choose varying levels of environmental scanning. To reduce risk and investment, many firms take on the role of the "follower," meaning that they limit their own investigations. Instead, they simply watch their competitors' moves and go where they go, assuming that the competitors have done their homework. Other firms go to considerable lengths to carefully gather data and examine options in the global arena.

Ideally, the firm should conduct global environmental analysis on three different levels: multinational, regional, and national. Analysis on the multinational level provides a broad assessment of significant worldwide trends—through identification, forecasting, and monitoring activities. These trends would include the political and economic developments of nations around the world, as well as global technological progress. From this information, managers can choose certain appropriate regions of the world to consider further.

Next, at the regional level, the analysis focuses in more detail on critical environmental factors to identify opportunities (and risks) for marketing the company's products, services, or technology. For example, one such regional location ripe for investigation by a firm seeking new markets is the EU.

Having zeroed in on one or more regions, the firm must, as its next step, analyze at the national level. Such an analysis explores in depth specific countries within the desired region for economic, legal, political, and cultural factors significant to the company. For example, the analysis could focus on the size and nature of the market, along with any possible operational problems, to consider how best to enter the market. In many volatile countries, continuous monitoring of such environmental factors is a vital part of ongoing strategic planning. Another important factor which must be considered in the environmental assessment at all levels is that of how institutions might affect potential opportunities to compete.

INSTITUTIONAL EFFECTS ON INTERNATIONAL COMPETITION[34] Various institutions can create opportunities or constraints for firms considering entry into specific global markets. Recently, researchers such as Peng have argued that " . . . firm strategies and performance are, to a large degree, determined by institutions popularly known as the 'rules of the game' in a society."[35] Institutions include both those formal institutions that promulgate laws, regulations and rules, as well as informal ones that exert influence through norms, cultures, and ethics (discussed elsewhere in this book.)[36]

Specific ways in which formal institutions affect international competition are (1) the attractiveness of overseas markets, (2) entry barriers and industry attractiveness, (3) antidumping, and (4) competitiveness of Indian IT/BPO firms.[37]

Attractiveness of Overseas Markets The extent to which countries have institutions to promote the rule of law affects the attractiveness of those economies to outside investors. Specifically, institutions provide a broad framework of liberty and democracy, as well as human rights protections. In addition, institutions contribute to a stable environment for firms by creating specific laws such as those protecting property rights. Countries with more developed institutions are seen as more stable and attractive to foreign firms.[38]

Entry Barriers and Industry Attractiveness Institutions create barriers to entry in certain industries and hence make those industries more attractive (profitable) for incumbent firms. For example, in the U.S. pharmaceutical industry, barriers are created by the U.S. Food and Drug Administration in the form of stringent drug approval requirements. Since new entrants (with potentially cheaper drugs) are restricted, Americans pay double what Canadians and Europeans pay for the same drugs produced in the United States. Americans spend about $240 billion a year on drugs, more than Britain, Canada, France, Germany, Italy, and Japan combined. In turn, U.S. firms in this industry earn above-average profits as the institutional barriers restrict entrants and reduce rivalry.[39]

Antidumping as an Entry Barrier A second example of an entry barrier is illustrated by current U.S. antidumping laws which place a foreign entrant at a disadvantage if accused of "dumping" (defined as selling a product below the cost of producing that product with the intent to later raise prices). Where a dumping charge is filed by a domestic firm with the International Trade Administration (a division of the U.S. Department of Commerce) against a foreign competitor, that foreign competitor will frequently lose the case. Many accused foreign firms fail to properly complete a questionnaire which is required as part of the legal proceedings. This questionnaire is lengthy and requires the foreign firm to submit extensive and sometimes proprietary information about its costs. In contrast, if a similar practice occurs domestically (predatory pricing), it is generally difficult to prove that the firm was selling below cost and engaging in predatory pricing. As such, while antidumping laws are a frequent deterrent to foreign entrants, the domestic equivalent strategy of predatory pricing is rarely a barrier for that new entrant. The suggestion here is that U.S. antidumping laws strongly favor domestic firms and place international firms at a disadvantage.[40]

Competitiveness of Indian IT/BPO Firms What explains the competitive advantages of the Indian IT/BPO industry compared to U.S. competitors? One explanation is that institutional changes in India, such as a greater emphasis on higher education, and legal and regulatory reforms that liberalized the economy, created a more open and competitive atmosphere in which these firms could flourish. These institutional changes have, however, created opportunities for Western firms which began to locate subsidiaries in India to take advantage of skilled but less costly human resources. This in turn forced the Indian IT/BPO companies to become more competitive to take on the new entrants.[41]

Clearly, there are many formal institutions affect international strategy. But, what explains successes of companies despite the failure or absence of these formal institutions? China is a common illustration of where domestic firms have built competitive advantages despite poorly developed formal institutions. The answer lies in the extensive use of informal institutions or networks of interpersonal connections known in Chinese as *guanxi*. These networks function as substitutes for the weaknesses of the formal institutions. Research has shown that these informal networks are common in a variety of emerging markets with different cultural traditions and are a response to transitions in many emerging markets where formal institutions are evolving.[42]

In summary, this process of environmental scanning, from the broad global level down to the local specifics of entry planning, is illustrated in Exhibit 6-3. The first broad scan of all potential world markets results in the firm being able to eliminate from its list those markets that are closed or insignificant or do not have reasonable entry conditions. The second scan of remaining regions, and then countries, is done in greater detail—perhaps eliminating some countries based on political instability, for example. Remaining countries are then assessed for competitor strengths, suitability of products, and so on. This analysis leads to serious entry planning in selected countries; managers start to work on operational plans, such as negotiations and legal arrangements.

EXHIBIT 6-3   Global Environmental Scanning and Strategic Decision-Making Process

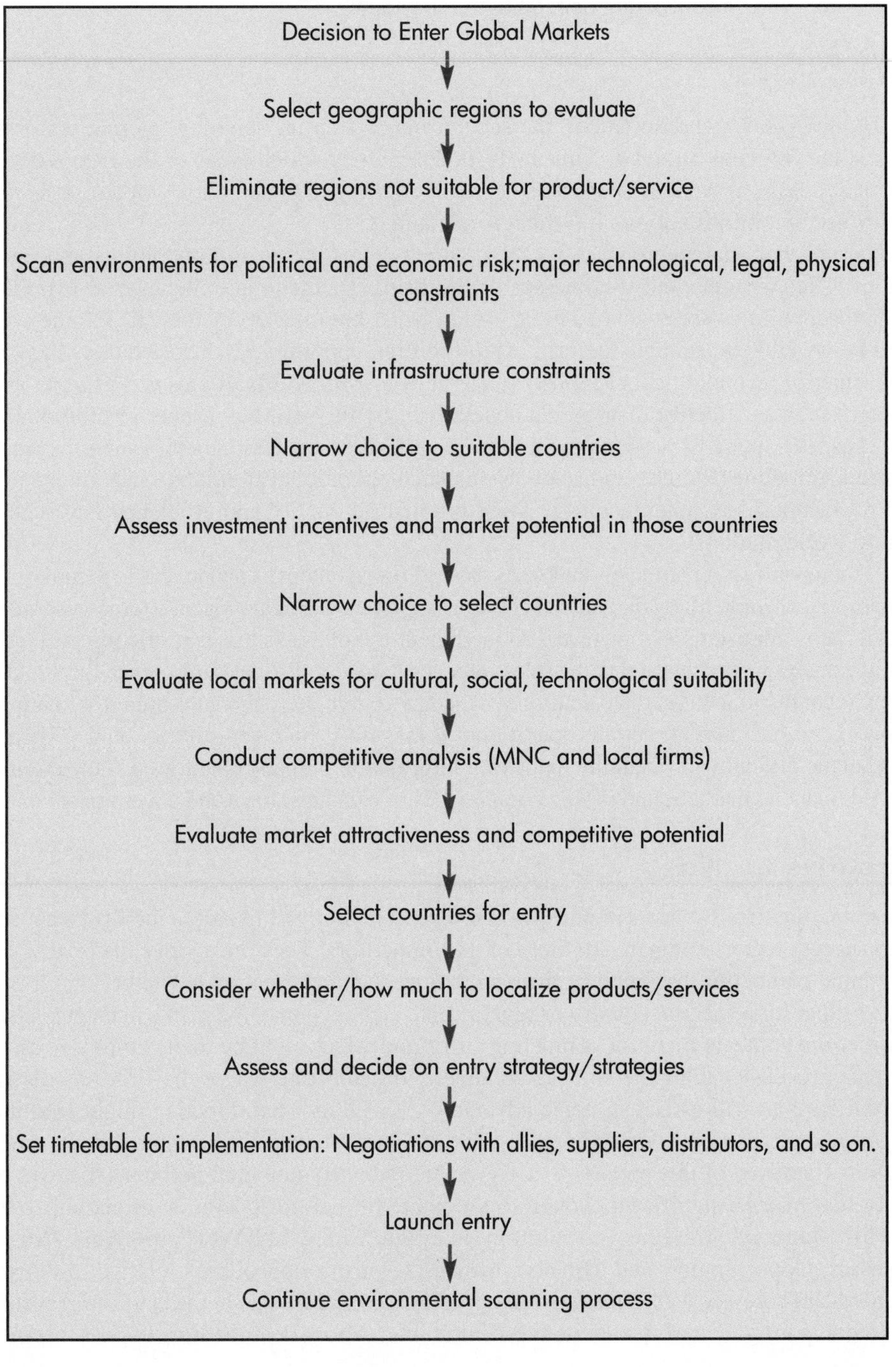

Decision to Enter Global Markets

↓

Select geographic regions to evaluate

↓

Eliminate regions not suitable for product/service

↓

Scan environments for political and economic risk;major technological, legal, physical constraints

↓

Evaluate infrastructure constraints

↓

Narrow choice to suitable countries

↓

Assess investment incentives and market potential in those countries

↓

Narrow choice to select countries

↓

Evaluate local markets for cultural, social, technological suitability

↓

Conduct competitive analysis (MNC and local firms)

↓

Evaluate market attractiveness and competitive potential

↓

Select countries for entry

↓

Consider whether/how much to localize products/services

↓

Assess and decide on entry strategy/strategies

↓

Set timetable for implementation: Negotiations with allies, suppliers, distributors, and so on.

↓

Launch entry

↓

Continue environmental scanning process

Sources of Environmental Information

The success of environmental scanning depends on the ability of managers to take a global perspective and to ensure that their *sources of information and business intelligence* are global. A variety of public resources are available to provide information. In the United States alone, more than 2,000 business information services are available on computer databases tailored to specific industries and regions. Other resources include corporate "clipping" services and information packages. However, internal sources of information are usually preferable—especially alert field personnel who, with firsthand observations, can provide up-to-date and relevant information for the firm. Extensively using its own internal resources, Mitsubishi Trading Company employs worldwide more than 50,000 people in 50 countries, as of January 2009, many of whom are market analysts, whose job it is to gather, analyze, and feed market information to the parent company.[43] Internal sources of information help to eliminate unreliable information from secondary sources, particularly in developing countries. As Garsombke points out, the "official" data from such countries can be misleading: "Census data can be tampered with by government officials for propaganda purposes or it may be restricted. . . . In South Korea, for instance, even official figures can be conflicting depending on the source."[44]

Internal Analysis

After the environmental assessment, the second major step in weighing international strategic options is the **internal analysis.** This analysis determines which areas of the firm's operations represent strengths or weaknesses (currently or potentially) compared to competitors, so that the firm may use that information to its strategic advantage.

The internal analysis focuses on the company's resources and operations and on global synergies. The strengths and weaknesses of the firm's financial and managerial expertise and functional capabilities are evaluated to determine what key success factors (KSFs) the company has and how well they can help the firm exploit foreign opportunities. Those factors increasingly involve superior technological capability (as with Microsoft and Intel), as well as other strategic advantages such as effective distribution channels (as with Wal-Mart), superior promotion capabilities (Disney), low-cost production and sourcing position (as with Toyota), superior patent and new product pipeline (Merck), and so on. Using such operational strengths to advantage is exemplified by Japanese car manufacturers. Their production quality and efficiency have catapulted them into world markets.

All companies have strengths and weaknesses. Management's challenge is to identify both and take appropriate action. Many diagnostic tools are available for conducting an internal resource audit. Financial ratios, for example, may reveal an inefficient use of assets that is restricting profitability; a sales-force analysis may reveal that the sales force is an area of distinct competence for the firm. If a company is conducting this audit to determine whether to start international ventures or to improve its ongoing operations abroad, certain operational issues must be taken into account. These issues include (1) the difficulty of obtaining marketing information in many countries, (2) the often poorly developed financial markets, and (3) the complexities of exchange rates and government controls.

Competitive Analysis

At this point, the firm's managers perform a *competitive analysis* to assess the firm's capabilities and key success factors compared to those of its competitors. They must judge the relative current and potential competitive position of firms in that market and location—whether that is a global position or that for a specific country or region. Like a chess game, the firm's managers also need to consider the strategic intent of competing firms and what might be their future moves (strategies). This process enables the strategic planners to determine where the firm has **distinctive competencies** that will give it strategic advantage as well as what direction might lead the firm into a sustainable competitive advantage—that is, one that will not be immediately eroded by emulation. The result of this process will also help to identify potential problems that can be corrected or that may be significant enough to eliminate further consideration of certain strategies.

This stage of strategic formulation is often called a **SWOT analysis** (Strengths, Weaknesses, Opportunities, and Threats), in which a firm's capabilities relative to those of its competitors are assessed as pertinent to the opportunities and threats in the environment for those firms. In comparing their company with potential international competitors in host markets, it is

EXHIBIT 6-4 Global Competitor Analysis

Comparison Criteria	A (U.S. MNC)	B (Korean MNC)	C (Local Malaysian Firm)	D (Japanese MNC)	E (Local Malaysian Firm)
Marketing capability	0	0	0	0	—
Manufacturing capability	0	+	0	0	0
R&D capability	0	0	0	—	0
HRM capability	0	0	0	0	0
Financial capability	+	—	0	0	—
Future growth of resources	+	0	—	0	—
Quickness	—	0	+	—	0
Flexibility/adaptability	0	+	+	0	0
Sustainability	+	0	0	0	—

Key:
+ = firm is better relative to competition.
0 = firm is same as competition.
— = firm is poorer relative to competition.

useful for managers to draw up a competitive position matrix for each potential location. For example, Exhibit 6-4 analyzes a U.S. specialty seafood firm's competitive profile in Malaysia. The U.S. firm has advantages in financial capability, future growth of resources, and sustainability, but a disadvantage in quickness. It also is at a disadvantage compared to the Korean MNC in important factors such as manufacturing capability and flexibility and adaptability. Because the other firms seem to have little **comparative advantage,** the major competitor is likely to be the Korean firm. At this point, then, the U.S. firm can focus in more detail on assessing the Korean firm's relative strengths and weaknesses.

Most companies develop their strategies around key strengths, or **distinctive competencies.** Distinctive—or "core"—competencies represent important corporate resources because, as Prahalad and Hamel explain, they are the "collective learning in the organization, especially how to coordinate diverse production skills and integrate multiple streams of technologies."[45] Core competencies—like Sony's capacity to miniaturize—are usually difficult for competitors to imitate and represent a major focus for strategic development at the corporate level.[46] Canon, for example, has used its core competency in optics to its competitive advantage throughout its diverse businesses: cameras, copiers, and semiconductor lithographic equipment.

Managers must also assess their firm's weaknesses. A company already on shaky ground financially, for example, will not be able to consider an acquisition strategy, or perhaps any growth strategy. Of course, the subjective perceptions, motivations, capabilities, and goals of the managers involved in such diagnoses frequently cloud the decision-making process. The result is that because of poor judgment by key players sometimes firms embark on strategies that are contraindicated by objective information.

Strategic Decision-Making Models

We can further explain and summarize the hierarchy of the strategic decision-making process described here by means of three leading strategic models. Their roles and interactions are conceptualized in Exhibit 6-5. At the broadest level are those global, regional, and country factors and risks discussed above and in Chapter 1 that are part of those considerations in an **institution-based theory** of existing and potential risks and influences in the host area.[48] For example, firms considering operating in Russia are realizing the potential vulnerability to a changing political attitude to the market reforms and openness from recent progress since President Putin's actions to exert control over key industries. Secondly, or concurrently, the firm's competitive position in its industry can be reviewed using Michael Porter's **industry-based model** of five forces that examines the dynamics within an industry. The forces refer to the relative level of competition already in the industry, the relative ease with which new competitors may or may not enter the field, how much power the suppliers and also the buyers have within the industry, and the extent of substitute products or services that prevail.[49]

These strategic models can provide the decision makers with a picture of the kinds of opportunities and threats that the firm would face in a particular region or country within its industry. This assumes, of course, that the locations that are under consideration have already been pinpointed as attractive and growing markets for the industry. However, that picture would be true for any firm within the particular industry. In other words, all firms within an industry face the same environmental and industrial factors; the difference among firms' performance is as a result of each firm's own resources, capabilities, and strategic decisions. The factors that determine a firm's unique niche or competitive advantage within that arena are a function of its own capabilities (strengths and weaknesses) as relative to those opportunities and threats which are perceived for that location; this is the **resource-based** view of the firm—when considering the unique value of the firm's competencies and that of its products or services.[50]

While these models may indicate varying choices, this strategic decision-making process should enable the managers to give an overall assessment of the strategic fit between the firm and the opportunities in that location and so result in a "go/no go" decision for that point in time. Those managers may want to start the process again relative to a different location in order to compare the relative levels of strategic fit. If it is determined that there is a good strategic fit and a decision is made to enter that market/location, the next step, as indicated in Exhibit 6-5, is to consider alternative entry strategies. A discussion of these entry strategies follows after we first examine the broader picture of the overall strategic approach that a firm might take toward world markets.

Global and International Strategic Alternatives

The strategic planning process involves considering the advantages (and disadvantages) of various strategic alternatives in light of the competitive analysis. While weighing alternatives, managers must take into account the goals of their firms and the competitive status of other firms in the industry. Depending on the size of the firm, managers must consider two levels of strategic alternatives. The first level, *global strategic alternatives* (applicable primarily to MNCs), determines what overall approach to the global marketplace a firm wishes to take. The second level, *entry strategy alternatives,* applies to firms of any size; these alternatives determine what specific entry strategy is appropriate for each country in which the firm plans to operate. Entry strategy alternatives are discussed in a later section. The two main global strategic approaches to world markets—global strategy and regional, or local, strategy—are presented in the following subsections.

Approaches to World Markets

GLOBAL STRATEGY   In the last decade, increasing competitive pressures have forced businesses to consider global strategies—to treat the world as an undifferentiated worldwide marketplace. Such strategies are now loosely referred to as **globalization**—a term that refers to the establishment of worldwide operations and the development of standardized products and marketing. Many analysts, like Porter, have argued that globalization is a competitive imperative for firms in global industries: "In a global industry, a firm must, in some way, integrate its activities on a worldwide basis to capture the linkages among countries. This includes, but requires more than, transferring intangible assets among countries."[51] The rationale behind globalization is to compete by establishing worldwide economies of scale, offshore manufacturing, and international cash flows. The term *globalization,* therefore, is as applicable to organizational structure as it is to strategy. (Organizational structure is discussed further in Chapter 8.)

The pressures to globalize include (1) increasing competitive clout resulting from regional trading blocs; (2) declining tariffs, which encourage trading across borders and open up new markets; and (3) the information technology explosion, which makes the coordination of far-flung operations easier and also increases the commonality of consumer tastes.[52] Use of Web sites has allowed entrepreneurs, as well as established companies, to go global almost instantaneously through e-commerce—either B2B or B2C.[53] Examples are eBay, Yahoo!, Lands' End, and the ill-fated E-Toys, which met its demise in 2001. In addition, the success of Japanese companies with global strategies has set the competitive standard in many industries—most visibly in the automobile

EXHIBIT 6-5 A Hierarchical Model of Strategic Decision Making

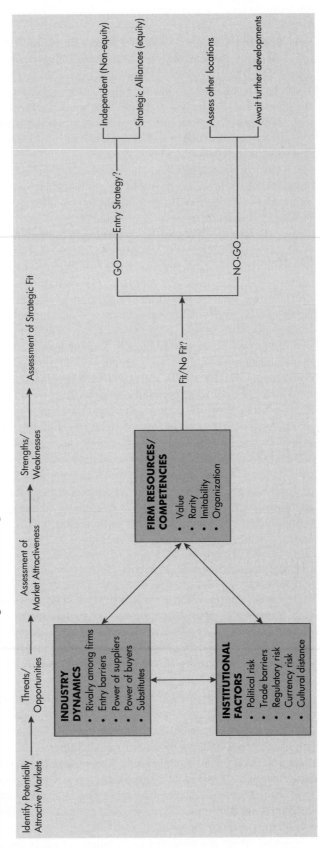

industry. Other companies, such as Caterpillar, ICI, and Sony, have fared well with global strategies. Another company bent on a global strategy is Lenovo, a Chinese computer-maker which became a global brand when it bought IBM's PC business in 2005 for $1.75 billion. Says Mr. Yang, Lenovo's Chairman:

> We are proud of our Chinese roots, but we no longer want to be positioned as a Chinese company. We want to be a truly global company."[54]

As a result, Lenovo has no headquarters and its senior managers rotate meetings around the world. The company's global marketing department is in Bangalore, and its development teams comprise people in several centers around the world, often meeting virtually. Mr. Yang himself moved his family to North Carolina in order to immerse himself in the culture and language of global business.[55]

One of the quickest and cheapest ways to develop a global strategy is through strategic alliances. Many firms are trying to go global faster by forming alliances with rivals, suppliers, and customers. The rapidly developing information technologies are spawning cross-national business alliances from short-term virtual corporations to long-term strategic partnerships.

Alliances are also sometimes formed in difficult times as a result of government interference. In April 2009, the U.S. government insisted that Chrysler accept the alliance with Fiat as a precondition to government financial assistance to remain viable. The new company would be set up with the best assets of Chrysler. Fiat of Italy would own 20 percent to 35 percent of the new Chrysler, with the government also holding a stake. Some of the equity in the new company would also be given to Chrysler's creditors as repayment, after Chrysler emerged from bankruptcy proceedings.[56] (Strategic alliances are discussed further in Chapter 7.)

A global strategy is inherently more vulnerable to environmental risk, however, than a regionalization (or "multi-local") strategy. Global organizations are difficult to manage because doing so requires the coordination of broadly divergent national cultures. It also means that firms must lose some of their original identity—they must "denationalize operations and replace home-country loyalties with a system of common corporate values and loyalties."[57] In other words, the global strategy necessarily treats all countries similarly, regardless of their differences in cultures and systems. Problems often result, such as a lack of local flexibility and responsiveness and a neglect of the need for differentiated products. Many companies now feel that regionalization/localization is a more manageable and less risky approach, one that allows them to capitalize on local competencies as long as the parent organization and each subsidiary retain a flexible approach to each other. Wal-Mart is one global company that has learned the hard way that it should have acted more "local" in some regions of the world, including Germany and South Korea, where it has had to abandon operations.

REGIONALIZATION/LOCALIZATION

> Nokia, Nestle, Google, and Wal-Mart have failed to adjust to the tastes of South Korean consumers. In contrast, the British retailer Tesco is a remarkable case of succeeding in localizing. Samsung Tesco is 89 percent owned by the British retail giant, but has relied heavily on local managers from Samsung. It is one of Tesco's biggest overseas success stories, generating a third of its overseas sales.
>
> NA HONG SEOK,
> Analyst in Seoul, South Korea, March 23, 2006.[58]

For those firms in multidomestic industries—those industries in which competitiveness is determined on a country-by-country basis rather than a global basis—regional strategies are more appropriate than globalization. The **regionalization strategy [multidomestic (or multilocal) strategy]** is one in which local markets are linked together within a region, allowing more local responsiveness and specialization. Top managers within each region decide on their own investment locations, product mixes, and competitive positioning; in other words, they run their subsidiaries as quasi-independent organizations.

While there are pressures to globalize—such as the need for economies of scale to compete on cost—there are opposing pressures to regionalize, especially for newly developed economies (NDEs) and developing economies. These localization pressures include unique consumer preferences resulting from cultural or national differences (perhaps something as simple as right-hand-drive cars for Japan), domestic subsidies, and new production technologies that facilitate product variation for less cost than before.[59] By "acting local," firms can focus individually in each country or region on the local market needs for product or service characteristics, distribution, customer support, and so on.

Ghemawat argues that strategy cannot be decided either on a country-by-country basis or on a one-size-fits-all-countries basis, but rather that both the differences and the similarities between countries must be taken into account. He bases his perspectives on the cultural administrative, geographic, and economic (CAGE) distances between countries. He concludes:

> *A semiglobalized perspective helps companies resist a variety of delusions derived from visions of the globalization apocalypse: growth fever, the norm of enormity, statelessness, ubiquity, and one-size-fits-all.*
> *Semiglobalization is what offers room for cross-border strategy to have content distinct from single-country strategy.*
>
> PANKAJ GHEMAWAT,
> *2007.*[60]

As with any management function, the strategic choice as to where a company should position itself along the globalization-regionalization continuum is contingent on the nature of the industry, the type of company, the company's goals and strengths (or weaknesses), and the nature of its subsidiaries, among many factors. In addition, each company's strategic approach should be unique in adapting to its own environment. Many firms may try to "Go Global, Act Local" to trade off the best advantages of each strategy. Matsushita, which grew to be Japan's largest electronics firm, and renamed itself the Panasonic Corporation in October 2008, is one firm with considerable expertise at being a "GLOCAL" firm (GLObal, LoCAL). Panasonic has operations in 60 countries and employs 305,828 people in its 556 domain companies; those companies follow policies to develop local R&D to tailor products to markets, to let plants set their own rules, and to be a good corporate citizen in every country.[61] Toyota, clearly a globally successful Japanese company, saw the value of being "Glocal" from early on and adopted regionalization as the basis of its strategy, subsequently passing General Motors as the world's largest automaker in 2009.

Google is another company that has had to step back from its ideal of being just "Global" to adapting to local markets. Ghemawat explains why the company had problems with a "one-size-fits-all-countries" strategy by using his CAGE distance framework, as follows:

Cultural distance: Google's biggest problem in Russia seems to have been associated with a relatively difficult language.

Administrative distance: Google's difficulties in dealing with Chinese censorship reflect the difference between Chinese administrative and policy frameworks and those in its home country, the United States.

Geographic distance: Although Google's products can be digitized, and it had trouble adapting to Russia from afar and has had to set up offices there.

Economic distance: The underdevelopment of payment infrastructure in Russia has been another handicap for Google relative to local rivals.[62]

Global Integrative Strategies

Many MNCs have developed their global operations to the point of being fully integrated—often both vertically and horizontally, including suppliers, productive facilities, marketing and distribution outlets, and contractors around the world. Dell, for example, is a globally integrated company, with worldwide sourcing and a fully integrated production and marketing system. It has factories in Ireland, Brazil, China, Malaysia, Tennessee, and Texas, and it has an assembly and delivery system from 47 locations around the world. At the same time, it has extreme flexibility. Since Dell builds computers to each order, it carries very little inventory and, therefore, can change its operations at a moment's notice. Thomas Friedman described the process that his notebook computer went through when he ordered it from Dell:

> *The notebook was co-designed in Austin, Texas, and in Taiwan. . . . The total supply chain for my computer, including suppliers of suppliers, involved about four hundred*

companies in North America, Europe, and primarily Asia, but with thirty key players. (It was delivered by UPS 17 days after ordering.).

THOMAS FRIEDMAN,
The World Is Flat, 2005.[63]

Although some companies move very quickly to the stage of global integration—often through merger or acquisition—many companies evolve into multinational corporations by going through the entry strategies in stages, taking varying lengths of time between stages. Typically, a company starts with simple exporting, moves to large-scale exporting with sales branches abroad (or perhaps begins licensing), then proceeds to assembly abroad (either by itself or through contract manufacturing), and eventually evolves to full production abroad with its own subsidiaries. Finally, the MNC will undertake the global integration of its foreign subsidiaries, setting up cooperative activities among them to achieve economies of scale. By this point, the MNC has usually adopted a geocentric orientation, viewing opportunities and entry strategies in the context of an interrelated global market instead of regional or national markets. In this way, alternative entry strategies are viewed on an overall portfolio basis to take maximum advantage of potential synergies and leverage arising from operations in multi-country markets.[64] While Procter & Gamble, for example, took around 100 years to fully go global, more recently many companies are **"born global"**—that is, they start out with a global reach, typically by using the internet capabilities and also through hiring people with international experience and contacts around the world.

> *Born globals globalize some aspects of their business– manufacturing, service delivery, capital sourcing, or talent acquisition, for instance – the moment they start up.*
> *. . . Standing conventional theory on its head, start-ups now do business in many countries before dominating their home markets.*

HARVARD BUSINESS REVIEW,
December 2008.[65]

Isenberg notes that successful entrepreneurs are able to establish multinational organizations from the outset by setting up and managing global supply chains and striking alliances from positions of weaknesses. The major challenges of born globals are those of accessing resources, and physical and cultural distances in their markets and operations.[66]

Using E-Business for Global Expansion

Companies of all sizes are increasingly looking to the Internet as a means of expanding their global operations. However, the Internet is not just about e-business:

> *The real story is that the Internet is driving global marketplace transformation and paradigm shift in how companies get things done, how they compete and how they serve their customers."*[67]

TABLE 6-1 World Internet Usage as of June, 2008.

Regions	Usage % of World	Usage Growth 2000–08
Africa	5.3	1,031.2
Asia	15.3	406.1
Europe	48.1	266.0
Middle East	21.3	1,176.8
North America	73.6	129.6
Latin America/Caribbean	24.1	669.3
Oceana/Australia	59.5	165.1
Total	29.9	305.5

Selected data from www.internetworldstats.com, accessed January 14, 2008.

The globalization of the web is evident, as Asia already has twice the number of Internet users as in North America, and is expected to have three times as many by 2012. Over half of Google's search queries come from outside the United States.

Many developing nations, in particular, are realizing the opportunities for e-commerce and are improving their infrastructure to take advantage of those opportunities. Governments and business are experiencing pressure to "go online" especially those companies that export goods to countries where a significant amount of business is conducted through the Internet, like the United States. Everest S.A., a family-run business in San Salvador, for example, sold a 69-kilogram lot (152 pounds) of coffee beans in an Internet auction from one of its five farms for a record price of $14.06 a pound.[68]

As a result, American technology giants are devoting great amounts of money and time to build and develop foreign-language Web sites and services. "Gone are the days in which you can launch a Web site in English and assume that readers from around the globe are going to look to you simply because of the content you're providing."[69]

While the benefits of e-business are many, including rapid entrance into new geographic markets (see Exhibit 6-6), less touted are the many challenges inherent in a global B2B or B2C strategy. These include cultural differences and varying business models, and governmental wrangling and border conflicts, in particular the question over which country has jurisdiction and responsibility over disputes regarding cross-border electronic transactions.[70] Potential problem areas that managers must assess in their global environmental analysis include conflicting consumer protection, intellectual property and tax laws, increasing isolationism even among democracies, language barriers, and a lack of tech-savvy legislators worldwide.[71]

Savvy global managers will realize that e-business cannot be regarded as just an extension of current businesses. It is a whole new industry in itself, complete with a different pool of competitors and entirely new sets of environmental issues. A reassessment of the environmental forces in the newly configured industry, using Michael Porter's five forces analytical model, should take account of shifts in the relative bargaining power of buyers and suppliers, the level of threat of new competitors, existing and potential substitutes, as well as a present and anticipated competitor analysis.[72] The level of e-competition will be determined by how transparent and imitable the company's business model is for its product or service as observed on its Web site.

It is clear that a competitive global B2B or B2C strategy must offer a technology solution that goes beyond basic transaction or listing service capabilities.[73] To assess the potential competitive position of the company, managers must ask themselves the following:

- Does the exchange provide a technology solution that helps industry trading partners to do business more efficiently?
- Is the exchange known to be among the top three to five within its vertical industry?
- Does the exchange offer industry-specific technology and expertise that gives it an advantage over generic exchange builders?[74]

EXHIBIT 6-6 Benefits of B2B

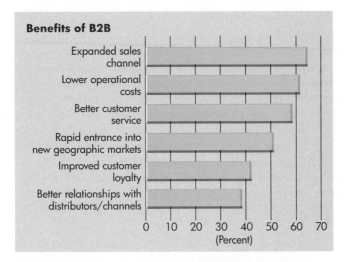

Source: Data from IDC Internet executive Advisory Council Surveys, 2001.

There is no doubt that the global e-business competitive arena is a challenging one, both strategically and technologically. But many companies around the world are plunging in, fearing that they will be left behind in this fast-developing global e-marketplace. In Melbourne, Australia, the Broken Hill Proprietary Company (BHP), which specializes in natural resources and regional steel for the global market, has launched its own one-stop global e-marketplace. The site provides logistics, sample products, and supply procurements to e-business producer market-places. BHP has conducted a series of Internet-based "reverse" auctions, where suppliers agree on starting prices and then bid against each other to lower prices for ferro-alloys.[75]

For companies like eBay, e-business is their business—services are provided over the Internet for end users and for businesses. With a unique business model, eBay embarked on a global e-strategy. The company has positioned itself to be global and giant: part international swap meet, part clearinghouse for the world's manufacturers and retailers. The international e-commerce market is evolving rapidly, and executives at eBay's annual financial conference in May 2006 discussed how eBay is responding effectively to challenges. "In Europe, eBay is on track to be a bigger business than it is in the United States, while Asia remains eBay's fastest growing region with tremendous long-term potential."[76]

> Across all of our businesses, we see greater opportunities for future growth than ever before. Each of our brands [Marketplaces, Payments and Communications] is the global leader in its space and well positioned to pursue new opportunities and accelerate growth. Together, they're working to turbo charge one another. Our multi-brand strategy is opening up entirely new vistas of opportunity for the company.
>
> MEG WHITMAN,
> (then) *CEO, eBay, Canada News Wire Group,*
> *May 4, 2006.*[77]

It has not all been easy for eBay's international ventures, however. For a discussion on the company's troubles in Japan, causing its exit from that market, and then its re-entry in 2007, see the Part 3 comprehensive case "eBay in Japan."

E-Global or E-Local?

> Alibaba has more than 8 million small and midsize companies using its business-to-business online marketplace. . . . The company has launched local versions of its B2B service in Japan, South Korea, and India.[78]
>
> BUSINESS WEEK,
> *April 9, 2009.*

Although the Internet is a global medium, the company is still faced with the same set of decisions regarding how much its products or services can be "globalized" or how much they must be "localized" to national or regional markets. Local cultural expectations, differences in privacy laws, government regulations, taxes, and payment infrastructure are just a few of the complexities encountered in trying to "globalize" e-commerce. Further complications arise because the local physical infrastructure must support e-businesses that require the transportation of actual goods for distribution to other businesses in the supply chain, or to end users. In those instances, adding e-commerce to an existing "old-economy" business in those international markets is likely to be more successful than starting an e-business from scratch without the supply and distribution channels already in place. However, many technology consulting firms, such as NextLinx, provide software solutions and tools to penetrate global markets, extend their supply chains, and enable new buyer and seller relationships around the globe.

Going global with e-business, as Yahoo! has done, necessitates a coordinated effort in a number of regions around the world at the same time to gain a foothold and to grab new markets before competitors do. Certain conditions dictate the advisability of going e-global:

> The global beachhead strategy makes sense when trade is global in scope; when the business does not involve delivering orders; and when the business model can be hijacked relatively easily by local competitors.[79]

This strategy would work well for global B2B markets in steel, plastics, and electronic components.

The e-local, or regional strategic, approach is suited to consumer retailing and financial services, for example. Amazon and eBay have started their regional approach in Western Europe. Again, certain conditions would make this strategy more advisable:

> *[The e-local/regional approach] is preferable under three conditions: when production and consumption are regional rather than global in scope; when customer behavior and market structures differ across regions but are relatively similar within a region; and when supply-chain management is very important to success.*[80]

The selection of which region or regions to target depends on the same factors of local market dynamics and industry variables as previously discussed in this chapter. However, for e-businesses, additional variables must also be considered, such as the rate of Internet penetration and the level of development of the local telecommunications infrastructure.

One company which learned the hard way how to localize its e-business is Handango, Inc., of Hurst, Texas—a maker of smart-phone and wireless-network software. As the company vice president of marketing, Clint Patterson, said, reflecting on their move into Asian markets several years ago: "We didn't understand what purchasing methods would be popular or even what kinds of content. We didn't have a local taste. We realized we needed someone on the street to hold our hand."[81] For example, Handango found it needed a local bank account to do business in Japan, because Japanese consumers use a method called *konbini* to make online payments. This means that when they place their order online, instead of paying with a credit card, they go to a local convenience store and pay cash to a clerk, who then transfers the payment into the online vendor's account. In order to adapt to this system Handango formed an alliance with @irBitway, a local consumer-electronics Web portal, which now acts as Handango's agent in the konbini system, and also has taken over Handango's local marketing and translation.[82] Handango ran into a similar problem in Germany, finding out that Germans do not like debt and prefer to pay for their online purchases with wire transfers from their bank accounts. To get around this, the company found a local partner to interface with local banks, and then adapted its Web site to the new payment method.[83]

Entry Strategy Alternatives

For a multinational corporation (or a company considering entry into the international arena), a more specific set of strategic alternatives, often varying by targeted country, focuses on different ways to enter a foreign market. Managers need to consider how potential new markets may best be served by their company in light of the risks and the critical environmental factors associated with their entry strategies. The following sections examine the various entry and ownership strategies available to firms, including exporting, licensing, franchising, contract manufacturing, offshoring, service-sector outsourcing, turnkey operations, management contracts, joint ventures, fully owned subsidiaries set up by the firm, and e-business. These alternatives are not mutually exclusive; several may be employed at the same time. They are addressed in order of ascending risk, although e-business is usually low-risk.

EXPORTING Exporting is a relatively low-risk way to begin international expansion or to test out an overseas market. Little investment is involved, and fast withdrawal is relatively easy. Small firms seldom go beyond this stage, and large firms use this avenue for many of their products. Because of their comparative lack of capital resources and marketing clout, exporting is the primary entry strategy used by small businesses to compete on an international level. Jordan Toothbrush, for example, a small company with one plant in Norway and with limited resources, is dependent on good distributors. Since Jordan exports around the world, the company recognizes the importance of maintaining good distributor relations. A recent survey by Dun and Bradstreet showed that more than half of small to medium-sized businesses anticipate growth in their export sales in the next few years.[84]

An experienced firm may want to handle its exporting functions by appointing a manager or establishing an export department. Alternatively, an export management company (EMC) may be retained to take over some or all exporting functions, including dealing with host-country regulations, tariffs, duties, documentation, letters of credit, currency conversion, and so forth. Frequently, it pays to hire a specialist for a given host country.

Certain decisions need special care when managers are setting up an exporting system, particularly the choice of distributor. Many countries have regulations that make it very hard to remove a distributor who proves inefficient. Other critical environmental factors include export-import tariffs and quotas, freight costs, and distance from supplier countries.

LICENSING An international licensing agreement grants the rights to a firm in the host country to either produce or sell a product, or both. This agreement involves the transfer of rights to patents, trademarks, or technology for a specified period of time in return for a fee paid by the licensee. Anheuser-Busch, for instance, has granted licenses to produce and market Budweiser beer in England, Japan, Australia, and Israel, among other countries. Many food-manufacturing MNCs license their products overseas, often under the names of local firms, and products like those of Nike and Disney can be seen around the world under various licensing agreements. Like exporting, licensing is also a relatively low-risk strategy because it requires little investment, and it can be a useful option in countries where market entry by other means is constrained by regulations or profit-repatriation restrictions.

Licensing is especially suitable for the mature phase of a product's life cycle, when competition is intense, margins decline, and production is relatively standardized. It is also useful for firms with rapidly changing technologies, for those with many diverse product lines, and for small firms with few financial and managerial resources for direct investment abroad. A clear advantage of licensing is that it avoids the tariffs and quotas usually imposed on exports. The most common disadvantage is the licensor's lack of control over the licensee's activities and performance.

Critical environmental factors to consider in licensing are whether sufficient patent and trademark protection is available in the host country, the track record and quality of the licensee, the risk that the licensee may develop its competence to become a direct competitor, the licensee's market territory, and legal limits on the royalty rate structure in the host country.

FRANCHISING Similar to licensing, **franchising** involves relatively little risk. The franchisor licenses its trademark, products and services, and operating principles to the franchisee for an initial fee and ongoing royalties. Franchises are well known in the domestic fast-food industry; McDonald's, for example, operates primarily on this basis. For a large up-front fee and considerable royalty payments, the franchisee gets the benefit of McDonald's reputation, existing clientele, marketing clout, and management expertise. The "Big M" is well recognized internationally, as are many other fast-food and hotel franchises, such as Holiday Inn, along with products such as Nike's and Disney's. A critical consideration for the franchisor's management is quality control, which becomes more difficult with greater geographic dispersion.

Franchising can be an ideal strategy for small businesses because outlets require little investment in capital or human resources. Through franchising, an entrepreneur can use the resources of franchisees to expand; most of today's large franchises started out with this strategy. An entrepreneur can also use franchisees to enter a new business. Higher costs in entry fees and royalties are offset by the lower risk of an established product, trademark, and customer base, as well as the benefit of the franchisor's experience and techniques.

CONTRACT MANUFACTURING A common means of using cheaper labor overseas is contract manufacturing, which involves contracting for the production of finished goods or component parts. These goods or components are then imported to the home country, or to other countries, for assembly or sale. Alternatively, they may be sold in the host country. If managers can ensure the reliability and quality of the local contractor and work out adequate means of capital repatriation, this strategy can be a desirable means of quick entry into a country with a low capital investment and none of the problems of local ownership. Firms like Nike use contract manufacturing around the world.

OFFSHORING Offshoring is when a company moves one or all of its factories from the 'home' country to another country, as is the case with some of Toyota's factories in the U.S. Offshoring provides the company with access to foreign markets while avoiding trade barriers, as well as, frequently, an overall lower cost of production. According to the U.S. Commerce Department, approximately 90 percent of the output from U.S.-owned offshore factories is sold to foreign consumers.[85]

However, some companies attribute their global success to their local connections for part or all of their manufacturing. An example is the BAG shoe company in Italy. Just over half the upper shoe parts are made in low-cost countries such as Serbia and Tunisia. The rest of the uppers and the soles are made locally. Having such a large part of its shoes made by local suppliers enables BAG's CEO, Mr. Bracalente, to emphasize the "Made in Italy" label as a big marketing advantage. And having suppliers close by means production problems are quickly solved. "Our technicians can go and visit the suppliers, often in just half an hour," Mr. Bracalente says; he feels that splitting the assembly functions between BAG and many outside companies is a strength, not a weakness.[86] He argues that this mix of production location gives the company a vital source of flexibility and the capacity to make rapid changes in shoe style.[87]

One means of gaining increased efficiencies and therefore lower costs is through **clustering**—used when contract manufacturing, offshoring, or service-sector outsourcing (explained below). Sirkin et al. note that many companies from emerging market economies—companies which they call "challengers"—have gained rapid success by clustering:

> *Challengers are particularly expert at keeping their costs low by clustering – operating in concentrations of related, interdependent companies within an industry that use the same suppliers, specialized labor, and distribution channels.[88]*

> HAROLD SIRKIN ET AL.,
> *Globality, 2008.*

Examples of industry clusters are an appliance cluster in Monterey, Mexico, which serves the North American market, serving firms both global and local, and including around two hundred local suppliers; the many manufacturing clusters in China, and service center clusters in India, as discussed elsewhere in this chapter.

SERVICE SECTOR OUTSOURCING   An increasing number of firms are outsourcing "white-collar" jobs overseas in an attempt to reduce their overall costs. Indeed, the practice is not limited to large firms. Research by Gregorio et al. found that "Offshore outsourcing enhances international competitiveness by enabling SMEs to reduce costs, expand relational ties, serve customers more effectively, free up scarce resources, and leverage capabilities of foreign partners."[89]

Firms which outsource services usually enter overseas markets by setting up local offices, research laboratories, call centers, and so on in order to utilize the highly skilled but lower-wage **"human capital"** that is available in countries such as India, the Philippines, and China, as well as the ability to offer global, round-the-clock service from different time zones. Some examples include the following:

General Electric: 20,000 people in India; a big China R&D center: services in finance, IT support, R&D for medical, lighting, aircraft

Accenture: 5,000 in the Philippines; accounting, software, back-office work

Oracle: Doubling India staff to 4,000; software design, customer support, accounting

Conseco: 1,700 in India, three more centers planned; insurance claim processing[90]

Overall, it seems that India has benefited in IT jobs; as noted by Bill Gates of Microsoft "India is the absolute leader in IT services offered on the world market."[91] (In fact, the preparation of this book for publishing was outsourced by Prentice Hall to a company in India—Integra Software Services Pvt.Ltd.) However, as India gets more sophisticated at taking over high-skilled jobs outsourced from European and U.S. multinationals, they are starting to turn away call-center work, saying that it doesn't pay well any longer. In addition, companies are finding that salaries in India are increasing with the demand for jobs from MNCs, and with the Indian technology companies themselves growing in global clout. Outsourcing of low-end office jobs may then start to migrate to other countries such as the Philippines or South Africa.[92] In turn, both Indian and American IT service providers are opening offices in Hungary, Poland, and the Czech Republic to take advantage of the German and English-speaking workforce for European clients. (For further discussion of this issue, see the chapter-ending case "Indian BPOs Waking up to the Philippines Opportunities.")

Whether the firms outsource (or "offshore") white-collar or blue-collar jobs, they must consider strategic aspects of that decision beyond immediate cost savings. According to Hewitt Associates, a global human resources consulting firm, the "global sourcing" strategy utilized by the firms it surveyed was often short-sighted:

Although cost reduction is the primary driver, less than half of companies analyze the tax environments of considered countries, only three-fourths measure the impact on supply chain costs, and only 34 percent assess the cost of plant or office shutdown.[93]

In addition to the lack of consideration for factors other than production costs, sending jobs to a particular country is typically a short-term cost-reduction strategy, because at some point competitive pressures will increase jobs there, necessitating moving those jobs again to still lower-cost countries (a transition known as "the race to the bottom.")

Even with its increasing outsourcing of jobs, IBM has acknowledged the need to consider factors other than cost, as it started a radical revamping of its 200,000 people services workforce in 2006, saying

The idea is to perform work for clients where it can be done most competitively. That means not only India and China, but Tulsa, Oklahoma, and Boulder, Colorado.

BUSINESS WEEK,
June 5, 2006.[94]

Managers are in fact broadening their strategic view of sending skilled work abroad, now using the term "transformational outsourcing" to refer to the growth opportunities provided by making better use of skilled staff in the home office which are brought about by the gains in efficiency and productivity through leveraging global talent.[95] The U.S.-based bank Wachovia Corp. (which became part of Wells Fargo in 2009), for example, signed a $1.1 billion deal in 2006 with India's Genpact to outsource finance and accounting jobs but at the same time the company outsourced administration of its human-resources programs to Hewitt Associates, based in the United States.[96] However, the risk of backlash from customers, community, and current employees necessitates careful consideration of the reasons for a company to go offshore. Managers also must consider the risk of losing control of proprietary technology and processes and decide whether to set up the company's own subsidiary offshore (a "captive" operation) instead of contracting with outside specialists. Bank of America, for example, split their strategy by opening their own subsidiary in India, but also allied with Infosys technologies and Tata Consultancy Services for 30 percent of its IT resources to be outsourced.[97]

TURNKEY OPERATIONS   In a so-called **turnkey operation**, a company designs and constructs a facility abroad (such as a dam or chemical plant), trains local personnel, and then turns the key over to local management—for a fee, of course. The Italian company Fiat, for example, constructed an automobile plant in the former Soviet Union under a turnkey agreement. Critical factors for success are the availability of local supplies and labor, reliable infrastructure, and an acceptable means of repatriating profits. There may also be a critical risk exposure if the turnkey contract is with the host government, which is often the case. This situation exposes the company to risks such as contract revocation and the rescission of bank guarantees.

MANAGEMENT CONTRACTS   A management contract gives a foreign company the rights to manage the daily operations of a business but not to make decisions regarding ownership, financing, or strategic and policy changes. Usually, management contracts are enacted in combination with other agreements, such as joint ventures. By itself, a management contract is a relatively low-risk entry strategy, but it is likely to be short term and provide limited income unless it leads to another more permanent position in the market.

INTERNATIONAL JOINT VENTURES   At a much higher level of investment and risk (though usually less risky than a wholly owned plant), joint ventures present considerable opportunities unattainable through other strategies. A joint venture involves an agreement by two or more companies to produce a product or service together. In an **international joint venture (IJV)** ownership is shared, typically by an MNC and a local partner, through agreed-upon proportions of equity. This strategy facilitates an MNC's rapid entry into new markets by means of an already established partner who has local contacts and familiarity with local operations. IJVs are a common strategy for corporate growth around the world. They also are a means to overcome trade barriers, to achieve significant economies of scale for development of a strong competitive position, to secure access to additional raw materials, to acquire managerial and technological skills, and to spread the risk associated with operating in a foreign environment.[98] Not surprisingly, larger companies are more inclined to take a high-equity stake in an IJV, to engage in global industries, and to be less vulnerable to the risk conditions in the host country.[99] The joint venture reduces the risks of expropriation and harassment by the host country. Indeed, it may be the only means of entry into certain countries, like Mexico and Japan that stipulate proportions of local ownership and local participation.

In recent years, IJVs have made up about 20 percent of direct investments by MNCs in other countries, including such deals as that between Mittal Steel of India and Arcelor of France in 2006—creating the world's biggest steel company.[100] Many companies have set up joint ventures with European companies to gain the status of an "insider" in the European Common Market. Most of these alliances are not just tools of convenience but are important—perhaps critical—means to compete in the global arena. To compete globally, firms have to incur, and defray, immense fixed costs—and they need partners to help them in this effort.[101]

Sometimes countries themselves need such alliances to improve economic conditions. The Russian Federation has recently opened its doors to joint ventures, seeking an infusion of capital and management expertise. IJVs are one of the many forms of strategic global alliances that are further discussed in the next chapter.

In a joint venture, the level of relative ownership and specific contributions must be worked out by the partners. The partners must share management and decision making for a successful alliance. The company seeking such a venture must maintain sufficient control, however, because without adequate control, the company's managers may be unable to implement their desired strategies. Initial partner selection and the development of a mutually beneficial working agreement are, therefore, critical to the success of a joint venture. In addition, managers must ascertain that there will be enough of a "fit" between the partners' objectives, strategies, and resources—financial, human, and technological—to make the venture work. Unfortunately, too often the need for preparation and cooperation is given insufficient attention, resulting in many such marriages ending in divorce. About 60 percent of IJVs fail, usually because of ineffective managerial decisions regarding the type of IJV, its scope, duration, and administration, as well as careless partner selection.[102] In 1998, the chief executive of Daimler-Benz, Jürgen Schrempp, said that its joint venture with Chrysler would be a "marriage made in heaven." But it ended in a messy divorce in 2007 because of cross-cultural conflicts and because the German company's luxury-car lineup had little in common with Chrysler's portfolio of vehicles.[103] In 2009, Chrysler, as well as General Motors and Ford, was seeking massive funding from the U.S. government in order to stem its losses as a result of the economic downturn; this in spite of the many joint ventures and alliances that those companies have around the world. Toyota, on the other hand surpassed GM in 2008 sales to become the world's number one automaker.

FULLY OWNED SUBSIDIARIES In countries where a **fully owned subsidiary** is permitted, an MNC wishing total control of its operations can start its own product or service business from scratch, or it may acquire an existing firm in the host country. The Tata Group, an Indian conglomerate for cars, steel, software, and tea, continues to make acquisitions around the world. In 2007 it acquired Corus, a European steel company, and in 2008 it paid Ford $2.3 billion for Jaguar and land Rover.[104] Such acquisitions by MNCs allow rapid entry into a market with established products and distribution networks and provide a level of acceptability not likely to be given to a "foreign" firm. These advantages somewhat offset the greater level of risk stemming from larger capital investments, compared with other entry strategies. Other examples of acquisitions to gain further growth and entry into global markets include that of the IBM Personal Computing Division by the Lenovo Group of China, creating a global business with worldwide reach;[105] and the Procter and Gamble acquisition of Gillette, which paved the way for the creation of the world's largest consumer goods company.[106]

At the highest level of risk is the strategy of starting a business from scratch in the host country—that is, establishing a new wholly owned foreign manufacturing or service company or subsidiary with products aimed at the local market or targeted for export. Japanese automobile manufacturers, such as Honda, Nissan, and Toyota, have successfully used this strategy in the United States to get around U.S. import quotas.

This strategy exposes the company to the full range of risk, to the extent of its investment in the host country. As evidenced by events in South Africa and China, political instability can be devastating to a wholly owned foreign subsidiary. Add to this risk a number of other critical environmental factors—local attitudes toward foreign ownership, currency stability and repatriation, the threat of expropriation and nationalism—and you have a high-risk entry strategy that must be carefully evaluated and monitored. There are advantages to this strategy, however, such as full control over decision making and efficiency, as well as the ability to integrate operations with overall company-wide strategy.

E-BUSINESS   Discussed earlier as a global strategy, e-business is an entry strategy at the local level. As such, the failure risk of entry depends greatly on the country or region, even though it is relatively low globally. Yahoo!, for example, bought the largest Arabic-language web portal in August 2009. Although fewer than 50 million of the world's 320 million Arabic-language speakers are on line, CEO Carol Bartz says that "emerging markets and new languages are a key part of the strategy. Acquisition costs are modest, and while advertising spending is too low for immediate payback, the medium-term prospects for significant growth are surer than in more mature markets."[107]

Exhibit 6-7 summarizes the advantages and critical success factors of these entry strategies, which must be taken into account when selecting one or a combination of strategies

EXHIBIT 6-7   International Entry Strategies: Advantages and Critical Success Factors

Strategy	Advantages	Critical Success Factors
Exporting	Low risk No long-term assets Easy market access and exit	Choice of distributor Transportation costs Tariffs and quotas
Licensing	No asset ownership risk Fast market access Avoids regulations and tariffs	Quality and trustworthiness of licensee Appropriability of intellectual property Host-country royalty limits
Franchising	Little investment or risk Fast market access Small business expansion	Quality control of franchisee and franchise operations
Contract manufacturing/Offshoring	Limited cost and risk Short-term commitment	Reliability and quality of local contractor Operational control and human rights issues
Service-sector outsourcing	Lower employment costs	Quality control
Turnkey operations	Access to high skills and markets Revenue from skills and technology where FDI restricted	Domestic client acceptance Reliable infrastructure Sufficient local supplies and labor Repatriable profits Reliability of any government partner
Management contracts	Low-risk access to further strategies	Opportunity to gain longer-term position
Joint ventures	Insider access to markets Share costs and risk Leverage partner's skill base technology, local contacts	Strategic fit and complementarity of partner, markets, products Ability to protect technology Competitive advantage Ability to share control Cultural adaptability of partners
Wholly owned subsidiaries	Realize all revenues and control Global economies of scale Strategic coordination Protect technology and skill base	Ability to assess and control economic, political, and currency risk Ability to get local acceptance Repatriability of profits
eBusiness	Rapid entry (or exit) into new markets (often through alliance or purchase of local websites); relatively low-risk	Differences in business models, culture, language, and laws regarding intellectual property, consumer protection, and taxes.

depending on the location, the environmental factors and competitive analysis, and the overall strategy with which the company approaches world markets.

Complex situational factors face the international manager as she or he considers strategic approaches to world markets, along with which entry strategies might be appropriate, as illustrated in Comparative Management in Focus: Strategic Planning for the EU Market.

COMPARATIVE MANAGEMENT IN FOCUS

Strategic Planning for the EU Market

There are big differences between European business today and 10 years ago. The largest impetus for change is the rise in foreign shareholders. While some further change may be necessary, such as in openness to takeovers - European companies should not get rid of the things that make them so successful.

FINANCIAL TIMES
(August 14, 2008).[108]

If you're investing in Hungary or Poland, you get access to the lower costs they offer, compared with, say, Germany or France or Britain. At the same time, if you're producing in Poland, you have an ability to move your goods and services around within the European Union.[109]

As shown in Table 6-2, European countries dominate in the 2009–2010 Global Competitiveness Index (GCI) rankings of the World Economic Forum. The United States slipped from its first position the previous year; the report attributed that to "weaker financial markets and less macroeconomic stability."[110] The GCI is based on 12 pillars of competitiveness which provide attractive conditions and incentives for both local and foreign companies to do business there: *Institutions, Infrastructure, Macroeconomic Stability, Health and Primary Education, Higher Education and Training, Goods Market Efficiency, Labor Market Efficiency, Financial Market Sophistication, Technological Readiness, Market Size, Business Sophistication*, and *Innovation.*[111]

Clearly, this 27-nation unified market of more than 400 million people in the expanded EU provides great business opportunities. This is particularly so for small and medium-sized enterprises (SMEs), to gain access to the EU market by taking advantage of the lower costs in the Central and Eastern European countries (CEE) compared to the rest of the EU, including cheaper wages, lower corporate taxes, and educated workforces. Those countries have strengthened their economies in order to meet EU accession requirements, including privatizing state-run business, improving the infrastructure, and revamping their finance and banking systems. Manea and Pearce researched the strategies of MNEs in Central and Eastern Europe and found that, because of uncertainty about investing in CEE, "initially market-seeking operations dominated in CEE, with little integration of CEE subsidiaries into global MNE networks."[112] The authors found that European MNEs tended to pursue country-centered strategies, while Asian MNEs invested more in exporting. They recommended that "product differentiation using CEE creative capabilities

TABLE 6-2	2009–10 Global Competitiveness Index Score (7 is the highest score)	
Rank	Country	Score
1	Switzerland	5.60
2	U.S.	5.59
3	Singapore	5.55
4	Sweden	5.51
5	Denmark	5.46
6	Finland	5.43
7	Germany	5.37
8	Japan	5.37
9	Canada	5.33
10	Netherlands	5.32

Selected data from www.worldeconomicforum.org, September 8, 2009.

(i.e. technology and engineering expertise) rather than cost-competitiveness, may ultimately secure a more sustainable and embedded entry into MNEs' wider European (or global) networks."[113]

It is noteworthy that the dominant theme of the past decade has been the internationalization of European companies, with "German, French, Spanish and Italian groups grasping the opportunity from emerging markets, probably better than most US companies."[114]

For firms within Europe, the euro eliminates currency risk, and so "Pan European thinking becomes not only practicable but essential."[115] The success of companies within Europe, then, depends on their efficiency in streamlining and consolidating their processes and in integrating product and marketing plans across Europe. The challenge is to balance the national and the continental view because a common currency does not bring about cultural or linguistic union.[116]

Clearly, both European and non-European companies must reconsider their European, and indeed global, strategies now that the enlarged EU has become a reality, complete with a common currency, the euro. "Foreign" managers, for example, need to develop an action program to ensure that their products have continued access to the EU and to adapt their marketing efforts to encompass the whole EU. The latter task is difficult, if not impossible, however, because the "citizen of Europe" is a myth; national cultures and tastes cannot be homogenized. With many different languages and distinctive national customs and cultures, companies trying to sell in Europe must thread their way through a maze of varying national preferences. These and other challenges lie ahead, along with numerous opportunities.

Meanwhile, adventurous European businesses are spreading their wings across neighboring countries as they realize that open markets can offer as much growth and profitability as does protectionism—probably more. Companies within the EU are gaining great advantages by competing in a continental-scale market and thereby avoiding duplication of administrative procedures, production, marketing, and distribution. The Italian company Benetton Group SPA is one such company—competing by being technologically efficient. For insiders, a single EU internal market means greater efficiencies and greater economic growth through economies of scale and the removal of barriers, with the consequent lowering of unit costs.

Companies based outside the EU enjoy the same advantages if they have a subsidiary in at least one member state, but they sometimes feel discrimination simply because they are outside what, for the member states, is a domestic market. In other words, the EU has a protectionist wall—of tariffs, quotas, local content laws, and competitive tactics—to keep out the United States and Japan. However, the EU has also created opportunities for nonmembers. Many companies, especially MNCs, start from a better position than some firms based inside the community because of (1) their superior competitiveness and research and development, (2) an existing foothold in the market, and (3) reduced operating expenses (one subsidiary for the whole EU instead of several). But European harmonized standards, while seeking to eliminate trade barriers within Europe, serve to limit access to EU markets by outside companies through the standardized specifications of products allowed to be sold in Europe. The harmonization laws set minimum standards for exports and imports that are EU-wide. However, those standards also frequently hinder European companies from efficient sourcing of raw materials or component parts from "foreign" companies.

Opinions differ about the long-term impact on U.S. firms: The EU could unify its markets, adversely affecting some U.S. industries; market access could be reduced; and demands for reciprocal market access in the United States might ensue. In November 2003, for example, when then President Bush imposed tariffs on steel imports, the WTO ruled that the tariffs were illegal and authorized European and Asian nations to impose retaliatory tariffs against the United States. Not long after, President Bush was forced to reverse himself and lift the tariffs.[117]

Others feel that the new single market provides little threat to and considerable opportunity for Americans. Many U.S. firms (in anticipation of protectionism) have invested in Europe since the beginning of the Common Market in 1958, and they now feel satisfied with their current positions. Indeed, U.S. companies (GE, Dow, 3M, Hewlett-Packard) that already have well-established European presences enjoy the same free flow of goods, services, capital, and people as Europeans. It is clear, though, that the EU Competition Commissioner is keeping a keen eye on any anticompetitive tactics from abroad. Microsoft and the EU have engaged in a running spat over competition issues for years, and as of 2009 the U.S. company has been fined more than one billion euros in all for allegedly abusing its 95 percent dominance of personal computer systems through its ubiquitous Windows software.[118] On January 16, 2009, the EU Commissioner ordered Microsoft to untie the browser from its operating system in the 27-nation union, enabling makers of rival browsers to compete fairly.

Indeed, foreign companies wishing to merge with or acquire companies in Europe, or even with companies outside of Europe, who plan to do business in the EU, need to be aware of the EU competition policies and merger control. In reviewing the failed GE-Honeywell merger, which was knocked down by the EU Commission, even though the proposed marriage was one of two U.S. companies, Anwar noted:

> Under the European Merger Control Regulation (MCR) 4064/89, the Commission can review and investigate any business concentration (mergers, takeovers, acquisitions) that exceeds a world-wide turnover (revenues) of $4.6 billion or $250 million sales in the European region.[119]

Whereas in the U.S. those acquisitions that may create a monopoly will not be allowed, within the EU the prohibition criterion is "a business concentration that strengthens a market position and impedes competition."[120]

Nevertheless, many firms are opting for joint ventures with European partners, sacrificing their usual preference of 100 percent ownership (or majority control) to extend operations around Europe. This strategy also opens doors to markets dominated by public procurement, as with the AT&T–Philips venture to produce telecommunications equipment. But for a number of firms—both foreign and European—operating in Western Europe, at least, has become cost prohibitive. The average Western European earns more, works fewer hours, takes longer vacations, and receives more social entitlements and job protection than workers in Asia and North America. European MNCs have the highest labor and taxation costs among the TRIAD nations.[121] Siemens AG of Germany, for example, shifted almost all its semiconductor assembly work from its plants in Germany—where it was not permitted to operate around the clock or on weekends—to a plant in Singapore, where it operates twenty-four hours a day, 365 days a year, and pays $4.40 an hour for workers.[122]

Suzuki, Toyota, Nissan, and other Japanese companies are also experiencing the dilemma of operating in Europe. They are reluctant to freely pour yen into Europe, but they want to keep a foothold in the market. Suzuki, for example, found that in its Spanish plant it took five times the number of workers and cost 46 percent more to produce a Suzuki Samurai than in its Japanese plants.

Strategic Choice

The strategic choice of one or more of the entry strategies will depend on (1) a critical evaluation of the advantages (and disadvantages) of each in relation to the firm's capabilities, (2) the critical environmental factors, and (3) the contribution that each choice would make to the overall mission and objectives of the company. Exhibit 6-7 summarized the advantages and the critical success factors for each entry strategy discussed. However, when it comes down to a choice of entry strategy or strategies for a particular company, more specific factors relating to that firm's situation must be taken into account. These include factors relating to the firm itself, the industry in which it operates, location factors, and venture-specific factors, as summarized in Exhibit 6-8.

After consideration of the factors for the firm as shown in Exhibit 6-8, as well as what is available and legal in the desired location, some entry strategies will no doubt fall out of the feasibility zone. With those options remaining, then, strategic planners need to decide which factors are more important to the firm than others. One method is to develop a weighted assessment to compare the overall impact of factors such as those in Exhibit 6-8 relative to the industry, the location, and the specific venture—on each entry strategy. Specific evaluation ratings, of course, would depend on the country conditions at a given point in time, the nature of the industry, and the local company.

Based on a study of more than 10,000 foreign entry activities into China between 1979 and 1998, Pan and Tse concluded that managers tend to follow a hierarchy of decision-sequence in choosing an entry mode. As depicted in Exhibit 6-9, managers first decide between equity based and non-equity based. Then, equity modes are split into wholly owned operations and equity joint ventures (EJVs); non-equity modes are divided into contractual agreements and export. Pan and Tse found that the location choice—specifically the level of country risk—was the primary influence factor at the level of deciding between equity and non-equity modes. Host-country government incentives also encouraged the choice of equity mode.[124]

Gupta and Govindarajan also propose a hierarchy of decision factors but consider two initial choice levels. The first is the extent to which the firm will export or produce locally; the second is the extent of ownership control over activities that will be performed locally in the

EXHIBIT 6-8 Factors Affecting Choice of International Entry Mode[123]

Factor Category	Examples
Firm factors	International experience
	Core competencies
	Core capabilities
	National culture of home country
	Corporate culture
	Firm strategy, goals, and motivation
Industry factors	Industry globalization
	Industry growth rate
	Technical intensity of industry
Location factors	Extent of scale and location economies
	Country risk
	Cultural distance
	Knowledge of local market
	Potential of local market
	Competition in local market
Venture-specific factors	Value of firm—assets risked in foreign location
	Extent to which know-how involved in venture is informal (tacit)
	Costs of making or enforcing contracts with local partners
	Size of planned foreign venture
	Intent to conduct research and development with local partners

EXHIBIT 6-9 A Hierachical Model of Choice of Entry Modes

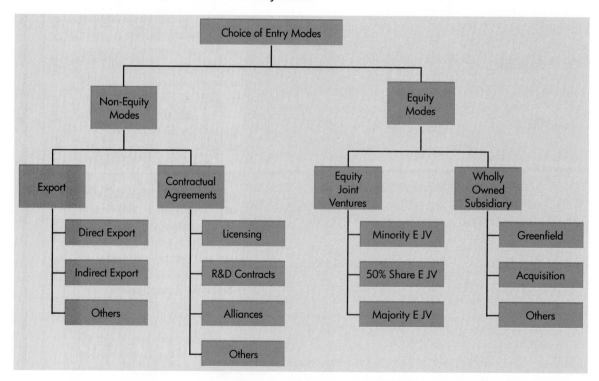

Source: Yigang Pan and David K. Tse, "The Hierarchical Model of Market Entry Modes," *Journal of International Business Studies* 31, no. 4 (4th Quarter 2000): 535–54.

EXHIBIT 6-10 Alternative Modes of Entry

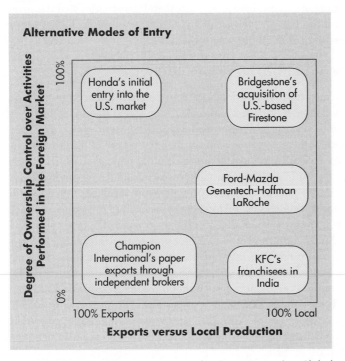

Source: Anil K. Gupta and Vijay Govindarajan, "Managing Global Expansion: A Conceptual Framework," *Business Horizons,* March/April 2000: 45–54.

target market.[125] As shown in Exhibit 6-10, there is an array of choice combinations within those two dimensions. Gupta and Govindarajan point out that, among the many factors to take into account, alliance-based entry modes are more suitable under the following conditions:

- Physical, linguistic, and cultural distance between the home and host countries is high.
- The subsidiary would have low operational integration with the rest of the multinational operations.
- The risk of asymmetric learning by the partner is low.
- The company is short of capital.
- Government regulations require local equity participation.[126]

The choice of entry strategy for McDonald's, for example, varies around the world according to the prevailing conditions in each country. As of September 2009, McDonalds had 31,000 restaurants in 118 countries, employing 58 million people.[127] In Europe, the company prefers wholly owned subsidiaries, since European markets are similar to those in the United States and can be run similarly. Those subsidiaries in the United States both operate company-owned stores and license out franchises. Approximately 70 percent of McDonald's stores around the world are franchised. In Asia, joint ventures are preferred so as to take advantage of partners' contacts and local expertise, and their ability to negotiate with bureaucracies such as the Chinese government. McDonald's has more than 1,000 stores in Japan; and continues its expansion in China, in spite of conflicts with the Chinese government, such as when it made McDonald's move from its leased Tiananmen Square restaurant. In other markets, such as in Saudi Arabia, McDonald's prefers to limit its equity risk by licensing the name—adding strict quality standards—and keeping an option to buy later. Some of McDonald's implementation policies are presented in Chapter 7.

Timing Entry and Scheduling Expansions

As with McDonald's, international strategic formulation requires a long-term perspective. Entry strategies, therefore, need to be conceived as part of a well-designed, overall plan. In the past, many companies have decided on a particular means of entry that seemed appropriate at the time, only to find later that it was shortsighted. For instance, if a company initially chooses to license a host-country company to produce a product, then later decides that the market is large enough to warrant its own production facility, this new strategy will no longer be feasible because the local host-country company already owns the rights.

The Influence of Culture on Strategic Choice

In addition, strategic choices at various levels often are influenced by cultural factors, such as a long-term versus a short-term perspective. Hofstede found that most people in such countries as China and Japan generally had a longer-term horizon than those in Canada and the United States.[128] Whereas Americans, then, might make strategic choices with a heavy emphasis on short-term profits, the Japanese are known to be more patient in sacrificing short-term results in order to build for the future with investment, research and development, and market share.

Risk orientation was also found to explain the choice between equity and non-equity modes.[129] Risk orientation relates to Hofstede's uncertainty avoidance dimension.[130] Firms from countries where, generally speaking, people tend to avoid uncertainty (for example, Latin American and African countries) tend to prefer non-equity entry modes to minimize exposure to risk. Managers from firms from low-uncertainty avoidance countries are more willing to take risks and are, therefore, more likely to adopt equity entry modes.[131]

Choice of equity versus non-equity mode has also been found to be related to level of power distance. According to Hofstede, a high power-distance country (such as Arab countries and Japan) is one where people observe interpersonal inequality and hierarchy.[132] Pan and Tse found that firms from countries tending toward high power distance are more likely to use equity modes of entry abroad.[133]

These are but a few of the examples of the relationships between culture and the choices that are made in the strategic planning and implementation phase. They serve to remind us that it is people who make those decisions and that the ways people think, feel, and act are based on their ingrained societal culture. People bring that context to work, and it influences their propensity toward or against certain types of decisions.

CONCLUSION

The process of strategic formulation for global competitiveness is a daunting task in the volatile international arena and is further complicated by the difficulties involved in acquiring timely and credible information. However, early insight into global developments provides a critical advantage in positioning a firm for future success.

When an entry strategy is selected, the international manager focuses on translating strategic plans into actual operations. Often this involves strategic alliances; always it involves functional level activities for strategic implementation. These subjects are covered in Chapter 7.

Summary of Key Points

1. Companies "go international" for many reasons, including reactive ones, such as international competition, trade barriers, and customer demands. Proactive reasons include seeking economies of scale, new international markets, resource access, cost savings, and local incentives. Those companies which are proactive in establishing a presence in many countries from their outset are referred to as "Born Globals."

2. International expansion and the resulting realization of a firm's strategy are the product of both rational planning and responding to emergent opportunities.

3. The steps in the rational planning process for developing an international corporate strategy comprise defining the mission and objectives of the firm, scanning the environment for threats and opportunities, assessing the internal strengths and weaknesses of the firm, considering alter-

native international entry strategies, and deciding on strategy. The strategic management process is completed by putting into place the operational plans necessary to implement the strategy and then setting up control and evaluation procedures.

4. Competitive analysis is an assessment of how a firm's strengths and weaknesses vis-à-vis those of its competitors affect the opportunities and threats in the international environment. Such assessment allows the firm to determine where the company has distinctive competences that will give it strategic advantage or where problem areas exist.

5. Corporate-level strategic approaches to international competitiveness include globalization and regionalization. Many MNCs have developed to the point of using an integrative global strategy. Entry and ownership

strategies are exporting, licensing, franchising, contract manufacturing, offshoring, outsourcing services, turnkey operations, management contracts, joint ventures, and fully owned subsidiaries, as well as the local level of e-business. Critical environmental and operational factors for implementation must be taken into account.

6. Companies of all sizes are increasingly looking to the Internet as a means of expanding their global operations, but localizing Internet operations is complex.

Discussion Questions

1. Discuss why companies "go international," giving specific reactive and proactive reasons.
2. What effects on company strategy have you observed as a result of the global economic downturn which began in 2008?
3. Discuss the ways in which managers arrive at new strategic directions—formal and informal. Which is the best?
4. Explain the process of environmental assessment. What are the major international variables to consider in the scanning process? Discuss the levels of environmental monitoring that should be conducted. How well do you think managers conduct environmental assessment?
5. How can managers assess the potential relative competitive position of their firm in order to decide on new strategic directions?
6. Discuss the relative advantages of globalization versus regionalization/localization.
7. What are the relative merits of the entry strategies discussed in this chapter? What is their role in an integrative global strategy?
8. Discuss the considerations in strategic choice, including the typical stages of the MNC and the need for a long-term global perspective.

Application Exercises

1. Choose a company in the microcomputer industry or a chain in the fast-food industry. In small groups, conduct a multilevel environmental analysis, describing the major variables involved, the relative impact of specific threats and opportunities, and the critical environmental factors to be considered. The group findings can then be presented to the class, allowing a specific time period for each group so that comparison and debate of different group perspectives can follow. Be prepared to state what regions or specific countries you are interested in and give your rationale.
2. In small groups, discuss among yourselves and then debate with the other groups the relative merits of the alternative entry strategies for the company and countries you chose in exercise 1. You should be able to make a specific choice and defend that decision.
3. For this exercise, research (individually or in small groups) a company with international operations and find out the kinds of entry strategies the firm has used. Present the information you find, in writing or verbally to the class, describing the nature of the company's international operations, its motivations, its entry strategies, the kinds of implementation problems the firm has run into, and how those problems have been dealt with.

Experiential Exercise

In groups of four, develop a strategic analysis for a type of company that is considering entry into Russia. Which entry strategies seem most appropriate? Share your results with the class.

Internet Resources

Visit the Deresky Companion Website at www.pearsonhighered.com/ Deresky for this chapter's Internet resources.

CASE STUDY

YouTube LLC: Going Global by Acting Local

On May 7, 2008, the world's largest online video community, YouTube, LLC (YouTube), announced the launch of its Indian site (YouTube.co.in). "We are very excited to bring a local version of YouTube to India considering the passion of users here for music and entertainment. For a culture that is steeped both in video and in storytelling, and where everyone has a voice—YouTube India will not only offer Indian users more relevant content but also provide a platform to share India's unique and diverse culture and lifestyle with the largest online video community in the world,"[1] said Steve Chen (Chen), chief technology officer (CTO) and co-founder of YouTube. The launch of the site did not come as a surprise considering the growing popularity of online social networking and video sharing sites in India. Moreover, there had been speculations of an imminent launch of a localized YouTube site ever since late 2007 when the company had bought the domain names YouTube.in and YouTube.co.in.

YouTube, a video sharing website where users can upload, view, and share video clips, is headquartered in San Bruno, California, USA. The company was founded in early 2005 by three employees of PayPal Inc.[2], Chen, Chad Hurley (who was the CEO as of 2008), and Jawed Karim. The site was launched in November 2006 with funding from venture capital firm Sequoia Capital. In October 2006, Google Inc.[3] (Google) announced that it would acquire YouTube for US$1.65 billion in Google stock and the deal came through the following month. YouTube then began operating as a subsidiary of Google. Though the company was yet to become profitable as of early 2008, analysts felt its user-base was growing rapidly. For instance, its user-base was increasing by around 200,000 every month as of early 2008.[4]

With the launch of YouTube India, India became the 20th country in which YouTube had launched a localized site.[5] The site contained local features such as promoted videos, featured videos, and homepage promotions, localized user interface and help center, user support, and community features. While the site had all the YouTube content, it was being customized to feature top Indian content. The site was initially to be in English, but was expected to expand in future to include some Indian languages as well. Sakina Arsiwala, International Manager, YouTube, said, "YouTube India would allow users to create and share videos, discover the most popular and relevant videos in India, and connect with other Indian and global users. Over time, YouTube India will benefit from an entirely local experience highlighting and featuring the content and functionality most desired by the Indian users."[6] She also added that the site was very user-friendly and users could upload their videos quite easily.

While YouTube had globally entered into various partnerships with content providers such as BBC, CBS, NBA, Sony Music Group, The Sundance Channel, Universal Music Group, Warner Music Group, etc., it had also struck deals with Eros Entertainment, the International Indian Film Academy (IIFA), India TV, Krishcricket, Ministry of Tourism (Government of India), NDTV, Rajshri Films, UTV, Zoom TV, etc. in India for providing India-specific content. The company said it was committed to protecting the intellectual property rights (IPRs) of content uploaded on the site and of protecting users against objectionable content. The company said that it used digital hash technology for copyright protection. This technology made it very difficult for others to copy and reload the same content.

The mid-2000s witnessed a trend of a section of youth in India increasingly becoming attracted to online social networking sites and video sharing sites. In fact, Google's social networking site Orkut had witnessed sound growth in India and was the most popular social networking site in the country. According to the company, YouTube too had developed a good following and India was one of the top 15 countries in terms of growth.[7] However, it had encountered some problems as well. For instance, a local music label in India had sued YouTube for hosting its product. Orkut too had been at the receiving end of criticism from fundamentalist groups regarding its content.[8]

YouTube expected to expand its user-base in India in a big way in the future by forging partnerships with various other companies and providing an offering that would suit the local tastes and preferences of the Indian users.[9] Once the user-base increased, the company planned to sell customized advertising on the site.[10] Analysts expected the competition for the Indian Internet space to heat up with major Internet companies such as Google and Yahoo! Inc.[11] trying

---

[1] "YouTube India is Launched," www.techtree.com, May 2008.
[2] PayPal, Inc., headquartered in Palo Alto, California, USA, is an e-commerce business allowing payments and money transfers to be made through the Internet.
[3] Google Inc., headquartered in Menlo Park, California, USA, is one of the world's leading Internet software companies.
[4] "YouTube Launched in India," www.economictimes.indiatimes.com, May 7, 2008.
[5] "YouTube Goes Bollywood," www.sfgate.com, May 7, 2008.
[6] "Now, Google Launches YouTube India," http://sify.com, May 8, 2008.
[7] "YouTube Goes Bollywood," www.sfgate.com, May 7, 2008.
[8] John Ribeiro, "YouTube Launches Site for India," http://computerworld.com.sg, May 7, 2008.
[9] "YouTube India Goes Live!" www.techshout.com, May 7, 2008.
[10] "YouTube Goes Bollywood," www.sfgate.com, May 7, 2008.
[11] Yahoo! Inc., headquartered in Sunnyvale, California, USA, is one of the world's leading Internet software companies.

to expand their user-base in the country by providing more local content. However, the global companies operating in this space would face competition from a number of Indian portals offering local content that had mushroomed in the recent years, they said.

Additional Readings and References

1. "YouTube Goes Bollywood," www.sfgate.com, May 7, 2008.
2. "YouTube India Goes Live!" www.techshout.com, May 7, 2008.
3. "YouTube Launched in India," www.economictimes.indiatimes.com, May 7, 2008.
4. John Ribeiro, "YouTube Launches Site for India," http://computerworld.com.sg, May 7, 2008.
5. "Now, Google Launches YouTube India," http://sify.com, May 8, 2008.
6. "YouTube India is Launched," www.techtree.com, May 2008.
7. www.en.wikipedia.org

Author Information: This case was written by Debapratim Purkayastha, ICMR. It was compiled from published sources, and is intended to be used as a basis for class discussion rather than to illustrate either effective or ineffective handling of a management situation.

Case Questions

1. Do a SWOT analysis of YouTube in India.
2. Assess YouTube's growth through alliances and partnerships.
3. Assess the company's localizing strategy. Do you recommend that YouTube "localize" when entering other countries?
4. What are the problems YouTube is experiencing in India?

Global Alliances and Strategy Implementation

OBJECTIVES:

1. To realize that much of international business is conducted through strategic alliances.

2. To understand the reasons that firms seek international business allies and the benefits they bring.

3. To understand the complexities involved in managing international joint ventures.

4. To appreciate the governmental and cultural factors that influence strategic implementation; as well as the impact of e-commerce.

5. To recognize the changing factors, opportunities and threats involved in joint ventures in the Russian Federation.

Opening Profile: Haeir Group: Growth Through Strategic Alliances, Acquisitions, and Global Networks.[1]

Chairman and CEO Zhang Ruimin took the reins of the Chinese government-controlled Qingdao Refrigerator Plant in 1984. He took over a company with 100 employees and poor quality products. To make matters worse, they were on the verge of bankruptcy. In his dramatic first act as CEO he smashed 76 poor-quality refrigerators with a hammer to drive home his intention to improve product quality. Ever pragmatic, Zhang Ruimin believes that Haeir has to think about talent management and performance management. They must focus on how they can change the mindset of the employees to get the needed results.

The foundation of Haier's human resource management strategy is rigorous performance management. They rank employees daily on results. Managers are evaluated monthly on performance and quarterly on potential. The system is fully transparent, and performance management is tightly linked to employee rewards and development. This system is highly differentiated from human resource practices used in other Chinese companies.

Today Haier Group is the fourth-largest white goods (refrigerators, washing machines, and other appliances) manufacturer in the world and is a very well known brand in China. As it grew, Haier acquired 18 companies that it identified as running at a loss. Haier acquired these companies because of their market potential, vitality and expected contributions once Haier's manufacturing processes and culture were adopted. Once acquired, Haier then restructured processes and procedures and converted idle tangible assets into productive assets at a minimum cost and in a short period of time.

Haier has established an extensive sales network around the globe primarily through strategic alliances with key partners in prospective global markets. Haier learned about the U.S. market by supplying small refrigerators to Wal-Mart Stores as Haier built their internationalization competencies.

Haier uses a three-pronged approach to internationalization that includes a localization strategy combining design, production and marketing network as the core of its global branding strategy. By the end of 2006, Haier owned 240 corporate subsidiaries and 18,000 sales outlets throughout the world. It has 5 research centers, 8 design centers, 6 design branches, 10 information stations, 30 manufacturing centers, 22 trading companies and almost 59,000 sales network outlets in more than 160 countries.

Haier has their eye on the high-tech future. Zhang believes that people must be connected to the world during the information era. He hopes that through this set of solutions, Haier can enable everybody, especially the Chinese, to enter the information era.

Source: Mary B. Teagarden and Dong Hong Cai, "Learning from Dragons who are Learning from Us: Developmental Lessons from China's Global Companies," *Organizational Dynamics* 38, no 1, (2009): 73–81 copyright 2009 Elsevier, used with permission of Elsevier.

STRATEGIC ALLIANCES

> *It is no longer an era in which a single company can dominate any technology or business by itself. The technology has become so advanced, and the markets so complex, that you simply can't expect to be the best at the whole process any longer.*

> FUMIO SATO,
> *CEO, Toshiba Electronics*[2]

As discussed in the opening profile, the Haeir Group gained rapid global growth through strategic alliances, acquisitions, and global networks, leading it to become one of *Fortune's* "China's Most Admired Companies of 2007."

Strategic alliances are partnerships between two or more firms that decide they can better pursue their mutual goals by combining their resources—financial, managerial, technological—as well as their existing distinctive competitive advantages. Alliances—often called *cooperative strategies*—are transition mechanisms that propel the partners' strategies forward in a turbulent environment faster than would be possible for each company alone.[3] Alliances typically fall under one of three categories: joint ventures, equity strategic alliances, and non-equity strategic alliances.

It should be noted that, while the last decade brought a surge in companies seeking growth through mergers and acquisitions (M&As), joint ventures, and other alliances, as of 2009 the global economic downturn was causing many companies to postpone or cancel out on such plans, often instead retrenching or "de-merging." Examples were General Motors and Citigroup having to spin off partners as well as retrench operations in order to maintain sufficient cash flow.

The rate of deals collapsing increased amid the credit crisis and global equity market volatility. An example cited in the Financial Times in January 2009 was the C$34.8bn ($28.2bn) leveraged buy-out of BCE, the Canadian telecoms giant, which was under threat after auditor KPMG said BCE might not meet solvency tests if it absorbed the C$32bn of debt required to finance the transaction.[4] Other proposed deals were going ahead, but with revised terms, such as Dow Chemical, the largest U. S. chemical group, in a deal to inject its low-growth plastics business into a joint venture with Kuwait's state oil company—but at a reduced price.

Still other deals, made under duress, involved government alliances in an attempt to save companies and industries from default, as with a number of banks which become subject to partial nationalization. As one example, the British Government struck a deal in March 2009 to increase its stake in Lloyds' Banking Group (LBG) to 65 percent from 43 percent. The Government guaranteed some $575 billion worth of toxic assets as part of the deal, which was brokered between bank and Treasury officials. Lloyds Banking Group was created early 2009 when Lloyds TSB bought rival lender HBOS, which faced collapse because it was struggling to raise funds due to the credit crunch.[5]

Joint Ventures

As discussed in Chapter 6, a **joint venture (JV)** is a new independent entity jointly created and owned by two or more parent companies. The JV form for a firm may comprise a majority JV (where the firm has more than 50 percent equity), a minority JV (less than 50 percent equity), or a 50-50 JV (where two firms have equal equity). An **IJV** is a joint venture among companies in different countries. In that case, the firm shares the profits, costs, and risks with a local partner, and benefits from the local partner's local contacts and markets. (Advantages and disadvantages of IJVs were discussed in Chapter 6). An example of a 50-50 equity IJV is that between France's PSA Peugeot-Citroen Group and Japan's Toyota at Kolin in the Czech Republic. As noted by Fujio Cho, president of the world's richest carmaker, Toyota Motors:

> Each company has brought its own style, culture and way of thinking to this partnership—but our different approaches have benefited our joint venture enormously.[6]

The benefits noted by the two companies are that Toyota "gains an insight into the mindset of one of Europe's biggest indigenous carmakers and knowledge of its suppliers and their capabilities."[7] And Peugeot-Citroen can gain experience from Toyota's lean manufacturing system. The companies acknowledge that the IJV has resulted in faster development and increased production capacity, and that costs are shared without either company renouncing its independence.[8]

Equity Strategic Alliances

> Abu Dhabi's state-owned Advanced Technology Investment Company, the latest entrant in the $20bn contract chipmaking industry, is proving it has the capital to back its ambition of making Abu Dhabi a chip industry heavyweight through yesterday's $1.8bn deal to buy a majority stake in Singapore's Chartered Semiconductor.
>
> FINANCIAL TIMES,
> September 9, 2009.[9]

Two or more partners have different relative ownership shares (equity percentages) in the new venture in an equity strategic alliance. As do most global manufacturers, Toyota has equity alliances with suppliers, sub-assemblers, and distributors; most of these are part of Toyota's network of internal family and financial links. Another example is TCL-Thompson Electronics. France's Thompson owns 33 percent of the combined company and China's TCL owns the remaining 67 percent.[10] Risk-sharing is often the motive behind equity alliances, as when Daiichi Sankyo, a Japanese pharmaceutical giant, bought a 51 percent equity share in India's Ranbaxy Laboratories in June 2008. The goal for Daiichi was to add value to its research and development expertise, to use Ranbaxy's low-cost manufacturing base; in turn Ranbaxy would gain access to Japan's markets.[11]

Sometimes an international, or global, joint venture is part of a desperate strategy. This was the case in January 2009 when Chrysler reached for another lifeline in its equity deal to join forces with Italy's Fiat. The plan was for Fiat to get a 35 percent ownership stake in Chrysler with the goal of bringing its Fiat and Alfa Romeo brands back to the United States through Chrysler's dealership network. In return Chrysler would get the opportunity to stay alive by presenting a strategic partnership as part of its plan to the U.S. government in its quest for an additional $3 billion loan to allow it to stay in business.[12] However, further developments led to a change in plan when some creditors did not make concessions, and President Obama announced on April 30, 2009:

> *Chrysler, the third-largest American auto company, will seek bankruptcy protection and enter an alliance with the Italian automaker Fiat, the White House announced Thursday.*[13]

However, the deal with Fiat would be intact after bankruptcy, with Fiat to take part in running Chrysler, provide technical operations, and build at least one vehicle in a Chrysler plant. Fiat did not put up any financing as part of the agreement. Considerable additional financing from the U.S. government was planned after Chrysler's restructuring, with the Canadian government also offering some financing.[14] (For an in-depth look at the Fiat-Chrysler alliance, see the Comprehensive Case 8, at the end of this section of chapters.)

Non-equity Strategic Alliances

Agreements are carried out through contract rather than ownership sharing in a non-equity strategic alliance. Such contracts are often with a firm's suppliers, distributors, or manufacturers, or they may be for purposes of marketing and information sharing, such as with many airline partnerships. UPS, for example, is a global supply-chain manager for many companies around the world, such as Nike, which essentially do not touch their own products but contract with UPS to arrange the entire process from factory to warehouse to customer to repair, even collecting the money.[15]

Global Strategic Alliances

Working partnerships between companies (often more than two) across national boundaries and increasingly across industries are referred to as global strategic alliances. A glance at the global airline industry, for example, tells us that global alliances have become a mainstay of competitive strategy. Not one airline is competing alone; each major U.S. carrier has established strategic links with non-U.S. companies. The Star Alliance, for example, has code sharing among 19 airlines around the world.

> *French Company Joins Indian Utility in a Deal for Nuclear Plants*
>
> www.nytimes,
> *February 5, 2009.*

Alliances are also sometimes formed between a company and a foreign government, or among companies and governments. In addition, changing regulations and policies by governments and institutions lead to new opportunities for alliances with national industries abroad. As an example, when the Nuclear Suppliers Group, a global consortium that regulates the sale of the items, voted in September 2008 to lift the ban on deals with India, that freed up any country to sign nuclear plant deals there. The company, Areva, which is owned mostly by the French government, joined with the state-run Nuclear Power Corporation of India to build at least two and possibly as many as six nuclear power plants in the energy-starved country. Their two-reactor project could be worth about $10 billion.[16]

Alliances may comprise full global partnerships, which are often joint ventures in which two or more companies, while retaining their national identities, develop a common, long-term strategy aimed at world leadership. The European Airbus Industrie consortium, for example, comprises France's Aerospatiale and Germany's Daimler-Benz Aerospace, each with 37.9 percent of the business; British Aerospace with 20 percent, and Spain's Construcciones Aeronauticas with 4.2 percent.

Whereas such alliances have a broad agenda, others are formed for a narrow and specific function, including production, marketing, research and development, or financing. More recently these have included electronic alliances, such as Covisint, which is redefining the entire system of car production and distribution through a common electronic marketplace. Covisint is an e-business exchange developed by Ford, General Motors, Nissan, Renault, and (then) DaimlerChrysler AG, to meet the needs of the automotive industry, and is focused on procurement, supply chain, and product development solutions.[17]

Global and Cross-Border Alliances: Motivations and Benefits

Some of the typical reasons behind cross-border alliances are as follows:

1. **To avoid import barriers, licensing requirements, and other protectionist legislation.** Japanese automotive manufacturers, for example, use alliances such as the GM–Toyota venture, or subsidiaries, to produce cars in the United States so as to avoid import quotas.

2. **To share the costs and risks of the research and development of new products and processes.** In the semiconductor industry, for example, where each new generation of memory chips is estimated to cost more than $1 billion to develop, those costs and the rapid technological evolution typically require the resources of more than one, or even two, firms. Intel, for example, has alliances with Samsung and NMB Semiconductor for technology (DRAM) development; Sun Microsystems has partners for its technology (RISC), including N. V. Philips, Fujitsu, and Texas Instruments. Toshiba, Japan's third-largest electronics company, has more than two dozen major joint ventures and strategic alliances around the world, including partners such as Olivetti, Rhone-Poulenc, GEC Alstholm in Europe, LSI Logic in Canada, and Samsung in Korea. Fumio Sato, Toshiba's CEO, recognized long ago that a global strategy for a high-tech electronics company such as his necessitated joint ventures and strategic alliances.

3. **To gain access to specific markets, such as the EU, where regulations favor domestic companies.** Firms around the world are forming strategic alliances with European companies to bolster their chances of competing in the European Union (EU) and to gain access to markets in Eastern European countries as they open up to world business. The EU's new law, passed in November 2003, was intended to increase the opportunities for cross-border mergers and takeovers, for companies both within and outside of the EU.[18] U.S. companies protested that the law did not go far enough to open up a "fortress Europe," because hostile bids would be more difficult to pursue.[19] However, seven of the ten largest deals that Citigroup completed around the world in 2003, for example, were in Europe—including the $2 billion acquisition of British tavern chain Pubmaster.[20] Chun Joo Bum, chief executive of the Daewoo Electronics unit, acknowledges that he is seeking local partners in Europe for two reasons: (1) to provide sorely needed capital and (2) to help Daewoo navigate Europe's still disparate markets, saying "I need to localize our management. It is not one market."[21]

   Market entry into some countries may only be attained through alliances—typically joint ventures. South Korea, for example, has a limit of 18 percent on foreign investment in South Korean firms.

4. **To reduce political risk while making inroads into a new market.**

Carefully orchestrated partnerships with governments and other business groups are crucial to the [Disney] entertainment group's thrust into China and the rest of southeast Asia.

BOB IGER,
President and COO, Walt Disney[22]

Hong Kong Disneyland is jointly owned by the Chinese government, which owns a 57 percent stake. Beijing is especially interested in promoting tourism through the venture, and in the employment for the 5,000 workers Disney employs directly, as well as the estimated 18,000 in related services.[23] Maytag Corporation, also determined to stay on the right side of the restrictive Chinese government while gaining market access, formed a joint venture with RSD, the Chinese appliance maker, to manufacture and market washing machines and refrigerators. Maytag also invested large amounts in jointly owned refrigeration products facilities to help RSD get into that market. Coca-Cola—a global player with large-scale alliances—is not beyond using some very small-scale alliances to be "political" in China. The company uses senior citizens in the party's neighborhood committees to sell Coke locally.

5. To gain rapid entry into a new or consolidating industry and to take advantage of synergies.

Disney now has 3.5m subscribers for content services, offered through Japan's largest mobile operators.

STEVE WADSWORTH,
President, Internet Division, Walt Disney[24]

Technology is rapidly providing the means for the overlapping and merging of traditional industries such as entertainment, computers, and telecommunications in new digital-based systems, creating an information superhighway. Disney's business model of cellular partnerships and content sales, for example, created Disney mobile operations in Hong Kong, Taiwan, South Korea, Singapore, and the Philippines.[25] The company uses joint venture partners such as the Hong Kong government, or licensees and distributors such as Oriental Land and NTT DoCoMo.[26]

In many cases, technological developments are necessitating strategic alliances across industries in order for companies to gain rapid entry into areas in which they have no expertise or manufacturing capabilities. Competition is so fierce that they cannot wait to develop those resources alone. Many of these objectives, such as access to new technology and to new markets, are evident in AT&T's network of alliances around the world. Agreements with Japan's NEC, for example, gave AT&T access to new semiconductor and chip-making technologies, helping it learn how to better integrate computers with communications. Another joint venture with Zenith Electronics led to the next generation of high-definition television (HDTV).[27]

Challenges in Implementing Global Alliances

Effective global alliances are usually tediously slow in the making but can be among the best mechanisms to implement strategies in global markets. In a highly competitive environment, alliances present a faster and less risky route to globalization. It is extremely complex to fashion such linkages, however, especially where many interconnecting systems are involved, forming intricate networks. Many alliances fail for complex reasons. Many also end up in a takeover in which one partner swallows the other. McKinsey & Company, a consulting firm, surveyed 150 companies that had been in alliances and found that 75 percent of them had been taken over by Japanese partners. Problems with shared ownership, differences in national cultures, the integration of vastly different structures and systems, the distribution of power between the companies involved, and conflicts in their relative locus of decision making and control are but a few of the organizational issues that must be worked out. When the joint venture between France Telecom and Deutsche Telekom was announced in September 2009, Tim Hottges, France Telecom finance director, said that the two sides had already agreed on a "solution mechanism" for potential problems in the United Kingdom. Noting that "This is a sign that even those who embark on such partnerships with optimism recognize that conflict about who is in charge is a constant risk," the *Financial Times* observed that "joint ventures start with smiles, but often end in tears."[28]

Often, the form of governance chosen for multinational firm alliances greatly influences their success, particularly in technologically intense fields such as pharmaceuticals, computers, and semiconductors. In a study of 153 alliances, researchers found that the choice of the means of governance—whether a contractual agreement or a joint venture—depended on a desire to control information about proprietary technology.[29] Thus, joint ventures are often the chosen form for such alliances because they provide greater control and coordination in high-technology industries.

Cross-border partnerships, in particular, often become a "race to learn"—with the faster learner later dominating the alliance and rewriting its terms. In a real sense, an alliance becomes a new form of competition. In fact, according to researcher David Lei,

Perhaps the single greatest impediment managers face when seeking to learn or renew sources of competitive advantage is to realize that co-operation can represent another form of unintended competition, particularly to shape and apply new skills to future products and businesses.[30]

All too often, cross-border allies have difficulty collaborating effectively, especially in competitively sensitive areas; this creates mistrust and secrecy, which then undermine the purpose of the alliance. The difficulty that they are dealing with is the dual nature of strategic alliances—the benefits of cooperation versus the dangers of introducing new competition through sharing their knowledge and technological skills about their mutual product or the manufacturing process. Managers may fear that they will lose the competitive advantage of the firm's proprietary technology or the specific skills that their personnel possess. One example of a situation of potential loss of proprietary technology affecting entire industries became apparent in January 2004 when China announced that foreign computer and chip makers selling various wireless devices there would have to use Chinese encryption software and co-produce their products with Chinese companies from a designated list.[31]

The cumulative learning that a partner attains through the alliance could potentially be applied to other products or even other industries that are beyond the scope of the alliance, and therefore would hold no benefit to the partner holding the original knowledge.[32] As noted by Lei, the Japanese have far overtaken their U.S. allies in developing and applying new technologies to other uses. Examples are in the power equipment industry (e.g., Westinghouse-Mitsubishi), the office equipment industry (Kodak-Canon), and the consumer electronics industry (General Electric-Samsung). Some of the trade-offs of the duality of cross-border ventures are shown in Exhibit 7-1.

The enticing benefits of cross-border alliances often mask the many pitfalls involved. In addition to potential loss of technology and knowledge or skill base, other areas of incompatibility often arise, such as conflicting strategic goals and objectives, cultural clashes, and disputes over management and control systems. Sometimes it takes a while for such problems to evidence themselves, particularly if insufficient homework has been done in meetings between the two sides to work out the implementation details. The alliance between KLM Royal Dutch Airlines and Northwest Airlines linking their hubs in Detroit and Amsterdam, for example, resulted in a bitter feud among the top officials of both companies over methods of running an airline business—the European way or the American way—and over cultural differences between the companies, as well as a power struggle at the top over who should call the shots.[33]

EXHIBIT 7-1 The Dual Role of Strategic Alliances

Cooperative	Competitive
Economies of scale in tangible assets (e.g., plant and equipment).	Opportunity to learn new intangible skills from partner, often tacit or organization embedded.
Upstream–downstream division of labor among partners.	Accelerate diffusion of industry standards and new technologies to erect barriers to entry.
Fill out product line with components or end products provided by supplier.	Deny technological and learning initiative to partner via outsourcing and long-term supply arrangements.
Limit investment risk when entering new markets or uncertain technological fields via shared resources.	Encircle existing competitors and preempt the rise of new competitors with alliance partners in "proxy wars" to control market access, distribution, and access to new technologies.
Create a "critical mass" to learn and develop new technologies to protect domestic, strategic industries.	Form clusters of learning among suppliers and related firms to avoid or reduce foreign dependence for critical inputs and skills.
Assist short-term corporate restructurings by lowering exit barriers in mature or declining industries.	Alliances serve as experiential platforms to "demature" and transform existing mature industries via new components, technologies, or skills to enhance the value of future growth options.

Source: David Lei, "Offensive and Defensive Uses of Alliances," in Heidi Vernon-Wortzel and L. H. Wortzel, *Strategic Management in Global Economy*, 3rd ed. (New York: John Wiley & Sons, 1997).

IMPLEMENTING ALLIANCES BETWEEN SMEs AND MNCs

All countries have a large proportion of business enterprises, as well as NGOs, which are small or medium-sized (SMEs). But, increasingly, MNCs are dominating the markets in which SMEs operate, often crowding them out of business altogether. However, astute managers of SMEs can often find opportunities for alliances with those multinationals, providing "complementary resources and capabilities that can lead to, for instance, an innovative product offering being rolled out on a global scale, or a worldwide licensing agreement."[34]

Exhibit 7-2 shows strategies for SMEs to take advantage of alliances with MNCs, as concluded by Prashantham and Birkinshaw from their research with 15 companies. For example, MNCs often partner with local small enterprises to capture new ideas and innovations. Sun Microsystems, for instance, engaged with a number of small enterprises in Scotland on RFID projects in order to bolster its competitiveness in this emerging area.[35] SMEs should seek out those opportunities to offer MNCs complementary technologies as well as local market networks.

EXHIBIT 7-2 Strategies for Dancing with Gorillas

Stage of Relationship	Traditional Model: MNCs Partnering with Each Other	New Model: Small Enterprises Partnering Locally with MNCs	Strategies for Small Enterprises Partnering with MNCs
Forming	A direct frontal approach through a dedicated alliance department or key individuals who are direct counterparts	Given asymmetry of access and attention, the direct approach is likely to fail; so *use indirect means of access*	• Use local allies such as regional institutions or partnering programs;"make your luck" by converting low-key interactions into concrete relationships • Use the MNC's reputational strength to gain support through written commitment and bringing to bear social sanctions
Consolidating	Well-established processes for structuring, governance, and staffing alliances	Given asymmetry of resources and long term objectives, these processes don't apply; so *plan for the short term with an eye on the long term*	• Capitalize on points of technology by proactively demonstrating skills and creating opportunities • Ensure modular or discrete knowledge transfer to ensure tangible outcomes (e.g., a product prototype) if the partnership is prematurely terminated
Extending	A relatively predictable pattern for the further development of alliances, including built-in contingencies for instability and dissolution	Given asymmetry and therefore dispensability of small enterprises, there's greater uncertainty vis-à-vis MNCs' own plans and priorities; so *be vague by design with an eye on the bigger prize*	• Proactively build networks within the MNC and add value (e.g., extending from technological to commercial activities, and from local to international business) • Adopt an ambiguous approach by design; pursue oblique goals without showing all cards initially, and keep options open for as long as possible

Source: **Shameen Prashantham and Julian Birkinshaw,** "Dancing with Gorillas: How Small Companies can Partner Effectively with MNCs," California Management Review, Fall 2008.

Guidelines for Successful Alliances

As discussed earlier, many global companies, such as IBM, The Tata Group, and Toyota, build extensive alliance portfolios that involve multiple concurrent alliances. Oracle's Partner Network, for example, includes 19,500 partners. Alliance partners can provide synergies and value to corporate performance by providing access to new resources and markets, generating economies of scale and scope, reducing costs, sharing risks, and enhancing flexibility.[36] Unfortunately, the complexities involved in managing many alliances often means that many— around half by most estimates—are unsuccessful, often because of poor partner selections initially, and then also because of poor management to ensure that the expected competencies and synergies are realized. Research by Dovev Lavie of 20,000 alliances involving about 8,800 unique partners provides some insight into how managers can manage their alliances in ways that will increase the likelihood of success. The results enabled the identification of "value-creation and value-capture strategies that can guide partner selection decisions, and developed alliance portfolio management practices to help managers extract more value from their alliance portfolios."[37] These strategies are detailed in Exhibit 7-3. One key factor in managing alliance portfolios, for example, is to consider not only what each alliance partner will bring to the company, but also how that partner will affect other partners in the portfolio.

It is clear that many difficulties arise in cross-border alliances in melding the national and corporate cultures of the parties, in overcoming language and communication barriers, and in building trust between the parties over how to share proprietary assets and management processes. Some basic guidelines, as follow, will help to minimize potential problems. However, nothing is as important as having a long "courtship" with a potential partner to establish compatibility strategically and interpersonally and set up a plan with the prospective partner. Even setting up some pilot programs on a short-term basis for some of the planned combined activities can highlight areas that may become problematic.

1. Choose a partner with compatible strategic goals and objectives and with whom the alliance will result in synergies through the combined markets, technologies, and management cadre.

EXHIBIT 7-3   Value Creation and Value Capture in Alliance Portfolios

Value Creation Strategies	Value Capture Strategies	Portfolio Management Practices

• **Complementarity**
  • Seek Partners that offer complementary resources
• **Enrichment Strategy**
  • Leverage network resources to extend your market opportunities
• **Combination Strategy**
  • Integrate network resources with your internal resources to create synergies
• **Absorption Strategy**
  • Learn and assimilate network resources in order to develop new skills and capabilities
	• **Coopetition**
	  • Watch out for opportunistic partners that value your business more than your partnership
	• **Bargaining Strategy**
	  • Seek partners that have greater stake in your joint alliances and fewer partnering alternatives
	• **Bilateral Competition Strategy**
	  • Avoid partners that compete in your industry if they enjoy superior bargaining power
	• **Multilateral Competition Strategy**
	  • Ally with multiple partners in particular industries to neutralize each partner's bargaining power
		• **Interdependencies**
		  • Consider how each alliance affects other alliances in the portfolio
		• **Separation**
		  • Set organizational and technological buffers between competing partners
		• **Segmentation**
		  • Benchmark partners and assign them to market opportunities
		• **Coordination**
		  • Align organizational units and create a coherent interface with each partner

Source: reprinted from: Dovev Lavie, "Capturing Value from Alliance Portfolios," *Organizational Dynamics* 38, no. 1 (2009): 26–36, copyright Elsevier, used with permission of Elsevier, www.elsevier.com

2. Seek alliances where complementary skills, products, and markets will result. If each partner brings distinctive skills and assets to the venture, there will be reduced potential for direct competition in end products and markets. In addition, each partner will begin the alliance in a balanced relationship.[38]

3. Work out with the partner how you will each deal with proprietary technology or competitively sensitive information—what will be shared and what will not, and how shared technology will be handled. Trust is an essential ingredient of an alliance, particularly in these areas; but this must be backed up by contractual agreements.

4. Recognize that most alliances last only a few years and will probably break up once a partner feels it has incorporated the skills and information it needs to go it alone. With this in mind, managers need to "learn thoroughly and rapidly about a partner technology and management: transfer valuable ideas and practices promptly into one's own operations."[39]

Some of the opportunities and complexities in cross-border alliances are illustrated in the following Comparative Management in Focus on joint ventures in the Russian Federation. Such alliances are further complicated by the different history of the two parties' economic systems and the resulting business practices.

COMPARATIVE MANAGEMENT IN FOCUS

Joint Ventures in the Russian Federation

Since the financial exodus from Russia in the wake of the world credit crisis and Moscow's heavy-handed military incursion into Georgia, the country's capacity to tap the tens of billions of dollars in foreign investment it needs to overhaul its creaking infrastructure has been thrown into doubt.[40]

www.ft.com,
September 30, 2008

Norwegian Stake in Russian Joint Venture Seized
   Already jittery investors were alarmed on Thursday when a Norwegian cellphone company (Telenor) announced that a Siberian court had seized its multibillion-dollar investment in a Russian joint venture and would turn it over to a company thought to be allied with a Russian oligarch.[41]

www.nytimes.com,
March 13, 2009

The seizure of Telenor in 2009 (see above) is the latest in a series of events shaking faith in the Russian market. Foreign companies have started to think twice about investing in international joint ventures (IJVs) in Russia since (then) President Putin's moves to take control of key industries, including banks, newspapers, and oil assets. He partly re-nationalized the Yukos oil company, Russia's biggest, after jailing its former chief Mikhail Khodorkovsky for eight years. In May 2008, President Putin signed the Strategic Industries Bill, which regulates foreign investment. The new law identifies 42 strategic sectors (compared to 16 in 2005) in which foreign investors have to seek special permission before investing. In June 2007, Putin forced BP (British Petroleum) to sell the largest gas field to Gazprom, the Russian natural gas monopoly, by threatening to revoke the license held by the TNK-BP joint venture.[42]

   All in all, investors are confused, though many are determined to take advantage of a more stable and now-convertible ruble, an underexploited natural resource potential, and a skilled, educated population of 145 million. Many MNCs claim that they must have a presence in Russia to be globally competitive. But a survey of 158 corporate investors and non-investors in Russia indicated that respondents thought that doing business in Russia was more risky and less profitable than China, India, or South-east Asia. Their main concerns were corruption and bribe-taking at all levels of the state bureaucracy and weak legislative and enforcement regimes.[43] Russia was ranked 147th out of 180 countries by Transparency International, based on clean government and business.[44] Indeed, Ikea, the Swedish retailer, has found that Russian graft on several levels has so far won out against the company's efforts to thwart extortion efforts by power companies; even the courts found in favor of the power companies.[45] The level of uncertainty by foreign investors is fueled by the experience of some companies in joint ventures in Russia, such as the General Motors joint venture with Russia's biggest car maker, OAO

MAP 7-1 Russia

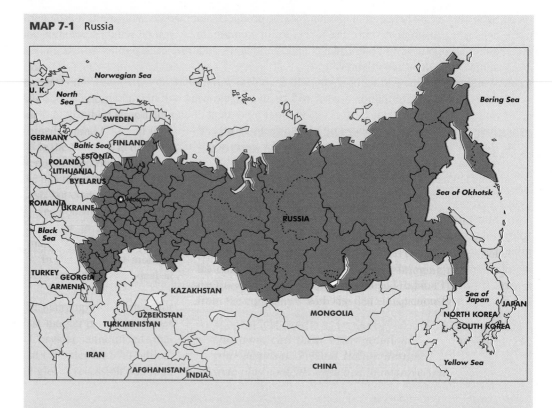

Avtovaz. The $340 million IJV was the first between a Russian and Western automaker; GM's strategy was to partner with a local producer to make a low-cost, locally developed model. The GM venture stopped making Chevrolet Niva sport-utility vehicles in 2006, after Avtovaz halted delivery of parts, demanding that GM pay more for them. Rosoboronexport, the Russian state arms trader, took control of Avtovaz from the management group that had run the company since the Soviet era. The takeover "appeared to be the start of a Kremlin drive to revive Russia's ailing auto industry—which is rapidly losing market share to Western imports and locally assembled foreign models—through direct state intervention. It would also highlight the Kremlin's tough new approach to foreign investment in industries deemed strategic."[46] Subsequent negotiations were focusing on an acceptable compromise.

In spite of the uncertainty, many companies feel that they should take advantage of the growth opportunities in Russia—the seventh biggest population in the world. According to the Foreign Investment Advisory Council (FIAC) Report in January 2009, Russia now boasts a US$1.3 trillion economy, foreign currency reserves approaching US$500 billion, and a Stabilization Fund exceeding US$150 billion.[47] However, the 50 executives representing large companies around the world who were surveyed by the FIAC expressed concern about political interference in business, arbitrariness in the application of laws, complexity of the tax system, and the lack of skilled staff. They also expressed concern that small companies would have difficulties in registering and start up, thus limiting economic growth.[48] Nevertheless, investment continues from companies such as Dutch brewer Heineken, and Citibank, which says its business in Russia is growing at an annual rate of 70 percent. Moscow and other major cities are experiencing a consumer boom, spurred on by rising incomes in the middle class, making Russia one of the fastest growing regions for global consumer giants such as Coca-Cola, Procter & Gamble, and Nestle.[49] They join those already taking advantage of those opportunities such as Caterpillar, IBM, GE, Ford, Hewlett-Packard, Pepsi-Co., Eastman Kodak, and AT&T, as well as thousands of smaller IJVs—primarily in software, hotels, and heavy industrial production. Many, like Bell Labs, are involved in research and development, taking advantage of the Russians' high-level education and technical capabilities. In addition, Russia is promoting its several special economic zones around the country; the government hopes to attract further investment by offering tax concessions, such as exemption from property and land tax for the first five years.[50]

Overall, managers of foreign companies planning to set up business in Russia should carefully consider the following:

- Investigate whether a joint venture is the best strategy. If a lot of real estate is needed, it may be better to acquire a Russian business, because of the difficulties involved in acquiring land.
- Set up meetings with the appropriate ministry and regional authorities well in advance. Have good communication about your business needs and build local relationships.

- Be sure to be totally above board in paying all relevant taxes to avoid crossing the Russian authorities.
- Set up stricter controls and accountability systems than usual for the company.
- Communicate clearly up front that your firm does not pay bribes.
- Assign the firm's best available managers and delegate to them enough authority to act locally.
- Take advantage of local knowledge by hiring appropriate Russian managers for the venture.
- Designate considerable funds for local promotion and advertising so as to establish the corporate image with authorities and consumers.[51]

Foreign managers' alliance strategy must also take into account the goals of potential Russian partners. For example, when viewed from the perspective of Russian managers, Hitt et al. found that:

> *The less stable Russian institutional environment has influenced Russian managers to focus more on the short term [than those in China], selecting partners that provide access to financial capital and complementary capabilities so as to enhance their firms' ability to weather that nation's turbulent environment.*[52]

An awareness and acceptance of the motivations of Russian firms for alliances with foreign companies will aid in finding and achieving a cooperative joint venture.

In December, 2008, researchers for the *Wall Street Journal* reported their findings about what local Russian firms want from an alliance with a foreign firm; they made it clear that they expect assistance with market entry through forming an alliance, and that they need assistance in solving bribes, kickbacks, and other under-the-table transactions. [53]

STRATEGIC IMPLEMENTATION

IMPLEMENTATION MCDONALD'S STYLE

- Form paradigm-busting arrangements with suppliers.
- Know a country's culture before you hit the beach.
- Hire locals whenever possible.
- Maximize autonomy.
- Tweak the standard menu only slightly from place to place.
- Keep pricing low to build market share. Profits will follow when economies of scale kick in.[54]

Decisions regarding global alliances and entry strategies must now be put into motion with the next stage of planning: strategic implementation. Implementation plans are detailed and pervade the entire organization because they entail setting up overall policies, administrative responsibilities, and schedules throughout the organization to enact the selected strategy and to make sure it works. In the case of a merger or IJV, this process requires compromising and blending procedures among two or more companies and is extremely complex. The importance of the implementation phase of the strategic management process cannot be overemphasized. Until they are put into operation, strategic plans remain abstract ideas: verbal or printed proposals that have no effect on the organization.

Successful implementation requires the orchestration of many variables into a cohesive system that complements the desired strategy—that is, a *system of fits* that will facilitate the actual working of the strategic plan. In this way, the structure, systems, and processes of the firm are coordinated and set into motion by a system of management by objectives (MBO), with the primary objective being the fulfillment of strategy. Managers must review the organizational structure and, if necessary, change it to facilitate the administration of the strategy and to coordinate activities in a particular location with headquarters (as discussed further in Chapter 8). In addition to ensuring the strategy-structure fit, managers must allocate resources to make the strategy work, budgeting money, facilities, equipment, people, and other support. Increasingly, that support necessitates a unified technology infrastructure in order to coordinate diverse businesses around the world and to satisfy the need for current and reliable information. An efficient technology infrastructure can provide a strategic advantage in a globally competitive environment. Jack Welch, while CEO of General Electric (he retired in late 2001), used to refer to his e-commerce initiative, saying, "It will change relationships with suppliers. Within 18 months, all our suppliers will supply us on the Internet, or they won't do business with us."[55]

An overarching factor affecting all the other variables necessary for successful implementation is that of leadership; it is people, after all, who make things happen. The firm's leaders must skillfully guide employees and processes in the desired direction. Managers with different combinations of experience, education, abilities, and personality tend to be more suited to implementing certain strategies. In an equity-sharing alliance, sorting out which top managers in each company will be in which position is a sensitive matter. Who in which company will be CEO is usually worked out as part of the initial deal in alliance agreements. This problem seems to be frequently settled these days by setting up joint CEOs, one from each company. Setting monitoring systems into place to control activities and ensure success completes, but does not end, the strategic management process. Rather, it is a continuous process, using feedback to reevaluate strategy for needed modifications and for updating and recycling plans. Of particular note here we should consider what is involved in effective management of the increasingly popular global sourcing strategy; then we will review what is involved in managing performance in international joint ventures, since they are such a common form of global alliance, and yet they are fraught with implementation challenges.

Implementing a Global Sourcing Strategy

> *Multinational corporations and their manufacturing partners in emerging markets need to rethink how they manage their relationships with each other in light of the global downturn.*
>
> HARVARD BUSINESS REVIEW,
> *Jul/Aug 2009.*[56]

The entry strategy of global sourcing was discussed in Chapter 6. Outsourcing abroad—alliances with firms in other countries to perform specific functions for the firm—is often in the news because of the politically charged issue of domestic jobs apparently being "lost" to others overseas. Beyond finding lower paid workers, however, the strategic view of global sourcing is developing into "transformational outsourcing"—that is, the view that, properly implemented, global sourcing can produce gains in efficiency, productivity, quality, and profitability by fully leveraging talent around the world.[57] Procter & Gamble, for example, having outsourced everything from IT infrastructure and Human Resources around the world, announced that CEO Alan G. Lafley wants 50 percent of all new P&G products to come from other countries by 2010, compared to 20 percent in 2006.[58] However, implementing such a strategy is more difficult than it is made to seem in the press, as many companies have encountered unexpected problems when outsourcing. Advice on implementation from experiences by companies such as Dell, IBM, and Reuters Group PLC lead us to the following guidelines:

1. **Examine your reasons for outsourcing.** Make sure that the advantages of efficiency and competitiveness will outweigh the disadvantages from your employees, customers, and community; don't outsource just because your competitors are doing it.
2. **Evaluate the best outsourcing model.** Opening your own subsidiary in the host country (a "captive" operation) may be better than contracting with an outside firm if it is crucial for you to keep control of proprietary technology and processes.
3. **Gain the cooperation of your management and staff.** Open communication and training is essential to get your domestic managers on board; uncertainty, fear, and disagreement from them can jeopardize your plans.
4. **Consult your alliance partners.** Consult with your partners and treat them with the respect that made you decide to do business with them.
5. **Invest in the alliance.** Plan to invest time and money in training in the firm's business practices, in particular those to do with quality control and customer relations.[59]

Further advice comes from Josh Green, CEO of Panjiva, an information resource for companies doing business across borders. Green asks "How healthy is your global partner?" as he noted in August 2009 that an increasing number of firms in developed economies were finding that their suppliers in Asia had gone out of business following the protracted global economic downturn which caused firms reduce their demand to the suppliers. He notes that both buyers and suppliers have learned the hard way that in future they need to carefully investigate and evaluate their potential partners. He suggests, for example, that both sides should do a background check on the financial health and future viability of the company; get references from other partners of the firm; be prepared to give those assurances and data about their own companies; and be prepared for problems by having alternate partners ready to fill in.[60]

Managing Performance in International Joint Ventures

Much of the world's international business activity involves international joint ventures (IJVs), in which at least one parent is headquartered outside the venture's country of operation. IJVs require unique controls. Ignoring these specific control requisites can limit the parent company's ability to efficiently use its resources, coordinate its activities, and implement its strategy.

The term **IJV control** refers to the processes that management puts in place so as to direct the success of the firm's goals. Most of a firm's objectives can be achieved by careful attention to control features at the outset of the joint venture, such as the choice of a partner, the establishment of a strategic fit, and the design of the IJV organization.

The most important single factor determining IJV success or failure is the choice of a partner. Most problems with IJVs involve the local partner, especially in less developed countries. In spite of this fact, many firms rush the process of partner selection because they are anxious to "get on the bandwagon" in an attractive market. In this process, it is vital to establish whether the partners' strategic goals are compatible (see Chapter 6). The strategic context and the competitive environment of the proposed IJV and the parent firm will determine the relative importance of the criteria used to select a partner.[61] IJV performance is also a function of the general fit between the international strategies of the parents, the IJV strategy, and the specific performance goals that the parents adopt.[62] Research has shown that, to facilitate this fit, the partner selection process must determine the specific task-related skills and resources needed from a partner, as well as the relative priority of those needs.[63] To do this, managers must analyze their own firms and pinpoint any areas of weakness in task-related skills and resources that can be overcome with the help of the IJV partner.

Partnerships with companies in India present both positive and negative examples of IJV performance, although overall IJVs there run into considerable problems. Although India still insists on joint ventures in sectors such as telecommunications, agriculture, retailing, and insurance, it has lifted restrictions for other industries, allowing wholly-owned operations in them. However, a number of recent IJVs have done poorly, especially for the Indian partner. TVS Motor, for example, which is the third-largest motorbike manufacturer in India (a market with around 8 million bikes a year), recently bought out its Japanese partner Suzuki. From Suzuki's perspective, the only entry strategy available to the company under government regulations at the time was a joint venture. However, after a while TVS complained that it was not able to develop the company's own capabilities because "Suzuki wanted to keep its technology for itself. It was a frustrating episode."[64] On the other hand, an IJV between Indian engineering group Kirloskar with Japan's Toyota, for vehicle production, has had more positive results, with Mr. Kirloskar acknowledging that Toyota has been open in sharing ideas and improving the productivity of his firm.[65]

Organizational design is another major mechanism for factoring in a means of control when an IJV is started. Beamish et al. discuss the important issue of the strategic freedom of an IJV. This refers to the relative amount of decision-making power that a joint venture will have, compared with the parents, in choosing suppliers, product lines, customers, and so on.[66] It is also crucial to consider beforehand the relative management roles each parent will play in the IJV because such decisions result in varying levels of control for different parties. An IJV is usually easier to manage if one parent plays a dominant role and has more decision-making responsibility than the other in daily operations. Alternatively, it is easier to manage an IJV if the local general manager has considerable management control, keeping both parents out of most of the daily operations.

International joint ventures are like a marriage: the more issues that can be settled before the merger, the less likely it will be to break up. Control over the stability and success of the IJV can be largely built into the initial agreement between the partners. The contract can specify who has what responsibilities and rights in a variety of circumstances, such as the contractual links of the IJV with the parents, the capitalization, and the rights and obligations regarding intellectual property. Of course, we cannot assume equal ownership of the IJV partners; where ownership is unequal, the partners will claim control and staffing choices proportionate to the ownership share. The choice of the IJV general manager, in particular, will influence the relative allocation of control because that person is responsible for running the IJV and for coordinating relationships with each of the parents.[67]

Where ownership is divided among several partners, the parents are more likely to delegate the daily operations of the IJV to the local IJV management—a move that resolves many potential disputes. In addition, the increased autonomy of the IJV tends to reduce many common human resource problems: staffing friction, blocked communication, and blurred organizational culture, to name a few, which all result from the conflicting goals and working practices of the parent companies.[68] Regardless of the number of parents, one way to avoid such potential problem situations is to provide special training to managers about the unique nature and problems of IJVs. The extent of control exercised over an IJV by its parent companies seems to be primarily determined by the decision-making autonomy that the parents delegate to the IJV management—which is largely dependent on staffing choices for the top IJV positions and thus on how much confidence the partners have in these managers. In addition, if top managers of the IJV are from the headquarters of each party, the compatibility of the managers will depend on how similar their national cultures are. This is because there are many areas of control decisions where agreement will be more likely between those of similar cultural backgrounds.[69]

Knowledge Management in IJVs

> *The most effective strategic leadership practices in the 21st century will be ones through which strategic leaders find ways for knowledge to breed still more knowledge.*[70]

Managing the performance of an IJV for the long term, as well as adding value to the parent companies, necessitates managing the knowledge flows within the IJV network. When managed correctly, "alliances serve as a source of new knowledge for the firm."[71] Sirmon et al. contend that if firms can access and "absorb" this new knowledge, it can be used to alter existing capabilities or create new ones.[72] Yet, as found by Hitt et al., "cultural differences and institutional deficits can serve as barriers to the transfer of knowledge in alliance partnerships"[73] Clearly, then, managers need to recognize that it is critical to overcome cultural and system differences in managing knowledge flows to the advantage of the alliance.

Knowledge management, then, is "the conscious and active management of creating, disseminating, evolving, and applying knowledge to strategic ends."[74] Research on eight IJVs by Berdrow and Lane led them to define these processes as follows and as shown in Exhibit 7-4.

1. **transfer:** managing the flow of existing knowledge between parents and from the parents to the IJV.
2. **transformation:** managing the transformation and creation of knowledge within the IJV through its independent activities.

EXHIBIT 7-4   Knowledge Management in IJVs

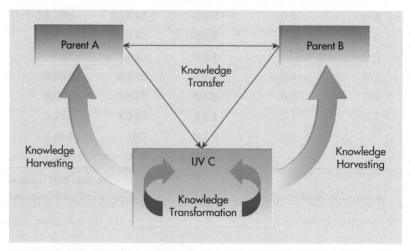

Note: Knowledge transfer usually follows the paths AB and/or BA and BC. Harvesting follows the paths CA and CB.

Source: I. Berdrow and H. W. Lane, "International Joint Ventures: Creating Value Through Successful Knowledge Management," *Journal of World Business*, Vol. 38, 1, February 2003, pp. 15–30, reprinted with permission from Elsevier.

3. harvest: managing the flow of transformed and newly created knowledge from the IJV back to the parents.[75]

In particular, the sharing and development of technology among IJV partners provides the opportunity for knowledge transfer among those individuals who have internalized that information, beyond any tangible assets; the challenge is to develop and harvest that information to benefit the parents through complementary synergies. Those IJVs that were successful in meeting that challenge were found to have personal involvement by the principals of the parent company in shared goals, in the activities and decisions being made, and in encouraging joint learning and coaching.[76]

The many operational activities and issues involved in strategic implementation—such as negotiating, organizing, staffing, leading, communicating, and controlling—are the subjects of other chapters in this book. Elsewhere we include discussion of the many variables involved in strategic implementation that are specific to a particular country or region, such as goals, infrastructure, laws, technology, ways of doing business, people, and culture. In the following sections, the focus is on three pervasive influences on strategy implementation: government policy, societal culture, and the Internet.

Government Influences on Strategic Implementation

Host governments influence, in many areas, the strategic choices and implementations of foreign firms. The profitability of those firms is greatly influenced, for example, by the level of taxation in the host country and by any restrictions on profit repatriation. Other important influences are government policies on ownership by foreign firms, on labor union rules, on hiring and remuneration practices, on patent and copyright protection, and so on. For the most part, however, if the corporation's managers have done their groundwork, all these factors are known beforehand and are part of the location and entry strategy decisions. However, what hurts managers is to set up shop in a host country and then have major economic or governmental policy changes after they have made a considerable investment.

Unpredictable changes in governmental regulations can be a death knell to businesses operating abroad. Recent changes in Russia causing uncertainty for foreign investors were already discussed. Another country that is often the subject of concern for foreign firms is China. Already one of the toughest countries for mergers and acquisitions, China recently added new restrictions on foreign investors, thus prolonging the time that a number of firms have to continue to wait to find out if their deals will go through.

> *[As of September 2006], more deal proposals will require approval by the national Ministry of Commerce, the body that is responsible for the Xugong impasse. Acquisitions that will require the ministry's approval include companies with a well-known brand or those that could have an impact on "China's economic security."*
>
> FINANCIAL TIMES,
> *August 10, 2006.*[77]

While China contends it is more committed to a market economy since it joined the World Trade Organization (WTO) in November 2001, history shows that foreign firms need to be cautious about entering China.

Political change in itself can, of course, bring about sudden change in strategic implementation of alliances of foreign firms with host-country projects. This was evident in May 1998 when President Suharto of Indonesia was ousted following economic problems and currency devaluation. The new government began reviewing and canceling some of the business deals linked with the Suharto family, including two water-supply privatization projects with foreign firms—Britain's Thames Water PLC and France's Suez Lyonnaise des Eaux SA. The Suharto family had developed a considerable fortune from licensing deals, monopolies, government "contracts," and protection from taxes.[78] Alliances with the family were often the only way to gain entry for foreign companies.

Cultural Influences on Strategic Implementation

When managers are responsible for implementing alliances among partners from diverse institutional environments, such as transition- and established-market economies, they are faced with the critical challenge of reconciling conflicting values, practices, and systems. Research by

EXHIBIT 7-5   **Key Differences in Managerial Values, Practices, and Systems Among Hungarian Managers and Western Expatriates**

Western	Hungarian	Perceived source of difference*
Key differences in values		
Extensive use of espoused values	Relative absence of espoused values	Systemic legacy
Focus on core competencies	Focus on empire building	Systemic legacy
Focus on a broad set of stakeholders	Focus on a narrow set of stakeholders	Systemic legacy
Market mentality	Production/volume mentality	Systemic legacy
Professional relationships	Personal relationships	Systemic legacy
Living to work	Working to live	Cultural and systemic legacy
Key differences in practices		
Team orientation/play by the rules	Individual orientation/beat the system	Cultural and systemic legacy
Consensual management style	Autocratic management style	Systemic legacy
High information/ knowledge sharing	Low information/ knowledge sharing	Systemic legacy
Plan for the future mentality	Survival mentality	Recent economic events
Key differences in managerial systems		
Market-driven technology	Volume-driven technology	Systemic legacy
Small, flat structures	Large, hierarchical structures	Systemic legacy
Formal, strategic HR systems	Informal, administrative HR systems	Systemic legacy
Transparent information systems	Opaque information systems	Systemic legacy

*Consensus of Hungarian and Western respondents.

Source: Reprinted from *Journal of World Business* 38, No. 3 (2003): 224–44. W. M. Danis, "Differences in Values, Practices, and Systems among Hungarian Managers and Western Expatriates: An Organizing Framework and Typology," reprinted with permission from Elsevier © 2003.

Danis shows those important differences among Hungarian managers and Western expatriates (see Exhibit 7-5).[79] Such advance knowledge can provide expatriate managers with valuable information to help them in successful local operations.

In other situations, the culture variable is often overlooked when deciding on and implementing entry strategies and alliances, particularly when we perceive the target country to be familiar to us and similar to our own. However, cultural differences can have a subtle and often negative effect. In fact, in a study of 129 U.K. cross-border acquisitions in continental Europe, Schoenberg found that 54 percent of the acquiring firms cited poor performance resulting from the implementation of their acquisitions, compared to their domestic mergers.[80] The researchers' study of those firms revealed six dimensions of national and corporate cultural differences between the management styles of the U.K. firms and the continental European firms:

- Organizational formality
- The extent of participation in decision making
- Attitude toward risk
- Systemization of decision-making
- Managerial self-reliance
- Attitudes toward funding and gearing.[81]

Among these dimensions, risk-orientation was the key factor that impacted the performance of the combined firm, because risk-taking propensity impacts managers' approach toward strategic options. Overall, risk-taking firms are likely to pursue aggressive strategies and deal well with change, whereas risk-averse companies are likely to tread more carefully and employ incremental strategies. Clearly, for companies entering into an IJV, successful implementation will depend largely on careful planning to take account of such differences, in particular that of risk-orientation, to improve organizational compatibility. The greater the cultural distance between the allied firms, the more likely problems will emerge such as conflict regarding the level of innovation and the kinds of investments each firm is willing to pursue.

Since many of Europe's largest MNCs—including Nestlé, Electrolux, Grand Metropolitan, and Rhone-Poulenc—experience increasing proportions of their revenues from their positions in the United States, and employ more than 2.9 million Americans, they have decided to shift the headquarters of some product lines to the United States. As they have done so, however, there is growing evidence that managing in the United States is not as easy as they anticipated it would be because of their perceived familiarity with the culture. Rosenzweig documents some reflections of European managers on their experiences of managing U.S. affiliates. Generally, he has found that European managers appreciate that Americans are pragmatic, open, forthright, and innovative. However, they also say that the tendency of Americans to be informal and individualistic means that their need for independence and autonomy on the job causes problems in their relationship with the head office Europeans. Americans simply do not take well to directives from a foreign-based headquarters.[82] Rosenzweig presents some comments from French managers on their activities in the United States:

French Managers Comment on Their Activities in the United States:

- "Americans see themselves as the world's leading country, and it's not easy for them to accept having a European in charge."
- "It is difficult for Americans to develop a world perspective. It's hard for them to see that what may optimize the worldwide position may not optimize the U.S. activities."
- "The horizon of Americans often goes only as far as the U.S. border. As a result, Americans often don't give equal importance to a foreign customer. If a foreign customer has a special need, the response is sometimes: 'It works here, why do they need it to be different?'"
- "It might be said that Americans are the least international of all people, because their home market is so big."[83]

Other European firms have had more successful strategic implementation in their U.S. plants by adapting to U.S. culture and management styles. When Mercedes-Benz of Germany launched its plant in Tuscaloosa, Alabama, U.S. workers and German "trainers" had doubts. Lynn Snow, who works on the car-door line of the Alabama plant, was skeptical whether the Germans and the Americans would mesh well. Now she proudly asserts that they work together, determined to build a quality vehicle. As Jürgen Schrempp, then CEO of Mercedes's parent, Daimler-Benz, observed, "'Made in Germany'—we have to change that to 'Made by Mercedes,' and never mind where they are assembled."[84]

The German trainers recognized that the whole concept of building a Mercedes quality car had to be taught to the U.S. workers in a way that would appeal to them. They abandoned the typically German strict hierarchy and instead designed a plant in which any worker could stop the assembly line to correct manufacturing problems. In addition, taking their cue from Japanese rivals, they formed the workers into teams that met every day with the trainers to problem solve. Out the window went formal offices and uniforms, replaced by casual shirts with personal names on the pocket. To add to the collegiality, get-togethers for a beer after work became common. "The most important thing is to bring together the two cultures," says Andreas Renschler, who has guided the M-Class since it began in 1993. "You have to generate a kind of ownership of the plant."[85] The local community has also embraced the mutual goals, often having beer fests and including German-language stations on local cable TV.

The impact of cultural differences in management style and expectations is perhaps most noticeable and important when implementing international joint ventures, mergers, or acquisitions. The complexity of such alliances requires that managers from each party learn to compromise to create a compatible and productive working environment, particularly when operations are integrated. Sometimes a cross-border alliance deal may in itself contradict cultural traditions, as explained in the following Management Focus.

In China, too, strategic implementation necessitates an understanding of the pervasive cultural practice of *guanxi* in business dealings. Discussed in previous chapters, *guanxi* refers to the relationship networks that "bind millions of Chinese firms into social and business webs, largely dictating their success."[96] Tapping into this system of reciprocal social obligation is essential to get permits, information, assistance to access material and financial resources, and tax considerations. Nothing gets done without these direct or indirect connections. In fact, a new term has arisen—**guanxihu**, which refers to a bond between specially connected firms that generates preferential treatment to members of the network. Without *guanxi*, even implementing

MANAGEMENT FOCUS

Mittal's Marriage to Arcelor Breaks the Marwari Rules

The biggest steel merger in history was consummated in June 2006 during a 20-minute meeting at a hotel near the Brussels Airport after a five-month takeover battle. The combination of India's Mittal Steel and Luxembourg steelmaker Arcelor creates the world's biggest steel company. The Arcelor acquisition brings Mittal's production to over 100 million tons, creating a company with 333,000 employees on four continents.[86]

The deal did not come about easily, but Lakshmi Mittal, Mittal Steel's founder and 90 percent owner, skillfully managed opposition from two fronts—strategically and culturally.

Strategically, Mr. Mittal worked hard to overcome overwhelming hostility by Arcelor to his initial proposal. Arcelor had planned a deal with Russian steelmaker Severstal in a bid to block the Mittal acquisition.[87] But after two rejected bids from Mittal Steel, Mr. Mittal reached an agreement to acquire Arcelor in a deal valued at $33.7 billion. Mittal, his son Aditya, and a team of negotiators gained agreement to a 2008 business plan and provided a comparison of their deal to the one from Severstal. Mittal also provided a plan for corporate governance rules to promote Arcelor's business model and a commitment that his family would vote its share to support the board's recommendations.[88] It was clear to Mr. Mittal that the Arcelor executives had an outdated view of Mittal Steel, but he spent a lot of time explaining and showing Arcelor executives how Mittal Steel operates. The Arcelor chairman, Joseph Kinsch, spent some time talking to the members of Mittal family and discussing the potential alliance. Finally a better relationship was acknowledged by both sides and the deal was sealed, with Kinsch saying "I hope it can become a love marriage between our teams."[89]

Apart from the strategic negotiations of the deal, which finally turned from hostile to friendly, there was opposition for other reasons. There was a battle from France, seemingly over a perception of losing control of a company that was already a European multinational, though there was no objection to Arcelor's effort to bring in the Russian company Severstal as a white knight.[90] In addition, critics in the French and Luxembourg governments seemed to view the takeover by a family-run company as "a betrayal of old continental European traditions to a new cost-cutting imperative of globalization."[91] A similar objection came from India, showing how growth can bring Indians into conflict with cultural traditions. The objection was that Lakshmi Mittal, Indian-born head of Mittal Steel, was breaking the Marwari rules. Mittal belongs to an ethnic group called Marwari that "traditionally believes it is critical for companies to maintain family ownership."[92] Three of the five major steel companies in India are controlled and run by Marwari families, as well as companies in a number of other industries. Various family members run the operations of those companies, managing separate factories and strategic deals with other firms. The Marwaris, often India's most affluent families whose businesses thrived under the old protective government policies, had considerable business networks among the families, favoring doing business with them over others. As an ethnic group, they developed their own business practices:

> Marwaris started business days with Hindu prayer and ended with an accounting of that day's cash flow. This practice, called partha, allowed them to respond quickly to market changes. Another, called modi, was a secret language that other Indians couldn't decipher and was used for trading data and business records.[93]

When Lakshmi Mittal, billionnaire steel tycoon—a global strategist based in London running a Dutch-registered company—launched a dramatic bid to take over Mittal Steel's chief rival, the reaction in India was one of shock. But Mittal said, "We have to put behind our family interest for the interest of the industry and the shareholders at large."[94] In giving up half of his 90 percent share of his company, to hold less than 45 percent of the combined company, he stated that he did not think his cultural traditions should deter the company from growth. In addition Arcelor-Mittal will be based in Luxembourg, not in London where Mr. Mittal lives. He will share the chairmanship and be able to appoint only one-third of the board's 18 seats. Mittal recognizes that to be globally competitive Marwari family businesses will have to change their governance policies.[95]

a strategy of withdrawal is difficult. Joint ventures can get hard to dissolve and as bitter as an acrimonious divorce. Problems include the forfeiture of assets and the inability to gain market access through future joint venture partners—all experienced by Audi, Chrysler, and Daimler-Benz. For example:

> *Audi's decision to terminate its joint venture prompted its Chinese partner, First Automobile Works, to expropriate its car design and manufacturing processes. The result was an enormously successful, unauthorized Audi clone, with a Chrysler engine and a First Automobile Works nameplate.*[97]

E-commerce Impact on Strategy Implementation

> *With subsidiaries, suppliers, distributors, manufacturing facilities, carriers, brokers and customers all over the globe, global trade is complicated and fragmented. Shipments cross borders multiple times a day. Are they compliant with all the latest trade regulations? Are they consistently classified for each country? Can you give your buyers, customers and service providers the latest information, on demand?*[98]

As indicated in this quote, global trade is extremely complicated. Deciding on a global strategy is one thing; implementing it through all the necessary parties and intermediaries around the world presents a whole new level of complexity. Because of that complexity, many firms decide to implement their global e-commerce strategy by outsourcing the necessary tasks to **e-commerce enablers**, companies that specialize in providing the technology to organize transactions and follow through with the regulatory requirements. These specialists can help companies sort through the maze of different taxes, duties, language translations, and so on specific to each country. Such services allow small and medium-sized companies to go global without the internal capabilities to carry out global e-commerce functions. One of these specialist e-commerce enablers is NextLinx, which applies technology to the wide range of services it provides for strategic implementation, allowing all trading partners to collaborate in a single online location, using the same information and processes. These kinds of Web-based services allow a company to manage an entire global trade operation, including automation of imports and exports by screening orders and generating the appropriate documentation, paying customs charges, complying with trade agreements, etc.[99]

CONCLUSION

Cross-border strategic alliances are becoming increasingly common as innovative companies seek rapid entry into foreign markets and as they try to reduce the risks of going it alone in complex environments. Those companies that do well are those that do their groundwork and pick complementary strategic partners. Too many, however, get "divorced" because "the devil is in the details"—which is what happens when "a marriage made in heaven" runs into unanticipated problems during actual strategic implementation, such as cultural clashes and government restrictions.

Summary of Key Points

1. Strategic alliances are partnerships with other companies for specific reasons. Cross-border, or global, strategic alliances are working partnerships between companies (often more than two) across national boundaries and increasingly across industries.

2. Cross-border alliances are formed for many reasons, including market expansion, cost- and technology-sharing, avoiding protectionist legislation, and taking advantage of synergies.

3. Technological advances and the resulting blending of industries, such as those in the telecommunications and entertainment industries, are factors prompting cross-industry alliances.

4. Alliances may be short or long term; they may be full global partnerships, or they may be for more narrow and specific functions such as research and development sharing.

5. Alliances often run into trouble in the strategic implementation phase. Problems include loss of technology and knowledge skill-base to the other partner, conflicting strategic goals and objectives, cultural clashes, and disputes over management and control systems.

6. Successful alliances require compatible partners with complementary skills, products, and markets. Extensive preparation is necessary to work out how to share management control and technology and to understand each other's culture.

7. Strategic implementation—also called *functional level strategies*—is the process of setting up overall policies, administrative responsibilities, and schedules throughout the organization. Successful implementation results from setting up the structure, systems, and processes of the firm, as well as the functional activities that create a *system of fits* with the desired strategy.

8. Differences in national culture and changes in the political arena or in government regulations often have unanticipated effects on strategic implementation.

9. Strategic implementation of global trade is increasingly being facilitated by *e-commerce enablers*—companies that specialize in providing the software and Internet technology for complying with the specific regulations, taxes, shipping logistics, translations, and so on for each country with which their clients do business.

Discussion Questions

1. Discuss the reasons that companies embark on cross-border strategic alliances. What other motivations may prompt such alliances?

2. Why are there an increasing number of mergers with companies in different industries? Give some examples. What industry do you think will be the next for global consolidation?

3. Discuss the problems inherent in developing a cooperative alliance to enhance competitive advantage, but also incurring the risk of developing a new competitor.

4. What are the common sources of incompatibility in cross-border alliances? What can be done to minimize them?

5. Explain what is necessary for companies to successfully implement a global sourcing strategy.

6. Discuss the political and economic situation in the Russian Federation with your class. What has changed since this writing? What are the implications for foreign companies to start a joint venture there now?

7. What is involved in strategic implementation? What is meant by creating a "*system of fits*" with the strategic plan?

8. Explain how the host government may affect strategic implementation—in an alliance or another form of entry strategy.

9. How might the variable of national culture affect strategic implementation? Use the Mittal Steel example to highlight some of these factors.

10. Discuss the importance of knowledge management in IJVs and what can be done to enhance effectiveness of that process.

Application Exercises

1. Research some recent joint ventures with foreign companies situated in Russia or China. How are they doing? Bring your information to class for discussion. What is the climate for foreign investors in Russia/China at the time of your reading this chapter?

Experiential Exercise: Partner Selection in an International Context

—BY PROFESSOR ANNE SMITH

Read the following three scenarios and think about the assigned questions before class. Although the names of the specific telecommunications firms have been disguised, each scenario is based on actual events and real companies in the telecommunications service industry.

Scenario 1: Toolbox and Frozen in Mexico

By October 30, 1990, managers from TOOLBOX (A Baby Bell[1] located in the eastern United States) and FROZEN (a Canadian telecommunications service and equipment provider) had been working for months on a final bid for the Telmex privatization. In two weeks, a final bid was due to the Mexican Ministry of Finance for this privatization; TOOLBOX's consortium was competing against four other groups.

Teléfonos de México (Telmex) was a government-run and owned telecommunications provider, which included local, long-distance, cellular, and paging services in Mexico. Yet, in late 1989, the Mexican government decided to privatize Telmex. Reasons for Telmex's privatization included its need for new technology and installation expertise and the large pent-up demand for phone service in Mexico (where only one in five households had a phone). In early 1990, managers from TOOLBOX's international subsidiary were in contact with many potential partners such as France Telecom, GTE, FROZEN, and Spain's Telefonica. By June 1990, TOOLBOX and FROZEN had

---

[1] Seven Baby Bells (also know as Regional Bell Operating Companies, or RBOCs for short) were created in 1984, when they were divested from AT&T. The term "Baby Bell" is really a misnomer given their large size, between $7 billion and $10 billion in revenues, at divestiture. In 1984, the Baby Bells were granted discrete territories where they offered local telephone service; these seven firms also were allowed to offer cellular service in their local service territories. From the AT&T divestiture settlement, the Baby Bells were allowed to keep the lucrative Yellow Pages and directory assistance services. Yet, these seven firms had no international activities or significant international managerial experience at divestiture.

chosen each other to partner and bid on the Telmex privatization. During the past six months, discussions had gone smoothly between the international managers at TOOLBOX and FROZEN. With a local Mexican partner (required by the Mexican government), the managers worked out many details related to their Telmex bid, such as who would be in charge of installations and backlog reduction, who would install new cellular equipment, who would upgrade the marketing and customer service function, and who would select and install the central office switches. A TOOLBOX international manager commented, "We got along extremely well with our neighbors to the north. Not surprisingly, given that we speak the same language, have similar business values . . . but, basically we liked their international people, which was essential for our largest international deal ever." A FROZEN international manager stated, "It was ironic that our top executive in charge of business development had been a summer intern at TOOLBOX when he was in college. So, he liked our selection of TOOLBOX for this partnering arrangement, even though he was not familiar with the current TOOLBOX top managers." By September 1990, investment bankers estimated that a winning bid would probably top $1.5 billion. On November 15, 1990, all final bids for the privatization would be due. Having worked out the operational details (contingent on a winning bid), managers from TOOLBOX and FROZEN returned to meet with their top managers one final time to get some consensus on a final bid price for Telmex.

Scenario 2: The Geneva Encounter

At the Telecom 1984 convention in Geneva, Robert and Jim (a GEMS senior vice president and a business development manager, respectively) had just finished hearing the keynote address and were wandering among the numerous exhibits. This convention, hosted every four years in Geneva, included thousands of exhibits of telecommunications services and hardware providers; tens of thousands of people attended. Though GEMS (a Baby Bell in the southwestern United States) did not have a booth at the 1984 convention, Robert and Jim were trying to learn about international telecommunications providers and activities. On the third day of the conference, Robert and Jim were standing at an exhibit of advanced wireless technologies when they struck up a conversation with another bystander who was from Israel.

"You can get lost in this convention," exclaimed Jim. Daniel from Israel agreed: "Yes, this is my first trip to the Telecom convention, and it is overwhelming . . . Tell me about GEMS. How is life freed from Ma Bell?" Robert, Jim, and Daniel continued their conversation over drinks and dinner. They learned that Daniel was an entrepreneur who was involved in many different ventures. One new venture that Daniel was pursuing was Yellow Pages directories and publishing. Daniel was

delighted to meet those high-level executives from GEMS because of the Baby Bells' reputations as high-quality telephone service providers. Several months after the conference, Robert and Jim visited Daniel in Israel to discuss opportunities there. Six months later, GEMS and Daniel's firm were jointly developing software for a computerized directory publishing system in Israel. GEMS had committed people and a very small equity stake ($5 to $10 million) to this venture.

Scenario 3: Layers and Jck in UK Cable

In early 1990, LAYERS (another Baby Bell from the western United States) was considering investing in an existing cable television franchise in the United Kingdom. In 1984, pioneer/pilot licenses had been awarded in some cities. Many of these initial licenses were awarded to start-up companies run by entrepreneurs with minimal investment capital. Unfortunately, "the 100 percent capital allowances that were seen as vital to make the financial structuring of the cable build a commercial reality" were abolished, creating a "break in the industry's development [from 1985 to 1989] whilst many companies that were interested in UK cable were forced to reexamine their financial requirements."[2]

Jack had obtained one of these early UK cable licenses in 1984, and his investment capital was quickly consumed from installing cable coupled with slow market penetration. By 1986, his efforts toward this venture had waned. In the 1990 Broadcast Act, the government relaxed its rule for cable operators and allowed non-EC control of UK cable companies. This created incentives for current cable operators to sell an equity stake in their ventures. This allowed U.S. and Canadian telephone companies to bring desperately needed cash as well as marketing and installation expertise to these cable ventures. Aware of the impending changes, Jack was once again focusing on his cable operations. He arranged a meeting with several LAYERS international managers in November 1989, in anticipation of the changes. Turning on his charm and sales abilities, Jack explained to the LAYERS international managers the potential for UK cable television.[3] He also shared with these managers that he was willing to sell a large equity stake in his company to get it growing again. The international managers from LAYERS were impressed by Jack's enthusiasm, but they were even more intrigued by the possibility of learning about the convergence of cable and telephone services from this UK "laboratory." The LAYERS international managers decided that they would discuss this deal with their executive in charge of unregulated activities. By June 1990, LAYERS had an equity stake, estimated to be between $30 and $50 million, in Jack's UK cable venture.

source: This exercise was written by Professor Anne Smith, University of New Mexico, based on her research of the firms discussed. Copyright Professor Anne Smith. Used with permission.

Questions

Think about these questions from the perspective of the Baby Bell in each scenario:

1. In your opinion, which one of these scenarios should lead to a long-term successful international partnering relationship? Based on what criteria?

2. In your opinion, which one of these scenarios has the least chance of leading to a long-term, successful international partnering relationship? Why?

Internet Resources

Visit the Deresky Companion Website at www.pearsonhighered.com/deresky for this chapter's Internet resources.

---

[2] The Cable Companion, The Cable Television Association, 1–12.

[3] In the UK, cable operators were allowed to offer both cable and telephone service.

CASE STUDY

Aditya Birla Group: Global Vision—Indian Values

In 2008, the Aditya Birla Group (ABG) was a US$28 billion corporation. It employed 100,000 people belonging to 25 nationalities and over 50% of its revenues were attributed to its overseas operations in countries like the US, the UK, China, Germany, Hungary, and Brazil, among others.[4]

The group's product portfolio comprised Aluminum (Hindalco-Indal), Copper (Birla Copper), Fertilizers (Indo Gulf Fertilizers Ltd.), Textiles and Cement (Grasim Industries Ltd.), Insulators (Birla NGK Insulators Pvt. Ltd.), Viscose Filament Yarn (Indian Rayon and Industries Ltd.), Carbon black (Birla Carbon), Insurance (Birla Sun Life Insurance Company Ltd.), Telecommunications (Idea Cellular Ltd.), and BPO (Minacs Worldwide Ltd.).

In 2007, the group acquired Novelis Inc., the Atlanta (US)-based aluminum producer to become the largest rolled-aluminum products manufacturers in the world.[5] The group had also acquired a majority stake in Indal from Alcan of Canada in the year 2000,[6] and this had positioned it in the value-addition chain of the business, from metal to downstream products. Birla Copper enjoyed a good market share in the country and the acquisition of mines in Australia in the year 2003[7] elevated it to an integrated copper producer. Indo-Gulf Fertilizers possessed a brand that commanded strong cash flows and a leadership position in the fertilizer industry. The group had entered into a 50:50 joint venture with NGK Corporation of Japan for its insulators division in 2002. This was expected to provide ABG access to the latest in product and manufacturing technology for the insulators division and also to open up the path to global markets. In 2006, the group purchased the equity holding of NGK and made the venture its subsidiary.[8] A Group company, Birla Sun Life, offered insurance and mutual fund products in the Indian market. In 2006, the group acquired Minacs Worldwide, a BPO company,[9] and acquired Tata's stake in Idea Cellular.[10] In 2007, the group acquired Trinethra, a chain of retail stores.[11]

The Group's strategy toward the business portfolio was to exit from those areas of business where they had a minor presence or where losses were being incurred and to consolidate and build upon operations where competencies and business strengths existed. For instance, the group's textiles division Grasim had consolidated its operations by closing down operations at its pulp and fiber plants located at Mavoor and had sold the loss making fabric operations at Gwalior in 2002.[12] ABG also divested itself of its stake in Mangalore Refinery and Petrochemicals Ltd. to the leading Indian oil company ONGC in 2002.[13]

Analysts felt that the group's ability to grow had stemmed largely from the emphasis placed on building meritocracy in the group. Under the leadership of Kumar Mangalam Birla (Birla), several initiatives were taken with the focus on learning and relearning, performance management, and organizational renewal. Birla also instituted steps to retire aged managers and replaced them with young managers who came in with fresh and 'out of the box' ideas.

ABG instituted *Gyanodaya*, the group's learning center, to facilitate transfer of best practices across the group companies. The training methodology comprised classroom teaching and e-learning initiatives and the training calendar was accessible to the group employees through the group-wide intranet. The company also put in place 'The Organizational Health Survey' aimed at tracking the satisfaction levels of the group's managers. The survey was seen as a gauge of the happiness at work index in the group. The implementation of these initiatives resulted in ABG becoming one of the preferred employers in Asia. Toward performance management, the group had instituted the Aditya Birla Sun awards to recognize the successes of the group companies. This resulted in information sharing and encouraged healthy competition among these companies.

---

[4] www.adityabirla.com/the_group/index.htm
[5] "Birla Group Acquires Novelis for $ 6 Billion," www.indiapost.com, February 19, 2007.
[6] "Hindalco Buys Out Alcan in Indal," www.hinduonnet.com, March 24, 2000.
[7] "Hindalco to Acquire Australia Mine," www.thehindubusinessline.com, January 25, 2004.
[8] "Aditya Birla Nuvo Pact with NGK," www.thehindubusinessline.com, November 21, 2006.
[9] "Aditya Birla Group to Acquire Minacs Worldwide," www.ciol.com, June 26, 2006.
[10] "Birlas Set to Buy Tata's Stake in Idea," http://in.ibtimes.com, April 14, 2006.
[11] "Trinethra: Birla's First Retail Takeover," http://economictimes.indiatimes.com, January 3, 2007.
[12] "Grasim to Sell Off Textile Division for Rs.15 Crores," www.financialexpress.com, February 27, 2002.
[13] "Birlas Sell MRPL Stake to ONGC," www.tribuneindia.com, August 2, 2002.

In addition to the stunning growth of ABG, Kumar Mangalam Birla has taken steps to root the company in its heritage and give back to India. Its mission in that regard is evidenced in the website description of its activities:

Beyond business—the Aditya Birla Group is:

- Working in 3,700 villages
- Reaching out to seven million people annually through the Aditya Birla Centre for Community Initiatives and Rural Development, spearheaded by Mrs. Rajashree Birla
- Focusing on: health care, education, sustainable livelihood, infrastructure and espousing social causes
- Running 41 schools and 18 hospitals (11)

Transcending the conventional barriers of business to send out a message that "We care."

Additional Readings and References

1. "Hindalco Buys Out Alcan in Indal," www.hinduonnet.com, March 24, 2000.
2. "Grasim to Sell Off Textile Division for Rs.15 Crores," www.financialexpress.com, February 27, 2002.
3. "Birlas Sell MRPL Stake to ONGC," www.tribuneindia.com, August 2, 2002.
4. "Hindalco to Acquire Australia Mine," www.thehindubusinessline.com, January 25, 2004.
5. "Birlas Set to Buy Tata's Stake in Idea," http://in.ibtimes.com, April 14, 2006.
6. "Aditya Birla Group to Acquire Minacs Worldwide," www.ciol.com, June 26, 2006.
7. "Aditya Birla Nuvo Pact with NGK," www.thehindubusinessline.com, November 21, 2006.
8. "Trinethra: Birla's First Retail Takeover," http://economictimes.indiatimes.com, January 3, 2007.
9. "Birla Group Acquires Novelis for $ 6 Billion," www.indiapost.com, February 19, 2007.
10. www.adityabirla.com/the_group/index.htm
11. Ibid.

Author Information: This case was written by **Debapratim Purkayastha** and **T. Seshasai**, ICMR. It was compiled from published sources, and is intended to be used as a basis for class discussion rather than to illustrate either effective or ineffective handling of a management situation.

Case Questions

1. Critically analyze the growth strategy adopted by the Aditya Birla Group. What are your views on the business portfolio adopted by the group?
2. Analyze the initiatives taken by the group on the personnel and culture front under the leadership of Kumar Mangalam Birla.
3. Discuss how ABG has addressed the second part of its mission— "Indian Values."

Organization Structure and Control Systems

OBJECTIVES:

1. To understand the importance of appropriate organizational structures to effective strategy implementation.

2. To become familiar with the types of organizational designs suitable for the level and scope of internationalization of the firm.

3. To be able to recognize why and when organizational restructuring is needed.

4. To understand the role of technology in the evolution of the networked structure; and to appreciate the role of "human networks" in achieving business goals.

5. To realize how organizational design affects the manager's job, for example on the level and location of decision making.

6. To emphasize the role of control and monitoring systems for suitable for specific situations and locations in the firm's international operations.

Opening Profile: Samsung Electronics Reorganizes to Fight Downturn[1]

Companies change their structures to align with new strategic directions and competition, but also to respond to developments in their operating environment. Such was the case early in 2009 when Samsung Electronics of Seoul, South Korea, implemented a radical reorganization in order to become more efficient to deal with worsening economic conditions.

Samsung Electronics is the world's leading manufacturer of memory chips, liquid crystal displays, and flat screen televisions, and is second in mobile phones after Finland's Nokia Corp. (Samsung Electronics is part of the Samsung Group, which includes dozens of companies with interests in shipbuilding, construction, life insurance and leisure.) But Samsung has been badly hit by the global economic downturn, resulting in falling prices for semiconductors and flat screens, and such a radically declining profitability as to "threaten its existence," according to a Samsung spokeswoman Hwang Eun-ju. She stated that the changes are needed to "effectively respond to the current global recession."[2]

As a result, Samsung Electronics Co. announced a major restructuring, consolidating business operations into two operating divisions, one focused on consumer products such as televisions and cellphones, and the other on components such as memory chips and displays. Thus the company integrated four business units—semiconductors, LCDs, mobile phones, and consumer electronics—into two divisions regarded as "parts" and "sets." This necessitated reassigning two-thirds of its executives and relocating 1,200 staff members, cutting executives' pay by 20 percent, and reducing other benefits. The company also replaced the heads of five of its eight overseas operations—North America, Europe, the CIS, and the Middle East and Africa.

Clearly, the company strategy has had to change from high-tech competition to controlling cash flow and profitability. The reorganization was expected to eliminate bureaucracy and speed decision making. Another goal of the restructuring was to help resolve conflicts that Samsung's components businesses serve customers who are competitive with its own consumer-products businesses. Samsung's CEO Lee Yoon-woo was selected to directly oversee the components division; and Mr. Choi Gee-sung will head the consumer products division.

Strategic plans are abstract sets of decisions that cannot affect a company's competitive position or bottom line until they are implemented. Having decided on the strategic direction for the company, international managers must then consider two of the key variables for implementing strategy: the organizational structure and the control and coordinating mechanisms. The necessity of adapting organizational structures to facilitate changes in strategy, competitive moves, and changes in the environment is illustrated in the opening profile describing Samsung Electronics' organizational response to global economic decline. The failure to adapt to changing market conditions both strategically and structurally is evidenced by the short life-span of even large companies. As one example of studies highlighting corporate mortality, only 160 out of 1008 large corporations studied by Foster and Kaplan survived between 1962 and 1998.[3] This is particularly apparent in times of radical change such as the economic relapse which started in 2008 and resulted in many firms going out of business. Even General Motors, one of the largest global companies, was tipped over the edge into bankruptcy after decades of poor management, surviving only with radical downsizing and government aid. Comparatively, IBM has adapted in various ways. After realizing that the company had missed opportunities for growth initiatives, the company developed its EBO (emerging business opportunities) model into three horizons— current core businesses, growth businesses, and future growth businesses.[4]

ORGANIZATIONAL STRUCTURE

> *There is no permanent organization chart for the world. . . . It is of supreme importance to be ready at all times to take advantage of new opportunities.*
>
> Robert C. Goizueta,
> *(Former) Chairman and CEO, Coca-Cola Company*[5]

Organizational structures must change to accommodate a firm's evolving internationalization in response to worldwide competition. Considerable research has shown that a firm's structure must be conducive to the implementation of its strategy.[6] In other words, the structure must "fit" the strategy, or it will not work. Managers are faced with how best to attain that fit in organizing the company's systems and tasks.

The design of an organization, as with any other management function, should be contingency based, taking into account the variables of that particular system at that specific point in time. Major variables include the firm's strategy, size, and appropriate technology, as well as the environment in those parts of the world in which the firm operates. Given the increased complexity of the variables involved in the international context, it is no easy task to design the most suitable organizational structure and subsystems. In fact, research shows that most international managers find it easier to determine what to do to compete globally (strategy) than to decide how to develop the organizational capability (structure) to do it.[7] Additional variables affecting structural choices—geographic dispersion as well as differences in time, language, cultural attitudes, and business practices—introduce further layers of complication. We will show how organizational structures need to, and typically do, change to accommodate strategies of increasing internationalization.

EVOLUTION AND CHANGE IN MNC ORGANIZATIONAL STRUCTURES

Historically, a firm reorganizes as it internationalizes to accommodate new strategies. The structure typically continues to change over time with growth and with increasing levels of investment or diversity and as a result of the types of entry strategy chosen. Internationalization is the process by which a firm gradually changes in response to international competition, domestic market saturation, and the desire for expansion, new markets, and diversification. As discussed in Chapter 6, a firm's managers weigh alternatives and decide on appropriate entry strategies. Perhaps the firm starts by exporting or by acting as a licensor or licensee, and then over time continues to internationalize by engaging in joint ventures or by establishing service, production, or assembly facilities or alliances abroad, moving into a global strategy. At each stage, the firm's managers redesign the organizational structure to optimize the strategy's chances to work, making changes in the firm's tasks and relationships and designating authority, responsibility, lines of communication, geographic dispersal of units, and so forth. This model of **structural evolution** has become known as the **stages model**, resulting from Stopford's research on 187 U.S. multinational corporations (MNCs).[8] Of course, many firms do not follow the stages model because they may start their internationalization at a higher level of involvement— perhaps a full-blown global joint venture without ever having exported, for example.

Even a mature MNC must make structural changes from time to time to facilitate changes in strategy—perhaps a change in strategy from globalization to regionalization (see Chapter 6) or an effort to improve efficiency or effectiveness. The reorganization of Aluminum Company of America (Alcoa), for example, split the company into smaller, more autonomous units, thereby giving more focus to growing businesses, such as automotive products, where the market for aluminum is strong. It also enabled Alcoa to link businesses with similar functions that are geographically divided—that is, to improve previously insufficient communication between Alcoa's aluminum operations in Brazil and its Australian counterparts. Alcoa, as with most MNCs, has found the need to continuously adapt its structure to accommodate global expansion and new ventures. Alcoa has a presence in 41 countries, employing 120,000 people worldwide.

The typical ways in which firms organize their international activities are shown in the following list. (Larger companies often use several of these structures in different regions or parts of their organization.) After the presentation of some of these structural forms, the focus will turn to transitional organizational arrangements.

- Domestic structure plus export department
- Domestic structure plus foreign subsidiary
- International division
- Global functional structure
- Global product structure
- Matrix structure

As previously stated, many firms—especially smaller ones—start their international involvement by exporting. They may simply use the services of an export management company for this, or they may reorganize into a simple *domestic structure plus export department.*

To facilitate access to and development of specific foreign markets, the firm can take a further step toward worldwide operations by reorganizing into a *domestic structure plus foreign subsidiary* in one or more countries (see Exhibit 8-1). To be effective, subsidiary

EXHIBIT 8-1 Domestic Structure Plus Foreign Subsidary

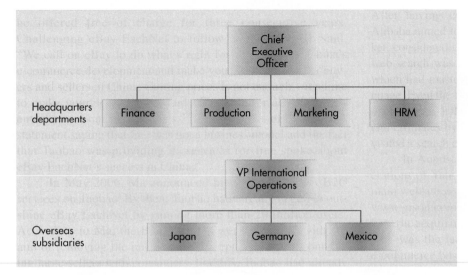

managers should have a great deal of autonomy and be able to adapt and respond quickly to serve local markets. This structure works well for companies with one or a few subsidiaries located relatively close to headquarters.

With further market expansion, the firm may then decide to specialize by creating an *international division*, organized along functional, product, or geographic lines. With this structure, the various foreign subsidiaries are organized under the international division, and subsidiary managers report to its head and are typically given the title Vice President, International Division. This vice president, in turn, reports directly to the CEO of the corporation. The creation of an international division facilitates the beginning of a global strategy. It permits managers to allocate and coordinate resources for foreign activities under one roof, and thus enhances the firm's ability to respond, both reactively and proactively, to market opportunities. Some conflicts may arise among the divisions of the firm because more resources and management attention tend to get channeled toward the international division than toward the domestic divisions and because of the different orientations of various division managers. Companies such as IBM and PepsiCo have international divisions called, respectively, IBM World Trade and PepsiCola International.

Integrated Global Structures

To respond to increased product diversification and to maximize benefits from both domestic and foreign operations, a firm may choose to replace its international division with an integrated global structure. This structure can be organized along functional, product, geographic, or matrix lines.

The **global functional structure** is designed on the basis of the company's functions—production, marketing, finance, and so forth. Foreign operations are integrated into the activities and responsibilities of each department to gain functional specialization and economies of scale. This form of organization is primarily used by small firms with highly centralized systems. It is particularly appropriate for product lines using similar technology and for businesses with a narrow spectrum of customers. This structure results in plants that are highly integrated across products and that serve single or similar markets.

Much of the advantage resulting from economies of scale and functional specialization may be lost if the managers and the work systems become too narrowly defined to have the necessary flexibility to respond to local environments. An alternative structure can be based on product lines.

For firms with diversified product lines (or services) that have different technological bases and that are aimed at dissimilar or dispersed markets, a **global product (divisional) structure** may be more strategically advantageous than a functional structure. In this structure, a single product (or product line) is represented by a separate division. Each division is headed by its own general manager, and each is responsible for its own production and sales functions. Usually, each division is a **strategic business unit** (SBU)—a self-contained business with its own functional departments and accounting systems. The advantages of this organizational form are market

EXHIBIT 8-2   Global Product (Divisional) Structure

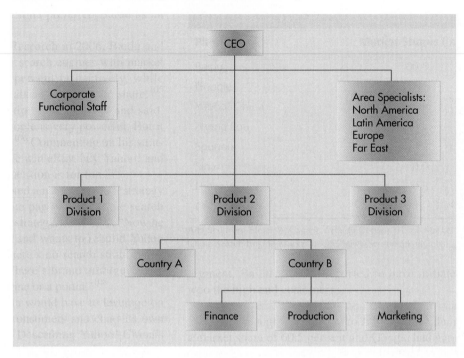

concentration, innovation, and responsiveness to new opportunities in a particular environment. It also facilitates diversification and rapid growth, sometimes at the expense of scale economies and functional specialization. H. J. Heinz Company CEO William R. Johnson came on board in April 1998 and decided that the company should restructure to implement a global strategy. He changed the focus of the company from a multidomestic international strategy using the global geographic area structure to a global strategy using the global product divisional structure. His goal was further growth overseas by building international operations; this structure also readily incorporated Heinz's Specialty Pet Food Division for marketing those products around the world.[9] Particularly appropriate in a dynamic and diverse environment, the global product structure is illustrated in Exhibit 8-2.

With the global product (divisional) grouping, however, ongoing difficulties in the coordination of widely dispersed operations may result. One answer to this problem, particularly for large MNCs, is to reorganize into a global geographic structure.

In the **global geographic (area) structure**—the most common form of organizing foreign operations—divisions are created to cover geographic regions (see Exhibit 8-3). Each regional manager is responsible for the operations and performance of the countries within a given region. In this way, country and regional needs and relative market knowledge take precedence over product expertise. Local managers are familiar with the cultural environment, government regulations, and business transactions. In addition, their language skills and local contacts facilitate daily transactions and responsiveness to the market and the customer. While this is a good structure for consolidating regional expertise, problems of coordination across regions may arise.

With the geographic structure, the focus is on marketing, since products can be adapted to local requirements. Therefore, marketing-oriented companies, such as Nestlé and Unilever, which produce a range of products that can be marketed through similar (or common) channels of distribution to similar customers, will usually opt for this structure. Nestlé SA, for example, uses this decentralized structure, which is more typical of European companies, because "it is not Nestlé's policy to generate most of its sales in Switzerland, supplemented by a few satellite subsidiaries abroad. Nestlé strives to be an insider in every country in which it operates, not an outsider."[10] In 2005, Nestlé reinforced its global business strategy of emphasizing its brands by making its head of marketing responsible for Nestlé's seven SBUs—dairy, confectionery, beverages, ice cream, food, pet care, and food services. Those SBUs help determine the

EXHIBIT 8-3   Global Geographic Structure

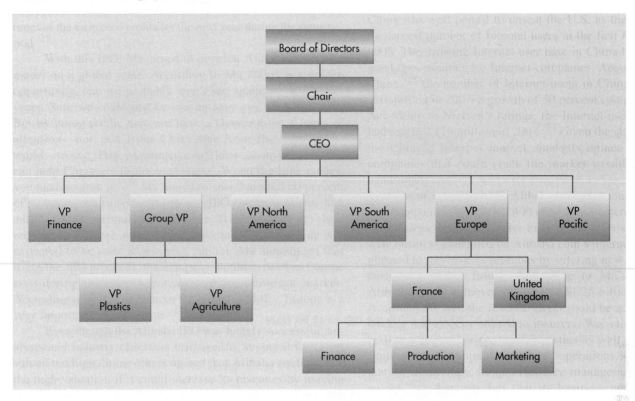

company's regional business strategy, which then shapes the local market business strategies.[11] Still Nestlé's marketing manager, Mr. Brabeck, insists that

> *There is no such thing as a global consumer, especially in a sector as psychologically and culturally loaded as food. . . . This means having a local character.*
>
> PETER BRABECK,
> *Nestlé Marketing Manager*[12]

Grouping a number of countries under a region doesn't always work out, however, as Ford experienced with its European Group. It soon discovered tensions among the units in Germany, Britain, and France resulting from differences in their national systems and cultures, and in particular management styles. Nevertheless, it has pursued its consolidation into five regionalized global centers for the design, manufacture, and marketing of 70 lines of cars around the world. In 2001, under Ford's CEO Jac Nasser—born in Lebanon and raised in Australia—Ford negotiated a presence in more than 200 countries, with 140 manufacturing plants.[13]

A **matrix structure** is a hybrid organization of overlapping responsibilities. The structure is developed to combine geographic support for both global integration and local responsiveness; also it can be used to take advantage of personnel skills and experience shared across both functional and divisional structures. In the matrix structure the lines of responsibility are drawn both vertically and horizontally as illustrated in Exhibit 8-4. While this method of management and organization maximizes the focus of skills and experience in the company to bring to bear on a particular product as well as region, it often brings confusion, communication problems, and conflict over having more than one boss to whom to report and stress over prioritizing time among overlapping and conflicting responsibilities. Indeed, in their research of 36 Dutch organizations, including subsidiaries of global firms, Strikwerda and Stoelhorst concluded from the majority of interviewees that:

> *executives associate the matrix organization with unclear responsibilities, a lack of accountability, and political battles over resources, resulting in risk-averse behavior and loss of market share*
>
> CALIFORNIA MANAGEMENT REVIEW,
> *Summer 2009.*[14]

EXHIBIT 8-4 Matrix Geographic Structure

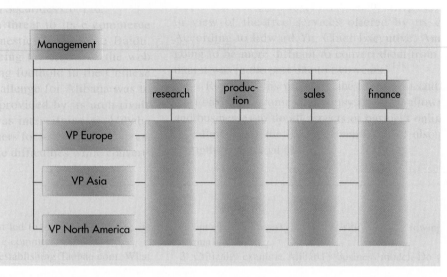

ORGANIZING FOR GLOBALIZATION

No matter what the stage of internationalization, a firm's structural choices always involve two opposing forces: the need for **differentiation** (focusing on and specializing in specific markets) and the need for **integration** (coordinating those same markets). The way the firm is organized along the differentiation–integration continuum determines how well strategies—along a local-ization-globalization continuum—are implemented. This is why the structural imperatives of various strategies such as globalization must be understood to organize appropriate worldwide systems and connections.

As previously presented, global trends and competitive forces have put increasing pressure on multinational corporations to adopt a strategy of **globalization**, a specific strategy that treats the world as one market by using a standardized approach to products and markets. The following are two examples of companies reorganizing to achieve globalization:

- **IBM.** Big Blue decided to move away from its traditional geographic structure to a global structure based on its 14 worldwide industry groups, such as banking, retail, and insurance, shifting power from country managers to centralized industry expert teams. IBM hopes the restructuring will help the company take advantage of global markets and break down internal barriers.
- **Asea-Brown Boveri (ABB).** A global leader in the power and the oil and gas industry, ABB is legendary in its record of changing its organizational structure to fit its new strate-gic directions and its competitive environment, such as the losses it incurred resulting from the East Asian currency crisis. Exhibit 8-5 illustrates two phases of the company's strategic direction and organization structure. For further details and developments, see the Part 3 Comprehensive Case on ABB.

Organizing to facilitate a globalization strategy typically involves rationalization and the development of strategic alliances. To achieve rationalization, managers choose the manufactur-ing location for each product based on where the best combination of cost, quality, and technolo-gy can be attained. It often involves producing different products or component parts in different countries. Typically, it also means that the product design and marketing programs are essentially the same for all end markets around the world—to achieve optimal economies of scale. The down-side of this strategy is a lack of differentiation and specialization for local markets.

Organizing for global product standardization necessitates close coordination among the various countries involved. It also requires centralized global product responsibility (one manager at headquarters responsible for a specific product around the world), an especially difficult task for multiproduct companies. Henzler and Rall suggest that structural solutions to this problem can be found if companies rethink the roles of their headquarters and their national subsidiaries. Managers should center the overall control of the business at

EXHIBIT 8-5 ABB's Old Versus New Corporate Strategy and Organizational Models During the Tenures of CEOs Percy Barnevik and Jürgen Dormann (1988–2004) and Fred Kindle (2005 on)

Old Corporate Strategy/Organizational Model
(Percy Barnevik, 1988–2001)

- Create a powerful global corporation
- Seek aggressive global expansion
- Design and implant matrix management structure
- Encourage entrepreneurship, decentralization, and multiculturalism in overseas subsidiaries
- Seek internal benchmarking and corporate parenting
- Keep local corporate identities while seeking globalization
- Seek cosmopolitan conglomerates
- Seek pan European and global strategies
- Concentrate on Asian markets

Net Output
- Global corp.
- Matrix structure

- Networking

- Horizontal structure

New Corporate Strategy/Organizational Model
(Jürgen Dormann, 2002–2004) and Fred Kindle (2005 on)

- Revise core competencies
- Sell off non-core businesses
- Seek corporate restructuring
- Improve financial health of company
- Seek more regional strategies
- Resolve old disputes such as asbestos liabilities.
- Simplify ABB's global structure; create two divisions (power technology and automation)
- Seek cost cutting; seek downsizing
- Unload unproductive units
- Improve credit rating

Net Output
- Rationalization
- Simplicity
- Avoid non-core businesses
- Downsizing
- Save money
- Redesign the company

Sources: Business Week; The Economist; Financial Times; The Wall Street Journal. Compiled by Syed Tariq Anwar, case study "ABB, Sweden: What Went Wrong?" in 6ed of this book.

headquarters, while treating national subsidiaries as partners in managing the business—perhaps as holding companies responsible for the administration and coordination of cross-divisional activities.[15]

Governments as well as firms may structure their holdings in order to attract and integrate strategic allies. Such was the case for Brazil's federal energy company Petrobas (NYSE: PBR) when it announced in February 2009 that it had created six wholly owned companies, along product lines, for the Rio de Janeiro Comperj petrochemical complex, commenting that:

> *Petrobras will hold a 100% stake in the companies and voting capital at the initial stage while it integrates and defines the relationship between Comperj's component parts. By establishing these companies Petrobras is laying the foundations for the potential involvement of partners. Planned investments in Comperj are expected to total US$8.4bn and operations are scheduled to begin in 2012.*
>
> BUSINESS NEWS AMERICAS,
> *February 5, 2009.*[16]

A problem many companies face in the future is that their structurally sophisticated global networks, built to secure cost advantages, leave them exposed to the risk of environmental volatility from all corners of the world. Such companies must restructure their global operations to reduce the environmental risk that results from multicountry sourcing and supply networks.[17] In other words, the more links in the chain, the more chances for things to go wrong.

Organizing to "Be Global, Act Local"

In their rush to get on the globalization bandwagon, too many firms have sacrificed the ability to respond to local market structures and consumer preferences. Managers are now realizing that—depending on the type of products, markets, and so forth—a compromise must be made along the globalization–regionalization continuum, and they are experimenting with various structural configurations to "be global and act local."

Levi Strauss is another example of a company attempting to maximize the advantages of different structural configurations. The company employs a staff of approximately 10,000 people worldwide, including approximately 1,010 people at its San Francisco, California, headquarters. It is a worldwide corporation organized into three geographic divisions:

Levi Strauss Americas (LSA), based in the San Francisco headquarters.

Levi Strauss Europe, Middle East, and North Africa (LSEMA), based in Brussels.

Asia Pacific Division (APD), based in Singapore.

In the LSEMA division there is a network of nine sales offices, six distribution centers, and three production facilities, employing a total of approximately 4,600 people. The headquarters are located in Brussels, Belgium. The company's European franchise partners bring the products to consumers throughout the region.[18]

Levi Strauss & Co.'s Asia Pacific Division is comprised of subsidiary businesses, licensees and distributors throughout Asia Pacific, the Middle East and Africa.

Thus, through these various structural global-local formats, the company has ensured its ability to respond to local needs by allowing its managers to act independently: Levi's success turns on its ability to fashion a global strategy that doesn't snuff out local initiative. It's a delicate balancing act, one that often means giving foreign managers the freedom needed to adjust their tactics to meet the changing tastes of their home markets.

One well-known global consumer products company, Procter & Gamble, is succeeding with its global–local "Four Pillars" structure, as described in the accompanying Management Focus.

MANAGEMENT FOCUS

Procter & Gamble's "Think Globally-Act Locally" Structure

On October 10, 2006, Procter & Gamble (P&G) Chairman of the Board, President and Chief Executive, A. G. Lafley, addressed shareholders at its annual meeting saying,

"We are now focused on delivering a full decade of industry-leading top and bottom line growth. We have the strategies, strengths and the structure to continue to transform our company in the face of unrelenting change and competition."[19]

Lafley was referring to their Four Pillars structure and to their recent merger with Gillette; both are described below.

With the Gillette merger, P&G now has over 135 employees working in over 80 countries around the world. P&G touches the lives of people around the world three billion times a day with its broad portfolio of leading brands, including Pampers®, Tide®, Charmin®, Downy®, Crest®, Gillette®, and Braun®.[20]

In January 2006, Gillette India announced its merger plans with Procter & Gamble India. The plan was for the Boston-based blades and razor company to adopt P&G's organizational structure and effective July 1, 2006, relocate its headquarters from Gurgaon to P&G Plaza in Mumbai, which would house all P&G subsidiaries in India. Zubair Ahmed, head of Gillette India, stated that "even as Gillette India stays as a separate legal entity in India, P&G's organizational structure, distribution, systems and facilities will help increase our reach, cost efficiencies, speed to market and our current growth momentum."[21]

By July 1, 2006—nine months after closing the Gillette deal—P&G had completed business systems integration in 31 countries spanning five of P&G's seven geographic regions. The company is now taking orders, shipping products, receiving payments, tracking financials, and handling payroll as a single company in these countries. Systems integration is continuing in another 14 countries, including the largest region, North America. When completed, nearly 80 percent of the company's sales will have been integrated.

P&G's organizational structure is broadly divided into three heads: GBU (Global Business Unit), MDO (Market Development Organization), and GBS (Global Business Services). Gillette will move from business units based on geographic regions to GBUs based on product lines. MDOs will develop market strategies to build business based on local knowledge and GBS will bring together business activities such as accounting, human resource systems, order management, and information technology, thus making it cost-effective.[22]

Since 2001, P&G has acquired three leading companies with leading brands in Clairol, Wella, and Gillette. The acquisition of Gillette added five brands with annual sales in excess of $1 billion. Lafley said he is confident the company can deliver on a full decade of growth because of P&G's strategies and strengths, and the company's unique organizational structure. P&G's structure makes it the only consumer products company with global business unit profit centers, global market development organizations, and global shared services, all supported by innovative corporate functions. Lafley reported that he's pleased with progress on the Gillette integration, which will result in $1.0 billion to $1.2 billion in annual cost synergies before taxes and about $750 million in revenue synergy growth by 2009.[23]

P&G's organization structure is described below as given in the company's corporate information description on their Web site.[24]

P&G's Global/Local Structure

Four pillars—Global Business Units, Market Development Organizations, Global Business Services, and Corporate Functions—form the heart of P&G's organizational structure.

- Global Business Units (GBUs) build major global brands with robust business strategies.
- Market Development Organizations (MDOs) build local understanding as a foundation for marketing campaigns.
- Global Business Services (GBS) provide business technology and services that drive business success.
- Corporate Functions (CFs) work to maintain our place as a leader of our industries.

P&G approaches business knowing that we need to Think Globally (GBUs) and Act Locally (MDOs). This approach is supported by our commitment to operate efficiently (GBS) and our constant striving to be the best at what we do (CFs). This streamlined structure allows us to get to market faster.

Global Business Units
Philosophy: Think Globally
General Role: Create strong brand equities, robust strategies, and ongoing innovation in products and marketing to build major global brands.
GBUs:

- Baby Care/Family Care
- Beauty Care/Feminine Care
- Fabric & Home Care
- Snacks & Beverage
- Health Care

Market Development Organizations (MDO)
Philosophy: Act Locally
General Role: Interface with customers to ensure marketing plans fully capitalize on local understanding, to seek synergy across programs to leverage corporate scale, and to develop strong programs that change the game in our favor at point of purchase.
MDO Regions:

- North America
- Asia/India/Australia
- Northeast Asia
- Greater China
- Central-Eastern Europe/Middle East/Africa
- Western Europe
- Latin America

Global Business Services (GBS)
Philosophy: Enabling P&G to win with customers and consumers
General Role: Provide services and solutions that enable the Company to operate efficiently around the world, collaborate effectively with business partners, and help employees become more productive.

GBS Centers:

- GBS Americas located in Costa Rica
- GBS Asia located in Manila
- GBS Europe, Middle East & Africa located in Newcastle

Corporate Functions (CF)
Philosophy: Be the Smartest/Best
General Role: Ensure that the functional capability integrated into the rest of the company remains on the cutting edge of the industry. We want to be the thought leader within each CF.
Corporate Functions:

- Customer Business Development
- External Relations
- Finance & Acct.
- Human Resources
- Information Technology
- Legal
- Marketing
- Consumer & Market Knowledge
- Product Supply
- Research & Development
- Workplace Services

Although strategy may be the primary means to a company's competitive advantage, the burden of realizing that advantage rests on the organizational structure and design; that structure, in turn, establishes the responsibilities and guides the decisions, actions, and communications, of its employees. Because of the difficulties experienced by companies trying to be "glocal" companies (global and local), researchers are suggesting new, more flexible organizational designs involving interorganizational networks and transnational design.

EMERGENT STRUCTURAL FORMS

Companies are increasingly abandoning rigid structures in an attempt to be more flexible and responsive to the dynamic global environment. Some of the ways they are adapting are by transitioning to formats known as interorganizational networks, global e-corporation network structures, and transnational corporation network structures, described below. Other new structural formats are evolving as emerging market companies make their rapid entré onto the global scene, as discussed in the following Comparative Management in Focus section.

COMPARATIVE MANAGEMENT IN FOCUS

Changing Organizational Structures of Emerging Market Companies

Rapidly changing competition and global business activities demand that companies run their worldwide operations efficiently and effectively, based on the right business models and organizational structures. Stable organizational structures and control systems are necessary to seek timely internationalization. The major variables involved in choosing the right organizational structure depend on a company's global involvement and degree of localization. In 2009, fast-growing companies from emerging markets (EMs), BRIC (Brazil, Russia, India and China), and rapidly developing economies (RDEs) continue to internationalize their operations.[25] Examples are CNOOC (China), Dr. Reddy's Laboratories (India), Embraer (Brazil), Gazprom (Russia), Haier Company (China), Infosys Technologies (India), Koc Holdings (Turkey), Lenovo Group (China), Tata Motors (India), and Wipro (India).[26] These emerging market companies are the first wave of highly successful firms benefiting from the globalization phenomenon.[27]

Interestingly, the expansion models sought by these new emerging market companies from Asia, Latin America, and Eastern Europe are unique and may not fit with today's mainstream multinational corporation (MNC) model because of the following three reasons: First, many emerging market companies are avoiding the traditional roadmap to internationalization and capitalizing on the "born-global phenomenon," which means running their operations and opening subsidiaries worldwide from the beginning. Second, they are finding niche businesses where competition is limited. Third, they are thriving in those old-economy industries that have been abandoned by established MNCs from developed countries.

A new breed of companies is emerging in those geographic areas that have excelled in global business because of their unique organizational structures and design. Like Korean chaebols (industrial conglomerates), most emerging market companies were started as family businesses and entrepreneurial entities where ownership and control of firms resided with the families. Therefore, the control mechanism is somewhat bureaucratic and headquarters-centered. Currently, a multitude of changes are in the pipeline that will force emerging market companies to redefine their family-based governance structures and rigid control systems. The ongoing changes include simplifying firms' traditional hierarchical structures, reducing the role of family members, providing more operational powers to international subsidiaries, and redesigning organizational systems that could follow the traditional MNC-model or company-specific forms.

Major structural changes include simplifying hierarchies, reducing family ownerships, providing more powers to subsidiaries, and seeking organizational structures based on either the traditional MNC model or company-specific hybrid structures. Interestingly, many emerging market companies have been following the model of "be global, act local" in becoming good citizens and adapting their products and services. Embraer, Haier Group, Lenovo, Mittal Steel, Orsacom, and others fit in this category. In addition, overseas Chinese business networks (OCBNs) are also changing to become part of the globalization phenomenon. Increasingly, emerging market companies from Asia, Latin America, and Eastern Europe will seek internationalization in their own unique ways, leading to hybrid structures and fast-growth entities. Of course, these newly emerging MNCs will continue to be part of global integration, multidomestic synergies, and international/global/transnational strategies. Their future goals and scope of operations will determine organizational structures and global initiatives.

Source: Written exclusively for this text by Syed Tariq Anwar, Professor, West Texas A&M University.

Interorganizational Networks

Whether the ever-expanding transnational linkages of an MNC consist of different companies, subsidiaries, suppliers, or individuals, they result in relational networks. These networks may adopt very different structures of their own because they operate in different local contexts within their own national environments. Similarly, the "I-form" is described by Miles et al. as a collaborative, multi-firm network along with community-based structures, used by innovative firms such as Taiwan's Acer.[28] By regarding the MNC's overall structure as a network of interconnected relations, we can more realistically consider its organizational design imperatives at both global and local levels. Royal Philips Electronics of the Netherlands, one of the world's biggest electronics companies, has operating units in 60 countries, using a network structure. These units range from large subsidiaries, which might be among the largest companies in a country, to very small single-function operations, such as research and development or marketing divisions for one of Philips's businesses. Some have centralized control at Philips's headquarters; others are quite autonomous. For some time, Philips had fallen far behind its Japanese competitors in productivity because of missteps and seemingly endless restructurings. However, when Philips' chief executive Gerard J. Kleisterlee—a 30-year Philips veteran—took over in 2001, he again reorganized the company. He divested $850 million in less important or unprofitable businesses and shuttered a dozen factories, and outsourced manufacturing for much of the electronics and appliance manufacturing as well as chip production.[29]

In yet another structural variation, Intel, in adapting to changes in the semiconductor industry, announced in early 2005 a wholesale reorganization of its businesses. Intel's executives decided that they wanted the company to focus more on what was going on outside the business, and developed a structural focus they call "Platformisation"—that is, customizing a range of chips in a combination suitable for a particular target market, as a response for the increasing need for speedy adaptation to the market.[30] As the world's biggest semiconductor maker, with

78,000 employees worldwide, the company's general description of its approach to organizing, in response to an inquiry by this author, is as follows:

> *Intel is not a very hierarchical company so a formalized organizational structure is not a particularly good representation of how the company works. At the highest level, Intel is organized into largely autonomous divisions. Intel uses matrix management and cross-functional teams including IT, knowledge management, human resources, finance, legal, change control, data warehousing, common directory information management, and cost reduction teams (to name a few) to rapidly adapt to changing conditions.*

> www.intel.com,
> *August 19, 2006.*[31]

The network framework makes clear that the company's operating units link vastly different environmental and operational contexts based on varied economic, social, and cultural milieus. This complex linkage highlights the intricate task of a giant MNC to rationalize and coordinate its activities globally to achieve an advantageous cost position while simultaneously tailoring itself to local market conditions (to achieve benefits from differentiation).[32]

The Global E-Corporation Network Structure

The organizational structure for global e-businesses, in particular for physical products, typically involves a network of virtual e-exchanges and "bricks and mortar" services, whether those services are in-house or outsourced. This structure of functions and alliances makes up a combination of electronic and physical stages of the supply chain network, as depicted in Exhibit 8-6.

As such, the network comprises some global and some local functions. Centralized e-exchanges for logistics, supplies, and customers could be housed anywhere; suppliers, manufacturers, and distributors may be in various countries, separately or together, wherever efficiencies of scale and cost may be realized. The final distribution system and the customer interaction

EXHIBIT 8-6   The Global E-Corporation Network Structure

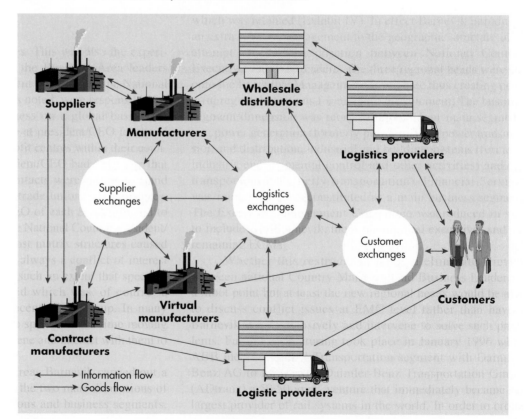

Source: John D. Daniels, Lee H. Radebaugh, and Daniel P. Sullivan, *Globalization and Business,* 1st ed., 2002. Electronically reproduced by permission of Pearson Education, Inc., Upper Saddle River, New Jersey.

must be tailored to the customer-location physical infrastructure and payment infrastructure, as well as local regulations and languages.[33]

The result is a global e-network of suppliers, subcontractors, manufacturers, distributors, buyers, and sellers, communicating in real time through cyberspace. This spreads efficiency throughout the chain, providing cost-effectiveness for all parties.[34] Dell Computer is an example of a company that uses the Internet to streamline its global supply systems. It has a number of factories around the world that supply custom-built PCs to customers in that region. Customers' orders are received through call centers or Dell's own Web site. The order for components then goes to its suppliers, which have to be within a 15-minute drive of its factory. The component parts are delivered to the factory, and the completed customers' orders are collected within a few hours. Dell maintains Internet connections with its suppliers and connects them with its customer database so that they have direct and real-time information about orders. Customers also can use Dell's Internet system to track their orders as they go through the chain.[35]

Dell's organizational structure to implement its business model has evolved to what is known as a virtual company, or value web, as shown in Exhibit 8-7. Dell's strategy is to conduct critical activities in-house, while outsourcing non-strategic activities.

The Transnational Corporation (TNC) Network Structure

To address the globalization-localization dilemma, firms that have evolved through the multinational form and the global company seek the advantages of horizontal organization in the pursuit of transnational capability—that is, the ability to manage across national boundaries, retaining local flexibility while achieving global integration.[36] This capability involves linking foreign operations to each other and to headquarters in a flexible way, thereby leveraging local and central capabilities. ABB (discussed earlier) is an example of such a decentralized horizontal organization. ABB operates in 100 countries with 120,000 employees, with only one management level separating the business units from top management. Its revenues in 2008 were $34,912 million. ABB prides itself on being a truly global company, with 11 board members representing seven nationalities. Thus, this structure is less a matter of boxes on an organizational chart and more a matter of a network of the company's units and their system of horizontal communication. This involves lateral communication across networks of units and alliances rather than in a hierarchy. The system requires the dispersal of responsibility and decision making to local

EXHIBIT 8-7   Dell's Value Web Model

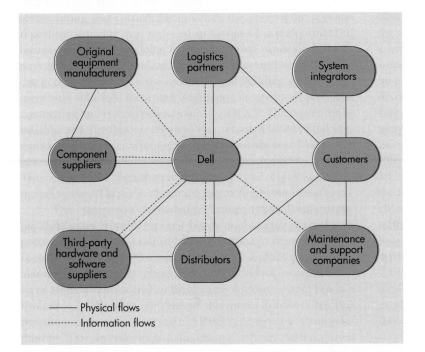

Source: Kenneth L. Kraemer and Jason Dedrick, "Dell Computer: Organization of a Global Production Network" (December 1, 2002). Globalization of IT. Paper 255, Center for Research on Information Technology and Organizations, University of California, Irvine, used with permission of the authors.

subsidiaries and alliances. The effectiveness of that localized decision making depends a great deal on the ability and willingness to share current and new learning and technology across the network of units. The matrix structure typical of the transnational company creates a complex coordination and control system as it attempts to combine

- The capabilities and resources of a multinational corporation
- The economies of scale of a global corporation
- The local responsiveness of a domestic company
- The ability to transfer technology efficiently typical of the international structure[37]

Whatever the names given to the organizational forms emerging to deal with global competition and logistics, the MNC organizational structure as we know it, with its hierarchical pyramid, subsidiaries, and world headquarters, is gradually evolving into a more fluid form to adapt to strategic and competitive imperatives. As is now well known, these more flexible forms are facilitated by the ever-developing technologies which enable various forms of electronic instant communication to connect elaborate networks of people and information around the world regardless of their locations. In this new global web, the location of a firm's headquarters is unimportant. Various alliances tie together units and subunits in the web. Corning Glass, for instance, changed from its national pyramidlike organization to a global web, giving it the capability of making optical cable through its European partner, Siemens AG, and medical equipment with Ciba-Geigy.

CHOICE OF ORGANIZATIONAL FORM

Two major variables in choosing the structure and design of an organization are the opportunities and need for (1) globalization and (2) localization. Exhibit 8-8 depicts alternative structural forms appropriate to each of these variables and to the strategic choices regarding the level and type of international involvement desired by the firm.

This figure thereby updates the evolutionary stages model to reflect alternative organizational responses to more recent environments and to the anticipated competitive environments ahead. The updated model shows that, as the firm progresses from a domestic to an international company—and perhaps later to a multinational and then a global company—its managers adapt the organizational structure to accommodate their relative strategic focus on globalization versus localization, choosing a global product structure, a geographic area structure, or perhaps a matrix form. The model proposes that, as the company becomes larger, more complex, and more sophisticated in its approach to world markets (no matter which structural route it has taken), it may

EXHIBIT 8-8 Organizational Alternatives and Development for Global Companies[38]

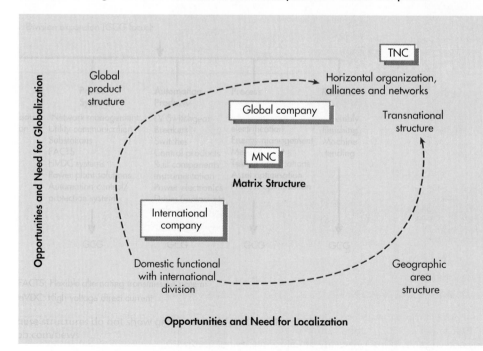

EXHIBIT 8-9   Global Strategy–Structure Relationships[39]

	Multidomestic Strategy	International Strategy	Globalization Strategy	Transnational Strategy
	Low ←————————→ Need for Coordination ←————————→ High			
	Low ←————————→ Bureaucratic Costs ←————————→ High			
Centralization of authority	Decentralized to national unit	Core competencies centralized; others decentralization to national units	Centralized at optimal global location	Simultaneously Centralized and Decentralized
Horizontal differentiation	Global area structure	International division structure	Global product group structure	Global matrix Structure
				"Matrix in the Mind"
Need for complex integrating mechanisms	Low	Medium	High	Very High
Organizational culture	Not important	Quite important	Important	Very important

evolve into a transnational corporation (TNC). The TNC strategy is to maximize opportunities for both efficiency and local responsiveness by adopting a transnational structure that uses alliances, networks, and horizontal design formats. The relationships between choice of global strategy and the appropriate structural variations necessary to implement each strategic choice are further illustrated in Exhibit 8-9.

Organizational Change and Design Variables

When a company makes drastic changes in its goals, strategy, or scope of operations, it will usually also need a change in organizational structure. However, other, less obvious indications of organizational inefficiency also signal a need for structural changes: conflicts among divisions and subsidiaries over territories or customers, conflicts between overseas units and headquarters staff, complaints regarding overseas customer service, and overlapping responsibilities are some of these warning signals. Exhibit 8-10 lists some indications of the need for change in organizational design.

At persistent signs of ineffective work, a company should analyze its organizational design, systems, and work flow for the possible causes of those problems. The nature and extent of any design changes must reflect the magnitude of the problem. In choosing a new organizational design or modifying an existing structure, managers must establish a system of communication and control that will provide for effective decision making. At such times, managers need to localize decision making and integrate widely dispersed and disparate global operations.

Besides determining the behavior of the organization on a macro level (in terms of what the different divisions, subsidiaries, departments, and units are responsible for), the organizational design must determine behavior on a micro level. For example, the organizational design affects the level at which certain types of decisions will be made. Determining how many and what types of decisions can be made and by whom can have drastic consequences; both the locus and the scope of authority must be carefully considered. This centralization-decentralization variable actually represents a continuum. In the real world, companies are neither totally centralized nor totally decentralized: The level of centralization imposed is a matter of degree. Exhibit 8-11 illustrates this centralization-decentralization continuum and the different ways that decision making can be shared between headquarters and local units or subsidiaries. In general, centralized decision making is common for some functions (finance, research and development) that are organized for the entire corporation, whereas other functions (production, marketing, sales) are more appropriately decentralized. Two key issues are the speed with which the decisions have to be made and whether they primarily affect only a certain subsidiary or other parts of the company as well.

As noted, culture is another factor that complicates decisions on how much to decentralize and how to organize the work flow and the various relationships of authority and responsibility. Part IV of this book more fully presents how cultural variables affect people's attitudes about working relationships and about who should have authority over whom. At this point, it is important merely to note that cultural variables must be taken into account when designing an organization.

EXHIBIT 8-10 When Is Change Needed?[40]

- A change in the size of the corporation—due to growth, consolidation, or reduction
- A change in key individuals—which may alter management objectives, interests, and abilities
- A failure to meet goals, capitalize on opportunities, or be innovative
- An inability to get things done on time
- A consistently overworked top management that spends excessive hours on the job
- A belief that costs are extravagant or that budgets are not being met
- Morale problems
- Lengthy hierarchies that inhibit the exercise of strategic control
- Planning that has become increasingly staff-driven and is thus divorced from line management
- Innovation that is stifled by too much administration and monitoring of details
- Uniform solutions that are applied to nonuniform situations. The extreme opposite of this condition—when things that should or could function in a routine manner do not—should also be heeded as a warning. In other words, management by exception has replaced standard operating procedures

The following are a few specific indicators of *international* organizational malaise:
- A shift in the operational scope—perhaps from directing export activities to controlling overseas manufacturing and marketing units, a change in the size of operations on a country, regional, or worldwide basis, or failure of foreign operations to grow in accordance with plans and expectations.
- Clashes among divisions, subsidiaries, or individuals over territories or customers in the field
- Divisive conflicts between overseas units and domestic division staff or corporate staff
- Instances wherein centralization leads to a flood of detailed data that is neither fully understood nor properly used by headquarters
- Duplication of administrative personnel and services
- Underutilization of overseas manufacturing or distribution facilities
- Duplication of sales offices and specialized sales account executives
- Proliferation of relatively small legal entities or operating units within a country or geographic area
- An increase in overseas customer service complaints
- Breakdowns in communications within and among organizations
- Unclear lines of reporting and dotted-line relationships, and ill-defined executive responsibilities

Delegating a high level of authority to employees in a country where workers usually regard "the boss" as the rightful person to make all the decisions is not likely to work well. Clearly, managers must think through the interactions of organizational, staffing, and cultural issues before making final decisions.

In summary, no one way to organize is best. Contingency theory applies to organizational design as much as to any other aspect of management. The best organizational structure is the one that facilitates the firm's goals and is appropriate to its industry, size, technology, and competitive environment. Structure should be fluid and dynamic, and highly adaptable to the changing needs of the company. The structure should not be allowed to get bogged down in the administrative heritage of the organization (that is, "the way we do things around here" or "what we've always done") to the point that it undermines the very processes that will enable the firm to take advantage of new opportunities.

Most likely, however, the future for MNC structure lies in a global web of networked companies. Ideally, a company tries to organize in a way that will allow it to carry out its strategic goals; the staffing is then done to mesh with those strategic goals and the way the organizational structure has been set up. In reality, however, the existing structural factors often affect strategic decisions, so the end result may be a trade-off of desired strategy with existing constraints.

EXHIBIT 8-11   Locus of Decision Making in an International Organization[41]

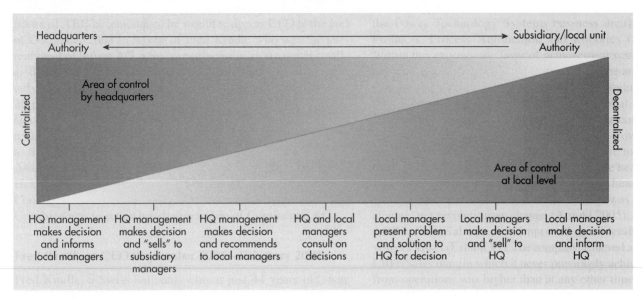

So, too, with staffing: "ideal" staffing plans have to be adjusted to reflect the realities of assigning managers from various sources and the local regulations or cultural variables that make some organizing and staffing decisions more workable than others.

What may at first seem a linear management process of deciding on strategy, then on structure, and finally on staffing is actually an interdependent set of factors that must be taken into consideration and worked out as a set of decisions. Chapter 9 explores how staffing decisions are—or should be—intricately intertwined with other decisions regarding strategy, structure, and so forth. A unique set of management cadre and skills in a particular location can be a competitive advantage in itself, and so it may be a smart move to build strategic and organizational decisions around that resource rather than risk losing that advantage. The following sections present some other processes that are involved in implementing strategy and are interconnected with coordinating functions through organizational structure.

CONTROL SYSTEMS FOR GLOBAL OPERATIONS

The establishment of a single currency makes it possible, for the first time, to establish shared, centralized accounting and administrative systems.

FRANCESCO CAIO,
CEO, Merloni Elettrodomestici[42]

To complement the organizational structure, the international manager must design efficient coordinating and reporting systems to ensure that actual performance conforms to expected organizational standards and goals. The challenge is to coordinate far-flung operations in vastly different environments with various work processes; rules; and economic, political, legal, and cultural norms. The feedback from the control process and the information systems should signal any necessary change in strategy, structure, or operations in a timely manner. Often the strategy, the coordinating processes, or both, need to be changed to reflect conditions in other countries.

The design and application of coordinating and reporting systems for foreign subsidiaries and activities can take any form that management wishes. MNCs usually employ a variety of direct and indirect coordinating and control mechanisms suitable for their organization structure. For example, in the transnational network structure, decision-making control is centralized to key network nodes, greatly reducing emphasis on bureaucratic control. Other specific mechanisms are summarized in the next sections.[43]

Direct Coordinating Mechanisms

Direct mechanisms that provide the basis for the overall guidance and management of foreign operations include the design of appropriate structures (discussed previously in this chapter) and the use of effective staffing practices (discussed in Chapters 9 and 10). Such decisions proactively set the stage for operations to meet goals, rather than troubleshooting deviations or problems after they have occurred. When McDonald's first opened its doors in Moscow in 1990, the biggest control problem was that of quality control for its food products. McDonald's anticipated that challenge and adopted a strategy of vertical integration for its sourcing of raw materials.[44] To control the quality, distribution, and reliability of its ingredients, McDonald's built a $40 million, 110,000-square-foot plant in a Moscow suburb to process the required beef, milk, buns, vegetables, sauces, and potatoes. In addition, the company brought the managers to Toronto, Canada, for five months of training.[45] Top management at McDonald's anticipated difficulties with the setup and daily operations of this IJV and, indeed, had been working toward the opening day for 13 years. Through careful planning for the control of crucial operational factors, they solved the sourcing, distribution, and employment problems inherent in the former Soviet Union.[46]

Other direct mechanisms are visits by head-office personnel and regular meetings to allow employees around the world to consult and troubleshoot. Increasingly those meetings comprise videoconferences to allow face-to-face, if not physical, interaction among managers around the world to enable faster and less expensive frequent meetings. Top executives from headquarters may use periodic visits to subsidiaries to check performance and help to anticipate future problems. The meetings allow each general manager to keep in touch with her or his associates, with the overall mission and strategy of the organization, and with comparative performance data and new problem-solving techniques. Increasingly, the tools of technology are being applied as direct mechanisms to ensure up front that operations will be carried out as planned, in particular in countries where processes such as efficient infrastructure and goods forwarding cannot be taken for granted. An example of this is the logistics monitoring system set up by Air Express International in Latin America to minimize its many problems there.[47]

Indirect Coordinating Mechanisms

Indirect coordinating mechanisms typically include sales quotas, budgets, and other financial tools, as well as feedback reports, which give information about the sales and financial performance of the subsidiary for the last quarter or year.

Domestic companies invariably rely on budgets and financial statement analyses, but for foreign subsidiaries, financial statements and performance evaluations are complicated by *financial variables in MNC reports,* such as exchange rates, inflation levels, transfer prices, and accounting standards.

To reconcile accounting statements, MNCs usually require three different sets of financial statements from subsidiaries. One set must meet the national accounting standards and procedures prescribed by law in the host country. This set also aids management in comparing subsidiaries in the same country. A second set must be prepared according to the accounting principles and standards required by the home country. This set allows some comparison with other MNC subsidiaries. The third set of statements translates the second set of statements (with certain adjustments) into the currency of the home country for consolidation purposes, in accordance with FASB Ruling Number 52 of 1982. A foreign subsidiary's financial statements must be consolidated line by line with those of the parent company, according to International Accounting Standard Number 3, adopted in the United States.

Researchers have noted comparative differences between the use of direct versus **indirect controls** among companies headquartered in different countries. One study by Egelhoff examined the practices of 50 U.S., U.K., and European MNCs over their foreign subsidiaries. It compared the use of two mechanisms—the assignment of parent-company managers to foreign subsidiaries and the use of performance reporting systems (that is, comparing behavior mechanisms with output reporting systems).[48] The results of this study show that considerable differences exist in practices across MNC nationalities. For example, U.S. MNCs monitor subsidiary outputs and rely more on frequently reported performance data than do European MNCs. The latter tend to assign more parent-company nationals to key positions in foreign subsidiaries and can count on a higher level of behavior control than their U.S. counterparts.[49]

These findings imply that the U.S. system, which measures more quantifiable aspects of a foreign subsidiary, provides the means to compare performance among subsidiaries. The European system, on the other hand, measures more qualitative aspects of a subsidiary and its environment, which vary among subsidiaries—allowing a focus on the unique situation of the subsidiary but making it difficult to compare its performance to other subsidiaries.[50]

MANAGING EFFECTIVE MONITORING SYSTEMS

Management practices, local constraints, and expectations regarding authority, time, and communication are but a few of the variables likely to affect the **appropriateness of monitoring (or control) systems**. The degree to which headquarters' practices and goals are transferable probably depends on whether top managers are from the head office, the host country, or a third country. In addition, information systems and evaluation variables must all be considered when deciding on appropriate systems.

The Appropriateness of Monitoring and Reporting Systems

One example of differences in the expectations regarding monitoring practices, and therefore in the need for coordination systems, is indicated by a study of Japanese and U.S. firms. Ueno and Sekaran state that their research shows that "the U.S. companies, compared to the Japanese companies, tend to use communication and coordination more extensively, build budget slack to a greater extent, and use long-term performance evaluations to a lesser extent."[51] Furthermore, Ueno and Sekaran conclude that those differences in reporting systems are attributable to the cultural variable of individualism in U.S. society, compared to collectivism in Japanese society. For example, U.S. managers are more likely to use formal communication and coordination processes, whereas Japanese managers use informal and implicit processes. In addition, U.S. managers, who are evaluated on individual performance, are more likely to build slack into budget calculations for a safety net than their Japanese counterparts, who are evaluated on group performance. The implications of this study are that managers around the world who understand the cultural bases for differences in control practices will be more flexible in working with those systems in other countries.

The Role of Information Systems

Reporting systems, such as those described in this chapter, require sophisticated information systems to enable them to work properly—not only for competitive purposes but also for purposes of performance evaluation. Top management must receive accurate and timely information regarding sales, production, and financial results to be able to compare actual performance with goals and to take corrective action where necessary. Most international reporting systems require information feedback at one level or another for financial, personnel, production, and marketing variables.

The specific types of functional reports, their frequency, and the amount of detail required from subsidiaries by headquarters will vary. Neghandi and Welge surveyed the types of functional reports submitted by 117 MNCs in Germany, Japan, and the United States.[52] They found that U.S. MNCs typically submit about double the number of reports than do German and Japanese MNCs, with the exception of performance reviews. German MNCs submit a few more reports than do Japanese MNCs. Thus U.S. MNCs seem to monitor much more via specific functional reports than do German and Japanese MNCs. The Japanese MNCs put far less emphasis on personnel performance reviews than do the U.S. and German MNCs—a finding consistent with the Japanese culture of group decision making, consensus, and responsibility.

Unfortunately, the accuracy and timeliness of information systems are often less than perfect, especially in less developed countries, where managers typically operate under conditions of extreme uncertainty. Government information, for example, is often filtered or fabricated; other sources of data for decision making are usually limited. Employees are not used to the kinds of sophisticated information generation, analysis, and reporting systems common in developed countries. Their work norms and sense of necessity and urgency may also confound the problem. In addition, the hardware technology and the ability to manipulate and transmit data are usually limited. The **MIS adequacy** in foreign affiliates is a sticky problem for headquarters managers in their attempt to maintain efficient coordination of activities and consolidation of results. Another problem is the **noncomparability of performance data across countries**—the control problem caused by the difficulty of comparing performance data across various countries because of the variables that make that information appear different—which hinders the evaluation process.

The Internet has, of course, made the availability and use of information attainable instantaneously. Many companies are starting to supply Internet MIS systems for supply-chain management. European partners Nestlé S.A. and Danone Group, world leaders in the food industry, set up Europe's first Internet marketplace for e-procurement in the consumer goods sector, called CPGmarket.com:

> *CPGmarket.com will enhance the efficiency of logistics while at the same time reducing procurement costs for businesses producing, distributing and selling consumer goods. CPG (based on mySAP.com e-business platform) allows companies not only to buy and sell, but also to access industry information. . . . Participants will benefit from a more efficient market, reducing costs through higher transaction efficiency and simplified processes.*[53]

Evaluation Variables Across Countries

A major problem that arises when evaluating the performance of foreign affiliates is the tendency by headquarters managers to judge subsidiary managers as if all of the evaluation data were comparable across countries. Unfortunately, many variables can make the evaluation information from one country look very different from that of another country, owing to circumstances beyond the control of a subsidiary manager. For example, one country may experience considerable inflation, significant fluctuations in the price of raw materials, political uprisings, or governmental actions. These factors are beyond the manager's control and are likely to have a downward effect on profitability—and yet, that manager may, in fact, have maximized the opportunity for long-term stability and profitability compared with a manager of another subsidiary who was not faced with such adverse conditions. Other variables influencing profitability patterns include transfer pricing, currency devaluation, exchange-rate fluctuations, taxes, and expectations of contributions to local economies.

One way to ensure more meaningful performance measures is to adjust the financial statements to reflect the uncontrollable variables peculiar to each country where a subsidiary is located. This provides a basis for the true evaluation of the comparative return on investment (ROI), which is an overall control measure. Another way to provide meaningful, long-term performance standards is to take into account other nonfinancial measures. These measures include market share, productivity, sales, relations with the host-country government, public image, employee morale, union relations, and community involvement.[54]

CONCLUSION

The structure, control, and coordination *processes* are the same whether they take place in a domestic company, a multinational company with a network of foreign affiliates, or a specific IJV. It is the extent, the focus, and the mechanisms used to organize those activities that differ. More coordination is needed in global companies because of uncertain working environments and information systems and because of the variable loci of decision making. Headquarters managers must design appropriate systems to take into account those variables and to evaluate performance.

Summary of Key Points

1. An organization must be designed to facilitate the implementation of strategic goals. Other variables to consider when designing an organization's structure include environmental conditions, the size of the organization, and the appropriate technology. The geographic dispersion of operations as well as differences in time, language, and culture affect structure in the international context.

2. The design of a firm's structure reflects its international entry strategy and tends to change over time with growth and increasing levels of investment, diversity, or both.

3. Global trends are exerting increasing pressure on MNCs to achieve economies of scale through globalization. This involves rationalization and the coordination of strategic alliances.

4. MNCs can be regarded as interorganizational networks of their own dispersed operations and other strategic alliances. Such relational networks may adopt unique structures for their particular environment, while also requiring centralized coordination.

5. The transnational structure allows a company to "be global and act local" by using networks of decentralized units with horizontal communication. This permits local flexibility while achieving global integration.

6. Indications of the need for structural changes include inefficiency, conflicts among units, poor communication, and overlapping responsibilities.

7. Coordinating and monitoring systems are necessary to regulate organizational activities so that actual perfor-

mance conforms to expected organizational standards and goals. MNCs use a variety of direct and indirect controls.

8. Financial monitoring and evaluation of foreign affiliates are complicated by variables such as exchange rates, levels of inflation, transfer prices, and accounting standards.

9. The design of appropriate monitoring systems must take into account local constraints, management practices and expectations, uncertain information systems, and variables in the evaluation process.

10. Two major problems in reporting for subsidiaries must be considered: (1) inadequate management information systems and (2) the noncomparability across countries of the performance data needed for evaluation purposes.

Discussion Questions

1. What variables have to be considered in designing the organizational structure for international operations? How do these variables interact, and which do you think are most important?

2. Explain the need for an MNC to "be global and act local." How can a firm design its organization to enable this?

3. What is a transnational organization? Since many large MNCs are moving toward this format, it is likely that you could at some point be working within this structure. How do you feel about that?

4. Discuss the implications of the relative centralization of authority and decision making at headquarters versus local units or

subsidiaries. How would you feel about this variable if you were a subsidiary manager?

5. As an international manager, what would make you suggest restructuring your firm? What other means of direct and indirect monitoring systems do you suggest?

6. What is the role of information systems in the reporting process? Discuss the statement "Inadequate MIS systems in some foreign affiliates are a control problem for MNCs."

Application Exercises

1. If you have personal access to a company with international operations, try to conduct some interviews and find out about the personal interactions involved in working with the organization's counterparts abroad. In particular, ask questions about the nature and level of authority and decision making in overseas units compared with headquarters. What kinds of conflicts are experienced? What changes would your interviewees recommend?

2. Do some research on monitoring and reporting issues facing an MNC with subsidiaries in (1) a country in Asia, and (2) a country in South America. Discuss problem areas and your recommenda-

tions to the MNC management as to how to control potential problems.

3. Find out about a foreign company with an IJV in the United States. Review some articles from the library, write to the company for information, and if possible visit the company and ask questions. Present your findings on the company's major control issues to the class—both at the beginning of the venture and now. What is the company doing differently in its control process compared to a typical domestic operation? Are the control procedures having the desired results? What recommendations do you have?

Experiential Exercise

In groups of four, consider a fast-food chain going into Eastern Europe. Decide on your initial level of desired international involvement and your entry strategy. Draw up an appropriate organizational design, taking into account strategic goals, relevant variables in the particular countries in which you will have opera-

tions, technology used, size of the firm, and so on. At the next class, present your organization chart and describe the operations and rationale. (You could finalize the chart on an overhead or flip chart before class begins.) What are some of the major control issues to be considered?

Internet Resources

Visit the Deresky Companion Website at www.pearsonhighered.com/deresky for this chapter's Internet resources.

CASE STUDY
Acer Restructures for Global Growth

Taiwan's Acer Inc. (Acer) was the third largest computer company in terms of world-wide personal computer (PC) shipments in 2007. With 2.43 million units shipped, the company enjoyed a market share of 7.6%. Its growth rate stood at 31% against the 30% of Hewlett-Packard Company (HP) and 21% of Lenovo Group Ltd.[1] In the first quarter of 2008, the company sustained its performance and its market share grew to 9.5%.[2] Its growth rate of 25.2% was higher than that of Dell Inc. (Dell) and Lenovo. Analysts felt that the company had come a long way since 1994 when it was the number eight player in the global PC market. On April 7, 2009, *Business Week* reported that:

> *"If Acer can keep the current momentum, it could pass second-place Dell in number of computers shipped this year (2009)—and close in on HP (Hewlett Packard). Acer has a strong chance of overtaking HP."*[3]

According to analysts, Acer's rapid growth could be attributed to the restructuring efforts the company had taken up since the year 2000. In December 2000, Acer split its PC-system manufacturing business unit into a new division and this was incorporated as a separate company, Wistron Corporation, in 2002. In 2001, the name of Acer Communications and Multimedia was changed to BenQ and it started operations as an independent BenQ brand. Acer focused on providing Acer-brand IT products like desktop PCs, home PCs, mobile PCs, servers, and Internet appliances. BenQ, on the other hand, offered digital life devices like mobile phones, LCD and CRT monitors, digital projectors, plasma displays, optical storage, and imaging products. In 2006, Acer left the board of BenQ in order to avoid conflicts.[4]

Acer's restructuring enabled the company to realize lower operating expenses which provided the twin advantages of allowing it to price the PC aggressively and offer higher incentives to its channel distributors.

Acer also refocused its marketing efforts from direct sales to indirect channel driven sales. The company opted for achieving growth through building strong relationships with its dealers, by offering lower prices to the consumers and providing unique product innovations.

As a part of its growth and expansion strategies, Acer acquired Gateway, Inc. (Gateway) in 2007.[5] This acquisition also resulted in the acquisition of Packard Bell (a major player in the Western European PC market) by Acer as Gateway had a controlling stake in Packard Bell. The acquisition also established Acer as the third largest computer company.

In India, Acer partnered with Wipro Infotech Ltd. in the initial years. In the year 1999, Acer opened its own full-fledged Indian subsidiary.[6] It initially concentrated on selling to government organizations and corporate customers. In 2003, Acer entered the consumer business by introducing consumer desktops and laptops which were to be sold through channel partners. The business was divided into the Enterprise Systems Group and the Consumer Systems Group. However, these groups were disbanded and replaced by a unified marketing and sales organization.

Acer was a strong player in the government and institutional sales in India. According to the company, it had strong relationships with 15 large system integrators and this had provided it with a presence in 40 customer verticals including the banking and financial services industry, education, telecom, and government.

---

[1] Yuga Chaudhari & Megha Bandhuni-Rai, "Competition Beware," www.channelbusiness.in.
[2] Yuga Chaudhari & Megha Bandhuni-Rai, "Competition Beware," www.channelbusiness.in.
[3] Bruce Einhorn, "How Acer is Burning its PC Rivals," Business Week, April 7, 2009.
[4] Dan Nystedt, "Acer Leaves Benq Board to Avoid Conflict," www.infoworld.com, April 17, 2006.
[5] "Acer Acquires Gateway, Packard Bell," www.eetindia.co.in, October 19, 2007.
[6] "Acer to Open Full Fledged Indian Subsidiary," www.rediff.com, April 9, 1999.

Acer had been aggressive in building its brand image in India. It signed up Hrithik Roshan, a popular Hindi film star, as its brand ambassador to promote its products. The advantage of having a brand ambassador like Hrithik Roshan was that he helped in brand recall and in associating Acer with high quality.

To have greater brand visibility, Acer began focusing on the retail outlets. As of May 2006, Acer had 225 retail outlets and 179 retail partners.[7] It intended to establish 350 retail outlets by 2008. Analysts felt that the retail network was a prime channel for the movement of premium products like notebooks, consumer desktops, and home theater solutions.

Acer's retail strategy was such that each retail outlet was allocated a geographical area in the city so that the individual retailers could grow their business without infringing on another Acer partner's customer base. The channel partners were provided training and emphasis was placed on channel communication and relationship management.

According to the company, in 2008, Acer's focus in India would be on education, youth, and retail. For the education segment, it was building solutions which fit the needs and budget of the students. On the retail front, it intended to tie up with large format retail stores such as Croma, Home Solutions, Next, and Metro. Acer's turnover in India in 2007 was Rs. 12 billion, with the goal of Rs. 18 billion for 2008.[8] In India, Acer trailed HP, HCL Infosystems Ltd[9] (HCL), and Lenovo in the overall PC market but had a significant share (10%) of the fast growing notebook segment in India, after HP (37%) and Lenovo (16%).[10]

The growth in India was spurred by an increase in the consumer demand for notebooks, which accounted for 27 percent of PC shipments in 2007. IDC[11] had predicted that the Indian PC market would grow at a compound annual growth rate of 20 per cent through 2012.[12] According to Piyush Pushkal, manager for PC research at IDC India, the growth in the market would be fueled by an increased demand for PCs by large enterprises, their increased usage in education, and the Indian government's push toward automation.[13] In addition to this, the increase in wages in India would also help in driving PC sales in the consumer market, analysts felt.

However, there were certain challenges that Acer faced in India. In addition to intensifying competition, the company had to deal with challenges such as how it could take advantage of the growing affluence of consumers in smaller cities and towns. The growth for Acer in India, thus far, had come from the big cities and it had a low market penetration rate in the small towns. Further, the service infrastructure in the small towns was also a cause for concern.

Additional Readings and References

1. "Acer to Open Full Fledged Indian Subsidiary," www.rediff.com, April 9, 1999
2. Dan Nystedt, "Acer Leaves Benq Board to Avoid Conflict," www.infoworld.com, April 17, 2006
3. "Acer's Retail Strategy Boosts Revenue," www.channeltimes.com, May 6, 2006
4. John Jacob, "Acer Revamps its Marketing Strategies in India," www.itvarnews.net, July 17, 2008
5. "Acer Acquires Gateway, Packard Bell," www.eetindia.co.in, October 19, 2007
6. "India's Computer Market Sees 20% Year-on-Year Growth," www.economictimes.indiatimes.com, February 27, 2008
7. John Rebeiro, "HP Holds Top Spot in Indian PC Market," www.infoworld.com, February 27, 2008
8. Yuga Chaudhari & Megha Bandhuni-Rai, "Competition Beware," www.channelbusiness.in

---

[7] "Acer's Retail Strategy Boosts Revenue", www.channeltimes.com, May 6, 2006.
[8] John Jacob, "Acer Revamps its Marketing Strategies in India", www.itvarnews.net, July 17, 2008.
[9] HCL Infosystems Ltd, headquartered in Noida India, is a hardware and systems integrator. Its revenue for the year March 31, 2007, was US$ 2.6 billion. It is a subsidiary of India's leading electronics, computing and information technology (IT) company, HCL Enterprises.
[10] "India's Computer Market Sees 20% Year-on-Year Growth," www.economictimes.indiatimes.com, February 27, 2008.
[11] IDC, based in Massachussetts, USA, is a market research and analysis firm specializing in information technology, telecommunications, and consumer technology markets.
[12] John Rebeiro, "HP Holds Top Spot in Indian PC Market," www.infoworld.com, February 27, 2008.
[13] "India's Computer Market Sees 20% Year-on-Year Growth," www.economictimes.indiatimes.com, February 27, 2008.

Case Questions

1. In your opinion, can Acer's growth in the global arena be attributed to the restructuring of its operations? Give reasons to support your answer.
2. Write a note on the growth path adopted by Acer in India. What should Acer do now to take advantage of the opportunities presented by the Indian market?
3. Do some research on Acer and give an update on the company's situation in India and also globally as of the time of your reading this case.

Author Information:

This case was written by Debapratim Purkayastha and T. Seshasai, ICMR. It was compiled from published sources, and is intended to be used as a basis for class discussion rather than to illustrate either effective or ineffective handling of a management situation.

CASE 6 EBAY IN JAPAN: STRATEGIC AND CULTURAL MISSTEPS

"I am not one for regrets, but I still regret we don't have a presence in Japan."[1]

—MEG WHITMAN,
CEO, eBay in 2008.

"When we arrived last year, the 800-pound gorilla [Yahoo Japan Auctions] was already positioned."[2]

—MERLE OKAWARA,
President and CEO, eBay Japan in 2001

"I think eBay learned what it did wrong in Japan. Because of the nature of the auction model, I think it now understands that you have to be the leader in the market. I think it's a smart move for the company to have closed its site in Japan and to wait for another time when it can go in and do what it takes to be the leader there."[3]

—LINDSAY HOOVER,
Vice President, Houlihan Lokey Howard & Zukin[4] *in 2002*

Ebay Reenters Japan

In December 2007, eBay Inc., the U.S.-based online auction company, announced its reentry into Japan, through an agreement with U.S.-based Internet services company, Yahoo! Inc.[5] eBay and Yahoo agreed to link their auction sites to facilitate cross-border bidding. This would enable the users of Yahoo Auctions Japan to bid for items listed on eBay's U.S. site using their Yahoo Japan ID, and eBay users in the U.S. to buy items auctioned on Yahoo Japan using their eBay ID. On Yahoo and eBay teaming up, Meg Whitman,[6] President and CEO, eBay, said, "We are excited to partner with Yahoo Japan in providing Japanese users with localized site designed to enable them to shop on the eBay marketplace with ease and convenience."[7]

As a part of the agreement, the companies decided to start a Japanese website, Sekaimon.[8] Apart from translating the names and details of the items listed on eBay's U.S. website into Japanese, the site would provide services like overseas shipping and customs clearance. According to Hiroko Sato, zanalyst at JP Morgan, Chase & Co, Tokyo, "the alliance will create a very

attractive service for U.S. and Japanese users as it allows them to purchase items simultaneously in both countries."[9]

After several highly successful international ventures, eBay first entered Japan in 2000. By then, Yahoo was already a well-established portal in the Japanese market and its online auctions site, which had started a few months before eBay's entry into Japan, had started tasting success. eBay found it difficult to establish itself in the Japanese market. Some of its practices like charging transaction fees and requiring the use of credit cards[10] made the going tough for it. By 2002, it was able to garner only a 3 percent share of the Japanese online auctions market. eBay decided to exit the country in 2002. While exiting the country, eBay spokesperson Kevin Pursglove said, "We may come back to Japan sometime when factors are a little more in our favor, but they are not at the current time."[11]

The news of eBay's reentry into the Japanese market in late 2007 was met with mixed reactions. Some analysts were of the view that eBay's return to Japan filled a major gap in its international business, while others were not too sure whether it would make any difference to eBay's fortunes.

Background Note

eBay was founded by Pierre Omidyar, a software programmer, in 1995 as AuctionWeb. eBay was incorporated in May 1996. It was a person-to-person trading community, where sellers could list the items they wanted to put on sale, and specify the minimum bid and duration of the auction. The items were shown under different categories and the buyers could bid for the items. eBay's revenues came through the fees it collected from the sellers. When an item was listed, a listing fee was charged, depending on the opening bid specified by the seller. This fee was non-refundable. Additional fees were charged for listing options like bold display or highlight. When the listed item was

This case was written by **Indu Perepu and Sachin Govind**, ICMR Center for Management Research (ICMR). It was compiled from published sources, and is intended to be used as a basis for class discussion rather than to illustrate either effective or ineffective handling of a management situation.

© 2008, ICMR Center for Management Research, used with permission.

[1] Erick Schonfeld, "Meg Whitman's Exit Interview," *TechCrunch*, January 24, 2008.
[2] "How Yahoo! Japan Beat eBay at Its Own Game," *BusinessWeek*, June 04, 2001.
[3] Joan Harrison, "Asian Advances, and a Retreat, for Online Auctioneer eBay," *Mergers & Acquisitions: The Dealmaker's Journal*, April 2002.
[4] Houlihan Lokey Howard & Zukin is a US-based investment bank. The services provided include mergers and acquisitions, financing, financing opinions, and advisory services. The firm was established in 1970 and has 13 offices spread across the world.
[5] Yahoo! Inc., is a leading Internet services company headquartered in Sunnyvale, California, USA. In 2007, its revenues were at $6.7 billion.
[6] Margaret C Whitman (Meg Whitman) announced that she would retire from eBay by March 2008. She was to be succeeded by John Donahoe.
[7] "eBay, Yahoo Japan Team up Services," www.taipeitimes.com, December 05, 2007.
[8] Sekaimon in Japanese means "Gateway to the world."

[9] Masaki Kondo, Kiyotaka Matsuda, "Yahoo Japan Shares Gain on Online-Auction Alliance with eBay," www.bloomberg.com, December 04, 2007.
[10] Japan was largely a cash-based society, and the use of credit cards was limited.
[11] "Sayonara: For eBay, Japan is the Land of Setting Sun," Seattlepi.com, February 27, 2002.

sold, a fee ranging from 1.25 to 5 percent of the final sale price was collected. At the end of the auction, eBay notified the buyer and the seller through e-mail, and they completed the transaction.

In 1996, Omidyar appointed Jimmy Griffith, who till then, had been voluntarily helping eBay users through their auction processes, as eBay's first customer support representative. By 1996 end, eBay had conducted 250,000 auctions and had 41,000 users.

In June 1997, Benchmark Capital, a leading venture capital firm, acquired a 22 percent stake in eBay by investing $4.5 million. By 1997 end, eBay had around 341,000 registered users.

In 1998, Harvard alumna Whitman joined the company as President and CEO. Whitman revamped the site to make it easier for users to participate in the auctions. The cumbersome payment process involving personal checks and money orders was changed and eBay began accepting payments through credit cards. In the same year, eBay entered into a three-year agreement with America Online[12] (AOL), under which it became AOL's exclusive online trading community. In September 1998, eBay raised $60 million through an IPO. By the end of the year, eBay had 2.1 million registered users and 138 employees.

In May 1999, eBay acquired Billpoint,[13] an online payment service company. Another acquisition in the year was of Butterfield & Butterfield,[14] a 134-year-old auction house based in San Francisco, for $260 million. In the same year, eBay acquired Indiana-based Kruse International, an automobile auction house. In 1999, it introduced a new service called Personal Shopper on its site. Through this service, buyers got e-mail alerts when the items they were searching for were put up for sale.

In 2000, eBay launched 53 regional sites, covering around 50 of the largest metropolitan areas in the US. These sites helped the company to encourage trade in items that were too bulky or expensive to ship, and in items of local interest.

In March 2000, eBay, in association with AutoTrader .com,[15] launched an online automotive site, eBayMotors.com. In the same year, it also formed a strategic alliance with Wells Fargo & Co.[16] to develop an online person-to-person payment platform. This resulted in the launch of a new payment option for eBay users, Electronic Check. In mid-2000, eBay acquired Half.com, a fixed price, person-to-person online trading site, for $300 million in stock. During the year, it launched the "eBay Anywhere" service, which made it accessible from any Internet-enabled mobile device. By the end of the year, eBay had 22 million registered users.

In January 2001, eBay launched eBay Premier, a site for antiques and collectibles. However, the performance of the site was dismal, and eBay entered into a deal with Sotheby's[17] which involved moving Sotheby's online business onto the eBay website. In 2002, eBay acquired PayPal,[18] for $1.5 billion. PayPal allowed consumers to make and accept payments over the Internet without the use of credit cards.

In August 2004, eBay acquired a 25 percent stake in craigslist,[19] an online classifieds site. In December 2004, it acquired rent.com,[20] a housing rental listing service, for $415 million. This acquisition marked eBay's entry into the online real estate and housing market.

In 2005, eBay set up its own online international classifieds group, Kijiji.com.[21] Kijiji later purchased leading online classified sites such as the London-based Gumtree.com and the Barcelona-based Loquo.com. In June 2005, eBay bought Shopping.com[22] for $620 million in cash. Another acquisition in the year was of Skype,[23] an Internet communications company, for $2.6 billion ($1.3 billion in cash and $1.3 billion in stock).

Some of the other acquisitions made by eBay were Tradera.com[24] for $48 million in April 2006, ViA-Online GmbH[25] in October 2007, StumbleUpon[26] for $75 million in May 2007, and StubHub.com,[27] for $307 million in February 2007.

In 2006, Yahoo and eBay announced a strategic partnership in the areas of search and graphical advertising, online payments, co-branded toolbar, and click-to-call advertising.[28] eBay also entered into an agreement with Google Inc.[29] wherein Google became the exclusive text-based advertising provider for eBay. Both the companies also planned to cooperate on click-to-call advertising.

Ebay's International Ventures

eBay's international ventures began in late 1998. Due to growing competition in the US from websites like Amazon, Yahoo, and AuctionWatch, eBay began exploring opportunities in other markets. At that time, eBay's US website was gaining popularity in Canada, the UK, and Germany. eBay launched country specific

---

[12] America Online Inc. is an Internet services company. In 2000, it merged with Time Warner. From April 2006, it has been known as AOL LLC.

[13] Although Billpoint was heavily promoted by eBay, it failed to capture market share from its rival PayPal.

[14] In 2002, eBay sold Butterfield & Butterfield to Bonhams.

[15] Autotrader.com deals with buying and selling used cars both offline and online.

[16] Wells Fargo & Co. is a financial services company based in the US.

[17] Sotheby's is one of the leading auction houses in the world, with auction centers at London, Geneva, New York, Hong Kong, Sydney, Melbourne, Milan, Paris, Zurich, Amsterdam, and Singapore. It mainly auctions collectibles, fine art, and antiques.

[18] California-based PayPal, founded in 1998, is an online payment company. Through PayPal, individuals and businesses can send or receive money over the Internet. As of 2002, PayPal was available in 38 countries and had revenues of $100 million, 17 million customers, and $1.5 million transactions.

[19] craigslist, founded in 1995, is an online community featuring classified listings for jobs, goods, personals, houses, events. Craigslist had dedicated sites for 45 cities all over the world.

[20] Launched in 2001, rent.com helped property buyers and sellers to come together to trade. Users could find properties for purchase, flats for rent, and even housemates.

[21] Kijiji means "village" in Swahili.

[22] Shopping.com is a website that provides price comparison services for goods sold on the web. It was founded in 1998 and had sites in the US, the UK, and France.

[23] Skype Technologies SA allows users to make voice calls through its peer-to-peer software. Skype was launched in 2003.

[24] Tradera.com, launched in 1999, is a Sweden-based online marketplace.

[25] Germany-based ViA-Online launched auction management software Afterbuy in 2002.

[26] StumbleUpon helps users to discover and share content online. The company was founded in 2001.

[27] StubHub.com enables customers to buy and sell tickets for sports, concerts, theaters, live entertainment, etc.

[28] Click-to-call advertising enables advertisers to generate customer leads using the Internet. The click-to-call capability allows users to click on a link or icon in the advertisements to call the advertisers directly to pursue a transaction.

[29] Google, Inc. was co-founded by Sergey Brin and Larry Page in 1998. It is the world's most popular Internet search engine and has a diversified range of products such as E-mail, blogs, etc.

websites for these countries in 1999. In the same year, eBay also acquired Germany-based alando.de,[30] for $50 million.

eBay entered Japan and France in 2000. Its next foray was into Australia, for which it partnered with eCorp.[31] In these countries, eBay customized the web pages and denominated the transactions in the local currency.

In January 2001, eBay entered Korea by acquiring a majority stake in Internet Auction Co. Ltd,[32] then the largest auction website in Korea. In May 2001, it acquired Paris-based iBazar SA,[33] the company that operated the leading auction sites in Europe, for $112 million. Through this acquisition eBay was able to enter several European countries including Belgium, the Netherlands, Spain, Portugal, Italy, and Sweden. The acquisition also helped eBay enter Brazil, where iBazar had a significant presence.

In October 2001, eBay and MercadoLibre, the company that operated the Latin American trading site, MercadoLibre.com, entered into an agreement under which MercadoLibre agreed to acquire the Brazilian subsidiary of iBazar; in return eBay received 19.5 percent ownership in MercadoLibre. This helped eBay establish a strong presence in the Latin American market. By the end of the year, eBay was the leading auction website in the US, the UK, Germany, Canada, and Australia.

eBay entered Taiwan in 2002, through the acquisition of Neocom Technology Co. Ltd.[34] Taiwan's leading auction website operator, for $9.5 million. During the year, it entered China by acquiring a 33 percent stake in EachNet Inc.,[35] a leading online Chinese e-commerce company, for $30 million. In 2003, it acquired the remaining 67 percent stake in EachNet, for $150 million.

In August 2004, eBay entered India through the acquisition of the online auction company, Bazee.com Inc. and its subsidiary Bazee.com India Pvt. Ltd.,[36] for $50 million. In the same year, it launched eBay Malaysia and eBay Philippines. In April 2004, eBay acquired Germany-based mobile.de,[37] a classifieds website for automobiles, for $149 million. In November 2004, it acquired Marktplaats.nl,[38] a Dutch classifieds website, from Het Goed Beheer BV (a company that owned a chain of

retail shops selling second-hand goods in the Netherlands) for $290 million.

In June 2005, Kijiji acquired Opusforum.org,[39] a Germany-based local classifieds website. By 2005, eBay was present in 29 countries across the world. In the year it recorded sales of $4.5 billion, with international sales accounting for 46 percent of the total sales. According to Whitman, "International [sic] is a very important part of the future growth. We're entering new countries that are at a much earlier stage of e-commerce development than the U.S. They should provide higher levels of growth for the foreseeable future."[40]

In 2007, eBay acquired a minority stake in GittiGidiyor.com, one of the leading players in the Turkish online trading market. In the same year, it entered into an agreement with the leading Internet portal in Thailand, Sanook!,[41] to launch a co-branded site. The site www.shopping.co.th was launched in January 2008.

Ebay in Japan

In February 2000,[42] eBay entered into a joint venture with NEC Corporation[43] (NEC), to form eBay Japan; NEC held a 30 percent stake in the company while the rest was held by eBay Inc. On the JV, Ichi Yoshikawa, Executive Vice President, NEC, said, "Our work with eBay will help bring the excitement of the online auction format to Japan and create a new marketplace for trading virtually anything."[44] Merle Okawara,[45] who till then had worked as the CEO of JC Foods Ltd., was chosen as CEO of eBay Japan.

Even before eBay was launched in Japan, its websites were popular among auction enthusiasts and collectors. eBay launched its Japanese website, www.ebayjapan.co.jp, on February 28, 2000. NEC began promoting the site through BIGLOBE, its Internet Service Provider. On the launch, Okawara said, "We feel that the launch of eBay Japan is a milestone in the company's international expansion, bringing the excitement and fun of the online auction format to the world's second biggest Internet market."[46]

The site was in Japanese, and the items were listed in the order of the Japanese alphabet. The items on the site, denominated in yen, were listed under more than 800 categories though this was much fewer than the number of categories on eBay's US

[30] Alando.de was a leading online person-to-person trading company. It had more than 80,000 listed items in 500 categories and had around 50,000 registered members, as of 1999.

[31] Australia-based eCorp is Australia is involved in Internet portals, ticketing services, financial services, career management services, and online gaming.

[32] Internet Auction Co. Ltd was established in April 1998, and was the first Korean company to offer online trading. In 2000, it had 2.8 million registered users and around 450,000 items on sale. The company was listed on the Korean stock exchange in June 2000.

[33] iBazar SA launched iBazar in 1998 as an online person-to-person trading website. By 2001, it had a presence in 8 countries and over 2.4 million registered users. iBazar is the leading online auction site in France, Italy, Spain, Brazil, the Netherlands, Belgium, and Portugal, and the second in Sweden.

[34] Neocom Technology Co. Ltd. was launched in 1998, and operated two websites uBid.com.tw and bid.com.tw.

[35] EachNet a leading online trading community in China was founded in 1999. As of 2002, it had more than 3.5 million registered users.

[36] Bazee.com India Pvt. Ltd, a subsidiary of US-based Bazee.com Inc., started operating in India in 2000. Bazee.com had over 1 million registered users at the time it was acquired by eBay.

[37] Mobile.de was founded in 1996. It was one of the first websites dedicated to buying and selling automobiles.

[38] Marktplaats.nl was launched in 1999 and enabled buyers and sellers to trade in various items like cars, clothing items, collectibles, etc.

[39] www.opusforum.org, founded in 2002 is a Germany-based classifieds website. As of 2005, it provided services in 45 cities in Germany and in 10 cities in Switzerland and Austria and had more than 1 million unique visitors (as of May 2005).

[40] Erick Scholfeld, "The World According to eBay," Business 2.0, January 2005.

[41] Sanook.com, is a subsidiary of the MH Group, which, in turn, is a subsidiary of Naspers Limited. Sanook! offered search engine, online marketplace, social networking, mobile services, search marketing, online advertising, and other services.

[42] In 2000, Japan was the second largest economy in the world.

[43] NEC Corporation is a Japan-based multinational. The company provides IT and network solutions to business enterprises, communication providers, and government.

[44] "eBay and NEC Announce Joint Venture in Japan," www.nec.co.jp, February 17, 2000.

[45] Okawara was one of the most prominent businesswomen in Japan. She was born in Hawaii and studied in Northwestern University in the US and the University of Geneva, Switzerland.

[46] "eBay Launches in Japan," www.ebay.com, February 28, 2000.

EXHIBIT I   **eBay Japan's Homepage**

Source: bbc.co.uk

site. This was because several categories on the Japanese site were combined; books, movies, and music were under a single category, as were travel and tickets. Apart from categories like computers and electronics which were common across eBay's international sites, the website also had some Japan-specific categories like Hello Kitty,[47] and Pokémon[48] merchandise.

The online help information about bidding and selling items was more detailed on the Japanese site compared to eBay's U.S. site. Details highlighting the safety of transactions on eBay were displayed prominently. Some links like using wireless phones to bid were highlighted as graphic links, while on the U.S. site, they were displayed as a part of the text. The website allowed the Japanese consumers to view the items listed on eBay websites across the world, along with their prices in yen. (Refer to Exhibit I for screenshot of the eBay Japan homepage.)

On the Japanese site, eBay had Supershops, a merchant-to-person section through which individual users could bid for items listed by companies. Several companies such as Mitsui Real Estate, Kinkou, Culture Convenience Club, @venture, and Marubeni Corporation, participated in the Supershops selling computers, electronics, real estate, jewelry, etc.

As in the other markets, in Japan too, eBay charged listing fees and final value fees. The listing fees were in the range of ¥30 to ¥240, and the final value fees ranged from 1.25 to 5 percent, depending on the final sale price of the listed item.

After one year in Japan, eBay was able to secure only a 3 percent share of the online auctions market, valued at $1.6 billion. Not finding many takers for its online auctions, it decided to scrap fees for online transactions in March 2001. On the

fee being waived, the marketing manager of eBay Japan said, "We are taking the business here as a marathon not a sprint. We are not focused on short-term profits."[49] eBay claimed that after it stopped levying the commissions it had witnessed an increase in the number of listings.

While millions of items were listed on eBay worldwide, in Japan there were only around 4,000 items listed on the website even in 2001. At that time, Yahoo Auctions was the leading auction site in Japan with more than 2 million items listed and around 180,000 transactions per day. In the second position was www.bidders.co.jp, with around 100,000 items. Online mall Rakuten, which had both B2C and C2C auctions, was in the third position.

eBay was unable to make any headway in Japan in 2002 too.,eBay spokesperson Chris Donlay said, "Over the past six months we've been taking a serious look at it. We've been doing a lot on the ground growing the business there, and it has been growing, but slowly."[50] In 2002, eBay was ranked fourth in the Japanese online auctions market. Yahoo Japan Auctions maintained its lead, followed by the Japanese players. At that time, analysts were of the view that eBay could improve its position only by acquiring one of the top three players.

In February 2002, eBay announced that its website in Japan would be closed by March 31, 2002. At that time, eBay Japan employed 17 people and had around 25,000 items[51] listed on the site. According to Pursglove, "Despite the hard work of eBay's team in Japan, we simply believe the issues eBay is facing there are insurmountable without changes in the Japanese market."[52] After the site was closed, customers accessing the site were redirected to eBay's website in the US.

[47] Hello Kitty is a fictional character created in 1974. Hello Kitty merchandise includes stationery products, clothing, bags, jewelry, etc.
[48] Pokémon (Poketto Monsutā101; in Japanese) is a media franchise owned by Nintendo, which was originally a Game Boy video game. Pokémon also refers to more than 450 fictional species that have appeared in Pokémon media. Pokémon merchandise includes trading cards, toys, and books.

[49] Gail Nakada, "eBay Japan Revenues Going, Going . . . ?" www.marketwatch.com, April 02, 2001.
[50] "eBay Mulls Japan Options, Including Site Sale," Bloomberg News, January 14, 2002.
[51] At that time Yahoo offered more than 3.5 million items on its auction website in Japan.
[52] Tiffany Kary, "eBay Exits Japan, moves into Taiwan," www.news.com, February 26, 2002.

What Went Wrong?

Several reasons were cited for eBay's failure in Japan. According to analysts, however, the main reason was the dominance of Yahoo Auctions in the Japanese online auctions market. Yahoo having entered Japan in 1996 through a joint venture with SoftBank[53] made the right moves to become the largest Internet access provider and the largest portal in Japan.

Before online auction sites started operations in Japan, analysts believed that these would not be successful in the country as the Japanese were image conscious, and would not buy second hand and used goods. Therefore, not many Japanese and international Internet companies were interested in entering the market. eBay, however, was keen on entering the market. In fact, it was the first company to announce its plans for Japan. When Yahoo in Japan learnt that eBay was planning to enter Japan, it decided to move ahead and get a head start by launching online auctions before eBay did. It immediately set out to develop a Japanese auctions site. According to Masahiro Inoue, President, CEO, Yahoo Japan, "We knew catching up with a front-runner is hard, because in auctions, more buyers bring more sellers."[54]

Yahoo Japan Auctions was launched in September 1999, just four months after Yahoo decided to launch the site. Being the first auction website in Japan, it was able to attract several sellers, which brought in many buyers. Initially, Yahoo Japan Auctions did not charge transaction fees and all its services were free. Analysts were of the view that the five-month lead which Yahoo got over eBay was crucial. In the absence of competition, Yahoo was able to establish itself firmly. According to an analyst from SoundView Technology Group, "The online marketplace really becomes difficult to prosper in when you don't secure the first-mover advantage."[55]

By the time eBay entered the market, Yahoo had developed a loyal customer base. Moreover, eBay's practices—especially that of charging listing fees and final value fees—also worked against the company. Most Japanese were not willing to pay for services that Yahoo Auctions had till then been providing free. Although eBay stopped levying fees in March 2001, the situation did not change much. And even when Yahoo Japan Auctions decided to charge transaction fees (a nominal monthly listing charge and commission in the range of 3–5 percent) from July 2001, it did not affect Yahoo adversely.[56]

Another factor that worked against eBay was the strength of the Yahoo brand in Japan. Yahoo was the best known online brand in Japan and was successful in channeling traffic from its other services like Yahoo mail, search, etc. toward Yahoo Auctions. eBay, on the other hand, was known only to those who were interested in online auctions. The Japanese generally trusted well-known and established brands, and this proved to be an advantage for Yahoo.

Analysts were of the view that eBay could have benefited if it had started its Japanese website earlier, for example, immediately after Yahoo launched its Japanese site. eBay had spent considerable time in establishing a subsidiary and in finding a country head. It had also spent a lot of time developing a site that would appeal to the Japanese. According to sources, eBay consumed a lot of time in developing add-ons such as a daily horoscope, detailed product descriptions, and newsletters for its Japanese site.

Moreover, even though Yahoo had a wide presence in the Japanese Internet market at the time, it spent money on advertising the launch of its online auction site in Japan. It advertised through billboards in some of the prominent locations across the country, and through magazines. Even after the launch, Yahoo continued to spend around 8 percent (on an average) of its annual revenues in the country on promotions. eBay, on the other hand, did not spend much on advertisements and relied on word-of-mouth publicity. And as very few users registered with eBay, this strategy did not work as anticipated.

Industry analysts pointed out that eBay had used its American-centric payment model in Japan, instead of modifying the service model to suit the needs of the Japanese. eBay charged user fees for listing and selling the items and users were required to submit their credit card information at the time of signing up, a process that did not go down well with most Japanese. Also, most of the Internet savvy people in Japan were young, and did not use credit cards. Even otherwise, Japan was largely a cash-based society, and the Japanese preferred to pay for purchases with cash or through bank transfers.

The design of the site also seemed to have contributed to eBay's troubles in Japan. On its Japanese site, eBay put in a search function instead of creating sub-categories under each category. This seemed to have annoyed many customers as they had to spend a lot of time finding items on the site. For example, a user in the US searching for external modems for desktop PCs could find them in Home > Buy > Computers & Networking > Desktop & Laptop Components > Modems for Desktop PC > External. On the Japanese website, however, as there were no sub-categories under Computers & Networking, users had to use the search function. And the results given by the search function often included items that were not relevant to the search request.

Analysts pointed out that eBay had also erred in its choice of country head. eBay was keen on having a country head who knew the local language and English. Okawara was made the CEO of eBay Japan as she was of Japanese origin and had entrepreneurial experience. The fact that she was new to the Internet business and may not have been aware of the trends in the business was not taken into consideration, and this, in hindsight, proved to be a serious mistake.

[53] SoftBank Corp. is a leading telecommunications and media company in Japan. Its businesses include broadband, fixed-line telecommunications, e-commerce, Internet, technology services, marketing, finance, and media. As of September 2007, Yahoo held a 33.42 percent stake while Softbank held 41.09 percent in Yahoo Japan.[54] "How Yahoo! Japan Beat eBay at Its Own Game," *BusinessWeek*, June 04, 2001.
[55] "eBay Pulls out of Japan," news.bbc.co.uk, February 27, 2002.
[56] According to Yahoo, though there was opposition from the users initially, after they learned about the security features of the escrow system, they agreed to pay the fees.

EXHIBIT II Internet and E-Commerce in Japan

Broadband penetration in Japan picked up from 2001 onward, soon after liberalization of the telecom sector. Broadband penetration was at 25 percent in 2002. As of 2005, Japan stood third in the world in terms of number of Internet users with 86.3 million users; only USA (197.8 million users) and China (119.5 million users) were ahead of Japan. At that time, broadband penetration in Japan was at 50 percent. With the growth of high-speed broadband, the e-commerce market in Japan also grew.

In 1999, after NTT DoCoMo introduced Internet-enabled wireless handsets in Japan, mobile phones began to be used to access the Internet. In 2000, the government issued 3G licenses. With the increase in mobile penetration, mobile phone-based Internet usage also increased. By 2005, the number of mobile Internet users was greater than the number of PC Internet users.

Consumers in Japan started trading using the Internet in 1999. After a slow start, online shopping picked up in Japan, led by Yahoo, which is also the largest general information website in Japan. Another popular destination for online shoppers in Japan is Raukten Ichiba. As of 2003, Japan was the third largest e-commerce market in the world at $255.7 billion, after USA at $733.4 billion, and Western Europe at $516.2 billion.

As of 2006, B2B e-commerce in Japan was valued at $1.3 trillion. The largest users of B2B e-commerce were manufacturing ($714 billion), wholesalers ($363 billion), and finance ($58 billion). The market size of B2C e-commerce was $37.8 billion. The largest users were IT/telecommunications ($10.2 billion), general retail ($8.5 billion), electric appliances ($4.9 billion), and travel ($4.4 billion), according to the Electronic Commerce Promotion Council in Japan. The value of B2B e-commerce in Japan is greater than in the U.S.; the value of B2C e-commerce in the U.S. is much greater in value than in Japan.

JAPANESE B2B MARKET

Year	US$ billion
2000	220
2001	360
2002	510
2003	670
2004	870
2005	1110

Source: Electronic Commerce Promotion Council, Japan

There are some barriers to the growth of B2C e-commerce in Japan like the limited usage of credit cards. Shopping is considered to be a social activity in Japan and a large majority of young people prefer to spend their free time visiting shopping areas and trying out new products, rather than buying new products on the Internet.

Compiled from various sources

The Aftermath

After its Japanese misadventure, eBay chose to expand into countries like China and Taiwan by acquiring leading auction websites, where it relied on local brands for growth and market share. According to Sherif Mityas, a vice president in the consumer business and retail practice at A.T. Kearney,[57] "Two important issues for companies like eBay are novelty and loyalty. In North America, where eBay was one of the first companies to institute the Internet auction model, it is enjoying both. Its experience in Japan, however, has taught it that if you're not the first one in a market, it is very difficult to get people to use your site. In those markets you have to buy the leaders, and the loyal customer bases attached to them."[58]

By 2007, eBay was able to establish a strong presence in other Asian markets like Taiwan, the Philippines, India, Malaysia, and Hong Kong. Despite that, it appeared that without Japan, the largest market in the region, eBay's Asian expansion would not be complete. Therefore, eBay decided to explore the available options to reenter Japan.

After Yahoo closed down its auction sites in the US and Canada, and agreed to collaborate with eBay in the US on online advertising, communication, payments, etc. in 2006,

---

[57] A T Kearney Inc. is a US-based management consulting firm.

[58] Joan Harrison, "Asian Advances, and a Retreat, For Online Auctioneer eBay," Mergers & Acquisitions: *The Dealmaker's Journal,* April 2002.

eBay decided to partner with Yahoo in its second attempt to enter the Japanese market. It entered into an agreement with Yahoo according to which, by March 2008, eBay would list its items on Yahoo Japan Auctions. By the end of 2008, items on Yahoo Japan Auctions were to be listed on eBay's US website. The sellers would get a wider platform to display their items, while the buyers would get more choice.

The website, Sekaimon, would be used to translate names and details of the items listed on eBay's website into Japanese, and also provide shipping and customs clearance services, etc. The website was to be operated by Shop Airlines—a unit of Netprice.com.[59] Shop Airlines would handle payment, customs clearance, and delivery. A fee of 15 percent of the sale price would be charged for these services. Analysts were of the opinion that the association would help both the companies benefit from the growing online auction markets, which were valued at $172 billion in the US and at $36.4 billion in Japan as of 2007.

In 2007, eBay announced that it planned to extend the deal with Yahoo in the future to include other markets and services like PayPal and Skype. According to Masahiro Inoue, President, Yahoo Japan, "We are also considering allying with eBay in countries where eBay has a strong foothold, but we will study this once the U.S. and Japanese business proves successful."[60]

Some analysts were, however, not very upbeat about the Yahoo-eBay joint venture. They felt that as it would involve highly complex shipment and payment processes, customers might not want to use the services on offer. According to Masato Araki, an analyst at Mitsubishi UFJ Securities,[61] "When you take into consideration shipping and transaction fees, participation may be limited."[62]

Case Questions:

1. Paul Anders Schwamm, an entrepreneur from Tokyo, said that the failure of eBay is a classic case study on how not to launch a business in Japan. Analyze eBay's entry strategies in Japan and examine what went wrong with its launch.

2. According to Masahiro Inoue, President and CEO of Yahoo Japan, "Yang [Jerry Yang, co-founder of Yahoo!] understood it was critical to be first. We knew catching up with a front-runner is hard, because in auctions, more buyers bring more sellers." Examine the disadvantages of not being the first mover in online auctions, with reference to eBay in Japan.

3. Discuss the cultural misunderstandings in this case.

4. What is eBay's status in Japan as of the time of your reading this case?

---

[59] Netprice.com is a Japanese online shopping company.
[60] Vivian Wai-yin Kwok, "Bids Across the Pacific: Yahoo! Japan and eBay Ally," www.forbes.com, December 04, 2007.
[61] Mitsubishi UFJ Securities is an investment arm of Mitsubishi UFJ Financial Group, which was formed in October 2005, through the merger of Mitsubishi Tokyo Financial Group and UFJ Holdings.
[62] Mayumi Negishi, "eBay, Yahoo Japan to Link up Auction Services," Reuters Canada, December 03, 2007.

CASE 7   THE 2009 CHRYSLER-FIAT STRATEGIC ALLIANCE

"Four years ago, Fiat was a laughingstock . . . We've come a long way since then. Our bottom line is solidly in the black, and our latest car— the Cinquecento, one of the smallest compacts in the world— is the talk of the industry.— My job as CEO is not to make business decisions— it's to push managers to be leaders".

SERGIO MARCHIONNE,
"Fiat's Extreme Makeover," Harvard Business Review (December 2008), 45.

Introduction

In May 2007, Chrysler LLC again became homeless when Daimler sold its 80 percent stake in the company to Cerberus Capital Management LP, a New York-based private equity firm, for $7.4 billion.[1] Interestingly, Daimler paid $36 billion to acquire Chrysler in 1998 and ended up losing $29 billion in the deal. DaimlerChrysler AG's de-merger was a major financial setback and a public relations blunder to the German Group. In the auto industry, the DaimlerChrysler break-up was called "Chrysler's private bailout." Although the DaimlerChrysler merger was hailed as the "merger of equals," both companies encountered problems in the areas of post-merger integration and corporate cultures. Kirk Kerkorian, a billionaire from Las Vegas, was equally interested in buying Chrysler for $4.5 billion, but Daimler sold Chrysler to Cerberus for a good price. However, Cerberus could not reap tangible benefits from the deal because of the 2008–09 global financial crisis and cost problems in the industry.[2] High oil prices and a recession in the U.S. was the last blow to Chrysler's demise.[3]

In May 2009, Chrysler was in dire straits because of its massive financial exigencies, disappearing market share, and limited clout in the global auto industry (see Tables I and IV). Earlier in April 2009, the company had negotiated and concluded a high-profile strategic alliance with Fabbrica Italiana Automobili Torino or Fiat SpA (hereafter Fiat) that was going to provide the Italian automaker 20 percent stake in Chrysler. Chrysler had held talks with other auto companies such as GM, Toyota, Volkswagen,

Nissan, Tata Motors, and Hyundai. Chrysler's strategic alliance with Fiat looked secure regarding the companies' global operations, corporate compatibility, and long-term synergies. In April 2009, on the recommendation of the U.S. Treasury Department, Chrysler filed for Chapter 11 in a New York court to have the bankruptcy proceedings started.[4] Chrysler's financial difficulties were the result of its de-merger, disappearing market share, and massive losses (see Table IV). Within the globalization debate, Chrysler's woes were also the result of changing global markets and the 2008–09 global financial crisis.[5] Of course, this attracted bidders from Europe to buy undervalued assets of Chrysler and other auto companies. European auto makers had been eyeing the North American auto industry because of future market opportunities and usable assets.[6]

TABLE I   Financial and market-related data of Chrysler and Fiat (2008)

	Chrysler	Fiat
Financial Data		
Sales	$59,700.0 mil.	$83,696.1 mil.
Net income	na	$ 2,425.7 mil.
One-year sales growth	(4.0%)	(2.8%)
One-year net income growth	na	(19.8%)
Price/earning ratio	na	(0.20); industry: (0.04)
Price/sales ratio	na	6.16; industry: 2.62
Price/cash flow ratio	na	0.62; industry: 0.17
Return on equity	na	15.5%
Market/Company Data		
Car Production (in units)	2 mil.	2.2 mil.
Market share	12.5% (U.S.)	8.2 % (Europe)
Total Employees	66,409	198,348

Source: Paul Betts and John Reed. "Driving on Regardless," *Financial Times*, May 4, 2009: 5; *Hoovers.com*, 2009. Fiat SpA. (http://premium.hoovers.com/subscribe/co/fin/factsheet.xhtml?ID=ffffcrkkkctx ffyfjh&ticker=F). Accessed on May 13, 2009.

Written exclusively for Helen Deresky, *International Management: Managing Across Borders and Cultures*, 7th edition, 2011. By **Syed Tariq Anwar**, West Texas A&M University. Copyright © 2009 by Syed Tariq Anwar. Used with permission.

[1] For more information on Cerberus, see: www.cerberus.com; Emily Thornton. "What's Bigger than CISCO, Coke, or McDonald's?" *Business Week* (October 3, 2005): 101–10.

[2] Chrysler's 1998 merger with DaimlerBenz and its 2007 de-merger is thoroughly analyzed and discussed by three widely used cases. See: Syed T. Anwar. "DaimlerChrysler, AG: The Making of a New Transnational Corp.," in Helen Deresky, *International Management: Managing Across Borders and Cultures* 4th ed., (Upper Saddle River, NJ: Prentice Hall, 2002): 340–56; Syed T. Anwar. "DaimlerChrysler AG in 2004: A Global Strategy Gone Sour," in Helen Deresky, *International Management: Managing Across Borders and Cultures*, 5th ed. (Upper Saddle River, NJ: Prentice Hall, 2005): 330–42; Syed T. Anwar. "DaimlerChrysler AG: A Decade of Global Strategic Challenges Leads to Divorce in 2007," in Helen Deresky, *International Management: Managing Across Borders and Cultures* 6th ed., (Upper Saddle River, NJ: Pearson/Prentice Hall, 2007): 323–37.

[3] For more discussion on the 2008–09 global financial crisis and relevant Web-based links, see: Syed T. Anwar (2009). *2008–2009 global financial crisis*, (http://www.wtamu.edu/~sanwar.bus/otherlinks.htm#GlobalFinCrisis). Accessed on May 13, 2009.

[4] Neil King and Jeffrey McCracken, "Chrysler Goes to Court," *The Wall Street Journal*, May 1, 2009; "Chrysler Pushed into Fiat's Arms," *The Wall Street Journal*, May 1, 2009.

[5] Syed T. Anwar. "Global Business and Globalization," *Journal of International Management* 13 no. 1 (2007): 78–89.

[6] John D. Stoll and Norihiko Shirouzu. "Detroit's Troubles Lure World of Bidders," *The Wall Street Journal*, May 7, 2009; Stacy Meichtry, "Chrysler in hand, Fiat Turns to Focus to Opel," *The Wall Street Journal*, May 4, 2009.

Chrysler as the "Number Three" Auto Manufacturer in North America

History reveals that Chrysler was never a leading player in the North American auto industry. The company always trailed both GM and Ford in market share, technology, and consumer satisfaction. Right from its inception, Chrysler was called the "Number Three" auto manufacturer and concentrated on producing inexpensive autos for middle-income consumers. The company was further downgraded in the auto industry with the arrival of Japanese companies such as Toyota, Honda, and Nissan. As of this day, Chrysler has remained synonymous with its "Number Three" status that often brought poor brand visibility and marginal quality. Of course, in minivans and the Jeep brand, the company was a competitive player in North America (see Table II).

TABLE II   History and Timeline of Chrysler (1924–2009)

Early Years

1924 Former president of Buick Motor Co./former vice president of General Motors Walter Chrysler introduces the Chrysler brand with a six-cylinder automobile targeting middle classes in the U.S. The car is an affordable luxury with good engineering features.

1925 Chrysler Corp. buys the assets of the Maxwell Motor Corp.

1928 Chrysler introduces two distinct brands, a low-priced Plymouth and a medium-priced DeSoto. Both brands become popular with the American public during the 1930's depression.

1940s During World War II, Chrysler manufactures trucks, tanks, and other armaments for the U.S. army.

1960s Chrysler enters into the European automobile market.

1970s Chrysler concentrates on full-sized cars, later known as "gas guzzlers" during the oil embargo of 1973. Between 1973 and 1974, Chrysler's production falls by 26 percent.

1979 Chrysler hires Lee Iacocca as the CEO who seeks a government-sponsored bailout for the company.

After the First Bail-Out

1980 The U.S. Congress authorizes a loan guarantee act for Chrysler providing the company a $1.5 billion loan.

1983 Chrysler pays off its loans and develops a new range of minivans (Plymouth Voyager and Dodge Caravan) that helps the company to find new markets in the U.S.

1987 Chrysler acquires American Motor Corporation (AMC), the fourth largest auto manufacturer in North America, for $800 million and takes control of the Jeep brand.

1996 Chrysler's brands compete successfully with other manufacturers in North America, fetching the company a 16.2 percent market share.

Merger with Daimler-Benz

1998 Chrysler seeks a $36 billion merger with Daimler-Benz and is called DaimlerChrysler AG; the company headquarter moves to Stuttgart, Germany.

2001 Because of tough competition, changing markets and quality issues, DaimlerChrysler announces laying-off 26,000 workers and stops assembly operations in six plants.

2005 Chrysler introduces a new range of products encompassing the Chrysler 300 sedan, the Dodge Magnum wagon, and the Dodge Ram pickup that brings $2 billion in profit to the Group.

2006 Because of competition and changing markets, Chrysler Group reports a net loss of $1.5 billion.

February 2007 Chrysler seeks a restructuring plan and lays off 16 percent of its work force (13,000 workers).

De-Merger of DaimlerChrysler

May 2007 DaimlerChrysler announces that a New York-based private equity firm Cerberus Capital Management will acquire 80 percent of Chrysler for $7.4 billion.

2008 Chrysler is impacted by 2008 global recession and high oil prices; Cerberus explores the possibilities of selling Chrysler to GM, Nissan, Fiat, and others. Fiat is a major contender to have a tie-up with Chrysler.

Bankruptcy and Strategic Alliance with Fiat

April 2009 Chrysler and Fiat announce a global strategic alliance and agree on a new ownership structure (see Exhibit II); Chrysler files for Chapter 11 bankruptcy in the U.S.

May 2009 Chrysler appears in a Bankruptcy Court in New York and starts the process of Chapter 11 leading to a company-wide restructuring.

June 2009 Chrysler emerges from its bankruptcy.

September 2009 Fiat owns 20 percent of Chrysler.

Source: Hoovers.com. (2009). Chrysler LLC, (http://premium.hoovers.com/subscribe/co/overview.xhtml?ID=ffffrfyycffryccstx). Accessed on May 13, 2009; *NPR.* (2009). Timeline: Tracing Chrysler's history, (http://www.npr.org/templates/story/story.php?storyId=10172953). Accessed on May 12, 2009; *Financial Times; The Wall Street Journal* (various issues).

Chrysler was founded in 1925 by Walter P. Chrysler, who had worked for Buick Motor Company. As stated earlier, Chrysler manufactured cars for the masses and particularly targeted the mainstream American consumer (for Chrysler's auto models since 1925, see Exhibit I). Between 1941 and 1960, Chrysler introduced a variety of newer models and took credit for technological innovations in North America. As the third largest auto manufacturer, Chrysler always remained behind GM and Ford and was rated one of the "late movers" in the industry. In the early eighties, the company was on the verge of bankruptcy but was rescued by the U.S. government. In the nineties, Chrysler vehicles started to get good ratings from analysts but continued to remain behind other manufacturers in quality and consumer satisfaction. When Daimler-Benz proposed the merger in January 1998, Chrysler's board of directors saw a major opportunity for future survival and access to new markets. In the next four months, both companies negotiated extensively and closed the deal in May 1998.

The next eight years witnessed many ups and downs for Chrysler because of the issues of post-merger problems, losses and lay-offs. In 2007, DaimlerChrysler announced that Cerberus would acquire 80 percent of Chrysler for $7.4 billion. As Chrysler dealt with the 2008–09 global recession and high oil prices, Cerberus kept on exploring the possibilities of either selling Chrysler or creating an alliance with GM, Nissan, Fiat, or Volkswagen. Early 2009, Fiat turned out to be the key contender for Chrysler. In April 2009, Chrysler and Fiat announced their strategic alliance and agreed on a new ownership structure (see Exhibit II). In May 2009, Chrysler filed for Chapter 11 bankruptcy in a New York court and started the process of a company-wide restructuring (see Table II).

Fiat's Tumultuous Corporate Growth and Survival in European Markets

Right from its inception, Fiat's corporate growth has been tumultuous, yet the company survived industry disruptions, labor crises, and technology shifts. Most of Fiat's problems have been attributed to Italian labor laws, business environment, and cost issues. Fiat has come a long way in Europe regarding dealing with its market share problems and reputation.[7] As of 2009, the company has reinvented itself by bringing new products to the European markets (see Table I and Exhibit I). This is evident from the company's Web site that conspicuously stated:

Our cars, call them smart solutions . . . Every Fiat, at your disposal. Typical Italian design, fresh and lively style plus contents designed to improve your life. Let the Fiat range surprise you: 16 models produced around the world, thinking of you.[8]

EXHIBIT I Brand Portfolios of Chrysler and Fiat (Past and Present)

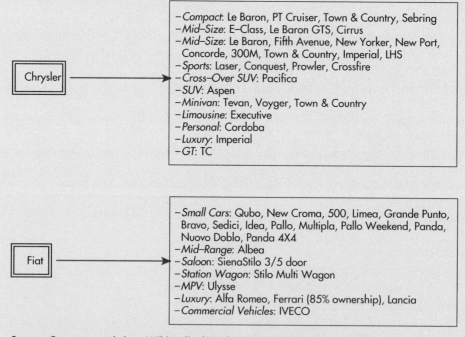

Chrysler →
- *Compact*: Le Baron, PT Cruiser, Town & Country, Sebring
- *Mid–Size*: E–Class, Le Baron GTS, Cirrus
- *Mid–Size*: Le Baron, Fifth Avenue, New Yorker, New Port, Concorde, 300M, Town & Country, Imperial, LHS
- *Sports*: Laser, Conquest, Prowler, Crossfire
- *Cross–Over SUV*: Pacifica
- *SUV*: Aspen
- *Minivan*: Tevan, Voyger, Town & Country
- *Limousine*: Executive
- *Personal*: Cordoba
- *Luxury*: Imperial
- *GT*: TC

Fiat →
- *Small Cars*: Qubo, New Croma, 500, Limea, Grande Punto, Bravo, Sedici, Idea, Pallo, Multipla, Pallo Weekend, Panda, Nuovo Doblo, Panda 4X4
- *Mid–Range*: Albea
- *Saloon*: SienaStilo 3/5 door
- *Station Wagon*: Stilo Multi Wagon
- *MPV*: Ulysse
- *Luxury*: Alfa Romeo, Ferrari (85% ownership), Lancia
- *Commercial Vehicles*: IVECO

Source: Company websites; *Wikipedia*. (2009). Template: Chrysler, (http://en.wikipedia.org/wiki/Template:Chrysler_timeline). Accessed on May 12, 2009; *Wikipedia*. (2009). Template: Fiat Automobiles, (http://en.wikipedia.org/wiki/Template:Fiat_Pre_War_Timeline). Accessed on May 12, 2009.

[7] For more discussion on Fiat's history and its evolutionary growth and company-related issues, see: Francesca Fauri, "The Role of Fiat in the Development of the Italian Car Industry in the 1950s," *Business History Review* 70 no. 1 (1996): 167–206; Francesco Garibaldo, "A Company in Transition: Fiat Mirafiori of Turin," *International Journal of Technology and Management* 8 no. 2 (2008): 185–193; Giuliano Maielli, "The Machine that Never Changed: Intangible Specialization and Output-mix Optimization at Fiat, 1960s–1990s," *Competition & Change* 9 no. 3 (2005): 249–76; Josh Whitford and Aldo Enrietti, "Surviving the Fall of King: The Regional Institutional Implications of Crisis at Fiat Auto," *International Journal of Urban and Regional Research* 29 no. 4 (2005): 771–95.
[8] See: Fiat. (2009). Fiat Web site, (http://www.fiat.com). Accessed on May 13, 2009.

TABLE III History and Timeline of Fiat (1899–2009)

Early Years

1899 Fabbrica Italiana Automobili Torino (Fiat) was founded.

1900 Fiat manufactures 24 cars and employs 35 workers.

1966 Former cavalry officer Gianni Agnelli becomes Fiat's chairman.

1969 Fiat acquires Lancia and 50 percent of Italian icon Ferrari. Fiat encounters massive labor strikes and assembly-line disruptions.

1970s and 1980s: Strikes and Layoffs

1973 Fiat witnesses first operating loss because of labor strikes and 1970's oil price shock.

1976 The Libyan government buys about 10 percent of Fiat. This is strongly opposed by Italian businesses.

1980–85 Fiat reduces its labor force by cutting 100,000 jobs.

1986 Fiat acquires Alfa Romeo from the Italian government and becomes largest automaker in Europe. Libya unloads its stake in Fiat and sells it to the Agnellis and a consortium headed by Mediobanca.

1996 Agnelli resigns as chairman and receives the position of an honorary chairman.

Acquisition by GM

2000 GM acquires 20 percent of Fiat Auto for $2.4 billion.

2002 Fiat puts the company on a crisis status; asks the Italian government for laying off 8,100 workers; closes its Sicilian plant.

January 2003 Gianni Agnelli dies; brother Umberto takes over the company holding; a year later, Umberto also passes away.

Arrival of Sergio Marchionne

June 2004 Fiat hires Sergio Marchionne to become its CEO. Accountant by profession, Marchionne has a master's in business administration from the University of Windsor.

February 2005 Fiat and GM dissolve their five-year partnership; GM pays Fiat $2 billion in cash to get out of the partnership.

July 2005 Spanish bank BNP Paribas buys 2 percent of Fiat.

July 2007 Fiat introduces a new version of its iconic Cinquecento 500 model after 32 years.

Major Global Initiatives in 2009

January–February 2009 Fiat announces a deal to acquire 20 percent of Chrysler in exchange for technology and overseas markets. Fiat receives a $1.26 billion line of credit from its banks to pursue the deal.

April 2009 Chrysler and Fiat announce a global strategic alliance and agree on a new ownership structure (see Exhibit II); Chrysler files for Chapter 11 bankruptcy in the U.S.

May 2009 Marchionne proposes to GM regarding acquiring Opel in Germany and Vauxhall in the UK.

September 2009 Fiat owns 20 percent of Chrysler.

Source: *Hoovers.com*. (2009). Fiat SpA. (http://premium.hoovers.com/subscribe/co/history.xhtml?ID=ffffcrkkkctxffyfjh). Accessed on May 13, 2009; *Reuters*. (2009). Timeline: Key events on Fiat's bumpy road, (http://uk.reuters.com/article/mergersNews/idUKL74393720090507). Accessed on May 12, 2009; *Financial Times*; *The Wall Street Journal* (various issues).

Like Chrysler, Fiat's evolutionary growth and survival had encountered problems in the areas of technology and quality standards. The company history has been unique and reflects Italy's industry-specific problems and rigid labor laws (see Table III). In 2009, Fiat sold 24 models and mostly assembled small vehicles. In 1899, Giovanni Agnelli founded the company by including other investors from Italy. Giovanni died in 1945, and Vittorio Valletta managed Fiat's corporate activities and achieved various accomplishments for the company. By 1910, Fiat had become the largest auto firm in Italy. During the World War II, Fiat manufactured military vehicles and other machinery for the government. Agnelli's grandson and former cavalry officer Gianni Agnelli took over the company in 1963 and eventually became chairman in 1996. In 2009, the Agnelli family still controlled 35 percent of Fiat.[9] During the

sixties and the seventies, Fiat witnessed massive labor strikes and assembly-line disruptions that resulted into 15 million lost worker hours. Between 1980 and 1985, the company reduced its labor force by cutting 100,000 jobs. In 1986, Fiat acquired Alfa Romeo from the Italian government and became the largest automaker in Europe. In 1996, Agnelli resigned as chairman and was given the position of an honorary chairman.

In 2000, GM acquired 20 percent of Fiat for $2.4 billion. In 2002, Fiat encountered financial problems and laid off thousands of workers. In 2003, Gianni Agnelli died and his brother Umberto took over the company.[10] In 2004, Fiat recruited a well known turnaround executive Sergio Marchionne to become its CEO. In 2005, Fiat and GM dissolved their five-year partnership when GM paid Fiat $2 billion in cash to get out of the

---

[9] Stacy Meichtry and John Stoll. "Fiat Nears Stake in Chrysler that Could Lead to Takeover," *The Wall Street Journal* January 20, 2009.

[10] Alessandra Galloni. "Death of Fiat's Agnelli's Marks the End of an Era," *The Wall Street Journal*, January 27, 2003.

EXHIBIT II   **Ownership Structure of Chrysler (2009 and Beyond)**

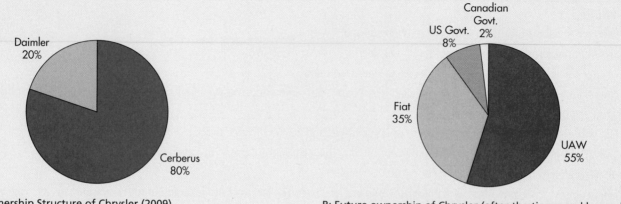

A: Ownership Structure of Chrysler (2009)

B: Future ownership of Chrysler (after the tie-up and beyond 2009)

Source: Neil King and Jeffrey McCracken Chrysler pushed into Fiat's arms, *The Wall Street Journal*, May 1, 2009.

Note: The United Auto Workers (UAW) is a combination of 800 local unions in the U.S. and Puerto Rico and represents diverse industries such as auto manufacturing, healthcare, casino gaming, higher education and others.

partnership.[11] In 2007, Fiat introduced its iconic Cinquecento 500 model after 32 years. In early 2009, Fiat announced a deal to acquire 20 percent of Chrysler in exchange for a technology sharing pact and distribution networks in Europe and North America. During the same period, Marchionne also showed interest in acquiring GM's Opel and Vauxhall brands in Germany and the UK (see Exhibit II).

The Global Auto Industry and its Changing Profile

The global auto industry has been one of the largest industries in the world that impacts countries as well as their socio-political environments. In the U.S., Japan, and Europe, auto companies often became part of their country-specific policies and national prides. Today's auto industry is totally different since it does not excite national emotions, although labor unions continue to exert pressure on their governments.[12] As of 2009, the global auto industry is a complex array of modular technologies and assembly line operations that encompass thousands of suppliers and parts manufacturers. These entities are highly intertwined at the global level. No wonder small disruptions can cause havoc in the auto industry's value chains.[13] In the last 20 years, the auto industry has witnessed hundreds of cross-border strategic alliances, joint ventures, and other tie-ups that aim at economies of scale

and other value chain efficiencies.[14] In 2009, only three American auto manufacturers prevailed in North America (General Motors, Ford, and Chrysler) while Japan had three major firms: Toyota, Honda, and Nissan. Interestingly Europe has been left with four large auto companies (Daimler, Volkswagen, Fiat, and Renault-Nissan). In 2008, revenues of the top five auto firms were as follows: Toyota—$230.20 billion, GM—$182.14 billion, Daimler—$177.16, Ford—$172.46 billion, and Volkswagen—$149.05 billion. During the same period, Fiat's revenues stood at $80.11 billion.[15] The auto industry has witnessed many structural changes in the forms of strategic alliances and collaborative activities in R&D, distribution agreements, joint ventures, and equity stakes. The reasons behind these changes are the industry's evolutionary processes, economies of scale in manufacturing, and consolidations (see Exhibit III).[16]

Changing demographics and rising costs have compelled large-scale auto manufacturers to move assembly plants to low cost economies. In addition, consumer demand in emerging

[11] Alessandra Galloni and Gregory L. White. "Fiat Head Sees GM Write-off as Tuneup to Bid," *The Wall Street Journal*, October 11, 2002.

[12] For more discussion on this topic, see: Maureen Dowd, "No More Hummer Nation," *New York Times*, April 1, 2009: Paul Ingrassia, "The UAW in the Driver's Seat," *The Wall Street Journal*, April 30, 2009; Paul Ingrassia, "How Ford Restructured without Federal Help," *The Wall Street Journal*, May 11, 2009.

[13] For detail, see: "Japan Makes More Cars Elsewhere," *New York Times*, August 1, 2005; "Fitting Together a Modular Approach," *Financial Times*, August 15, 2002: "FT—Motor Industry," *Financial Times*, September 28, 2006; Matthew Symonds. "A Global Love Affair: A Special Report on Cars in Emerging Markets," *The Economist*, November 15, 2008, 1-20.

[14] For more discussion on cross-border strategic alliances, joint ventures, and mergers and acquisition, see the following recent studies: Ruth V. Aguilera, "Translating Theoretical Logics Across Borders: Organizational Characteristics, Structural Mechanisms and Contextual Factors in International Alliances," *Journal of International Business Studies* 38 (2007): 38–46; Mary Y. Brannen and Mark F. Paterson. "Merging without Alienating: Interventions Promoting Cross-cultural Organizational Integration and Their Limitations," *Journal of International Business Studies* 40 (2009): 468–89; Nicolas Coeurdacier et al.,"Cross-border Mergers and Acquisitions and European Integration," *Economic Policy* 24 no. 57 (2009): 55–106; Xu Jiang, Yuan Li, and Shanxing Gao, "The Stability of Strategic Alliances: Characteristics, Factors, and Stages," *Journal of International Management* 14 (2008): 173–89; Brane Kalpic, "Why Bigger is not Always Better: The Strategic Logic of Value Creation through M&As," *Journal of Business Strategy* 29 no. 6 (2008): 4–13; Melissa A. Schilling, "Understanding the Alliance Data," *Strategic Management Journal* 30: 233–60; Tony W. Tong, Jeffrey J. Reur, and Mike Peng, "International Joint Ventures and the Value of Growth Options," *Academy of Management Journal* 51 no. 5 (2008): 1014–29.

[15] "World's Largest Corporations," *Fortune*, July 21, 2008., (July 21): 165.

[16] "Chrysler Gains Edge by Giving New Flexibility to its Factories," *The Wall Street Journal*, April 11, 2006.

EXHIBIT III Chrysler and Fiat Compared with Major Global Auto Manufacturers (as of December 2009)

Chrysler	General Motors	Ford	Volkswagen	Toyota	Daimler	Fiat
Sales: $59 bil* Units Sold: 1.95 mil**	Sales: $182 bil* Units Sold: 7.51 mil**	Sales: $172 bil* Units Sold: 6.34 mil**	Sales: $149 bil* Units Sold: 5.99 mil**	Sales: $230 bil* Units Sold: 5.99 mil**	Sales: $177 bil* Units Sold: NA	Sales: $83 bil* Units Sold: 5.99 mil**
Strengths: * Established brand in North America; sells sub-compact vehicles and utility trucks * Established distribution and sales network in North America * Major manufacturer of utility trucks * Jeep brand and minivans are popular in North America	**Strengths:** * Established brand in the U.S.; also the largest automaker in the U.S. * Major player in global markets with good brand variety; largest exporter of vehicles from the U.S. * Maintains a good distribution system worldwide	**Strengths:** * Ford is the third largest automaker in the world. * Maintains visible brands and supplier networks * Big player in utility trucks in the U.S. * Hired a new CEO in 2007	**Strengths:** * Good brand recognition and sales in Europe * Strong presence in small cars * Excellent distribution network in Europe	**Strengths:** * In 2009, Toyota surpassed GM in sales * Aggressively expanding in global markets * Maintains outstanding manufacturing plants worldwide; Toyota production system (TPS) continues to be the world-wide quality benchmark in quality * Toyota products are rated highly in North America and other parts of the world * Toyota is a leader in hybrid cars	**Strengths:** * Established manufacturer in luxury brands and trucks * Quality standards are well known * Strong brand visibility in Europe, Asia, and North America * Highly focused on R&D and product development * Expanding in North America and Asia	**Strengths:** * Fiat has made a tremendous recovery under the leadership of Sergio Marchionne * Fiat has been reinvigorated in Europe * One of the most visible brands in small cars in Europe * Many new small car models have been introduced by Fiat * Quality has improved; turnaround strategy is in progress * Fiat alliances with other auto companies have paid-off * Fiat's corporate culture and business practices have improved under the new management
Weaknesses: * The de-merger of DaimlerChrysler has created problems for the company * Viable synergy is limited because of quality issues * Chrysler has limited models in sub-compact cars; do not get good quality ratings	**Weaknesses:** * Market share has weakened; big losses were incurred in 2008 * Slow to change because of company size; bureaucratic structure is a problem * Cost and expensive labor contracts are the roadblock * Product development cost is high * Brand Portfolio is too diverse.	**Weaknesses:** * Ford faced major problems in 2008–09 * Mortgaged company assets to get loans worth $23 billions * Distribution system is weak in overseas markets * Has lost market share in North America; Toyota surpassed Ford in sales	**Weaknesses:** * Key models in the sub-compact segments are aging * Suffers from cost over-runs * Limited brand visibility in North America, especially in the sub-compact market; dealer network is weak. * Limited product offerings and brand portfolio * Sales and marketing outside of Europe is weak * Volkswagen does not attract a mass market outside of Europe	**Weaknesses:** * Corporate culture is somewhat myopic; plans on making leadership changes * Some of the product designs continue to be unappealing; may need an overhaul in product portfolio * Limited market share in the European luxury segments	**Weaknesses:** * Daimler has a limited presence in some markets of Asia and Latin America * Product portfolio lacks variety * Limited diversification and expansion in the auto sector * Daimler lost billions of dollars in its merger with Chrysler	**Weaknesses:** * In global markets, Fiats still lacks marketing charisma to compete with other auto manufacturers * The company has a limited product portfolio in global markets
Current/Future Plans: * Filed for bankruptcy in 2009; reorganization is in progress * Alliances with Mitsubishi and Hyundai were unproductive. * In 2008–09, Chrysler's global strategy stalled because of losses * Alliance with Fiat is on schedule * More restructuring and reorganization will take place in the coming years.	**Current/Future Plans:** * A new CEO was recruited in early 2009 * As of 2009, GM is in the process of a major restructuring * A new range of models are possible * More emphasis is placed on flexible manufacturing. * Continue to overhaul its small car segments. * Will introduce new hybrid cars after 2010	**Current/Future Plans:** * Major reorganization is being undertaken to address new brands and other recovery issues * Concentrating more on sub-compacts * A limited number of hybrid models are available	**Current/Future Plans:** * Reorganization is in progress; product development issues are being addressed. * Plans on expanding in the Chinese market * Entry into the high-end market will continue in the coming years	**Current/Future Plans:** * Continues to expand worldwide; will be a major player in the coming years * Overseas manufacturing is a major part of Toyota's global strategy	**Current/Future Plans:** * Future expansion is somewhat on hold after de-merging with Chrysler * Concentrating on its core luxury brands * Plans on bringing new luxury vehicles in Europe and North America	**Current/Future Plans:** * Strategic alliance with Chrysler is expected to be a good long-term strategy for the company * Company-wide reorganization is on track; making big efforts in product development is a top priority

Notes: * 2008 data; ** Light vehicles sales in 2008.

Source: Syed T. Anwar, "DaimlerChrysler AG: A Decade of Global Strategic Challenges Leads to Divorce in 2007," in Helen Deresky, *International Management: Managing Across Borders and Cultures*, 6th ed. (Upper Saddle River, NJ: Pearson/Prentice Hall: 2007): 323–37; Oliver Wyman, *The Harbour Report 2008*; *The Economist; Financial Times; Value Line; The Wall Street Journal* (various issues).

markets (EMs) has forced large auto manufacturers to move facilities abroad to take advantage of cheaper labor and market opportunities.[17] Auto analysts believe that in the coming years, only a small number of auto manufacturers will be left at the global level because of consolidations and mergers. Companies maintaining strong brand identities with competitive technologies and quality will be able to compete effectively. This may result in plant and dealer closings, disruptions in sales, and labor problems (for 2008–09 sales and market shares, see Table IV). It is one of the reasons that restructuring may result in efficiencies in flexible manufacturing, faster product development, and supplier

networks.[18] The global auto industry is a classic example in the areas of competition, industry evolutions, and creative destruction. About the future auto industry, *The Harbour Report 2008* convincingly predicted:[19]

> *A painful realignment made tougher by falling sales . . . Change is coming, and it's coming with gut-wrenching speed . . . This time no one is calling a downturn, but a permanent change in direction of the North American industry.*

TABLE IV Selected Sales (Cars and Trucks) and Market Shares in the U.S. Auto Industry (2008–09)

Company*	Units Sold (2008)	Units Sold (2009)**	% Change	Market Share(%) 2008	Market Share(%) 2009
General Motors Corp.	1,049,966	578,028	-44.9%	21.8%	19.1%
Toyota	789,448	486,212	-38.4	16.4	16.1
Ford Motor	733,296	440,045	-40.0	15.2	14.6
Chrysler LLC	601,622	323,890	-46.2	12.5	10.7
American Honda Motor	487,822	332,014	-31.9	10.1	11.0
Nissan North America	345,600	221,957	-35.8	7.2	7.3
Volkswagen of America	137,105	106,652	-22.2	2.8	3.5
Hyundai Motor America	134,618	129,806	-3.6	2.8	4.3
Mazda Motor of America	101,449	69,934	-31.1	2.1	2.3
Kia Motors America	98,280	94,499	-3.8	2.0	3.1
BMW	85,100	58,436	-31.3	1.8	1.9
Mercedes-Benz	77,960	54,827	-29.7	1.6	1.8
Subaru of America, Inc.	57,652	57,181	-0.8	1.2	1.9
American Suzuki Motor Corp.	36,095	17,674	-51.0	0.7	0.6
Mitsubishi Motor NA, Inc.	35,959	17,753	-50.6	0.7	0.6
Volvo	31,942	17,127	-46.4	0.7	0.6
Audi of America	28,286	22,818	-19.3	0.6	0.8
Mini	14,877	12,170	-18.2	0.3	0.4
Land Rover	11,289	7,890	-30.1	0.2	0.3
Porsche Cars NA Inc.	9,640	6,778	-29.7	0.2	0.2
Saab	8,048	3,824	-52.5	0.2	0.1
Jaguar	5,264	4,030	-23.4	0.1	0.1
Isuzu Motors America Inc.	2,464	165	-93.3	0.1	–
Bentley	1,162	375	-67.7	–	–

Note: Companies are ranked by 2008 sales data;** 2009 sales are from April 2008 to April 2009.

Source: The Wall Street Journal. (2009). Auto sales, (http://online.wsj.com/mdc/public/page/2_3022-autosales.html). Accessed on May 15, 2009.

---

[17] See: "Detroit, Far South," *New York Times,* July 21, 2006: "China's Fast Gains in Auto Parts Reflect New Manufacturing Edge," *The Wall Street Journal,* August 1, 2006:. "Toyota Races to Rev Up Production for a boom in emerging markets," *The Wall Street Journa,,* November 13, 2006.

[18] For more discussion, see: The Harbour Associates. (2008). *The Harbour Report 2008,* Chicago, Illinois: Oliver Wyman; *Standard & Poor's Industry Survey.* (2008). Autos and auto parts, (December 25): 1-26.
[19] Oliver Wyman. (2008). *The Harbour Report 2008,* Chicago, Illinois: Oliver Wyman: 6,11&198.

The 2009 Chrysler-Fiat Strategic Alliance and Corporate Tie-Up

Strategic alliances link two or more companies' operations by combining manufacturing resources and knowledge. These tie-ups combine R&D, product development, distribution networks, and other areas in knowledge sharing. Strategic alliances mostly aim at seeking economies of scale and raising productivity.[20] Inter-organizational cooperation is a unique competitive weapon that helps companies to expand their managerial and financial resources.[21] This is also the case with the Chrysler-Fiat strategic alliance that is a part of hundreds of tie-ups created in the auto industry. As announced by the companies, as well as the Obama Administration, Fiat Group plans on providing technology-related expertise and assembly platforms to Chrysler. The main aim of this alliance is to allow Chrysler to survive and develop small and fuel-efficient autos in North America. The Chrysler-Fiat alliance does not involve any cash injection by the Italian company. In its initial phase, Fiat would own 20 percent of Chrysler and could raise its stake to 35 percent. After 2013, there is a possibility that Fiat may raise its share of Chrysler to 51 percent after meeting certain conditions such as introducing fuel-efficient cars and manufacturing small auto engines in North America.[22]

The Chrysler-Fiat strategic alliance is heavily influenced by today's global competition in the auto industry that continues to seek consolidations. The industry has witnessed downsizing, massive losses, and weak consumer demand. The auto manufacturers from North America have been heavily burdened with debt and expensive labor union contracts. Chrysler was in the most dire situation and saw Fiat as the only available partner for survival. Other factors that helped form this alliance are R&D opportunities, access to markets, and long-term rationalization in manufacturing. The major issues of the strategic alliance are as follows:

1. **Strengths and weaknesses of the Chrysler-Fiat strategic alliance:** Within today's business conditions, Chrysler's tie-up with Fiat was not only a matter of survival but became a part of bankruptcy proceedings. Fiat can take care of some of the retooling activities by sharing its technology with Chrysler for building small cars in North America. This will help them receive additional loans from the U.S. government. In addition Chrysler will have Fiat's readily available distribution network in the European markets. For Fiat, the alliance is a quick access to the North American market that the company exited in the eighties. An initial 20 percent stake in Chrysler is a good market entry strategy for Fiat and could reach to 51 percent. In the coming years, both companies' combined production capacity could reach to five million cars based on "tangible economies of scale" and "geographical reach." Some of the weaknesses of the alliance could show up in corporate integration, technology sharing, and mismatch of brand portfolios. In most of the alliances, companies' goals and changing markets can pose problems. Also areas that may create predicaments in cross-border alliances are knowledge sharing in R&D, control, regulatory and antitrust issues, and distribution and ownership problems.[23]

2. **Company-specific issues:** In the nineties, Chrysler was known as a low-cost a manufacturer. Most of the changes that took place during that time were the result of Chrysler's legendary CEO Lee Iacocca, who joined the company in the late seventies. After the departure of Iacocca, Chrysler took a different approach because of changing markets and losses. The company lost most of its competitive advantage because of global competition and expensive labor contracts. On the other hand, Fiat made a good recovery by reinventing itself, resulting in fuel-efficient small cars and a lean and well-integrated organization. In 2009, Fiat assembled quality vehicles and carried a good learning curve in R&D, manufacturing, and dealer networks. Both companies are looking at future opportunities regarding their tie-up that aim at saving millions in R&D know-how and joint technology platforms. The strategic alliance is envisioning major savings in the area of joint product development as well.

3. **U.S. government's 2009 auto bailout:** In February 2009, the Obama Administration initiated the auto bailout by specifically targeting GM and Chrysler. Ford did not participate in the government financial rescue. In 2008, Chrysler's losses amounted to $8 billion and GM's to $30.9 billion. Under the auto bailout plan, Chrysler was given $4 billion and GM received $13.4 billion. The U.S. government also demanded that the company implement two major changes: file bankruptcy and seek a long-term partnership with an auto manufacturer for future survival. Fiat was the only auto company that aggressively showed interest in a strategic alliance.[24]

4. **Availability of Fiat's technology platforms:** One of the major clauses of the alliance is technology sharing. Fiat plans on supplying four technology platforms and two types of engines to Chrysler. This will help Chrysler to get involved in small cars technology.[25] In Europe, Fiat is known for its "small car production model" that particularly helped the company to seek recovery since 2004.[26]

[20] For more discussion on the concepts, theories and problems of strategic alliances, see: Yves L. Doz and Gary Hamel, *Alliance Advantage: The Art of Creating Value through Partnering*" (Boston: Harvard Business School Press, 1998); Jeffrey H. Dyer and Nile W. Hatch. "Relation-Specific Capabilities and Barriers to Knowledge Transfers: Creating Advantage through Network Relationships," *Strategic Management Journal* 27: 701–19 (2006); Fred A. Kuglin, *Building, Leading, and Managing Strategic Alliances*, (New York: AMACOM, 2002).

[21] Robert P. Lynch, *Business Alliances Guide: The Hidden Competitive Weapon*, New York: John Wiley, 1993.

[22] See: Neal E. Boudette. "Fiat Could Own 51% of Chrysler," *The Wall Street Journal*, May 14, 2009; *Hoovers.com*. (2009). Fiat SpA, (http://premium.hoovers.com/subscribe/co/overview.xhtml?ID=ffffcrkkkctxffyfjh). Accessed on May 13, 2009; Daniel Schafer and John Reed. "Starting Grid Fills Up in Race for GM's European Business," *Financial Times*, May 14, 2009.

[23] Meichtry and Stoll, op cit.

[24] *The New York Times*; *The Wall Street Journal* (various issues).

[25] Bernard Simon. "Time is Tight for Chrysler in Drive for Reinvention," *Financial Times*, May 4, 2009.

[26] Vincent Boland, "Rome Throws Weight Behind Fiat Pact," *Financial Times*, May 2/3, 2009.

5. **Sergio Marchionne as a turnaround artist:** As a CEO of Fiat, 56-year old Sergio Marchionne joined the company in 2004. Marchionne was trained as a chartered accountant and solicitor who received a master's degree in business administration from the University of Windsor and worked for SGS-SA, a Swiss company that dealt with trade goods.[27] Under his short tenure at Fiat, Marchionne was able to turn around the company in difficult times. Marchionne sought a planned and systematic restructuring of the company by concentrating on new technologies and consumer issues and has realigned its management structure. Because of Marchionne's leadership, Fiat in 2008 showed a profit, and its new product development cycle was cut from four years to 18 months.[28]

6. **Availability of the North American market:** Fiat left the North American market in the eighties because of its limited market share, quality problems and mismanagement. To re-enter the North American market, Fiat needed a well established partner that knew the market. Chrysler was the best choice available for this tie-up. No wonder Marchionne had been seeking this strategic alliance to sell Fiat cars in North America.

7. **Globalization and the global auto industry:** Globalization is a major force impacting countries and their industries.[29] The same applies to the global auto industry that continues to be dynamic yet highly competitive in sales and market shares (see Table IV). Regardless of the auto industry's consolidations and mergers and acquisitions, there are opportunities available to those companies that bring new technologies and auto models. Chrysler and Fiat may have a good opportunity to target small car and hybrid segments. If planned accurately, both companies have the potential in targeting middle classes in North America, Europe, and emerging markets.

8. **Brand portfolios and branding issues:** Chrysler and Fiat's brand portfolios seem compatible (see Exhibit I). Both manufacture small cars that are in demand because of high gasoline prices. In their strategic alliance, the companies can pool resources together to consolidate brand portfolios aiming at significant savings in R&D and technology platforms. The companies' joint dealer networks can bring enormous savings in the long-term.

What Lies Ahead for the Chrysler-Fiat Strategic Alliance?

As of 2009, Chrysler and Fiat are expected to have a long-term strategic alliance leading to common technology platforms, distribution networks, and management expertise. Since Chrysler has suffered from its leadership vacuum, Marchionne

is expected to become CEO of Chrysler. The company's losses may be brought under control if the alliance pays off. Of course this also depends on the bankruptcy proceedings and restructuring of Chrysler. Major structural changes in manufacturing and management are expected in Chrysler. This could lead to job cuts, plant closings, and consolidation in dealer networks. In the long-term (4–6 years), the alliance may face challenges in the following areas: (1) recasting the brand image of Chrysler and Fiat products; (2) dealing with labor unions in Europe and North America; (3) redesigning management structures; and (4) formulating new global synergies for long-term survival.

According to Marchionne, Chrysler and Fiat need a strong global presence, competitive brands, and efficient technology platforms. Fiat has been successful in Europe but lacks visibility in North America. Chrysler has a brand name in North America but does not carry a strong dealer network in the European markets. Both companies' brand portfolios (passenger cars and commercial vehicles) can be reinvigorated in the alliance structure. Of course, this will be a daunting task in the short-term. Chrysler and Fiat carry acceptable brands but lag in quality and global integration. In the next four years, if Chrysler and Fiat achieve their alliance objectives in the areas of cost cutting, technology sharing, global integration, product rationalizations, and R&D savings, the tie-up will definitely be rated as a major achievement. Within Chrysler's bankruptcy proceedings and Fiat's North American expansion, both companies will be credited for crafting a successful transatlantic auto alliance. According to academic and practitioner-related research, cross-national alliances often cause problems in the areas of corporate cultures, control, and value chain operations.[30] Because of Chrysler's financial problems, its weakened corporate structure and Marchionne's aggressive leadership style as well as ambitious agenda, *The Economist* correctly observed:[31]

> *If Mr. Marchionne pulls it off, he will create a new company consisting of Fiat Auto (without Ferrari and Maserati or the rest of the Fiat Group), Chrysler and GM Europe. Among the probable stakeholders would be the Agnelli family (which controls Fiat), the United Auto Workers Union health-care fund (until it cashes out) and GM . . . In a normal year that combination could expect revenues of $100 billion from the sale of 6m cars— just above Mr. Marchionne's viability threshold.*

Epilogue

As of September 2009, Fiat owns 20 percent of Chrysler that emerged from its bankruptcy in June 2009. Although Chrysler idled some of its manufacturing facilities and lost a big chunk of sales by closing dealerships, the company is on the road to recovery by launching new models with Fiat's technology

[27] For more information on Sergio Marchionne, see: "Pedal to the Metal," *The Economist*. April 25, 2009: Stacy Meichtry,. "Fiat CEO Builds Record of Bold Strategic Moves," *The Wall Street Journal* January 20, 2009; John Reed and Vincent Boland, "Fiat's Front-seat Driver," *Financial Times* January 24–25, 2009; Leslie Wayne, "New Leaders Hold Detroit's Prospects in their Hands," *New York Times*, March 31, 2009.

[28] Sergio Marchionne. "Fiat's Extreme Makeover," *Harvard Business Review* (December 2008): 45–48.

[29] Anwar, op cit, 78.

[30] Timothy Sturgeon, Johannes V. Biesebroeck, and Gary Gereffi. "Value Chains, Networks, and Clusters; Reframing the Global Automobile Industry," *Journal of Economic Geography* 8 (2008): 297–321.

[31] "The Italian Solution," *The Economist* (May 9, 2009): 72.

platforms and R&D resources. In June 2009, Sergio Marchionne became the CEO of Chrysler and implemented various short-term and long-term plans. In the next three years, Chrysler is expected to be a totally different auto company with new plans and global strategy. Chrysler is also expected to sell its shares to the public in 2011. If all goes well in the Chrysler-Fiat strategic alliance, Fiat may own 35 percent of Chrysler by 2013 and could ultimately acquire 51 percent of the company. This will be a major achievement on the part of Marchionne, who intends to become a major player in the North American auto market.

Case Questions

1. What are your views of the 2009 Chrysler-Fiat strategic alliance and its future prospects in the auto industry?
2. Analyze and evaluate Chrysler and Fiat's strengths and weaknesses before and after their 2009 strategic alliance (see Tables II and III).
3. Compare and contrast Chrysler and Fiat with five other global auto manufacturers (GM, Ford, Toyota, Volkswagen, and Daimler) in the areas of global operations and manufacturing issues (see Table IV and Exhibit III).
4. Analyze Chrysler and Fiat's brand portfolios in the world auto industry. How do you see both companies revamping and overhauling their brands in the short- (1–2 years) and long-terms (5–6 years) (see Exhibit I)?
5. What did you learn from the Chrysler-Fiat Strategic Alliance regarding managing multinationals in the changing global business? What role did the U.S. government play in the formation of this alliance?
6. What has happened to the company since this case was written as the alliance was being formed? Give an update as of the time of your reading this case.

CASE 8   ALIBABA: COMPETING IN CHINA AND BEYOND

Alibaba has a first-mover advantage that makes it very hard for competitors to chip away at their lead in the market.[1]

— DICK WEI,
Analyst, J.P. Morgan Securities Inc.,[2] *in 2007.*

For us, the goal has been to build a company that lasts 102 years and a company that changes China. We're only six years old, so while other people may call us a success, we still do not consider ourselves successful yet. We have a long way to go and the intense competition is what keeps us sharp. The success we've had so far has not made us lose our edge.[3]

— JACK MA,
Founder and CEO of Alibaba.com, in 2006.

If there's a company outside of America that can introduce a new business model to the world, it's Alibaba.[4]

— MASAYOSHI SON,
Founder and CEO, Softbank Corporation,[5] *Japan, in 2005.*

Introduction

In February 2008, Alibaba.com Corporation, China's leading e-commerce company, was ranked 8th in the World's Most Innovative Companies list by *Fast Company*[6] Magazine, a U.S.-based business publication[7] (Refer to Exhibit I for a list of World's most innovative companies). Alibaba was recognized for its simple website that provided easy-to-use features connecting buyers and suppliers all over the world.

Author Information:

Alibaba had several Internet businesses focused on various e-commerce business models such as Business-to-Business[8] (B2B), Consumer-to-Consumer[9] (C2C), and Business-to-Consumer[10] (B2C). It also had a presence in the

EXHIBIT I   World's Most Innovative Companies

Rank	Company
1	Google
2	Apple
3	Facebook
4	GE
5	Ideo
6	Nike
7	Nokia
8	**Alibaba**
9	Amazon
10	Nintendo

Adapted from "Alibaba.com Named One of the World's Most Innovative Companies," www. resources.alibaba.com, February 21, 2008.

intensely competitive web search market. Being one of the first companies to enter the Chinese Internet industry, Alibaba played a major role in bringing about an Internet revolution in the country (Refer to Exhibit II for a brief note on the Internet market in China). Alibaba was launched with the vision of serving the small and medium enterprises (SMEs) in China and across the world. As of 2007, it had 24.6 million registered users spread across more than 200 countries.[11]

According to Analysys International,[12] Alibaba had been the clear market leader in the rapidly growing Chinese e-commerce market with a market share of 69.04 percent in the second quarter of 2007.[13] However, the company lagged behind in the Chinese online search engine market despite having acquired

This case was written by **Hadiya Faheem**, under the direction of **Debapratim Purkayastha**, ICMR. It was compiled from published sources, and is intended to be used as a basis for class discussion rather than to illustrate either effective or ineffective handling of a management situation.

[1] Bei Hu and John Liu, "Alibaba.com Offers $1.3 Billion Share Sale," www.iht. com, October 15, 2007.
[2] J.P. Morgan Securities Inc., New York City, New York, USA is the non-banking subsidiary of JPMorgan Chase. It focuses on activities related to investment banking.
[3] Chua Chin Hon, "Yahoo! Jack Wants it to be No.1 in China," www.asiamedia. ucla.edu, April 28, 2006.
[4] "Meet Jack Ma, Who Will Guide Yahoo in China," www.bdachina.com, August 12, 2005.
[5] Softbank Corporation, headquartered in Tokyo, Japan, is a leading Japanese telecommunications and media company. It has investments in e-commerce, financial services, Internet infrastructure, IT-related distribution services, publishing and marketing, and technology services.
[6] *Fast Company* is a monthly magazine that reports on innovation, digital media, technology, change management, leadership, design, and social responsibility.
[7] "Alibaba.com Named One of the World's Most Innovative Companies," www. resources.alibaba.com, February 21, 2008.
[8] B2B or Business-to-Business e-commerce is trading between two businesses using the Internet.
[9] C2C or Consumer to Consumer e-commerce is trading between two consumers through the Internet.

[10] B2C or Business to Consumer e-commerce relates to business transactions between a company and a customer using the Internet.
[11] Amy Or, Lorraine Luk, and Sky Canaves, "China IPO Frenzy Rolls on with Alibaba.com Debut—Shares of B2B Site Skyrocket as Investors Buy its Growth Story," www.resources.alibaba.com, November 7, 2007.
[12] Analysys International, headquartered in Beijing, China, is a leading advisor of technology, media, and telecom industries in China.
[13] "Analysys International Says Alibaba, Global Sources and Made-in-China.com Led China Online B2B Market in Q2 2007," www.english.analysys. com, September 2007.

EXHIBIT II   Internet Market in China

As of 2007, China was the world's second-largest Internet market after the U.S. According to BDA China, the number of Internet users in China had reached 210 million in 2007 and the country had 163 million broadband connections as of 2007.[14] The Internet users in China comprised only a meager portion of the country's population of 1.3 billion, which meant that there was a huge potential for future growth. China was important for Internet companies not only because of its large market size but also for its vast talent pool.

Apart from the main business activities of Internet companies such as online search, online auctions, online communications, and online advertising, special features like blogging and SMS (Short Messaging Service) were also gaining popularity in China. Blogging was a popular feature, especially among Chinese youth. They were attracted to blogs[16] and the Bulletin Board System[15] (BBS) because of the freedom they offered to them to express their opinions and get to know those of others. These blogs were posted on a variety of topics, like what clothes to buy, what music to listen to, and what movies to watch, product reviews, comparison of products and advertisements, etc. Analysts opined that people expressed their likes and dislikes more strongly in blogs than they would otherwise. Blogs also generated a huge amount of information about customer choices and customer feedback throughout the country, which could be of great use for companies and the government. SMS was another popular practice in China, generating heavy revenue for Internet portals. According to Gartner Inc.,[17] messaging via cell phones and hand-held devices was a common practice in China and local Internet companies like Sina Corporation, Sohu.com Inc., and NetEase.com, Inc. received a good amount of revenue from the SMSs delivered through their portals.[18]

Despite the huge opportunities it offered, the Chinese Internet market was not without its challenges. The political environment in China had a bearing on the existence and performance of Internet companies in China. The Chinese Internet market was strictly regulated by the government. The government imposed a censorship on pornographic content and content related to controversial topics like Tiananmen Square,[19] Taiwan independence,[20] the Dalai Lama,[21] etc. According to media reports, the Chinese government employed around 30,000 people to ensure that such restricted content did not spread in the Chinese Internet space.

In addition to complying with the government rules, it was important for Internet companies in China to know how to successfully launch a Chinese language website or design a search engine that would suit the complex Chinese language. The Chinese language made extensive use of pictograms[22] and ideograms.[23] The characters were written without spaces between them, which made it hard to distinguish one word or phrase from the next. Due to all these political, cultural, and linguistic factors, many international Internet companies had to seek local help to understand the Chinese consumers and deal with the local nuances. Industry experts felt that many domestic Internet companies had managed to gain popularity and market share because of their familiarity with the local environment and customers. Because of their intimate knowledge of the local language, culture, and dealings with the government, the local players had an edge over their foreign counterparts in the Chinese Internet market.

Compiled from various sources.

Yahoo! China's operations in 2005. The Chinese search engine market was dominated by players like Baidu.com, Inc.[24] and Google Inc.[25] with market shares of 74.5 percent and 14.3 percent respectively in September 2007.[26] Moreover, with Baidu announcing its plans of foraying into the rapidly growing e-commerce market in 2008, competition was expected to intensify for Alibaba. Commenting on Baidu's entry into the e-commerce market, Robin Li, Chairman and CEO of Baidu, said, "Baidu's extensive user base and rich experience in Chinese language search makes e-commerce a natural step for expansion."[27] Baidu aimed to build an e-commerce platform by leveraging on its strong search engine capability. However, some industry observers were of the opinion that Alibaba had nothing to fear from Baidu because of its dominance and market leadership position in the Chinese e-commerce market.

[14]"210 Million Internet Users in China," www.english.peopledaily.com, January 21, 2008.

[15]A blog is a user-generated website where entries are made in journal style and displayed in chronological order.

[16]A Bulletin Board System allows users to dial into the system over a phone and using a terminal program, perform functions such as downloading software and data, uploading data, reading news, and exchanging messages with other users.

[17]Gartner Inc. is a US-based business consulting firm established in 1979. It delivers technology-related insights to around 10,000 clients around the world.

[18]Elizabeth Millard, "The Mushrooming Chinese Internet Market," www.ecommercetimes.com, January 11, 2007.

[19]Between April 15, 1989, and June 4, 1989, there were protests in China against the Communist Party of China government. The protests, which were centered at Tiananmen Square in Beijing, were led by students, intellectuals, and labor activists. On June 4, 1989, the Chinese government dispersed the mobs at Tiananmen Square using military force, which led to the deaths of hundreds of protesters. The incident came to be known as the "Tiananmen Square massacre."

[20]For years, the Taiwan independence movement was opposed by China, which described it as a separatist movement that would divide the nation and people. The pro-independence groups described it as a nationalist movement.

[21]The literal meaning of "Dalai Lama" is "spiritual leader." The Dalai Lama is considered the supreme head of Tibetan Buddhism. The 14th Dalai Lama demanded greater autonomy for Tibet, which is under the Chinese control.

[22]A pictogram is a character that represents an object, a concept, or an activity through a picture.

[23]An ideogram is a character that represents an idea.

[24] Baidu.com, headquartered in Beijing, China, is a leading Chinese search engine. Its revenues for the fiscal year 2006 were $107.4 million.

[25] Google Inc., headquartered in Mountain View, California, USA, is one of the leading Internet companies in the world. Its revenues for the fiscal year 2007 were $16.59 billion.

[26] "CNNIC Reports Baidu with 74.5% Market Share," www.chinatechstory.blogspot.com, September 25, 2007.

[27] "Baidu to Enter Chinese E-Commerce Market," www.ir.baidu.com, October 17, 2007.

In October 2007, Alibaba went in for one of the biggest Initial Public Offerings (IPO) in the history of Internet companies the world over. The IPO helped it raise $1.5 billion, which was next only to the Google's IPO in 2004 which had raised $1.7 billion. With a lot of funds coming in, Alibaba was looking to strengthen its position in China further and also to increase its global footprint.

Background Note

Jack Ma, the founder of Alibaba, was born in Hangzhou, a city in China's Zhejiang province, in 1964. At the age of twelve, Ma developed a fascination for the English language. He began learning English by listening to the Voice of America[28] and acting as a free guide to foreigners who visited Hangzhou. Another event that changed Ma was when he traveled to Australia to visit a friend in 1985. He had grown up believing that the world outside China was a terrible place to live in. He was taught that China was the richest country in the world and that the Chinese were the most contented people in the world. According to Ma, "Everything I'd learned in China was that China was the richest country in the world. When I arrived in Australia, I realized it's totally different. I started to think you have to use your own mind to judge, to think."[29]

In 1988, Ma earned a degree in English from the Hangzhou Teacher's Institute and began teaching English and international trade at the Hangzhou Electronic and Engineering Institute. In 1992, he founded an English translation agency in Hangzhou and soon built up a good reputation for his language skills.

In 1995, Ma was sent to Malibu, near Los Angeles, by a Chinese businessman. Ma was to mediate in a dispute between the businessman and his American counterpart who had not put in the money he had promised into the man's firm. Ma approached the American ready to mediate but to his shock, he was locked up for a couple of days in the American's house. Ma was released only after he promised the American that he would start an Internet company in China in association with him. Though this joint venture never actually happened, Ma was able to leave. The same year, Ma went to Seattle for a trade delegation as an interpreter. It was to become a turning point in his life. During the visit, a friend introduced him to the Internet. Ma typed in "beer" in the search engine. It yielded results like German beer, Japanese beer, and American beer. Nothing called Chinese beer came up. He then typed in "China" and "beer" but this gave no results. This made Ma decide to start a company to bring information regarding Chinese companies to the Internet. After returning to Hangzhou, Ma resigned his teaching job, borrowed $2,000 from his relatives, and launched China Pages, China's first commercial website, in 1995. About launching this website, Ma said, "At 9:30 we launched the home page, and by 12:30 I had six e-mails. I said, 'Whoa! Interesting!' If I could help Chinese companies list on the Internet and help foreigners find their websites, that might be a good thing."[30] The website contained a list of companies

operating in China. The Hong Kong media called Ma the "father of the Chinese Internet" and credited him with bringing about an Internet revolution in China.

In 1998, Ma moved to Beijing to work for the Chinese Ministry of Foreign Trade and Economic Cooperation (MOFTEC) as the Head of the Information Department of the China International Electronic Commerce Center[31] (CIECC). He designed a website for MOFTEC and this became the first government website in China.

Alibaba in its Initial Years

In 1998, Ma left MOFTEC and returned to Hangzhou to fulfill his dream of establishing his own e-commerce company. He said, "I realized that you can never expect a government company to grow. So I left to set up my own."[32] Ma gathered 18 people in his apartment to explain his vision to them. He warned his colleagues who wanted to join him that his venture was a risky one and that they would be paid only Renminbi[33] (RMB) 500 every month. He gave them three days to think it over. He was touched when finally, all 18 of them decided to follow him to Hangzhou. Ma and his colleagues put in some money. This money, which came up to $60,000, was used to start Alibaba from Ma's apartment in Hangzhou in March 1999. Asked why Alibaba had been chosen as the name, Ma said, "The name [Alibaba], taken from the Arabian Nights, was chosen because it's universally well known and is easy to spell."[34]

In August 1999, the Chinese Bureau of Industrial and Commercial Administration registered Alibaba as a computer company since the company's business could not be classified under any other category. Because of the strict IPO regulations in Beijing, Alibaba was registered in Hong Kong. At the same time, Ma started looking out for potential investors for the venture. But since the business model was new, the investors initially didn't believe in the venture.

However, by September 1999, a few venture capitalists approached Ma, attracted by the novel concept of the business. Ma told them frankly that launching Alibaba was a risky proposition and that he expected it to make hardly any profits during the initial years. Some of the prospective investors were still eager to lend. Ma said, "I told them at the very first meeting, Don't push us. We know what we are doing."[35] Initially, Ma rejected offers from 38 venture capitalists. Later, he accepted an offer from a group of investors such as The Goldman Sachs

---

[28] Started in 1942, Voice of America is an international radio and television broadcasting service of the US government.

[29] Sonia Kolesnikov-Jessop, "Spotlight: Jack Ma, Co-founder of Alibaba.com," www.iht.com, January 5, 2007.

[30] Clay Chandler, "China's Web King," *Fortune*, December 10, 2007.

[31] China International Electronic Commerce Center (CIECC) was founded in 1996 to build and operate a secure network for government communications and commerce. It provided services related to e-commerce and e-government that are used by government agencies in China.

[32] Sumie Kawakami, "China's Visionary B2B: Who Says the Dot-com Era is over? Alibaba.com Thrives as Chinese Imports and Exports Boom. CEO Jack Ma has a Vision: Helping SMEs Buy and Sell Goods through his Sites - Upfront - Company Profile," www.encyclopedia.com, May 2003.

[33] Renminbi is the currency of the mainland of the People's Republic of China. Its principal unit is called the Yuan. As of mid-2008, US$1 was approximately equal to RMB 6.83.

[34] "Open Sesame to the Net Highway," www.crienglish.com, April 17, 2005.

[35] Sumie Kawakami, "China's Visionary B2B: Who Says the Dot-com Era is over? Alibaba.com Thrives as Chinese Imports and Exports Boom. CEO Jack Ma has a Vision: Helping SMEs Buy and Sell Goods through his Sites – Upfront— Company Profile," www.encyclopedia.com, May 2003.

Group Inc.,[36] Fidelity Investments,[37] Investor AB,[38] Templeton Dragon Fund Inc.,[39] and Transpac Industrial Holdings Limited[40] and was able to raise $5 million from them in October 1999.[41] In January 2000, Ma successfully persuaded Softbank Corporation to invest $20 million in his venture.[42] Softbank was, at that time, the largest global investor in Internet businesses, owning stakes in hundreds of Internet companies such as Yahoo! Inc.,[43] Chinadotcom Corporation[44] (CDC), etc. In return, Peter Sutherland, Chairman of Goldman Sachs, and Masayoshi Son, CEO of Softbank, were made members of Alibaba's board of advisors. In 2000, Ma moved its headquarters from Hangzhou to a new building in Shanghai.

Alibaba concentrated on small and medium-sized Chinese firms which aspired to go global but found it very expensive to do so. Ma aimed at connecting these Chinese manufacturers with small and medium-sized buyers from across the world. Ma said, "We want to help SMEs from all over the world grow their business and benefit from cross border trade. Alibaba.com is like the World Trade Organization for SMEs."[45] Alibaba's mission was "to help small and medium enterprises (SMEs) grow." Commenting on its focus on SMEs, Ma said, "SMEs are the future of Asia, and the future of China. Many people believe in big companies, saying we should get more money from big companies, we should do transactions with them, et cetera. But I disagree. Asia is Asia. China is China. Unfortunately, in Asia, the market is too fragmented that we have no standard. There is no standard for e-commerce, SMEs, or B2B. Our job is to establish the standard. We cannot create beautiful Power Points, but we know how to listen to our customers."[46]

During the late 1990s and early 2000s, the Internet was not very popular in China and banks were not networked. Credit card usage was limited and providing logistics service in the country was difficult, to say the least. In this scenario, Alibaba thought it wisest to limit its business model to connecting buyers and suppliers. Suppliers were allowed to list their products on the website while buyers could post their requests on the bulletin boards. The deals were struck through e-mails or offline messages. The services were offered for free and no other value-added services were offered. Ma believed that Alibaba was still in its infancy stage and had to build a loyal customer base before it started charging for its services.

Initially, Alibaba had two websites—www.alibaba.com, an English website for international B2B trade, and www.china.alibaba.com for B2B trade in China. However, the company soon noticed that despite Japan being China's biggest trading associate, the online business carried out from that country was less compared to enterprises from the U.S., South Korea, India, and Europe. Alibaba therefore launched www.alibaba.co.jp, a Japanese site for Japanese traders, in 2002. According to Ma, "Chinese and Japanese entrepreneurs have a digital ditch on the Internet. We want to help them stride this ditch with Alibaba Japan Website."[47] Also, the Japanese preferred to use the site in Japanese. David Wei, CEO of Alibaba, said, "They prefer to use the Japanese language as their commercial language, and with China and Japan as each other's second-largest trading partner, there was a big demand."[48]

Ma found that SMEs were hesitant about using the Internet, as they assumed that it would require some expertise in computer use. Ma ensured that Alibaba's websites were simple and easy to browse through. He considered himself a non-technical person, and this, he believed, helped him keep the websites more user-friendly. According to Ma, "I use my computer for two things, e-mail and surfing the Web. Most of our customers are not high-tech people, so we have always tried to make the technology invisible. When a member goes on Alibaba.com to find a supplier, we want the website to be very simple and user-friendly. We have a great engineering team, but their job is to make sure everything passes the 'Jack test.' If I can understand our website, then I am sure our customers can too."[49] In May 2000, Ma brought in John Wu, the creator of the Yahoo! search engine, and appointed him as the Chief Technology Officer of Alibaba.

Another major concern for Ma was that many SMEs distrusted the idea of online payments. Ma managed to convince them about the safety of the practice by stressing the fact that Alibaba's system for online transactions was managed in partnership with a leading bank in China.

By the end of the first year in business, Alibaba had become the largest online global trading website in Asia with about 200,000 members from 194 countries (70 percent of the members were Chinese), and approximately 1,000 new members joining every day.[50] On the whole, the websites were receiving about 1,500 new subscribers every day.[51] Nearly half the requests were from companies based in the U.S., Europe, and India while the remaining were from Greater China. In March 2000, Alibaba started catering to the European market and also planned to expand its operations in North and South America, Japan, etc. Buyers from any country could locate and strike deals with sellers in any country/ies across the world.

[36] The Goldman Sachs Group Inc., headquartered in New York City, New York, USA, is a leading investment banking, securities, and investment management firm.

[37] Fidelity Investments, headquartered in Boston, Massachusetts, USA is an investment products and services company.

[38] Investor AB, headquartered in Stockholm, Sweden, is an investment company whose key products include core equity, private equity, operating and financial investments.

[39] Templeton Dragon Fund Inc., headquartered in Fort Lauderdale, Florida, USA, is a non-diversified, closed-ended investment company.

[40] Transpac Industrial Holdings Limited, headquartered in Singapore, is an investment holding company providing venture capital to private companies.

[41] "Fast as a Rabbit, Patient as a Turtle," www.resources.alibaba.com, July 3, 2000.

[42] "Fast as a Rabbit, Patient as a Turtle," www.resources.alibaba.com, July 3, 2000.

[43] Yahoo! Inc., headquartered in Sunnyvale, California, USA, is one of the leading online portals with a network of websites—news, search engine, entertainment, e-commerce etc. Its primary source of revenues is through online advertising but it also offers commercial services such as online marketing, etc. Its revenues for the fiscal year 2007 were $7 billion (Source: http://en.wikipedia.org).

[44] Chinadotcom Corporation, headquartered in Hong Kong, China is a leading provider of business solutions, enterprise software solutions, and mobile and Internet applications.

[45] "Alibaba.com Opens its First European Office in Geneva," www.alibaba.com, October 2, 2007.

[46] Sumie Kawakami, "China's Visionary B2B: Who Says the Dot-com Era is over? Alibaba.com Thrives as Chinese Imports and Exports Boom. CEO Jack Ma has a Vision: Helping SMEs Buy and Sell Goods through his Sites - Upfront - Company Profile," www.encyclopedia.com, May 2003.

[47] "Alibaba is to Land at Japan, as Planned," www.resources.alibaba.com, October 17, 2002.

[48] Fara Warner, "Alibaba.com's Helm," www.forbes.com, November 26, 2007.

[49] Chua Chin Hon, "Yahoo! Jack Wants it to be No.1 in China," www.asiamedia.ucla.edu, April 28, 2006.

[50] Justin Deobele, "B2B for the Little Guys," www.forbes.com, July 24, 2000.

[51] "Alibaba.com," www.lupaworld.com, 2001.

Alibaba aimed to have a global presence and expand in the U.S. and hence the company's R&D was mainly done at Silicon Valley. It did not spend any money on marketing its website—its membership was the result of the exceptional services that it offered to its customers.

During the early 2000s, the huge manufacturing potential of Asia, especially China, and the rising popularity of Alibaba attracted a number of other companies to start e-commerce ventures in China. In the early 2000s, Hutchison Whampoa Limited[52] launched a web portal called www.tom.com. A group of businessmen from Hong Kong partnered with America's B2B major Commerce One.[53] Hong Kong-based Global Sources Limited[54] and San Francisco-based MeetChina.com also announced their plans to enter the Chinese e-commerce market. MeetChina planned an aggressive expansion in Asia. While some of these firms concentrated on particular industries, others such as Commerce One and Ariba[55] concentrated on big businesses in Europe and the U.S.

Ma refused to worry about the rising competition. Instead, he set to work to make plans to provide various products targeting the SMEs in various countries. He made several efforts to differentiate Alibaba from others by providing innovative features like wireless access to its services in partnership with Motorola Inc.[56] To attract more users, Alibaba also started offering additional services for registered members (registration was free) such as e-mail, etc.

In March 2000, when the dotcom bubble[57] burst, a number of dotcom and e-commerce companies filed for bankruptcy. A vast majority of dotcom companies could not withstand the sharp fall in revenues from Internet advertising. Web-based retailers failed to gauge the infrastructure they required to carry on with their retailing activities on the Internet and so many companies were forced to shut down their businesses. Commerce One was also affected and it filed for bankruptcy in October 2004.[58] A few companies such as Ariba merged with FreeMarkets Inc.,[59] a leading B2B in June 2004.[60] Alibaba,

however, was able to withstand the dotcom crash since its business was not dependent on advertising revenues.

To deal with the dotcom crash, Alibaba reformulated its strategies. By September 2000, Ma was left with hardly any revenues and so had no choice but to curb his expansion plans. He told his employees that Alibaba would be in trouble if it did not adopt the right strategies. He announced three B2C strategies. These were:

- "Back to China," under which Alibaba would concentrate mainly on improving its business in China rather than focusing on global markets.
- "Back to Central," under which the headquarters was moved back from Shanghai to Hangzhou.
- "Back to the Coast," under which Alibaba would concentrate on improving its presence in the coastal areas, the richest region of China.

In July 2000, Alibaba started selling its advertising space. However, the revenues generated were very limited. Alibaba also began selling reports and statistics on various sellers. For the year 2000, Alibaba revenues were just $1 million and the company had not made any profits.[61] According to Ma, "The year 2000 was a difficult year. Our team was young—only a year old. We saw things were still going up, but knew it would surely go down. We didn't know how deep the fall would be, how bad it would be. Besides which, we had virtually no revenue."[62]

In early 2001, Alibaba started offering a customized online marketplace for its members called "Alibabies" for a premium. However, this generated only a small amount of revenue—$0.3 million a year.[63] Several analysts were quick to write off Alibaba. They expressed doubts about its survival in the long run in light of the dotcom crash. The increasing competition from other B2B companies targeting the Chinese B2B markets was also building up tremendous pressure on Alibaba to merge or to fall. In the same year, Ma brought in Savio Kwan, general manager of GE's equipment China division, as Chief Operating Officer of Alibaba with the aim of turning around the company. Kwan said, "We need to ground [Alibaba] in reality and make it into a business."[64]

In late 2001, Alibaba began charging its members for its services. The fee was $3,000 per year for a membership in "China Supplier"—an online community for qualified Chinese exporters who were verified by third party credit agencies. In mid-2002, the membership fee was gradually increased to $8,000.

By March 2002, Alibaba's members had touched the one million mark (Refer to Exhibit III for different types of membership). In 2002, Ma set a target of $1 profit for Alibaba. Commenting on this, Ma said, "We said, 'Let's make one dollar in profits for the whole year. We spend five million

---

[52] Hutchison Whampoa Limited, headquartered in Hong Kong, China, is a diversified conglomerate with business interests in ports and related services; telecommunications; property and hotels; retail and energy, etc.

[53] Commerce One, headquartered in Westbury, New York, USA was an e-commerce solutions provider and a leading marketplace for B2B transactions.

[54] Global Sources Limited, headquartered in Hong Kong, China, is a leading B2B media company. Its revenues for the fiscal year 2007 were $182.1 million.

[55] Ariba, headquartered in Sunnyvale, California, USA, is a provider of Intranet and e-commerce solutions. The Ariba B2B Commerce Platform allows online transactions between buyers and suppliers.

[56] Motorola Inc., headquartered in Schaumburg, Illinois, USA, is an electronics and telecom goods company.

[57] The increase in popularity of the Internet fueled the growth of dotcom companies—firms that provided products and services related to or by using the Internet. They grew rapidly in number between 1995 and 2000 as many individuals started their own companies. Most of these companies offered similar products and services. The uncontrolled proliferation of such companies ended with the bubble busting in March 2000, leading to the closure of many of these companies.

[58] Commerce One was later acquired by Perfect Commerce in February 2006. Perfect Commerce is one of the largest providers of On-Demand Supplier Relationship Management (SRM) solutions.

[59] FreeMarkets Inc., headquartered in Pittsburgh, Pennsylvania, USA is a leading e-commerce company.

[60] The merged entity was called Ariba Inc. and since then has been a leading provider of Spend Management solutions to help companies analyze, understand, and manage their corporate spending.

[61] "Alibaba's Magic Carpet is Losing Altitude," www.businessweek.com, April 9, 2001.

[62] Sumie Kawakami, "China's Visionary B2B: Who Says the Dot-com Era is over? Alibaba.com Thrives as Chinese Imports and Exports Boom. CEO Jack Ma has a Vision: Helping SMEs Buy and Sell Goods through his Sites - Upfront - Company Profile," www.encyclopedia.com, May 2003.

[63] "Alibaba's Magic Carpet is Losing Altitude," www.businessweek.com, April 9, 2001.

[64] "Alibaba's Magic Carpet is Losing Altitude," www.businessweek.com, April 9, 2001.

EXHIBIT III Types of Membership at Alibaba.Com

- **Free Membership:** Free members were offered basic services, free of cost. Sellers registered under this category could post products they wanted to sell, search for buyers, and contact them. Buyers were allowed to post buying leads and send inquiries to the suppliers. However, Chinese companies had to join as "Gold Supplier" members in order to become a seller.
- **TrustPass Membership:** It consisted of supplier members from outside Hong Kong, Macau, and Mainland China. TrustPass Membership was a paid service where the member had to pay $299 and would be authenticated and verified by a third-party credit reporting agency.[65] He would display a TrustPass icon symbolizing credibility to online buyers. However, this facility was available for Chinese companies only if they were "Gold Suppliers." TrustPass members were allowed to have their own websites which contained information about the company, its products, etc.
- **Gold Supplier:** This membership was primarily for export-oriented suppliers. It consisted of premium suppliers from Hong Kong, Macau, and Mainland China. The process of authentication and verification was more rigorous for such membership. The suppliers were classified into 27 industries which enabled buyers to locate the companies conveniently. The member would display the TrustPass icon and a Gold Supplier icon to symbolize the highest level of seller qualification. Some of the advantages that such members enjoyed were listing of products on Alibaba's home page and unrestricted access to buyers' trade leads.

Source: www.alibaba.com

U.S. dollars, we should make at least one back. If we spend 10 million, we should still earn one dollar.' So, we spent the whole year trying to make one dollar. When we set the target, everyone said I was stupid. But the whole company had a clear target throughout the year. The young people in the company had never had experience making money. Even if we say we are going to make 10 million dollars, how are we going to make it? But the one dollar target is something we could make if we just saved electricity, for example."[66]

In March 2002, Alibaba set a TrustPass membership fee of $299 for companies wanting to join Alibaba, after which they were verified and authenticated. However, this fee did not deter companies from joining; about 200 Chinese companies were registering themselves every day.

Business Portfolio

Despite its struggles, by the year 2000, the Alibaba Group had emerged as the largest e-commerce company in China and was one of the leading players in the international e-commerce market. Alibaba was the flagship company of the Alibaba Group with marketing and sales offices across Beijing, Seoul, Silicon Valley, London, and Latin America. Alibaba's business portfolio included the following:

Alibaba China: Launched in 1999, Alibaba China (www.china.alibaba.com) was a website in the Chinese language serving domestic B2B trade in China. It had a registered user base of

21 million users paying an annual subscription fee for posting their products on the website.[67] The authenticity of the members was verified by a third party credit-reporting agency.

Alibaba International: Launched in 1999, Alibaba International (www.alibaba.com) was an English website which connected a number of Chinese SMEs with a number of businesses worldwide. It had over 2.5 million registered users from around 200 countries as of January 2007.[68] More than 500,000 international users visited the website every day to find and trade with manufacturers in China and other countries.[69]

Taobao: Taobao (www.taobao.com) was launched in May 2003. It was China's most popular C2C trading site. As of May 2006, Taobao had more than 26 million product listings, the highest number of listings among C2C websites in China, and more than 100 million page views per day.[70] In July 2007, it had more than 39.9 million registered users.[71] According to iResearch Consulting Group,[72] Taobao had garnered a market share of 72 percent in the first quarter of 2007.[73]

AliPay: Launched in 2004, AliPay was an online payment solution which enabled the users to carry out online money transactions easily, quickly, and safely.

[65]Sumie Kawakami, "China's Visionary B2B: Who Says the Dot-com Era is over? Alibaba.com Thrives as Chinese Imports and Exports Boom. CEO Jack Ma has a Vision: Helping SMEs Buy and Sell Goods through his Sites – Upfront— Company Profile," www.encyclopedia.com, May 2003.

[66] Sumie Kawakami, "China's Visionary B2B: Who Says the Dot-com Era is over? Alibaba.com Thrives as Chinese Imports and Exports Boom. CEO Jack Ma has a Vision: Helping SMEs Buy and Sell Goods through his Sites - Upfront - Company Profile," www.encyclopedia.com, May 2003.

[67] "China's Alibaba.com Aims to Expand in Europe through Acquisitions—CEO," www.forbes.com, December 28, 2007.

[68] "China's Alibaba.com Aims to Expand in Europe through Acquisitions—CEO," www.forbes.com, December 28, 2007.

[69] Sonia Kolesnikov-Jessop, "Spotlight: Jack Ma, Co-founder of Alibaba.com," www.iht.com, January 5, 2007.

[70] "Taobao.com Launches B2C Services," www.resources.alibaba.com, May 10, 2006.

[71] "Taobao.com Triples to Beat eBay," www.chinaeconomicreview.com, July 25, 2007.

[72] iResearch Consulting Group is a market research company based in China. It offers companies market research services related to e-commerce, the Internet, online games, etc.

[73] "Internet in China: Taobao Transaction Volume Tripled in First Half of 2007," www.designative.info, 2007.

Yahoo! China: Yahoo! China (www.yahoo.com.cn) was China's third most popular search engine after Baidu and Google. It was started in October 2005 after Yahoo! merged its China operations with Alibaba in August 2005. Alibaba had the exclusive rights to use the Yahoo! brand and technologies in China.

Alisoft: In January 2007, Alibaba launched Alisoft, a software services company that catered to the needs of several SMEs in China. Alisoft allowed customers to use various services like Customer Relationship Management (CRM), Marketing information management, Sales force management, Inventory management, and Financial tools. Other services provided were e-mail, information management, inquiries, bookkeeping, and invoicing. Alisoft also provided an instant communication tool called 'Aliwangwang', which was offered to users as TradeManager[74] on Taobao. As of January 2007, Alisoft had operations in Shanghai and Hangzhou.

Alimama: In November 20, 2007, Alibaba launched Alimama, an online advertising exchange company. The company allowed advertisers and publishers on the web to trade advertising inventory online. It was intended to serve the more than one million SMEs in China that accounted for 80 percent of web traffic in China.[75]

The Competition

B2B Market

Alibaba was launched at a time when the Chinese Internet industry was in its infancy. Considering the growth potential of the budding e-commerce market, other players like Global Sources and MeetChina were launched in 1999. These players were expected to intensify competition in the emerging B2B market. Global Sources had an advantage over Alibaba because of its search technology and detailed information about the products listed on its site. Moreover, the company had an employee strength of 1,600 people with several salespeople across the world to build its supplier community, in 1999. There was also the threat of many new players entering this space. In order to gain a strong foothold in the B2B market, Ma announced that it would not charge any transaction fees. Commenting on Ma's strategy, Craig Pepples, CEO, Global Sources, said, "Some players are focusing on building as much 'community' as possible in a short period of time, usually by giving things away. The problem with this approach is . . . the free sites have very little depth. What customers need is detailed [information] and the tools to slice, dice, and compare."[76] Unfazed by the competition, Ma said that he was unaware of his competitors' existence. Ma said, "The world is changing so fast, you don't know what each other is thinking about, you don't even know what you are thinking yourselves. How do you know who are your competitors?"[77]

Despite several attempts made by Alibaba's competitors to carve out a place for themselves in the rapidly growing B2B

TABLE I   Market Shares of B2B Players in China (Q2 2007)

Players	Market Share (in %)
Alibaba	69.04
Global Sources	8.37
Made-in-China.com	5.45
HC360	3.02
emedChina	2.43
ChemNet	2.34
MainOne	2.24
315	1.95
Sell Great	0.19
Others	4.97

Adapted from "Analysys International Says Alibaba, Global Sources and Made-in-China.com Led China Online B2B Market in Q2 2007," www.english.analysys.com, September 2007.

market, they failed to make a mark, largely because of Alibaba's dominance in that market. On the other hand, Alibaba continued to enjoy phenomenal growth. According to a China B2B Market Quarterly Tracker Q2 2007 report by Analysys in 2007, the size of the B2B market in China had reached RMB 1.027 billion in the second quarter of 2007. Alibaba was the market leader in the Chinese B2B market with a market share of 69.04 percent (Refer to Table I for market shares of B2B players in China).

C2C and B2C Market

Alibaba's increasing popularity and the burgeoning Chinese e-commerce market attracted several foreign competitors to China (Refer to Exhibit IV for e-commerce market in China). In 2002, US-based eBay Inc.[78] entered China by acquiring a 33 percent equity stake in the Shanghai-based e-commerce website EachNet.com,[79] at an investment of $30 million. eBay launched its Chinese site based on its business model in the U.S.. By 2002, it had emerged as one of the leading online auction sites in China with 3.5 million registered users.[80] By 2003, eBay had cornered a 79 percent market share in the Chinese online auction market.[81]

eBay's success in China and the good prospects offered by the budding e-commerce market, spurred Ma on to team up again with Son to start a rival website to compete with eBay. Ma raised funds up to $56 million from Softbank. Ma's decision to team with Son was due to Son's experience in defeating eBay in Japan by

---

[74] TradeManager is an instant communication tool that is offered to buyers and sellers for interaction.

[75] "Corporate Overview," www.alibaba.com, 2008.

[76] "Alibaba.com," www.lupaworld.com, May 29, 2007.

[77] "Alibaba.com," www.lupaworld.com, May 29, 2007.

[78] eBay Inc., headquartered in San Jose, California, USA, is the world's largest online auction company and had around 233 million online auction users in June 2007. In addition to providing online auction markets, eBay also has an online payment service called PayPal and a communications business under Skype, which offers Voice-over-Internet Protocol (VoIP) services. Its revenues for the fiscal year 2007 were $7.67 billion.

[79] Founded in August 1999 by Chinese entrepreneurs Bo Shao and Haiyin Tan, EachNet was a major electronic commerce company based in China. It was later acquired by eBay in July 2003.

[80] "eBay and EachNet Team up in China," www.investing.ebay.com, March 17, 2002.

[81] "eBay's Exit from China Opens the Door for News Corp.," www.seekingalpha.com, December 21, 2006.

EXHIBIT IV e-Commerce Market in China

Though the concept of e-commerce was introduced in China in 1993, it took some time for it to catch on. But once it did, e-commerce in China began to grow at a frantic pace. For instance, the market scale for e-commerce in China grew from RMB 120 billion in 2001 to RMB 680 billion in 2005.[82] In comparison to the overall e-commerce market, the C2C market was smaller but had kept pace with the growth in the overall market.

The e-commerce market was a surging market in China. According to iResearch, the online shopping market was estimated at RMB 12.26 billion for the second quarter of 2007.

Despite huge opportunities, the Chinese e-commerce market was not without its challenges. It was influenced by government regulations, logistics, and payment systems. The Chinese government enforced regulations related to Internet access, content regulation, encryption, and domain name.

The government also set certain provisions related to Internet access. There was a four-tier system for accessing the Internet. The first tier consisted of the Ministry of Information Industry[83] (MII) that acted as the main gateway for transmission of information to and from the World Wide Web. The MII operated an international gateway at the top of this system.

The second tier comprised four government-owned Internet Service Providers (ISPs), which were called the interconnected networks. The third tier comprised privately owned ISPs that were linked through the interconnected networks to the Internet. The final tier included the Internet users. The users could gain access to the Internet either through the government or privately owned ISPs. Internet users were instructed to register themselves with local public securities authorities as part of Internet security regulations.

The regulations related to security involved censoring the content and preventing dissemination of sensitive information relating to the Chinese economy. Under this regulation, all Internet companies were obliged to censor sensitive content.

Domain regulations required e-commerce companies to register their domain names with the CNNIC. The encryption regulation forced e-commerce companies to obtain approval from the National Commission on Encryption Code Regulations (NCECR), an encryption regulation agency, for using Chinese products and encrypted imported products.

Payment systems were another problem as Chinese consumers were used to paying cash rather than using credit cards. The consumers raised doubts over the security of the payment systems, the quality of the purchased products, and after sales service.

An inefficient logistics system was considered as another major constraint in the development of e-commerce. This was due to the underdeveloped transportation systems, inadequate use of technology, and inconsistent distribution systems which resulted in an unreliable logistics system.

Compiled from various sources.

collaborating with Yahoo! Japan. Subsequently, eBay had to move out of Japan in 2002. Ma, in association with his experienced employees, drafted a plan for launching a consumer auction website in his apartment in Hangzhou. Finally, they came up with the idea of launching Taobao, which means "digging for treasure."

In May 2003, Ma launched Taobao as a wholly-owned subsidiary of Alibaba. Taobao aimed to create an online trading platform for both B2C and C2C models. Taobao differentiated itself from rival eBay by allowing free listings on its website. eBay charged for listings on its website so as to ensure quality. According to Ma, a loyal customer base had to be built before could Taobao start charging for its services.

Analysts were uncertain about Taobao's success since the C2C market was still in its infancy in China. On the other hand, Ma was confident and cited the fact that EachNet had only five million users among the 82 million odd Internet users in China (Refer to Exhibit V for the growing Internet usage in China). Ma said, "We launched Taobao not to make money, but because in the US, eBay gets a lot of its revenue from small businesses. We knew that some day, eBay would come in our direction."[84]

To gain a strong foothold in the Chinese e-commerce market and combat competition from Taobao, eBay bought the remaining equity stake in EachNet for $150 million in July 2003. The website was called eBay EachNet.[85] Yibo Shao, one of the founders of EachNet who remained with eBay, believed that there

---

[82]"China E-commerce Profit Model Report, 2006-2007," www.researchinchina.com, January 2007.
[83]MII has the authority to regulate the software and communications industry and is accountable for the manufacture of electronic and information products. It is also responsible for information dissemination related to the Chinese economy.

[84] Susan Kuchinskas, "Jack Ma, CEO, Alibaba," www.venturetdf.com, October 22, 2004.
[85] eBay EachNet is a subsidiary of eBay Inc. in China.

EXHIBIT V Growing Internet Usage in China

Year	User	% of Population Using the Internet
2000	22,500,000	1.7
2001	33,700,000	2.6
2002	59,100,000	4.6
2003	69,000,000	5.4
2004	94,000,000	7.3
2005	103,000,000	7.9
2006	137,000,000	10.4
2007	162,000,000	12.3
2009	338,000,000	25.3

Adapted from "China Internet Usage Stats and Telecommunications Market Report," www.internetworldstats.com, 2007, and 2009.

could only be one big consumer auction site in China and predicted that eBay would win the race against Taobao. Soon after, Ma announced his plans to invest another $12 million in Taobao. He said that it would be unwise to wait until the market matured and hinted at using the money on building infrastructure, recruitment, and an online credit system for the customers.

Analysts have observed that the growth in the Chinese e-commerce market was hampered due to the absence of the trust factor between buyers and sellers while trading online. Buyers refused to send money to sellers before they had received the goods while sellers were unwilling to ship the goods until they had received payment. To counter this problem, Alibaba launched an online payment platform called "AliPay" based on the lines of eBay's payment system, Paypal, in 2004. AliPay was an escrow[86]-based payment solution which allowed customers to safely and quickly send and receive money online. Once a deal had been finalized, the buyer paid the money through AliPay. The money was held in an AliPay account and was sent to the seller only after the buyer intimated AliPay about the receipt of the product. Alibaba partnered with a number of Chinese banks such as China Merchants Bank, Agricultural Bank of China, etc. to provide AliPay services.

Alibaba devised an aggressive promotional strategy for Taobao in order to compete with eBay EachNet. Taobao advertised itself online by placing ads on the websites and through billboards in major city centers. All these promotional strategies were ignored by eBay EachNet. In the first quarter of 2004, eBay EachNet garnered a 90 percent market share in the Chinese online C2C market against Taobao's 9 percent. By the fourth quarter of 2004, Taobao's market share had jumped to 41 percent while eBay EachNet's had declined to 53 percent.[87] While eBay EachNet had about 10 million users,[88] Taobao quickly gained four million users[89] in 2004. Further, Taobao's easy-to-use features on the website attracted a number of users and resulted in users shifting to Taobao. Taobao provided additional features like e-mail and chat facilities to users on its site. It also allowed the buyers to call the sellers before buying a product while eBay EachNet concealed the seller's identity until the end of the auction and allowed communication only through offline messages that could be left on the site. Another reason cited for users shifting to Taobao was the difficulty they faced while using the new eBay website that was created after it fully acquired EachNet. The number of product listings decreased from 780,000 to 250,000 after the website was changed.[90] Further, the lack of a secure online payment system like AliPay hindered eBay EachNet's growth.

In 2005, eBay EachNet's market share slipped further to 29.1 percent compared to Taobao's 67.3 percent.[91] Taobao was ahead of eBay EachNet on various counts. Some of the parameters included the number of page views per user, which was 10.7 for Taobao and 7.4 for eBay EachNet in August 2005. At the same time, Taobao's listings generated a Gross Merchandise Volume[92] (GMV) of $120 million compared to eBay EachNet's GMV of $90 million.[93] Porter Erisman, Vice President for International Marketing of Alibaba, said in 2006, "The real source of eBay's woes in Asia is its inability to understand local market conditions in this part of the world."[94]

According to Ma, eBay's business model might work well in other countries of the world, but it would face difficulties in China because the Chinese consumers and their preferences were very different from those in other countries. Commenting on the rivalry with eBay, Ma said, "Taobao didn't win the first battle, but eBay lost it. eBay may be a shark in the ocean, but I am a crocodile in the Yangtze River. If we fight in the ocean, we lose—but if we fight in the river, we win."[95] Ma also had plans to link Alibaba and Taobao to facilitate trade between the members of the two sites.

---

[86] Escrow is a financial instrument held by a third party on behalf of the other two parties in a transaction. The funds are held by the escrow service until it receives the appropriate written or oral instructions or until obligations have been fulfilled (Source: www.dictionary.com).

[87] "China's Online Auction Market," www.bbb.typepad.com, March 2005.

[88] "eBay Outlines Global Business Strategy at 2005 Analyst Conference," www.investor.ebay.com, February 10, 2005.

[89] "China's Online Auction Market," www.bbb.typepad.com, March 2005.

[90] "Ebay Oversold Recently Standing up to a Giant," www.marketmillionaires.com, April 2005.

[91] "China Online Shopping Market Survey Report," www.cnnic.cn, May 2006.

[92] Gross Merchandise Volume refers to the total value derived from closed listings in the online trading market.

[93] Bill Powell and Jeffrey Resner, "Why Ebay Must Win in China," www.time.com, August 22, 2005.

[94] Ina Steiner, "Competitor Comments on eBay China Rumors," www.auctionbytes.com, November 8, 2006.

[95] Justin Doebele, "Standing up to eBay," www.forbes.com, March 18, 2005.

In October 2005, Ma announced a new strategy to phase out eBay EachNet from China—the services at Taobao would be offered free of charge for three consecutive years. Challenging eBay EachNet to follow its strategy, Ma said, "We call on eBay to do what's right for this phase of China's e-commerce development and make your services free for buyers and sellers in China. Cutting prices is not enough—it's time to make your services free and affordable for all of China's entrepreneurs and consumers."[96] In response, eBay issued a statement saying that free was not a business model and the fact that Taobao was providing its services for free spoke about eBay EachNet's success in China.

In May 2006, Ma announced his plans to launch B2C services on Taobao. By then, Taobao had already begun to outshine eBay EachNet by gaining more than 20 million users. According to Ma, the B2C services were launched with the aim of removing the middleman concept by directly connecting large sellers with consumers. For this, Taobao had already tied up with companies such as Motorola, the Haier Group, Nokia Corporation, Adidas Group, etc., and was aggressively planning to expand its product offerings. Analysts opined that a large number of Alibaba's 10 million members would join Taobao.

Sensing the need for the support of a local company to control its declining market share, eBay EachNet entered into a joint venture (JV) with TOM Online Inc.[97] (TOM Online) to form TOM eBay in December 2006. Subsequently, the company also stopped charging its sellers listing fees and decided that free was a business model. Despite all these efforts, TOM eBay continued to lose market share. According to Analysys, TOM eBay's market share plummeted from 16 percent in the first quarter of 2007 to 7.2 percent in the second quarter of 2007.[98] In sharp contrast, Taobao reported a market share of 82.95 percent in the second quarter of 2007 compared to its 74 percent market share in the first quarter of 2007.[99]

Industry observers opined that foreign companies failed to make a mark in China because of their lack of understanding of the language and culture. Shaun Rein, Managing Director, China Market Research Group (CMR),[100] said, "Alibaba and Taobao have been much more successful in China than their competitors because they were able to cater their services specifically for the China market. eBay, on the other hand, tried to bring what worked in the United States. But many other global- brand companies, like eBay or Google, run into this problem when they enter China: They simply do not adjust to local realities enough."[101]

Web Search Market

After having conquered the lucrative e-commerce market, Alibaba aimed to enter the lucrative Chinese online search market, considered the most popular Internet business. The Chinese web search was dominated by the strong local company Baidu which had mastered the Internet search market in the local language. Even the international leader in the search market, Google, could not crack the Chinese web search market. According to certain estimates by iResearch, around 49 percent of the C2C users visited a search engine before visiting C2C sites.[102]

In August 2005, Alibaba struck a deal to acquire the operations of Yahoo! in China. Alibaba acquired Yahoo! China's main website www.cn.yahoo.com and search engines including www.yisou.com and www.3721.com. Yahoo! invested $1 billion on acquiring an equity stake of 40 percent in Alibaba. This was the largest investment by a foreign company in an e-commerce business in China. With this deal, Alibaba expected to gain a strong foothold in the web search market while having its presence in the B2B, B2C, C2C e-commerce, and online payments segments, through its online payment solution, AliPay. Ma said, "With the addition of Yahoo! China to Alibaba.com's business, we're expanding our services to provide a leading search offering to China's Internet users. According to analysts, by defeating its arch-rival eBay and with Yahoo! China's acquisition, Alibaba had become the dominant player in the Chinese Internet market."

In addition to having a presence in the web search market, Alibaba's announcement that it would acquire Yahoo! China came after Baidu, China's leading online search engine launched an IPO in the US. According to Ma, the addition of Yahoo!'s Chinese operations would allow Alibaba to expand in the rapidly growing Chinese search engine market. Further, Ma aimed to use Yahoo!'s search engine to direct customers to its online commerce sites that linked foreign buyers with Chinese wholesalers. Alibaba aimed to expand its search engine by leveraging on its huge customer base coming from its B2B, B2C, and C2C sites.

In August 2005, Ma stopped the operations of yisou, a search engine built by Zhou Hongyi, former President, Yahoo! China. The search engine offered search facilities to users in addition to the Yahoo! China portal. In the same year, Ma also stopped using 3721, a search engine bought by Zhou in 2003. With all these changes, Ma developed a simple search page that was quite in contrast to the portal like features offered by Yahoo! China, in order to make Yahoo! China the number one search engine in China. However, this looked an uphill task as Yahoo! China continued to lose market share. Contrary to Ma's beliefs, Yahoo! China's acquisition did not help Alibaba gain a larger portion of the pie in the web search market since it was already dominated by strong players such as Baidu and Google. According to an internal research study by Yahoo! China, Baidu was the most favored choice among college students, Google and Yahoo! China were preferred by affluent and business-oriented customers. According to a survey by China

[96] Ina Steiner, "Alibaba Calls on eBay to Make China Site Free, eBay Responds," www.auctionbytes.com, October 20, 2005.
[97] TOM Online Inc., headquartered in Beijing, China was a leading internet company in China.
[98] Simon Burns, "Going Local no Help for eBay in China," www.vnunet.com, August 23, 2007.
[99] Simon Burns, "Going Local no Help for eBay in China," www.vnunet.com, August 23, 2007.
[100] China Market Research Group is a market research company based in Shanghai. It provides companies with data, strategic recommendations, and analyses that help companies understand consumer behavior and evaluate opportunities for long-term growth (Source: www.researchcmr.com).
[101] Sonia Kolesnikov-Jessop, "Spotlight: Jack Ma, Co-founder of Alibaba.com," www.iht.com, January 5, 2007.

[102] "Baidu to Enter Chinese E-Commerce Market," www.baidu.com, October 17, 2007.

Internet Network Information Center[103] (CNNIC), around 74.5 percent of Internet users in China preferred Baidu as an online search engine.[104]

According to estimates by iResearch in 2006, Baidu and Google were the two most popular search engines with market shares of 46.5 percent and 26.9 percent respectively, while Yahoo! China had a share of just about 15.6 percent share.[105] However, Ma dismissed competition from Google and said, "For the search engine, I think Google is very powerful. But it is not that powerful in China now."[106] Commenting on his strategy to defeat Google, Ma said, "We win eBay, buy Yahoo! and stop Google. That is for fun. Competition is for fun."[107]

In September 2006, Ma adopted a new homepage strategy by promoting Yahoo! China's home page as a separate search engine page. Commenting on Ma's strategy, Zhou said, "Now he [Ma] has completely flipped back and wants to rebuild Yahoo China into a portal. As a result, there's no search strategy. He continues to lose market share. There's brand ambiguity. No one's sure whether it's a search engine or a portal."[108]

Ma opined that Yahoo! China would have to leverage on its understanding of the Chinese consumers and chart its own path in the online search market. Describing Yahoo! China's future course of action, Ma said, "If you follow Google's way, you will always be a follower . . . We have to make the Yahoo! search engine more human, more interactive . . . something for the 1.3 billion people in China who aren't technology-oriented, who don't know how to ask the right questions to a search engine—for people who are like me."[109]

In January 2007, Ma announced his new strategy to reorganize the Yahoo! China portal into a business-oriented search engine. As part of its new strategy, Yahoo! China's search results were to be directed more toward corporate or business-oriented websites. Describing the new strategy, Ma said, "We don't want those not interested in business or making money. They can go to Baidu. Our main focus is the high-end. We don't need to compare ourselves with Baidu in market share."[110] Ma was confident that the new strategy would help Yahoo! China gain leadership and succeed in the highly competitive Chinese Internet market. Industry experts felt that by positioning itself in the high end segment, Yahoo! China would be on a different platform when compared to Baidu. But it would have to compete with Google, a dominant player in that

TABLE II Market Shares of Search Engine Players in China (Q3 2007)

Players	Market Shares (in %)
Baidu	60.5
Google	23.7
Yahoo! China	10.4
Zhong Sou	2
Sougou	1.4
Sina	0.5
Netease	0.5
Others	1

Adapted from Elmer W Cagape, "Baidu Corners 61.5% Market Share in China Search Engine Market in Q3," www.seo-hongkong.com, 2007.

segment. Baidu too was reported to have initiated efforts to woo the high end customers.

However, Yahoo! China continued to lose market share to Baidu and Google. According to Analysys, Baidu had cornered a market share of 60.5 percent and Google had garnered a market share of 23.7 percent while Yahoo! China lagged behind with 10.4 percent (Refer to Table II for market shares of search engine players in China). However, Ma had no plans to give up since the Chinese web search market had reached RMB 811.7 million in third quarter of 2007.[111]

The Much Awaited IPO

In October 2007, Alibaba went public on the Hong Kong stock exchange by launching an IPO. The IPO was arranged (underwritten) by Deutsche Bank AG,[112] Goldman Sachs, and Morgan Stanley.[113] [114] Over 85 percent of the shares in the IPO were marked for institutional investors. The IPO received very good response from both individual and institutional investors and the individual portion was oversubscribed by 257 times. The response prompted a reallocation of the individual-investor portion to 25 percent up from the initial 15 percent. The company raised US$1.5 billion from the IPO, the second largest IPO after Google with US$1.7 billion in 2004.[115] Alibaba sold a 17 percent stake consisting of 858.9 million shares at US$1.75 per share. Alibaba's shares opened at HK$30 on the first day of trading, almost double the price of their IPO of HK$13.5, and reached HK$39.55, a raise of nearly 200 percent at close. The share closing at HK$39.55 gave Alibaba a market value of US$25.7 billion. The IPO was the most expensive trading stock at the Hong Kong stock exchange where shares were valued at HK$17.5 billion.[116] The shares of

[103] The China Internet Network Information Center (CNNIC) is the state network information center of China, founded as a non-profit organization in June 1997. The Computer Network Information Center of the Chinese Academy of Sciences runs CNNIC. CNNIC looks after everything related to the Internet in China like domain names registration, IP addresses, relevant researches, surveys and information services, and international liaison and policy research.
[104] "Baidu Faces off Alibaba in Online Trading Market," www.ict.tdctrade.com, October 18, 2007.
[105] www.baiduyahoogoogle.com.cn
[106] "Alibaba's Chief Vows to Beat Google in China," www.blog.searchenginewatch.com, November 17, 2005.
[107] "Watch Jack Ma," www.battellemedia.com, November 19, 2005.
[108] Matt Marshall, "China Wars: Zhou Fights Back, Says Alibaba's Ma is Desperate," www.venturebeat.com, November 5, 2006.
[109] John Heilemann, "Jack Ma Aims to Unlock the Middle Kingdom," www.money.cnn.com, October 2, 2006.
[110] Christopher Bodeen, "Yahoo China Portal to Be Reorganized," www.washingtonpost.com, January 8, 2007.

[111] Elmer W Cagape, "Baidu Corners 61.5% Market Share in China Search Engine Market in Q3," www.seo-hongkong.com, 2007.
[112] Deutsche Bank AG, headquartered in Frankfurt, Germany is an international financial institution whose main products include banking and insurance.
[113] Morgan Stanley, headquartered in New York City, New York, USA, is a leading investment banking and financial services corporation in the world.
[114] "Alibaba IPO Approved in Hong Kong," www.tagedge.com, October 6, 2007.
[115] "Alibaba IPO Boosts Yahoo!" www.seekingalpha.com, November 7, 2007.
[116] Amy Or, Lorraine Luk, and Sky Canaves, "China IPO Frenzy Rolls on with Alibaba.com Debut—Shares of B2B Site Skyrocket as Investors Buy its Growth Story," www.resources.alibaba.com, November 7, 2007.

Alibaba traded almost 155 times the estimated earnings of Alibaba for the next year. The shares of Google were trading at 36 times of the estimated profits for the next year during the same period.[117]

With this IPO, Ma aimed to position Alibaba's business model on a global scale. According to Ma, "This is a golden opportunity, one we probably won't see again for another 20 years. Sure we could just be like an easy guy and enjoy life. But by going public now, we have a chance to be a focus of attention—not just from China but from the rest of the world—to say, 'Hey, e-commerce in China can make money; it can help China get to the next stage.' When the time comes, you have to grab it."[118] Ma aimed to spend around 60 percent of the earnings raised through the IPO on acquisitions and enhancing its technologies, another 20 percent for development of its Chinese and international sites. The remaining was expected to be used as working capital. Ma announced that using the IPO proceeds, the company would expand in Europe considering the growth potential in the European market. According to Wei, "With more than 20 mln SMEs, Europe is a very important market for us."[119]

Even though the Alibaba IPO was hugely successful, analysts and industry observers criticized it, saying it had been valued too high. Some others opined that Alibaba could justify the high valuation if it could increase its revenues by making its customers pay for its services. Commenting on the high valuation, Rafe Xu, an analyst at Sinopac Securities Asia Ltd., a financial services company, said, "It's a high valuation but if Alibaba can use its leadership position in the e-commerce market to get more Chinese businesses to pay for its services, it will justify it. They have a lot of work to do."[120] However, the investors justified the price considering the huge growth outlook of the company. Ma also justified the pricing by showing the post IPO performance of its shares on the stock market. The other senior executives of the company too defended the higher valuation in view of the huge future growth potential of the company. Some analysts even attributed the spectacular success of the Alibaba IPO to the rise in the demand for the Chinese companies' shares.

According to certain estimates by Goldman Sachs, the IPO was expected to boost Alibaba's earnings to US$166 million with profits estimated at RMB 1.02 billion in 2008.[121] However, they were also of the view that Alibaba had to tap a huge customer base since only a percent of the 24.6 million registered users it had were paying members. The rest were using the services free of charge. With this IPO, Alibaba aimed to focus on increasing its community of users while providing enhanced services to customers who were paying a premium in the range RMB 2800 to 60,000. The company also had ambitious plans to tap the Asian markets like India and Japan.

Outlook

China was well poised to unseat the U.S. as the country with the largest number of Internet users in the first few months of 2008. The growing Internet user base in China had thrown up good opportunities for Internet companies. According to BDA China,[122] the number of Internet users in China had reached 210 million in 2007, a growth of 50 percent compared to 2006. According to Nielsen's ratings, the Internet users in the U.S. had reached 216 million in 2007.[123] Given the attractiveness of the Chinese Internet market, analysts opined that Internet companies that could crack the market would be rewarded handsomely.

As of June 30, 2007, Alibaba had grown into a $125 million company with about 4,400 employees generating business from across the world (Refer to Exhibit VI for country/region wise business generated on Alibaba.com's international site). It planned to increase its revenues by offering new services to its customers in the future. According to Ma's projections, Alibaba would achieve revenues of $1.25 billion in 2009.[124] According to Wei, the revenue target could be achieved by extending the services offered to its users. Wei said, "There will be new services for payment, logistics as well as services to support small companies' internal operations, such as information technology, human resource management, and legal advice."[125] Analysts felt that its business model provided Alibaba with enough space for future growth. "Alibaba is the largest B2B e-commerce portal on the mainland. Room for organic growth is still enormous. Given the nature of Alibaba's business model that connects business to business, rather than business to consumer, the competition is less intense, allowing

EXHIBIT VI   Country/Region Wise Business on Alibaba.com's International Site

Country/Region	Business (in %)
USA	21
Europe	21
India	7
South-east Asia	5
China	4
Hong Kong	4
Singapore and Malaysia	4
Canada	4
Australia	3
Others	27

Adapted from "Alibaba.com Company Introduction," www.asocio.org.

---

[117] Mark Lee and John Liu, "Alibaba Shares Triple in Hong Kong Trading Debut (Update8)," www.bloomberg.com, November 6, 2007.
[118] Clay Chandler, "China's Web King," *Fortune*, December 10, 2007.
[119] "China's Alibaba.com Aims to Expand in Europe through Acquisitions—CEO," www.forbes.com, December 28, 2007.
[120] Mark Lee and John Liu, "Alibaba Shares Triple in Hong Kong Trading Debut (Update8)," www.bloomberg.com, November 6, 2007.
[121] Mark Lee and John Liu, "Alibaba Shares Triple in Hong Kong Trading Debut (Update8)," www.bloomberg.com, November 6, 2007.

[122] BDA China is an advisory firm offering advisory services to companies to invest in telecommunications, media, and technology (TMT) sector.
[123] "China Overtakes U.S. as Largest Internet Market," www.eetasia.com, March 17, 2008.
[124] Jean-Philippe Massin, "Alibaba Thinks Big: US$ 1.25 Billion Revenue in 2009," www.massin.nl.
[125] Jean-Philippe Massin, "Alibaba Thinks Big: US$ 1.25 Billion Revenue in 2009," www.massin.nl.

a more stable and lucrative income stream,"[126] said Kenny Tang, Associate Director, Tung Tai Securities Co. Ltd.,[127]

Alibaba, however, faced a threat to its e-commerce business from other strong domestic players like Baidu. According to analysts, Baidu being the leader in the web search market could gain a strong foothold in the Chinese e-commerce market. Another challenge for Alibaba was to compete with the free services provided by its arch-rivals Baidu and Google. The threat was intensifying as Alibaba was planning to charge its customers for some of its services. The company was expected to face difficulties while convert-

ing its free model into a paid model. Analysts said that it would become difficult for Alibaba to charge for its services in view of the free services offered by its competitors. According to Edward Yu, Chief Executive, Analysys, "It's going to be more difficult to convert them from free to paid than it was in the past one to two years."[128]

Regarding his vision for the future, Ma said, "My vision is to build an e-commerce ecosystem that allows consumers and businesses to do all aspects of business online."[129] Flush with funds from the IPO, the company was also preparing to strengthen its global footprint.

Questions for Discussion

1. Critically analyze the factors that led to Alibaba sustaining its leadership position in the Chinese e-commerce market.
2. Discuss the rationale behind Ma establishing Taobao.com. What are the factors that led to Taobao's success as compared to eBay in the Chinese online auctions market? With Baidu's entry into the e-commerce market, discuss the challenges that Alibaba faces

with regard to sustaining its position in the growing e-commerce market in China.
3. Critically examine Alibaba's business model. Do you think it is sustainable? After having captured the Chinese e-commerce market, what steps should Alibaba take to expand globally?

References and Suggested Readings

1. "Fast as a Rabbit, Patient as a Turtle," www.resources.alibaba.com, July 3, 2000.
2. Justin Deobele, "B2B for the Little Guys," www.forbes.com, July 24, 2000.
3. "Alibaba's Magic Carpet is Losing Altitude," www.businessweek.com, April 9, 2001.
4. "eBay and EachNet Team up in China," www.investing.ebay.com, March 17, 2002.
5. "Alibaba is to Land at Japan, as Planned," www.resources.alibaba.com, October 17, 2002.
6. Sumie Kawakami, "China's Visionary B2B: Who Says the Dot-com Era is over? Alibaba.com Thrives as Chinese Imports and Exports Boom. CEO Jack Ma Has a Vision: Helping SMEs Buy and Sell Goods through his Sites—Upfront—Company Profile," www.encyclopedia.com, May 2003.
7. Susan Kuchinskas, "Jack Ma, CEO, Alibaba," www.venturetdf.com, October 22, 2004.
8. "eBay Outlines Global Business Strategy at 2005 Analyst Conference," www.investor.ebay.com, February 10, 2005.
9. Justin Doebele, "Standing up to eBay," www.forbes.com, March 18, 2005.
10. "China's Online Auction Market," www.bbb.typepad.com, March 2005.
11. "Open Sesame to the Net Highway," www.crienglish.com, April 17, 2005.
12. "Ebay Oversold Recently Standing up to a Giant," www.marketmillionaires.com, April 2005.
13. "Meet Jack Ma, Who Will Guide Yahoo in China," www.bdachina.com, August 12, 2005.
14. Bill Powell and Jeffrey Resner, "Why Ebay Must Win in China," www.time.com, August 22, 2005.
15. Ina Steiner, "Alibaba Calls on eBay to Make China Site Free, eBay Responds," www.auctionbytes.com, October 20, 2005.
16. "Alibaba's Chief Vows to Beat Google in China," www.blog.searchenginewatch.com, November 17, 2005.
17. "Watch Jack Ma," www.battellemedia.com, November 19, 2005.
18. Chua Chin Hon, "Yahoo! Jack Wants it to be No.1 in China," www.asiamedia.ucla.edu, April 28, 2006.
19. "Taobao.com Launches B2C Services," www.resources.alibaba.com, May 10, 2006.
20. "China Online Shopping Market Survey Report," www.cnnic.cn, May 2006.
21. John Heilemann, "Jack Ma Aims to Unlock the Middle Kingdom," www.money.cnn.com, October 2, 2006.
22. Matt Marshall, "China Wars: Zhou Fights Back, Says Alibaba's Ma is Desperate," www.venturebeat.com, November 5, 2006.
23. "eBay's Exit from China Opens the Door for News Corp.," www.seekingalpha.com, December 21, 2006.
24. Sonia Kolesnikov-Jessop, "Spotlight: Jack Ma, Co-founder of Alibaba.com," www.iht.com, January 5, 2007.
25. Christopher Bodeen, "Yahoo China Portal to Be Reorganized," www.washingtonpost.com, January 8, 2007.
26. Elizabeth Millard, "The Mushrooming Chinese Internet Market," www.ecommercetimes.com, January 11, 2007.
27. "China E-commerce Profit Model Report, 2006–2007," www.researchinchina.com, January 2007.
28. "Alibaba.com," www.lupaworld.com, May 29, 2007.
29. "Taobao.com Triples to Beat eBay," www.chinaeconomicreview.com, July 25, 2007.
30. Simon Burns, "Going Local No Help for eBay in China," www.vnunet.com, August 23, 2007.

---

[126] Karen Cho, "Alibaba Bumps up IPO Price," www.chinadaily.com, October 23, 2007.
[127] Tung Tai Securities Co. Ltd. headquartered in Hong Kong, China, is an investment expertise and stock brokerage services firm.

[128] Fara Warner, "Alibaba.com's Helm," www.forbes.com, November 26, 2007.
[129] "How I Did It: Jack Ma, Alibaba.com," www.inc.com, January 2008.

31. "CNNIC Reports Baidu with 74.5% Market Share," www. chinatechstory.blogspot.com, September 25, 2007.

32. "Analysys International Says Alibaba, Global Sources and Made-in-China.com Led China Online B2B Market in Q2 2007," www. english.analysys.com, September 2007.

33. "Alibaba.com Opens its First European Office in Geneva," www. alibaba.com, October 2, 2007.

34. "Alibaba IPO Approved in Hong Kong," www.tagedge.com, October 6, 2007.

35. Bei Hu and John Liu, "Alibaba.com Offers $1.3 Billion Share Sale," www.iht.com, October 15, 2007.

36. "Baidu to Enter Chinese E-Commerce Market," www.baidu.com, October 17, 2007.

37. "Baidu Faces off Alibaba in Online Trading Market," www.ict. tdctrade.com, October 18, 2007.

38. Karen Cho, "Alibaba Bumps up IPO Price," www.chinadaily.com, October 23, 2007.

39. Mark Lee and John Liu, "Alibaba Shares Triple in Hong Kong Trading Debut (Update8)," www.bloomberg.com, November 6, 2007.

40. Amy Or, Lorraine Luk, and Sky Canaves, "China IPO Frenzy Rolls on with Alibaba.com Debut—Shares of B2B Site Skyrocket as Investors Buy its Growth Story," www.resources.alibaba.com, November 7, 2007.

41. "Alibaba IPO Boosts Yahoo!" www.seekingalpha.com, November 7, 2007.

42. Fara Warner, "Alibaba.com's Helm," www.forbes.com, November 26, 2007.

43. Clay Chandler, "China's Web King," *Fortune*, December 10, 2007.

44. "China's Alibaba.com Aims to Expand in Europe through Acquisitions – CEO," www.forbes.com, December 28, 2007.

45. "Internet in China: Taobao Transaction Volume Tripled in First Half of 2007," www.designative.info, 2007.

46. Elmer W Cagape, "Baidu Corners 61.5% Market Share in China Search Engine Market in Q3," www.seo-hongkong.com, 2007.

47. "210 Million Internet Users in China," www.english.peopledaily. com, January 21, 2008.

48. "How I Did It: Jack Ma, Alibaba.com," www.inc.com, January 2008.

49. "Alibaba.com Named One of the World's Most Innovative Companies," www.resources.alibaba.com, February 21, 2008.

50. "China Overtakes U.S. as Largest Internet Market," www. eetasia.com, March 17, 2008.

51. "Corporate Overview," www.alibaba.com, 2008.

52. Jean-Philippe Massin, "Alibaba Thinks Big: US$ 1.25 Billion Revenue in 2009," www.massin.nl.

53. www.baiduyahoogoogle.com.cn

54. www.researchcmr.com

A. Strategic rise: Building a global powerhouse (January 1988–December 1996)

ABB Asea Brown Boveri (ABB) was formed on 5th January 1988 from the merger of Asea AB (Sweden) and BBC Brown Boveri (Switzerland). Each company took a 50 percent holding in ABB. However, because of ABB's higher profitability and market capitalisation, BBC agreed to contribute $508m in addition to its main assets. Initially, the merger created an organisation of 700 companies, 2,500 factories in 25 countries, 160 000 employees and revenues of almost $18bn. By the end of 1996 employees and revenue had grown to 215,000 and $34bn respectively and could meet customer requirements in the global arena.

Situational factors leading to the merger

The effect of the GATT rounds after WW2 contributed significantly to economic expansion in the developed industrialised countries and in some SE Asian countries. This economic expansion led to a significant rise in the demand for the generation, transmission and distribution of electricity to fuel the increasing demands of growing industries and domestic populations particularly in the 1960s and the early 1970s. Initially such demand was served by companies located within their own national boundaries developing capacity to meet this increased demand. Economic growth rates slowed from the mid-1970s due to the four-fold increase in the price of oil leading to higher inflation rates and periodic economic downturns thereafter. These factors inevitably led to lower demand rates for power generation and supply resulting in over capacity within many companies particularly within Europe. However, developments within the European Community began to offer companies a way out of this impasse. These may be determined as:

1. The lowering and eventual elimination of internal tariff barriers thus offering opportunities and flexibility in pricing strategies across national borders.
2. Public procurement policies began to indicate that any company involved in power generation, transmission and distribution contacts could bid for electricity utility contracts across their national borders thus offering such companies greater geographic freedom within the area of public procurement.
3. The continuing effect of the GATT rounds in the lowering of global tariffs also offered opportunities in areas outside the European Community notably North America.

This case was written by Dr Robert M Mulligan, Richmond of the American International University in London. It is intended to be used as the basis for class discussion rather than to illustrate either effective or ineffective handling of a management situation. The case was compiled from published sources.

© 2008, Richmond The American International University in London.

No part of this publication may be copied, stored, transmitted, reproduced or distributed in any form or medium whatsoever without the permission of the copyright owner. *Printed with permission from the author and www.ecch.com*

These economic and political drivers offered proactive electricity utility supply companies a way to rationalise spare capacity in the European Community and to build international strategies to meet and match major competitors.

Internally the main executive driving force for the merger was the CEO of Asea, Percy Barnevik who was born in 1941 in Skåne, southern Sweden, where his parents operated a small printing shop. He had a varied career with Sandvik between 1969–79 ending up as CEO of Sandvik Steel in the USA from 1975–79 during which time he tripled revenues to $250m and turned the company into profit. In 1979 he joined Asea, a leading Swedish industrial company where he was CEO from 1979–88. His understanding of the environmental forces affecting the heavy engineering industry in Europe and beyond and his ability to communicate and influence colleagues to see his point-of-view enabled the merger to be completed in January 1988. Barnevik became president and CEO of the merged entity in 1988 supported by a deputy and eleven executive vice presidents. The merger created an organisation of 700 companies, 160,000 employees in 25 countries with combined revenue of $18bn. and an initial free cash flow of $4bn, which was used for expansion and acquisition purposes. In the six years to 1994 ABB acquired more than 150 companies worldwide and by 1996 was transformed by such acquisitions, joint ventures, and internal expansion into a global company operating in all the major regions of the world i.e. Europe, Middle East, Africa, Asia and the Americas with some 215,000 employees generating $34bn in revenue. By this time the company had been organised into a matrix structure comprising eight major business segments (power generation plants, power transmission, power distribution, industrial engineering, transportation, environmental control, financial services and other activities), 65 major business areas spread between business segments and 1300 SBUs.

Core business segments were seen as power generation plants, high voltage power transmission of electricity, medium and low voltage distribution of electricity and industrial engineering. These four areas contributed over 50 percent of total revenue (Johnson and Scholes 2002).

The Percy Barnevik management philosophy

It was Percy Barnevik's inimitable management style that forged the rapid strategic expansion of ABB over these years. There is no doubt that his management philosophy was heavily influenced by the entrepreneurial experience gained in his parent's small printing shop and his expansionist style in Sandvik. His goal was to build a company that could conduct business in each of the major areas of the world. To do this Barnevik's focus was on:

1. **The development of a group-wide umbrella culture**: This was fostered by the use of English as the common language and the use of the US dollar as the global reporting currency. Most importantly, from the very beginning ABB established a common set of values, policies and operational guidelines to safeguard and promote

this umbrella culture. Not withstanding this approach, Barnevik recognised that ABB had deep roots in many countries and, as such, fostered respect for national cultures and differences by forging strong local identities in each of ABB's many home markets.

2. **The development of core technologies and core competencies**: This meant being a technology leader and market share leader in as many of the eight major business segments as possible. Such positions would, in time, bring lower operating costs and wider profit margins than experienced by competitors together with an ability to combat competitive attacks on their customer base.

3. **The development and use of multinational teams:** The main idea was to build a company that cut across cultural differences and solved problems quickly: The use of such teams started at the top after the merger with ABB's supervisory board of eight people made up of four nationalities and its eight-man executive committee consisting of German, Swedish, Swiss, American and Danish executives. Barnevik believed that the use of such teams throughout the company gave a deeper insight into global and local business problems. For example, the benchmarking of global operational performance became routine; the rotation of specialists across borders helped transfer best practices to different parts of the world and unique complementary skills and backgrounds were used to develop new markets e.g. Austrian team members helped develop access to Hungarian and Slovakian markets; Scandinavian team members helped develop markets in the Baltic states; Chinese-speaking team members from Singapore, Hong Kong, and Taiwan helped in the development of Chinese markets and Brazilians and Argentines helped in ABB's Latin American expansion.

4. **Application to the development of effective global managers:** Competence was the key to selection not creed or culture. Barnevik was of the opinion that few people have the ability to work well in and lead multicultural teams because it takes patience, cultural understanding and the ability to communicate in addition to having the other required managerial competencies. He also believed that global managers were made, not born. Therefore to affect such skills he opined and developed within ABB the transfer of such management potential to different countries for some years to learn deeper insights into different cultures. Such measures he believed were important for the development of effective global managers and multinational team members.

5. **Building a multi-domestic or federal organisation along a global-local continuum:** This essentially meant that some companies would be super-local (electrical installation and service) and some would be super-global (combined-cycle power plants and high-voltage DC stations). Most, however, would fall between the two extremes. However, wherever ABB conducted business it strived to develop deep local roots to get close to customers.

6. **The development of effective communication, understanding, and patience:** These were common denominators to fuse all the other elements discussed above throughout the group. There was no question in Barnevik's mind that the price to pay for a high degree of "multi-nationality" was a major investment in two-way communication and consensus building across all borders: such investment would allow communication not only by making full use of technology but also by the organisation of face-to-face meetings and team work.

7. **The development of a customer focus programme:** The main focus here was to permanently change the company's value system and orient every employee towards the customer. Raising quality and service levels was a key part of this programme. Secondary benefits from this were increased employee participation in running SBUs and the raising of competence levels via continuous training programmes. Barnevik believed that only skilled motivated people who understood the importance of their customers would deliver long- lasting competitive advantage.

For Barnevik, openness, trust and respect were the key words in all of this. At the end of the day, all people were 'local' with their roots in some home country. He was in no doubt that it would take a major, systematic and sustained effort to bridge all borders, build multi-national teams and thereby create a truly international organisation. Barnevik believed that all the above factors were essential and worthwhile (Taylor 1991).

Organisational structure

Initially Percy Barnevik and the Executive Management Committee (EMC) organised ABB as a decentralised matrix structure with the matrix organised along two dimensions viz; business segments and geographic regions (Exhibit I).

The purpose of this decentralised structure was to:

• Identify and analyse the total needs of the customer and the market in which they operated.
• Improve communication within the company such that the company could respond quickly to customer. To this

EXHIBIT I Outline matrix structure

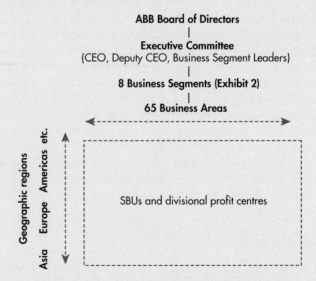

Source: Johnson and Scholes (1992), *Exploring Corporate Strategy*, Prentice Hall, 358

end the matrix structure was relatively flat incorporating only four layers from the CEO to each national SBU.

- Increase and improve company responsiveness to customer requirements.
- Improve product and service quality.
- Decrease operating cycle times.
- Assess and evaluate the company in terms of outcomes as seen from the viewpoint of the customer.

To try to ensure that all these objectives were achieved each business segment along the first dimension had an ECM executive responsible and accountable for it. Business Area (BA) executives within each business segment responded to the ECM for that segment. For example, the 'Industry' segment, (segment 4) had 7 BAs (Exhibit II). These BA leaders reported to an ECM member that was initially a German who worked out of Stamford, Connecticut. Each BA executive was responsible for optimising the business on a global basis. The BA executive was responsible and accountable for global strategy, product and product development, marketing, production and R&D without regard to national borders. For example initially the BA executive for power transformers (segment 2) was responsible for 25 factories in 16 countries and worked out of Germany but was not necessarily German; the BA executive for electric metering (segment 2) worked out of North Carolina in the USA and was not necessarily American. Along the second geographic dimension was a set of traditionally functionally organised national companies (SBUs and divisional profit centres) each serving its home market. Each SBU consisted of no more than 50 employees and was responsible for its own product development, production, sales and its own balance sheet. By 1991 there were 1100 such local country SBUs around the world. Within each main country a national company was formed of which each SBU in that country was a subsidiary. This national company had its own CEO or president. Thus the BA structure (first dimension) met the national country structure (second dimension) at the level of the ABB member SBUs (Taylor 1991). This can be represented in a short schematic (Exhibit III).

The success of the overall structure essentially depended on the leadership skills of the BA executives. It was they who were responsible for optimizing the business on a global basis. He/she devised and championed the global strategy of their respective business area; held factories around the world to cost and quality; allocated export markets to each factory and shared expertise by rotating people across borders thereby creating mixed nationality teams to solve problems and build a culture of communication and trust. The main components of this structure can thus be seen as providing for multi-cultural management, focused flexibility, tight decentralised control, flat structure (4-layers) for more effective communication, strict decentralisation, closeness to customer and a focus on quality, R&D and cycle times. All conducted along a global-to-local continuum.

Period of expansion

In the six year period between October 1988 and 1994 ABB acquired over 150 companies worldwide. Although the merger between Asea and Brown Boveri created a cash pile of $4bn the

extent of the acquisitions cost ABB around $12bn in the key Power (principally power generation) and Industry business segments of its business. Additionally, a series of joint ventures, mainly in the Power segments (principally power generation and transmission) but also in the Transportation segment (railway) added to the network. Some of these acquisitions and JVs were made in the mature markets of Western Europe (Germany, Italy, UK, Denmark, Sweden, and Finland) but acquisitions and JVs were also made in the faster growing areas of Eastern Europe and Asia. A significant acquisition was also made in the USA in 1989: this was Combustion Engineering (CE), an unprofitable manufacturer of power generation equipment such as boilers, nuclear plants and related equipment. The acquisition cost ABB $1.6bn and was made at a premium of 57 percent over CE's share price. It was an acquisition which was to cause ABB a lot of grief later on and will be discussed later at length. Barnevik's rationale for the expansion strategy was to move away from too heavy a dependency on mature Western European, build a greater presence in the key North American markets and expand into faster growing and less mature markets of Eastern Europe (East Germany, Poland, Czechoslovakia, Ukraine, Romania and Russia) and Asia. In essence this was classic strategy in that it sought to spread economic risk and build a balanced global portfolio of SBUs in ABB's key segments such that the company could become a global player for the long term. Thus by the end of 1995 ABB had established a network of 60 companies in Eastern Europe and the former Soviet Union giving it the largest manufacturing operation of any western company in the region. The expansion in Asia was more cautious. In 1992 more than 20 new manufacturing and service operations were established in the region through investments, acquisitions and JVs (Barham and Heimer 1998). This process continued in 1993 and 1994 including a $1bn investment in Malaysia to build a power plant. By 1995 ABB's Asian operations had 30,000 employees and 100 plants, engineering, servicing and marketing centres (www.fundinguniverse.com)

Period of major restructuring

Barnevik realised that such expansion could create problems in the matrix structure as originally designed for two basic reasons. Firstly, the world was becoming more regionalised by 1993. He reasoned that the EU was becoming a strong economic entity and could achieve economic parity with the USA as more European countries joined in the years ahead. Additionally, the North American Free Trade Association (NAFTA) was formed and the Asian countries were becoming more of an economic entity with economic power. These three geographic regions of the world were often referred to as "Triad economies" and were responsible for a vast and increasing proportion of world GDP (currently in excess of 80 percent). ABB needed to have strong representation in each of these three regions and needed structural systems in place that catered for this increased geographic spread and operational complexity. Secondly, the matrix structures of such size and reach can cause control and communication problems. In particular the dual reporting nature of matrix structures has always

EXHIBIT II Business segments and major business areas within

1 Power Plants	2 Power Transmission	3 Power Distribution	4 Industry	5 Transportation	6 Environmental Control	7 Financial Services	8 Other activities
Gas turbine	Cables & capacitors	Low-voltage gear	Drives	Rolling stock	Air pollution control	Treasury	Power lines
	Transformers	LV systems	Automation	Mass transit	Indoor climate	Financing	Contracting
Industrial Steam	Electric Metering	Installation	Marine, oil, and gas	Fixed railway installations	Resource recovery	Insurance	Installation
Pressurised Fluidized bed combustion systems	High-voltage switchgear	Medium-voltage equipment	Process engineering	Signalling	Colling	Trading and trade finance	Service
Hydro-power Plans	Network control	Distribution plants	Instrumentation	Complete rail systems	Industrial environmental services	Stockbrokerage	Motors & Robotics
Nuclear plants	Power systems		Metallurgy	Railway maintenance	Industrial drying	Investment management	Robotics
Control systems	Power transformers		Semiconductors		Paint finishing systems		Supercharges
Fossil Combustion Services & Systems	Relays						Telecommunications District heating IT systems

Source: Developed from Johnson and Scholes (1992), Exploring Corporate Strategy, Prentice Hall 363–64.

EXHIBIT III   Business Segment/Business Area/Country SBU: Control parameters

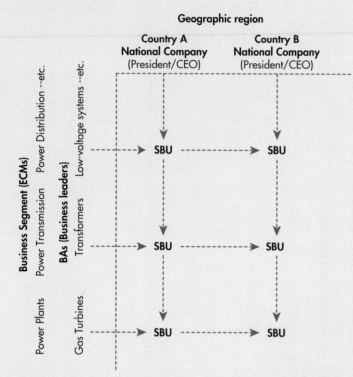

Note: The CEO of each SBU would in this structure report to two bosses—the BA Leader, located usually outside the country, and the President/CEO of the national company of which the local company would be a subsidiary (SBU). At this intersection, the ABB "multi-domestic" structural concept became a reality.

Source: Author's compilation

EXHIBIT IV   Restructured matrix 1993

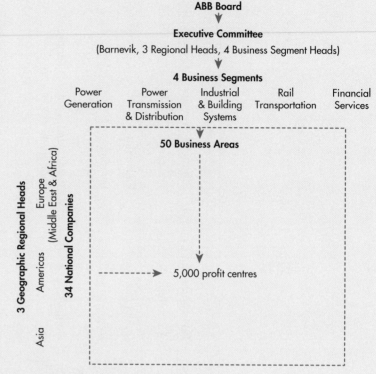

Source: Author's compilation

created friction between executives. This was also the experience within ABB. In particular the Business Area leaders (BAs) within each Business Segment clashed with the National Country executives. BA leaders, as noted, were responsible for optimising their particular business on a global basis. The National Country executives were at president/CEO level and were responsible for SBUs and profit centres within their country. Each National Country president/CEO had to ensure that regional targets were met and contacts were established and strengthened with governments, trade unions, communities, customers and the media. The CEO of each SBU then had to report to both the BA leader and the National Country president/CEO. This arrangement, as in most matrix structures caused friction between them. There was always a conflict of interest and tugs-of war between them to such an extent that speed of communication became damaged which was, of course, a key requirement of the highly decentralised group. In many instances, Barnevik himself had to spend a lot of time moving back and forth to personally intervene and interact with them to sort out conflicts.

To counter these problem areas Barnevik carried out a major restructuring in 1993 along the two main dimensions of the structure i.e. geographic regions and business segments. The geographic dimension was reorganised into three geographic regions viz; Europe (including the Middle East and

Africa), the Americas and Asia and three Geographic Regional Heads were appointed to oversee the national country structure which was retained (Exhibit IV). In effect Barnevik introduced an extra layer of management to the geographic structure in an attempt to limit the friction between National Country Executives and BA Leaders. The three regional heads were put onto the Executive Management Committee thus creating powerful regional positions for regional management. The business segment dimension was reorganised into four main segments viz; power generation (formerly power plants), power transmission and distribution, industrial and building systems (formerly industry, environmental control and other activities) and rail transportation (formerly transportation). Financial Services was retained but not constituted as a main business segment. The Executive Management Committee was reduced in size to include only Barnevik, the three regional executives and the remaining ECMs.

Whether this restructuring would eliminate friction between national Country Managers and Business Leaders is a moot point but at least the new regional heads would be able to discuss conflict issues at EMC level rather than having Barnevik travel extensively and intervene to solve such problems. Further restructuring took place in January 1996 when ABB merged its Rail Transportation segment with Daimler-Benz AG to form ABB Daimler-Benz Transportation GmbH (ADtranz) a 50:50 joint- venture that immediately became the largest provider of rail systems in the world. In order to create the 50:50 element of the merger Daimler Benz paid ABB some $900m in cash (www.fundinguniverse.com.) On the

1st January 1997 Barnevik relinquished his position as CEO of ABB but became Chairman. The new CEO was Göran Lindahl, a 25-year company veteran and previously head of the Power Transmission & Distribution segment. During Barnevik's time as CEO ABB's revenue nearly doubled from $17.8bn to $33.77bn. Although Barnevik's stated goal of 10 percent operating margin was not achieved: it did achieve a peak operating margin of 9.7 percent in 1995 before it fell back to 8.8 percent in 1996. However, through acquisition strategy, joint ventures and organic growth, he achieved a global reach for the company to a far greater extent than either ASEA or Brown Boveri could have achieved by acting independently. However, the achievement of this objective was not enough to save his reputation.

B. Strategic decline: Operational problems and shift to a "knowledge" company (January 1997 – September 2002)

Göran Lindahl as CEO (January 1997—December 2000)

During the late 1990s and into 2000, Lindahl left his mark on ABB through a number of initiatives. These were concerned with major restructuring and a planned change to a so-called "knowledge" company. In October 1997 he announced a major restructuring in which he planned to move thousands of manufacturing jobs from Europe and USA to Asia. The plan was to cut 10,000 jobs over an 18- month period. This move was planned despite the heavy downturn of Asian economies during this period. ABB executives reasoned that the Asian economic crisis would be short-term and the company could benefit from devalued currencies in the Asian region which would reduce manufacturing costs and improve exports from the region. To cover the costs of this move ABB took a charge of $850million in the fourth quarter of 1997. In August 1998 another major restructuring was carried out in which the geographic regional reporting structure was reduced in favour of a realignment of business activities on global lines. In addition, some of the business segments were broken up into smaller and more focused categories. In particular the industrial and building systems segment was split into three new segments: automation, products/contracting and oil/gas/petrochemicals (OGC). The power transmission and distribution segment was returned to its initial segments of power transmission and power distribution. The power generation and financial services segment remained unchanged. This essentially meant that ABB now had eight segments including the ADtranz joint venture (www.fundinguniverse.com).

The change to a "knowledge" company involved a strategic shift away from traditional heavy engineering activities of power generation and railway transportation systems towards a focus on high-tech "knowledge-based" sectors particularly automation, industrial robots and factory control systems. ABB were already represented in these areas to some extent but in a limited way (Exhibit II). One of the internal drivers for this transformation was to increase ABB's revenues by about one-third by 2001. In order to give this change impetus ABB acquired Elsag Bailey Process Automation N.V. a Netherlands-based manufacturer of industrial control systems for $2.1bn. in October 1998. It was the largest acquisition in ABB's history.

This deal made ABB's automation segment the world's leading manufacturer of robotics and automated control systems with annual revenues of $8.5bn. (ABB Annual Report 2001) Rationalisation out of heavy engineering occurred when in January 1999 ABB divested its 50 percent share of ADtranz to DaimlerChrysler AG in for $472mn. In March 1999 it merged its power generation segment with ALSTOM of France to form ABB ALSTOM Power[1] but subsequently sold its 50 percent interest in May 2000 to ALSTOM for $1.2bn. In May 2000 ABB sold its nuclear power business to the UK's BNFL for $485 mn.

All these changes meant that ABB now had six business segments comprising Power Transmission, Power Distribution, Automation, Products/Contracting, Oil/Gas/Petrochemicals and Financial Services (Exhibit VA). The matrix structure was essentially run down when the regional dimension was discontinued. Essentially the global nature of the structure was product focused. These changes were favourably received at the time. Lindahl shared Barnevik's thinking in moving ABB to a knowledge- based organisation primarily through industrial automation and Barnevik's reputation was such that it was accepted that these dramatic changes were necessary for future growth and profitability of ABB. However, at the end of 2000 Lindahl was forced to resign as CEO in an internal power struggle that favoured Jörgen Centerman, the head of ABB's automation segment. In retrospect the strategic shift initiated by Barnevik and Lindahl into higher technology sectors was essentially correct and has been followed by subsequent leading executives since. However, whilst the use of the phrase "knowledge-based" seemed apt at the time, it was a misnomer in the company's areas of operation and was confusing to many stakeholders.

Barnevik era comes to an end (November 2001)

Barnevik resigned as chairman of ABB in November 2001 as the results of his and Lindahl's strategic moves unravelled into a nightmare. The main drivers for this strategic unravelling were concerned with problems in Financial Services, lack of quality control in Power Generation, attempts at un-related diversification and continuing problems with Combustion Engineering in the USA. Within the Financial Services segment ABB reported a loss of $729million for the year 2001 and the share price fell in value by about two-thirds in a single year. The loss reported for 2001 included an exceptional loss of $433 million in the company's insurance business located in the Financial Services segment. This loss was due to a non-cash charge of $295 in estimating insurance loss reserves and $138 million in underwriting losses. Before taking this exceptional loss into account, financial services accounted for one-third of ABB's profits despite employing only one percent of the total ABB workforce: a serious state of affairs in a business where most of the sales were generated by electrical engineering products. A close look at ABB's balance sheet revealed that by the end of 2001 it had total debt outstanding of $9.79bn and

---

[1] For transferring to this 50:50 joint venture operation that generated some $8bn in annual revenues, ABB received some $1.5bn in cash.

EXHIBIT V   Structural developments

A. Lindahl: Downgrading matrix to Global Products Group (GPG) divisions.

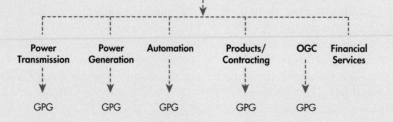

Power Transmission	Power Generation	Automation	Products/ Contracting	OGC	Financial Services
GPG	GPG	GPG	GPG	GPG	

B. Centerman: Global Customer Group (GCG) divisions.

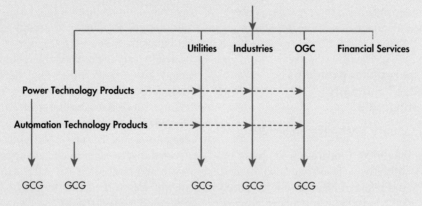

C. Dormann: Global Power and Automation divisions (GCG focus)

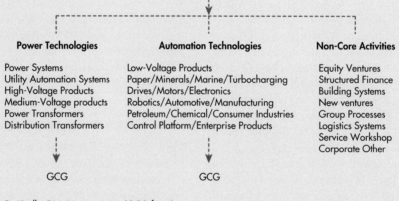

Power Technologies

Power Systems
Utility Automation Systems
High-Voltage Products
Medium-Voltage products
Power Transformers
Distribution Transformers

GCG

Automation Technologies

Low-Voltage Products
Paper/Minerals/Marine/Turbocharging
Drives/Motors/Electronics
Robotics/Automotive/Manufacturing
Petroleum/Chemical/Consumer Industries
Control Platform/Enterprise Products

GCG

Non-Core Activities

Equity Ventures
Structured Finance
Building Systems
New ventures
Group Processes
Logistics Systems
Service Workshop
Corporate Other

D. Kindle: Division expansion (GCG focus).

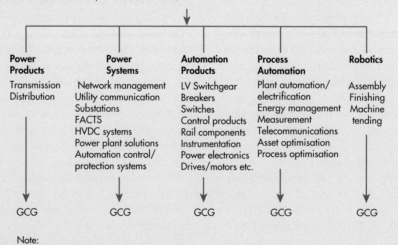

Power Products

Transmission
Distribution

GCG

Power Systems

Network management
Utility communication
Substations
FACTS
HVDC systems
Power plant solutions
Automation control/
protection systems

GCG

Automation Products

LV Switchgear
Breakers
Switches
Control products
Rail components
Instrumentation
Power electronics
Drives/motors etc.

GCG

Process Automation

Plant automation/
electrification
Energy management
Measurement
Telecommunications
Asset optimisation
Process optimisation

GCG

Robotics

Assembly
Finishing
Machine
tending

GCG

Note:
   FACTS: Flexible alternating transmission systems
   HVDC: High-voltage direct current

Note: These structures do not show group central functions. For these see
www.abb.com/news

$3.3bn (about one-third of its total debt) was in short-term loans which had been raised at relatively low interest rates. In addition ABB developed a net debt (borrowings minus cash and cash equivalents and marketable securities) of $4bn compared to $1.76bn at 31st December 2000. This increase in net debt arose due to the need to fund acquisitions (Entrelec, a French supplier of industrial automation and control products was purchased in April 2001 for $310m), provide significant investments to the Financial Services segment and to buy back $1.4bn of its own shares. The moves to support Financial Services were understandable but dangerous since any continuing downturn in this segment's profitability would expose the low-profitability of ABB's engineering core. What was essentially needed was a move out of Financial Services into making the engineering core much more profitable long-term. With respect to quality issues within power generation, Lindahl's stated objective to increase ABB's revenues by about one-third by 2001—within a period of three years since his appointment—began to be seen as not achievable as the time approached and doubts were expressed about the focus on sales growth in the short-term at the expense of other factors in the long-term, particularly with respect to product and service quality. For example, in 1998 around 80 new gas turbines were sold before quality testing procedures could be enacted and costing the company millions of dollars in repair and compensation costs. In 1999 ABB attempted to get into the telecommunication business as part of a consortium that bid for a third-generation (3G) mobile phone licence. This was unsuccessful but the move was indicative of Lindahl's and Barnevik's "knowledge-based" thinking at the time. In 1989 ABB made 40 acquisitions primarily in automation and instrumentation. However one of these acquisitions was one of which was Combustion Engineering (CE), a loss-making manufacturer of boilers and nuclear plants. Barnevik paid $1.6bn for the company, a premium of 57 percent over CE's share price. In the midst of all this acquisition activity ABB managers failed to carry out due diligence on CE which, prior to the mid-1970's, was a supplier of products containing asbestos and therefore failed to recognise the extent of potential asbestos liabilities in the company, a future obligation that had risen to approximately $1000 million by 2000[2] (BBC News 2002). It's a paradox to note that at the time that ABB wanted to re-focus on knowledge-based industries and sold many of its capital intensive companies that had ceased growing but it did not sell Combustion Engineering or the asbestos liabilities.

These strategic moves coupled with a rapidly deterring financial situation caused stakeholders to question the strategic fitness of both Barnevik and Lindahl to lead the company. This feeling was reinforced in early 2001 when it was learned that Lindahl and Barnevik had awarded themselves total retirement benefits of $143million between them. These extraordinary payments led to uproar and they were required to pay back $82 million of these monies. This episode raised questions in the minds of key investors and stakeholders about the competence

of top management to control the company. The secrecy of the deal also raised questions about corporate governance issues generally. Indeed this feeling was amplified with the fact that ABB did not have a CFO until 1996. Barnevik resigned his chairmanship of ABB in November 2001 (www.fundinguniverse.com). After his resignation Barnevik was succeeded by Jürgen Dormann as non-executive chairman. He was then currently full-time executive chairman of Aventis S.A—a pharmaceuticals company - but had been on the board of ABB for three years.

Jörgen Centerman as CEO (January 2001–September 2002)

During his short tenure (20 months) as CEO Centerman initiated a number of actions. These were mainly concerned with major restructuring, new acquisitions and issues relating to reducing costs and repairing the balance sheet. In January 2001 he replaced the six existing business segments with seven business division structures along customer groups. Four divisions—Utilities, Process Industries, Manufacturing and Consumer Industries, and Oil/Gas/Petrochemicals, were established to serve end- user customers. Two divisions, Power Technology Products and Automation Technology Products were established to serve the four end-user divisions as well as external customers. The Financial Services division still served the ABB Group's businesses and external customers. Centerman reasoned that this new structure was needed to accelerate ABB away from heavy industrial products towards new technologies and services. This thinking essentially continued with the Barnevik and Lindahl strategy. In April 2002 the company announced its intention to sell its Building Systems business (part of Manufacturing and Consumer Industries division) and placed it into a discontinued operations category. The remaining business areas of the Manufacturing and Consumer Industries were combined with the Process Industries division to form a new Industries division (Exhibit VB). Through this restructuring ABB hoped to realise annual savings of $800mn. In June 2001 AB acquired Entrelec Group for $284 million. Entrelec, based in Lyon, France, was a supplier of industrial automation and control products. The rationale of the acquisition was that it would strengthen ABB's market position in its key European and North American markets. During the first six months of 2001 ABB's operating earnings declined by 21 percent and revenues remained flat as key markets suffered from economic slowdown. Centerman moved to reduce the workforce by 12,000 (8 percent) over 18 months in order to reduce operating cost by some $500 million. In January 2002 ABB was forced to take a charge of $470 million for asbestos liabilities stemming from its 1989 acquisition of Combustion Engineering (www.abb.com/cawp/seitp202) This charge together with asset write-downs, a change to USA accounting practices in 2000 (which resulted in reduced reported earnings and prompted concerns about underlying profitability) and losses on some projects led to the company reporting a net loss of $729 million on revenues of $18.334bn. for the year ending 31st December 2001 (www.fundinguniverse.com). These results sent the shares substantially lower. With $4bn in debt and the company pushed to the brink of bankruptcy and near to collapse Centerman moved to repair the balance sheet by first

---

[2] More specifically, costs related to the potential asbestos obligations of Combustion Engineering were $470mn in 2001, $420mn in 2002 and $145mn in 2003, a total of $1035mn.

restructuring a $3bn of the debt and selling its Structured Finance business (part of the Financial Services division) to General Electric for $2.5bn. In September 2002 Centerman was replaced as CEO by Jürgen Dormann who then became Chairman and CEO of ABB. The reason given was that Dormann was unhappy at the pace of reforms and wanted to initiate action himself (www.fundinguniverse.com). In effect, however, ABB was by this time a crumbling mess. It had been brought to its knees by declining markets in core businesses, over-diversification, acute financial strain, adverse interest rate movements, severe loss of investor confidence (the share price had declined from SFr54 in May 2000 to SFr1.61 soon after Dormann was appointed CEO in September 2002), declining morale in employees due to constant re-structuring, ill-judged exposure to asbestos litigation and, most importantly, consistent poor management at the top level (Bream 2003)

C. Strategic renewal: Global focus on power, automation and robotic technologies. (September 2002 to present)

Jürgen Dormann as Chairman and CEO (December 2001–April 2007)

Jürgen Dormann trained as an economist and has spent his entire life in industry. As CEO of Hoechst until 1999, he steered the German company into the merger with Rhône-Poulenc of France that created Aventis which is now widely seen as Europe's more successful cross-border collaborations. He went on to become chairman of the supervisory board of this combined group. He was a specialist in bridging cultures as he is in turning around sleepy troubled companies. His exposure in such senior positions has given him more experience than most in handling difficult boardrooms. Welding together Hoechst and Rhône-Poulenc required diplomacy and cultural know how in addition to the application of strategic industrial skills[3] (Business Biographies 2008). Within months of his appointment Mr Dormann began a strategy that gradually returned the focus of ABB to its two core strengths of power and automation technologies. Fringe businesses were rapidly sold and the workforce reduced from 150,000 to 113,000. More specifically, on assuming executive power at ABB he initiated actions relating to a so-called step-change programme, Combustion Engineering, continuing balance sheet repair a major restructuring. The step-change programme was first announced in October 2002. Its goals were to increase the competitiveness of ABB's core businesses, reduce overhead costs and streamline operations by about $900 million on an annual basis up to 2005. In order to achieve this over 1,400 specific initiatives were established and monitored. About 40 percent of the savings were planned to come from a reduction of about 12,000 employees and subsequent costs thereto; 20 percent of savings were planned to come from improved production

methods, consolidation of office space and manufacturing facilities and the closure of non-profitable units and the final 40 percent of savings were expected to come from outsourcing of selected activities e.g. outsourcing a major part of its IT infrastructure services to IBM Corporation. In October 2002 ABB determined that expected asbestos- related costs of Combustion Engineering would exceed the value of the assets ($812 million as of September 2002). In its determination to resolve the asbestos liability Combustion Engineering was reorganised under Chapter 11, the principal business reorganisation chapter of the U.S. Bankruptcy Code. This reorganisation was structured as a "pre-packaged plan" in January 2003 and offered to resolve its asbestos liability through a deal that would cap payments at $1.2bn. for 110,000 asbestos claims. The main idea was to protect Combustion Engineering through Chapter 11 and pay claimants from the company's liquid assets. Acceptances of the plan were to be solicited prior to the filing of the Chapter 11 case, thus reducing the duration and expense of the bankruptcy proceedings. This plan was approved by a US court but was appealed by a small group of plaintiffs. Dormann continued to attack the asset side of the balance sheet with vigour. In December 2002, he sold ABB's water and electricity metering business to Ruhrgas Industries GmbH for $223million. In August 2003 ABB sold its Building Systems business in Sweden, Norway, Denmark, Finland, Russia and the Baltic states for $233 million to YIT Corporation of Helsinki. In December 2003 its Sirius re-insurance business was sold to White Mountains of Bermuda. In January 2004 ABB reached an agreement to sell the upstream part of its Oil/Gas/Petrochemical (OGP) division to a private equity consortium led by Candover Partners, a European buyout specialist, for around $925 million. He improved the liquidity of ABB by securing a $1.5bn credit facility in December 2002 and a further $1bn unsecured credit facility in 2003. He improved the capital base in 2003 via a $2.5bn rights issue and a $750 million bond issue. Finally, in January 2003 he streamlined the divisional structure, developed by Centerman, into just two core businesses and one Non-Core business. He combined the Power Technology Products division with the Utilities Division to create a new Power Technologies division and combined the Automation Technology Products division with the Industries division to create a new Automation technologies division. The Oil/Gas/Petrochemical division, along with a number of other businesses, were reclassified as a discontinued operation and put up for sale. The remaining activities were grouped into a Non-Core Activities division. (Exhibit VC). At the end of 2003 ABB posted total consolidated revenues of $18,795bn with Power technologies taking 38 percent, Automation technologies taking 49 percent and Non-Core Activities taking 13 percent (ABB Ltd United States SEC 2004 Form 20-F) By February 2004 the company's two core units had turned in stronger than forecast returns and the share price had risen to SFr6.50. Despite a net loss of $767 million on revenues of $18.795bn at 31st December 2003, first quarter results in 2004 showed that his plan was working as the company posted a net income of $4 million. Dormann stated that 2003 was the company's turnaround year and continued growth could be expected in the future (Simonian 2004a). Thus after three years

---

[3] In 2004 Sanofi-Aventis, the French "national champion" drug maker was formed after the takeover of Aventis by Sanofi-Synthélabo. Dormann sat on the board of this new group. At age 64 he also became an independent board member of Adecco (the world's biggest temporary employment group) with a brief to improve its corporate governance.

of losses swollen by one-off restructuring charges the group had finally been brought into profit. With confidence in the future of ABB he announced he would resign as CEO at the end of December 2004 in favour of Fred Kindle who was the current head of Sulzer AG, a Swiss engineering group much smaller than ABB. He planned to remain as chairman but would only devote 50 percent of his time to the company in 2005 and 25 percent in 2006 (Simonian 2004b). A new CFO, Michel Demare, was also appointed in January 2005. With ABB now returning to the frame, Fred Kindle and his team would be able to focus on competing on an even keel with Siemens, GE, and Alstom in the daily battle for new business. A new Chairman, Hubertus von Grünberg, Chairman of tyre manufacture Continental AG, succeeded Jürgen Dormann in May 2007. Mr von Grünberg was to retain his chairmanship of Continental AG.

Fred Kindle as CEO (September 2004—February 2008)

Fred Kindle, a Swiss national, who at just 44 years old, was appointed CEO of ABB in February 2004 but did not take up his duties until September 2004. Kindle's CEO experience was limited to Sulzer, a smaller Swiss engineering group that was once a by-word for Swiss engineering excellence and a main competitor to Brown Boveri before its merger with Asea to form the ABB conglomerate. Once a by- word for engineering excellence, Sulzer, like ABB, hit hard times and was forced to restructure (almost constantly) under its CEO Fritz Fahrni. Once Kindle was CEO he slimmed down Sulzer further to concentrate on four disparate core divisions. This strategy resulted in employees being reduced from 25,000 to 9,000 and sales from SFr4.5bn ($3.5bn) to SFr1.9bn ($1.48bn.). The strategy resulted in improved but modest earnings. Prior to joining Sulzer Fred Kindle spent four years as a management consultant with McKinsey. Before that he attended Zurich's prestigious technical university. Therefore, whilst his experience is seen as being in a mid-sized company, he is also seen as competent, convincing and relevant to ABB. His appointment was expected to bring some stability to ABB that had seen a succession of CEO's depart after the long tenure of Percy Barnevik. Moreover, his lack of experience in big business would be compensated by Dormann's continued presence as part-time Chairman (Simonian 2004c). Under Kindle future strategy would concentrate on improving operational excellence and margins via organic growth. Problems with asbestos litigation would be brought to conclusion and final touches to ABB's disposal programme rapidly concluded. With these goals in mind we can state that Kindle's tenure as CEO produced action relating to Combustion Engineering, divestitures, major restructuring and improvements in financial performance. In 2006 ABB resolved the bulk of asbestos claims with a $1.43bn settlement plan. Overall, this ill-fated venture cost ABB more than $2bn in asbestos-related claims. In November 2007 ABB sold its U.S.-based oil and gas production unit, Lummus Global, to Chicago Bridge & Iron Co. for $950 million. This sale put a cap on six years of ABB divestitures and was referred to by Kindle as a 'final milestone' in ABB's divestiture programme. In January 2006 Kindle eliminated the two core power and automation technology divisions (Exhibit VC) and replaced them with five divisions known as Power Products (formerly the Power Technology Products business area), Power Systems (formerly the Power Technology Systems business area), Automation Products, Process Automation and Robotics (Exhibit VD). Within this process one layer of management was removed and two new functions introduced at the centre: one at the Executive Committee level to integrate the regional organisation more strongly and one at the Group level, Global Markets and Technology, designed to drive execution of the company's strategy across national and regional borders. Power Products, Power Systems and Automation Products were to be headquartered in Zurich; Process Automation was to be headquartered in Norwalk, Connecticut and Robotics to be headquartered in Shanghai. For Kindle, this restructuring was evolutionary change, not revolutionary change (Arnold 2005). Under Kindle ABB's financial situation improved considerably from four years of losses (Exhibit VI). The company achieved a double- figure EBIT/Sales margin which it never previously achieved. Net cash from operations was higher than at any other time in its history. For the immediate future Kindle was confident that the company could achieve annual earnings growth of up to 20 percent in power-related activities and 10 percent in automation-related businesses. Such growth would be achieved organically and through acquisitions. Future demand for the products and services now at the heart of ABB's business—increasing energy efficiency, delivering reliable power and improving industrial productivity—was, Kindle believed, extremely positive.

It came as a complete surprise to analysts when Fred Kindle was pushed out of ABB unexpectedly in mid-January 2008 due to "irreconcilable differences relating to the strategic direction of the company" (Associated Press 2008). Such differences may have emanated between Kindle and the new Chairman, Hubertus von Grünberg. It's speculated that the differences of opinion referred to acquisition strategy (Bloomberg 2008). Kindle, it appears, favoured small acquisitions of around $2bn each whereas von Grünberg favoured a major acquisition such as Rockwell Automation of USA (market capitalisation of $8.5bn) or Legrand of France (market capitalisation of $7.6bn). Additionally it is speculated that von Grünberg became frustrated with Kindle's lack of appetite for pushing growth in Asian markets (Marsh et al. 2008). On 16th July 2008, von Grünberg announced that ABB, armed with a war chest of $5.6bn, planned to acquire US transformer company Kuhlman Electric Corporation but no acquisition price was given. This deal—the first significant one since 1998—favoured Kindle's strategy of securing bolt-on acquisitions to complement the existing product range and geographical presence. On 17th July 2008, ABB announced that Joseph Hogan was to become its new CEO.

Joseph Hogan as CEO (September 2008 to present)

Joe Hogan, formerly CEO of GE Healthcare and a member of GE's Senior Executive Council, commenced his appointment as CEO of ABB on 1st September 2008. It is believed that his appointment will lead to accelerated growth for ABB in Asian markets (Dow Jones 2008). Growth will come principally from bolt-on acquisitions—since Hogan developed an impressive

EXHIBIT VI ABB Group: Change in consolidated financial performance (1988 – 2007) ($bn)

	1988	1990	1991	1992	1993	1994	1995	1996	1997	1998	1999	2000	2001	2002	2003	2004	2005	2006	2007
Revenues	17.6	26.7	28.9	29.6	27.5	29.7	32.8	33.8	31.3	22.9	24.5	19.4	19.4	19.5	20.3	20.6	20.9	23.3	29.2
EBIT	0.85	1.79	1.91	1.81	1.31	2.62	2.18	2.13	1.14	1.33	1.12	1.17	0.16	0.20	0.29	1.05	1.71	2.56	4.01
Net profit (loss)	0.36	0.59	0.61	0.51	0.07	0.76	0.37	0.39	0.57	0.48	1.36	1.43	(0.73)	(0.82)	(0.78)	(0.035)	0.74	1.39	3.76
Stockholders equity	3.12	4.25	4.50	4.10	3.84	4.02	5.58	6.22	5.28	6.0	4.27	5.17	1.97	1.01	2.92	2.84	3.48	6.04	10.96
Total assets	19.0	30.2	30.8	25.9	24.9	29.1	32.1	30.1	29.8	32.8	30.6	30.9	29.5	32.3	30.4	24.7	22.8	25.1	31.0
Net cash from operations	0.57	0.89	2.00	1.45	1.52	2.14	2.08	0.83	1.79	0.80	1.58	0.75	1.98	0.019	(0.51)	0.90	1.01	1.94	3.1
Employees (nearest k)	170	215	214	213	206	208	210	215	213	199	161	161	157	139	116	102	104	108	112
Ratios (%):																			
EBIT/Revenues	4.8	6.7	6.6	6.1	4.8	8.8	6.7	6.3	3.6	5.8	4.6	6.0	0.8	1.0	1.4	5.1	8.2	11.0	13.7
Return/Capital Employed	13.6	19.7	17.1	17.9	16.1	17.6	21.8	19.9	12.2	21.1	21.8	n/a	n/a	n/a	n/a	8.0	14.0	21.0	35.0

Vice-Chairman structure

Barnevik as CEO

Barnevik as Chairman

Lindahl as CEO

Dormann as Chairman

Centerman as CEO

Dormann as CEO

Kindle as CEO

Grünberg as Chairman

Source:

1. Financial performance compiled from ABB consolidated financial statement at www.abb.com/news.

2. Author's notes.

record of securing growth through such acquisitions in his time at GE - but also from organic methods. To this end in the fourth quarter of 2008 ABB acquired Ber-Mac Electrical Instrumentation Ltd a supplier of industrial automation and field services to the oil and gas sector.

2008 proved to be a record-breaking year for ABB. Revenue was billed at $34.9bn (20 percent above 2007); EBIT was struck at $4.6bn (13 percent above 2007), and operating cash flow at $4.0bn (30 per cent above 2007). Additionally, orders logged at the end of 2008 were $38.9bn (an 11 percent improvement on 2007). Net cash shown on the balance sheet was $5.4bn at the end of 2008—the same as for 2007. These results are impressive and confirm the sound strategic direction developed by Centerman, Dormann, and Kindle to develop the company globally in power, automation technologies (including robotics) with customer focus. However, the global economic downturn in the latter stages of 2008 impacted adversely on the group particularly in new orders and EBIT. This pattern has continued into the first quarter of 2009 with revenues at $7.2bn down by 9 percent and EBIT at $862mn down by 36 percent both compared to the first quarter of 2008. Operating cash flow has also moved negative at ($104mn) compared to $464mn in the first quarter of 2008: this is due mainly to lower EBIT and the timing of project payments. All divisions except Process Automation experienced revenue declines in Q1 2009 compared to Q1 2008. However it should be noted that the first quarter of 2008 was one of the strongest ever quarters recorded by ABB (www.abb.com/cawp/seitp202). A positive note is that the order backlog for the group as a whole was $25bn at the end of March 2009 with no projected cancellations. Notwithstanding the current economic climate ABB's balance sheet remains rock solid with an A rating by S&P (outlook stable) and an A3 rating by Moody's (outlook stable).

For 2009 Joe Hogan, the new CEO has stated that "visibility" in its markets was "limited" because of significant uncertainty surrounding the key demand drivers for the company's products and systems. These drivers he put as (1) cost and scarcity of project funding which has delayed many power investment decisions (2) demand in ABB's industrial end markets being affected by lower GDP growth and capital spending (3) the level of commodity prices and (4) the need for its customers to steadily improve efficiency and productivity to meet increasing competition. Additionally ABB may be affected by costs associated with compliance activities. These relate to various suspect payments in the USA which have been disclosed to the U.S. Department of Justice and the U.S. Securities and Exchange Commission and various anti-trust authorities, including the European Commission, regarding allegedly anti-competitive practices in the power transformer business. To meet these uncertainties Joe Hogan will need to ensure that ABB has the flexibility to respond quickly to changing market conditions. He will be helped with this challenging endeavour by ABB's global footprint in key leading technologies, strong balance sheet, cost competitiveness enhanced by its cost take-out plan, strong corporate culture and improved corporate governance. There is no doubt that the challenges to be faced will test his managerial abilities to the full.

Case Questions

1. CEO Percy Barnevik's ideals in building ABB into a global corporate presence were well founded. Identify these ideals and discuss the factors which caused key areas to go awry and affect the performance of the business.
2. Identify and discuss the key strategic initiatives implemented by the various CEOs appointed after Barnevik's tenure to take the company out of the "crumbling mess" within which it found itself in 2001. In your opinion which CEO performed the better and why?
3. Percy Barnevik laid great store in the use of a matrix structure. Discuss the pros and cons of matrix structures and compare and contrast with those of so-called product/market structures and divisional structures. What particular structure has ABB now developed and why did it take five major restructurings from October 1997 to January 2006 to achieve it?
4. Assess ABB's current corporate culture. Do you think that it has changed since Percy Barnevik's time?
5. ABB's current growth strategy is to seek small "bolt-on" acquisitions to existing product areas rather than via major acquisitions that could take the company into new areas (e.g., aerospace). Comment on these strategic options.

References

1. ABB Ltd. United States Securities and Exchange Commission, Form 20-F (2004) 16–33, www.excite.brand.edgar.com Accessed 12th June 2008.
2. ABB press release (2002), ABB's operational and financial restructuring on track." www.abb.com/cawp/seitp202. Accessed 10th June 2008
3. ABB Annual Report (2001). www.abb.com/cawp/seitp255. Accessed 8th July 2008
4. P. Arnold, "ABB Announces Major Changes in Corporate Structure." www.reliableplant.com. Accessed 27th June 2008.
5. K. Barham and C. Heimer (1998) ABB-The Dancing Giant: Creating the Globally Connected Corporation. Upper Saddle River, NJ: Prentice Hall, 1998.
6. BBC News (2002). "ABB doubles asbestos liabilities." www.news.bbc.co.uk Accessed 10th June 2008
7. Bloomberg press release (2008). ABB's Kindle quits over irreconcilable differences. www.bloomberg.com/apps/news. Accessed 14th February 2008.
8. Rebecca Bream. "Plummeting Orders Casts Doubt Over ABB." *Financial Times,* February 28, 2003.
9. Business Biographies from www.answers.com/topic/j-rgen-dormann?cat=biz-fin. Accessed 10th June 2008
10. Dow Jones press release. ABB Appoints GE Executive Joseph Hogan as New CEO. www.beurs.nl/nieuws/artikel Accessed 17th July 2008.

11. G. Johnson and K. Scholes *Exploring Corporate Strategy*, Upper Saddle River, NJ: Prentice Hall, 1992: 358.

12. Ibid 363–64

13. J. Baer and P. Marsh, "ABB Signals Expansionary Plans by Recruiting GE Veteran as Chief," *Financial Times*, July 18 2008.

14. Simonian Haig, "ABB Appoints Fred Kindle as New CEO." *Financial Times* March 2, 2004.

15. Simonian Haig, "Dormann to Leave the Lights On." *Financial Times* July 12, 2004.

16. Simonian Haig, "ABB Optimistic it has Turned the Corner." *Financial Times* July 30, 2004.

17. William Taylor, "The Logic of Global Business: An Interview with ABB's Percy Barnevik." *Harvard Business Review* 69, no. 2.(1991).

18. The Associated Press (2008). "ABB posts fourfold jump in quarterly profit." www.iht.com. Accessed 10th June 2008.

19. www.abb.com/news. Accessed June-July 2008.

20. www.fundinguniverse.com/company-histories/ABB-LTD-Company-History.html. Accessed 17th July 2008.

Note: All financial data and company history can be accessed from ABB's website at www.abb.com

Global Human Resources Management

Staffing, Training, and Compensation for Global Operations

OBJECTIVES:

1. To understand the strategic importance to the firm of the IHRM function and its various responsibilities.

2. To learn about the major staffing options for global operations and the factors involved in those choices.

3. To emphasize the need for managing the performance of expatriates through careful selection, training, and compensation.

4. To discuss the role of host country managers and the need for their training and appropriate compensation packages.

5. To distinguish among various IHRM practices around the world.

Opening Profile: Staffing Company Operations in Emerging Markets[1]

The ability to staff subsidiaries in emerging market economies with local managers has become a major challenge in the race for recruiting and retaining local talent. Emerging economies such as Brazil, Russia, India, and China (often referred to as the BRIC countries) have been developing so rapidly and have attracted increasing overseas investment that they have outpaced the supply of suitable mid- and upper-level managers in their own markets. Foreign firms wishing to expand their investments there are competing for what talent is available with both local companies and other global companies; however they are falling behind the curve in not recognizing that they need different approaches than those they use domestically.

The problem is so acute that many companies have had to reconsider how fast they can expand in developing economies. A study by the McKinsey Global Institute predicts that 75,000 business leaders will be needed in China in the next ten years. It estimates the current availability at just 3,000 to 5,000, and that many of those are simply not at the skill level required by foreign companies.[2] According to *The Economist*:

> In a recent survey, 600 chief executives of multinational companies with businesses across Asia said a shortage of qualified staff ranked as their biggest concern in China and South-East Asia. It was their second-biggest headache in Japan (after cultural differences) and the fourth-biggest in India (after problems with infrastructure, bureaucracy and wage inflation).[3]

Reasons for the shortage of upper-level managers vary by country. Research by Ready, et al shows that while Brazil has an influx of new graduates available to staff at the low- to mid-management level, there is a deficit at the upper levels. In India there is also a surplus at the lower level, but a deficit starting at the middle levels; one additional explanation is the brain drain, in particular in the technology industry. In Russia, there is a deficit at all management levels as a result of decades of operating under a planned economy, together with the great increase in demand by foreign companies. In China, there is a sizable surplus at the entry level, though of varying quality, but a considerable deficit at all levels up from there.[4]

Clearly the competition for talent has become global, as has the competition for jobs. The brain drain from emerging economies has contributed to the dearth of local talent available. Over a million Chinese went to the United States to study between 1978 and 2006, and 70 percent of them did not go back. Exacerbating the problem is the high-turnover of those highly-sought managers, and, as a result of that, the escalating salary requirements.[5] For example, "for a chief finance officer the average pay is now $194,000 in China, $159,000 in Thailand, $157,000 in Malaysia and $73,000 in India."[6]

For these reasons, the challenge to companies operating around the world is not only to recruit capable local managers, but to be able to retain them. Advice from professionals includes "growing your own"—that is to provide sufficient training and career mentoring to elicit loyalty with managers; and, in particular, to balance local human resource needs with global standards. This may require tailoring employment packages to local markets to attract and keep top talent, rather than applying global policies for the sake of global consistency.[7]

Ready et al. suggest a framework for attracting and retaining talent which recognizes that managers in developing markets are motivated by factors which are a function of their culture, business practices, and personal goals, and which are usually dissimilar to what is expected in the home office. They conclude that successful companies offer more than a good salary and that they comprise four distinguishing characteristics which provide meaning for potential recruits in emerging markets:[8]

1. Brand—that is a global "name brand" known for its excellence and with a distinctive competence in a particular area, for example technology, in which new recruits would have confidence in their future.
2. Purpose—that is a company that is breaking into new markets with new models and strategy, giving new employees a chance to be part of something meaningful.
3. Opportunity—that is a company that provides a fast-track training and career path for new recruits
4. Culture—that is a company that has an organizational culture of openness and transparency for employees, with support for their work and career development.[9]

A GMAC Relocation Trends survey released in May 2008 found that despite a slowing economy, 68 percent of multinational corporations continued to relocate employees at record levels. Experts say it is too early to tell how the current crisis will affect global work force mobility.

THE NEW YORK TIMES, *December 2, 2008.* [10]

This chapter's opening profile describes the challenges involved in recruiting and retaining suitable managers to staff operations in emerging markets, where the burgeoning demand by both foreign and local companies is outstripping the supply. Other challenges for companies around the world include growing workforce mobility and the increasing trend of outsourcing employees as service and professional jobs have now joined manufacturing jobs in the category of "boundaryless" human capital (discussed in previous chapters).

Clearly the need to outsource employees is a complex issue for international human resource (IHR) managers as they seek to support strategic mandates (see Chapter 6). Global firms are finding that their practices of outsourcing skilled and professional jobs have implications for their human resource practices at home and around the world. Consequently, a firm such as Infosys, one of India's top outsourcing companies, also experiences complex human resource challenges involved in recruiting, training, and compensating increasingly sophisticated employees in its attempt to meet the escalating demand for its services.

It is clear, then, that a vital component of implementing global strategy is *international human resource management* (IHRM). IHRM is increasingly being recognized as a major determinant of success or failure in international business. In a highly competitive global economy, where the other factors of production—capital, technology, raw materials, and information—are increasingly able to be duplicated, "the caliber of the people in an organization will be the only source of sustainable competitive advantage available to U.S. companies."[11] Corporations operating overseas need to pay careful attention to this most critical resource—one that also provides control over other resources. In fact, increasing recognition is being given to the role of *Strategic Human Resource Management (SHRM)*—that is the two-way role of HRM in both helping to determine strategy as well as to implement it. That role in helping the organization to develop the necessary capabilities to be able to enact the desired strategy includes the reality that strategic plans are developed in large part based on the resources possessed by the firm, including the human resources capabilities.[12]

The IHRM function comprises varied responsibilities involved in managing human resources in global corporations, including recruiting and selecting employees, providing preparation and training, and setting up appropriate compensation and performance management programs. Of particular importance is the management of **expatriates**—employees assigned to a country other than their own. An overview of those functions is provided here, while further IHRM challenges in developing a global management cadre and working within host-country practices and laws are discussed in the following chapter.

At the first level of planning, decisions are required on the staffing policy suitable for a particular kind of business, its global strategy, and its geographic locations. Key issues involve the difficulty of control in geographically dispersed operations, the need for local decision making independent of the home office, and the suitability of managers from alternate sources.

The interdependence of strategy, structure, and staffing is particularly worth noting. Ideally, the desired strategy of the firm should dictate the organizational structure and staffing modes considered most effective for implementing that strategy. In reality, however, there is usually considerable interdependence among those functions. Existing structural constraints often affect strategic decisions; similarly, staffing constraints or unique sets of competences in management come into play in organizational and sometimes strategic decisions. It is thus important to achieve a system of fits among those variables that facilitates strategic implementation.

STAFFING FOR GLOBAL OPERATIONS

Globalization in the 21st century has resulted in an even higher demand for businesses to send the right talent to the right place at the right time.

KPMG 2008 GLOBAL ASSIGNMENT SURVEY,
www.kpmglink.com.

Despite concerns over the weaker global economy and the costs of international assignment programs, international assignments remain on the upswing, according to the results of KPMG's 2008 Global Assignment Policies and Practices Survey. Of the 430 human resources executives surveyed, 83 percent said they expected the number of international assignees from their organizations to remain the same or increase over the next five years.[13] Those executives made it clear that when competing in global markets, global experience and expertise are critical to the success of the organization and employee.

The traditional options available to the firm for managerial staffing abroad are discussed below. However, we see trends toward more flexible assignment policies for expatriates. Those found by the KPMG survey are: an increase in short-term assignments of less than 12 months, with 81 percent using this option; commuter assignments—assignments where employees work in a different country than where they reside—were utilized by 22 percent of the companies surveyed, especially in European-headquartered companies in order to take advantage of improved mobility within the European Union.[14]

Depending on the firm's primary strategic orientation and stage of internationalization, as well as situational factors, managerial staffing abroad falls into one or more of the following staffing modes—ethnocentric, polycentric, regiocentric, and global approaches. When the company is at the internationalization stage of strategic expansion, and has a centralized structure, it will likely use an **ethnocentric staffing approach** to fill key managerial positions with people from headquarters—that is, **parent-country nationals (PCNs)**. Among the advantages of this approach, PCNs are familiar with company goals, products, technology, policies, and procedures—and they know how to get things accomplished through headquarters. This policy is also likely to be used where a company notes the inadequacy of local managerial skills and determines a high need to maintain close communication and coordination with headquarters. For German companies, the most important reason for assigning expatriates was "to develop international management skills." For companies in Japan and the United Kingdom, it was "to set up a new operation," and in the United States it was "to fill a skill gap."[15]

Frequently, companies use PCNs for the top management positions in the foreign subsidiary—in particular, the chief executive officer (CEO) and the chief financial officer (CFO)—to maintain close control. PCNs are usually preferable when a high level of technical capability is required. They are also chosen for new international ventures requiring managerial experience in the parent company and where there is a concern for loyalty to the company rather than to the host country—in cases, for example, where proprietary technology is used extensively.

Disadvantages of the ethnocentric approach include (1) the lack of opportunities or development for local managers, thereby decreasing their morale and their loyalty to the subsidiary; and (2) the poor adaptation and lack of effectiveness of expatriates in foreign countries. Procter & Gamble, for example, routinely appointed managers from its headquarters for foreign assignments for many years. After several unfortunate experiences in Japan, the firm realized that such a practice was insensitive to local cultures and also underutilized its pool of high-potential non-American managers.[16] Furthermore, an ethnocentric recruiting approach does not enable the company to take advantage of its worldwide pool of management skill. This approach also serves to perpetuate particular personnel selections and other decision-making processes because the same types of people are making the same types of decisions.

With a **polycentric staffing approach**, local managers—**host-country nationals (HCNs)**—are hired to fill key positions in their own country. This approach is more likely to be effective when implementing a multinational strategy. If a company wants to "act local," staffing with HCNs has obvious advantages. These managers are naturally familiar with the local culture, language, and ways of doing business, and they already have many contacts in place. In addition, HCNs are more likely to be accepted by people both inside and outside the subsidiary, and they provide role models for other upwardly mobile personnel.

With regard to cost, it is usually less expensive for a company to hire a local manager than to transfer one from headquarters, frequently with a family and often at a higher rate of pay. Transferring from headquarters is a particularly expensive policy when the manager and her or his family do not adjust and have to be prematurely transferred home. Rather than building their own facilities, some companies acquire foreign firms as a means of obtaining qualified local personnel. Local managers also tend to be instrumental in staving off or more effectively dealing with problems in sensitive political situations. Some countries, in fact, have legal requirements that a specific proportion of the firm's top managers must be citizens of that country.

One disadvantage of a polycentric staffing policy is the difficulty of coordinating activities and goals between the subsidiary and the parent company, including the potentially conflicting loyalties of the local manager. Poor coordination among subsidiaries of a multinational firm could constrain strategic options. An additional drawback of this policy is that the headquarters managers of multinational firms will not gain the overseas experience necessary for any higher positions in the firm that require the understanding and coordination of subsidiary operations.

In the **global staffing approach,** the best managers are recruited from within or outside of the company, regardless of nationality. This practice—recruiting **third country nationals (TCNs)**—has been used for some time by many European multinationals. A global staffing approach has several important advantages. First, this policy provides a greater pool of qualified and willing applicants from which to choose, which, in time, results in further development of a global executive cadre. As discussed further in Chapter 10, the skills and experiences that those managers use and transfer throughout the company result in a pool of shared learning that is necessary for the company to compete globally.

Second, where third country nationals are used to manage subsidiaries, they usually bring more cultural flexibility and adaptability to a situation, as well as bilingual or multilingual skills, than parent-country nationals, especially if they are from a similar cultural background as the host-country coworkers and are accustomed to moving around. In addition, when TCNs are placed in key positions, they are perceived by employees as acceptable compromises between headquarters and local managers and thus appointing them works to reduce resentment.

Third, it can be more cost-effective to transfer and pay managers from some countries than from others because their pay scale and benefits packages are lower. Indeed, those firms with a truly global staffing orientation are phasing out the entire ethnocentric concept of a home or host country. In fact, as globalization increases, terms such as *TCNs, HCNs,* and *expatriates* are becoming less common, because of the kind of situation where a manager may leave her native Ireland to take a job in England, then be assigned to Switzerland, then to China, and so on, without returning to Ireland. As part of that focus, the term **transpatriate** is increasingly replacing the term *expatriate.* Firms such as Philips, Heinz, Unilever, IBM, and ABB have a global staffing approach, which makes them highly visible and seems to indicate a trend.

Overall, firms still tend to use expatriates in key positions in host countries that have a less familiar culture and also in less-developed economies. Clearly, this situation arises out of concern about uncertainty and the ability to control implementation of the corporation's goals. However, given the generally accepted consensus that staffing, along with structure and systems, must "fit" the desired strategy, firms desiring a truly global posture should adopt a global staffing approach. That is easier said than done. As shown in Exhibit 9-1, such an approach requires the firm to overcome barriers such as the availability and willingness of high-quality managers to

EXHIBIT 9-1   Maintaining a Globalization Momentum

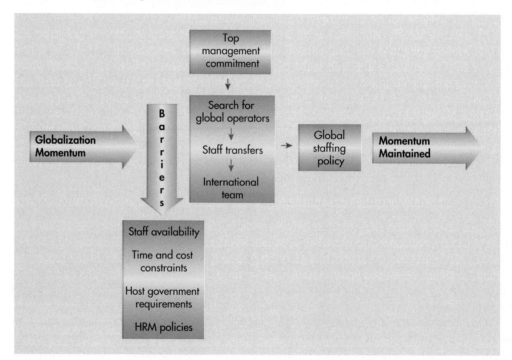

Source: Adapted from D. Welch, "HRM Implications of Globalization," *Journal of General Management* 19, no. 4 (Summer 1994): 52–69.

transfer frequently around the world, dual-career constraints, time and cost constraints, conflicting requirements of host governments, and ineffective human resource management policies.

In a **regiocentric staffing approach**, recruiting is done on a regional basis—say within Latin America for a position in Chile. This staffing approach can produce a specific mix of PCNs, HCNs, and TCNs, according to the needs of the company or the product strategy.

What factors influence the choice of staffing policy? Among them are the strategy and organizational structure of the firm, as well as the factors related to the particular subsidiary (such as the duration of the particular foreign operation, the types of technology used, and the production and marketing techniques necessary). Factors related to the host country also play a part (such as the level of economic and technological development, political stability, regulations regarding ownership and staffing, and the sociocultural setting).[17] As a practical matter, however, the choice often depends on the availability of qualified managers in the host country. Most MNCs use a greater proportion of PCNs (also called expatriates) in top management positions, staffing middle and lower management positions with increasing proportions of HCNs ("inpatriates") as one moves down the organizational hierarchy. The choice of staffing policy has a considerable influence on organizational variables in the subsidiary, such as the locus of decision-making authority, the methods of communication, and the perpetuation of human resource management practices. These variables are illustrated in Exhibit 9-2. The conclusions drawn by the researchers some time ago are still valid today. The ethnocentric staffing approach, for example, usually results in a higher level of authority and decision making in headquarters compared to the polycentric approach.[18]

A study by Rochelle Kopp found that ethnocentric staffing and policies are associated with a higher incidence of international human resource management problems.[20] In addition, Kopp found that Japanese firms scored considerably lower than European and American firms in their practice of implementing policies such as preparing local nationals for advancement and keeping inventory of their managers around the world for development purposes. As a result of these ethnocentric practices, Japanese firms seem to experience various IHRM problems, such as high turnover of local employees, more than European and American firms.

Without exception, all phases of IHRM should support the desired strategy of the firm. In the staffing phase, having the right people in the right places at the right times is a key ingredient to success in international operations. An effective managerial cadre can be a distinct competitive advantage for a firm.

The initial phase of setting up criteria for global selection, then, is to consider which overall staffing approach or approaches would most likely support the company's strategy, as previously discussed—such as HCNs for localization, the (multilocal) strategic approach, and transpatriates for a global strategy. These are typically just starting points using idealized criteria, however. In reality, other factors creep into the process, such as host-country regulations, stage of internationalization, and—most often—who is both suitable and available for the position. It is also vital to integrate long-term strategic goals into the selection and development process, especially when rapid global expansion is intended. Insufficient projection of staffing needs for global assignments will likely result in constrained strategic opportunities because of a shortage of experienced managers suitable to place in those positions.

A more flexible approach to maximizing managerial talent, regardless of the source, would certainly consider more closely whether the position could be suitably filled by a host-country national, as put forth by Tung, based on her research.[21] This contingency model of selection and training depends on the variables of the particular assignment, such as length of stay, similarity to the candidate's own culture, and level of interaction with local managers in that job. Tung concludes that the more rigorous the selection and training process, the lower the failure rate.

The selection process is set up as a decision tree in which the progression to the next stage of selection or the type of orientation training depends on the assessment of critical factors regarding the job or the candidate at each decision point. The simplest selection process involves choosing a local national because minimal training is necessary regarding the culture or ways of doing business locally. However, to be successful, local managers often require additional training in the MNC company-wide processes, technology, and corporate culture. If the position cannot be filled by a local national, yet the job requires a high level of interaction with the local community, careful screening of candidates from other countries and a vigorous training program are necessary.

EXHIBIT 9-2   Relationships Among Strategic Mode, Organizational Variables, and Staffing Orientation[19]

Aspects of the Enterprise	Orientation			
	Ethnocentric	**Polycentric**	**Regiocentric**	**Global**
Primary strategic orientation/stage	International	Multidomestic	Regional	Transnational
Perpetuation (recruiting, staffing, development)	People of home country developed for key positions everywhere in the world	People of local nationality developed for key positions in their own country	Regional people developed for key positions anywhere in the region	Best people everywhere in the world developed for key positions everywhere in the world
Complexity of organization	Complex in home country; simple in subsidiaries	Varied and independent	Highly interdependent on a regional basis	"Global Web": complex, independent, worldwide alliances/network
Authority; decision	High in headquarters	Relatively low in headquarters	High in regional headquarters and/or high collaboration among subsidiaries	Collaboration of headquarters and subsidiaries around the world
Evaluation and control	Home standards applied to people and performance	Determined locally	Determined regionally	Globally integrated
Rewards	High in headquarters; low in subsidiaries	Wide variation; can be high or low rewards for subsidiary performance	Rewards for contribution to regional objectives	Rewards to international and local executives for reaching local and worldwide objectives based on global company goals
Communication; information flow	High volume of orders, commands, advice to subsidiaries	Little to and from headquarters; little among subsidiaries	Little to and from corporate headquarters, but may be high to and from regional headquarters and among countries	Horizontal; network relations; "virtual" teams
Geographic identification	Nationality of owner	Nationality of host country	Regional company	Truly global company, but identifying with national interests ("glocal")

Most MNCs tend to start their operations in a particular region by selecting primarily from their own pool of managers. Over time, and with increasing internationalization, they tend to move to a predominantly polycentric or regiocentric policy because of (1) increasing pressure (explicit or implicit) from local governments to hire locals (or sometimes legal restraints on the use of expatriates) and (2) the greater costs of expatriate staffing, particularly when the company has to pay taxes for the parent-company employee in both countries.[22] In addition, in recent years, MNCs have noted an improvement in the level of managerial and technical competence in many countries, negating the chief reason for using a primarily ethnocentric policy in the past. One researcher's comment represents a growing attitude: "All things being equal, a local national who speaks the language, understands the culture and the political system, and is often a member of the local elite should be more effective than an expatriate alien."[23] However, concerns about the need to maintain strategic control over subsidiaries and to develop managers with a global perspective remain a source of debate about staffing policies among human resource management professionals. A globally oriented company such as ABB (Asea Brown Boveri), for example, has 500 roving transpatriates who are moved every two to three years, thus developing a considerable management cadre with global experience.[24]

For MNCs based in Europe and Asia, human resource policies at all levels of the organization are greatly influenced by the home-country culture and policies. For Japanese subsidiaries in Singapore, Malaysia, and India, for example, promotion from within and expectations of long-term loyalty to and by the firm are culture-based practices transferable to subsidiaries. At Matsushita, however, selection criteria for staffing seem to be similar to those of Western companies. Its candidates are selected on the basis of a set of characteristics the firm calls SMILE: specialty (required skill, knowledge), management ability (particularly motivational ability), international flexibility (adaptability), language facility, and endeavor (perseverance in the face of difficulty).[25]

MANAGING EXPATRIATES

The survey identified three significant challenges facing corporations: finding suitable candidates for assignments, helping employees—and their families—complete their assignments, and retaining these employees once their assignments end.[26]

GMAC GLOBAL RELOCATION
2008 Survey.

An important responsibility of IHR managers is that of managing expatriates—those employees who they assign to positions in other countries—whether from the headquarters country or third countries. Most multinationals underestimate the importance of the human resource function in the selection, training, acculturation, and evaluation of expatriates. The 2008 GMAC Global Relocation Survey—a worldwide survey of 154 multinational firms—found that 68 percent of corporations are boosting their employee assignment efforts. Of those, 95 percent say they plan to either increase the number of employees being transferred or stay at the same level as last year.

While the number of employers sending staff abroad is on the rise, only half actually have policies in place to govern these assignments, research shows.

Of the 200 MNCs surveyed by HR consultancy Mercer, 44 percent have increased the number of international assignments in the past two years, but only 56 percent of those companies said they have strategies in place to help ensure their success.[27]

Expatriate Selection

The selection of personnel for overseas assignments is a complex process. The criteria for selection are based on the same success factors as in the domestic setting, but additional criteria must be considered, relative to the specific circumstances of each international position. Unfortunately, many personnel directors have a long-standing, ingrained practice of selecting potential expatriates simply on the basis of their domestic track records and their technical expertise.[28] The need to ascertain whether potential expatriates have the necessary cross-cultural awareness and interpersonal skills for the position is too often overlooked. In their research of 136 large MNCs based in four countries—Germany, Japan, the United Kingdom, and the United States—Tungli and Peirperl examined the differences in frequency of using various selection criteria for expatriates; their results are shown in Exhibit 9-3, though of course they are not mutually exclusive criteria. While all four highly rated "Technical/professional skills," the highest score for the German companies was the expatriate's willingness to go (let's assume that's a relative term, since presumably all those being considered must be willing to go); for the Japanese sample, it was "experience in the company," reflecting their traditional long-term employment contract. Note, also, that "personality factors," which seems the closest "cultural adaptability" test, was given a far lower rating in the United States companies than those in Japan.[29]

EXHIBIT 9-3 **Frequency of use of Expatriate Selection Criteria**

	Germany	U.K.	Japan	U.S.	Total	N	F	p(F)
Technical/professional skills	4.50	5.75	5.55	5.43	5.28	130	15.07	***
Expatriate's willingness to go	5.42	5.28	5.05	5.09	5.22	129	1.60	ns
Experience in the company	5.27	4.94	5.65	5.13	5.20	131	3.67	*
Personality factors (e.g., open mind, flexibility, resilience)	5.16	5.13	5.47	4.24	4.87	126	9.54	***
Leadership skills	5.06	4.66	5.11	4.78	4.87	130	2.09	ns
The ability to work in teams	5.19	4.84	5.20	4.47	4.85	129	5.32	**
Previous performance appraisals	4.91	4.34	5.17	4.76	4.75	128	2.88	*
Family's willingness to go	4.66	4.69	3.32	4.42	4.38	128	5.45	***
Educational qualifications	4.58	4.09	3.89	3.98	4.15	128	2.04	ns
Previous international experience	3.88	4.03	4.67	3.72	3.96	128	3.26	*
Language proficiency	4.39	3.47	5.22	3.11	3.83	128	22.23	***
Loyalty to the company	4.58	3.26	4.11	3.07	3.67	125	10.05	***
Knowledge of new locality	3.30	3.23	4.32	2.89	3.29	128	9.35	***
Age	3.45	2.78	4.84	1.78	2.91	129	57.91	***
Gender	2.69	2.10	3.89	1.70	2.38	126	19.20	***

Each item was rated on a 6-point scale (1=never to 6=always).
*$p<.05$
**$p<.01$
***$p<.001$

Source: Zsuzsanna Tungli and Mauri Peiperl, "Expatriate Practices in German, Japanese, U.K., and U.S. Multinational Companies: A Comparative Survey of Changes," *Human Resources Management Journal* 48 no. 1 (2009): 153–71. Copyright 2009 John Wiley. Reproduced with permission of John Wiley.

Research by Mansour Javidan points to three major global mind-set attributes that successful expatriates possess:

- Intellectual capital, or knowledge, skills, understanding and cognitive complexity.
- Psychological capital, or the ability to function successfully in the host country through internal acceptance of different cultures and a strong desire to learn from new experiences.
- Social capital, or the ability to build trusting relationships with local stakeholders, whether they are employees, supply chain partners or customers.[30]

It is also important to assess whether the candidate's personal and family situation is such that everyone is likely to adapt to the local culture. Studies have shown there are five categories of success for expatriate managers: job factors, relational dimensions such as cultural empathy and flexibility, motivational state, family situation, and language skills. However, deciding before the expatriate goes on assignment whether he or she will be successful in those dimensions poses considerable problems for recruitment and selection purposes. Whereas language skills, for example, may be easy to ascertain, characteristics such as flexibility and cultural adjustment—widely acknowledged as most vital for expatriates—are difficult to judge beforehand. Human Resource managers wish for ways to prejudge such capabilities of candidates for assignments in order to avoid the many problems and considerable expense that can lead to expatriate failure (discussed further in this chapter and the next).

In order to address the problem of predicting how well an expatriate will perform on an overseas assignment, Tye and Chen studied factors that HR managers used as predictors of expatriate success. They found that the greatest predictive value was in the expatriate characteristics of stress tolerance and extraversion, and less on domestic work experience, gender, or even international experience. The results indicate that a manager who is extraverted (sociable, talkative) and who has a high tolerance for stress (typically experienced in new, different contexts such as in a "foreign" country) is more likely to be able to adjust to the new environment, the new job, and interacting with diverse people than those without those characteristics.

HR selection procedures, then, often include seeking out managers with those characteristics because they know there will be a greater chance for successful job performance, and a lesser turnover likelihood.[31]

These expatriate success factors are based on studies of American expatriates. One could argue that the requisite skills are the same for managers from any country—and particularly so for third country nationals. A study of expatriates in China, for example, found that expatriate success factors included performance management, training, organizational support, willingness to relocate, and strength of the relationship between the expatriate and the firm.[32]

Expatriate Performance Management

> *While 89 percent of companies formally assess a candidate's job skills prior to a foreign posting, less than half go through the same process for cultural suitability. Even fewer gauge whether the family will cope.*[33]

Deciding on a staffing policy and selecting suitable managers are logical first steps, but they do not alone ensure success. When staffing overseas assignments with expatriates, for example, many other reasons, besides poor selection, contribute to *expatriate failure* among U.S. multinationals. A large percentage of these failures can be attributed to poor preparation and planning for the entry and reentry transitions of the manager and his or her family. One important variable, for example, often given insufficient attention in the selection, preparation, and support phases, is the suitability and adjustment of the spouse. The inability of the spouse to adjust to the new environment has been found to be a major—in fact, the most frequently cited— reason for expatriate failure in U.S. and European companies.[34] In the 2005 Global Relocation Trends Survey, 67 percent of respondents cited family concerns as the main cause for assignment failure. They cited spouse dissatisfaction as the primary reason, which they attributed to cultural adjustment problems and lack of career opportunities in the host country.[35] Yet only about half of those companies studied had included the spouse in the interviewing process. In addition, although research shows that human relational skills are critical for overseas work, most of the U.S. firms surveyed failed to include this factor in their assessment of candidates.[36] The following is a synthesis of the factors frequently mentioned by researchers and firms as the major causes of expatriate failure:

- selection based on headquarters criteria rather than assignment needs
- inadequate preparation, training, and orientation prior to assignment
- alienation or lack of support from headquarters
- inability to adapt to local culture and working environment
- problems with spouse and children—poor adaptation, family unhappiness
- insufficient compensation and financial support
- poor programs for career support and repatriation.

After careful selection based on the specific assignment and the long-term plans of both the organization and the candidates, plans must be made for the preparation, training, and development of expatriate managers. In the following sections we discuss training and development and then compensation. However, it is useful to note that these should be components of an integrated performance management program, specific to expatriates, which includes goal setting, training, performance appraisal, and performance-related compensation.

Hsi-An Shih et al. conducted a study in which they interviewed expatriates and human resource professionals in global information technology companies headquartered in five different countries. These were Applied Materials (American) with 16,000 employees in 13 countries, Hitachi High Technologies (Japanese) with 470,000 employees in 23 countries, Philips Electronics (Dutch) with 192,000 employees in 60 countries, Samsung (Korean) with 173,000 employees in 20 countries, and Winbond Electronics (Taiwanese) with 47,000 employees in six countries. Shih et al. found that those companies used standardized forms from headquarters, rather than tailoring them to the host environment; as such they reflected the company culture but not the local culture in which those expatriates were operating. There also was lack of on-the-job training from those companies.[37] The differences in procedures for goal setting, performance appraisal, training, and performance-related pay among those five companies are detailed in Exhibit 9-4.

EXHIBIT 9-4 Expatriate Performance Management from MNEs of Five National Origins

Company	Goal setting	Performance appraisal	Training and development	Performance-related pay
AMT (American)	Short-term: sending unit's general manager Long term: host country's general manager	Annual performance appraisal Open feedback Interview	Applied global university Seldom take training programs while on assignment No clear connection between performance result and career development	Clear link between performance and compensation Cash bonuses and stock options
Hitachi (Japanese)	Self-setting, then finalized by host-country manager	Annually for managerial purposes, biannually for development purposes; One-way feedback discussion	Orientation Language training Seldom take training programs while on assignment Can apply to host location supervisor No clear connection between performance result and career development	Link between performance and compensation not clear Seniority-based pay system Cash bonuses
Philips (Dutch)	Self-setting, then finalized by host-country manager	Biannual performance appraisal; Open feedback in interview	Orientation Seldom take training programs while on assignment No clear connection between performance result and career development	Clear link between performance and compensation Cash bonuses and stock options
Samsung (Korean)	Self-setting, then finalized by host-country manager	Biannually for managerial purposes, annually for development purposes; Open feedback in interview	Orientation Language training Can apply to host location supervisor No clear connection between performance result and career development	Clear link between performance and compensation Senior managers: cash bonuses and stock options Ordinary expatriates; cash bonuses
Windbond (Taiwanese)	Self-setting, then finalized by host-country manager	Biannual performance appraisal; Feedback depends on manager	Orientation Seldom take training programs while on assignment Can apply to host location supervisor No clear connection between performance result and career development	Clear link between performance and compensation Cash bonuses and stock options

Source: Adapted from His-An Shih, Yun-Hwa Chiang, In-Sook Kim, "Expatriate Performance Management from MNEs of Different National Origins," *International Journal of Manpower* 26, no. 2 (2005): 161–62. Reprinted with permission of Emerald Group Publishing Ltd.

EXPATRIATE TRAINING AND DEVELOPMENT

It is clear that preparation and training for cross-cultural interactions are critical. The Global Relocation Trends Survey revealed that attrition rates for expatriates were more than double the rate of non-expatriates. They found that 21 percent of expatriates left their companies during the assignments, and another 23 percent left within a year of returning from the assignment.[38] Moreover, about half of those remain longer in their overseas assignment function at a low level of effectiveness. The direct cost alone of a failed expatriate assignment is estimated to be from

$200,000 to $1.2 million. The indirect costs may be far greater, depending on the expatriate's position. Relations with the host-country government and customers may be damaged, resulting in a loss of market share and a poor reception for future PCNs.

Both cross-cultural adjustment problems and practical differences in everyday living present challenges for expatriates and their families. Examples are evident from a survey of expatriates when they ranked the countries that presented the most challenging assignments to them, along with some pet peeves from their experiences:

China: a continuing problem for expatriates; one complained that at his welcome banquet he was served duck tongue and pigeon head.

Brazil: Expatriates stress that cell phones are essential because home phones don't work.

India: Returning executives complain that the pervasiveness of poverty and street children is overwhelming.

Indonesia: Here you need to plan ahead financially because landlords typically demand rent two to three years in advance.

Japan: Expatriates and their families remain concerned that, although there is excellent medical care, the Japanese doctors reveal little to their patients.

After these five countries, expatriates rank Russia, Mexico, Saudi Arabia, South Korea, and France as challenging.[39]

Even though cross-cultural training has proved to be of high value in making the assignment a success, as indicated by 73 percent of the respondents in the 2005 Global Relocation Survey, only 20 percent of companies had formal cross-cultural training for expatriates.[40] Much of the rationale for this lack of training is an assumption that managerial skills and processes are universal. In a simplistic way, a manager's domestic track record is used as the major selection criterion for an overseas assignment.

In most countries, however, the success of the expatriate is not left so much to chance. Foreign companies provide considerably more training and preparation for expatriates than U.S. companies. Therefore, it is not hard to understand why Japanese expatriates experience significantly fewer incidences of failure than their U.S. counterparts, although this may be partially because fewer families accompany Japanese assignees. Japanese multinationals typically have recall rates of below 5 percent, signifying that they send abroad managers who are far better prepared and more adept at working and flourishing in a foreign environment.[41] While this success is largely attributable to training programs, it is also a result of intelligent planning by the human resource management staff in most Japanese organizations, as reported by Tung.[42] This planning begins with a careful selection process for overseas assignments, based on the long-term knowledge of executives and their families. An effective selection process, of course, will eliminate many potential "failures" from the start. Another factor is the longer duration of overseas assignments, averaging almost five years, which allows the Japanese expatriate more time to adjust initially and then to function at full capacity. In addition, Japanese expatriates receive considerable support from headquarters and sometimes even from local divisions set up for that purpose. At NEC Corporation, for example, part of the Japanese giant's globalization strategy is its permanent boot camp, with its elaborate training exercises to prepare NEC managers and their families for overseas battle.[43]

The demands on expatriate managers have always been as much a result of the multiple relationships that they have to maintain as they are of the differences in the host-country environment. Those relations include family relations; internal relations with people in the corporation, both locally and globally, especially with headquarters; external relations (suppliers, distributors, allies, customers, local community, etc.); and relations with the host government. It is important to pinpoint any potential problems that an expatriate may experience with those relationships so that these problems may be addressed during predeparture training. Problem recognition is the first stage in a comprehensive plan for developing expatriates. The three areas critical to preparation are cultural training, language instruction, and familiarity with everyday matters.[44] In the model shown in Exhibit 9-5, various development methods are used to address these areas during predeparture training, postarrival training, and reentry training. These methods continue to be valid and used by many organizations. Two-way feedback between the executive and the trainers at each stage helps to tailor the level and kinds of training to the individual manager. The desired goal is the increased effectiveness of the expatriate as a result of familiarity with local conditions, cultural awareness, and an appreciation of his or her family's needs in the host country.

EXHIBIT 9-5   IHRM Process to Maximize Effectiveness of Expatriate Assignments

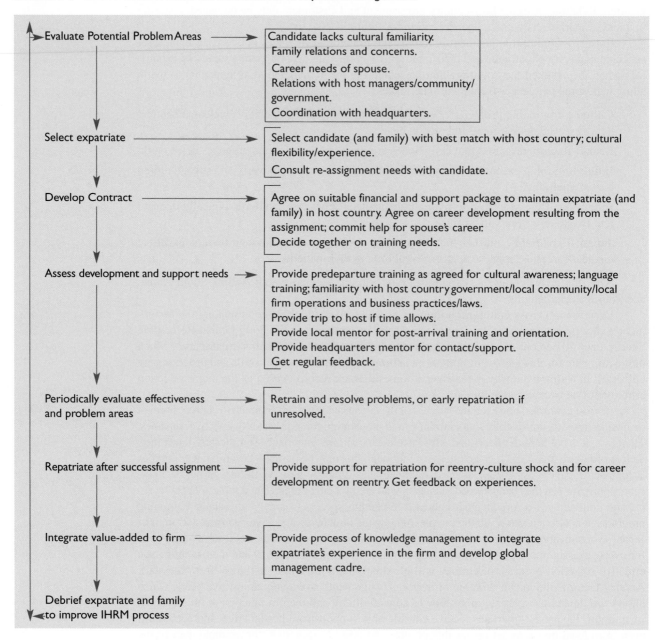

Cross-cultural Training

Training in language and practical affairs is quite straightforward, but cross-cultural training is not; it is complex and deals with deep-rooted behaviors. The actual process of cross-cultural training should result in the expatriate learning both content and skills that will improve interactions with host-country individuals by reducing misunderstandings and inappropriate behaviors.

CULTURE SHOCK   The goal of training is to ease the adjustment to the new environment by reducing **culture shock**—a state of disorientation and anxiety about not knowing how to behave in an unfamiliar culture. The cause of culture shock is the trauma people experience in new and different cultures, where they lose the familiar signs and cues that they had used to interact in daily life and where they must learn to cope with a vast array of new cultural cues and expectations.[45] The symptoms of culture shock range from mild irritation to deep-seated psychological panic or crisis. The inability to work effectively, stress within the family, and hostility toward host nationals are the common dysfunctional results of culture shock—often leading to the manager giving up and going home.

It is helpful to recognize the stages of culture shock to understand what is happening. Culture shock usually progresses through four stages, as described by Oberg: (1) *honeymoon*, when positive attitudes and expectations, excitement, and a tourist feeling prevail (which may last up to several weeks); (2) *irritation and hostility*, the crisis stage when cultural differences result in problems at work, at home, and in daily living—expatriates and family members feel homesick and disoriented, lashing out at everyone (many never get past this stage); (3) *gradual adjustment*, a period of recovery in which the "patient" gradually becomes able to understand and predict patterns of behavior, use the language, and deal with daily activities, and the family starts to accept their new life; and (4) *biculturalism*, the stage in which the manager and family members grow to accept and appreciate local people and practices and are able to function effectively in two cultures.[46] Many never get to the fourth stage—operating acceptably at the third stage—but those who do report that their assignment is positive and growth oriented.

SUBCULTURE SHOCK   Similar to culture shock, though usually less extreme, is the experience of **subculture shock.** This occurs when a manager is transferred to another part of the country where there are cultural differences—essentially from what she or he perceives to be a "majority" culture to a "minority" one. The shock comes from feeling like an "immigrant" in one's own country and being unprepared for such differences. For instance, someone going from New York to Texas will experience considerable differences in attitudes and lifestyle between those two states. These differences exist even within Texas, with cultures that range from roaming ranches and high technology to Bible-belt attitudes and laws and to areas with a mostly Mexican heritage.[47]

Training Techniques

Many training techniques are available to assist overseas assignees in the adjustment process. These techniques are classified by Tung as (1) *area studies*, that is, documentary programs about the country's geography, economics, sociopolitical history, and so forth; (2) *culture assimilators*, which expose trainees to the kinds of situations they are likely to encounter that are critical to successful interactions; (3) *language training*; (4) *sensitivity training*; and (5) *field experiences*— exposure to people from other cultures within the trainee's own country.[48] Tung recommends using these training methods in a complementary fashion, giving the trainee increasing levels of personal involvement as she or he progresses through each method. Documentary and interpersonal approaches have been found to be comparable, with the most effective intercultural training occurring when trainees become aware of the differences between their own cultures and the ones they are planning to enter.[49]

Similarly categorizing training methods, Ronen suggests specific techniques, such as workshops and sensitivity training, including a field experience called the *host-family surrogate*, where the MNC pays for and places an expatriate family with a host family as part of an immersion and familiarization program.[50]

Most training programs take place in the expatriate's own country prior to leaving. Although this is certainly a convenience, the impact of host-country (or in-country) programs can be far greater than those conducted at home because crucial skills, such as overcoming cultural differences in intercultural relationships, can actually be experienced during in-country training rather than simply discussed.[51] Some MNCs are beginning to recognize that there is no substitute for on-the-job training (OJT) in the early stages of the careers of those managers they hope to develop into senior-level global managers. Colgate-Palmolive—whose overseas sales represent two-thirds of its yearly revenue—is one company whose management development programs adhere to this philosophy. After training at headquarters, Colgate employees become associate product managers in the United States or abroad—and, according to John R. Garrison, then manager of recruitment and development at Colgate, they must earn their stripes by being prepared to country-hop every few years. In fact, says Garrison, "That's the definition of a global manager: one who has seen several environments firsthand."[52] Exhibit 9-6 shows some other global management development programs for junior employees.

EXHIBIT 9-6 Corporate Programs to Develop Global Managers

- ABB (Asea Brown Boveri) rotates about 500 managers around the world to different countries every two to three years in order to develop a management cadre of transpatriates to support their global strategy.
- PepsiCo has an orientation program for its foreign managers, which brings them to the United States for one-year assignments in bottling division plants.
- British Telecom uses informal mentoring techniques to induct employees into the ways of their assigned country; existing expatriate workers talk to prospective assignees about the cultural factors to expect (www.FT.com).
- Honda of America Manufacturing gives its U.S. supervisors and managers extensive preparation in Japanese language, culture, and lifestyle and then sends them to the parent company in Tokyo for up to three years.
- General Electric likes its engineers and managers to have a global perspective whether or not they are slated to go abroad. The company gives regular language and cross-cultural training for them so that they are equipped to conduct business with people around the world (www.GE.com).

MANAGEMENT FOCUS

Citibank Gives Advice on Career Planning

Be Mobile: to Get Somewhere, You Have to go Places!

As Citibank continues to expand globally, there is a growing need for a cadre of professionals with the global perspective to lead the organization. Two-thirds of Citibank's current management team have already had international experience. While living and working in other countries are probably the most direct ways to gain a global perspective, there are alternate routes to accomplish this objective. These are well worth exploring if your road to career growth lies over Citibank's global horizons.

A Global Move is a Good Career Move

Expatriate assignments offer an extraordinary opportunity for experience, learning, and personal and career enrichment. Our goal is to have each expatriate assignment fulfill a business need and to provide each person who accepts an expatriate assignment with professional as well as personal growth opportunities.

Some Career Advantages Offered by an Expatriate Assignment

- Develop a global business outlook and an understanding of how to leverage the bank's global position.
- Gain the broader perspective through working in different cultures, geographies, businesses, and functions.
- Interact with a wide range of customers and work with globally focused managers and colleagues, so you can stretch beyond your current environment and add breadth and depth to your work experience.
- Apply your solutions to truly unique problems within different cultures and environments.
- Take on new challenges that stretch and develop your skills by requiring you to take educated risks.

Other Ways to Gain a Global Perspective

While advantageous for some, international assignments aren't right for everyone. Only you and those close to you can decide if you want to live and work in a different country, and if so, at which point in time. If success on your career path requires international experience and you are unable to take on an international assignment at this time for any reason, there are other ways to gain global exposure. These might include short-term assignments in other locations, jobs that involve cross-border interaction, or a task force made up of a global team.

Source: www.Citibank.com

The importance of developing a global orientation in one's career development is illustrated by the advice offered to potential applicants to Citibank given on their Web site, as described in the accompanying Management Focus: Citibank Gives Advice on Career Planning. Citibank is now part of Citigroup—a global financial and insurance institution—since the merger of Citicorp and Travelers Insurance in 1998.

INTEGRATING TRAINING WITH GLOBAL ORIENTATION   In continuing our discussion of "strategic fit," it is important to remember that training programs, like staffing approaches, be designed with the company's strategy in mind. Although it is probably impractical to break down those programs into a lot of variations, it is feasible to at least consider the relative level or stage of globalization that the firm has reached because obvious major differences would be appropriate, for example, from the initial export stage to the full global stage. Exhibit 9-7 suggests levels of rigor and types of training content appropriate for the firm's managers, as well as those for host-country nationals, for four globalization stages—export, multidomestic, multinational, and global. It is noteworthy, for example, that the training of host-country nationals for a global firm has a considerably higher level of scope and rigor than that for the other stages and borders on the standards for the firm's expatriates.

As a further area for managerial preparation for global orientation—in addition to training plans for expatriates and for HCNs separately—there is a particular need to anticipate potential problems with the interaction of expatriates and local staff. In a study of expatriates and local staff (inpatriates) in Central and Eastern European joint ventures and subsidiaries, Peterson found that managers reported a number of behaviors by expatriates that helped them to integrate with local staff, but also some which were hindrances (see Exhibit 9-8).[54] Clearly, this kind of feedback from MNC managers in the field can provide the basis for expatriate training and also help HCNs to anticipate and work with the expatriates in order to meet joint strategic objectives.

EXHIBIT 9-7   Stage of Globalization and Training Design Issues[53]

Export Stage	**MNC Stage**
Training Need: Low to moderate	*Training Need:* High moderate to high
Content: Emphasis should be on interpersonal skills, local culture, customer values, and business behavior.	*Content:* Emphasis should be on interpersonal skills, two-way technology, transfer, corporate value transfer, international strategy, stress management, local culture, and business practices.
Host-Country Nationals: Train to understand parent-country products and policies.	*Host-Country Nationals:* Train in technical areas, product and service systems, and corporate culture.
MDC Stage	**Global Stage**
Training Need: Moderate to high	*Training Need:* High
Content: Emphasis should be on interpersonal skills, local culture, technology transfer, stress management, and business practices and laws.	*Content:* Emphasis should be on global corporate operations and systems, corporate culture transfer, customers, global competitors, and international strategy.
Host-Country Nationals: Train to familiarize with production and service procedures.	*Host-Country Nationals:* Train for proficiency in global organization production and efficiency systems, corporate culture, business systems, and global conduct policies.

EXHIBIT 9-8 Factors That Help or Hinder the Integration of Expatriate Staff with Local Staff

Factors Helping	Factors Hindering
Forming close working relationships	Not using team concept
Learning local language	Not learning local language
Transferring technical/business knowledge	Arrogance
Ability to integrate into local life	Spouse and family problems in adjusting
Professionalism in behavior	Being autocratic
Cultural sensitivity	Low level of delegating by expatriate
Willingness to learn	Expatriate not being talented
Providing model of competitiveness	Lack of cultural sensitivity
Adaptability	Reluctance to change and adapt
Team-building skills	We–they mentality
Introducing effective management control system	Too short expatriate assignment to nation
Focus on service dimension	"Home-country" mentality
Teaching locals about market economy	Poor cross-cultural mentality
Marketing know-how	Lack of curiosity
Friendliness/openness	Acting like back home
Deep financial knowledge	Different way of thinking than local staff
Self-confidence	
Strong work ethic	
Previous assignments in the region	
Treating local staff with respect	
Listening skills	
Acceptance of local culture	

Source: Reprinted from R. B. Peterson, *Journal of World Business* 38 (2003): 55–69. "The Use of Expatriates and Inpatriates in Central and Eastern Europe Since the Wall Came Down," with permission from Elsevier.

Compensating Expatriates

> *If you're an expatriate working alongside another expatriate and you're being treated differently, it creates a lot of dissension.*
>
> CHRISTOPHER TICE,
> *Manager, Global Expatriate Operations, DuPont Inc.*[55]

The significance of an appropriate compensation and benefits package to attract, retain, and motivate international employees cannot be overemphasized. Compensation is a crucial link between strategy and its successful implementation: There must be a fit between compensation and the goals for which the firm wants managers to aim. So that they will not feel exploited, MNC employees need to perceive equity and goodwill in their compensation and benefits, whether they are PCNs, HCNs, or TCNs. The premature return of expatriates or the unwillingness of managers to take overseas assignments can often be traced to their knowledge that the assignment is detrimental to them financially and usually to their career progression. One company which recognizes the need for a reasonable degree of standardization in its treatment of expatriates is DuPont. The company has centralized programs for its approximately 400 international relocations in its Global Transfer Center of Expertise, so its expatriates know that everyone is getting the same package. The company seems to be on the cutting edge, however, since a recent study by Mercer Human Resource Consulting found that "25 percent of multinational corporations do not have a benefits policy for globally mobile employees; 30 percent have no formal governance procedures, and 11 percent have never reviewed their policies."[56]

From the firm's perspective, the high cost of maintaining appropriate compensation packages for expatriates has led many companies—Colgate-Palmolive, Chase Manhattan Bank, Digital Equipment, General Motors, and General Electric among them—to find ways to cut the cost of PCN assignments as much as possible. "Transfer a $100,000-a-year American executive to London—and suddenly he [or she] costs the employer $300,000," explains the *Wall Street Journal*. "Move him to Stockholm or Tokyo, and he [or she] easily becomes a million-dollar [manager]."[57]

Firms try to cut overall costs of assignments by either extending the expatriate's tour, since turnover is expensive—especially when there is an accompanying family to move—or to assign expatriates to a much shorter tour as an unaccompanied assignment.[58]

Designing and maintaining an appropriate compensation package is more complex than it would seem because of the need to consider and reconcile parent- and host-country financial, legal, and customary practices. The problem is that although little variation in typical executive salaries at the level of base compensation exists around the world, a wide variation in net spendable income is often present. U.S. executives may receive more in cash and stock, but they have to spend more for what foreign companies provide, such as cars, vacations, and entertainment allowances. In addition, the manager's purchasing power with that net income is affected by the relative cost of living. The cost of living is considerably higher in most of Europe than in the United States. In designing compensation and benefit packages for PCNs, then, the challenge to IHRM professionals is to maintain a standard of living for expatriates equivalent to their colleagues at home, plus compensating them for any additional costs incurred. This policy is referred to as "keeping the expatriate whole."[59]

To ensure that expatriates do not lose out through their overseas assignment, the **balance sheet approach** is often used to equalize the standard of living between the host country and the home country and to add some compensation for inconvenience or qualitative loss.[60] However, recently some companies have begun to base their compensation package on a goal of achieving a standard of living comparable to that of host-country managers, which does help resolve some of the problems of pay differentials.

In fairness, the MNC is obliged to make up additional costs that the expatriate would incur for taxes, housing, and goods and services. The tax differential is complex and expensive for the company, and MNCs generally use a policy of tax equalization. This means that the company pays any taxes due on any type of additional compensation that the expatriate receives for the assignment; the expatriate pays in taxes only what she or he would pay at home. The burden of foreign taxes can be lessened, however, by efficient tax planning—a fact often overlooked by small firms. The timing and methods of paying people determine what foreign taxes are incurred. For example, a company can save on taxes by renting an apartment for the employee instead of providing a cash housing allowance. All in all, MNCs have to weigh the many aspects of a complete compensation package, especially at high management levels, to effect a tax equalization policy. The total cost to the company can vary greatly by location; for example:

> *Expatriates in Germany may incur twice the income tax they would in the U.S., and they are taxed on their housing and cost-of-living allowances as well. This financial snowball effect is a great incentive to make sure we really need to fill the position with an expatriate.*
>
> JOHN DE LEON,
> *Vice President IHRM, CH2MHill, 2003.*[61]

Managing PCN compensation is a complex challenge for companies with overseas operations. All components of the compensation package must be considered in light of both home- and host-country legalities and practices. Those components include:

Salary: Local salary buying power and currency translation, as compared with home salary; bonuses or incentives for dislocation

Taxes: Equalize any differential effects of taxes as a result of expatriate's assignment

Allowances: Relocation expenses; cost-of-living adjustments; housing allowance for assignment and allowance to maintain house at home; trips home for expatriate and family; private education for children

Benefits: Health insurance; stock options.

Most important, to be strategically competitive, the compensation package must be comparatively attractive to the kinds of managers the company wishes to hire or relocate. Some of those managers will, of course, be local managers in the host country. This, too, is a complex situation requiring competitive compensation policies that can attract, motivate, and retain the best local managerial talent. In many countries, however, it is a considerable challenge to develop compensation packages appropriate to the local situation and culture, while also recognizing the differences between local salaries and those expected by expatriates or transpatriates (that difference itself often being a source of competitive advantage).

TRAINING AND COMPENSATING HOST-COUNTRY NATIONALS

Training HCNs

> *We found that the key human resource role of the MNC [in Central and Eastern Europe] was to expose the local staff to a market economy; to instill world standards of performance; and provide training and functional expertise.*
>
> RICHARD PETERSON[62]

The continuous training and development of HCNs and TCNs for management positions is also important to the long-term success of multinational corporations. As part of a long-term staffing policy for a subsidiary, the ongoing development of HCNs will facilitate the transition to an indigenization policy. Furthermore, multinational companies like to have well-trained managers with broad international experience available to take charge in many intercultural settings, whether at home or abroad, and, increasingly in developing countries. Kimberly-Clark, for example, with over 60,000 employees around the world, has steadily increased its talent development and training programs in all countries, but more recently has focused on developing markets. "In Latin America, the average employee has gone from receiving practically no training time to about 38 hours each year. By contrast, workers in Europe now receive 40 hours per year—eight hours more than in 1996."[63]

Training for HCNs by foreign companies operating in the United States can be quite surprising for managers operating in their own country when they have to learn new ways. Toyota is an example of how employees at all levels must be trained in "the Toyota Way." As recounted by Ms. Newton, a 38-year-old Indiana native who joined Toyota after college 15 years ago and now works at the North American headquarters in Erlanger, Kentucky:

> *For Americans and anyone, it can be a shock to the system to be actually expected to make problems visible. Other corporate environments tend to hide problems from bosses.*[64]

What Ms. Newton is referring to is the colored bar charts against a white bulletin board, which represent the work targets of individual workers, visibly charting their successes or failures to meet those targets. This is part of the Toyota Way. The idea is not to humiliate, but to alert co-workers and enlist their help in finding solutions. Ms. Newton, now a general manager in charge of employee training and development at Toyota's North American manufacturing subsidiary, said it took a while to fully accept that but now she is a firm believer.[65]

Certainly, there is no arguing with success—in 2009 Toyota became the largest global automaker in sales. The training institute in Mikkabi has trained over 700 foreign executives, including cultural orientation, with the same intensity as its training in the production processes. Core concepts such as ownership of problems and visibility are impressed upon new employees. A shared sense of shared purpose is conveyed with open offices—often without even cubicle partitions between desks.[66]

Many multinationals, in particular "chains," wish to train their local managers and workers to bridge the divide between the firm's successful corporate culture and practices, on the one hand, with the local culture and work practices on the other. One example of how to do this in China is the Starbucks firm, featured in the Management Focus: "Success! Starbucks' Java Style Helps to Recruit, Train, and Retain Local Managers in Beijing."

Many HCNs are, of course, receiving excellent training in global business and Internet technology within their home corporations. For example, Kim In Kyung, twenty-four, has a job involving world travel and high technology with Samsung Electronics Company of Seoul, South Korea. Part of Samsung's strategy is to promote its new Internet focus, and this strategy has landed the farmer's daughter a $100,000 job. Her situation reflects Seoul's sizzling tech boom, where IT comprises 11 percent of its $400 billion economy and is expected to reach 20 percent by 2010.[68]

Whether in home corporations, MNC subsidiaries, or joint ventures in any country, managerial training to facilitate e-business adoption is competitively taking on increasing importance in order to take advantage of new strategic opportunities. While large companies are well ahead on the curve for information and communication technologies (ICT), there is considerable need for small and medium-sized enterprises (SMEs) to adopt such knowledge-creating capabilities.

Managerial training in ICT is particularly critical for firms in new economy and emerging markets, and, in the aggregate, can provide leverage for rapid economic growth in regions such as Eastern Europe. Research in 2003 by Damaskopoulos and Evgeniou addressed these needs by

MANAGEMENT FOCUS

Success! Starbucks' Java Style Helps to Recruit, Train, and Retain Local Managers in Beijing

Starbucks in Shanghai's historic Yu Yuan Garden area is one of the first Starbucks in China; it opened in 2000.

Source: Shanghai China Store Front. Exterior shot of retail store in international market. CSR FY05 Annual Report; compliments of Starbucks Inc., November 2006, used with permission.

When we first started, people didn't know who we were and it was rough finding sites. Now landlords are coming to us.

DAVID SUN,
President of Beijing Mei Da Coffee Company (former Starbucks' partner for Northern China,) The Economist, October 6, 2001.

As we see from the above quote, Starbucks has achieved a remarkable penetration rate in China, given that it is a country of devoted tea drinkers who do not take readily to the taste of coffee.

Starbucks is no stranger to training leaders from around the world into the Starbucks style As of March 2009, Starbucks has both store-owned and licensed locations in 44 countries, as detailed below.

Starbucks' Global Presence as of March 2009.

UNITED STATES STORES

50 states, plus the District of Columbia.

7,087 Company-operated stores.

4,081 Licensed stores.

INTERNATIONAL STORES

43 countries outside the United States.

Company-operated: 1,796 stores, including company-operated, in Australia, Canada, Chile, China (Northern China, Southern China), Germany, Ireland, Puerto Rico, Singapore, Thailand and the United Kingdom.

Joint Venture and Licensed stores: 2,792 in Austria, Bahamas, Bahrain, Brazil, Canada, China (Shanghai/Eastern China), Cyprus, Czech Republic, Denmark, Egypt, France, Greece, Hong Kong, Indonesia, Ireland, Japan, Jordan, Kuwait, Lebanon, Macau S.A.R., Malaysia, Mexico, the

Netherlands, New Zealand, Oman, Peru, Philippines, Qatar, Romania, Russia, Saudi Arabia, South Korea, Spain, Switzerland, Taiwan, Turkey, United Arab Emirates and the United Kingdom.[67]

Company managers nevertheless have had quite a challenge in recruiting, motivating, and retaining managers for its Beijing outlets (and, more recently in its Qunguang Square outlet in Central China). Starbucks' primary challenge has been to recruit good managers in a country where the demand for local managers by foreign companies expanding there is far greater than the supply of managers with any experience in capitalist-style companies. Chinese recruits have stressed that they are looking for opportunity to get training and to advance in global companies rather than for money. They know that managers with experience in Western organizations can always get a job. The brand's pop-culture reputation is also an attraction to young Beijingers.

In order to expose the recruits to java-style culture as well as to train them for management, Starbucks brings them to Seattle, Washington, for three months to give them a taste of the West Coast lifestyle and the company's informal culture, such as Western-style backyard barbecues.

Then they are exposed to the art of cappuccino-making at a real store before dawn and concocting dozens of fancy coffees. They get the same intensive training as anyone else anywhere in the world. One recruit, Mr. Wang, who worked in a large Beijing hotel before finding out how to make a triple grand latte, said that he enjoys the casual atmosphere and respect. The training and culture are very different from what one would expect at a traditional state-owned company in China, where the work is strictly defined and has no challenge for employees.

Starbucks has found that motivating their managers in Beijing is multifaceted. They know that people won't switch jobs for money alone. They want to work for a company that gives them an opportunity to learn. They also want to have a good working environment and a company with a strong reputation. The recruits have expressed their need for trust and participation in an environment where local nationals are traditionally not expected to exercise initiative or authority. In all, what seems to motivate them more than anything else is their dignity.

Sources: www.Starbucks.com Corporate Information, March 5, 2009; Press Release, October 11, 2006; J. Adamy, "Starbucks Raises New-Stores Goal, Enters iTunes Deal," *Wall Street Journal,* October 6, 2006; "China: Starbucks Opens New Outlet in Beijing," Info-Prod (Middle East) Ltd., July 20, 2003; "Coffee with Your Tea? Starbucks in China," *The Economist*, October 6, 2001.

surveying more than 900 SME managers in Slovenia, Poland, Romania, Bulgaria, and Cyprus. While most managers recognized the opportunities in implementing e-business strategies, they also noted the urgent need of training in order to take advantage of those opportunities. Exhibit 9-9 shows, in order of priority, the training needs and issues as perceived by those SME managers. Some of these factors are at the firm level, while other issues relate to the market and regulatory levels, such as the need to increase security for commercial activity on the Internet.[69] Such findings highlight the need to recognize the strategy-staffing-training link, and the importance to the overall growth of emerging economies.

In another common scenario also requiring the management of a mixture of executives and employees, American and European MNCs presently employ Asians as well as Arab locals in their plants and offices in Saudi Arabia, bringing together three cultures: well-educated Asian managers living in a Middle Eastern, highly traditional society who are employed by a firm reflecting Western technology and culture. This kind of situation requires training to help all parties effectively integrate multiple sets of culturally based values, expectations, and work habits.

Compensating HCNs

How do firms deal with the question of what is appropriate compensation for host-country nationals, given local norms and the competitive needs of the firm? According to a survey of 90 MNCs by Mercer Human Resource Consulting in 2005:

> *Eighty-five percent of multinationals have a global pay strategy in place, and the remaining 15 percent plan to introduce one by 2007. These global strategies consistently include policies on positioning pay relative to the market, short-term and long-term incentive design and methodologies for job grading. More than half incorporate fixed guidelines.*
>
> WORKFORCE MANAGEMENT,
> *April 10, 2006.*[70]

Of course, no one set of solutions can be applicable in any country. Many variables apply—including local market factors and pay scales, government involvement in benefits, the

EXHIBIT 9-9   SME Managers in Eastern Europe: Training Priorities for E-Business Development

Addressing security and privacy concerns
Developing a business plan
Developing an e-business strategy
Understanding of electronic payment methods
Financing e-business initiatives
Personalization and customer relationship management on the Internet
Sourcing e-business solutions and expertise
Developing the right partnerships for e-business
Training in technology management
Implementation of e-business strategy
Learning how to collect marketing intelligence online
Crafting the right business model for the Internet
Developing marketing strategies for the Internet
Collecting marketing intelligence online
Opportunities and pitfalls of online advertising
Understanding mobile commerce
Devising a sustainable revenue model
Understanding business-to-business marketplaces and virtual value chains

Source: Reprinted from Panagiotis Damaskopoulos and Theodoros Evgeniou, "Adoption of New Economy Practices by SMEs in Eastern Europe," *European Management Journal* 21, no. 2 (2003): 133–45. With permission from Elsevier.

role of unions, the cost of living, and so on. In Eastern Europe, for example, Hungarians, Poles, and Czechs spend 35 to 40 percent of their disposable income on food and utilities, which may run as high as 75 percent in the Russian Federation.[71] Therefore, East European managers must have cash for about 65 to 80 percent of their base pay, compared to about 40 percent for U.S. managers (the rest being long-term incentives, benefits, and perks). In addition, they still expect the many social benefits provided by the "old government." To be competitive, MNCs can focus on providing goods and services that are either not available at all or are extremely expensive in Eastern Europe. Such upscale perks can be used to atttract high-skilled workers.

> *Nestlé Bulgaria offers a company car and a cellular phone to new recruits. . . . Fuel prices are about $2 per gallon and cell phones cost $1,200 a year—equivalent to half a year's salary.*[72]

In Japan, companies are revamping their HRM policies to compete in a global economy, in response to a decade-long economic slump. The traditional lifetime employment and guaranteed tidy pension are giving way to the more Western practices of competing for jobs, of basing pay on performance rather than seniority, and of making people responsible for their own retirement fund decisions.[73]

In China, too, change is underway. University graduates may now seek their own jobs rather than be assigned to state-owned companies, though nepotism is still common. In a study of HRM practices in China, Bjorkman and Lu found that a key concern of Western managers in China was the compensation of the HCNs. In Beijing and Shanghai, top Chinese managers have seen their salaries increase by 30 to 50 percent in the last few years. They have also received considerable fringe benefits, such as housing, company cars, pensions, and overseas training. The difficulty, too, was that in Western-Chinese joint ventures, the Chinese partner opposed pay increases.[74] Yet when trying to introduce performance-based pay, the Western companies ran into considerable opposition and usually gave up, using salary increases instead. Setting up some kind of housing scheme, such as investing in apartments, seemed to be one way that foreign-owned firms were able to compete for good managers. Those managers were, understandably, maximizing their job opportunities now that they did not have to get permission to leave the Chinese state-owned companies.[75]

According to Citigroup, it is also imperative to make clear what benefits, as well as salary, come with a position because of the way compensation is perceived and regulated around the world.[76] In Latin America, for example, an employee's pay and title are associated with what type of car they can receive.

COMPARATIVE MANAGEMENT IN FOCUS

IHRM Practices in Australia, Canada, China, Indonesia, Japan, Latin America, Mexico, South Korea, Taiwan, and the United States

In a comparative long-term study of how the major IHRM functions are performed around the world, a team of 37 researchers in ten locations, led by Mary Ann von Glinow, studied how and in what environments various organizations conducted those functions. Exhibit 9-10 is a summary of their findings from their "Best International Human Resource Management Practices Project." For the practice of compensation, for example, the first column shows those practices the researchers found to be universal within the cultures studied. The second column shows countries or regions where those practices are similar. The third column shows where those practices were specific to certain countries. For the practice of selection, for example, a major tool in Korea is the employment test, whereas in Taiwan the job interview is considered the most important criterion. Korea and Taiwan also "cluster" in de-emphasizing proven work experience; whereas the Anglo cluster showed the job interview, technical skill, and work experience to be the most important selection criteria. Those "universals" found for the selection function, were "getting along with others" and "fit with the corporate values."[77]

EXHIBIT 9-10 Trends in International Human Resource Management Practices Across Selected Countries and Regions

Practice	Universal Derived ETICS "Best Practices"	Regional or Country Clusters	Country Specific
Compensation	Pay incentives should not comprise too much of an employee's compensation package. Compensation should be based on individual job performance. There should be a reduced emphasis on seniority. Benefits should comprise an important part of a compensation package.	Seniority-based pay, pay based on group/team or organizational goals, and pay based on future goals—all are used to a larger extent in the Asian and Latin countries now.	U.S. and Canada has less use of pay incentives than expected. China and Taiwan had above-average use of pay incentives, and wanted more based on individual contributions.
Selection	"Getting along with others", and "Fit with the Corporate Values" signals a shift in selection from "West meets East."	Selection practices were remarkably similar among the Anglo countries. Specifically, job interview, technical skill, and work experience are the most important selection criteria. How well the person fits the company's values replace work experience as one of the top selection criteria for future selection practices. Selection practices are quite similar in Korea, Japan, and Taiwan. Specifically, proven work experience is de-emphasized as a selection practice in these countries. In the Anglo and Latin American countries, allowing subordinates to express themselves is perceived as an important future appraisal practice.	In Japan, a heavy emphasis is placed on a person's potential (thus hiring new graduates) and his/her ability to get along with others. A relatively low weight was given to job-related skills, and experience as a selection criterion. In Korea, employment tests are considered crucial and are used to a large extent as a selection tool, as well as hiring new graduates. Koreans de-emphasize experience. In Taiwan, the job interview is considered the most important criterion in the selection process.

EXHIBIT 9-10 *(Continued)*

Performance appraisal	In all countries, "should-be" scores were higher on every purpose, suggesting that the purposes of PA have fallen short in every country. All countries indicated that a greater emphasis be placed on development and documentation in future PA practices. In particular, recognizing subordinates, evaluating their goal acheivement, planning their development activities, and (ways to) improving their performance are considered the most important appraisal practices for the future.	In contrast, in the Asian countries expression is used to a low extent, particularly in Korea. In the Latin American countries, the administrative purposes of performance appraisal are considered important in future practice.	In Taiwan, the administrative purposes of performance appraisal are considered important in future practice.
T&D	In most countries, T&D practices are used to improve employees' technical skills. There is a growing trend toward using T&D for team building and "soft management practices."	In the Anglo countries, the softer T&D practices such as team building, understanding business practices and corporate culture, and the pro-active T&D practices such as preparation for future assignment and cross-training are used moderately; however, a significant increase in these practices is desired. In the Latin countries, an increase in the extent to which all T&D practices are used is desired.	In Mexico, T&D as a reward to employees is considered a highly desirable practice. In the U.S. and Korea, preparing employees for future job assign-ments is used to a lesser extent. U.S. is using outsourcing more. In the Asian countries, most T&D practices are used moderately and are consistently considered satisfactory. In Japan, remedying past performance is used to a small extent, however, a significant increase in this practice is desired. In Korea, team building is used extensively and emphasized in all T&D practices.
Relation to business strategy	Across most countries, the HRM practices most closely linked to organizational capability are training and development and performance appraisal.	In the Asian countries, linkages were indicated between both low cost and differentiation strategies and HRM practices.	In Mexico, no linkages were indicated between organizational capability and HRM practices.
Status of HRM function			In Japan and Taiwan few linkages were indicated between organizational capability and HRM practices. Status of HRM was highest in Australia and lowest in Indonesia.

Source: Mary Ann Von Glinow, Ellen A. Drost, and Mary B. Teagarden, "Converging on IHRM Best Practices: Lessons Learned from a Globally Distributed Consortium on Theory and Practice," *Human Resource Management* 41, no. 1 (2002): 133–35.
Reprinted with permission of John Wiley and Sons, Inc.

CONCLUSION

The effectiveness of managers at foreign locations is crucial to the success of the firm's operations, particularly because of the lack of proximity to and control by headquarters executives. The ability of expatriates to initiate and maintain cooperative relationships with local people and agencies will determine the long-term success, even the viability, of the operation. In a real sense, a company's global cadre represents its most valuable resource. Proactive management of that resource by headquarters will result in having the right people in the right place at the right time, appropriately trained, prepared, and supported. MNCs using these IHRM practices can anticipate the effective management of the foreign operation, the fostering of expatriates' careers, and ultimately, the enhanced success of the corporation.

Summary of Key Points

1. Global human resource management is a vital component of implementing global strategy and is increasingly being recognized as a major determinant of success or failure in international business.
2. The main staffing alternatives for global operations are the ethnocentric, polycentric, regiocentric, and global approaches. Each approach has its appropriate uses, according to its advantages and disadvantages, and, in particular, the firm's strategy.
3. The causes of expatriate failure include the following: poor selection based on inappropriate criteria, inadequate preparation before assignment, alienation from headquarters, inability of manager or family to adapt to local environment, inadequate compensation package, and poor programs for career support and repatriation.
4. The three major areas critical to expatriate preparation are cultural training, language instruction, and familiarity with everyday matters.
5. Common training techniques for potential expatriates include area studies, culture assimilators, language training, sensitivity training, and field experiences.
6. Appropriate and attractive compensation packages must be designed by IHRM staffs to sustain a competitive global expatriate staff. Compensation packages for host-country managers must be designed to fit the local culture and situation, as well as the firm's objectives.

Discussion Questions

1. What are the major alternative staffing approaches for international operations? Explain the relative advantages of each and the conditions under which you would choose one approach over another.
2. Why is the HRM role so much more complex, and important, in the international context?
3. Explain the common causes of expatriate failure. What are the major success factors for expatriates? Explain the role and importance of each.
4. What are the common training techniques for managers going overseas? How should these vary as appropriate to the level of globalization of the firm?
5. Explain the balance sheet approach to international compensation packages. Why is this approach so important? Discuss the pros and cons of aligning the expatriate compensation package with the host-country colleagues compared to the home-country colleagues.
6. Discuss the importance of a complete program for expatriate performance management. What are the typical components for such a program?

Application Exercises

1. Make a list of the reasons you would want to accept a foreign assignment and a list of reasons you would want to reject it. Do they depend on the location? Compare your list with a classmate and discuss your reasons.
2. Research a company with operations in several countries and ascertain the staffing policy used for those countries. Find out what kinds of training and preparation are provided for expatriates and what kinds of results the company is experiencing with expatriate training.

Experiential Exercise

This can be done in groups or individually. After the exercise, discuss your proposals with the rest of the class.

You are the expatriate general manager of a British company's subsidiary in Brazil, an automobile component parts manufacturer.

You and your family have been in Brazil for seven years, and now you are being reassigned and replaced with another expatriate—Ian Fleming. Ian is bringing his family—Helen, an instructor in computer science, who hopes to find a position; a son, age twelve; and a daughter, age fourteen. None of them has lived abroad before. Ian has asked you what he and his family should expect in the new assignment. Remembering all the problems you and your family experienced in the first couple of years of your assignment in Brazil, you want to facilitate their adjustment and have decided to do two things:

1. Write a letter to Ian, telling him what to expect, both on the job and in the community. Tell him about some of the cross-cultural conflicts he may run into with his coworkers and employees, and how he should handle them.

2. Set up some arrangements and support systems for the family and design a support package for them, with a letter to each family member telling them what to expect.

Internet Resources

Visit the Deresky Companion Website at www.pearsonhighered.com/ deresky for this chapter's Internet resources.

CASE STUDY

Kelly's Assignment in Japan

Well, it's my job that brought us here in the first place . . . I am going to have to make a decision to stick with this assignment and hope I can work things out, or to return to the United States and probably lose my promised promotion after this assignment—maybe even my job.

As she surveyed the teeming traffic of downtown Tokyo from her office window, Kelly tried to assess the situation her family was in, how her job was going, and what could have been done to lead to a better situation four months ago when she was offered the job.

As a program manager for a startup internet services company, she had been given the opportunity to head up the sales and marketing department in Tokyo. Her boss said that "the sky's the limit" as far as her being able to climb the corporate ladder if she was successful in Tokyo. She explained that she did not speak Japanese and that she knew nothing about Japan. But he said he had confidence in her since she had done such a great job in Boston and in recent short assignments to London and Munich. Moreover, the company offered her a very attractive compensation package which included a higher salary, bonuses, a relocation allowance, a rent free apartment in Tokyo, and an education allowance for their two children, Lisa and Sam, to attend private schools. She was told she had two days to decide, and that they wanted her in Tokyo in three weeks because they wanted her to prepare and present a proposal for a new account opportunity there as soon as possible. Her boss said they would hire a relocation company to handle the move for her.

That night Kelly excitedly discussed the opportunity with her husband, Joe. He was glad for her and thought it would be an exciting experience for the whole family. However, he was concerned about his own job and what the move would do to his career. She told him that her boss said that Joe would probably find something or get transferred there, but that her boss did seem unconcerned about that. In the end, Joe felt that Kelly should have this opportunity, and he agreed to the move. He talked to his boss about a transfer and was told that they would look into that and get back to him. However, he knew that his company was having layoffs because of the economic decline which was taking its toll on profits in 2009. The problem was that Kelly had to make a decision before he could fully explore his options, so Kelly and Joe decided to go ahead with the plans. To sweeten the deal, Kelly's company had offered to buy her house in Boston since the housing market decline had her concerned about whether she could sell without taking a loss.

After the long trip, they arrived at their apartment in Tokyo; they were tired but excited, but did not anticipate that the apartment would be so tiny, given the very high rent that the company was paying for it. Kelly realized at once that they had included way too much in their move of personal belongings to be able to fit into this apartment. Undaunted, they planned to spend the weekend sightseeing and looked forward to some travel. Japan was beautiful in the spring and they were anxious to see the area.

On Monday, Kelly took a cab to the office. She had emailed requesting a staff meeting at 9 a.m. She knew that her immediate staff would include seven Japanese, two Americans and two Germans—all men. Her assistant, Peter, was an American who had also just arrived, coming from an assignment in London, and to whom she had not yet spoken. He greeted her at the elevator, looking surprised, and they proceeded to the conference room, where everyone was awaiting "the new boss." Kelly exchanged the usual handshake greetings with the westerners, and then bowed to the Japanese; an awkward silence and exchange took place, with the Japanese looking embarrassed. While she attempted a greeting in her limited Japanese that she had studied on the plane, she was relieved to find that the Japanese spoke English, but they seemed very quiet and hesitant. Peter then told her that they all thought that "Kelly" was a man, and they all attempted a laugh.

After that, Kelly decided that she would just meet with Peter, and postpone the general meeting until the next day. She asked them to each prepare a short presentation for her on their ideas for the new account. While the Americans and Germans said they would have it ready, the Japanese seemed reluctant to commit themselves.

Meanwhile, at home Joe was looking into the schools for the children and also trying to make some contacts to look for a job. Travelling, getting information, and shopping for groceries proved bewildering, but they decided that they would soon get acquainted with local customs.

At the office the next day, Kelly received a short presentation from the westerners on the staff, but when it came to the Japanese they indicated that they had not yet had a chance to meet with their groups and other contacts in order to come to their decisions. Kelly asked them why they had not told her the day before that they needed more time, and when could they be ready. They seemed unwilling to give a direct answer and kept their eyes lowered. In an attempt to lighten the atmosphere and get to know her staff, Kelly then began chatting casually and asked several of them about their families. The Americans chatted on about their children's achievements, the Germans talked about their family positions, and the Japanese went silent, seemingly very confused and offended.

Still attempting to get everyone's ideas for an initial proposal to the potential new client, Kelly later asked one of the Americans who had been there for some time what he thought was the problem and delay in getting presentations from the Japanese. He told her that they did not like to do individual presentations, but rather wanted to gain consensus among themselves and their contacts and present a group presentation. Having learned her lesson, but feeling irritated, she asked him to intervene and have the presentations ready for the next week. When that time came, the rest of the presentations were made by the Japanese, but, oddly, they seemed to be addressed primarily to Peter. Later, Kelly decided to finalize her own presentation to put forth a proposal for the client, which she set up for the following week.

At home, Joe said that he had not heard anything from his company in Boston and asked Kelly to again contact her company to request some networking in Tokyo that might lead to job opportunities for him. Kelly said she would do that, but that there didn't seem to be any one person "back home" who was keeping up with her situation or giving any support about that or about her job.

The children, meanwhile, complained that, although their schools were meant to be bi-lingual English-Japanese, a majority of the children were Japanese and did not speak English; Lisa and Sam felt confused and left out. They were disoriented by the different customs, classes, and foods for lunch. At home they complained that there was no back yard to go out to play, and that they could not get their programs on the television, or understand the Japanese programs.

Back at the office, Kelly worked with her staff to finalize the proposal, but noticed a strained atmosphere. Peter told her that some of them would drop by a local bar for a drink after work, which helped the whole group to relax together. However, she felt that she could not do that, nor that she would be accepted as a female.

The next week, as arranged, Kelly and Peter went to the offices of the client; she knew that a lot was riding on getting this big new contract. She had asked Peter to let them know ahead of time that she is a woman, yet the introductions still seemed strained. She planned to get straight down to business, so when the client company's CEO handed her his business card, she put it in her pocket without a glance, and did not give him her card. Again she noticed some shock and embarrassment all around. (She found out much later that a business card is very important to a Japanese businessman because it conveys all his accomplishments and position without having to say it himself.) Flustered, she tried to make light of the situation, patted him on the back and asked him what his first name was, saying, rather loudly, that hers' was Kelly. He went quiet again, backed away from her, and, with his head bowed, whispered "Michio." He glanced around at his Japanese colleagues rather nervously.

After a period of silence, Michio pointed to the table of refreshments, and indicated that they sit and eat; however, Kelly was anxious to present her power-point slides and went to the end of the table where the equipment was and asked Peter to set up the slides. As she proceeded to go through the proposal, telling them what her company could do for them, she paused and asked for questions. However, when Michio and his two colleagues asked questions, they directed them to Peter, not to her. In fact, they made little eye contact with her at all. She tried to remain cool, but insisted on answering the questions herself. In the end, she sat down and asked Michio what he thought of the proposal. He bowed politely and said "very good" and that he would discuss it with his colleagues and get back to her. However, Kelly did not hear from them, and after a couple of weeks she asked Peter to follow up with them. He did that, but reported that they were not going to pursue the contract. Frustrated, she said, "Well, why did Michio say that it looked very good, then?" She knew that it was a very competitive proposal and felt that something other than the proposed contract was to blame for the loss of the contract.

Disillusioned, but determined not to give up without success in the assignment, Kelly took a cab to go home and think about it, but the driver misunderstood her and went the wrong way and got stuck in traffic. She felt discouraged and wished that she had some female American friends to in whom to confide her problems.

When Kelly got home, Peter was angrily trying to fix dinner, complaining about the small appliances and not being able to understand the food packages or how to prepare the food. He said he needed something else to do but that there did not seem to be a job on the horizon for him. He was also concerned about continuing to live in such a high cost city on only one salary.

Kelly went to the other room to see the children; they were fighting and complaining that they had nothing to do and wanted to go home. Kelly felt that the three months that they had been there was not a fair trial, and was wondering what to do. She wished she had had more time to prepare for this assignment, and whenever she contacted the home office no-one seemed able to advise her.

Case Questions

1. Explain the clashes in culture, customs, and expectations that occurred in this situation.
2. What stage of culture shock is Kelly's family experiencing?
3. Turn back the clock to when Kelly was offered the position in Tokyo. What, if anything, should have been done differently, and by whom?
4. You are Kelly. What should you do now?

Source: Helen Deresky. Adapted and updated from a similar piece by J. Stewart Black and used with his permission.

Developing a Global Management Cadre

OBJECTIVES:

1. To emphasize the critical role of expatriates in managing in host subsidiaries and in transferring knowledge to and from host operations.

2. To acknowledge the importance of international assignments in developing top managers with global experience and perspectives.

3. To recognize the need to design programs for the careful preparation, adaptation, and repatriation of the expatriate and any accompanying family, as well as programs for career management and retention.

4. To become familiar with the use of Global Management Teams to coordinate cross-border business.

5. To recognize the varying roles of women around the world in international management.

6. To understand the variations in host-country labor relations systems and the impact on the manager's job and effectiveness.

Opening Profile: The Expat Life[1]

What is it like to take an assignment abroad? Would you like to be an "expat" (expatriate)? Is it an adventure or a hardship? Experiences of those who have done a stint abroad are mixed. But it is clear that it is very likely an opportunity that will present itself at some point during your career. Most companies with global business transactions want their top employees to have overseas experience. At Procter and Gamble, for example, 39 of the company's top 44 global officers have had an international assignment and 22 were born outside the United States. Most multinational companies are moving from 0.5 to 1 percent of their employees abroad, and about 68 percent expect that to increase, according to the 2008 GMAC Relocation Survey.

Experiences vary by job type, and especially by location. Adjustment is easier for those who go to places where the culture and business practices are similar to their own. Those transitioning between Western Europe and the United States or Canada, for example, typically adapt easier than those going to China or Yemen, as related below. Some expatriates enjoy perks that they do not get at home, and others find they fare worse financially, either while overseas or when they return home. Most expect the assignment to be career-broadening and hope it will leverage them to a promotion. Some expat experiences are described below.

As an example of how quickly the changing global environment can affect expats, we can look at the typical expat life for Wall Street executives as described in the *New York Times* as recently as 2008. "When Wall Streeters pack their bags for Dubai or Shanghai, for example, they get much more than a plane ticket and coverage of per-diem expenses. These days, moving abroad can mean scoring a nanny, a driver or even a bodyguard. In some locations, it means a tax-free income, depending on how you read the rules."[2] In Shanghai, there are 70,000 expatriates around the world, in various capacities. For those in the finance industry the expat package typically includes round trips home a year; fees for a real estate agency, moving expenses, at least one month of temporary accommodation; and language classes, if required. For an accompanying family, fees for private schools, for example, are usually included, and help for the spouse to find a job. A cost of living adjustment is typically included, as well as adjustment for tax equalization. A very nice assignment—however, in spring 2009, the *New York Times* was then reporting about the number of expats in the banking and finance industry who were getting laid off:

> *"Losing your job anywhere is disorienting, but imagine being laid off when you work in a foreign country. Not only is your source of income, and perhaps a good part of your identity, suddenly yanked away, but often you lose your right to remain in the country."*[3]

That was an unusual development, however; for most the overseas assignment has been very rewarding in terms of both personal and job experience.

In many circumstances the adventure which started out with many concerns turns out to be one that the expats and their families do not want to end. According to the GMAC Global Relocation survey, 26% of expats opt to continue their overseas assignment when the original term ends. Those people have settled in to their position and life in the host country and enjoy their situations.

One reporter assigned to Beijing commented, "That's why we recently decided to extend our stay for a fourth year. For me, it was an easy decision. The three years that seemed so ominous turned out to be not nearly enough time to settle into a new life, enjoy an extended stretch of normalized day-to-day home and work life and do everything we want to in terms of travel, absorbing the culture of Beijing and really meditating on what it means to live so far from home."[4]

Assignments in some locations can turn out to be more challenging. One example is that of Mr. Deffontaines, who moved to Yemen in 2008 as the local manager for Total, the French oil giant, along with his family. Since then, Mr. Deffontaines has seen his main export pipeline damaged by terrorists, endured devastating flash floods, and sent expatriate families back home because of security concerns.

Recounting some of the interesting challenges he had faced there Mr. Deffontaines, a 43-year-old Parisian, described "negotiating with tribal leaders and sending actors to remote villages to stage a play about the hazards of gas pipelines. In meetings with government officials to thrash out problems, participants typically chew khat, a mildly narcotic plant that is widely consumed in Yemen but banned in many places around the world."[5]

A particularly difficult decision, in response to growing security concerns, was to send the families of his workers back to France. His own wife, son, and twin daughters were among those forced to depart.

Robert Kneupfer, a lawyer, reflects that, in spite of inconveniences like the 17-year wait for a telephone line and the absence of any McDonald's, the five years he spent in Budapest with his family on behalf of international law firm Baker & McKenzie were a "defining moment both personally and professionally." The 56-year-old partner, now based in Chicago, didn't speak the language, and his children had been reluctant to leave family and friends. His advice: "Don't sweat the small stuff. You need to appreciate the bigger-picture experience."[6] His advice follows that of many others:

- Learn the customs of a new country before arriving, be flexible and maintain a lifeline to your home office. You don't want to become out of sight, out of mind.
- Learn the language, or at least practice a few key phrases.
- Prepare for the cultural differences as a family.
- Develop a support network with the local expatriate community.
- Set up a routine for the whole family as soon as possible.[7]
- Be aware of the potential negative effects on the whole family. The initial excitement can turn to culture shock, loneliness, identity loss and depression, and it is often the employee's spouse and children—without the familiar routine of work—who are most affected.

Further advice from a well-travelled expat comes from Philip Shearer, Group President, Clinique, Estee Lauder. His mother was French, his father British, and he was born in Morocco. After going to college in France and then business school in the United States, he worked at a pharmaceutical company in Minneapolis. Then he worked in France, Mexico, Britain, Japan, and again in the United States for companies like L'Oréal and the Elizabeth Arden division of Eli Lilly. He relates his experiences and suggests that" you learn common themes when you live all over the world. Most important: you have to remain yourself. People will trust you and relate to you whatever your culture is, provided you are trustworthy and credible. Still, you have to get used to other cultures." He warns that Americans generally show off too much. "But in the end, you have to deliver. And that's the same all over the world."[8]

A crucial factor in global competitiveness is the ability of the firm to maximize its global human resources in the long term. In the globalized economy, the knowledge and management resources, as well as the skilled and non-skilled employee resources, required for the firm to succeed are no longer concentrated in a single region but are distributed around the world. There are various categories of those resources—both people and processes—that IHR managers and others must develop and maintain; in particular it is essential for them to:

1. Maximize long-term retention and use of international cadre through career management so that the company can develop a top management team with global experience.
2. Develop effective global management teams.
3. Understand, value, and promote the role of women in international management in order to maximize those underutilized resources.
4. Work with the host-country labor relations system to effect strategic implementation and employee productivity.

EXPATRIATE CAREER MANAGEMENT

Nearly 80 percent of FTSE 100 chief executives in 2005 had had overseas assignments, compared with only 42 percent in 1996.

HEIDRICK & STRUGGLES, *2006*
(International Headhunting Firm)[9]

It is clear from the above quote that the road to the top necessitates that managers have overseas experience. For the firm the ability to develop a top management team, globally experienced, depends largely on the success of expatriates' assignments, and that depends on the ability to well manage the transitions for the expatriate and any accompanying family members.

Preparation, Adaptation, and Repatriation

Family concerns were cited as the most common reason for assignment refusal (89 percent), followed by spouse career concerns (62 percent). Family-related issues play a key role throughout the duration of international assignments; 28 percent of respondents cited family concerns as the top reason for early returns from assignments.

GMAC *Global Relocation*
2008 Survey.[10]

Effective human resource management of a company's global cadre does not end with the overseas assignment. It ends with the successful repatriation of the executive into company headquarters. A study by Heidrick & Struggles, the international headhunting firm, revealed that international experience has become much more important to get to the top of FTSE

(London Stock Exchange) 100 companies than a decade ago. "Chief executives such as Mark Tucker at Prudential, who has experience in the United States and Asia, and Unilever's Patrick Cescau, who has worked in Europe, Asia and the United States., are becoming the norm in top companies."[11] Clearly, those executives and their companies have paid careful attention to what is necessary for successful assignments, career management, and repatriation of their experiences and skills. Such firms realize that long-term, proactive management of such critical resources should begin with the end of the current assignment in mind—that is, it should begin with plans for the repatriation of the executive as part of his or her career path. The management of the reentry phase of the career cycle is as vital as the management of the cross-cultural entry and training. Otherwise, the long-term benefits of that executive's international experience may be negated. Shortsightedly, many companies do little to minimize the potential effects of **reverse culture shock** (return shock). The 2008 KPMG Global Assignment Policies and Practices Survey found that currently, just four percent of the 430 HRM executives surveyed agreed that they handle the repatriation process well and only 12 percent offer a formal mentoring/career coaching plan for their assignees. In fact, the survey results concluded that "25 percent of organizations surveyed do not know if assignees have left the organization within 12 months of returning from international assignment. For repatriated assignees that are tracked as leaving the organization soon after returning from assignment, the overriding reason cited is the lack of an appropriate job after repatriation."[12] For smaller companies, little, if any pre- or post-assignment counseling was provided.

A study by Lazarova and Cagligiuri with 58 expatriates from four North American companies found that repatriates who received supportive practices from their firms felt that their companies had an interest in their careers and well-being and so were more likely to stay with the firm upon reentry. The expatriates were asked their opinions about the importance of various factors to them, using the 11 HRM practices most frequently associated with successful repatriation. Exhibit 10-1 presents the average importance rating for each practice and the extent

EXHIBIT 10-1   Availability and Perceived Importance of Repatriation Practices

Repatriation Support Practices	Mean Importance Score[a]	Std. Dev.	Average Availability (%)
1. Predeparture briefings on what to expect during repatriation	3.16	1.09	45.6
2. Career planning sessions	3.57	0.75	36.2
3. Guarantee/agreement outlining the type of position expatriates will be placed in upon repatriation	3.28	0.88	23.2
4. Mentoring programs while on assignment	2.96	0.98	19.3
5. Reorientation program about the changes in the company	2.81	1.07	10.3
6. Repatriation training seminars on the emotional response following repatriation	2.67	1.07	13.8
7. Financial counseling and financial/tax assistance	3.17	0.94	36.8
8. Lifestyle assistance and counseling on changes likely to occur in expatriates' lifestyles upon return	2.51	1.04	17.9
9. Continuous communications with the home office	3.38	0.81	50.9
10. Visible signs that the company values international experience	3.70	0.50	28.1
11. Communications with the home office about the details of the repatriation process	3.47	0.68	46.3

Note: Based on a scale from (0) not important at all to (4) very important.

Source: M. Lazarova, Paula Caligiuri, "Retaining Repatriates: The Role of Organizational Support Practices," *Journal of World Business* 36, no. 4 (2001), 389–401, reprinted with permission of Elsevier.

to which each practice was available within the participating companies. Number 4, "Career Planning Sessions," for example, was rated very important (3.57 out of 4), yet was offered only 36.2 percent of the time.[13]

The long-term implications of ineffective repatriation practices for any particular company are clear—few good managers will be willing to take international assignments because they will see what happened to their colleagues. If a certain manager lost out on promotion opportunities while overseas and is now, in fact, worse off than before he or she left, the only people willing to take on foreign assignments in the future will be those who have not been able to succeed on the home front or those who think that a stint abroad will be like a vacation. Research has shown that employees commonly see overseas assignments as negative career moves in some U.S. multinational companies.[14] In contrast, such moves are seen as positive in most European, Japanese, and Australian companies because they consider international experience necessary for advancement to top management. In a study of dual-career couples, "the perceived impact of the international assignment upon returning to the U.S." was one of the most important issues stated by managers regarding their willingness to relocate overseas.[15]

Reverse culture shock occurs primarily because of the difficulty of reintegrating into the organization but also because, generally speaking, the longer a person is away, the more difficult it is to get back into the swing of things. Not only might the manager have been overlooked and lost in the shuffle of reorganization, but her or his whole family might have lost social contacts or jobs and feel out of step with their contemporaries. These feelings of alienation from what has always been perceived as "home"—because of the loss of contact with family, friends, and daily life—delay the resocialization process. Such a reaction is particularly serious if the family's overall financial situation has been hurt by the assignment and if the spouse's career has also been kept "on hold" while he or she was abroad.

For companies to maximize the long-term use of their global cadre, they need to make sure that the foreign assignment and the reintegration process are positive experiences. This means careful career planning, support while overseas, and use of the increased experience and skills of returned managers to benefit the home office. Research into the practices of successful U.S., European, Japanese, and Australian multinational corporations (MNCs) indicates the use of one or more of the following support systems, as recommended by Tung, for a successful repatriation program:

- A mentor program to monitor the expatriate's career path while abroad and upon repatriation.
- As an alternative to the mentor program, the establishment of a special organizational unit for the purposes of career planning and continuing guidance for the expatriate.
- A system of supplying information and maintaining contacts with the expatriate so that he or she may continue to feel a part of the home organization.[16]

The Role of the Expatriate Spouse

We began to realize that the entire effectiveness of the assignment could be compromised by ignoring the spouse.

STEVE FORD,
Corporation Relocations,
Hewlett-Packard[17]

Many companies are beginning to recognize the importance of providing support for spouses and children—in particular because both spouses are often corporate fast trackers and demand that both sets of needs be included on the bargaining table. The 2008 Global Relocation Trends Survey found that 83 percent of married expatriates were accompanied by their spouses. However, while 54 percent of the spouses were employed before the assignment, only 12 percent were employed during the assignment.[18] "Not surprisingly, children's education, family adjustment, partner resistance and difficult locations were identified as the top four critical family challenges in this year's (2008) survey," GMAC's Schwartz said. "That's underscored by the fact that 61 percent of respondents noted that the impact of family issues on early returns from assignment was very critical or of high importance."[19]

Firms often use informal means, such as intercompany networking, to help find the trailing spouse a position in the same location. They know that, with the increasing number of dual-career couples (65 percent in the United States), if the spouse does not find a position the manager will very likely turn down the assignment. They decline because they cannot afford to lose the income or because the spouse's career may be delayed entirely if he or she is out of the workforce for a few years. As women continue to move up the corporate ladder, the accompanying ("trailing") spouse is often male—estimated at more than 25 percent.[20] Companies such as Hewlett-Packard, Shell, Medtronic, and Monsanto offer a variety of options to address the dual-career dilemma.

Clearly, then, the selection process must include spouses, partners and entire families. Global assignments must take account of the expatriate's personal concerns and future career; otherwise the company will they face the possibility of early return and a possible doubling of the chances for employee attrition. The GMAC survey revealed that the annual turnover rate is 13 percent for all employees, compared to 25 percent for expatriate employees during assignments, and 27 percent within one year of completing assignments. Those assignees indicated that they felt their firms did not appreciate the difficulties of their overseas stints; nor did they fully utilize the expatriates' skills on return to the home country.[21]

At Procter & Gamble, employees and spouses destined for China are sent to Beijing for two months of language training and cultural familiarization. Nissho Iwai, a Japanese trading company, gets together managers and spouses who are leaving Japan with foreign managers and spouses who are on their way there. In addition, the firm provides a year of language training and information and services for Japanese children to attend schools abroad. Recent research on 321 American expatriate spouses around the world shows that effective cross-cultural adjustment by spouses is more likely (1) when firms seek the spouse's opinion about the international assignment and the expected standard of living and (2) when the spouse initiates his or her own predeparture training (thereby supplementing the minimal training given by most firms).[22]

Expatriate Retention

> *Managers returning from expatriate assignments are two to three times more likely to leave the company within a year because attention has not been paid to their careers and the way they fit back into the corporate structure back home.*[23]

Firms must design support services to provide timely help for the manager and, therefore, are part of the effective management of an overseas assignment. The overall transition process experienced by the company's international management cadre over time is shown in Exhibit 10-2. It comprises three phases of transition and adjustment that must be managed for successful socialization to a new culture and resocialization back to the old culture. These phases are (1) the exit transition from the home country, the success of which will be determined largely by the quality of preparation the expatriate has received; (2) the entry transition to the host country, in which successful acculturation (or early exit) will depend largely on monitoring and support; and (3) the entry transition back to the home country or to a new host country, in which the level of reverse culture shock and the ease of re-acculturation will depend on previous stages of preparation and support.[24]

A company may derive many potential benefits from carefully managing the careers of its expatriates. By helping managers make the right moves for their careers, the company will be able to retain people with increasing global experience and skills.

But from the individual manager's perspective, most people understand that no one can better look out for one's interests than oneself. With that in mind, managers must ask themselves, and their superiors, what role each overseas stint will play in career advancement and what proactive role each will play in one's own career. Retaining the returning expatriate within the company (assuming he or she has been effective) is vitally important in order to gain the knowledge and benefit from the assignment. Yet, as discussed earlier, the attrition rate for expatriates is about double that of non-expatriates. Researchers in the 2008 Global Relocation trends Survey found the reasons for this to be that:

- Expatriates are more marketable and receive more attractive offers from other employers.
- Expatriates find that their compensation packages on overseas assignments are more generous than at home and go from one company to another to take advantage of that.
- Expatriates feel unappreciated and dissatisfied both during and after the assignment and leave the company.[25]

It is essential, therefore, that the company pays careful attention to maintaining and retaining the expatriate by managing both the assignment and the repatriation of the expatriate and the family.

EXHIBIT 10-2   The Expatriate Transition Process.

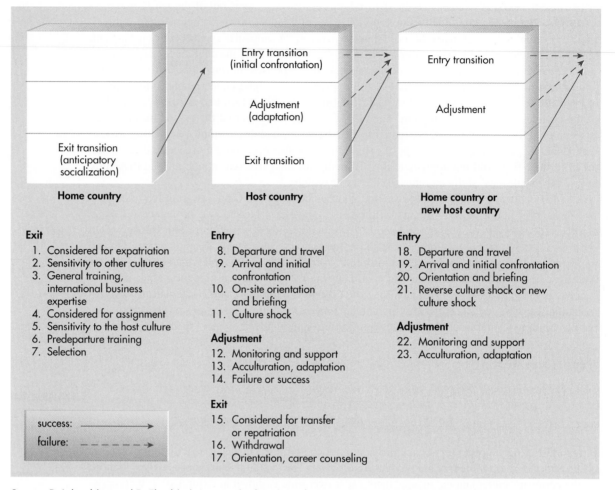

Home country

Host country

Home country or new host country

Exit
1. Considered for expatriation
2. Sensitivity to other cultures
3. General training, international business expertise
4. Considered for assignment
5. Sensitivity to the host culture
6. Predeparture training
7. Selection

Entry
8. Departure and travel
9. Arrival and initial confrontation
10. On-site orientation and briefing
11. Culture shock

Adjustment
12. Monitoring and support
13. Acculturation, adaptation
14. Failure or success

Exit
15. Considered for transfer or repatriation
16. Withdrawal
17. Orientation, career counseling

Entry
18. Departure and travel
19. Arrival and initial confrontation
20. Orientation and briefing
21. Reverse culture shock or new culture shock

Adjustment
22. Monitoring and support
23. Acculturation, adaptation

success: ⎯⎯⎯⎯→

failure: – – – – →

Source: P. Asheghian and B. Ebrahimi, *Internationl Business* (New York: Harper Collins, 1990), 470.

THE ROLE OF REPATRIATION IN DEVELOPING A GLOBAL MANAGEMENT CADRE

In the international assignment, both the manager and the company can benefit from the enhanced skills and experience gained by the expatriate. Many returning executives report an improvement in their managerial skills and self-confidence. Some of these acquired skills, as reported by Adler, include the following:

- **Managerial skills, not technical skills:** learning how to deal with a wide range of people, to adapt to their cultures through compromise, and not to be a dictator.
- **Tolerance for ambiguity:** making decisions with less information and more uncertainty about the process and the outcome.
- **Multiple perspectives:** learning to understand situations from the perspective of local employees and businesspeople.
- **Ability to work with and manage others:** learning patience and tolerance—realizing that managers abroad are in the minority among local people; learning to communicate more with others and empathize with them.[26]

In addition to the managerial and cross-cultural skills acquired by expatriates, the company benefits from the knowledge and experience those managers gain about how to do business overseas, and about new technology, local marketing, and competitive information. Expatriates have long served as facilitators of intra-firm knowledge transfer and application. Traditionally, it has been assumed that the role of expatriates is partly to bring knowledge from the corporate headquarters to subsidiaries; however, it is clear that there is a potential strategic advantage when expatriates acquiring knowledge while on international assignment bring it back to the center of the organization or disseminate it across other subsidiaries.[27] For example, Berthoin described five types of knowledge gained abroad: knowledge about what (e.g., differences in customer preferences), why (e.g., understanding how culture differences affect cross-cultural understanding), how (e.g., management skills such as delegating responsibilities), when (e.g., knowledge about the effect of timing), and who (e.g., relationships created over the life of an assignment). They point out that expatriate experience not only brings about knowledge about culture differences but also creates insights about HQ-subsidiary relations, from which ideas about improving business could be derived.[28] However, as found by Lazarova and Tarique, "repatriates' motivation to contribute to collective organizational learning is primarily driven by the fit between their individual career objectives and the career development opportunities offered by the organization upon return."[29] Lazarova and Tarique found that several conditions have to be met in order to successfully transfer knowledge: first that the repatriates have to: (a) have valuable knowledge to transfer and (b) be motivated to transfer that knowledge; secondly, that organizations need to (a) have the right tools to capture knowledge, and (b) create the right incentives for repatriates to share their knowledge. Knowledge transfer is optimized when the type of knowledge gained by repatriates is matched by the right knowledge transfer mechanisms—for example by assigning repatriates to strategic teams—and when career opportunities provided by the organization are congruent with repatriate career goals and aspirations.[30] Exhibit 10-3 illustrates the conditions and process by which knowledge may be successfully integrated into the organization.

The company should therefore position itself to benefit from that enhanced management knowledge if it wants to develop a globally experienced management cadre—an essential ingredient for global competitiveness—in particular where there is a high degree of shared learning among the organization's global managers. If the company cannot retain good returning managers, then their potential shared knowledge is not only lost but also conveyed to another organization that hires that person. This can be very detrimental to the company's competitive stance. Some companies are becoming quite savvy about how to use technology to utilize shared knowledge to develop their global management cadre, to better service their customers, and—as a side benefit—to store the knowledge and expertise of their managers around the world in case they leave the company. That knowledge, it can be argued, is an asset in which the company has invested large amounts of resources. One such savvy company is Booz-Allen & Hamilton, which instituted a Knowledge On-Line (KOL) intranet as a means to enhance knowledge sharing

EXHIBIT 10-3 • Conditions for Knowledge Transfer upon Repatriation.

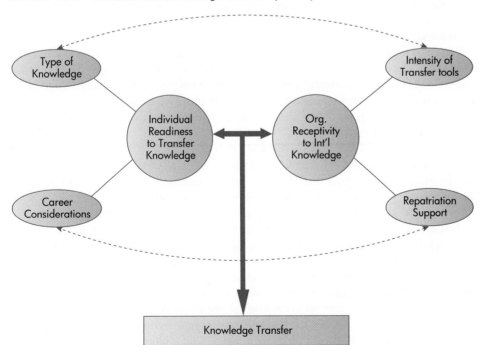

Source: Mila Lazarova and Ibraiz Tarique, "Knowledge Transfer upon Repatriation," *Journal of World Business* 40 no. 4 (2005): 361–373, reprinted with permission of Elsevier.

among its employees worldwide and to improve client service. By using its intranet to link islands of information separated by geography and platform-specific applications, the renowned consulting firm has enabled its 2,000 private sector consultants to collect and share firm-wide their best thoughts and expertise.[31]

Black and Gregersen's research of 750 U.S., European, and Japanese companies concluded that those companies that reported a high degree of job satisfaction and strong performance, and that experienced limited turnover, used the following practices when making international assignments:

- They focus on knowledge creation and global leadership development.
- They assign overseas posts to people whose technical skills are matched or exceeded by their cross-cultural abilities.
- They end expatriate assignments with a deliberate repatriation process.[32]

A successful repatriation program, then, starts before the assignment. The company's top management must set up a culture that conveys the message that the organization regards international assignments as an integral part of continuing career development and advancement, and that it values the skills of the returnees. The company's objectives should be reflected in its long-range plans, commitment, and compensation on behalf of the expatriate. GE sets a model for effective expatriate career management. With its 500 expatriates worldwide, it takes care to select only the best managers for overseas jobs and then commits to placing them in specific positions upon reentry.

GLOBAL MANAGEMENT TEAMS

MNCs realize it is essential to maximize their human assets in the form of global management teams so they can share resources and manage the transnational transfer of knowledge. The term **global management teams** describes collections of managers in or from several countries who must rely on group collaboration if each member is to experience optimum success and goal achievement. Whirlpool International, for example, is a U.S.-Dutch joint venture, with administrative headquarters in Comerio, Italy, where it is managed by a Swede and a six-person management team from Sweden, Italy, Holland, the United States, Belgium, and Germany. To achieve the individual and collective goals of the team members, international teams must "provide the means to communicate corporate culture, develop a global perspective, coordinate and integrate the global enterprise, and be responsive to local market needs."[33] The role and importance of international teams increase as the firm progresses in its scope of international activity. Similarly, the manner in which multicultural interaction affects the firm's operations depends on its level of international involvement, its environment, and its strategy.

The team's ability to work effectively together is crucial to the company's success. In addition, technology facilitates effective and efficient teamwork around the world. This was found by the Timberland U.K. sales conference planning team. In the past, the company's large sales conferences were cumbersome to organize because their offices were in France, Germany, Spain, Italy, and the United Kingdom. Then the team started using the British Telecom (BT) Conference Call system for the arrangements, which saved them much travel and expense. The company subsequently adopted the BT Conference Call system for the executive team's country meetings.[34] Teleconferencing and videoconferencing are now much of the way of life for global businesses. However, research indicates that face-to-face meetings are the best way to kick off a virtual team project so that the members can agree on goals and schedules and who is responsible for what. IBM project teams start with all members in a personal meeting to help to build an understanding of the other members' cultures and set up a trusting relationship.[35]

For global organizations and alliances, the same cross-cultural interactions hold as in MNCs, and, in addition, considerably more interaction takes place with the external environment at all levels of the organization. Therefore, global teamwork is vital, as are the pockets of cross-cultural teamwork and interactions that occur at many boundaries.[36] For the global company, worldwide competition and markets necessitate global teams for strategy development, both for the organization as a whole and for the local units to respond to their markets.

When a firm responds to its global environment with a global strategy and then organizes with a networked "glocal" structure (see Chapter 8), various types of cross-border teams are necessary for global integration and local differentiation. These include teams between and among headquarters and subsidiaries; transnational project teams, often operating on a "virtual" basis; and teams coordinating alliances outside the organization.[37] In joint ventures, in particular, multicultural teams work at all levels of strategic planning and implementation, as well as on the production and assembly floor.

"Virtual" Transnational Teams

Virtual groups, whose members interact through computer-mediated communication systems (such as desktop video conferencing systems, e-mail, group support systems, internets, and intranets), are linked together across time, space, and organizational boundaries.[38]

Increasingly, advances in communication now facilitate **virtual global teams,** a horizontal networked structure, with people around the world conducting meetings and exchanging information via the Internet, enabling the organization to capitalize on 24-hour productivity. In this way, too, knowledge is shared across business units and across cultures.[39] The advantages and cost savings of virtual global teams are frequently offset by their challenges—including cultural misunderstandings and the logistics of differences in time and space, as shown in Exhibit 10-4. Group members must build their teams while bearing in mind the group diversity and the need for careful communication.[40]

Many of these challenges have been noted by virtual team leaders from Alcoa Company's operations in 20 diverse countries. (Alcoa is the world leader in the production of aluminum and has 63,000 employees in 31 countries.) The teams are called parallel Global Virtual Teams (pGVTs)—teams which operate outside the formal structure, focusing on innovation and improvement. All their meetings are conducted electronically through videoconferencing,

EXHIBIT 10-4 Operational Challenges for Global Virtual Teams[41]

Geographic Dispersal:	The complexity of scheduling communications such as teleconferences and videoconferences across multiple time zones, holidays, and so on.
	Lack of face-to-face meetings to establish trust or for cross-interaction processes such as brainstorming.
Cultural Differences:	Variations in attitudes and expectations toward time, planning, scheduling, risk taking, money, relationship building, and so on.
	Differences in goal sets and work styles arising out of such variables as individualism/collectivism, the relative value of work compared with other life factors; variable sets of assumptions, norms, patterns of behavior.
Language and Communications:	Translation difficulties, or at least variations in accents, semantics, terminology, or local jargon.
	Lack of personal and physical contact, which greatly inhibits trust and relationship building in many countries; the social dynamics change.
	Lack of visibility of nonverbal cues makes interpretation difficult and creates two-way noise in the communication process.
Technology:	Variations in availability, speed, acceptability, cost of equipment necessary for meetings and communications through computer-aided systems.
	Variable skill levels and willingness to interact through virtual media.

teleconferencing, discussion boards, e-mail, instant messaging, knowledge repositories, and planning and scheduling tools.

> *There is clearly a cross-cultural issue here—one that is particularly important to the success of pGVTs as, more than other forms of team, their success vitally depends on all members contributing and debating ideas.*

"Lessons from Alcoa,"
Organizational Dynamics 38,
no. 3., 2009.[42]

In Cordery et al.'s studies of Alcoa's teams, leadership problems were highlighted. One GVT leader described the problems in not being able to always interpret or understand the subtleties of language being expressed and to respond accordingly when sharing ideas, because of not being able to observe the body language of members. She observed, "People from some cultures will say, 'yes' even if they have not understood. They do not feel comfortable asking you to repeat what they have not understood, being in such a large group. Others will commit to do almost anything (quite willingly) in the meeting, but it doesn't get done."[43]

A survey of 200 of Alcoa's virtual team members by Cordery et al. revealed that they view successful team leaders as having the following skills: *Interpersonal facilitation*—the ability to build teams and resolve conflicts; *task facilitation*—the ability to convey goals and train team members to effectively use the collaborative technology; *resource acquisition;* and *external alignment/vision*—that is being able to mesh the team's activities with the organization's goals.[44]

A survey of 440 training and development professionals across a variety of industries was conducted by Rosen, Furst, and Blackburn. The respondents indicated which training techniques for virtual teams were more effective than others, and reported which of those programs were most needed in the future. The relative priority of the training modules is shown in Exhibit 10-5.

EXHIBIT 10-5   Virtual Training Future Needs

Importance of Virtual Team Training Modules (in order of value and effectiveness)
Training on how to lead a virtual team meeting
Leader training on how to coach and mentor team members virtually
Training on how to monitor team progress, diagnose team problems, and take corrective actions
Training to use communications technologies
Leader training on how to manage team boundaries, negotiate member time commitments with local managers, and stay in touch with team sponsors
Training on how to establish trust and resolve conflicts in virtual teams
Communications skills training— cultural sensitivity, etc.
Team-building training for new virtual teams
Training to select the appropriate technologies to fit team tasks
Leader training on how to evaluate and reward individual contributions on the virtual team
Training on how to select virtual team members, establish a virtual team charter, and assign virtual team roles
Realistic preview of virtual team challenges
Training on what qualities to look for in prospective virtual team members and leaders

Source: Based on B. Rosen, S. Furst, and R. Blackburn, "Training for Virtual Teams: An Investigation of Current Practices and Future Needs," *Human Resources Management* 45, no. 2 (2006): 229–247.

On the top of the list considered very valuable, for example, was "Training on how to lead a virtual team meeting" and "Leader training on how to coach and mentor team members virtually," as well as "how to monitor team progress, diagnose problems and take corrective action."[45]

Managing Transnational Teams

The ability to develop and lead effective transnational teams (whether they interact "virtually," physically, or, as is most often the case, a mixture of both) is essential in light of the increasing proliferation of foreign subsidiaries, joint ventures, and other transnational alliances. The primary corporate question is how to integrate a diverse pool of cultural values, traditions, and norms in order to be competitive. These challenges were experienced when Nomura, Japan's largest investment bank, acquired most of Lehman Brothers' operations in Asia, Europe, and the Middle East in October 2008, after Lehman's collapse, and so had to absorb hundreds of Lehman employees immediately. Although Nomura is the acquirer, it is trying to transform its own culture to be more globally competitive. As observed by one manager:

> Nomura has "a completely domestic culture" . . . one based on Japanese customs of employment, and where company loyalty is strong, decision-making is slow and tolerance for risk is low.

> www.ft.com,
> *September 17, 2009.*[46]

The cultural divide was being felt by both the Japanese and the Americans trying to work together. In particular, the Japanese were shocked when Nomura's management introduced American-style pay and career structures.[47]

Teams comprising people located in far-flung operations are faced with often-conflicting goals of achieving greater efficiency across those operations, responding to local differences, and facilitating organizational learning across boundaries; conflicts arise based on cultural differences, local work norms and environments, and varied time zones. A recent study by Joshi et al. of a 30-member team of human resource (HR) managers in six countries in the Asia-Pacific region showed that network analysis of the various interactions among team members can reveal when and where negative cross-cultural conflicts occur and so provide MNC top management with information for conflict resolution so that a higher level of synergy may be attained among the group members. The advantages of synergy include a greater opportunity for global competition (by being able to share experiences, technology, and a pool of international managers) and a greater opportunity for cross-cultural understanding and exposure to different viewpoints. The disadvantages include problems resulting from differences in language, communication, and varying managerial styles; complex decision-making processes; fewer promotional opportunities; personality conflicts, often resulting from stereotyping and prejudice; and greater complexity in the workplace.[48] In the Joshi study, the greatest conflict, and therefore lack of synergy, was not, as one would expect, resulting from the headquarters-subsidiary power divide. Rather, the critical conflicts were between the Country A subsidiary and Country B subsidiary, given the required communication and workflow patterns between them. (Country names were kept confidential so that individuals in the study would not be identified.)

What are other ways that management can ascertain how well its international teams are performing and what areas need to be improved?

In recognizing the areas needing better team management, executives in a study by Govindarajan and Gupta ranked five key tasks based on their level of importance, as below:

Tasks for Global Business Teams[49]

Cultivating trust among members

Overcoming communication barriers

Aligning goals of individual team members

Obtaining clarity regarding team objectives

Ensuring that the team possesses necessary knowledge and skills.

The managers also rated the level of difficulty to accomplish that task. The researchers concluded from their study that the ability to cultivate trust among team members is critical to the success of global business teams if they want to minimize conflict and encourage cooperation.[50]

Following are some general recommendations the researchers make for improving global teamwork:

- Cultivating a culture of trust: one way to do this is by scheduling face-to-face meetings early on, even if later meetings will be "virtual."
- Rotating meeting locations: this develops global exposure for all team members and also legitimizes each person's position.
- Rotating and diffusing team leadership.
- Linking rewards to team performance.
- Building social networks among managers from different countries.[51]

What other techniques do managers actually use to deal with the challenge of achieving cross-cultural collaboration in multinational horizontal projects? A comparative study of European project groups in several countries by Sylvie Chevrie revealed three main strategies:[52]

- **Drawing upon individual tolerance and self-control:** In this R&D consortium, the Swiss manager treated all team members the same, ignoring cultural differences, and the team members coexisted with patience and compromise. Many of the members said they were used to multinational projects and just tried to focus on technical issues.
- **Trial-and-error processes coupled with personal relationships:** This is a specific strategy in which the project manager sets up social events to facilitate the team members getting acquainted with one another. Then, they discover, through trial and error, what procedures will be acceptable to the group.
- **Setting up transnational cultures:** Here the managers used the common professional, or occupational, culture, such as the engineering profession, to bring the disparate members together within a common understanding and process.

The managers in the study admitted their solutions were not perfect, but met their needs as best they could in the situation. Chevrie suggests that, where possible, a "cultural mediator" should be used who helps team members interpret and understand one another and come to an agreement about processes to achieve organizational goals.[53]

Whether in global management teams, as expatriates, or as host-country nationals, the importance of women as a valuable, and often-underutilized, resource, should not be overlooked in IHRM efforts to maximize the company's global management cadre. Their role is explored in the following Management Focus section.

MANAGEMENT FOCUS

The Role of Women in International Management

The world's expatriate workforce is becoming increasingly female.[54]

While it is clear that women are increasingly making their way into the international management cadre, their numbers and clout vary greatly around the world.

The 2009 ranking by *Fortune* magazine of the most powerful women in business in the United States lists Indra Nooyi, 53, as number one, for the fourth consecutive year. She is Pepsi's CEO, the Indian-born strategist and former CFO and president.[55] The article also includes a separate list called "International Power 50" (the first twenty of those are listed in Exhibit 10-6). The *Fortune* surveyors conclude that "power knows no bounds for this diverse group. Included on our list: the woman who built Australia's biggest bank (No.2) and the Siemens executive (No.6) who is the first woman to sit on that company's board in its 160-year history."[56]

Other women around the world in powerful positions include those in the Arab world, two of whom were described in a Financial Times article in June 2008:

Soha Nashaat, 41, in Dubai, who was appointed head of Barclays Private Bank, Middle East in 2006, tasked with building the business from the ground up. Half-Egyptian, half-Syrian, she was raised in Kuwait and educated in the U.S., and her career has echoed the international flavor of her upbringing, beginning in New York as an intern with Merrill Lynch in 1991.

EXHIBIT 10-6   Women in Top Business Positions Around the Globe

Cynthia Carroll, CEO Anglo American, Britain
Gail Kelly, Managing Director and CEO, Westpac, Australia
Marjorie Scardino, CEO, Pearson, Britain
Anne Lauvergeon, CEO, Areva, France
Barbara Dalibard, President and CEO, Orange Business Services, France
Barbara Kux, Head of Supply Chain Management, Siemens, Germany
Annika Falkengren, President and CEO, SEB, Sweden
Guler Sabanci, Chairman and Managing Director, Sabanci Holding, Turkey
Maria Ramos, Group CEO, ABSA, South Africa
Marina Berlusconi, Chairman, Fininvest, Italy
Ana Patricia Botin, Executive Chairman, Banesto, Spain
Maureen Kempston Darkes, President, GM Latin America, Africa & Middle East, U.S.
Nancy McKinstry, Chairman and CEO, Wolters Kluwer, Netherlands
Chua Sock Koong, CEO, Singapore Telecommunications, Singapore
Chandra Kochhar, Deputy Managing Director, ICICI Bank, India.
Patricia Barbizet, CEO Artemis Holding, France
Yang Mianmian, President Haier Group, China
Dominique Senequier, CEO Axa Private Equity, France
Deb Henretta, Group President, Asia, Procter & Gamble, Singapore
Sun Yafang, Chairman, Huawei Technologies, China

Source: Based on the selections of "The International Power 50," *Fortune,* September 28, 2009, and the Web sites of the listed companies.

Sheikha al-Bahar, in Kuwait, described as "the billion dollar banker", has reached the summit of the Gulf's financial community. She started as a trainee at NBK and now, as group general manager, corporate banking, oversees more than $12bn of assets and almost 150 employees.[57]

However, while women's advancement in global companies is impressive, it is still true that where there are limitations on managerial opportunities for women in their own country—some more than others—there are even more limitations on their opportunities for expatriate assignments. Research on expatriate assignments continues to show that females are disproportionately underrepresented in expatriate assignments.[58]

Opportunities for indigenous female employees to move up the managerial ladder in a given culture depend on the values and expectations regarding the role of women in that society. In Japan, for example, the workplace has traditionally been a male domain as far as managerial careers are concerned (although rapid changes are now taking place). To the older generation, a working married woman represented a loss of face to the husband because it implied that he was not able to support her. Women were usually only allowed clerical positions, under the assumption that they would leave to raise a family and perhaps later return to part-time work. Employers, thus, made little effort to train them for upper level positions.[59] As a result, very few women workers have been in supervisory or managerial posts—thus limiting the short-term upward mobility of women through the managerial ranks.[60]

The younger generation and increased global competitiveness have brought some changes to traditional values regarding women's roles in Japan. More than 60 percent of Japanese women are now employed, including half of Japanese mothers. But how and when these cultural changes will affect the number of Japanese women in managerial positions remains to be seen. Currently, only about 9 percent are in managerial positions, compared with about 45 percent in the United States and 30 percent in Sweden, for example. One can understand the problems Japanese women face when trying to enter and progress in managerial careers when we review the experiences of Yuko Suzuki who went into business for herself after the advertising company she worked for went bankrupt. However, she could not gain respect or even attention from customers, who often asked her who her boss was after she finished a presentation. She eventually hired a man to accompany her, which increased her sales. But, to her dismay, customers would only establish eye contact with him, even though she was doing the talking and he had nothing to do with the company.[61] Japanese labor economists observe that "Japan has gone as far as it can go with a social model that consists of men filling all of the economic, management and political roles."[62]

Overall, more managerial opportunities are available for American women than for women in most other countries. However, even for American women, who now fill more than 46 percent of the managerial positions at home, commensurate opportunities are still limited to them abroad. Also, in Germany, while in the 1990s less than 3 percent of German expatriates were women, this figure has steadily increased.[63] However, opportunities for women at the top ranks in Germany remain very limited. In a Deutsche Bank lecture in May 2004, statistics were discussed that showed that, although women accounted for 47 percent of the total labor force, only 3.7 percent of senior managers in Germany are women.

> *More than any other European economy, Germany has stunted the development of its female business community. None of the DAX index of Germany's top companies has a woman on the board.*
>
> *Financial Times*[64]

The reasons for the different opportunities for women among various countries can often be traced to the cultural expectations of the host countries—the same cultural values that keep women in these countries from the managerial ranks. In Germany, for example, the disparity in opportunities for women can be traced in part to the lifestyles and laws. For example, children attend school only in the mornings, which restricts the ability for both parents to work. Cultural expectations may also contribute to different opportunities for women at the top levels between northern and southern Europe.

> *The North-South Divide in Europe, Inc. . . . . Women are far more likely to serve on the boards of Scandinavia's biggest companies than Italy's or Spain's, and attitudes to their promotion remain deeply split.*
>
> *Financial Times*[65]

While top boardrooms in Spain and Italy remain almost exclusively male, women occupy 22 percent of board seats in the largest companies in Norway and 20 percent in Sweden. While this phenomenon can be attributed to complex social and cultural issues, firms ought to be aware of the effects on their bottom line. Research by Catalyst, published in 2004, showed that—of the 353 Fortune 500 companies they surveyed—the quartile with the largest proportion of women in top management had a return on equity of 35.1 percent higher than the quartile with the lowest female representation.[66]

The lack of expatriates who are female or represent other minority groups does not reflect their lack of desire to take overseas assignments. Indeed, studies indicate women's strong willingness to work abroad and their considerable success on their assignments. For example, Adler's major study of North American women working as expatriate managers in countries around the world showed that they are, for the most part, successful.[67]

The most difficult job seems to be getting the assignment in the first place. North American executives are reluctant to send women and minorities abroad because they assume they will be subject to the same culturally based biases as at home, or they assume a lack of understanding and acceptance, particularly in certain countries. Research on 52 female expatriate managers, for example, shows this assumption to be highly questionable. Adler showed, first and foremost, that foreigners are seen as foreigners; furthermore, a woman who is a foreigner (a *gaijin* in Japan) is not expected to act like a local woman. According to Adler and Izraeli, "Asians see female expatriates as foreigners who happen to be women, not as women who happen to be foreigners." The other women in the study echoed this view. One woman based in Hong Kong noted, "'It doesn't make any difference if you are blue, green, purple, or a frog. If you have the best product at the best price, they'll buy."[68]

Women and minorities represent a significant resource for overseas assignments—whether as expatriates or as host-country nationals—a resource that is underutilized by U.S. companies. Adler studied this phenomenon regarding women and recommends that businesses (1) avoid assuming that a female executive will fail because of the way she will be received or because of problems experienced by female spouses; (2) avoid assuming that a woman will not want to go overseas; and (3) give female managers every chance to succeed by giving them the titles, status, and recognition appropriate to the position—as well as sufficient time to be effective.[69]

WORKING WITHIN LOCAL LABOR RELATIONS SYSTEMS

If you have to close a plant in Italy, in France, in Spain or in Germany, you have to discuss the possibility with the state, the local communities, the trade unions; everybody feels entitled to intervene . . . even the Church.

JACOB BITTORELLI,
Former Deputy Chairman of Pirelli[70]

An important variable in implementing strategy and maximizing host-country human resources for productivity is that of the labor relations environment and system within which the managers of a multinational enterprise (MNE) will operate in a foreign country. Differences in economic, political, and legal systems result in considerable variation in labor relations systems across countries. It is the responsibility of the IHRM function to monitor the labor relations systems in host countries and advise local managers accordingly. In fact that information should be considered as one input to the strategic decision of whether to operate in a particular country or region.

The Impact of Unions on Businesses

European businesses, for example, continue to be undermined by their poor labor relations and by inflexible regulations. As a result, businesses have to move jobs overseas to cut labor costs, resulting from a refusal of unions to grant any reduction in employment protection or benefits in order to keep the jobs at home. In addition, non-European firms wishing to operate in Europe have to carefully weigh the labor relations systems and their potential effect on strategic and operational decisions. However, some change may be on the horizon to provide relief to businesses in Europe as some unions grant concessions to firms in order to keep their jobs. Recently, unions in Germany, France, and Italy have been losing their battle to derail labor-market reforms by the governments in those countries who are increasingly concerned that excess regulation and benefits to workers are smothering growth opportunities.

The term **labor relations** refers to the process through which managers and workers determine their workplace relationships. This process may be through verbal agreement and job descriptions, or through a union's written labor contract, which has been reached through negotiation in **collective bargaining** between workers and managers. The labor contract determines rights regarding workers' pay, benefits, job duties, firing procedures, retirement, layoffs, and so on.

The prevailing labor relations system in a country is important to the international manager because it can constrain the strategic choices and operational activities of a firm operating there. The three main dimensions of the labor-management relationship that the manager will consider are (1) the participation of labor in the affairs of the firm, especially as this affects performance and well-being; (2) the role and impact of unions in the relationship; and (3) specific human resource policies in terms of recruitment, training, and compensation.[71] Constraints take the form of (1) wage levels that are set by union contracts and leave the foreign firm little flexibility to be globally competitive, (2) limits on the ability of the foreign firm to vary employment levels when necessary, and (3) limitations on the global integration of operations of the foreign firm because of incompatibility and the potential for industrial conflict.[72]

Organized Labor Around the World

The percentage of the workforce in trade unions in industrialized countries has declined in the last decade, most notably in Europe. In the U.S., union membership fell from a third in 1950 to about 12 percent in 2006.[73] This global trend is attributable to various factors, including an increase in the proportion of white-collar and service workers as proportionate to manufacturing workers, a rising proportion of temporary and part-time workers, off shoring of jobs to gain lower wage costs, and a reduced belief in unions in the younger generations.[74] In addition, the global economic decline and loss of jobs in 2009 put downward pressure on union demands and power when the focus changed to job retention rather than increased benefits.

The numbers do not show the nature of the system in each country. In most countries, a single dominant industrial relations system applies to almost all workers. Both Canada and the United States have two systems—one for the organized and one for the unorganized. Each, according to Adams, has "different rights and duties of the parties, terms and conditions of employment, and structures and processes of decision making." Basically, in North America, an agent represents unionized employees, whereas unorganized employees can only bargain individually, usually with little capability to affect major strategic decisions or policies or conditions of employment.[75]

The traditional trade union structures in Western industrialized societies have been in *industrial unions*, representing all grades of employees in a specific industry, and *craft unions*, based on certain occupational skills. More recently, the structure has been conglomerate unions, representing members in several industries—for example, the metal workers unions in Europe, which cut across industries, and general unions, which are open to most employees within a country.[76] The system of union representation varies among countries. In the United States, most unions are national and represent specific groups of workers—for example, truck drivers or airline pilots—so a company may have to deal with several different national unions. A single U.S. firm—rather than an association of firms representing a worker classification—engages in its own negotiations. In Japan, on the other hand, it is common for a union to represent all workers in a company. In recent years, company unions in Japan have increasingly coordinated their activities, leading to some lengthy strikes.

Industrial labor relations systems across countries can only be understood in the context of the variables in their environment and the sources of origins of unions. These include government regulation of unions, economic and unemployment factors, technological issues, and the influence of religious organizations. Any of the basic processes or concepts of labor unions, therefore, may vary across countries, depending on where and how the parties have their power and achieve their objectives, such as through parliamentary action in Sweden. For example, collective bargaining in the United States and Canada refers to negotiations between a labor union local and management. However, in Europe collective bargaining takes place between the employer's organization and a trade union at the industry level.[77] This difference means that North America's decentralized, plant-level, collective agreements are more detailed than Europe's industry-wide agreements because of the complexity of negotiating myriad details in multi-employer bargaining. In Germany and Austria, for example, such details are delegated to works councils by legal mandate.[78]

The resulting agreements from bargaining also vary around the world. A written, legally binding agreement for a specific period, common in Northern Europe and North America, is less prevalent in Southern Europe and Britain. In Britain, France, and Italy, bargaining is frequently informal and results in a verbal agreement valid only until one party wishes to renegotiate.[79]

Other variables of the collective bargaining process are the objectives of the bargaining and the enforceability of collective agreements. Because of these differences, managers in MNEs overseas realize that they must adapt their labor relations policies to local conditions and regulations. They also need to bear in mind that, while U.S. union membership has declined by about 50 percent in the last 20 years, in Europe, overall, membership is still quite high, particularly in Italy and the United Kingdom—though it, too, has been falling but from much higher levels.

Most Europeans are covered by collective agreements, whereas most Americans are not. Unions in Europe are part of a national cooperative culture between government, unions, and management, and they hold more power than in the United States. Increasing privatization will make governments less vulnerable to this kind of pressure. It is also interesting to note that some labor courts in Europe deal separately with employment matters from unions and works councils.

In Japan, labor militancy has long been dead, since labor and management agreed 40 years ago on a deal for industrial peace in exchange for job security. Unions in Japan have little official clout, especially in the midst of the Japanese recession. In addition, not much can be negotiated, since wage rates, working hours, job security, health benefits, overtime work, insurance, and the like have traditionally been legislated. However, global competition is putting pressure on companies to move away from guaranteed job security and pay. Often, however, the managers and labor union representatives are the same people, a fact that serves to limit confrontation, as well as does the cultural norm of maintaining harmonious relationships.

In the industrialized world, tumbling trade barriers are also reducing the power of trade unions because competitive multinational companies have more freedom to choose alternative productive and sourcing locations. Most new union workers—about 75 percent—will be in emerging nations, like China and Mexico, where wages are low and unions are scarce. However, in some countries like India, outmoded labor laws are very restrictive for MNEs, making it difficult to lay off employees under any circumstances forcing foreign companies to be very careful in their selection of new employees.

In China, for example, in a surprising move, the government has passed a new law that will grant power to labor unions, in spite of protests by foreign companies with factories there. The order was in response to a sharp rise in labor tension and protests about poor working conditions and industrial accidents.[80] The All-China Federation of Trade Unions claimed that foreign employers often force workers to work overtime, pay no heed to labor-safety regulations, and deliberately find fault with the workers as an excuse to cut their wages or fine them. The move, which underscores the government's growing concern about the widening income gap and threats of social unrest, is setting off a battle with American and other foreign corporations that have lobbied against it by hinting that they may build fewer factories in China.[81]

Protests arose after Wal-Mart Stores, the world's biggest retailer, was forced to accept unions in its Chinese outlets; other MNCs then joined the effort to get the Chinese government to reverse its decision. State-controlled unions in China have traditionally not wielded much power; however after years of reports of worker abuse, the government seems determined to give its union new powers to negotiate worker contracts, safety protection and workplace ground rules.[82] However, in spite of such well-publicized incidences, the union situation in China is generally regarded as stated in *The Economist* as follows:

In name, the All-China Federation of Trade Unions (ACFTU) is a vast union bureaucracy running from the national level to small enterprises. In practice it is controlled by the Communist Party at the national level and, in companies, is mostly a tool of the management.

THE ECONOMIST,
August 1, 2009.[83]

Workers' basic rights for reasonable working conditions, safety, and even the right to get paid are often ignored by Chinese managers. Hopefully, as discussed in Chapter 2, the improved social responsibility of foreign firms operating there might exert pressure for better working conditions for Chinese employees.

Convergence Versus Divergence in Labor Systems

The world trade union movement is poised to follow the lead of transnational companies, by extending its reach and throwing off the shackles of national boundaries. Unions are about to go global.[84]

In October 2006 the International Trade Union Confederation (ITUC) was formed in Vienna, comprising the affiliated organizations of the former ICFTU and WCL, plus eight other national trade union organizations, to form a global body.[85] The ITUC represents 166 million workers through its 309 affiliated organizations in 156 countries and territories. Its objective is to provide "a countervailing force in a society that has changed enormously, with workers' rights being flouted under the pressure created by the current trajectory of 'race to the bottom' globalization."[86]

Political changes, external competitive forces, increased open trade, and frequent moves of MNCs around the world are forces working toward convergence in labor systems. **Convergence** occurs as the migration of management and workplace practices around the world reduce workplace disparities from one country to another. This occurs primarily as MNCs seek consistency and coordination among their foreign subsidiaries and as they act as catalysts for change by "exporting" new forms of work organization and industrial relations practices.[87] It also occurs as harmonization is sought, such as for the EC countries, and as competitive pressures in free-trade zones, such as the NAFTA countries, eventually bring about demands for some equalization of benefits for workers.[88] It would appear that economic globalization is leading to labor transnationalism and will bring about changes in labor rights and democracy around the world.[89]

Other pressures toward convergence of labor relations practices around the world come from the activities and monitoring of labor conditions worldwide by various organizations. One of these organizations is the International Labor Organization (ILO)—comprising union, employer, and government representation—whose mission is to ensure that humane conditions of labor are maintained. Other associations of unions in different countries include various international trade secretariats representing workers in specific industries. The activities and communication channels

EXHIBIT 10-7 Trends in Global Labor Relations Systems

Forces for Global Convergence ← **Current System** →	**Forces to Maintain or Establish Divergent Systems**
Global competitiveness	National labor relations systems and traditions
MNC presence or consolidation initiatives	Social systems
Political change	Local regulations and practices
New market economies	Political ideology
Free-trade zones: harmonization	Cultural norms
(EU), competitive forces (NAFTA)	
Technological standardization, IT	
Declining role of unions	
Agencies monitoring world labor practices	

of these associations provide unions and firms with information about differences in labor conditions around the world.[90] Exhibit 10-7 shows the major forces for and against convergence in labor relations systems.

ADAPTING TO LOCAL INDUSTRIAL RELATIONS SYSTEMS   Although forces for convergence are found in labor relations systems around the world, as discussed previously, for the most part, MNCs still adapt their practices largely to the traditions of national industrial relations systems, with considerable pressure to do so. Those companies, in fact, act more like local employers, subject to local and country regulations and practices. Although the reasons for continued divergence in systems seem fewer, they are very strong: Not the least of these reasons are political ideology and the overall social structure and history of industrial practices. In the European Union (EU), where states are required to maintain parity in wage rates and benefits under the Social Charter of the Maastricht Treaty, a powerful defense of cultural identity and social systems still exists, with considerable resistance by unions to comply with those requirements. Managers in those MNCs also recognize that a considerable gap often exists between the labor laws and the enforcement of those laws—in particular in less developed countries.

THE NAFTA AND LABOR RELATIONS IN MEXICO   About 40 percent of the total workforce in Mexico is unionized, with about 80 percent of workers in industrial organizations that employ more than 25 workers unionized. However, government control over union activities is very strong, and although some strikes occur, union control over members remains rather weak.[91] MNCs are required by government regulation to hire Mexican nationals for at least 90 percent of their workforce; preference must be given to Mexicans and to union personnel. In reality, however, the government permits hiring exceptions.

Many foreign firms set up production in Mexico at least in part for the lower wages and overall cost of operating there—utilizing the advantages of the NAFTA—and the Mexican government wants to continue to attract that investment, as it has for many years before NAFTA. Mexican workers claim that some of the large U.S. companies in Mexico violate basic labor rights and cooperate with pro-government labor leaders in Mexico to break up independent unions. Workers there believe that MNCs routinely use blacklists, physical intimidation, and economic pressure against union organization and independent labor groups that oppose Mexican government policies or the pro-government Confederation of Mexican Workers (CTM).

This example illustrates the complexities of labor relations when a firm operates in other countries—particularly with linkages and interdependence among those countries, such as through the NAFTA or the EU. Of interest are the differences among NAFTA nations in labor law in the private sector. For example, while the minimum wage in Mexico is far less than that in Canada or the United States, a number of costly benefits for Mexican workers are required, such as 15 days of pay for a Christmas bonus and 90 days of severance pay. For comparison, the following Comparative Management in Focus examines labor relations in Germany.

COMPARATIVE MANAGEMENT IN FOCUS

Labor Relations in Germany

This is really a paradigm change. Traditionally, collective bargaining was focused at the industry level. Now companies and the workplace level [bargaining unit] are much more important.

> DETLEF WETZEL,
> *Head of IG Metall,*
> *January 6, 2006*[92]

Germany's **codetermination** law *(mitbestimmung)* is coming under pressure from German companies dealing with global competition, and as a result of global trends of outsourcing, industrial restructuring and the expansion of the service sector.[93] That pressure is increasingly taking the form of concession bargaining to keep jobs at home. Still some companies, tired of restrictions on their strategic decisions and necessary job cuts, are sidestepping those restrictions by registering as public limited companies in the United Kingdom.[94]

Mitbestimmung refers to the participation of labor in the management of a firm. The law mandates representation for unions and salaried employees on the supervisory boards of all companies with more than 2,000 employees and "works councils" of employees at every work site. Those companies with 2,000 or more staff have to give employees half the votes; those with 500 employees or more have to give a third of supervisory board seats to union representatives.[95] Unions are well integrated into managerial decision making and can make a positive contribution to corporate competitiveness and restructuring; this seems different from the traditional adversarial relationship of unions and management in the United States. However, the fact is that firms, in the form of affiliated organizations of companies, have to contend with negotiating with powerful industry-wide unions. Employment conditions that would be negotiated privately in the United States, for example, are subject to federal mandates in Germany—a model unique in Europe. The average metalworker, for example, earns around $2,500 a month, works a 35-hour week, and has six weeks of annual vacation. Germans on average work fewer hours than those in any other country than the Netherlands.[96] Under pressure from global competition, German unions have incurred huge membership losses in the last decade—7 million members, 40 percent fewer than in 1990; only 20 percent of employees in Germany are union members, compared to 29 percent in the United Kingdom and 75 percent in Denmark.[97] As a result, the unions are now more willing to make concessions and trade flexibility for increased job security. This was the case in 2005 when the German engineering group Linde decided to build a factory in Eastern Europe to take advantage of lower wages there. However, Linde reversed the decision after the IG Metall trade union local decided to match the savings by working longer hours and taking less pay.[98]

Union membership in Germany is voluntary, usually with one union for each major industry, and union power traditionally has been quite strong. Negotiated contracts with firms by the employers' federation stand to be accepted by firms that are members of the federation, or used as a guide for other firms. These contracts, therefore, result in setting the pay scale for about 90 percent of the country's workers.[99]

The union works councils play an active role in hiring, firing, training, and reassignment during times of reorganization and change.[100] Because of the depth of works council penetration into personnel and work organization matters, as required by law, their role has been described by some as "co-manager of the internal labor market."[101] This situation has considerable implications for how managers of MNCs plan to operate in Germany. IG Metall, for example, which is Germany's largest metalworking union with 2.6 million workers, has traditionally negotiated guidelines regarding pay, hours, and working conditions on a regional basis. Then, works councils use those guidelines to make local agreements. In 2006 the bargaining role started to devolve to the local unit. IG Metall's proactive role on change illustrates the evolving role of unions by leading management thinking instead of reacting to it. In addition, management and workers tend to work together because of the unions' structure. Indeed, such institutional accord is a powerful factor in changing deeply ingrained cultural traits. However, as of 2009, with an increasingly competitive business environment, IG Metall's traditional and inflexible views on labor relations, has led to a decline in membership and bargaining power.

Codetermination has clearly helped to modify German managerial style from authoritarian to something more akin to humanitarian, without, it should be noted, altering its capacity for efficiency and effectiveness.[102] This system compares to the lack of integration and active roles for unions in the U.S. auto industry—for example, conditions that limit opportunities for change.

Pay for German production workers has been among the highest in the world, about 150 percent of that in the United States and about ten times that in Mexico. German workers also have the highest number of paid vacation days in the world and prefer short workdays. However, in July 2004, Jürgen

Peters, chairman of Germany's powerful IG Metall engineering trade union, announced the agreement with what was then DaimlerChrysler to accept smaller raises and increased working hours after the company threatened to move 6,000 jobs elsewhere.[103] (Chrysler was since taken over by Cerebus, and, as of April 2009, was fighting to stay solvent by accepting an alliance with Fiat.[104]) The agreement followed one by 4,000 Siemens employees in June 2004 to extend their work week.

Foreign companies operating in Germany also have to be aware that termination costs are very high—including severance pay, retraining costs, time to find another job, and so on—and that is assuming the company is successful in terminating the employee in the first place, which is very difficult to do in Europe. This was brought home to Colgate-Palmolive when it tried to close its factory in Hamburg in 1996. The company offered the 500 employees an average of $40,000 each, but the union would not accept, and eventually Colgate had to pay a much higher (undisclosed) amount.

The German model, according to Rudiger Soltwedel of the Institute for the World Economy at Kiel, holds that competition should be based on factors other than cost.[105] Thus, the higher wage level in Germany should be offset by higher-value goods like luxury cars and machine tools, which have been the hallmark of Germany's products. To the extent that the West German unions have established the high-wage, high-skill, and high-value-added production pattern, they have also become dependent on the continued presence of that pattern.[106] In recognition of that dependency, German auto firms are in the process of remaking themselves after the Japanese model—reducing supplies and cutting costs so they can compete on a global scale. However, this social contract, which has underpinned Germany's manufacturing success, is fraying at the edges as Germany's economy weakens under the $100 billion cost of absorbing East Germany and under competitive EU pressures.[107]

Conflicting opinions over the value of codetermination are increasingly evident, as business practices become increasingly subject to EU policies. A major concern was that firms from other countries which were considering cross-border mergers would be discouraged by the EU statute, which would oblige them to incorporate codetermination if the new company includes significant German interests.

CONCLUSION

The role of the IHRM department has expanded to meet the strategic needs of the company to develop a competitive global management cadre. Maximizing human resources around the world requires attention to the many categories and combinations of those people, including expatriates, host-country managers, third country nationals, female resources, global teams, and local employees. Competitive global companies need top managers with global experience and understanding. To that end, attention must be paid to the needs of expatriates before, during, and after their assignments in order to maximize their long-term contributions to the company.

Summary of Key Points

1. Expatriate career management necessitates plans for retention of expatriates during and after their assignments. Support programs for expatriates should include information from and contact with the home organization, as well as career guidance and support after the overseas assignment.

2. The expatriate's spouse plays a crucial role in the potential retention and effectiveness of the manager in host locations. Companies should ensure the spouse's interest in the assignment, include him or her in the predeparture training, and provide career and family support during the assignment and upon return.

3. Global management teams offer greater opportunities for competition—by sharing experiences, technology, and international managers—and greater opportunities for cross-cultural understanding and exposure to different viewpoints. Disadvantages can result from communication and cross-cultural conflicts and greater complexity in the workplace.

4. Virtual global teams enable cost effective, rapid knowledge sharing and collaboration, but are fraught with cross-cultural and logistical challenges.

5. Women represent an underutilized resource in international management. A major reason for this situation is the assumption that culturally based biases may limit the opportunities and success of female managers and employees.

6. The labor relations environment, system, and processes vary around the world and affect how the international manager must plan strategy and maximize the productivity of local human resources.

7. Labor unions around the world are becoming increasingly interdependent because of the operations of MNCs worldwide, the outsourcing of jobs around the world, and the "leveling of the playing field" for jobs.

Discussion Questions

1. What steps can the company's IHRM department take to maximize the effectiveness of the expatriate's assignment and the long-term benefit to the company?

2. Discuss the role of reverse culture shock in the repatriation process. What can companies do to avoid this problem? What kinds of skills do managers learn from a foreign assignment, and how can the company benefit from them? What is the role of repatriation in the company's global competitive situation?

3. What are the reasons for the small numbers of female expatriates? What more can companies do to use women as a resource for international management?

4. What is a virtual global management team? How do the members interact? Discuss the advantages and the challenges faced by these teams. Give some suggestions as to how to maximize the effectiveness of virtual teams across borders.

5. Discuss the reasons behind the growing convergence and interdependence of labor unions around the world.

Application Exercise

Interview one or more managers who have held positions overseas. Try to find a man and a woman. Ask them about their experiences both in the working environment and in the foreign country generally. How did they and their families adapt? How did they find the stage of reentry to headquarters, and what were the effects of the assignment on their career progression? What differences do you notice, if any, between the experiences of the male and the female expatriates?

Experiential Exercise

Form groups of six students, divided into two teams, one representing union members from a German company and the other representing union members from a Mexican company. These companies have recently merged in a joint venture, with the subsidiary to be located in Mexico. These union workers, all line supervisors, will be working together in Mexico. You are to negotiate six major points of agreement regarding union representation, bargaining rights, and worker participation in management, as discussed in this chapter. Present your findings to the other groups in the class and discuss. (It may help to read the Comparative Management in Focus on Motivation in Mexico in Chapter 11.)

Internet Resources

Visit the Deresky Companion Website at www.pearsonhighered.com/deresky for this chapter's Internet resources.

CASE STUDY

Avon in Global Markets in 2009: Managing and Developing a Global Workforce

I was recently in Turkey, where only 10 percent of the population has Internet access at home. Yet almost 95 percent of our sales in Turkey are submitted online—our representatives go to Internet cafes.

ANDREA JUNG,
CEO, Avon Products.,
October 2006.[1]

Avon, the company for women, is a leading global beauty company, with over $10 billion in annual revenue. As the world's largest direct seller, Avon markets to women in more than 100 countries through 5.8 million independent Avon Sales Representatives and has 42,500 employees as of 2009.[2] Avon's product line includes beauty products, fashion jewelry and apparel.

The company is one of the well-established brands in the $90 billion toiletries/cosmetics and household nondurables industry.[3]

---

[1] Andrea Jung, "Now is the Time to Invest," *Fortune*, October 16, 2006.
[2] www.avon.com, September 15, 2009.
[3] See Company Web site (www.avon.com); "Industry Surveys: Household Nondurables," *Standard & Poor's Industry Surveys,* December 18, 2003, 1–25.

In 1999, Andrea Jung was named the first female CEO of the company. Since taking charge, Jung has reinvigorated the company and implemented many timely changes in the U.S. and global markets. It is no longer the same company that faced sluggish sales and debt problems in the 1980s.[4] In 2008, Avon's revenues surpassed $10.7 billion.[5] Approximately 70 percent of the company's revenues come from selling its products in international markets. According to *Fortune* magazine's annual business rankings, the company is one of the most admired companies in the area of household nondurables and personal products and consistently receives good ratings from the industry (see Table 1 and Exhibit 1). Regarding brand identity, corporate reputation, and sales network, Avon is truly a global brand for the masses. In addition, in the area of minority recruitment, Avon always receives good ratings by the analysts.[6]

TABLE 1   Avon Products, Inc.: Selected Company Data

A. Company data (2009):

Senior Management:

ANDREA JUNG	Chairman and Chief Executive Officer, Avon Products, Inc.
ELIZABETH A. SMITH	President, Avon Products, Inc.
CHARLES CRAMB	Vice Chairman, Chief Finance & Strategy Officer, Avon Products, Inc.
LUCIEN ALZIARI	Senior Vice President, Human Resources, Avon Products, Inc.
GERALYN R. BREIG	Senior Vice President & President, North America, Avon Products, Inc.
JERI B. FINARD	Senior Vice President, Global Brand President, Avon Products, Inc.
BENNETT R. GALLINA	Senior Vice President, Asia Pacific, China, Western Europe, the Middle East and Africa, Avon Products, Inc.

Financial Data (2008 Annual Report):

Sales: $10,588.9 bil. (up 8% from 2007)
Net income: $875.3 mil.
Assets: $6.074 bil.
Company type: Public (listed on NYSE)
Global Segments Selected Results: (Figures in millions)

Total Revenue & Operating Profit-2008

	Total Revenue	Operating Profit
North America		
U.S.	$2,492.7	$ 213.9
International		
Europe	1,719.5	346.2
Latin America	3884.1	690.3
Asia Pacific	891.2	102.4
Total from operations	10,690.1	1,491.5
Global expenses	–	(152.2)
Total	$10,690.1	$1,339.3

Source: company website, March 3, 2009 (www.avon.com).

---

[4] "Despite the Face-lift, Avon is Sagging," *Business Week*, December 2, 1991, 101–02; "Scents and sensibility," *The Economist*, July 13, 1996, 57–58.
[5] www.avon.com
[6] For more detail, "Fortune Global 500," *Fortune*, April 5, 2004, F1–F72; "America's Most Admired Companies," Fortune, March 8, 2004, 112.

EXHIBIT 1   Avon's Global Operations in 2009

North America:

Antigua (West Indies), Aruba, Bahamas, Barbados, Bermuda, Canada, Cayman Island, Curacao, Dominica (West Indies), Dominican Republic, Grenada, Guadeloupe (French Antilles), Haiti, Jamaica, Martinique, Mexico, Puerto Rico, St. Croix (U.S. Virgin Islands), St. Kitts & Nevis (West Indies), St. Lucia (West Indies), St. Maarten (Netherlands Antilles), St. Pierre Et Miquelon, St. Thomas (U.S. Virgin Islands), St. Vincent (West Indies), Tortola (British Virgin Islands), Trinidad & Tobago, Turks & Caicos Islands, and United States.

Latin America:

Argentina, Bolivia, Brazil, Chile, Colombia, Costa Rica, Ecuador, El Salvador, French Guyana, Guatemala, Honduras, Nicaragua, Panama, Paraguay, Peru, Uruguay, and Venezuela.

Europe, Middle East, and Africa:

Abu Dhabi, Austria, Bahrain, Belgium, Bulgaria, Congo, Croatia, Cyprus (North), Cyprus (South), Czech Republic, Denmark, Dubai, Egypt, Estonia, Finland, France, Germany, Greece, Hungary, Iceland, Ireland, Israel, Italy, Ivory Coast, Jordan, Kazakhstan, Kuwait, Latvia, Lebanon, Lithuania, Madagascar, Malta, Mauritius, Moldova, Morocco, Norway, Oman, Poland, Portugal, Qatar, Reunion Island, Romania, Russia, Saudi Arabia, Senegal, Seychelles, Slovakia, Slovenia, South Africa, Spain, Sweden, Tunisia, Turkey, Ukraine, United Arab Emirates, United Kingdom, and Yugoslavia.

Asia Pacific:

American Samoa, Australia, China, Fiji, French Polynesia, Guam, Hong Kong, India, Indonesia, Japan, Malaysia, Micronesia, Nepal, New Caledonia, New Zealand, Palau, Philippines, Saipan, Singapore, South Korea, Taiwan, and Thailand.

Source: company website (www.avon.com).

Right from its inception, direct selling has been Avon's major strength in the U.S. and global markets. Other companies (Mary Kay and Amway) that capitalized on the direct selling model equally excel in their target markets and have made phenomenal expansion overseas.[7] In global markets, Avon's major competitors include Procter & Gamble, Johnson & Johnson, Pfizer, Sara Lee, Gillette, Wyeth, Estée Lauder, L'Oreal, and Unilever.[8] Avon also sells through catalogs, mall kiosks, and a Web-based store. Beyond its personal care products and cosmetics, the company has expanded in other areas that include fragrances, toiletries, jewelry, apparel, and home furnishings. Avon's products/brand names include Avon Color, Avon Skincare, Avon Bath & Body, Avon Hair Care, Avon Wellness, Avon Fragrance, and Mark.[9]

Avon—Managing and Developing a Global Workforce

In global business, a company's workforce and sales people are the main representatives, taking orders and dealing with customers on a daily basis in consumer and industrial markets. Avon's managers realized that becoming aware of intercultural differences and getting the appropriate training play an important role in the development of a productive sales force. Areas that are important in the development of a good workforce include cultural sensitivity, motivation, ethical standards, relationship building, and organizational skills.[10] In addition, valuing workplace

---

[7] In 2003, Mary Kay's worldwide revenues surpassed $1.2 billion and maintained operations in 30 countries. Amway, on the other hand, had operations in eighty countries and its sales totaled $4.5 billion. For more information, see www.marykay.com; www.amway.com.

[8] For detail, see: Hoover's.com (www.hoover.com); "Industry Surveys: Household Nondurables," *Standard & Poor's Industry Surveys*, December 18, 2003, 1–25.

[9] For more detail, see company website (www.avon.com).

[10] Masaaki Kotabe and Kristiaan Helsen. (2004).*Global Marketing Management*, 3rd edition, New York: John Wiley, 2004.

TABLE 2 Human Resource Issues of Market Entry and Workforce Management

Pre-market entry/short-term issues:
- Availability of local management and workforce
- Expatriate recruiting
- Recruitment methods and selection
- Sales force training
- Cultural sensitivity/cross-cultural training
- Cost issues
- Dealing with labor relations/laws
- Intercultural considerations
- Perceptions of equality and equal opportunity issues
- Dealing with local labor relations/laws
- Sales force strategy (territorial, product, and customer)

Post-market entry/long-term issues:
- Job training/professional development
- Retention
- Knowledge management
- Sales force productivity issues
- Control, trust, and commitment issues
- Implanting organizational culture
- Relationship marketing
- Acculturation/adaptation issues
- Supervision/mentoring (motivation and ethical perceptions)
- Building global/local management teams
- Managing diversity/multiculturalism

Sources: Helen Deresky,.*International Management: Managing across Borders and Cultures*, 6th edition, Upper Saddle River, NJ: Prentice Hall, 2008; Masaaki Kotabe and Kristiaan Helsen. *Global Marketing Management*, 3rd edition, New York: John Wiley, 2004.

diversity and providing equal opportunity is important to the company. Avon's salespeople and company representatives become even more critical in their door-to-door selling in diverse markets. Organizing the workforce in the new markets and dealing with a variety of industrial labor relations around the world can be a daunting task. Equally important areas are hiring, training, and, above all, retaining the best employees (see Table 2). In the case of Avon, effective management of its global workforce is crucial to the company's strategy since it maintains 5.8 million independent representatives and approximately 42,500 associates in over a hundred countries (see Exhibit 1). In international business, consumer companies cannot operate efficiently without having the best and most well-trained workforce. Like other companies, Avon runs leadership programs and on-the-job training seminars on a regular basis. The company particularly maintains high standards in four areas that affect the sales force productivity and future retention (i.e., compensation, fringe benefits, professional development, and workforce environment). Avon's five values and principles include trust, respect, belief, humility, and integrity. Interestingly, Avon has also been one of the first-movers in workforce diversity and minority recruitment in the United States and over 86 percent of management positions in the company are held by women. The company conspicuously follows what it preaches in its corporate philosophy. Avon's vision states:

To be the company that best understands and satisfies the product, service and self-fulfillment needs of women— globally.[11]

In addition, five of the company's top ten executives are female.[12] In international markets the majority of the company staff and independent representatives is female, making the company a good employer and a role model in women's well-being and employment opportunities. Of course, the nature of the company's product lines and operations deal with areas that attract women from all walks of life.[13] Furthermore, through the Avon Foundation, the company generously provides funding for cancer research, education, and other charitable programs. The company has been one of the major supporters of women's issues in North America and overseas. This creates commitment, harmony, and a supportive work environment that has been beneficial to the company. The Avon Foundation's projects include breast cancer programs in the areas of education, outreach and support services, screening, diagnostic and treatment services, and medical research and clinical care. Besides this, the company supports various programs in women's empowerment and in the arts and humanities.[14]

Avon's Future Growth and Workforce Development in Multicultural Markets

The toiletries/cosmetics and household nondurables industry has done well in the United States and global markets. In international markets, methods of production, manufacturing, and competition have become truly global, producing additional opportunities and growth.[15] This is also attributed to the globalization phenomenon, strong consumer demand, changing

---

[11] See company website (www.avon.com).
[12] See company website (www.avon.com).
[13] For a good discussion on this topic, see Joanne Martin, Kathleen Knopoff, and Christine Beckman. "An Alternative to Bureaucratic Impersonality and Emotional Labor: Bounded Emotionality at the Body Shop," *Administrative Science Quarterly* 43 (2001): 429–69.
[14] For more detail see company website (www.avon.com).
[15] Lynn K. Mytelka, "Local Systems of Innovation in a Globalized World Economy," *Industry and Innovation* 7, no. 1 (2000), 15–32.

demographics, better household income, and supply chain efficiencies.[16] Avon's market share is growing in China, Russia, Eastern Europe, emerging markets, and selected developing countries. In the coming years, from population and growth perspectives, countries such as China, India, Indonesia, Brazil, Pakistan, Bangladesh, and Russia carry huge opportunities for Avon and other players in the toiletries/cosmetics and household nondurables industry. These countries either have a large population or maintain a well-educated middle class, which is a prerequisite for the toiletries/cosmetics industry. Like other companies, Avon may have to adapt its business model because of local considerations and supply chain issues. Consequently, these forces will help expand Avon's workforce as well as its market share.

In global markets, Avon is in a better position to attract a productive workforce because of its well-established sales network and a strong brand identity. Avon is particularly interested in expanding operations in China, and in March 2006 China granted Avon a national direct selling license, reversing its 1998 ban of door-to-door selling.[17] As a result Avon has built a sales force of 399,000 in China.[18] The General Manager of Avon China, Mr. S. K. Kao, stated:

The high numbers of licensed Sales Promoters in such a short time reflects the great appeal of the Avon earnings opportunity in the Chinese market, enhancing our confidence in the future of our business in China. We are very pleased that nearly 90 percent of our Beauty Boutiques have qualified to act as Service Centers under the government's regulations, indicating that our Beauty Boutique owners want to be involved in direct selling.

S. K. KAO,
General Manager,
Avon China[19]

Because of shorter life cycles and a rising middle class, new products and markets are the key to success in the emerging markets. According to Jung,

India is the other top priority [after China]. Right now we have about 60,000 representatives in India. . . . India has more than 300 million women between ages 15 and 64, and a rising middle class. . . . a market creation waiting to happen.

ANDREA JUNG,
October 16, 2006.[20]

Since the company continues to grow in international markets, it will keep hiring and training the new workforce in its door-to-door selling model. The company's distribution strategies may have to be adapted to the local needs because of working women or other cultural and logistical considerations and include mail, phone, fax, retail outlets, and Web sites.[21] One priority for training Avon's international representatives is to move faster to get the representatives online. Ms. Jung says that Avon's IT team has developed a global Internet platform, and that she has put a top strategist on the case.[22] Market entry issues and workforce management will have a big impact on Avon's future expansion in international markets.

In conclusion, Avon definitely carries a significant advantage over its rivals because of a well-organized and trained global management cadre, and 5.8 million independent representatives in local markets. Those representatives are self-managed Host Country Nationals who know the culture and ways to do their business in their home turf. It is also noteworthy that the Avon business model is promoting women as managers in areas where they probably have little other opportunity for such independence. Clearly, Avon is a company which excels in all the areas of IHRM.

---

[16] Pankaj Ghemawat, "Globalization: The Strategy of Differences," *HBS Working Knowledge*, November 10, 2003, 1–4 (www.hbswk.hbs.edu).
[17] Andrea Jung, "Now is the Time to Invest," *Fortune*, October 16, 2006.
[18] Nanette Byrnes, "Avon: More than Cosmetic Changes," *Business Week*, March 12, 2007.
[19] www.avon.com, July 17, 2006.
[20] *Fortune*, October 16, 2006.
[21] Ibid.
[22] Ibid.

Case Questions

1. Referring to this chapter and Chapter 9, evaluate Avon's Strategic International Human Resources practices in global markets regarding development of a global management cadre, HCNs, and building company associates and independent representatives in host countries.

2. Describe how Avon's business model has changed in light of demographic and social changes in the United States and abroad. What role has IHRM played in the company's global expansion?

3. Since 70 percent of Avon's revenues are generated outside the United States, what recommendations would you provide to the company regarding dealing with a culturally diverse workforce and a multicultural marketplace in the coming years?

4. Avon's future global expansion is contingent on hiring and retaining the best workforce and salespeople in global markets. What training and cross-cultural practices would you recommend to the company to deal with this area?

5. China is expected to be a major market for Avon. If you were to advise Avon, how would you develop a competitive IHR plan for the company?

6. What is the role of IT in Avon's markets, in particular in developing areas? What are the implications for training its representatives?

7. What do you think are Avon's prospects in India, given that the per capita spending on beauty there is only $1, compared to between $100 and $200 in developed markets?

Source: Updated and adapted by Helen Deresky, March 2009, from a case written exclusively for this book by Syed Tariq Anwar, 2004. The material in this case is intended to be used as a basis for classroom/academic discussion rather than to illustrate either effective or ineffective handling of a managerial situation or business practices.

Motivating and Leading

CHAPTER OBJECTIVES:

1. To understand the complexity and the variables involved in cross-cultural motivation and leadership

2. To learn to use the research on cultural dimensions as tools to understand how to motivate people in different cultural contexts

3. To become familiar with some common features of Mexican culture and context and how to motivate employees

4. To understand how leadership styles and practices vary around the world

5. To emphasize what makes a successful "global leader"

6. To gain familiarity with the variables of context, people, and situations affecting the leadership role

Opening Profile: The EU Business Leader—Myth or Reality?

Research results label French captains of industry as "autocrats," Germans as "democrats," and British as "meritocrats."

DDI,
*International Human Resources Consultants,
January 9, 2006*[1]

Is "the EU business leader" a myth or reality? The European Union now comprises a 27-nation unified market of over 400 million people. Can a businessperson have an effective leadership style across such diverse contexts and people? Not according to a survey of 200 chief executives in France, Germany, and the United Kingdom. Steve Newhall, managing director of DDI Europe, an International Human Resources Consultancy, notes that "the danger for any leader is only being able to operate within one of these styles. If you take an autocratic style into a culture that expects a more democratic or meritocratic style, the chances are that you will trip up."[2]

Perhaps some people can lead well in firms that stretch across countries in the EU. But, consider the complexity in its many forms: different histories and languages, government systems, business practices, educational systems, religions, organizations, and, not the least, national cultures. We have already examined, in this book, the many dimensions of culture along which societies differ and which determine how people behave on the job—their attitudes towards work and their superiors, their perspectives on time and scheduling, their level of motivation, and so on. In addition, countries in the EU are fiercely defensive of any incursions on national culture and identity. Given those factors, the prospect of convergence of leadership styles across the EU countries seems dim. On the other hand, argue Kets de Vries and Korotov:

> *Can European organizations afford not to have some form of European leadership? Can an organization remain Belgian, or Polish, or Italian and not include a "toolset" of European capabilities?*[3]

The strategic argument for convergence of leadership styles for EU business executives is that, while the Japanese or Americans, for example, can succeed with their predominantly "local" leadership style, it is not a good option for executives in most EU companies. For them, retaining "national styles and processes" will not lead to those companies being competitive in the EU and global markets because of the blending of labor, goods, and services, and processes across the EU countries. Rather, EU leaders need an "EU style" which will work across their markets.[4]

With that lofty goal in sight—whether one considers that goal desirable or undesirable—research shows that differences in leadership style still dominate. The DDI survey on leadership in 2006 asked 200 executives what they liked or disliked about being a leader. It was found that, for example, the French are three times more likely than the British and eight times more likely than the Germans to regard being in a position of power as important.[5] In other words, there are differences in attitude towards being a leader and making decisions. Whereas French leaders like to make decisions unilaterally, German executives indicated their concern about the responsibility of their decisions; leaders in the United Kingdom seemed less troubled about their decisions.[6]

Research on the German culture, for example, tells us that German leaders most likely will evidence high assertiveness and high individualism, but low humane orientation.[7] Their primary focus is on structured tasks and performance, and less on relationships. While very organized, based on technical expertise, they have been criticized for lack of innovation as leaders.[8]

The status of leaders in France is known to be based on position and the educational institutions that they attended—known as the "grand écoles." Title and position are attained through this elite status and thus are paramount over advancement through skills or training. French leadership style is very hierarchical and autocratic. French managers do not typically use a participative leadership style.[9] These conclusions about French leaders are supported by Javidan et al., who found that:

> *To French managers, people in positions of leadership should not be expected to be sensitive or empathetic, or to worry about another's status because such attributes would weaken a leader's resolve and impede decision making. Leaders should make decisions without being distracted by other considerations.*

JAVIDAN,
Dorfman, de Luque, and House, 2006[10]

We also see a predominantly autocratic style in the United Kingdom. Top positions of leadership are usually attained through the "old boy network" as a function of the tripartite class system that still permeates British society (upper-, middle-, and "working"-class). In this respect, leadership is based on traits, not skills, and there tends to be a highly cynical attitude throughout this style.[11]

These brief glimpses of leadership style in three of the EU countries indicate the difficulty, at least for now, of being an EU leader. Clearly, however, any leaders in positions where they deal with people and processes in several EU countries need to consider the context and cultures where they are operating and try to be flexible with their leadership style.

As the opening profile illustrates, leadership, at any level and in any location, is complicated by the norms and expectations of the people involved and by the local business practices. A successful leader must be an effective motivator, a process which is also culturally-contingent. We review the processes of motivating and leading in this chapter, bearing in mind the fact that they are intricately intertwined.

Motivating

The Westerners can't understand that we need the fork on our neck, not all these nice words and baby techniques. The Technique is the fork.

RUSSIAN MIDDLE MANAGER[12]

After managers set up a firm's operations by planning strategy, organizing the work and responsibilities, and staffing those operations, they turn their attention to everyday activities. This ongoing behavior of individual people carrying out various daily tasks enables the firm to accomplish its objectives. Getting those people to perform their jobs efficiently and effectively is at the heart of the manager's challenge.

Motivation—and therefore appropriate leadership style—is affected by many powerful variables (societal, cultural, and political). When considering the Japanese culture, for example, discussed throughout this book, it is not surprising to find that Fujitsu uses some motivational techniques very different from those in the West, such as when it cut the salaries of around 14,000 managers to motivate them and their subordinates to work harder. Fujitsu management said that if the company met their profit goal for the year the managers might have their full salaries restored. The logic was to build a sense of urgency and team spirit. Japanese workers typically feel a strong kinship to their employers and will work harder if they see their managers making similar sacrifices for the group goals.[13] Clearly Fujitsu's decision to cut pay is based on the Japanese tradition of "sink or swim" with co-workers and employer, and its collectivist culture.

Our objective in this chapter is to consider motivation and leadership in the context of diverse cultural milieus. We need to know what, if any, differences exist in the societal factors that elicit and maintain behaviors leading to high employee productivity and job satisfaction. Are effective motivational and leadership techniques universal or culture based?

CROSS-CULTURAL RESEARCH ON MOTIVATION

Motivation is very much a function of the context of a person's work and personal life. That context is greatly influenced by cultural variables, which affect the attitudes and behaviors of individuals (and groups) on the job. The framework of this context was described in Chapter 3 and illustrated in Exhibit 3-1. In applying Hofstede's research on the cultural dimensions of individualism—uncertainty avoidance, masculinity, and power distance, for example—we can make some generalized assumptions about motivation, such as the following:

- High uncertainty avoidance suggests the need for job security, whereas people with low uncertainty avoidance would probably be motivated by more risky opportunities for variety and fast-track advancement.
- High power distance suggests motivators in the relationship between subordinates and a boss, whereas low power distance implies that people would be more motivated by teamwork and relations with peers.

- High individualism suggests people would be motivated by opportunities for individual advancement and autonomy; collectivism (low individualism) suggests that motivation will more likely work through appeals to group goals and support.
- High masculinity suggests that most people would be more comfortable with the traditional division of work and roles; in a more feminine culture, the boundaries could be looser, motivating people through more flexible roles and work networks.

More recent research, reported in 2008, and based on Hofstede's dimensions of individualism and masculinity was conducted by Gelade, Dobson, and Auer. They compared what 50,000 workers in a global pharmaceutical company in 29 nations valued most in their jobs and that positively impacted their company. The results, based on Hofstede's individualism dimension, showed that the higher the level of national individualism (such as is typical in the United States) the more employees valued their autonomy, opportunities for personal achievements, and a worklife balance. This compared with employees in the more collectivistic countries (such as in China and Singapore) who apparently are more motivated when they felt that their jobs fully utilized their skills, and when they felt that the company was providing them with good working conditions, fringe benefits, and training.[14] The findings based on the masculinity dimension were that the higher the level of "masculinity" (such as in Japan and Mexico), the more motivated employees were by being given opportunities for high pay, personal accomplishment, and job advancement. This compared with those from more "feminine" cultures (such as in Denmark and Sweden), who claimed that factors related to their relationships with their managers and co-workers provided more commitment to the organization. The authors conclude that:

> *These findings show that the sources of organizational commitment are culturally conditioned and that their effects are predictable from Hofstede's value dimensions*
>
> JOURNAL OF CROSS-CULTURAL PSYCHOLOGY
> *39, no. 5 (2008).*[15]

Misjudging the importance of these cultural variables in the workplace may result not only in a failure to motivate but also in demotivation. Rieger and Wong-Rieger present the following example:

> *In Thailand, the introduction of an individual merit bonus plan, which runs counter to the societal norm of group cooperation, may result in a decline rather than an increase in productivity from employees who refuse to openly compete with each other.*[16]

In considering what motivates people, we have to understand their needs, goals, value systems, and expectations. No matter what their nationality or cultural background, people are driven to fulfill needs and to achieve goals. But what are those needs, what goals do they want to achieve, and what can motivate that drive to satisfy their goals?

The Meaning of Work

Because the focus in this text is on the needs that affect the working environment, it is important to understand first what work means to people from different backgrounds. For most people, the basic meaning of work is tied to economic necessity (money for food, housing, and so forth) for the individual and for society. However, the additional connotations of work are more subjective, especially about what work provides other than money—achievement, honor, social contacts, and so on.

Another way to view work, however, is through its relationship to the rest of a person's life. The Thais call work *ngan,* which is the same as the Thai word for "play," and they tend to introduce periods of play in their workdays. On the other hand, most people in China, Germany, and the United States have a more serious attitude toward work. Especially in work-oriented China, seven-day work weeks with long hours and few days off are common. A study of average work hours in various countries conducted by Steers found that Koreans worked longer hours and took fewer vacation days than workers in Thailand, Hong Kong, Taiwan, Singapore, India, Japan, and Indonesia.[17] The study concluded that the Koreans' hard work was attributable to loyalty to the company, group-oriented achievement, and emphasis on group harmony and business relationships.

Studies on the meaning of work in eight countries were carried out by George England and a group of researchers who are called the Meaning of Work (MOW) International Research Team.[18] Their research sought to determine a person's idea of the relative importance of work compared to that of leisure, community, religion, and family. They called this concept of work **work centrality**, defined as "the degree of general importance that working has in the life of an individual at any given point in time." The results showed, for example, that the Japanese hold work to be very important in their lives; the Brits, on the other hand (in this author's birth country) seem to like their leisure time more than those in the other countries surveyed. However, given the complexity of cultural and economic variables involved in people's attitude toward work, the results are difficult to generalize, in particular as concerns the implications of on-the-job work motivation. More relevant to managers (as an aid to understanding culture-based differences in motivation) are the specific reasons for valuing work. What kinds of needs does the working environment satisfy, and how does that psychological contract differ among populations?

The MOW research team provided some excellent insights into this question when it asked people in the eight countries what they valued about work and what needs are satisfied by their jobs. Their research results showed the relative order of importance overall as follows:

1. A needed income
2. Interest and satisfaction
3. Contacts with others
4. A way to serve society
5. A means of keeping occupied
6. Status and prestige.[19]

Note the similarities of some of these functions with Maslow's need categories and Herzberg's categories of motivators and maintenance factors. Clearly, these studies can help international managers to anticipate what attitudes people have toward their work, what aspects of work in their life context are meaningful to them, and therefore what approach the manager should take in setting up motivation and incentive plans.

In addition to the differences among countries within each category—such as the higher level of interest and satisfaction derived from work by the Israelis as compared with the Germans—it is interesting to note the within-country differences. Although income was the most important factor for all countries, it apparently has a far greater importance than any other factor in Japan. In other countries, such as the Netherlands, the relative importance of different factors was more evenly distributed.

The broader implications of such comparisons about what work means to people are derived from considering the total cultural context. The low rating given by the Japanese to the status and prestige found in work, for instance, suggests that those needs are more fully satisfied elsewhere in their lives, such as within the family and community. In the Middle East, religion plays a major role in all aspects of life, including work. The Islamic work ethic is a commitment toward fulfillment, and so business motives are held in the highest regard.[20] The origin of the Islamic work ethic is in the Muslim holy book, the Qur'an, and the words of the Prophet Mohammed:

> *On the day of judgment, the honest Muslim merchant will stand side by side with the martyrs.*
>
> MOHAMMED

Muslims feel that work is a virtue and an obligation to establish equilibrium in one's individual and social life. The Arab worker is defined by his or her level of commitment to family, and work is perceived as the determining factor in the ability to enjoy social and family life.[21] A study of 117 managers in Saudi Arabia by Ali found that Arab managers are highly committed to the Islamic work ethic and that there is a moderate tendency toward individualism.[22]

Exhibit 11-1 shows the results of the study and gives more insight into the Islamic work ethic. Another study by Kuroda and Suzuki found that Arabs are serious about their work and that favoritism, give-and-take, and paternalism have no place in the Arab workplace. They contrasted this attitude to that of the Japanese and Americans, who consider friendship to be an integral part of the workplace.[23]

EXHIBIT 11-1   The Islamic Work Ethic: Responses by Saudi Arabian Managers[24]

*Item	Mean*
Islamic Work Ethic	
1. Laziness is a vice.	4.66
2. Dedication to work is a virtue.	4.62
3. Good work benefits both one's self and others.	4.57
4. Justice and generosity in the workplace are necessary conditions for society's welfare.	4.59
5. Producing more than enough to meet one's personal needs contributes to the prosperity of society as a whole.	3.71
6. One should carry work out to the best of one's ability.	4.70
7. Work is not an end in itself but a means to foster personal growth and social relations.	3.97
8. Life has no meaning without work.	4.47
9. More leisure time is good for society.	3.08
10. Human relations in organizations should be emphasized and encouraged.	3.89
11. Work enables man to control nature.	4.06
12. Creative work is a source of happiness and accomplishment.	4.60
13. Any man who works is more likely to get ahead in life.	3.92
14. Work gives one the chance to be independent.	4.35
15. A successful man is the one who meets deadlines at work.	4.17
16. One should constantly work hard to meet responsibilities.	4.25
17. The value of work is derived from the accompanying intention rather than its results.	3.16

*On scale of 1–5 (5 highest)

Other variables affect the perceived meaning of work and how it satisfies various needs, such as the relative wealth of a country. When people have a high standard of living, work can take on a meaning different from simply providing the basic economic necessities of life. Economic differences among countries were found to explain variations in attitudes toward work in a study by Furnham et al. of over 12,000 young people from 41 countries on all five continents. Specifically, the researchers found that young people in Far East and Middle Eastern countries reported the highest competitiveness and acquisitiveness for money, while those from North America and South America scored highest on work ethics and "mastery" (that is, continuing to struggle to master something).[25] Such studies show the complexity of the underlying reasons for differences in attitudes toward work—cultural, economic, and so on—which must be taken into account when considering what needs and motivations people bring to the workplace. All in all, research shows a considerable cultural variability affecting how work meets employees' needs.

The Needs Hierarchy in the International Context

How can a manager know what motivates people in a specific country? Certainly, by drawing on the experiences of others who have worked there and also by inferring the likely type of motivational structure present by studying what is known about the culture in that region.

People's opinions of how best to satisfy their needs vary across cultures also. One clear conclusion is that managers around the world have similar needs but show differing levels of satisfaction of those needs derived from their jobs. Variables other than culture may be at play, however. One of these variables may be the country's stage of economic development. With regard to the transitioning economy in Russia, for example, a study by Elenkov found that Russian managers stress security and belongingness needs as opposed to higher-order needs, such as self-actualization.[26] Whatever the reason, many companies that have started operations in other countries have experienced differences in the apparent needs of the local employees and how they expect work to be recognized. Mazda, of Japan, experienced this problem in its Michigan plant. Japanese firms tend to confer recognition in the form of plaques, attention, and applause, and Japanese workers are likely to be insulted by material incentives because such rewards imply that they would work harder to achieve them than they otherwise would. Instead, Japanese firms focus on group-wide or company-wide goals, compared with the American emphasis on individual goals, achievement, and reward.

When considering the cross-cultural applicability of Maslow's hierarchy of needs theory, then, it is not the needs that are in question as much as the ordering of those needs in the hierarchy. The hierarchy reflects the Western culture where Maslow conducted his study; he concluded that people progress from satisfying basic needs, on to belongingness and esteem needs, and then to self-actualization needs.[27] However, different hierarchies might better reflect other cultures. For example, Eastern cultures focus on the needs of society rather than on the needs of individuals. It is difficult to observe or measure the individual needs of a Chinese person because, from childhood, these are intermeshed with the needs of society. Clearly, however, along with culture, the political beliefs at work in China dominate many facets of motivation. As the backbone of the industrial system, cadres (managers and technicians) and workers are given exact and detailed prescriptions of what is expected of them as members of a factory, workshop, or work unit. This results in conformity at the expense of creativity. Workers are accountable to their group, which is a powerful motivator. Because being "unemployed" has not been an option in China traditionally, it is important for employees to maintain themselves as cooperating members of the work group.[28] Money is also a motivator, stemming from the historical political insecurity and economic disasters that have perpetuated the need for a high level of savings.[29]

Although more cross-cultural research on motivation is needed, one can draw the tentative conclusion that managers around the world are motivated more by intrinsic than by extrinsic factors. Considerable doubt remains, however, about the universality of "western" theories because it is not possible to take into account all of the relevant cultural variables when researching motivation. Different factors have different meanings within the entire cultural context and must be considered on a situation-by-situation basis. The need to consider the entire national and cultural context is shown in the Comparative Management in Focus: Motivation in Mexico, which highlights motivational issues for Mexican workers and indicates the meaning of work to them.

COMPARATIVE MANAGEMENT IN FOCUS
Motivation in Mexico

In Mexico, everything is a personal matter; but a lot of managers don't get it. To get anything done here, the manager has to be more of an instructor, teacher, or father figure than a boss.

ROBERT HOSKINS,
Manager, Leviton Manufacturing, Juarez

To understand the cultural milieu in Mexico, we can draw on research that concludes that Latin American societies, including Mexico, rank high on power distance (the acknowledgment of hierarchical authority) and on uncertainty avoidance (a preference for security and formality over risk). In addition, they rank low on individualism, preferring collectivism, which values the good of the group, family, or country over individual achievement.[30] It is important for managers to recognize that Mexican society is very hierarchical, with a clear power structure for family, religion, business, politics and other areas of life. People are accorded respect according to their age, sex, and rank or position.[31]

The Mexican culture, generally, is "being-oriented," compared to the "doing-oriented" culture which prevails in the rest of North America; business takes a back seat to socializing.[32] Integral to the being-orientation is the high-context and implicit communication style of most Mexicans; much takes place on the level of non-verbal cues; the assumption of unspoken communication is based on the personal relationships and trust developed with colleagues. Implicit communication is also based on the importance attached to respect, whereas any conflict would lose face for all concerned.[33] On the other hand, they maintain a small personal space with others and are a "touching" society. They are also frequently very expressive and passionate communicators. In addition, that being-orientation leads to a rather fluid attitude towards time whereas relationships and commitment to individuals frequently take precedence over scheduled time commitments.[34]

It is said that Mexicans "work to live" compared to those in the United States, for example, who "live to work." One reason for that is that in Mexico the family is of central importance; loyalty and commitment to family and friends frequently determine employment, promotion, or special treatment for contracts. Decisions and actions are usually based on what is good for the family and the group. Unfortunately, it is this admirable cultural norm that often results in motivation and productivity problems on the job by contributing to very high absenteeism and turnover, especially in the *maquiladoras*. This high turnover and absenteeism are costly to employers, thereby offsetting the advantage of relatively low labor cost per hour. "Family reasons" (taking care of sick relatives or elderly parents) are the most common reasons given for absenteeism and for failing to return to work.[35] Workers often simply do not come back to work after vacations or holidays. For many Mexican males, the value of work lies primarily in its ability to fulfill their culturally imposed responsibilities as head of household and breadwinner rather than to seek individual achievement. Machismo (sharp role differentiation based on gender) and prestige are important characteristics of the Mexican culture.

As a people, speaking very generally, Mexicans are very proud and patriotic; *respeto* (respect) is important to them, and a slight against personal dignity is regarded as a grave provocation.[36] Mexican workers expect to be treated in the same respectful manner that they use toward one another. As noted by one U.S. expatriate, foreign managers must adapt to Mexico's "softer culture"; Mexican workers "need more communication, more relationship-building, and more reassurance than employees in the U.S."[37] The Mexican people are very warm and have a leisurely attitude toward time; face-to-face interaction is best for any kind of business, with time allowed for socializing and appreciating the Mexicans' cultural artifacts, buildings, and so forth. Taking time to celebrate a worker's birthday, for instance, will show that you are a *simpático* boss and will increase workers' loyalty and effort. The workers' expectations of small considerations that seem inconsequential to U.S. managers should not be discounted. In one *maquiladora,* when the company stopped providing the annual Halloween candy, the employees filed a grievance to the state Arbitration Board—Junta de Conciliación y Arbitraje.

Personal relationships are of utmost importance to the Mexican people, usually taking priority over work goals. Trust in friends and family takes precedence over purely business relationships, so that networking through personal contacts is the best way to do business. Following are some general guidelines on the Mexican culture to guide "foreign" managers in Mexico:

- Family and friends are first priority; maintaining those relationships and trust takes precedence over "outsiders" and so are important for business success
- Works to live; scheduling and time management is secondary.
- Fatalistic, based on strong religious influence
- Nationalistic; importance of history and tradition
- Work harmony is important; sensitive to conflict situations; need to maintain "face"
- Very proud; status is evidenced by title, position, formality in dress and etiquette.

Most managers in Mexico find that the management style that works best there is authoritative and paternal. Paternalism is expected; the manager is regarded as *el patrón* (pronounced pah-trone), or the father figure, whose role it is to take care of the workers as an extended family.[38] Employees expect managers to be the authority; they are the "elite"—power rests with the owner or manager and other prominent community leaders. Frequently, if not told to do something, the workers will not do it, nor will they question the boss or make any decisions for the boss.[39] Nevertheless, employees perceive the manager as a person, not as a concept or a function, and success often depends on the ability of a foreign manager to adopt a personalized management style, such as by greeting all workers as they arrive for their shifts.

Generally speaking, many Mexican factory workers doubt their ability to personally influence the outcome of their lives. They are apt to attribute events to the will of God, or to luck, timing, or relationships with higher authority figures. For many, decisions are made on the basis of ideals, emotions, and intuition rather than objective information. However, individualism and materialism are increasingly evident, particularly among the upwardly mobile high-tech and professional Mexican employees.

Corrective discipline and motivation must occur through training examples, cooperation, and, if necessary, subtle shaming. As a disciplinary measure, it is a mistake to directly insult a Mexican; an outright insult implies an insult to the whole family. As a motivation, one must appeal to the pride of the Mexican employees and avoid causing them to feel humiliated. Given that, "getting ahead" is often associated more with outside forces than with one's own actions; the motivation and reward system becomes difficult to structure in the usual ways.

Past experiences have indicated that, for the most part, motivation through participative decision making is not as effective as motivation through the more traditional and expected autocratic methods. With careful implementation, however, the mutual respect and caring that the Mexican people have for one another can lead to the positive team spirit needed for the team structure to be used successfully by companies, such as GM in its highest-quality plant in the world in Ramos Arizpe, near Saltillo, Mexico.[40] Although a study by Nicholls, Lane, and Brechu concluded cultural constraints are considerable when it comes to using self-managing teams in Mexico, the Mexican executives surveyed suggested that the relative success depends on the implementation. The conflicts are between the norms of behavior in self-managed teams typical of U.S. and Canadian culture (such as initiative and self-leadership, bottom-up decision making), and typical values in Mexican business culture (such as resistance to change, adherence to status roles, and top-down hierarchical structure). These differences in work-role norms seem to create a behavioral impasse, at least initially, when it comes to the potential for setting up self-managed teams.[41]

Although self-managed teams require individual leaders to take risks by spearheading team initiatives, those behaviors, according to the survey of Mexican executives, "are in sharp contrast to the behavioral norms of the paternalistic and hierarchical tradition of managers and workers in the Mexican work place." The workers expect the managers to give instructions and make decisions.[42] The business culture in Mexico is also attributable to prevailing economic conditions in Mexico of low levels of education, training, and technical skills. The Mexican executives surveyed gave some suggestions for implementing work teams and cautioned that the process of implementation will take a long time. They suggested the following:

- Foster a culture of individual responsibility among team members.
- Anticipate the impact of changes in power distribution.
- Provide leadership from the top throughout the implementation process.
- Provide adequate training to prepare workers for teamwork.
- Develop motivation and harmony through clear expectations.
- Encourage an environment of shared responsibility.[43]

For the most part, Mexican workers expect that authority will not be abused but rather that it will follow the family model in which everyone works together in a dignified manner according to their designated roles.[44] Any event that may break this harmony, or seems to confront authority, will likely be covered up. This may result in a supervisor hiding defective work, for example, or, as in the case of a steel conveyor plant in Puebla, a total worker walkout rather than using the grievance process.[45] Contributing to these kinds of problems is the need to save face for oneself and to respect others' place and honor. Public criticism is regarded as humiliating. Employees like an atmosphere of formality and respect. They typically use flattery and call people by their titles rather than their names to maintain an atmosphere of regard for status and respect.

A context of continuing economic problems and a relatively low standard of living for most workers help explain why Maslow's higher-order needs (self-actualization, achievement, status) are generally not very high on most Mexican workers' lists of needs. In discussing compensation, Mariah de Forest, who consults for American firms in Mexico, suggests the following:

> Rather than an impersonal wage scale, Mexican workers tend to think in terms of payment now for services rendered now. A daily incentive system with automatic payouts for production exceeding quotas, as well as daily/monthly attendance bonuses, works well.[46]

Global economic problems and cutbacks in auto manufacturing in 2009 have also affected Mexico, making money a pressing motivational factor for most employees. Benefits that most workers cannot afford are prized. For example, since workers highly value the enjoyment of life, many companies in Mexico provide recreation facilities—a picnic area, a soccer field, and so forth. Bonuses are expected regardless of productivity. In fact, it is the law to give Christmas bonuses of 15 days of pay to each worker. Fringe benefits are also important to Mexicans; because most Mexican workers are poor, the company provides the only source of such benefits for them. In particular, benefits that help to manage family-related issues are positive motivators for employees at least to turn up for work. To this end, companies often provide on-site health care facilities for workers and their families, nurseries, free meals, and even small loans in crisis situations.[47] In addition, those companies that understand the local infrastructure problems often provide a company bus to minimize the pervasive problems of absenteeism and tardiness.

The foregoing statements are broad generalizations about Mexican factory workers. Increasing numbers of American managers are in Mexico because the NAFTA has encouraged more U.S. businesses to move operations there. For firms on U.S. soil, managers may employ many Mexican-Americans in an intercultural setting. As the second-largest and fastest-growing ethnic group in the United States, Mexican-Americans represent an important subculture requiring management attention as they take an increasing proportion of the jobs there.

Research shows that little conclusive information is available to answer a manager's direct question of exactly how to motivate in any particular culture. The reason is that we cannot assume the universal applicability of the motivational theories, or even concepts, that have been used to research differences among cultures. Furthermore, the entire motivational context must be taken into account. For example, Western firms entering markets in Eastern Europe invariably run into difficulties in motivating their local staffs. Those workers have been accustomed to working under entirely different circumstances and usually do not trust foreign managers. Typically, then, the work systems and responsibilities must be highly structured because workers in Eastern Europe are not likely to use their own judgment in making decisions and because managerial skills are not developed.[48]

> *A principal rule in the [Russian] workplace is "Superiors know better."*
>
> SNEJINA MICHAILOVA[49]

A study by Michailova found that most Russian employees are still used to the management style that prevailed in a centrally planned economic system. This context resulted in vertically managed hierarchies, one-man authority, and anti-individualism. The employees in the study experienced conflict when faced with different managerial styles from their Russian and Western managers in joint venture situations. Those employees were in traditional industries, were on average 45 years old, and were more motivated by the authoritarianism of their Russian managers than the attempts at empowerment by their Western managers. More importantly, the conflicting motivational techniques left them in a "double bind," as shown in Exhibit 11-2.

In sum, motivation is situational, and savvy managers use all they know about the relevant culture or subculture—consulting frequently with local people—to infer the best means of motivating in that context. Furthermore, tactful managers consciously avoid an ethnocentric attitude in which they make assumptions about a person's goals, motivation, or work habits based on their own frames of reference, and they do not make negative value judgments about a person's level of motivation because it differs from their own.

Many cultural variables affect people's sense of what is attainable, and thus affect motivation. How much control people believe they have over their environment and their destiny—whether they believe that they can control certain events, and not just be at the mercy of external forces—is one example. Although Americans typically feel a strong internal locus of control, others attribute results to, for example, the will of God (in the case of Muslims) or to the good fortune of being born in the right social class or family (in the case of many Latin Americans). For example, whereas Americans feel that hard work will get the job done, many Hong Kong Chinese believe that outcomes are determined by *joss,* or luck. Clearly, then, managers must use persuasive strategies to motivate employees when they do not readily connect their personal work behaviors with outcomes or productivity.

The role of culture in the motivational process is shown in Exhibit 11-3. An employee's needs are determined largely by the cultural context of values and attitudes—along with the

EXHIBIT 11-2 Conflicting Motivational Techniques in Western–Russian Joint Ventures

Western Managers to Russian Employees	**Russian Managers to Russian Employees**
Take initiative and come with suggestions	Do what you are supposed to do and obey the established rules
Learn from the mistakes and don't repeat them	Mistakes are not allowed and should be punished
Be longer term and future oriented	Concentrate on here and now (and don't forget how it was before)
Think of the company as an integrated entity	Act according to your own job description and don't interfere in other people's job

Source: Reprinted from S. Michailova, "When Common Sense Becomes Uncommon: Participation and Empowerment in Russian Companies with Western Participation," *Journal of World Business* 37 (2002): 180–87, with permission from Elsevier.

EXHIBIT 11-3   The Role of Culture in Job Motivation

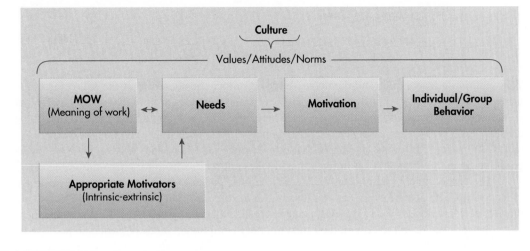

national variables—in which he or she lives and works. Those needs then determine the meaning of work for that employee. The manager's understanding of what work means in that employee's life can then lead to the design of a culturally appropriate job context and reward system to guide individual and group employee job behavior to meet mutual goals.

Reward Systems

Incentives and rewards are an integral part of motivation in a corporation. Recognizing and understanding different motivational patterns across cultures leads to the design of appropriate reward systems. In the United States, there are common patterns of rewards, varying among levels of the company and types of occupations and based on experience and research with Americans. Rewards usually fall into five categories: financial, social status, job content, career, and professional. The relative emphasis on one or more of these five categories varies from country to country. In Japan, for example, reward systems are based primarily on seniority, and much emphasis is put on the bonus system. In addition, distinction is made there between the regular workforce and the temporary workforce, which usually traditionally comprises women expected to leave when they start a family. As is usually the case, the regular workforce receives considerably more rewards than the temporary workforce in pay and benefits and the allocation of interesting jobs.[50] For the regular workforce, the emphasis is on the employee's long-term effectiveness in terms of behavior, personality, and group output. Rewarding the individual is frowned on in Japan because it encourages competition rather than the desired group cooperation. Therefore, specific cash incentives are usually limited. In Taiwan, recognition and affection are important; company departments compete for praise from top management at their annual celebration.

In contrast, the entire reward system in China is very different from that of most countries. The low wage rates are compensated for by free housing, schools, and medical care. While egalitarianism still seems to prevail, the recent free-enterprise reform movements have encouraged *duo lao, duo de* ("more work, more pay"). One important incentive is training, which gives workers more power. One approach used in the past—and one that seems quite negative to Americans—is best illustrated by the example of a plaque award labeled "Ms. Wong—Employee of the Month." While Westerners would assume that Ms. Wong had excelled as an employee, actually this award given in a Chinese retail store was for the worst employee; the plaque was designed to shame and embarrass her.[51] Younger Chinese in areas changing to a more market-based economy have seen a shift toward equity-based rewards, no doubt resulting from a gradual shift in work values.[52]

No doubt culture plays a significant role in determining the appropriate incentive and reward systems around the world. Employees in collectivist cultures such as Japan, Korea, and Taiwan would not respond well to the typical American merit-based reward system to motivate employees because that would go against the traditional value system and would disrupt the harmony and corporate culture.

Leading

Le patron, der Chef, and the Boss.

DDI,
Leaders on Leadership Survey, 2006[53]

This section on leadership (and the above quote) prompts consideration of the following questions: To what extent, and how, do leadership styles and practices around the world vary? What are the forces perpetuating that divergence? Where, and why, will that divergence continue to be the strongest? Is there any evidence for convergence of leadership styles and practices around the world? What are the forces leading to that convergence, and how and where will this convergence occur in the future? What implications do these questions have for cross-cultural leaders?

The task of helping employees realize their highest potential in the workplace is the essence of leadership. The goal of every leader is to achieve the organization's objectives while achieving those of each employee. Today's global managers realize that increased competition requires them to be open to change and to rethink their old culturally conditioned modes of leadership.

THE GLOBAL LEADER'S ROLE AND ENVIRONMENT

The greatest competitive advantage global companies in the twenty-first century can have is effective global leaders. Yet this competitive challenge is not easy to meet. People tend to rise to leadership positions by proving themselves able to lead in their home-country corporate culture and meeting the generally accepted behaviors of that national culture. However, global leaders must broaden their horizons—both strategically and cross-culturally—and develop a more flexible model of leadership that can be applied anywhere—one that is adaptable to locational situations around the world.[54]

The critical factors necessary for successful leadership abroad have come to be known as the "Global Mindset." Typically that mindset compares with the traditional mindset in the areas of general perspective, organizational life, work style, view of change, and learning.[55] Some of the typical actions and attitudes of a leader with a global mindset are shown in Exhibit 11-4.

One successful leader with a "global mindset" is Carlos Ghosn, a French businessman and CEO of Nissan and Renault. He was born in Brazil of Lebanese parents and educated in France. While at Renault, he was sent to Japan to turnaround the ailing auto company, Nissan, which he did very successfully, surprising everyone that he could work so well within the intricate culture of Japanese business. (For further details see the Part 4 Comprehensive Case Study on Carlos Ghosn.) Ghosn was voted man of the Year 2003 by *Fortune* magazine's Asian edition, he also sits on the boards of Alcoa, Sony, and IBM. This global leader and multicultural manager conveyed his high CQ when interviewed by *Newsweek:*

> *Companies are going global, but the teams are divided and scattered all over the planet. . . . You have to know how to motivate people who think very differently than you, who have different kinds of sensitivities, so I think the most important message is to get prepared to deal with teams who are multicultural, who do not think the same way.*[57]

EXHIBIT 11-4 The Global Mindset of Successful Leaders[56]

Personal work style	High "cultural quotient" (CQ)
	Open-minded and flexible
	Effective cross-cultural communicator and collaborator
	Team player in a global matrix
	Supports global objectives and balances global with local goals and practices.
General Perspective	Broad, systems perspective
	Personal autonomy and emotional resilience
	Change is welcomed and facilitated
	Enables boundaryless organizations
	Operates easily in cross-cultural and cross-functional environment
	Global learning is sought and used for career development

Further information regarding leadership effectiveness abroad was found by Morrison, Gregersen, and Black; their research involved 125 global leaders in 50 companies. They concluded that effective leaders must have global business and organizational savvy. They explain global business savvy as the ability to recognize global market opportunities for a company and having a vision of doing business worldwide. Global organizational savvy requires an intimate knowledge of a company's resources and capabilities in order to capture global markets, as well as an understanding of each subsidiary's product lines and how the people and business operate on the local level. Morrison, Gregersen, and Black outline four personal development strategies through which companies and managers can meet these requirements of effective global leadership: travel, teamwork, training, and transfers (the four "T's").[58]

Travel, of course, exposes managers to various cultures, economies, political systems, and markets. Working on global teams teaches managers to operate on an interpersonal level while dealing with business decision-making processes that are embraced by differences in cultural norms and business models. Although formal training seminars also play an important role, most of the global leaders interviewed said that the most influential developmental experience in their lives was the international assignment. Increasingly, global companies are requiring that their managers who will progress to top management positions must have overseas assignment experience.[59] The benefits accruing to the organization depend on how effectively the assignment and repatriation are handled, as discussed in Chapter 10.

Effective global leadership involves the ability to inspire and influence the thinking, attitudes, and behavior of people anywhere in the world. The importance of the leadership role cannot be overemphasized because the leader's interactions strongly influence the motivation and behavior of employees, and ultimately, the entire climate of the organization. The cumulative effects of one or more weak managers can have a significant negative impact on the ability of the organization to meet its objectives.

Managers on international assignments try to maximize leadership effectiveness by juggling several important, and sometimes conflicting, roles as (1) a representative of the parent firm, (2) the manager of the local firm, (3) a resident of the local community, (4) a citizen of either the host country or of another country, (5) a member of a profession, and (6) a member of a family.[60]

The leader's role comprises the interaction of two sets of variables—the content and the context of leadership. The content of leadership comprises the attributes of the leader and the decisions to be made; the context of leadership comprises all those variables related to the particular situation.[61] The increased number of variables (political, economic, and cultural) in the context of the managerial job abroad requires astute leadership. Some examples of the variables in the content and context of the leader's role in foreign settings are given below.[62] The multicultural leader's role thus blends leadership, communication, motivational, and other managerial skills within unique and ever-changing environments. We will examine the contingent nature of such leadership throughout this section.

THE LEADER AND THE JOB:[63]

- Leadership experience and technical knowledge
- Cultural adaptability
- Clarity of information available in host area
- Level of authority and autonomy
- Level of cooperation among partners, government and employees.

THE JOB CONTEXT:

- Level of authority granted to leader
- Physical location and local resource availability
- Host professional contacts, and community relations
- Organizational structure, scope of internationalization, technology, etc.
- Business environment: social-cultural, political-economic, level of risk
- Systems of staffing, coordination, reward system and decision making, locally and in home office.

The E-Business Effect on Leadership

An additional factor—technology—is becoming increasingly pervasive in its ability to influence the global leader's role and environment and will, perhaps, contribute to a lessening of the differences in motivation and leadership around the world. More and more often, companies like Italtel Spa are using technology such as the intranet to share knowledge and product information throughout their global operations. In the case of Italtel, this required wide delegation and empowerment of their employees so that they could decentralize.

Individual managers are realizing that the Internet is changing their leadership styles and interactions with employees, as well as their strategic leadership of their organizations. They have to adapt to the hyperspeed environment of e-business, as well as to the need for visionary leadership in a whole new set of competitive industry dynamics. Some of these new-age leadership issues are discussed in the Management Focus: Leadership in a Digital World.

MANAGEMENT FOCUS

Leadership in a Digital World

What does leadership mean in a digital world in which organizations are flexible and fluid and the pace of change is extremely rapid? What's it like to lead in an e-business organization? Jomei Chang of Vitria Technology describes it as follows: "There's no place to hide. [The Internet] forces you to be on your toes every minute, every second." Is leadership in e-businesses really all that different from traditional organizations? Managers who've worked in both think it is. How? Three differences seem to be most evident: the speed at which decisions must be made, the importance of being flexible, and the need to create a vision of the future.

Making Decisions Fast. Managers in all organizations never have all the data they want when making decisions, but the problem is multiplied in e-business. The situation is changing rapidly and the competition is intense. For example, Meg Whitman, then president and CEO of eBay, said, "We're growing at 40 percent to 50 percent per quarter. That pace absolutely changes the leadership challenge. Every three months we become a different company. In one year, we went from 30 employees to 140, and from 100,000 registered users to 2.2 million. At Hasbro [where she was previously an executive], we would set a yearlong strategy, and then we would simply execute against it. At eBay, we constantly revisit the strategy—and revise the tactics."

Leaders in e-businesses see themselves as sprinters and their contemporaries in traditional businesses as long-distance runners. They frequently use the term "Internet time," which is a reference to a rapidly speeded-up working environment. "Every [e-business] leader today has to unlearn one lesson that was drilled into each one of them: You gather data so that you can make considered decisions. You can't do that on Internet time."

Maintaining Flexibility. In addition to speed, leaders in e-businesses need to be highly flexible. They have to be able to roll with the ups and downs. They need to be able to redirect their group or organization when they find that something doesn't work. They have to encourage experimentation. This is what Mark Cuban, president and co-founder of Broadcast.com, had to say about the importance of being flexible. "When we started, we thought advertising would be the core of our business. We were wrong. We thought that the way to define our network was to distribute servers all over the country. We were wrong. We've had to recalibrate again and again—and we'll have to keep doing it in the future."

Focusing on the Vision. Although visionary leadership is important in every organization, in a hyperspeed environment, people require more from their leaders. The rules, policies, and regulations that characterize more traditional organizations provide direction and reduce uncertainty for employees. Such formalized guidelines typically don't exist in e-businesses, and it becomes the responsibility of the leaders to provide direction through their vision. For instance, David Pottruck, co-CEO of Charles Schwab, gathered nearly 100 of the company's senior managers at the southern end of the Golden Gate Bridge. He handed each a jacket inscribed with the phrase "Crossing the Chasm" and led them across the bridge in a symbolic march to kick off his plan to turn Schwab into a full-fledged Internet brokerage. Getting people to buy into the vision may require even more radical actions. For instance, when Isao Okawa, chairman of Sega Enterprises, decided to remake his company into an e-business, his management team resisted—that is, until he defied Japan's consensus-charged, lifetime-employment culture by announcing that those who resisted the change would be fired, risking shame. Not so amazingly, resistance to the change vanished overnight.

Source: S. P. Robbins and M. Coulter, *Management*, 7ᵗʰ ed. (Upper Saddle River, NJ: Prentice Hall, 2001), used with permission.

CROSS-CULTURAL RESEARCH ON LEADERSHIP

Numerous leadership theories focus in various ways on individual traits, leader behavior, interaction patterns, role relationships, follower perceptions, influence over followers, influence on task goals, and influence on organizational culture.[64] Here it is important to understand how the variable of societal culture fits into these theories and what implications can be drawn for international managers as they seek to provide leadership around the world. Although the functions of leadership are similar across cultures, anthropological studies, such as those by Margaret Mead, indicate that while leadership is a universal phenomenon, what makes effective leadership varies across cultures.[65]

In addition to research studies that indicate variations in leadership profiles, the generally accepted image that people in different countries have about what they expect and admire in their leaders tends to become a norm over time, forming an idealized role for these leaders. Industry leaders in France and Italy, for example, are highly regarded for their social prominence and political power. In Latin American countries, leaders are respected as total persons and leaders in society, with appreciation for the arts being important. In Germany, polish, decisiveness, and a wide general knowledge are respected, with their leaders granted a lot of formality by everyone. Foreigners are often surprised at the informal off-the-job lifestyles of executives in the United States and would be surprised to see them pushing a lawn mower, for example.

Most research on U.S. leadership styles describes managerial behaviors on, essentially, the same dimension, variously termed *autocratic* versus *democratic, participative* versus *directive, relations-oriented* versus *task-oriented,* or *initiating structure* versus *consideration continuum.*[66] These studies were developed in the West, and conclusions regarding employee responses largely reflect the opinions of U.S. workers. The democratic, or participative, leadership style has been recommended as the one more likely to have positive results with most U.S. employees.

CONTINGENCY LEADERSHIP: THE CULTURE VARIABLE

Modern leadership theory recognizes that no single leadership style works well in all situations.[67] A considerable amount of research, directly or indirectly, supports the notion of cultural contingency in leadership. This means that, as a result of culture-based norms and beliefs about how people in various roles should behave, what is expected of leaders, what influence they have, and what kind of status they are given vary from nation to nation. Clearly, this has implications for what kind of leadership style a manager should expect to adopt when going abroad.

The GLOBE Project

Research by the Global Leadership and Organizational Behavior Effectiveness (GLOBE) research program comprised a network of 170 social scientists and management scholars from 62 countries for the purpose of understanding the impact of cultural variables on leadership and organizational processes. Using both quantitative and qualitative methodologies to collect data from 18,000 managers in those countries, representing the majority of the world's population, the researchers wanted to find out which leadership behaviors are universally accepted and which are culturally contingent. Not unexpectedly, they found that the positive leadership behaviors generally accepted anywhere are behaviors such as being trustworthy, encouraging, an effective bargainer, a skilled administrator and communicator, and a team builder; the negatively regarded traits included being uncooperative, egocentric, ruthless, and dictatorial.[68] Those leadership styles and behaviors found to be culturally contingent are charismatic, team-oriented, self-protective, participative, humane, and autonomous.

The results for some of those countries researched are shown in Exhibit 11-5. The first column *(N)* is the sample size within that country. The scores for each country on those leadership dimensions are based on a scale from 1 (the opinion that those leadership behaviors would not be regarded favorably) to 7 (that those behaviors would substantially facilitate effective leadership). Note that reading from top to bottom on a single dimension allows comparison among those countries on that dimension. For example, being a participative leader is regarded as more important in Canada, Brazil, and Austria than it is in Egypt, Hong Kong, Indonesia, and Mexico. In addition, reading from left to right for a particular country on all dimensions allows development of an effective leadership style profile for that country. In Brazil, for example, one can conclude that an effective leader is expected to be very charismatic, team-oriented and participative, and relatively humane but not autonomous.

EXHIBIT 11-5 Culturally Contingent Beliefs Regarding Effective Leadership Styles[69]

Country	N	Charisma	Team	Self-Protective	Participative	Humane	Autonomous
Australia	345	6.09	5.81	3.05	5.71	5.09	3.95
Brazil	264	6.01	6.17	3.50	6.06	4.84	2.27
Canada (English-speaking)	257	6.16	5.84	2.96	6.09	5.20	3.65
China	160	5.57	5.57	3.80	5.05	5.18	4.07
Denmark	327	6.01	5.70	2.82	5.80	4.23	3.79
Egypt	201	5.57	5.55	4.21	4.69	5.14	4.49
England	168	6.01	5.71	3.04	5.57	4.90	3.92
Greece	234	6.02	6.12	3.49	5.81	5.16	3.98
India	231	5.85	5.72	3.78	4.99	5.26	3.85
Ireland	157	6.08	5.82	3.01	5.64	5.06	3.95
Israel	543	6.23	5.91	3.64	4.96	4.68	4.26
Japan	197	5.49	5.56	3.61	5.08	4.68	3.67
Mexico	327	5.66	5.75	3.86	4.64	4.71	3.86
Nigeria	419	5.77	5.65	3.90	5.19	5.48	3.62
Philippines	287	6.33	6.06	3.33	5.40	5.53	3.75
Poland	283	5.67	5.98	3.53	5.05	4.56	4.34
Russia	301	5.66	5.63	3.69	4.67	4.08	4.63
Singapore	224	5.95	5.77	3.32	5.30	5.24	3.87
South Korea	233	5.53	5.53	3.68	4.93	4.87	4.21
Spain	370	5.90	5.93	3.39	5.11	4.66	3.54
Sweden	1,790	5.84	5.75	2.82	5.54	4.73	3.97
Thailand	449	5.78	5.76	3.91	5.30	5.09	4.28
Turkey	301	5.96	6.01	3.58	5.09	4.90	3.83
USA	399	6.12	5.80	3.16	5.93	5.21	3.75

Scale 1 to 7 in order of how important those behaviors are considered for effective leadership (7 = highest).

The charismatic leader shown in this research is someone who is, for example, a visionary, an inspiration to subordinates, and performance-oriented. A team-oriented leader is someone who exhibits diplomatic, integrative, and collaborative behaviors toward the team. The self-protective dimension describes a leader who is self-centered, conflictual, and status conscious. The participative leader is one who delegates decision making and encourages subordinates to take responsibility. Humane leaders are those who are compassionate to their employees. An autonomous leader is, as expected, an individualist, so countries that ranked participation as important tended to rank autonomy in leadership as relatively unimportant. In Egypt, participation and autonomy were ranked about equally.[70]

This broad, path-breaking research by the GLOBE researchers can be very helpful to managers going abroad, enabling them to exercise culturally appropriate leadership styles. In another stage of this ongoing research project, interviews with managers from various countries led the researchers, headed by Robert House, to conclude that the status and influence of leaders vary a great deal across countries or regions according to the prevailing cultural forces. Whereas Americans, Arabs, Asians, the English, Eastern Europeans, the French, Germans, Latin Americans, and Russians tend to glorify leaders in both the political and organizational arenas; those in the Netherlands, Scandinavia, and Germanic Switzerland have very different views of leadership.[71] Following are some sample comments made by managers from various countries:

- Americans appreciate two kinds of leaders. They seek empowerment from leaders who grant autonomy and delegate authority to subordinates. They also respect the bold, forceful, confident, and risk-taking leader, as personified by John Wayne in his movies.
- The Dutch place emphasis on egalitarianism and are skeptical about the value of leadership. Terms like *leader* and *manager* carry a stigma. If a father is employed as a manager, Dutch children will not admit it to their schoolmates.

EXHIBIT 11-6 Cultural Views of Leadership Effectiveness

Behaviors and Traits Universally Considered Facilitators of Leadership Effectiveness

• Trustworthiness (integrity)
• Visionary (charismatic-visionary)
• Inspirational and motivating (charismatic-inspirational)
• Communicative (team builder)

Behaviors and Traits Universally Considered Impediments to Leadership Effectiveness

• Being a loner and asocial (self-protective)
• Non-cooperative (malevolent)
• Dictatorial (autocratic)

Culturally Contingent Endorsement of Leader Attributes

• Individualistic (autonomous)
• Status-conscious (status-conscious)
• Risk-taking (charismatic III: self-sacrificial)

Source: Based on Mansour Javidan, Peter W. Dorfman, Mary Sully de Luque, and Robert J. House, "In the Eye of the Beholder: Cross Cultural Lessons in Leadership from Project GLOBE," *The Academy of Management Perspectives* 20, no. 1 (2006): 75.

• Arabs worship their leaders—as long as they are in power!
• Iranians seek power and strength in their leaders.
• Malaysians expect their leaders to behave in a manner that is humble, modest, and dignified.
• The French expect leaders to be "cultivated"—highly educated in the arts and in mathematics.[72]

Subsequently, further conclusions were drawn from the GLOBE results by Javidan et al. as to which leadership variables are found to be universally effective, which are found to be universal impediments to effectiveness, and which are considered to be culturally contingent attributes. Their findings are listed in Exhibit 11-6, with the corresponding GLOBE dimension in parentheses.

Earlier Leadership Research

Other research also provides insight on the relative level of preference for autocratic versus participative leadership styles. For example, Hofstede's four cultural dimensions (discussed in Chapter 3) provide a good starting point to study leader–subordinate expectations and relationships. We can assume, for example, that employees in countries that rank high on power distance (India, Mexico, the Philippines) are more likely to prefer an autocratic leadership style and some paternalism because they are more comfortable with a clear distinction between managers and subordinates rather than with a blurring of decision-making responsibility.

Employees in countries that rank low on power distance (Sweden and Israel) are more likely to prefer a consultative, participative leadership style, and they expect superiors to adhere to that style. Hofstede, in fact, concludes that participative management approaches recommended by many American researchers can be counterproductive in certain cultures.[73] The crucial fact to grasp about leadership in any culture, he points out, is that it is a complement to subordinateship (employee attitudes toward leaders). In other words, perhaps we concentrate too much on leaders and their unlikely ability to change styles at will. Much depends on subordinates and their cultural conditioning, and it is that subordinateship to which the leader must respond.[74] Hofstede points out that his research reflects the values of subordinates, not the values of superiors.

In another part of his research, Hofstede ranked the relative presence of autocratic norms in the following countries, from lowest to highest: Germany, France, Belgium, Japan, Italy, the United States, the Netherlands, Britain, and India. India ranked much higher than the others on autocracy.[75]

Expectations about managerial authority versus participation were also among the managerial behaviors and philosophies studied by Laurent, a French researcher. In a study conducted in nine Western European countries, the United States, Indonesia, and Japan, he concluded that national origin significantly affects the perception of what is effective management.[76] For example, Americans and Germans subscribe more to participation than do Italians and Japanese; Indonesians are more comfortable with a strict autocratic structure. Managers in Sweden, the

EXHIBIT 11-7 Comparative Leadership Dimensions: Participation and Initiative[79]

Managerial Initiative, Managers' Sense of Drive and Responsibility		Extent to Which Leaders Delegate Authority	
0 = low; 100 = high		0 = low; 100 = high	
USA	73.67	Sweden	75.51
Sweden	72.29	Japan	69.27
Japan	72.20	Norway	68.50
Finland	69.58	USA	66.23
Korea	67.86	Singapore	65.37
Netherlands	67.11	Denmark	64.65
Singapore	66.34	Canada	64.38
Switzerland	65.71	Finland	62.92
Belgium/Luxembourg	65.47	Switzerland	62.20
Ireland	64.76	Netherlands	61.33
France	64.64	Australia	61.22
Austria	62.56	Germany	60.85
Denmark	62.79	New Zealand	60.54
Italy	62.40	Ireland	59.53
Australia	62.04	UK	58.95
Canada	61.56	Belgium/Luxembourg	54.55
Spain	61.55	Austria	54.29
New Zealand	59.46	France	53.62
Greece	58.50	Italy	46.80
UK	58.25	Spain	44.31
Norway	54.50	Portugal	42.56
Portugal	49.74	Greece	37.95

Netherlands, the United States, Denmark, and Great Britain believe that employees should participate in problem solving rather than simply be "fed" all the answers by managers, compared with managers in those countries on the higher end of this scale, such as Italy, Indonesia, and Japan. Laurent's findings about Japan, however, seem to contradict common knowledge about Japan's very participative decision-making culture. In fact, research by Hampden-Turner and Trompenaars places Japan as second highest, after Sweden, in the extent to which leaders delegate authority.[77] Findings regarding the other countries are similar—shown in Exhibit 11-7. However, participative leadership should not mean a lack of initiative or responsibility.

Other classic studies indicate cross-cultural differences in the expectations of leadership behavior. Haire, Ghiselli, and Porter surveyed more than 3,000 managers in 14 countries. They found that, although managers around the world consistently favored delegation and participation, those managers also had a low appreciation of the capacity and willingness of subordinates to take an active role in the management process.[78]

In addition, several studies of individual countries or areas conclude that a participative leadership style is frequently inappropriate. Managers in Malaysia, Indonesia, Thailand, and the Philippines were found to prefer autocratic leadership, whereas those in Singapore and Hong Kong are less autocratic.[80] Similarly, the Turks have been found to prefer authoritarian leadership, as do the Thais.[81]

In the Middle East, in particular, little delegation occurs. A successful company there must have strong managers who make all the decisions and who go unquestioned. Much emphasis is placed on the use of power through social contacts and family influence, and the chain of command must be rigidly followed.[82]

The effects of participative leadership can vary even in one location when the employees are from different cultural backgrounds—from which we can conclude that a subordinate's culture is usually a more powerful variable than other factors in the environment. Research that supports this conclusion includes a study conducted in Saudi Arabia that found participative leadership to be more effective with U.S. workers than with Asian and African employees,

EXHIBIT 11-8   The Culture Contingency in the Leadership Process: An Integrative Model

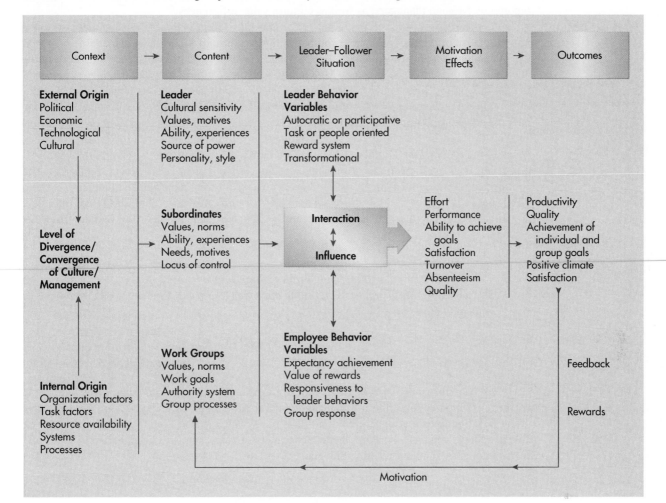

and a study in a U.S. plant that found that participative leadership resulted in greater satisfaction and communication among U.S. employees than among Mexican employees.[83]

Exhibit 11-8 depicts an integrative model of the leadership process that pulls together the variables described in this book and in the research on culture, leadership, and motivation—and shows the powerful contingency of culture as it affects the leadership role. Reading from left to right, Exhibit 11-8 presents contingencies from the broad environmental factors to the outcomes affected by the entire leadership situation. As shown, the broad context in which the manager operates necessitates adjustments in leadership style to all those variables relating to the work and task environment and the people involved. Cultural variables (values, work norms, the locus of control, and so forth), as they affect everyone involved—leader, subordinates, and work groups—then shape the content of the immediate leadership situation.

The leader-follower interaction is then further shaped by the leader's choice of behaviors (autocratic, participative, and so on) and by the employees' attitudes toward the leader and the incentives. Motivation effects—various levels of effort, performance, and satisfaction—result from these interactions, on an individual and a group level. These effects determine the outcomes for the company (productivity, quality) and for the employees (satisfaction, positive climate). The results and rewards from those outcomes then act as feedback (positive or negative) into the cycle of the motivation and leadership process.

Clearly, then, international managers should take seriously the culture contingency in their application of the contingency theory of leadership: They must adjust their leadership behaviors according to the context, norms, attitudes, and other variables in that society. One example of the complexity of the leadership situation involving obvious contextual as well as cultural factors can be seen in the results of a study of how Russian employees responded to the participative management practices of North American managers. It was found that the performance of the

Russian workers decreased, which the researchers attributed to a history of employee ideas being ignored by Russian managers, as well as cultural value differences.[84]

As noted, leadership refers not just to the manager-subordinate relationship, but also to the important task of running the whole company, division, or unit for which a manager is responsible. When that is a global responsibility, it is vital to be able to adapt one's leadership style to the local context on many levels. Nancy McKinstry, an American leader in Europe, is very sensitive to that imperative. Since she moved to Europe, charged with the task of turning around the troubled Wolters Kluwer, the Dutch publishing group, she "has had plenty of experience of the way national and cultural differences can both bedevil and enliven business."[85] One immediate difference she noticed is that she is one of few women in senior management in Holland. That fact, added to the focus of the Dutch media on the executive as a person and the views of the employees, rather than the focus on the company as in the United States, was surprising to her. As she continues her restructuring plan, Ms. McKinstry (whose physician husband commutes every two weeks between his hospital job in New York and his family in Amsterdam) has found that there is a misconception that she is going to apply an American, bottom-line leadership style. However, she says:

> There isn't that one-size-fits-all approach, not even within Europe. . . . If you have a product or a customer problem in France, there might be an approach that works extremely well. But if you took that same approach and tried to solve the exact same problem in Holland, you might fail.[86]

NANCY MCKINSTRY,
Chairman and CEO, Wolters Kluwer Publishing Group,
Holland, July 15, 2004[87]

Ms. McKinstry explains that in southern Europe, there is far more nuance to what people are saying compared to northern Europe and in particular compared to the direct, optimistic style of the U.S. She finds that they often don't want to say "No" to her, even though they may not be able to achieve what she is asking them. Her leadership approach is to listen hard and say "How are you going to go about meeting this goal?"[88]

CONCLUSION

Because leadership and motivation entail constant interactions with others (employees, peers, superiors, outside contacts), cultural influences on these critical management functions are very strong. Certainly, other powerful variables are intricately involved in the international management context, particularly those of economics and politics. Effective leaders carefully examine the entire context and develop sensitivity to others' values and expectations regarding personal and group interactions, performance, and outcomes—and then act accordingly.

Summary of Key Points

1. Motivation and leadership are factors in the successful implementation of desired strategy. However, while many of the basic principles are universal, much of the actual content and process are culture-contingent—a function of an individual's needs, value systems, and environmental context.

2. One problem in using content theories for cross-cultural research, such as that created by Maslow, is the assumption of their universal application. Because they were developed in the United States, even the concepts, such as achievement or esteem, may have different meanings in other societies, resulting in a noncomparable basis of research.

3. Implicit in motivating an employee is an understanding of which of the employee's needs are satisfied by work. Studies on the "meaning of work" indicate considerable cross-cultural differences.

4. A reexamination of motivation relative to Hofstede's dimensions of power distance, uncertainty avoidance, individualism, and masculinity provides another perspective on the cultural contexts that can influence motivational structures.

5. Incentives and reward systems must be designed to reflect the motivational structure and relative cultural emphasis on five categories of rewards: financial, social status, job content, career, and professional.

6. Effective leadership is crucial to the ability of a company to achieve its goals. The challenge is to decide what is effective leadership in different international or mixed-culture situations.

7. The perception of what makes a good leader—both traits and behaviors—varies a great deal from one society to another. The GLOBE leadership study across 62 countries provides considerable insight into culturally appropriate leadership behaviors.

8. Contingency theory is applicable to cross-cultural leadership situations because of the vast number of cultural and national variables that can affect the dynamics of the leadership context. These include leader–subordinate and group relations, which are affected by cultural expectations, values, needs, attitudes, perceptions of risk, and loci of control.

9. Joint ventures with other countries present a common but complex situation in which leaders must work together to anticipate and address cross-cultural problems.

Discussion Questions

1. What have you learned from the research on work centrality and the relative importance of work dimensions to people around the world?

2. What are the implications for motivation of Hofstede's research findings on the dimensions of power distance, uncertainty avoidance, individualism, and masculinity?

3. Explain what is meant by the need to design culturally appropriate reward systems. Give some examples.

4. Develop a cultural profile for workers in Mexico and discuss the management style you would use.

5. Describe the variables of content and context in the leadership situation. What additional variables are involved in cross-cultural leadership? What are the major elements of a "Global Mindset?"

6. Explain the theory of contingency leadership and discuss the role of culture in that theory.

7. How can we use Hofstede's four dimensions—power distance, uncertainty avoidance, individualism, and masculinity—to gain insight into leader–subordinate relationships around the world? Give some specific examples.

8. Describe the autocratic versus democratic leadership dimension. Discuss the cultural contingency in this dimension and give some examples of research findings indicating differences among countries.

9. Discuss how you would develop a profile of an effective leader from the research results from the GLOBE project. Give an example.

10. Can there be an effective "EU Leader?" Is this a realistic prospect? Discuss the factors involved with this concept.

Application Exercises

1. Using the material on motivation in this chapter, design a suitable organizational reward system for the workers in your company's plant in Mexico.

2. Choose a country and do some research (and conduct interviews, if possible) to create a cultural profile. Focus on factors affecting behavior in the workplace. Integrate any findings regarding motivation or work attitudes and behaviors. Decide on the type of approach to motivation you would take and the kinds of incentive and reward systems you would set up as manager of a subsidiary in that country. Use the theories on motivation discussed in this chapter to infer motivational structures relative to that society. Then decide what type of leadership style and process you would use. What major contingencies did you take into account?

3. Try to interview several people from a specific ethnic subculture in a company or in your college regarding values, needs, expectations in the workplace, and so on. Sketch a motivational profile of this subculture and present it to your class for discussion.

Experiential Exercises

1. Meet with another student, preferably one whom you know well. Talk with that person and draw up a list of leadership skills you perceive him or her to possess. Then consider your research and readings regarding cross-cultural leadership. Name two countries where you think the student would be an effective leader and two where you think there would be conflict. Discuss those areas of conflict. Then reverse the procedure to find out more about yourself. Share with the class, if you wish.

Internet Resources

Visit the Deresky Companion Website at www.pearsonhighered.com/deresky for this chapter's Internet resources.

CASE STUDY

Sir Richard Branson: Global Leader in 2010—Planes, Trains, Resorts, and Space Travel

Sir Richard Branson, long considered king of the über-stretch, has successfully wrapped his core Virgin brand (which began as a student magazine and small mail order record company in the 1970s) around everything from wine to bridal to travel and financial services. No matter what type of business it is, the autographed Virgin identity and/or signature red and white colors are prominently incorporated within the business unit's visual identity.

ALYCIA DE MESA,
www.brandchannel.com[1]

In today's competitive world, running a global company requires strong leadership skills based on creative thinking, sound judgment, and visionary attitude. Clearly, there is no doubt that Sir Richard is visionary, as his Virgin Galactic company planned to take passengers into space in 2009 for $200,000 each in the world's first spaceline. It is also clear that his vision has global breadth, as he seals a string of deals in Asia to expand Virgin's global presence, such as a joint-venture agreement in telecommunications in China.[2] Increasingly, it also entails being a down-to-earth good corporate citizen. In that regard, also, Sir Richard Branson, serial entrepreneur, has demonstrated his commitment to the world.

With his usual promotional flair and with former President Bill Clinton at his side, Sir Richard Branson announced last week that over the next decade he would put $3 billion in personal profits toward development of energy sources that do not contribute to global warming.

WALL STREET JOURNAL,
September 22, 2006[3]

What makes Sir Richard a good leader—both strategically and personally? Motivating company employees who may be located in far-flung corners of the world can be a daunting task. Companies may have powerful brands, but weaker leadership can impinge smooth operations. In any company, corporate leadership requires two important areas: content leadership (leader's attributes and decision making skills) and context leadership (variables dealing with a particular situation).[4] Corporate leadership in global business becomes even more complex when companies enter into other markets. Global managers understand that the magic formula for success is how to adapt their organizational skills to local cultures. This may include changing corporate and functional strategies on a regular basis. The challenge of working and dealing with people in the international environment can be a complex task. Virgin Group's Chairman, President, and CEO Sir Richard Branson is a good example, who in many categories fits well with the qualities needed to be a role model in global leadership. As a founder of the group, he continues to inspire and lead Virgin and has made the company one of the top global brands. Under the leadership of Sir Richard, Virgin Group has over 200 companies in more than 30 countries, selling books, music, colas, and mobile phones, and aggressively competing in large industries such as airlines, trains, resorts, finance, and intergalactic travel. Virgin is an $10 billion successful empire and employs 50,000 workers all over the world (see Table 1).[5] Virgin's success can be attributed to Sir Richard's charismatic personality and down-to-earth leadership style, often using common sense strategies and openness. Often called flamboyant and charismatic, Sir Richard is a highly effective leader and tough negotiator. His outward-oriented approach was a big plus in the establishment of the company. Media often called him a "walking billboard" and a "one man brand."

---

[1] Alycia de Mesa, "How Far Can a Brand Stretch?" BrandChannel.com, February 23, 2004, 1.
[2] Tucker Sundeep, "Today Shanghai, Tomorrow the Universe," *Financial Times,* December 12, 2005; www.virgingalactic.com, September 15, 2009.
[3] S. Beatty, "Giving Back: Branson's Big Green Investment,"*Wall Street Journal,* September 22, 2006.
[4] Helen Deresky. *International Management: Managing Across Borders and Cultures,* 5ed (Upper Saddle River, New Jersey: Prentice Hall, 2006): 305.
[5] For more detail, see "Virgin Group, Ltd.," *Hoover's Online,* (April 2004): 1, (www.hoover.com).

TABLE 1 Virgin Group Brands			
Travel and tourism	**Leisure and pleasure**	**Shopping**	**Media and telecommunications**
Virgin Atlantic	Virgin Games	Virgin Books	Virgin 1
Virgin Holidays	V Festival	Virgin Drinks	Virgin Broadband Australia
Virgin Trains	• Virgin Festival South Africa	Virgin Megastore USA	Virgin Connect
Virgin Blue	• V Festival UK	Virgin Vie at Home	Virgin Media
Blue Holidays	• V Festival Aus	Virgin Wines	Virgin Mobile
Virgin Limited Edition	• Virgin Festival Canada		• Virgin Mobile Australia
Virgin Vacations	• Virgin Festival USA		• Virgin Mobile Canada
Virgin America	The Virgin Voucher		• Virgin Mobile France
Virgin Charter	Virgin Experience Days		• Virgin Mobile India
Virgin Nigeria	• Virgin Active Italy		• Virgin Mobile South Africa
	• Virgin Active South Africa		• Virgin Mobile UK
Virgin Holidays Cruises			• Virgin Mobile USA
Virgin Holidays Hip Hotels			Virgin Radio International
Virgin Limobike			
Virgin Balloon Flights			
Virgin Limousines			
Virgin Galactic			

Finance and money	**Health**	**Social and Environment**
Virgin Money	Virgin Life Care	Virgin Earth
• Virgin Money UK	Virgin Active	Virgin Green Fund
• Virgin Money USA	• Virgin Active UK	Virgin Unite
• Virgin Money Australia	• Virgin Active Spain	
• Virgin Money South Africa	Virgin Health Bank	
	Virgin Health Miles	
	Virgin Healthcare	
	Virgin Spa	

As a tireless worker, Sir Richard has converted Virgin into a top-tier brand in Europe and other parts of the world.[6] One analyst commented:

> *Yet Branson himself is the opposite of elitist; his company is one of the least hierarchical one could come across. To the annoyance of his senior managers, Branson seems to pay as much attention to a chat with a clerk in the airline's mailroom as to a memorandum from his marketing director. Letters from his staff are always read first. . . . He manages and motivates his staff by example. Branson is highly energetic.[7]*

Another analyst observed:

> *In the modern world of business, Richard Branson is an anomaly. In an era dominated by strategists, he is an opportunist. Through his company, the Virgin Group, he has created a unique business phenomenon. Never before has a single brand been so successfully deployed across such a diverse range of goods and services.[8]*

---

[6] For more detail, see BrandChannel.com, "Brand of the Year 2003," (www.brandchannel.com); "Mature, Experienced Virgin Seeks Out Bright City Lights," *Financial Times* (May 7, 2002).

[7] Tim Jackson. *Richard Branson—Virgin King: Inside Richard Branson's Business Empire,* (Rocklin, CA: Prima Publishing, 1996): 6–7.

[8] Des Dearlove. *Business the Richard Branson Way: 10 Secrets of the World's Greatest Brand-Builder* (New York: American Management Association, 1999), 1.

From the corporate perspective, Sir Richard is famous for his team-building skills and consultative approach in day-to-day business. On many occasions, he quietly but firmly initiated new ventures from scratch and built them into large and profitable entities (see Table 1). Virgin Atlantic Airways, the flagship of the group, fits in this category, having started as a small entity and later becoming a huge success. As a company's main spokesperson, Sir Richard is always "visible" and does not miss any opportunity to promote the Virgin brand, often seeking "daring personal exploits."[9] For example, on many occasions, Sir Richard attempted daredevil stunts and balloon rides across the globe to get free publicity for the company. At the micro level, Sir Richard is highly involved with the management for corporate growth and expansion. At the macro level, Sir Richard personally gets involved in the risky yet profitable ventures that the company starts. Virgin Group avoids large acquisitions and aggressively develops smaller companies for future growth in new industries. For this reason, Virgin's corporate culture keeps Sir Branson busy and well informed about the company's global operations.

Customer service is Sir Richard's utmost priority. It is one of the reasons that in customer service, Virgin Atlantic Airways is among the top brands in the airline industry. To be a successful corporate leader, one has to deal with the day-to-day activities of their companies. Sir Richard is good at leading his empire in a variety of industries and markets where environments are dynamic and changing (see Table 1). Sir Richard's Virgin is one of the highly rated companies in the areas of airlines, resorts, auto rentals, mobile phones, financial services, health services, media, environment, and other products. Virgin Mobile's operations are booming in the United Kingdom and have entered into the U.S. by making a joint venture with Sprint. In Australia, Virgin Blue, a low-cost airline, is doing well. In 2009, Branson continued his daredevil, unexpected ventures:

> *At a time when others are exiting the mortgage space, leaving consumers with fewer financing options, Virgin Money is jumping in with its wholesale mortgage program, said Sir **Richard Branson**, founder and chairman of the Virgin Group*
>
> PR NEWSWIRE,
> *February 12, 2009.*[10]

In conclusion, Sir Richard has created an umbrella of companies where cooperation rather than intra-company competition is encouraged. Although Virgin Group does face problems in some of its new ventures and markets, the company as a whole is a classic case in the areas of global leadership—in fact, one could say "outerworld leadership" with his latest venture into space travel, Virgin Galactic LLC. Sir Branson's common sense leadership skills and strategies are a great asset to Virgin. The company's Web site accurately affirms this corporate philosophy that states:

> *Our companies are part of a family rather than a hierarchy. They are empowered to run their own affairs, yet other companies help one another, and solutions to problems come from all kinds of sources. In a sense, we are a community, with shared ideas, values, interests, and goals. The proof of our success is real and tangible.*[11]

Case Questions

1. Discuss the key components of Sir Richard Branson's leadership style and his motivational skills. Apply the research results in this chapter as you develop your answer.
2. Analyze and discuss the transformation and future prospects of the company in global markets under the leadership of Sir Richard Branson. Do you agree with his overall strategy?
3. What do you think of Sir Richard's pledge toward renewable energy sources? Is this all about charity alone?

Source: Written especially for this book by Syed Tariq Anwar, updated by Helen Deresky in 2007 and 2009.

---

[9] Manfred Vries and F. R. Kets. "Charisma in Action: The Transformational Abilities of Virgin's Richard Branson and ABB's Percy Barnevik," *Organizational Dynamics,* (Winter 1998): 9. For a good discussion on global leadership, see: Maxine Dalton et al. *Success for the New Global Manager: How to Work Across Distances, Countries, and Cultures* (San Francisco: Jossey-Bass, 2002); Morgan McCall and George P. Hollenbeck. *Developing Global Executives* (Boston: Harvard Business School Press, 2002).
[10] "Virgin Money Becomes A Lender for the First Time," *PR Newswire,* Feb 12, 2009.
[11] See company website (www.virgin.com).

ICMR
Center for
Management Research

CASE 10   RATAN TATA: LEADING THE TATA GROUP INTO THE 21ST CENTURY

"He [Ratan Tata] comes across as an individual with clarity and conviction, a business leader with vision. Ratan Tata has steered the Tata ship in turbulent times. . . . above all, I have an immense admiration for Ratan Tata, the man, for his unassuming and warm nature, an outstanding business leader imbued with social concerns and committed to uphold ethics and values."[1]

MUKESH AMBANI,
Chairman and Managing Director of Reliance Industries,[2]
December 29, 2001

"[Ratan] Tata understood what needed to be done and how it needed to be done."[3]

HENRY SCHACHT,
former chairman of Cummins Engine, USA

Introduction

On April 9, 2009, bookings opened for the Nano, an entry-level small car developed by Tata Motors, a Tata Group[4] company. The standard or base version of the car was priced at Rs. 120,960, the middle version (CX) was priced at Rs. 145,725 and the top-end (LX) was priced Rs. 170,335.[5] At around US$2,400[6] the Nano, the dream project of Ratan Naval Tata, the Chairman of Tata Sons[7] (Refer to Exhibit I for the businesses of the Tata Group), was the cheapest car in the world.

According to Ratan Tata, the inspiration for developing the Nano had come to him on a rainy day when he had seen a family of four traveling precariously perched on a two-wheeler. This gave him the idea of creating a vehicle for the masses that would make travel for the middle class less dangerous.

The Nano was not the only reason why Ratan Tata was in the news. He was also instrumental in Tata Motors acquiring Jaguar and Land Rover,[8] from Ford. And under his leadership,

Tata Steel acquired the Anglo-Dutch steel maker Corus[9] in 2007. The Corus deal, valued at US$12 billion, was reported to be the largest takeover of a foreign company by an Indian company.[10]

Ratan Tata took over the reins of the Tata Group from J. R. D. Tata in 1991 (Refer to Exhibit II for information on J. R. D. Tata and to Exhibit III for the Pioneers of the Tata Group). It was around this time that the Indian government had begun to initiate a series of reforms to open up the economy. However, for the Tata Group companies, like for most other Indian companies, it was a testing time as economic liberalization also increased the threat of competition from multinational companies.[11] Having operated in a protected environment for decades, the Tata Group companies were not globally competitive. Also, the Group lacked focus, being present in several unrelated businesses.

Ratan Tata was responsible for overseeing a transformation of the Tata Group to prepare the conglomerate to face the pressures of globalization. He took several initiatives – rightsizing, exiting some businesses, injecting fresh talent, and changing the culture—to effect a transformation. By the mid-2000s, the Group was firmly on the path to growth. The Group's turnover grew from US$3.10 billion in 1991 to US$28.8 billion in 2006–07.[12] Analysts attributed much of its success to Ratan Tata, who with his vision and conviction, had managed to transform a once unwieldy collection of companies in diverse businesses into a relatively nimble and efficient conglomerate.

However, there were several challenges that still remained. The Group continued to be present in too many unrelated businesses and some of its products faced quality issues. In the case of Tata Motors, as of 2009, because of the global recession, the demand for its vehicles (commercial and passenger) had fallen sharply, even as its debt levels remained high. These and many

This case was written by **V Namratha Prasad**, **Sachin Govind** and **T. Sesha Sai**, ICMR Center for Management Research (ICMR). It was compiled from published sources, and is intended to be used as a basis for class discussion rather than to illustrate either effective or ineffective handling of a management situation.

© 2008, ICMR Center for Management Research, used with permission.

[1] "Mukesh Ambani on Ratan Tata," www.timesofindia.indiatimes.com, December 29, 2001.
[2] Reliance Industries, founded by Dhirubhai Ambani in 1977, is India's largest private sector enterprise and a Fortune 500 company. It has a major presence in the energy, textiles, and retail businesses.
[3] Robyn Meredith, "Tempest in a Teapot," www.forbes.com, February 14, 2005.
[4] The Tata Group is one of India's largest and oldest business conglomerates. Tata Motors is a Tata Group company and manufactures cars, trucks, buses, etc.
[5] "Tata Motors keeps its Nano price promise," www.tata.com, March 23, 2009.
[6] As of April 2, 2009, 1 US$=Rs. 50.36.
[7] Tata Sons is the premier promoter company of the Tata Group. It was established as a trading enterprise by Group founder Jamsetji Tata in 1868. It is the promoter of all key companies of the Tata Group. The chairman of Tata Sons has traditionally been the chairman of the Tata Group. Tata Sons is the owner of the Tata brand and the Tata trademark, which are registered in India and several other countries. These are used by various Tata companies in relation to their products and services. (Source: www.tata.com)
[8] Jaguar was founded by William Lyons in Coventry, UK, in 1922. Land Rover, initially the name of a vehicle launched by the Rover Car Company in 1948, became a part of Leyland Motors Ltd. in 1967. As of early 2008, both Jaguar and Land Rover (together with Volvo) were part of the Premier Automotive Group, a company owned by Ford Motor Company.

[9] Corus was formed in October 1999 through the merger of British Steel and Koninklijke Hoogovens. It manufactures, processes, and distributes metal products as well as provides design, technology, and consultancy services. Its plants are spread across the UK, Belgium, The Netherlands, Norway, and France. (Source: www.corusgroup.com)
[10] "Corus Accepts Takeover Bid by Tata," www.rediff.com, October 20, 2006.
[11] "Complementing for Complexity: Leading through Managing," www.etmgr.com, January-March, 2005.
[12] www.tata.com.

EXHIBIT I **The Business Sectors of Tata Group as of 2008**

S. No	Industry	Sector	Tata Company	Subsidiaries/ Associates/ Joint Ventures
1	ENGINEERING	Automotive	Tata AutoComp Systems	Automotive Composite Systems International, Automotive Stampings and Assemblies, Knorr Bremse Systems for Commercial Vehicles, Tata AutoComp GY Batteries, TACO Engineering, TACO Faurecia Design Centre, TACO Hendrickson Suspension Systems, TACO Interiors and Plastics Division, TacoKunststofftechnik, TACO MobiApps Telematics, TACO Supply Chain Management, TACO Tooling, TACO Visteon Engineering Center, Tata Ficosa Automotive Systems, Tata Johnson Controls Automotive, Tata Toyo Radiator, Tata Yazaki AutoComp, TC Springs, Technical Stampings Automotive
			Tata Motors	Concorde Motors, HV Axels, HV Transmissions, Nita Company, TAL Manufacturing Solutions, Tata Cummins, Tata Daewoo Commercial Vehicles Company, Tata Engineering Services, Tata Precision Industries, Tata Technologies, Telco Construction Equipment
		Engineering Services	Tata Projects	
			Tata Consulting Engineers	
			Voltas	
		Engineering Products	TAL Manufacturing Solutions	
			Telco Construction Equipment Company	
			TRF	
2	MATERIALS	Composites	Tata Advanced Materials	
		Metals	Tata Steel	Hooghly Met Coke and Power Company, Jamshedpur Injection Powder (Jamipol), Jamshedpur Utility and Service Company Limited (JUSCO), Lanka Special Steel, mjunction services, NatSteel, Sila Eastern Company, Tata BlueScope Steel, Tata Metaliks,

EXHIBIT I *(Continued)*

				Tata Pigments, Tata Refractories, Tata Ryerson, Tata Sponge Iron, Tata Steel (Thailand), Tata Steel KZN, Tayo Rolls, The Dhamra Port Company, The Indian Steel and Wire Products, The Tinplate Company of India, TM International Logistics, TRF
3	**ENERGY**	**Power**	Tata BP Solar India.	
			Tata Power	Tata Ceramics, Tata Power Trading, North Delhi Power Limited
		Oil & Gas	Tata Petrodyne	
4	**CHEMICALS**	**Chemicals**	Rallis India	
			Tata Chemicals	
			Tata Pigments	
5	**PHARMA**		Advinus Therapeutics	
6	**HOTELS AND REALTY**	**Hotels**	Indian Hotels	Taj Air, Roots Corporation (Ginger Hotels)
			THDC	
		Realty	Tata Realty and Infrastructure	
7	**FINANCIAL SERVICES**	**Insurance**	Tata AIG General Insurance	
			Tata AIG Life Insurance	
		Other Financial Services	Tata Asset Management	
			Tata Capital	
			Tata Financial Services	
			Tata Investment Corporation	
8	**OTHER SERVICES**		Tata Quality Management Services	
			Tata Services	
			Tata Strategic Management Group	
9	**CONSUMER PRODUCTS**	**Retail**	Infiniti Retail	
			Trent	
		Tea	Tata Tea	Tetley Group, Tata Coffee, Tata Tetley, Tata Tea Inc
		Ceramics	Tata Ceramics	
		Publishing	Tata McGrawHill Publishing Co.	
		Watches, Jewelry, and eyewear	Titan Industries	

(Continued)

EXHIBIT I   (*Continued*)

S. No	Industry	Sector	Tata Company	Subsidiaries/ Associates/ Joint Ventures
10	**INFORMATION SYTEMS AND COMMUNICATIONS**	**Information Systems**	Nelito Systems	
			TCS	APONLINE, Airline Financial Support Services, Aviation Software Development Consultancy, CMC, CMC Americas Inc, Conscripti, HOTV, Tata America International Corporation, WTI Advanced Technology
			Tata Elxsi	
			SerWizSol	
			Tata Interactive Systems	
			Tata Technologies	
		Communication	Tata Teleservices	Tata Teleservices (Maharashtra)
			Tata Sky	
			VSNL	
			Tatanet	
11	**INDUSTRIAL AUTOMATION**		Nelco	

Source: www.tata.com.

EXHIBIT II   About J. R. D. Tata

> J. R. D. Tata became the chairman of the Tata Group in 1938. During his tenure, the Group operated under the license raj. J. R. D. was interested in starting new business ventures and was a vocal champion of free enterprise. As a person, he was charming and flamboyant. He developed a team of exceptional managers and empowered them to build companies with entrepreneurial zeal. J. R. D. also delinked ownership from management of the companies. He never had to assert himself over the team as the team acknowledged him as the leader. J. R. D. clearly visualized the relationship between business and society and promoted a sense of ownership and initiative amidst the managers. The Group's business portfolio when J. R. D. took over in 1938 included steel, power, cement, insurance, and aviation. The Tata Group ventured into Automobiles (TELCO), Chemicals (Tata Chemicals), Tea (Tata Tea), and Software (Tata Consultancy) under his stewardship. The revenues of the Tata Group grew from a few millions in 1947 to Rs.130 billion in 1991.

Compiled from various sources

other critical issues had the potential to derail Ratan Tata's plan. In addition, Ratan Tata had also not yet named his successor.

The Early Days

Ratan Tata was born in Mumbai (then Bombay) on December 28, 1937, to Soonoo and Naval Hormusji Tata, both Gujarati[13]-speaking Parsis.[14] He was the grandson of Jamsetji Tata, founder of the Tata Group. Ratan Tata had a troubled childhood as his parents separated when he was only seven. He was then raised by his grandmother Lady Navajibai. After schooling in Mumbai, he went to Cornell University in the United States to

---

[13] Gujarati is the official language of the Indian state of Gujarat.

[14] The Parsis (or Parsees) are Zoroastrians who are believed to have emigrated to the Indian subcontinent (especially to Sind and Gujarat) some 1,000 years ago from Persia and Central Asia.

EXHIBIT III   The Pioneers of Tata Group

The Tata Group was founded by Jamsetji Tata in 1868. He began with a textile mill and his vision led to the creation of the Tata Iron and Steel Company (Tata Steel) in Bihar. Jamsetji Tata was a man of high principles and he ensured that schools and gardens were provided for the children of the employees. He founded the Indian Institute of Science in Bangalore. He also built The Taj Mahal Hotel in Mumbai.

On his demise in 1904, his elder son Sir Dorabji Tata took over control of the business. He was the driving force in operationalizing the steel plant and the power project as envisioned by his father. He also established the Sir Dorabji Tata Trust that was to become the premier charitable endowment of the Tata Group. The trust provides institutional grants and individual grants.

Sir Ratan Tata, younger son of Jamsetji Tata was a philanthropist all his life. He created a trust fund for "the advancement of learning and for the relief of human suffering and other works of public utility." The Sir Ratan Tata Trust makes institutional grants for land and water development, micro-finance, education, health, arts and culture, and civil society and governance.

J. R. D. Tata entered the Tata Group as an unpaid apprentice in December 1925 when Sir Dorabji was the chairman of the Group. In 1932, J. R.D. created the Tata Aviation service, which later led to the creation of Air India. Under him, the Group made forays into a diverse set of businesses ranging from automobiles to tea over a period of fifty years. J. R. D. was responsible for the creation of the Tata Institute of Fundamental Research, the Tata Memorial Hospital, the Tata Institute of Social Sciences, the National Institute of Advanced Sciences, and the National Center for the Performing Arts, each an exemplar of excellence in its field. J. R. D. died in 1993.

Compiled from various sources

earn a degree in architecture and structural engineering. He was then offered a position at IBM,[15] which he turned down on the advice of his uncle, J. R. D. Tata. He joined the Tata Group in 1962 in Tata Iron and Steel Company[16] (TISCO, later renamed Tata Steel) and started his career working on the shop floor, alongside blue-collar employees (Refer to Exhibit IV for the Group companies in 1962). He was made Director-in-charge of the National Radio and Electronics Company (NELCO) in 1971 and continued in that position till 1974. In 1975, he completed an advanced management program at Harvard Business School. In 1977, Ratan Tata was made the Chairman of TISCO. He became the Chairman of Tata Engineering and Locomotive Company[17] (TELCO, later renamed Tata Motors) and Tata Industries[18] in 1981. In the 1980s, he drafted a strategic plan for the Tata Group, which, however, was rejected by the board at Tata Sons.

In 1991, Ratan Tata became the Chairman of Tata Sons. When he took over as Chairman, there was widespread

EXHIBIT IV   Business Portfolio of Tata Group in 1962

S. No.	Company	Sector
1	Central India Spinning, Weaving and Manufacturing Company	Textile
2	Tata Iron and Steel Company	Iron & Steel
3	Tata Hydro Electric Power Supply company	Energy
4	Tata Oil Mills Company	
5	Tata Chemicals	Chemicals
6	Tata Engineering and Locomotive Company	Automobile
7	Tata Industries	
8	Voltas	
9	Tata Finlay	
10	Tata Exports	

Source: www.tata.com/history/milestones

[15] International Business Machines or IBM Corp. is a multinational information technology and consulting corporation based in New York, USA.
[16] Tata Iron and Steel Company was established in 1907. As of 2008, it was one of India's largest steel companies with crude steel production capacity of more than 28 million tons.

[17] Tata Engineering and Locomotive Company was established in 1945 to manufacture locomotives and other engineering products. (Source: www.tata.com)
[18] Tata Industries was set up by Tata Sons in 1945 as a managing agency for the businesses it promoted. Following the abolition of the managing agency system, Tata Industries' mandate was recast in the early 1980s to promote the

skepticism about whether he would be effective in the position, and whether he would be able to fill the outsized shoes of JRD Tata, the outgoing Chairman. Undaunted, he set about implementing his vision for the Group.

A Change Agent

When Ratan Tata took over as chairman, the Tata Group seemed on its way to disintegration, with powerful CEOs running some of the Group companies like their personal fiefdoms and challenging the core structure of the Group. However, Ratan Tata soon enforced a mandatory retirement age policy and over a period of four years, managed to expel most of these CEOs, and bring in fresh talent to replace the senior executives in the Group companies. For example, Tata replaced Rusy Mody, the long-time chief of TISCO. The shake-up was not without its critics, with one leading Indian news magazine even describing him as the "Insecure Tata." However, explaining what Ratan Tata was trying to do, Amar Bose, Chairman of Bose Corp., the US-based manufacturer of high-end audio products, and a longtime friend of his, said, "He saw a very closed society that he was part of, and he had to find a way to open that up."[19]

To bring in greater integration among the Group companies, Ratan Tata created the Group Executive Office, whose members were represented on the boards of the Tata companies. He also increased the stake of Tata Sons in the Group companies to at least 26%, to protect them from hostile takeovers.

Prior to Ratan Tata assuming leadership, the work culture at the Group companies had resembled that of the Indian public sector units where job security was assured and lethargy tolerated. While India had embraced liberalization in 1991 and the business environment had been undergoing significant changes, Ratan Tata felt that the Tata Group remained stuck in the pre-liberalization era. So he decided to shake things up. In 1998, at a gathering of heads and senior officials of Group companies, he made a speech talking of the changes in the external environment and cautioning the senior management that inaction would cost them dearly. He spoke about the Tata Business Excellence Model, which was to become the Tata Group's largest change initiative and was to be introduced in each of the Group companies.

The Tata Business Excellence Model (TBEM) framework was implemented through Tata Quality Management Services, a Tata organization "mandated to help Tata companies achieve their business objectives through specific processes." Once a company signed up, it was annually evaluated on seven criteria—Leadership, Strategic Planning, Customer and Market Focus, Information and Analysis, Process Management, Human Resource Focus, and Business Results. Each of these criteria was allotted points, totaling 1,000. Each participating company

aimed to earn 600 points, at the least, over five years. Some companies such as Indian Hotels and Tata International set a target of achieving the 600 points in just three years. Xerxes Desai, then CEO of Titan Industries, said, "What the model evaluates firms on is the least that any company with even a pretense toward excellence should be doing." Ratan Tata also established the Group Corporate Center—an apex body that was to review Group operations on a monthly basis.

Using the TBEM framework, Ratan Tata was able to transform the Tata Group's behemoths into much leaner and nimbler companies. For example, TISCO, in the early 1990s, had surplus manpower, obsolete equipment and blast furnaces, and quality problems. In fact, the situation was so bad that McKinsey & Co.[20] advised Ratan Tata to dispose of the company. Under the TBEM framework, Ratan Tata initiated measures to enhance productivity at Tata Steel by closing down outdated factories and modernizing mines and steelworks. He also reduced the workforce at Tata Steel.[21] All these measures helped the company record productivity gains; productivity rose from 78 tons of steel per worker per year in 1993 to 264 tons in 2004.

Similarly, TELCO was seeing escalating costs and falling market share. It had quality issues as well. There were far more employees and suppliers than required. Ratan Tata introduced rigorous quality assurance measures in the company's factories and a voluntary retirement scheme to reduce the number of employees. He also took measures to reduce the number of suppliers by half. Ratan Tata tried to shift the focus of the company from manufacturing to marketing. A range of passenger vehicles was launched after the Sierra, a SUV, in 1991, including the Sumo, a multi-utility vehicle, in 1994 and the Safari, a SUV, in 1998 and the indigenous passenger car, Indica, also in 1998 (Refer to Exhibit V for the product portfolio milestones at Tata Motors under Ratan Tata).

However, after 1997, growth stagnated owing to the worsening business environment. In 2001, the company's financial situation deteriorated and losses of Rs. 5 billion (US$106 million) were posted. Tata Motors then took up several cost-cutting measures and made restructuring efforts. By 2003, the company was making profits. In the same year, TELCO was renamed Tata Motors. As of early 2008, Tata Motors, with revenues of Rs. 287 billion (US$7.2 billion), was India's largest automobile company and the leader in commercial vehicles. On a global scale, it was the fifth largest medium and heavy commercial vehicle manufacturer.

When Ratan Tata assumed leadership of the Group, the Tata Group was involved in many businesses—steel, tea, oil mills, cosmetics, chemicals, power, and automobiles among them. In 1997, the Group had 84 companies; however, only a few large companies contributed significantly to the Group's revenues and profits. " . . . just a handful of the 84 companies account for the bulk of [sales], and Tata needs to focus on those,"[22] said Bharat Shah, chief investment officer of Birla

---

[18] (*continued*) Group's entry into new and high-tech areas. Tata Industries has, in the 1990s and 2000s, initiated and promoted the Group's ventures into several sectors, including control systems, information technology, financial services, auto components, advanced materials, and telecom hardware. It is the key player in the Group's entry into telecommunication services. (Source: www.tata.com)

[19] Robyn Meredith, "Tempest in a Teapot," www.forbes.com, February 14, 2005.

[20] Founded in 1926 by James O. Mckinsey, McKinsey & Co. is a privately owned management consulting firm.

[21] The number of employees at Tata Steel was brought down to 46,350 in 2001–02, from 76,436 in 1993–94.

[22] "The New Raj at Tata," *Business Week*, www.tata.com, November 27, 1997.

EXHIBIT V Product Portfolio Milestones at Tata Motors under Ratan Tata

Year	Product Launch/ Milestone
1983	Manufacture of Heavy Commercial Vehicle begins
1985	First Hydraulic excavator produced in collaboration with Hitachi
1986	Production of First Light Commercial Vehicle (LCV) Tata 407, indigenously designed, followed by Tata 608
1989	Introduction of Tata Mobile-206, the 3rd LCV
1991	Tata Sierra launched. Tac 20 crane produced. Millionth vehicle rolled out.
1992	Launch of Tata Estate
1993	Joint venture entered into with Cummins Engine for the manufacture of high power and emission free engines
1994	Launch of Tata Sumo and LPT 709 Joint venture entered into with Daimler-Benz for manufacture of Mercedes-Benz cars in India
1995	Mercedes Benz Car E220 launched
1996	Tata Sumo Deluxe launched
1997	Tata Sierra Turbo launched 100,000th Tata Sumo rolled out
1998	Tata Safari utility vehicle launched Two millionth vehicle rolled out Indica, India's first fully indigenous passenger car launched
1999	Commercial production of Indica starts
2000	Launch of CNG Buses 160 Indicas shipped to Malta Launch of 1109 intermediate commercial vehicle
2001	100,000th Indica rolled out exit from JV with DaimlerChrysler launch of Tata Safari Ex
2002	Unveiling of the Tata Sedan 200,000th Indica rolled out 500,000th passenger vehicle rolled out. Product agreement with MG Rover of the UK signed
2003	Launch of the Tata Safari Limited Edition Tata Indigo Station Wagon unveiled at the Geneva Motor Show First City Rover rolled out
2004	Tata Motors unveils new product range at Auto Expo '04 New Tata Indica V2 launched Indigo Advent unveiled at Geneva Motor Show Tata Motors completes acquisition of Daewoo Commercial Vehicle Company Tata LPT 909 EX launched Tata Daewoo Commercial Vehicle Co. Ltd. (TDCV) launches the heavy duty truck Novus in South Korea Sumo Victa launched Indigo Marina launched Tata Motors lists on the NYSE
2005	The Tata Xover unveiled at the 75th Geneva Motor Show; branded buses and coaches— Starbus and Globus—launched Tata Motors acquires a 21% stake in Hispano Carrocera SA, a Spanish bus manufacturing Company Tata Ace, India's first minitruck launched Safari Dicor is launched New factory inaugurated at Jamshedpur for Novus

(Continued)

EXHIBIT V   (Continued)

Year	Product Launch/ Milestone
2006	Tata TL 4X4, India's first Sports Utility Truck (SUT) is launched
	Launch of Novus range of medium trucks in South Korea by TDCV
	Indica V2 Xeta launched
	Tata Motors and Marcopolo, Brazil, announce joint venture to manufacture fully-built buses and coaches for India and markets abroad
	Tata Motors extends CNG options on its hatchback and estate range
	TDCV develops South Korea's first LNG-Powered Tractor-Trailer
	Tata Motors introduces a new Indigo range
2007	Tata Motors' integrated Customer Relationship Management (CRM)-Dealer Management System (DMS) initiative crosses the significant milestone of covering 1,000 locations in India and abroad.
	Tata Motors introduces Magic & Winger, creating new segments in urban and rural passenger transportation.

Source: www.tatamotors.com.

Capital Asset Management. In order to bring in greater focus, Ratan Tata started offloading businesses that he felt did not fit in with his vision for the Group.

In 1998, the Group sold its 50 percent stake in Merind (including Tata Pharma), a pharmaceutical company, to Wockhardt.[23] In 1999, it sold its 28 percent stake in Goodlass Nerolac, a paint company, to Kansai.[24] The same year Lakmé, a cosmetics company, was sold to Hindustan Lever[25] (HLL, now renamed Hindustan Unilever). In 1999–2000, the Group also exited the cement industry by selling its stake in ACC, a cement company, to Gujarat Ambuja Cements (now renamed Ambuja Cements).

Speaking about the rationale behind exiting certain businesses, Ratan Tata said, "At Tatas, we believe that if we are not among the top three in an industry, we should look seriously at what it would take to become one of the top three players—or think about exiting the industry."[26]

In addition, Ratan Tata instituted performance goals and a group-wide standard of conduct for the Group's executives. Talking about his leadership style, R. Gopalakrishnan, Executive Director of Tata Sons said, "Rather than telling them [executives] what to do, he [Ratan Tata] asked them what they liked to do and how they would advance that [goal]. It's a very empowering form of leadership, rather than a directive form of leadership."[27]

Ratan Tata also endeavored to increase the "dare quotient" of his executives. He prodded his managers to be bold and more aggressive in their planning, even as he remained available to help them. Alan Rosling, Executive Director of Tata Sons, said, "When you come to him for a critical decision—which will always be in some negotiations—he will give you a very quick answer. The answers would be something along these lines: 'Yes, I agree that we should offer this price' or 'Yes, I agree we should withdraw' (the group has done that on occasions.) His involvement in cross-border deals could be quite significant."[28]

In order to create a single brand image, all the Group companies, which had earlier had individual logos, began to use one common logo in 1999. Some of the Group companies were also renamed. The Tata Group also started sponsoring major events such as music concerts by Bob Dylan and Zubin Mehta and tennis tournaments, where the new logo was prominently displayed.

Tata's plan for the Group envisaged two broad directions for growth. One was targeting the emerging mass market in India through product development and innovation. The other was the international route, where the Group planned to expand the markets for its existing products.

Product Development and Innovation

Ratan Tata strongly believed that to achieve growth at the Tata Group, it was necessary to create technologically superior and exciting products. According to him, the Tata Group would have to distinguish itself from other companies through innovation and low costs.

Under his leadership, the Group companies came up with several new and innovative products. For example, Tata Steel patented several new equipments such as a fuel and reducing

[23] Wockhardt is a global pharmaceutical and biotechnology company with its headquarters in India and has 15 manufacturing plants in India, the UK, France, Ireland, and USA. (Source: wockhardtin.com)

[24] Kansai Paint Co. Ltd. is a Japanese paint company whose principal activity is to manufacture and sell paints. The company has operations in the UK, USA, Canada, China, Thailand, Taiwan, Singapore, the Philippines, Indonesia, Malaysia, India, Korea, Mexico, and Japan. (Source: www.kansai.co.jp)

[25] Hindustan Unilever is India's largest fast moving consumer products company, with several successful brands such as Lux, Surf, Rexona, etc. In 2007, it recorded revenues of Rs.100 billion. (Source: www.hll.com)

[26] "We Need a Consortium of Like-Minded Companies to Face the Multinationals," www.tata.com, November 2001.

[27] "India's Ratan Tata Is On A Roll" http://battakiran.wordpress.com, June 20, 2008.

[28] M Anand, "Global leadership, the Ratan Tata way," http://business. outlookindia.com, November 17, 2007.

gas generator,[29] an emulsion atomizer,[30] and processes such as the inert gas shrouding process[31] and the corrosion resistant steel production process. More importantly, the company started selling its products, which till then were sold as commodities, under the Tata brand.

The Indica was a major step forward for Tata Motors, a company that had been known for its bulky trucks. Initially, Ratan Tata had requested the Indian automotive industry to join hands to create a car that would be designed, developed, and produced in India. However, his proposal was met with skepticism. Ratan Tata particularly remembered an instance when an official in the industry body said, "Why doesn't Mr. Tata produce a car that works before he talks about an Indian car."[32] Tata Motors then started work to develop the car on its own. The Indica was launched in December 1998. Although, initially, there were quality issues, the Indica soon became one of the largest selling models in the country.

The Nano car project too required Tata Motors to come up with innovative solutions to bring down costs so that the car could be priced at Rs. 100,000—an almost unimaginably low price for other car companies. For example, the company designed a smaller engine for the Nano that would fit snugly under the rear seat, allowing for a compact car while providing extra space for the passengers. The company also used digital validation techniques[33] extensively so as to hasten the product development process. Although the Nano was not a path-breaking product in terms of customer utility, the company brought about small changes in how cars were built that would allow huge cost savings and thus allow for aggressive pricing. "There are no radical changes in the manufacturing; it is the traditional system. But there is a whole host of small issues that go into putting together the package,"[34] said Ratan Tata.

Ratan Tata also challenged suppliers and engineers to think differently. Daryl Rolley, Senior Vice President of Ariba Inc., a supply-chain adviser to Tata, said, "They took a clean sheet of paper and said, 'How are we going to create a vehicle that is one lakh?' It's easier to start with an existing product and pull costs out."[35]

On April 9, 2009, bookings were opened for the Nano, to an overwhelmingly positive response from the Indian public. Auto analysts were also quite impressed with the car and most car reviews said that even though the basic model of the car lacked features like a radio and air conditioning and had only a 33-horsepower engine and one windshield wiper, it was stylish, could seat five people, and provided value-for-money. Moreover, they were quite impressed with the fact that Ratan Tata had delivered on his promise of keeping the price of the car at around Rs. 100,000.

The Nano was acclaimed to be innovative on multiple levels—from its engineering to its manufacturing to its marketing. *Time* magazine listed Nano among the top 12 cars in the world after 1908. Analysts said that the Nano had created an entirely new segment in the Indian and global auto industry. Vikas Sehgal, vice-President at management consulting firm, Booz & Co. said, "The Nano shows that a new world order is possible in the auto industry. It shows a glimpse of what's to come."[36]

Even after it became clear that the global economy was in trouble, Ratan Tata maintained that innovation in business remained a priority. He said, "When one has the companies attempting to differentiate themselves from their competitors, there would be innovation, new product launches, and an attempt made to do business differently. That is what happens in any highly competitive environment. It is driven more when you have the kind of crisis that you have."[37]

Going Global

Although Jamsetji Tata, the pioneer of the Tata Group, had tried to establish European operations, the Tata Group's overseas ventures had never been large enough to be worth a mention. Ratan Tata, however, was keen on the Group companies entering new markets as he felt that global operations would make them more competitive and efficient. He also believed that a company should be able to take advantage of global opportunities. "The objective of globalization is to move towards becoming globally competitive and to expand your market,"[38] he said.

However, the more compelling reason for going global was risk mitigation. As Ratan Tata said, "Perhaps the most graphic moment came in 1997–1998 or 2000 when we had that economic downturn and when Tata Motors, at that time, produced that Rs 500 crore [Rs 5 billion] loss. That told me that we had to do something where we would not in the future be dependent on one economic cycle, but we had to have more irons in the fire in different economies and if one economic cycle was down, the chances are that the other might be up. That accelerated the move to go and search, not for acquisitions, but for markets in a serious way."[39]

According to Rosling, Ratan Tata had waited for the Group to become more competitive before trying to expand globally; he had also ensured that his global expansion theme was adopted by all the companies in the Tata Group. Rosling

[29] An apparatus for heating and mixing industrial tail gases with a reducing gas by burning a mixture of fuel, air, and steam in a combustion chamber.

[30] An emulsion atomizer helps in efficient combustion of liquid fuel for blast furnace operations. (*Source*: www.tata.com)

[31] A method for providing a protective gaseous atmosphere around a liquid stream during transfer between containers.

[32] "The making of the Nano," http://tatanano.inservices.tatamotors.com, 2008.

[33] Digital validation techniques unite a number of computer-based tools that rapidly analyze and validate design alternatives. Prior to the use of digital validation techniques, engineers would manually assess the potential impact of every proposed change in an automobile's design. Digital validation techniques have allowed Tata Motors to find the best components or a combination of them even before any parts are actually built, thus reducing the time required to develop the Nano drastically.

[34] Kunal N. Talgeri and Sriram Srinivasan, "The Countdown Begins Now . . ." www.outlookbusiness.com, February 9, 2008.

[35] "India's Ratan Tata Is On A Roll" http://battakiran.wordpress.com, June 20, 2008.

[36] Jessie Scanlon, "What Can Tata's Nano Teach Detroit?" www.businessweek.com, March 18, 2009.

[37] "Biz innovation more during crises: Ratan Tata," www.moneycontrol.com, December 18, 2008.

[38] "Driving Global Strategy," www.tata.com.

[39] "I Always Envisaged Tata Could be a Global Group: Ratan Tata," http://markets.moneycontrol.com

said, "Tata identified the theme of going global very early on, but his initial judgment was that the group was not yet ready to move on to this agenda. To begin with, Tata focused on competitiveness. We have to earn the right to survive, he would say."[40]

The route adopted by Ratan Tata to go global was acquisition of foreign companies and he started the process of global acquisitions in the year 2000, when Tata Tea, a Group company, acquired Tetley, a British company. In the 2000s, the Group acquired companies across a wide range of industries, from hotels to steel and from automobiles to communication. Stating his rationale for making an international acquisition, Ratan Tata said, "We look for the acquisition of companies that fill a product gap or have a strategic connection with what we do, wherever that company might be."[41]

In 2001, Tata acquired a controlling stake in VSNL, a government company. In 2004, VSNL (now renamed Tata Communications), purchased Tyco International's[42] undersea telecom cables. This made it the world's biggest carrier of international phone calls. In the same year, the Tata Group made history when Tata Motors acquired Daewoo's commercial vehicles operations, making it the first Indian company to have acquired a major foreign automobile company.

In 2005, the Group acquired Incat International,[43] a major vendor for American auto and aerospace companies. In this period, India Hotels Company, the Group's hotel business, acquired renowned hotels like The Pierre,[44] the Ritz-Carlton Boston,[45] and Camden Place.[46] The Group also acquired businesses and made investments in several third world countries like Bangladesh, Morocco, Uganda, Senegal, etc. Ratan Tata said, "We look at countries where we can play a role in development. Our hope in each is to create an enterprise that looks like a local company, but happens to be owned by a company in India."[47]

In January 2007, Tata achieved a landmark for the Group when Tata Steel acquired the Anglo-Dutch steel company, Corus. With this acquisition, the Tata Group, worth US$40 billion, became the largest business group in India. By 2007, international revenues accounted for over 50% of the Group's revenues. Ratan Tata said, "Both Indian and global stakeholders are increasingly seeing us as a group that is making big plays, taking

more risks than it was known to do in the past and managing large global takeovers with reasonable grace and finesse and, hopefully, success."[48] In March 2008, Tata Motors acquired Jaguar-Land Rover for US$2.3 billion (Refer to Exhibit VI for the acquisitions and mergers at the Tata Group under Ratan Tata).

Ratan Tata also had plans to develop a Nano variant for the European and U.S. markets that was set to be launched by 2011. He said, "It [the Nano] would not be a $2,000 or $3,000 vehicle, but it will encompass all the features required as per European regulations and by the customers like protective airbags. It would also have a more powerful engine and comply with all the emission norms applicable in Europe. Given the present indications, we plan to further develop the European model for the US markets."[49]

A Risk Taker

Ratan Tata was instrumental in changing the Tata Group's attitude toward risk. Earlier, the Group had been risk averse, and had had very few ambitious projects. By the mid-2000s, the Group companies had become more aggressive, with most of them entering new markets and developing new products.

Perhaps one of Ratan Tata's greatest gambles was the Indica project. This project was viewed with skepticism and analysts doubted whether Tata Motors could ever become a carmaker. The critics were of the view that "a good truck business was about to be destroyed for the sake of an ill-conceived vanity project."[50] However, after a tough start, Tata Motors went on to become India's second largest carmaker by sales.[51]

Ratan Tata's bid to acquire Corus was seen by many as "risky". Some felt that the price that Tata Steel eventually agreed to pay was way above the 'comfort zone' and that Ratan Tata had put the company in jeopardy in the process. However, from Ratan Tata's perspective, the limit set on the deal was never reached and hence the acquisition was a good business decision. "Ratan was the chief architect of the Corus deal," said B. Muthuraman, chairman, Tata Steel, "I was worried about the magnitude and the amount of money. But he instilled confidence."[52] Although the Corus deal went through successfully, the net benefits that Tata Steel would derive from the company would only be known with time.

However, the Group met with a few reversals too. Ratan Tata's efforts to take Indica to foreign markets in 2003 did not succeed. Tata Motors had entered into a deal with MG Rover in 2003 to sell the Indica under the City Rover brand in the UK. However, the demand for the car was unsatisfactory and the deal was called off in 2005. Tata Steel's foray in 2004 into

---

[40] M Anand, "Global leadership, the Ratan Tata way," http://business.outlookindia.com, Novemeebr 17, 2007

[41] Alex Perry, "How Ratan Tata turned the country's oldest conglomerate into a global force," www.time.com, June 12, 2006.

[42] Tyco International is a highly diversified global company that provides a large range of products and services considered important to residential and commercial customers. (Source: www.tyco.com)

[43] INCAT is the world's leading independent global professional services company engaged in Engineering & Design Services, Product Lifecycle Management, Enterprise Solutions, and Plant Automation. (Source: www.incat.com)

[44] The Pierre opened in 1930 as a luxury hotel. Located on Fifth Avenue and opposite to Central Park, this 41-story hotel consists of 201 rooms, 40 suites, and 12 grand suites. (Source: www.tajhotels.com)

[45] Ritz-Carlton Boston first opened its doors in 1927. Located on Arlington Road and three miles from Logan International Airport, it is one of the leading hotels in the world. (Source: www.ritzcarlton.com)

[46] Camden Place is located along Stockton Street in San Francisco and is more than 100 years old. The hotel is housed in a 15-storied building constructed in the classical European style and has 110 rooms. (Source: www.tajhotels.com)

[47] Alex Perry, "How Ratan Tata turned the country's oldest conglomerate into a global force," www.time.com, June 12, 2006.

[48] M Anand, "Global leadership, the Ratan Tata way," http://business.outlookindia.com, Novemeebr 17, 2007.

[49] "Ratan Tata plans Nano launch in Europe, US," www.thaindian.com, March 24, 2009.

[50] Arzan Sam Wadia," The shy architect: Ratan Tata," http://parsikhabar.net, January 13, 2007.

[51] "The Shy Architect," www.economist.com, January 13, 2007.

[52] Pete Engardio and Nandini Lakshman, "The Last Rajah," www.businessweek.com, August 13, 2007.

EXHIBIT VI   Acquisition and Mergers at the Tata Group under Ratan Tata

Year	Tata Company	Acquired Company	Country	Stake acquired	Value
February 2000	Tata Tea and Tata Sons	Tetley Group	UK	100 percent	GB£271 million
November 2001	Tata Sons (TCS)	Computer Maintenance Corporation (CMC)	India	51 percent	Not disclosed
2002					
February	Tata Sons	VSNL	India	25 percent	Rs. 14.39 billion
September	Indian Hotels	Regent Hotel (renamed Taj Lands End)	India	100 percent	Rs. 4.50 billion
December	Tata Teleservices	Hughes Telecom (India)	India	50.83 percent	Rs. 8.58 billion
2003					
May	TCS	Airline Financial Support Services India (AFS)	India	75.1 (thereby taking TCS' stake to 100 percent)	Not disclosed
July	VSNL	Gemplex	US	Assets and networks	Not disclosed
2004					
March	Tata Motors	Daewoo Commercial Vehicle Company	Korea	100 percent	KRW 120 billion (US$102 million)
March	VSNL	Dishnet DSL's ISP division	India	-	Rs. 2.7 billion
March	TCS	Aviation Software Development Consultancy India (ASDC) Phoenix Global Solutions	India	51 percent (thereby taking Tata Group's stake to 100 percent)	Rs. 140.2 million
July	TCS		India	100 percent	Not disclosed
November	VSNL	Tyco Global Network	US	100 percent	US$130 million
2005					
February	Tata Steel	NatSteel Asia Pte Ltd	Singapore	100 percent	US$468.10 million
February	Tata Motors	Hispano Carrocera	Spain	21 percent	€12 million (Rs.70 crore)
March	Tata Chemicals	Indo Maroc Phosphore S.A. (IMACID)	Morocco	33 percent	US$38 million (Rs. 1.66 billion)
July	Indian Hotels	The Pierre	US	Lease of the property	US$9 million
July	Tata Industries	Indigene Pharmaceuticals Inc	US	< 30 per cent	Not disclosed
July	VSNL	Teleglobe International	US	100 percent	US$239 million
August	Tata Tech	INCAT International	UK		
August	Trent	Landmark Ltd	India	76 per cent	US$24.09 million (Rs. 103.60 crore)
September	Tata AutoComp Systems	Wündsch Weidinger	Germany	100 percent	£7 million
October	Tata Tea through Tata Tea (GB)	Good Earth Corporation & FMali Herb Inc	US	100 per cent	US$31 million
October	TCS	Financial Network Services	Australia	100 percent	US$26 million
October	TCS	Pearl Group	UK	Structured deal	
November	TCS	Comicrom	Chile	10 percent	US$23 million
December	Indian Hotels	Starwood Group (W Hotel)	Sydney	100 per cent	US$29 million
December	Tata Chemicals	Brunner Mond	UK	63.5 per cent (December 2005) 36.5 per cent (March 2006)	Rs. 5.08 billion (December 2005) Rs. 2.90 billion (March 2006)

(Continued)

EXHIBIT VI *(Continued)*

2006					
January	Tata Metaliks	Usha Ispat, Redi Unit	India	100 per cent	Rs. 1.15 billion
January	Tata Interactive	Tertia Edusoft Gmbh	Germany	90 per cent	Not disclosed
		Tertia Edusoft AG	Switzerland	90.38 per cent	
April	Tata Steel	Millenium Steel	Thailand	67.11 per cent (Baht 6.5 billion)	US$167 million
May	Tata Tea through Tata Tea (GB)	JEMCA	Czech Republic	Assets: intangible and tangible	GB£11.60 million
June	Tata Coffee	Eight O' Clock Coffee Company	US	100 per cent	US$220 million (Rs 1015 crore)
September	Tata Tea through Tata Tea (GB)	Joekels Tea Packers	South Africa	33.3 per cent	GBP 0.91 million
2007	Tata Steel	Corus	UK	100 percent	US$12 billion
2008	Tata Motors	Jaguar-Land Rover	UK	100 percent	US$2.3 billion

Source: www.tata.com.

Ukraine also proved unsuccessful and Tata Chemicals failed in its bid to acquire Egyptian Fertilizers in 2005.

Elucidating his ideas on risk, Ratan Tata said, "You can be risk-averse and take no risks, in which case you will have a certain trajectory in terms of your growth. Or you can, while being prudent, take greater risk in order to grow faster. I think, as a Group, we were risk averse and we hardly grew because either it was not safe or no one else had done it before. I view risk as an ability to be where no one has been before. I view risk to be an issue of thinking big, something we did not do previously. We did everything in small increments so we always lagged behind."[53]

Value Driven

From the beginning, the management at Tata Group had sought to function with ethics, integrity, social consciousness, and fairness. According to Ratan Tata, these values were an integral part of the Tata Group and the questions one needed to ask while making decisions were: "Does this stand the test of public scrutiny in terms of what I said earlier? As you think the decision through, you have to automatically feel that this is wrong, incorrect, or unfair. You have to think of the advantages or disadvantages to the segments involved, be it employees or stakeholders."[54]

Ratan Tata was keen that the Group companies show the way when it came to business ethics. According to him, "The kind of company one would want to emulate is one where products and technology are at the leading edge, dealings with customers are very fair, services are of a high order, and business ethics are transparent and straightforward. A less tangible issue involves the work environment, which should not be one where you are stressed and driven to the point of being drugged."[55]

Ratan Tata felt that acquiring assets in India could be an exercise fraught with frustration due to the role of the bureaucracy. He said, "It takes more time in India to undertake projects or to set up or develop mergers and acquisitions. A deal [like] Corus in India may not have been possible [because of government bureaucracy]."[56] Despite that, he tried to ensure that Group companies did not indulge in malpractices such as giving bribes to quicken the pace of work or secure permissions. Rajeev Chandrasekhar, Chairman and CEO of the BPL Innovision Business Group, who interacted closely with Ratan Tata on various government task forces, said, "Ratan Tata has set an example with his transparency and integrity. In a milieu haunted by wheeler-dealers and a business climate where companies will stop at nothing to pouch contracts, [Ratan] Tata is an inspiration for young entrepreneurs."[57]

As Ratan Tata turned his Group global, it was but natural that comparisons were drawn with Jack Welch[58] of GE.[59] However, Ratan Tata did not subscribe to the ideas of mass layoffs that the latter was famous for. He said he liked to believe that the Group companies were not driven to grow "over everybody's dead bodies."[60]

Ratan Tata's perspective on going global was not just to increase the turnover; it was also to creatively engage in the development of the countries in which the Group entered. Keeping this perspective in view, the Group ventured into countries such as Bangladesh and Sri Lanka.

Ratan Tata was an environmentalist (Refer to Exhibit VII to know more about Ratan Tata). Under his leadership, the Group

---

[53] "Vision of the Future," www.tata.com, August 2006.
[54] "View from the Top," www.tata.com. June 2002.
[55] www.tata.com.

[56] Elliot Wilson, "Tata's Global Ambitions Show No Sign of Abating," www.asiamoney.com, July 2007.
[57] "Tata Juggernaut Stirring," Business India, www.tata.com, April 30-May 13, 2001.
[58] Jack Welch was the Chairman and CEO of General Electric from 1981 to 2001. (Source: en.wikepedia.org)
[59] GE or General Electric is a diversified technology, media, and financial services company. (*Source*: www.ge.com)
[60] George Wehrfritz and Ron Moreau, "A Kinder Gentler Conglomerate," www.newsweek.com, October 31, 2005.

EXHIBIT VII   Ratan Tata—The Man

Ratan Tata is a simple, soft-spoken, and considerate person who leads a frugal life. He is media- and publicity-shy. He is not married. He does not drink or smoke and keeps himself in shape. He loves dogs. He has designed and built his own house in Alibaug, a fishing hamlet 130 kilometers south of Mumbai.

Ratan Tata has been conferred Honorary Doctorates by Ohio State University, the University of Warwick, and the Asian Institute of Technology.

He chairs the Indian government's investment commission and serves on the international advisory boards of Mitsubishi Corp., JPMorgan Chase, and the American International Group, on the International Investment Council set up by the president of the Republic of South Africa, and on the Asia Pacific Advisory committee to the board of directors of the New York Stock Exchange.

Ratan Tata also serves on the board of trustees of the Ford Foundation and the Program Board of the Bill & Melinda Gates Foundation's India AIDS Initiative. He chairs the advisory board of RAND's Center for Asia Pacific Policy, and two of India's largest philanthropic trusts, the Sir Dorabji Tata Trust and the Sir Ratan Tata Trust. He is an independent director at Fiat S.p.A

Ratan Tata received the Padma Vibhushan (India's second highest civilian award) from the Indian government in 2008.

Compiled from various sources

companies took up a number of projects that had a direct influence on the societal environment in which they existed. Tata Pipes Parivaar Water Conservation Project, a nationwide campaign to create awareness on water conservation, was launched in 2004 on the occasion of World Environment Day. The idea was to awaken society to the need for using water sensibly, avoiding mismanagement and wastage.

The Tata Group had always been known for its philanthropic activities. During Ratan Tata's tenure, the Group's philanthropic initiatives focused on grassroots level projects such as microfinance to keep people out of the clutches of money-lenders, savings programs in villages, education, and hygiene awareness. Through the philanthropic trusts,[61] which owned two thirds of Tata Sons, the Group gave away 8–14 percent of its profits in the form of institutional grants (endowment grants, program grants, small group grants) and individual grants (medical grants and educational grants) every year.

In 2008, the Tata Group was ranked third in the list of the World's Most Accountable and Transparent Businesses, by One World Trust, a British non-profit research firm. However, although Ratan Tata and the Tata Group were appreciated for their record on business ethics, his detractors pointed out the limited representation of women at senior levels in the Tata companies as one of the Group's failures.

Handling Controversies

2008 proved to be year of controversies for Ratan Tata, testing his ability to make the right decisions to protect the Tata Group's interests.

The Nano project faced a setback during the year, when the site for the plant at Singur, West Bengal, became the stage for a political war game. The Tata Group was provided 1000 acres of farmland in Singur to construct the plant. However, there were sporadic incidents of protests from some of the farmers who were reluctant to part with the land. The situation took on a political hue in August 2008, when Mamata Banerjee, the leader of Trinamool Congress, an opposition political party, launched an agitation against setting up the plant at the site. She stated that she was protesting on behalf of some of the farmers whose land was taken over 'forcibly' by the West Bengal government and given to the Tatas.

As the protests turned violent, Ratan Tata threatened to pull out of Singur, if the situation was not brought under control by the West Bengal government. He said, "There is a sense of tension, violence and disruption (at Singur). Obviously it is not a conducive atmosphere. The compound wall is broken down, materials stolen. We are deeply concerned at the violence and disruption and at the safety of our employees, equipment and investments at the project site at Singur. Whatever be the cost, we will move out if the situation demands so."[62]

By that time, the Tata Group had already invested Rs. 150 billion in the plant. However, as the situation at Singur continued to deteriorate with no clear solution at hand, Ratan Tata decided to withdraw from Singur in October 2008. The same month, Ratan Tata decided to construct a new production facility for the Nano in Sanand, Gujarat.

[61] The Tata Group runs several philanthropic trusts – Sir Ratan Tata Trust, Sir Dorabji Tata Trust, Tata Social Welfare Trust, Tata Education Trust, Jamsetji Tata Trust, JRD Tata Trust, JRD Tata and Thelma Tata Trust, etc. The Sir Ratan Tata Trust, established in 1919, makes grants in areas of Rural Livelihoods & Communities, Education, Enhancing Civil Society & Governance, Health and Arts & Culture. The Sir Dorabji Tata Trust, established in 1932, has set up several institutions such as Tata Institute of Social Sciences, Tata Memorial Centre for Cancer Research and Treatment, Tata Institute of Fundamental Research, National Centre for Performing Arts, and makes grants to to five major sectors of social development: Management of Natural resources, Livelihood, Education, Health, and Social Development Initiatives.

[62] "Tata threatens to pull out of Singur . . . . . . ," www.pressnote.in, August 22, 2008.

As a stop-gap arrangement, Ratan Tata planned to produce the Nano at its facility in Pantnagar, UP, until the construction of its new facility at Sanand became operational at the start of 2010. However, the Pantnagar facility had the capacity to produce only 5000 Nanos per month, which industry observers felt was not enough to meet the expected demand. The new plant would have the capacity to produce 250,000 cars a month.

In November 2008, the Taj Mahal Palace Hotel in Mumbai owned by Indian Hotels Company, a Tata Group subsidiary, was one of a number of buildings attacked by terrorists. More than 170 people were killed in the attacks. Following the attacks, Ratan Tata criticized the Indian government over its lack of crisis management infrastructure and urged his fellow countrymen to rebuild whatever was destroyed. He said, "We must show that we cannot be disabled or destroyed, but that such heinous acts will only make us stronger. It is important that we do not allow divisive forces to weaken us. We need to overcome these forces as one strong unified nation."[63]

In December 2008, in a report on the Mumbai terror attack, *Forbes* magazine's Senior Editor (Asia) Robyn Meredith compared Ratan Tata to U.S. President Barack Obama. Merdith said, "India could have an Obama moment—one in which a leader, whose personal history epitomizes the country's principles, marches forward to unite the country during its very moment of trauma. India has a chance now to get it right, but it needs a strong, credible leader to step up. As an American, I don't get a vote in India, but if I did, mine would go to Ratan Tata. A fractured India would benefit immeasurably from his acumen, his managerial skills, and his very obvious—but always constructive—patriotism."[64]

What Next?

Ratan Tata believed that the biggest challenge for the Group was finding the right talent and retaining the Group's value systems as it grew bigger and more diverse. He believed that the Group had to expand the managerial perspective while retaining the same ethical and moral standards. That made his failure to designate a successor all the more disconcerting. Some criticized the move to extend his tenure as the chairman till 2012. Others wondered whether his departure might result in the Group's break-up, asking "Who will be the glue? Will there even be a central leader?"[65] There was also concern that the value systems of the Tata Group might be lost, as Ratan Tata might be the last Tata to oversee the Group. Some were of the view that after Ratan Tata, the future managers of the Group might view the development projects and philanthropy as burdens which they would like to get rid of during difficult times.

Critics of Ratan Tata pointed out that he had not been successful in bringing a focus to the business portfolio of the Group. The Group still had a presence in a wide range of disparate businesses ranging from salt to jewelry, retailing to computer software, trucks to tea, and insurance to steel. Analysts pointed out that Ratan Tata had, in fact, added to the diversity by entering new businesses such as direct-to-home services (Tata Sky) and consumer electronics retail (Croma).

By 2009, Ratan Tata and the Tata Group, and Tata Motors in particular, were facing a number of key challenges. This included the repayment of the US$2.3 billion loan which Tata Motors had taken to purchase Jaguar and Land Rover; the production issues that arose after the abandonment of the Nano assembly facility in Singur; and the falling demand of both commercial and passenger vehicles in the Indian and global markets.

Critics of Ratan Tata were waiting to see how successful the integration of Corus' operations would be with that of Tata Steel and how widespread the acceptance of the Nano before giving their verdict on his performance as the Group head.

Also, the acquisition of Jaguar-Land Rover together with the Nano project put a lot of financial pressure on Tata Motors. While Jaguar was a loss-making entity, the Nano was not expected to make profits for a long time, unless the sales picked up really fast. "It is unlikely that profits will materialize until production volumes exceed 400,000 units per annum. Margins will be razor thin—negative in the short term—and it will only make a meaningful contribution to Tata Motors' overall profits once volumes exceed 500,000 units,"[66] said London-based auto analyst, Ashvin Chotai.

However, Ratan Tata was very positive about the future prospects of the Nano. He said, "What has happened in the changing economic situation globally reinforces, if nothing else, the fact that a low-cost car has a place."[67]

As of March 2009, the total debt of the Tata Group was over Rs. 1 trillion, of which Rs. 117 billion was due for repayment/refinance in March 2010. Some analysts felt that the financial situation of the Tata Group was not precarious and the debt obligations could be met through the cash flows generated by various group companies and proceeds from stake sales by the holding company Tata Sons.

Many analysts felt that the Tata Group under Ratan Tata had prospered. They pointed out that he had been instrumental in transforming the focus of a large conglomerate from domestic to global. They believed that Ratan Tata would be remembered as a man who had the conviction, belief, and determination to convert his vision for the Group into reality, while retaining the ethical values of his predecessors.

Talking about his future vision for the Tata Group, Ratan Tata said, "One hundred years from now, I expect the Tatas to be much bigger than it is now. More importantly, I hope the Group comes to be regarded as being the best in India . . . best in the manner in which we operate, best in the products we deliver, and best in our value systems and ethics. Having said that, I hope that a hundred years from now we will spread our wings far beyond India."[68]

---

[63] Ratan Tata hits out following Mumbai terror attacks," www.campdenfb.com, December 1, 2008.

[64] "Forbes Thinks Tata Can Be India's Obama," www.business-standard.com, December 5, 2008.

[65] Pete Engardio and Nandini Lakshman, "The Last Rajah", www.businessweek.com, August 13, 2007.

[66] Kunal N.Talgeri and Sriram Srinivasan, "The Countdown Begins Now . . . ," www.outlookbusiness.com, February 09, 2008.

[67] Arun Kumar, "Little Nano makes big splash in US media," www.thaindian.com, March 24, 2009.

[68] "One hundred years of fortitude," www.tata.com, June 2004.

References and Suggested Readings

1. Kunal N. Talgeri and Sriram Srinivasan, "The Countdown Begins Now . . . " www.outlookbusiness.com, February 09, 2008.
2. Pete Engardio and Nandini Lakshman "The Last Rajah," www.businessweek.com, August 13, 2007.
3. Elliot Wilson, "Tata's Global Ambitions Show No Sign of Abating," www.asiamoney.com, July 2007.
4. "The Shy Architect," www.economist.com, January 13, 2007.
5. "Corus Accepts Takeover Bid by Tata," www.rediff.com, October 20, 2006.
6. "Vision of the Future," www.tata.com, August 2006
7. George Wehrfritz and Ron Moreau, "A Kinder Gentler Conglomerate," www.newsweek.com, October 31, 2005.
8. Robyn Meredith, "Tempest in a Teapot," www.forbes.com, February 14, 2005.
9. "Complementing for Complexity: Leading through Managing," www.etmgr.com, January-March, 2005.
10. "View from the Top," www.tata.com. June 2002.
11. "Mukesh Ambani on Ratan Tata," www.timesofindia.indiatimes.co, December 29, 2001.
12. "Tata Juggernaut Stirring," Business India, www.tata.com, April 30-May 13, 2001.
13. "The New Raj at Tata," Business Week, www.tata.com, November 27, 1997.
14. "Driving Global Strategy," www.tata.com.
15. "I Always Envisaged Tata Could be a Global Group: Ratan Tata," http://markets.moneycontrol.com
16. www.tata.com.

Case Questions

1. The Tata Group has been transformed from a risk-averse, slow-moving giant into a more dynamic and aggressive conglomerate. How much of such a transformation can be attributed to one individual? Discuss the role of the leader in initiating and managing change.
2. The Tata Group had a presence in a wide range of businesses since its early days. Later, Ratan Tata managed to streamline the Tata Group. What advantages and disadvantages did the Group gain through the streamlining of businesses? Do you think, as of 2009, the Group is still present in too many businesses?
3. The Tata Group has acquired many companies in the last few years. Critically discuss the benefits and the risks associated with Ratan Tata's growth-through-acquisition strategy, especially in the global context.

CASE 11   CARLOS GHOSN: MULTICULTURAL LEADER AS CEO OF NISSAN AND RENAULT

We knew some people were concerned about the potential for culture clashes between the French and the Japanese, but it was not an issue. Cultural differences should be used as a catalyst for change, not as a crutch that inhibits change. You can learn a lot from somebody who is not like you.[1]

— CARLOS GHOSN,
CEO, Nissan

Make sure you are focused on your own people. Bring in them motivation and sense of ownership, then you can do your miracle.[2]

— CARLOS GHOSN,
CEO, Nissan

Introduction

In 2002, Louis Schweitzer, CEO of Renault, announced that Carlos Ghosn (Carlos), the president and CEO of Nissan, would also take over the reigns at Renault in April 2005, while Louis Schweitzer would remain the chairman of the board. With the new position, Carlos would lead two companies Nissan and Renault. As of 2004, Renault held 44% stake in Nissan which owned around 15% of Renault's shares. "Turnaround artist," as Carlos was called, was behind the industry's most remarkable turnaround at Nissan. After he became the CEO of Nissan in 1999, he had brought in many un-Japanese changes in the Japanese company and had actively persuaded the employees to accept change. Carlos was credited for reviving the company from $254 million losses and $19 billion debt in 1999 into profits within 2 years.

After taking up his position as the CEO of Renault in April 2005, Carlos faced many challenges. Heading two different automobile companies from two different countries was first of its kind and industry observers expressed doubts whether Carlos would be able to take up the pressure and rework the "Nissan magic." Although Renault witnessed an increase in its net income from €2,836 million in 2005 to €3,376 million in 2006, it witnessed decrease afterwards.[3]

Carlos Ghosn: The "Nissan Magic"

In March 1999, Renault, the then ninth carmaker in the world announced its alliance with Nissan, investing $5.4 billion. Nissan had losses for many years from 1990–99 except for profits reported in 1997 (Exhibit I) and looked out for partners

EXHIBIT I   The Nissan Crisis

Year	Annual Sales ($)million)	Annual net income ($) million)
1995	67,401.6	(1,918.4)
1996	56,972.7	(834.1)
1997	53,700.6	627.0
1998	49,732.1	(106.1)
1999	54,380.2	(229.0)
2000	56,387.5	(6,456.3)
2001	49,109.8	2,670.0
2002	46,588.3	2,799.0
2003	56,904.9	4,126.4
2004	70,087.0	4,751.6

Source: www.hoovers.com.

to recover from the troubles. The brand recognition was very low and it was estimated that Nissan was losing $1,000 for every car it sold in US. By the end of 1990s, Nissan exported cars to Europe and Australia and some parts of Asia. The company had losses to the tune of $5.5 billion, had debts totalling around $19 billion and was suffering from a poor product portfolio and diminishing brand value. Nissan's market share had dropped from 6.6% in 1991 to 4.9% by late 1990s.

Renault at the same time was expanding internationally through acquisitions. After the unsuccessful merger with Volvo, Renault under Louis Schweitzer entered into an alliance with Nissan acquiring a 36% stake in the company. Triggering the alliance was Nissan's strength in product designs and sophisticated manufacturing that blended well with the engineering quality at Renault. For Renault, the alliance would help in international expansions in the long term while for Nissan; it was to get rid of its short-term troubles that had accumulated.

Initially, industry observers were sceptical about a non-Japanese manager successfully leading a Japanese firm. While Carlos was successful in cutting costs and had sometimes imposed hard regimes during his tenure at Michelin,[4] many

This case was written by D. Gayatri, under the direction of T. Phani Madhav, Icfai Business School Case Development Centre. It is intended to be used as the basis for class discussion rather than to illustrate either effective or ineffective handling of a management situation. This case was compiled from published sources.

© 2009, Icfai Business School Case Development Centre. HYPERLINK "http://www.ibscdc.org" www.ibscdc.org. Used with permission.

[1] Carlos Ghosn's interview, "Interview: The road to ruin," www.themanufacturer.com, December 2002.
[2] Parachkevova Anna, "CEO outlines Nissan's resurgence," www.thedartmouth.com, May 12th 2004.
[3] "Financial Statements for Renault SA (RENA)," http://investing.businessweek.com/businessweek/research/stocks/financials/financials.asp?ric=RENA.PA.

[4] Carlos Ghosn joined Michelin in 1974, where he was chairman and CEO of North American operations and had undertook several cost-cutting initiatives.

were apprehensive if he would be successful in Japan. He was 46 when he joined Nissan and was far younger than the middle-level managers in the company. Carlos knew nothing about Japan and had no knowledge of the culture there. He once said that he had a "very vague" idea about the country and accepted, "I did not try to learn too much about Japan before coming, because I didn't want to have too many preconceived ideas. I wanted to discover Japan by being in Japan with Japanese people."[5] On the first day, when Carlos arrived at Nissan, he took an elevator to reach his office. As he entered the lift, which was already packed with workers who were coming up from garage, everyone knew he was the new CEO. To his surprise, at every floor the lift stopped, none got down. Finally, when he got down, the employees bowed as he left and went back to their floors. After such an unexpected incident which reflected major cultural difference, Carlos realised how important it was to understand them. Since the first day, Carlos had made the cultural diversity a catalyst rather than a crutch for the company.[6]

However, since the beginning, Carlos was in a Catch-22 situation as Japanese were not used to dictatorship kind of leadership. He knew that if he tried to dictate terms that could lead to bruising employee morale and if he remained lenient, it could hinder the required change. Instead of imposing change, Carlos brought about the need for urgency in operations by mobilising the managers. Carlos identified that the basic flaw with Nissan's culture when he took over was that employees were reluctant to accept the failures and held other departments or economic conditions responsible for them. This resulted in a lack of urgency among employees as everyone assumed the other would take action. He found that instead of solving the problems, they were trying to live with them. Nissan, throughout 1990s, had been concentrating on short-term market share growth rather than long-term growth and instead of investing its profits towards product portfolio improvement, it was spending them towards equity purchases of other companies especially its suppliers. Its product profile was comparatively outdated with old designs when customers craved for stylish designs while competitors were steadily

focusing on new product designs. By 1999, it had around \$4 billion held in the form of shares while its purchasing costs remained very high, around 20%–25% more than that of Renault's.

The employees openly resisted cross-functional teams as they strongly believed in territories and sectionalism, which was a major part of their culture. Carlos explained, "Engineers work very well together, financial people work very well together, salespeople work very well together. But when you start to add an engineer, a marketer, a salesperson, and a manufacturer, here all the strengths of Japan in teamwork disappear."[7] To overcome the resistance, he had to explain to the employees why the cross-functional teams were important and how they would impact the overall benefits. Carlos believed that the general human tendency was to resist anything different. He considered that by accepting change people tend to become stronger, as they understand the differences and try to analyse the causes for such differences. Cross-functional teams were formed and employees were involved in the revival process. This helped Carlos explain his plans and gain acceptance easily. Through these cross-functional teams, employees were made to look beyond their line of responsibilities, understanding the nitty-gritties of the other departments as well. After the cross-functional teams were in place, people owned up responsibility whenever something went wrong. "The solution to Nissan's problems was inside the company. The main (idea) we would have for revival of the company would be a rebuilt motivation of Nissan employees and partners," he explained.[8]

Immediately after appointing the teams, they were asked to submit plans to achieve the maximum possible output in each area and within a week decisions were made. The outcome was the Nissan Revival Plan (NRP) (Exhibits IIa and IIb). After the NRP was announced, every aspect from the timing, the plan schedules and the commitments as well as targets were clearly stated. Shiro Tomii, vice president, Nissan Japan remarked, "He establishes high yet attainable goals; makes everything clear to all roles and levels of responsibility, works with speed; checks on progress; and appraises results based on fact."[9]

EXHIBIT IIA   The Nissan Restructuring Plan (NRP) and Results . . .

Carlos Ghosn explaining the NRP, once remarked that if people at Nissan were still in school, the Nissan's final exam would have the following multiple-choice question:

>How do you revive Nissan?

a) Implement Nissan Revival Plan

b) All the above

Cross Functional Teams at Nissan

The cross functional teams were established to meet the objective of bringing in around 200 senior executives at all levels of the organisation to discuss the problems and the opportunities for each particular area: business development, marketing and sales, purchasing, manufacturing & logistics, research & development, and general & administrative costs, finance cost, product phasing out, organisation, cost of Investment (Exhibit VIII). They were given a single goal: To develop business and reduce costs and were given time of three months to come up with a plan. The result was NRP.

(*Continued*)

[5] "Carlos Ghosn: standing at the global crossing," http://web-japan.org, April 5th 2002.
[6] "Throwing away the culture crutch," *2000 Automotive News World Congress*, January 18th 2000.
[7] "Carlos Ghosn: standing at the global crossing," op.cit.

[8] Saadi Dania, "Nissan's miracle man offers clues to solving national economic woes," www.lebanonwire.com.
[9] David Magee, *Turnaround: How Carlos Ghosn Rescued Nissan*, HarperCollins, 2003.

EXHIBIT IIA *(Continued)*

NRP	Results
Goals . . .	*Progress . . .*
Profitability by March 31st 2001 and achieve an operating margin of 4.5% by March 31st 2001.	Group net profit forecast at Yen 250 billion for full year to March 2001. Operating margin of 4.5% achieved for the half year ending October 30 th 2000.
Reduce debt from Yen 1.4 trillion to Yen 700 billion by March 31st 2003	Debt reduced to Yen 1.15 trillion by October 30th 2000.
Cut 14% of the workforce-around 21,000 jobs by March 31st 2003	12,000 jobs eliminated by March 31st 2001
Close 3 assembly plants and two power train factories by March 31st 2002 - a 30% reduction in manufacturing capacity. Reduce number of platforms from 24 to 15	All three proposed plants winding off operations by summer of 2000
Reduce the purchasing costs by 20% and decrease the number of suppliers from 1,145 to 600 by March 31st 2002	Savings of Yen 192 billion from cost reduction in sales, purchasing and administrative expenses by October 30th 2000
Sell off assets in non-core affiliates and assets. Achieve a 30% cut in inventory to sales	Sold the stake in Fuji Heavy Industries, Akebono Brake Industries, Ichiko Industries and Ikeda Bussan

Source: Gold R. Allan, et al., "An outsider takes on Japan", www.mckinseyquarterly.com.

EXHIBIT IIB **The Results in Key Performance Areas**

	FY99 results	FY00 results	Preliminary results of 1st half of FY01	Forecast for FY01	Revival plan objectives for FY02
Operating margin	1.4%	4.75%	6.2%	5.5%	**more than 4.5%**
Operating profit	$6.8 million	$2.4 billion	$1.6 billion	$2.9 billion	N/A
Net profit (loss)	($5.7 billion)	**positive result of $2.8 billion**	$1.9 billion	$2.8 billion	N/A
Net automotive debt	$11.2 billion	$7.9 billion	$6.7 billion	Less than $6.25 billion	**less than $5.8 billion**
Capacity utilization (Japan)	53%	51.1%	75.7%	74.1%	82%
Purchasing cost reduction	N/A	11%	N/A	More than 18%	20%
Number of parts suppliers	1,145	810 (30% reduction)	750 (35% reduction)	N/A	600 (50% reduction)
Number of employees	148,000	133,800	128,100	N/A	127,000

The conversion rate used was ¥120=$1

Source: Carlos Ghosn, "Saving the Business without Losing the Company," *Harvard Business Review*, January 2002.

Listening to the employees and facilitating their participation in the decision-making process, was key aspect of Carlos' leadership. By avoiding impersonal meetings through mails, he stressed the need for face-to-face communication. He believed that the people close to the company could come out with better solutions than an outsider like him. In contrast, the Japanese were polite, reticent and never spoke about the plans to their boss. Carlos had to repeatedly explain to the employees that he needed their viewpoints and would not mind if they speak out. This, according to him was the greatest hurdle. While in France at Renault, he emphasised on teamwork, in Japan he believed it was not required and instead individuality was given more prominence. PriceWaterhouseCoopers in a report on change management listed Carlos' key human resource management techniques calling them very simple and straightforward (Exhibit III).

By maintaining transparency from the stage of planning to action, he aimed at the best possible outcomes while also l-ifting the morale of the employees who were particularly distressed after the crisis at the company. He invited suggestions from every influential individual from suppliers, Nissan's ex-employees, dealers, etc. He explained, "As you know credibility has two legs, performance, and transparency. Performance, we had none to show at the time, so we were determined to be highly transparent."[10] He called the NRP an "organisation's collective effort" involving thousands of employees at every managerial level. To show his commitment to the plan, he declared that he would resign along with other top executives if the plan fails in bringing in the benefits. Carlos wanted immediate results by fixing short-term targets. While he called the passive style of management-by-consensus a killer, an active and constructional version could work miracles, according to him. He believed that an 85% consensus was enough and 100% was not always essential.

While cultural adaptability had been his key, he was also at the same time affirmative about giving more priority to the bottom line growth rather than just to the cultural aspects. He remarked, "I do not want to intentionally offend people, but I am more concerned about making Nissan profitable again than being culturally sensitive."[11] The first phase of NRP focused on cutting the costs and improving profits. The first major step Carlos undertook was divestments from subsidiaries to reduce the debt. Suppliers accounted for major

part of costs of production and the age-old *Keiretsu* system[12] and the obligations that came with it were adding to heavy costs. Deviating from the system, Carlos opened the purchasing offer to all the suppliers encouraging new suppliers who were ready to supply at low prices. As part of the revival plan, suppliers were forced to offer discounts to the tune of 20%–30% and the number of suppliers was brought down to 600 from 1,145 while the purchasing costs were reduced by 20%. During a meeting with the dealers of Nissan, Carlos announced, "I don't want any excuses. I want to know what you are going to do to make things better."[13] Cost cutting at each stage began to be regarded as the need of the hour as the employees were encouraged to reduce expenses through all possible ways. The cross-functional teams were given one month time to identify areas to cut costs and increase the profits through bottom line growth.

The most un-Japanese practices like closing plants and cutting work force, in a country, which believed in lifetime employment, were the biggest of all challenges. When he planned to close five plants which included both assembly plants and powertrain plants, the board of directors were not informed until the night before, as Carlos knew some people within the company wanted his plans to fail. After he announced, he was reported to have threatened, "If this leaks out, I'll close seven plants, not five."[14] For Carlos, convincing the labour unions over the disadvantages of rigid job definition was a big task.

The seniority-based promotion that was entrenched in the Japanese firm was replaced by a performance-based and merit-based incentive system. Instead of sacking people, which was against the culture in Japan, 21,000 jobs were cut through retirements, pre-retirements and golden handshakes out of which 16,500 were in Japan alone. The plants were closed, while offering alternative jobs to the employees in other plants of the company. The complex manufacturing structure, which involved 24 platforms at seven assembly plants, was brought down to 12 platforms, which were shared by four plants. Around 10% of the retail outlets were closed and 20% of the dealer affiliates was streamlined to further reduce selling and marketing expenses. After the phase one of the revival plan was over, Nissan reported profits of $1.5 billion for 6 months between April to September, which was the best result the company had ever seen.

At the same time, Carlos began to be called an iconoclast, who had brought in some un-Japanese, western style of culture in the company's operations. In contrast to the traditional Japanese business etiquettes, he shook hands with his partners and other executives. As a result, there was discontent among the traditionalists and other industry associations in the country. And his bold decisions, like closing plants, had invited repugnance among many including the insiders and Carlos began to take along a bodyguard wherever he went.

The cross-cultural alliance between a French and a Japanese firm, raised several other challenges. The alliance aimed at cost savings through sharing of platforms and

---

EXHIBIT III **Carlos Ghosn's Human Resource Management**

> • Listen (if you can't listen, you can't lead)
> • Make and keep commitments
> • Encourage focused input, make fact-based decisions
> • Be consistent
> • Instill motivation and urgency.

Source: "Change management insights", www.pwc.com.

---

[10] Ibid.
[11] Larimar Tim, "Japan, Nissan and Ghosn revolution," www.gsb.columbia.edu
[12] The *Keiretsu* system in which the companies maintained partnership with each of its suppliers, holding shares in those companies, transferring managers characterised the big family of companies and its suppliers were both shared relationships.

[13] "Japan, Nissan and Ghosn revolution," op.cit.
[14] "Nissan's boss," www.businessweek.com, October 4th 2004.

engineering capabilities. Initially though the employees and the design engineers were convinced over the superiority of the platforms brought in from the Renault plants, they were reluctant to adopt them. To overcome resistance, regular meetings were conducted among the Nissan and Renault employees. At the same time, Carlos began to recruit more designers from Japan to design new models. He maintained that the best way to solve the cultural differences was to avoid forcing the cultural blend. Rather, he believed in appreciating the differences between the cultures and minimising the cultural clashes by bringing in a performance-driven management. To ensure that the Japanese staff understands what the French managers spoke, English was made the common language in the company. A dictionary of 100 keywords used by the management was prepared to solve the differences that came in the way as work was interpreted by French as well as Japanese. The words included 'commitment,' 'transparency,' 'objectives,' 'targets,' etc.

In Japan, attending all formal parties of suppliers was very important and one was not supposed to miss them unless there was a strong reason. When Carlos missed the New Year party hosted by the suppliers' association, it was considered as a sign of disrespect to their culture. Carlos attended all such gatherings since then. Carlos understood all these subtle aspects, which were an essential part of the culture, as he began adapting to them.

In the second phase of the revival plan, which started in 2001, Carlos stressed selling more cars, improving the top line growth as well. Dropping non-performing products from its portfolio, the company introduced trendy new models in SUVs and minivans category. An updated Z sports coupe was

reintroduced in the market. The phase two increased sales by 1 million and debt was brought down to zero.

With his unconventional leadership style and charisma, he began to win praises from the employees of the company as well as from the industry and the public. Sometimes, people in streets would stop him and wish him success saying, "Gambatte (go for it)." *Time* magazine named him the most influential global business executive and more and more Japanese companies were embarking on the *gaijin* (Foreigner) – Carlos style for attaining maximum benefits in a short time. His colleagues at Nissan were particularly impressed by his dedication towards achievement of targets and his 24/7 work ethics reinforcing the importance of hard work. His devotion towards the revival of the company from problems, for which he was not in any way responsible, encouraged his peers to work hard and contribute towards a common goal. Toshiyuki Shiga who was made in charge of the Nissan's expansions in China had once remarked, "He told me to make a clear strategy for Nissan in China, and he gave me two months to do it."[15] While he ensured that the progress was undertaken without holding any individual responsible for the past crisis, he was also at the same time particular about results. Dominique Thormann, senior vice president, Nissan Europe, said, "To people who don't accept that performance is what is at stake, he can be ruthless."[16]

Calling his turnaround at Nissan a "near death experience," Carlos said he had experienced extensive cultural diversities during his tenure at Renault, Nissan, Nissan's North American business and Samsung Motors, a Korean-based company acquired by Renault. His management style is woven around two attributes—"value and motivation." He believed in motivating

EXHIBIT IV   The True Life of Carlos Ghosn

Source: www2.gol.com

---

[15] Ibid.

[16] "Nissan's boss," op.cit.

EXHIBIT V   Carlos Ghosn: Le Cost Killer

Born in Brazil on March 9th 1954 and educated in France. Graduated in engineering from polytechnic. Career

Michelin, tyre maker (1978–96)
- Plant manager in Le Puy, France (1981–84)
- R&D head in Ladoux, France (1984–1985)
- COO of South American operations (1985–99)
- President and COO of North American operations (1989–90)
- Chair, president and CEO of Michelin in North America (1990–96)

Renault (1996–99)
- Executive VP. In charge of advanced research, car engineering and development, car manufacturing, power train operations and purchasing.

Nissan (1999 onwards) as president and CEO

Speaks five languages: English, French, Italian, Portuguese and Spanish

Compiled by the author

employees and demanding performance by empowering them. "Your employees must be interested in what is going on in the company. Nothing is more inefficient than a boring company. You have to create an interesting environment where people are interested in the story you are creating and want to hear the happy ending," he said. He was called "Ice Breaker" by DaimlerChrysler's chairman Jurgen E. Schrempp because of his unconventional thinking and implementing western style of management in Japan breaking the prevalent myth in the industry.

The biweekly comic series *The True Life of Carlos Ghosni* (Exhibit IV) featured Nissan's CEO Carlos, depicting his popularity in the industry as well as the country. Some others called him "an ambassador of change," "the troubleshooter" and considered him as a role model for all those business executives who were seeking solutions to the poor state of their companies in Japan (Exhibit V).

After the implementation of the Nissan Revival Plan (NRP), within 2 years, the company recovered from the losses and reported a 10.2% increase in its revenues and nearly 84%

increase in its operating profits (Exhibits VIa, VIb, VIc, VId). Though the sales had not considerably improved, the cost cuttings contributed towards improving the bottom line. In May 2001, the company reported its largest net profit of $2.7 billion. Carlos was named the "Businessman of the Year" by *Fortune* magazine in 2002 and *Automobile* magazine called him 'Man of the Year' for his contributions to Nissan. Renault increased its stake in Nissan to 44.4% while Nissan owned 13.5% of Renault's share capital.

However, by 2003, Nissan started experiencing a downward trend in its sales, as the volume of goods that passed out from dealers was dropping in size. Customers regularly complained of quality defects and Nissan's rank in overall quality (as per a survey by J.D. Power Associates) dropped to 11 th in 2004 from 6th in 2003. It looked as the rigorous emphasis on the faster execution of the restructuring had resulted in these quality defects while Carlos assured he would fix them. To counter the situation, in May 2004, he sent a quality control team of 220 engineers to the Nissan plant in Smyrna (Tennessee) and every part of the assembly line went through a

EXHIBIT VIA   Nissan's Net Sales (1999–2007)

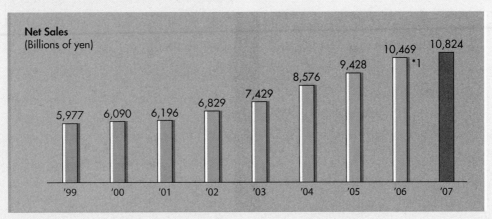

*1 – Due to the fiscal year unification, includes 15 months result in FY 2006.

Source: "Historial Financial Data," http://www.nissan-global.com/EN/IR/SUMMARY/

EXHIBIT VIB Nissan's Consolidated Operating Profit Margin (1999–2007)

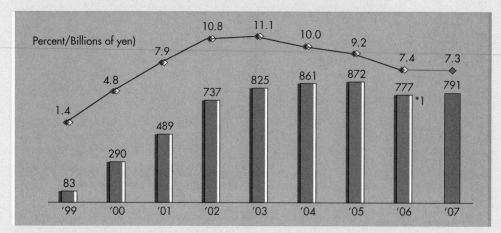

*1 – Due to the fiscal year unification, includes 15 months result in FY 2006.

Source: "Historial Financial Data", http://www.nissan-global.com/EN/IR/SUMMARY/

EXHIBIT VIC Nissan's Net Income (1999–2007)

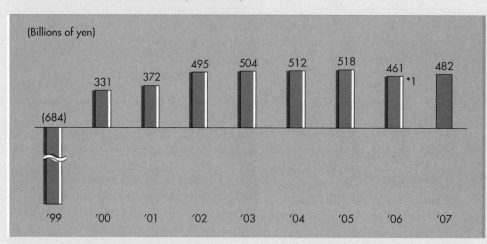

*1 – Due to the fiscal year unification, includes 15 months result in FY 2006.

Source: "Historial Financial Data", http://www.nissan-global.com/EN/IR/SUMMARY/

EXHIBIT VID Nissan's Financial Performance (2006–2008) ($ million)

Year	Revenue	Gross Profit	Operating Income	Total Net Income
March 2008	109,324.8	24,410.1	7,987.4	4,870.8
March 2007	88,716.8	20,689.8	6,584.2	3,905.1
March 2006	80,583.7	20,404.3	7,451.6	4,427.8

Source: "Financial Information: Nissan Financials," http://www.hoovers.com/nissan/—ID 41879,target financial_information—/free-co- samples-index.xhtml

detailed scrutiny. Subtle issues like the workers who wore studded jeans and rings causing scratches to the freshly painted cars, etc., came to light. Carlos was amazed at some very obvious ones, which could be rectified at the plant like defective doors and reading lights, etc. Carlos had already achieved two of the three goals that were set for NRP, the debt was cleared and profitability was achieved.

The Nissan 180, an extension of NRP was launched and aimed at additional sales volume of 1 million annually from 2005, the third objective of NRP. The US market was considered to play a key role in achieving the goal of additional 1 million sales. A new plant was set up in Canton, the first in North America where Nissan was facing challenges from other Japanese automakers, Toyota and Honda. Meanwhile, Nissan was planning an alliance with Mitsubishi after DaimlerChrysler gave up its plans of partnership with Mitsubishi. The partnership would help Nissan enter the minicar segment while Mitsubishi would be able to reduce cost burden of new product development.

The shortage of steel supplies forced Nissan to reduce its production in 2004, affecting production of 15,000 units amounting to $58.5 million of loss in sales. Nissan closed its plants for 5 days following the shortage of supplies, as steel prices increased with demand for steel increasing after the economic boom in China. While halting production was considered a sign of mismanagement, many felt that Carlos' attempt to bring down the number of suppliers as part of NRP had resulted in over-reliance on few suppliers. However, Carlos defended himself saying that the savings achieved during that phase were far more ($9.7 billion) than the losses incurred due to loss of sales.

Renault—The French Automaker

Renault was a state-owned government enterprise since 1945. It was started as a motorised vehicle assembler in 1898. Renault built trucks, airplane engines and heavy vehicles during the World War II and after the war along with the economic boom, Renault achieved high volume sales with its low-cost cars like 4CV, Renault 4 and Renault 5 through the 1970s and 1980s. During early 1980s, Renault expanded into US by acquiring half the shares of American Motor Corporation. However, the deal was unprofitable and the company had to withdraw from the market in 1987. A similar deal failed in Mexico and with both the deals financed through debts, Renault was left with huge debts accumulated by the end of 1980s. It reported losses of $3.5 billion between 1984 and 1986. Further, because it was a state-owned business, obligations with labour unions led to more costs for the company.

When Louis Schweitzer joined Renault in 1986, Renault had accumulated debts to the tune of $9 billion and was in huge losses. Its proposed merger with Sweden-based AB Volvo in 1993 failed due to unfavourable French political climate and with Swedish shareholders expressing reservation. The company continued to have losses till 1996, when Louis Schweitzer brought in Carlos as the executive vice president. Under the duo, product quality was improved, outsourcing secondary activities and overheads were reduced along with reduction in workforce. At the same time, French government started setting ground for its IPO when Louis Schweitzer discovered that privatisation of the company could only save it. In July 1996, the IPO was completed. By 1998, with the midsize model Scenic, Renault was successful in the European market and, in 1998 alone, it made profits of $1.4 billion from $40 billion sales.[17]

While Renault became the No. 1 automaker in Europe, to be a global player, it had to expand its operations further. By the end of 1990s, it had a very small presence in Asia and was totally absent in the North American market. After the merger of Daimler and Chrysler in 1998, for Renault, expansions became a requisite. And, Nissan seemed a lucrative opportunity, as an alliance with Nissan could help in easier market expansion for Renault in developing markets. While others, including Ford and DaimlerChrysler, had earlier attempted a deal with Nissan, they later withdrew keeping in view the huge debt that Nissan held and its culture that was inflexible. After the alliance, Renault managed to reduce its launching and warranty costs for new product introductions by recruiting managers from Nissan to undertake the launch. At the same time, it sent its employees to Nissan to oversee manufacturing, to achieve cost-efficient production. Later, Renault acquired Samsung Motors in South Korea and Roman automaker Dacia, as part of its international expansion. With the launch of multi-purpose vehicles, Laguna II and Avantime in 2001 and Espace IV in 2002 (Exhibit VII), and after its association with Formula One racing between 1992 and 1997, its brand popularity improved.

By 2004, Renault held strong foothold in European market and reported a 6.5% increase in sales by the first half of 2004 and was the fourth-largest auto company in the world. It held nearly 11% market share in Western European market in passenger car and light vehicle cars. At the same time, Renault performance in large cars segment was sluggish and was struggling to achieve operating margin of 4%, when the demand for cars in the European market was low. Some of the new launches like the Vel Satis, a tall saloon luxury model, were not very successful in the market. A relaunch in the US market was also underway. Renault was facing other challenges along with Nissan and other automakers. Environmentally friendly cars, which seemed a likely potential opportunity, were costly to manufacture at the price the customers were ready to pay. Renault was planning for expansions in the Chinese market and South Korea and other parts of Asia through alliance with Nissan.

Carlos Ghosn as CEO of Renault and Nissan

By 2010, Nissan and Renault would build their cars using the common building blocks. Carlos viewed the alliance as "managing contradiction between synergy and identity"[18] and confirmed that, while gaining synergies, the individual identity of each brand would be safeguarded. The other major alliances in the industry, the DaimlerChrysler and the GM/Fiat, had not proved to be very successful because of improper management of merged assets, trans-atlantic product development, and failed attempts in understanding the local market; Carlos confirmed that Nissan's alliance with Renault would creatively achieve it. At the same time the alliance would avoid merger and would maintain "a spirit of partnership."[19] The alliance would be the fourth-largest automobile group in the world. In October 2004, the first car was built using a common platform of Nissan and Renault. Modus, a subcompact minivan of Renault shared its base with Nissan's Micra saving $500 million for Renault every year.

After taking over from Louis Schweitzer at Renault's in April 2005, Carlos would also continue as the CEO of Nissan. Carlos was affirmative that he would not leave the company unless he finds the right person who would succeed him at Nissan. He stressed the need for a Japanese as the CEO of Nissan in such a culture-sensitive country. While at Nissan, he had transformed himself into a Japanese, adapting to the culture, analysts feared that he would breach the French business etiquette as he takes the rein at Renault.[20] Carlos took up the reins at both the companies when they also underwent senior level

[17] "For Renault, a new chance to take on the world," www.businessweek.com, November 15th 1999.

[18] "Renault's alliance with Nissan," www.economist.com, August 16th 2001.
[19] "CEO outlines Nissan's resurgence," op.cit.
[20] "Carlos Ghosn-Nissan motor," www.businessweek.com, January 8th 2001.

EXHIBIT VII   Renault Product Portfolio

Category	Brands
Passenger Cars	• Twingo
	• Clio
	• Clio V6
	• Clio Saloon
	• Clio Renault Sport
	• Modus(small car)
	• Kangoo
	• Kangoo 4x4
	• Megane Hatch Megane
	• sports Hatch Megane
	• Coupe-Cabriolet Megane
	• Sports Saloon Megane
	• Sport Tourer Megane
	• Renault Sport Scenic
	• Grand Secnic(7 seater version of Scenic)
	• Laguna
	• Laguna Sport Tourer
	• Espace
	• Grand Espace
	• Vel Satis
	• Trafic Generation
	• Kangoo Express
Light Commercial Vehicles	• Trafic
	• Master
	• Master RWD

Source: www.renault.com

Nissan Product Portfolio

Category	Brands			
Cars	Sentra	Altima	Maxima	350Z
Trucks	Frontier	Titan		
SUVs	Xterra	Murano	Pathfinder	Armada
Van Concepts	Quest	Actic	Qashgai	Tone
	C-note	Dunehawk(2003)	Jikoo	

Source: www.nissan.com

management changes. At the same time, many wondered whether the sense of urgency brought through NRP would continue at Nissan or the company would slip back to its old habits when Carlos left. The pressure was considered to be very high, as an analyst stated, "He will be less present at Renault than he was at Nissan, and less present at Nissan that he used to be. I believe this challenge will be more difficult."[21]

The alliance had helped both the companies equally, in terms of cost savings from not requiring to construct new plants where the alliance can use common buildings, common platforms, etc. This had also helped them enter new markets faster and gain other synergies (Exhibits VIIa and VIIb). The

purchasing power had also increased as they ordered and bought components through Renault-Nissan purchasing organisation for both the companies at a time. The alliance had from the beginning ensured that the inter-company cultural clashes do not exist, by maintaining individual cultural identities. While a merger had been avoided since the beginning, Carlos confirmed that it would be its agenda in future also.

Carlos remarked that taking up the two positions would blend the strengths of the people at the companies, the innovation excellence of the French and the dedication towards manufacturing of the Japanese.[22] He affirmed that his tenure at Nissan had allowed him to learn the real essence of successful

[21] Tierney Christine, "Leadership, bold moves help Renault save Nissan," www.detnews.com, October 24th 2003.

[22] Smith DuVergne Nancy, "Nissan Renault alliance faces down few challenges," http://web.mit.edu, November 18th 2004.

EXHIBIT VIIIA   Nissan Renault Alliance – The Synergies

2003	
January	The Alliance Vehicle Evaluation System (AVES) is applied in Nissan and Renault plants.
January	The Renault 1.5 dCi engine (K9K) is used on Nissan Micra.
January	Sales of Renault vehicles through local Nissan sales network in Kuwait begin.
January	Sales of Nissan vehicles through local Renault sales network in Romania begin.
February	Sales of Renault vehicles through local Nissan sales network in Bahrain begin.
March	Production of Nissan Xterra, the third model produced at Curitiba LCV plant, begins.
May	Establishment of common working group to improve supply plant management for logistics.
May	Sales of Renault vehicles through local Nissan sales network in Qatar begin.
May	Distribution of Nissan vehicles by Renault importer ARTES in Tunisia begins.
May	Establishment of fourth Single Legal Entity (SLE) in Austria.
June	Renault and Nissan announce the creation of common regional parts warehouse in Hungary, to cover the activities of both groups in Central Europe from end of 2004.
July	The Renault 200Nm manual transmission (JR) is used on Nissan Micra.
October	The Renault Kangoo is adapted and sold by Nissan under the Kubistar name.
December	The Alliance Worldwide Backbone (AWB) broadband network, the new high level network infrastructure of the Alliance, is operational.
2004	
January	The Renault Nissan Purchasing Organisation (RNPO) enlarges the scope of its operations from 43% to 70% of Alliance turnover, or an increase from $21.5 billion to $33 billion. Geographical responsibilities are also expanded.
January	A new financing programme in Mexico begins.
January	New SLEs in Slovenia and Croatia begin operations.
March 29th	Announcement of the Alliance Vision – Destination on the occasion of the fifth anniversary of the Alliance.
May	Unveiling of the new Modus, the first Renault model to use the common B Platform, to be marketed largely in Europe from September 2004.

Source: Nissan Annual Report 2003, www.nissan-global.com

leaders and would drive his success in future also. He called himself, "not a theorist of citizenship but an expert in multinationality."[23] However, under Carlos, Renault has witnessed a flat growth in its total revenues and fall in its net income (Exhibit IX).

Carlos had done wonders blending his innovative management practices with a unique understanding of international business and world cultures. He accomplished this through empowering company employees, and developing internal, cross-communication process that broke down barriers between corporate divisions.

Carlos called the three major attributes, 'Value, Transparency, and Performance' as the ones that would determine the competence of any CEO. He believed that they act as standards for leadership in global business, in the light of growing corporate scandals, when the top executives of the companies were increasingly coming under scrutiny. He explained that the actual results that are delivered, along with simultaneous value creation to the customers and the other stakeholders through maintaining transparency, reflect an efficient leadership. By communicating every strategy to every person concerned, he maintained that it would facilitate a faster reaction to dynamics in the fiercely competitive global marketplace. An analyst once called Carlos , 'a manager without borders, polyglot and cosmopolitan'. Talking about his dual roles and the cultural barriers that he had to face as he moved to Renault while also heading Nissan, Carlos said, "Global is global. In my opinion, this is going to be the story of the twenty-first century. This is what's going to happen in the twenty-first century—you're going to see the emergence of more 'global' standards, some kind of global references; you're going to see more and more of it. But 'globality' doesn't mean 'uniformity.' It doesn't mean that. You'll still have different cultures, you'll still have different tastes, and you'll still have some adaptations to make to different countries, but you'll have some basic things that will be common globally, especially in the economic area."[24]

---

[23] Abescat Bruno, "I am an expert of multinationality," http://livres.lexpress.fr

[24] "Carlos Ghosn: standing at the global crossing," op.cit.

EXHIBIT VIIIB   Cross Functional Teams

Team	Business Development	Purchasing	Manufacturing & Logistics	Research & Development	Sales & Marketing	General & Administrative	Finance & Cost	Phaseout of Products & Parts Complexity Management	Organization
CFT Leaders	• executive VP of overseas sales & marketing • executive VP of product planning	• executive VP of purchasing • executive VP of engineering	• executive VP of manufacturing • executive VP of product planning	• executive VP of purchasing • executive VP of engineering	• executive VP of overseas sales & marketing • executive VP of	• executive VP of finance (CFO) • senior VP of finance (DCFO)	• executive VP of finance (CFO) • senior VP of finance (DCFO)	• executive VP of domestic sales & marketing • executive VP of product planning	• executive VP of finance (CFO) • executive VP of manufacturing
CFT Pilot	• general manager of product planning	• general manager of purchasing	• deputy general manager of manufacturing	• general manager overseas of engineering	• manager of sales & marketing	• manager of finance	• deputy general manager of finance	• manager of product planning	• manager of human resources
Functions Represented	• product planning • engineering • manufacturing • sales & marketing	• purchasing • engineering • manufacturing • finance	• manufacturing • logistics • product planning • human resources	• engineering • purchasing • design	• sales & marketing • purchasing	• sales & marketing • manufacturing • finance • human resources	• finance • sales & marketing	• product planning • sales & marketing • manufacturing • engineering • finance • purchasing	• product planning • sales & marketing • manufacturing • engineering • finance • purchasing
Team Review Focus	• profitable growth • new product opportunities • brand identity • product development lead time	• supplier relationships • product specifications and standards	• manufacturing efficiency and cost effectiveness	• R&D capacity	• advertising structure • distribution structure • dealer organisation • incentives	• fixed overhead costs	• shareholdings and other on-core assets • financial planning structure • working capital	• manufacturing efficiency and cost effectiveness	• organisational structure • employee incentive and pay packages
Objectives Based on Review	• launch 22 new models by 2002 • introduce a minicar model by 2002 in Japan	• cut number of suppliers in half • reduce costs by 20% over three years	• close three assembly plants in Japan • close two power-train plants in Japan • improve capacity utilisation in Japan from 53% in 1999 to 82% in 2002	• move to a globally integrated organisation • increase output efficiency by 20% per project	• move to a single global advertising agency • reduce SG&A costs by 20% • reduce distribution subsidiaries by 20% in Japan • close 10% of retail outlets in Japan • create prefecture business centres or common back offices	• reduce SG&A costs by 20% • reduce global head count by 21,000	• dispose of noncore assets • cut automotive debt in half to $5.8 billion net • reduce inventories	• reduce number of plants in Japan from seven to four by 2002 • reduce number of platforms in Japan from 24 to 15 by 2002 • reduce by 50% the variation in parts (due to differences in engines or destination, for example) for each model	• create a worldwide corporate headquarters • create regional management committees • empower programme directors • implement performance-oriented compensation and bonus packages, including stock options

Source: Ghosn Carlos, "Saving the Business without losing the company," *Harvard Business Review,* January 2002.

EXHIBIT IX Renault's Financial Performance (2005–2008) (€ million)

Financials	January 2nd 2005 Restated	January 2nd 2006 Restated	January 2nd 2007 Restated	Jan. 2nd 2008
Total Revenues	40,292.0	40,246.0	40,332.0	40,682.0
Gross Profit	8,290.0	8,240.0	8,004.0	8,153.0
Operating Income	2,115.0	1,323.0	1,063.0	1,354.0
Net Income	2,836.0	3,376.0	2,886.0	2,669.0

Source: "Financial Statements for Renault SA (RENA)," http://investing.businessweek.com/ businessweek/research/stocks/financials/financials.asp?ric=RENA.PA

Carlos, who has never lacked for confidence, explained in an interview, "In 1999 Nissan was in trouble and Renault was a very small regional company. Joining forces and working together, today [Renault Nissan] has the second-largest market capitalization in the car industry and the second-most-profitable car conglomerate in the industry."[25]

However, the automobile industry faces collapse due to the global financial crisis which started in 2008 without rapid intervention from governments. This affected Renault too. Carlos explained how to survive a crisis and prosper, saying, "First, you need to [weather] the next two years. That's a basic condition. To get through them, you need to make sure that you have a positive free cash flow. Or to put it another way, avoid burning cash. That's very fundamental. [You must be able to] still generate cash, even with a market as treacherous as the one we'll be facing. There is an end to any crisis, and this one is no exception. There will be an end. And you want to be ready. You want to have innovative products, strong fundamentals, a team that believes in the brand and believes the company will be ready to fight again. I don't think everybody is going to make it through this period of time, but those who survive will have a boulevard in front of them because people will still need to buy cars."[26] It remains to be seen whether Carlos would do the turnaround magic again.

Case Questions

1. What are the different management practices that are unique to Japanese organisations?
2. Do the management practices followed by Japanese organizations enable a company to remain competitive in a changing global economic environment?
3. What were the reasons behind the problems at Nissan? Was it wise to appoint an outsider as the CEO of Nissan?
4. What steps did Carlos initiate to bring about change in the organization?
5. Why did Renault decide to enter into an alliance with a troubled company like Nissan? How did the alliance benefit both the companies?
6. What are the challenges in heading two diverse cultures at Renault and Nissan?
7. Research and give an update on this alliance and on Carlos Ghosn as of the time of your reading this case.
8. Evaluate the global leadership skills of Carlos Ghosn.

[25] Taylor III Alex, "The world according to Ghosn," http://money.cnn.com/ magazines/fortune/fortune_archive/2006/12/11/8395466/index.htm, November 30th 2006.

[26] Bartiromo Maria, "Carlos Ghosn on Detroit and the Future of the Auto Business," http://www.businessweek.com/magazine/content/08_48/ b4110000510031_page_2.htm, November 19th 2008.

INTEGRATIVE SECTION – Project and Integrative Case

INTEGRATIVE TERM PROJECT

This project requires research, imagination, and logic in applying the content of this course and book.

In groups of three to five students, create an imaginary company that you have been operating in the domestic arena for some time. Your group represents top management, and you have decided it is time to go international.

- Describe your company and its operations, relative size, and so forth. Give reasons for your decision to go international.
- Decide on an appropriate country in which to operate, and give your rationale for this choice.
- State your planned entry strategy, and give your reasons for this strategy.
- Describe the environment in which you will operate and the critical operational factors that you must consider and how they will affect your company.
- Give a cultural profile of the local area in which you will be operating. What are the workers going to be like? What kind of reception do you anticipate from local governments, suppliers, distributors, and so on?

- Draw up an organization chart showing the company and its overseas operations, and describe why you have chosen this structure.
- Decide on the staffing policy you will use for top-level managers, and give your rationale for this policy.
- Describe the kinds of leadership and motivational systems you think would be most effective in this environment. Give your rationale.
- Discuss the kinds of communication problems your managers might face in the host-country working environment. How should they prepare for and deal with them?
- Explain any special control issues that concern you for this overseas operation. How do you plan to deal with them?

Identify the concerns of the host country and the local community regarding your operations there. What plans do you have to deal with their concerns and to ensure a long-term cooperative relationship?

UNIVERSITÉ
DE GENÈVE

FACULTÉ DES SCIENCES
ÉCONOMIQUES ET SOCIALES
Section des Hautes Études
Commerciales (HEC)

ICRC

INTEGRATIVE CASE THE INTERNATIONAL COMMITTEE OF THE RED CROSS: MANAGING ACROSS CULTURES

Source: ICRC, Comite' International de la Croix-Rouge

Introduction

Jacques Stroun, M.D., Director of Human Resources at the ICRC was at his desk thinking about the future of the Red Cross. In the past 140 years of its existence, ICRC had provided humanitarian relief in most of the major crises, helping millions of people around the world, he noted with pride. Dr. Stroun, an ICRC veteran of 28 years, had worked in Cambodia and El Salvador before coming to headquarters (HQ) in Geneva. Back at HQ, he had successively taken up posts as Head of Detention Division and as Deputy Director of Operations. In 1999 he was appointed Director of Human Resources and Finance. J. Stroun had witnessed over the years the evolution of the ICRC into a "humanitarian" multinational organization. More and more staff, in the field as well as at HQ, now came from around the world. In 2008, the total workforce of the organization was over 14,000 representing over 100 nationalities.[1]

Until recently, the Red Cross was considered to be "very Swiss," even some would say "very Genevoise." Due to its founding fathers and Geneva home base, values of neutrality, independence, discretion, and humanism were firmly implanted. In 1992, expatriate positions became open to all nationalities. Still, 93% of expatriates remained "westerners," although the number of expatriates from Africa, Asia, and Latin America was beginning to rise.

This case was written by Sowon Kim, Ph.D. candidate, and Susan Schneider, Chaired Professor of Human Resources Management at HEC—University of Geneva. The case was made possible through the generous cooperation of the International Committee of the Red Cross. The case is intended as a basis for class discussion rather than to illustrate either effective or ineffective handling of a management situation.

[1] From this number 807 work at HQ in Geneva, 1,498 are expatriates (delegates and professionals) and 10,850 are Host Delegation Employees (HDE). In addition there are 131 staff seconded from National Societies.

Nearly all those recruited in Geneva were sent to the field as expatriates and were expected to "hit the ground running," a "learning by doing" approach. Field managers, operating under sense of danger and urgency, were mostly concerned with meeting the immediate challenges. The focus was on the short term and on taking action in crisis situations. Operating in these conditions quickly develops and reinforces the importance of teamwork and team loyalties. However, as expatriates change positions every 12 months (representing more than 1,000 rotations per year[2]) teams form and re-form very quickly, rarely keeping the same personnel for an entire year. Thus there was neither the time for formal training nor the continuity for developing people.

In the past, careers evolved informally, with little planning, and were mainly developed through interpersonal networks and driven by opportunities. As most recruits stayed for only two to three years, not much thinking was given to management development: "Working for the ICRC was like an initiation rite taking place after the completion of general education and prior to assuming full career and family responsibilities."[3] Those who remained with the organization and reached the top at HQ were mostly male Swiss delegates ("operations" types) who had developed strong bonds from having been in the field together. Now, there was greater diversity in the management ranks including more professionals, foreigners, and women.

The new strategic plan for 2007–10 made clear the challenges for human resource management. The plan established three management priorities: multidisciplinary action, greater accountability, and increased efficiency through results based management. The plan also called into question the role of HQ. What should be centralized or decentralized? What policies and procedures needed to be standardized to achieve efficiency and

[2] The rotation depends on the position/function of the expatriate. In the first two years expatriates change position every 12 months. Managers in the field change position every 18–24 months. Professionals may change every 3 months.

[3] Saner, 1990: 764.

coherence across operations while ensuring the flexibility needed to respond swiftly and appropriately?

The challenges specific to HR included clarifying roles and responsibilities and putting in place a results based performance management system. The action plan also called for increasing the number of staff available for rapid deployment as well as reinforcing the geographical and hierarchical mobility for staff members. Furthermore what was needed was to provide management development and career planning to align individual interests and competencies with the organizational needs and priorities. The HR challenge was also to take into account the growing diversity, but particularly with regard to promoting women to top management positions. According to Jacques Stroun,

Nous étions une entreprise constituée de collaborateurs suisses généralistes, nous devenons une entreprise multi-culturelle et professionnelle. (We were an organization made up of Swiss generalists. We are becoming a multi-cultural and professional enterprise.)

Facing these challenges, he wondered what would be necessary to ensure that the ICRC adapted to these strategic demands while preserving the culture that he believed was critical to upholding its mission of neutral, independent humanitarian action (NIHA). He believed strongly in the ICRC culture and that it would override any concerns related to the growing diversity. Yet he worried to what extent the ICRC culture might get in the way of implementing the new strategic plan and the HR policies that would be required. Just then JS heard a knock at the door; his HR team was waiting for their scheduled meeting to discuss these challenges.

The Humanitarian Sector

Evolution and Trends

In the last decade, the world has witnessed a massive increase of both natural and man-made disasters. Following 9/11, these confrontations have taken on a global dimension (as seen in the globalization of terrorist activities). In 2003, 200 million people were affected by natural disasters[4] and 45 million by complex emergencies (civil wars being the most common example) which required life-saving assistance.[5]

While the extent of warfare has not changed significantly, the nature of conflicts has. The disengagement of the superpowers following the end of the Cold War led to the emergence of a more intractable type of war. Also, there is greater political instability due to the weak governance capacity of many nation states. Today, armed conflicts are characterized by active and deliberate targeting of civilians, widespread human rights abuses, and the use of crimes of violence as weapons of war.[6] Humanitarian

action itself has become more politicized. Even providing water could be interpreted as an act of war, for example, seen as supporting a new regime. And humanitarian workers are increasingly becoming targets if not victims of violence.

The number of agencies and organizations working in the humanitarian sphere has significantly proliferated bringing to the scene more and more players with differing objectives, activities and principles. Over the last ten years, securing funding has become more difficult. Although net aid from Development Aid Committee (DAC) had gradually increased from 1997, when it was at its lowest level, foreign aid (as measured in terms of percentage of Gross National Income (GNI) had fallen sharply for the previous five consecutive years. The main donor governments thus engaged in a process of collective reflection in order to encourage professionalism, coordination, results and greater accountability towards donors as well as beneficiaries.

The United Nations (UN) humanitarian system has embarked on a process of reform. In 1992, former UN Secretary General, Boutros Boutros-Ghali proposed *An Agenda for Peace*[7] which aimed to integrate humanitarian activities, the political agenda and military operations under a common direction. Although the original policies are still in place, implementation remains selective, on a case by case basis, as no universal criteria for military humanitarian intervention has yet been agreed upon. Still, the vision remains as the UN Office for the Coordination of Humanitarian Affairs (OCHA) hopes to integrate all (UN and non-UN) operations to be managed as a global humanitarian system.

For some actors, involvement of military actors in humanitarian operations is seen as a natural evolution caused by the growing number of peacekeeping operations[8] as well as the growing need for protection of aid workers. However, other actors have a strong conviction that independent humanitarian action is necessary to achieve impartiality and neutrality and therefore should be institutionally separated from the UN's political-military activities. They strive not only to maintain their autonomy but also to be clearly differentiated from UN or UN affiliated organizations reinforcing the strength and importance of their "unique" organizational identity.

Many activities initiated by the UN agencies, for example in refugee camps, are decided at headquarters in New York to be implemented in the field—a centralized and top down approach. The ICRC prides itself with starting in the field in order to identify local needs and then deciding what to do—a bottom up approach. Thus, not only does the field take initiative by making proposals to hierarchy, but also has more autonomy compared with other organizations which are to varying degrees affiliated with or financially dependent on the UN.

Working in the humanitarian sector implies being ready to respond to continuous crises. In the case of armed conflict,

---

[4] As a specific example, in 1998, floods, droughts, storms and earthquakes caused more than 50,000 deaths and economic losses exceeding $90 billion. The figure for that year alone exceeds the disaster costs for the entire 1980s. More than 90% of all disaster victims live in developing countries. For more see OCHA (ochaonline.un.org).
[5] OCHA (ochaonline.un.org).
[6] OCHA (ochaonline.un.org).

[7] *Agenda for Peace* set out the main principles by which the UN intended to take the lead on preventive diplomacy, peacemaking, peace-keeping and post-conflict peace-building through the usage of the UN military force in order to implement these strategies.
[8] Macrae, 2002: 9.

its very nature—danger, unpredictable precipitous change, hardship, and chaos—contributes to a level of stress and burn-out that is seen in few other types of organizations. Performance is not about profit, but about the survival and integrity of individuals and groups of people. Discussions about "employee security" are not about keeping position (status, salary, or benefits) but about keeping life and limbs. Not surprisingly, this may lead to a high turnover rate of expatriate staff which may limit staff experience and institutional memory. In the last twenty years, humanitarian operations have become less characterized by "crisis and emergency" and more by rehabilitation and development aimed at developing local competencies.

The International Red Cross and Red Crescent Movement

The International Red Cross and Red Crescent Movement is the largest humanitarian network in the world. Also known as the *International Red Cross* or the *Red Cross Movement*, it embodies the *International Committee of the Red Cross* (ICRC), the *International Federation of Red Cross and Red Crescent Societies* (IFRC) and over 180 *National Red Cross and Red Crescent Societies* (a.k.a. National Societies or NS) (see exhibit I).

Though the functions of the three entities (ICRC, IFRC, NS) differ, the Red Cross Movement is bound by a common heritage and a commitment to the seven Fundamental Principles: humanity, impartiality, neutrality, independence, voluntary service, unity and universality (see exhibit II). These principles were first proclaimed at the 20th International Conference of the Red Cross and Red Crescent in 1965. While independent, the organizations often work as partners in implementation of certain policies.

The IFRC (International Federation) differs from the ICRC in that it focuses on natural or technological disasters. They offer support to the public sector through social service activities and/or assistance during disasters (relief operations). Furthermore they aim to strengthen the NS (National Societies) which are responsible for both relief and development activities in their respective countries. The cooperation with the network of National Societies, gives the ICRC and IFRC a uniquely broad base of action as it includes tens of millions of members worldwide.

Established in 1863, the ICRC is at the origin of the International Red Cross and Red Crescent Movement. The ICRC has been given the role of guardian of the Red Cross Principles and of International Humanitarian Law.[9] In order to be admitted to the Red Cross Movement, potential National

EXHIBIT I   The International Red Cross and Red Crescent Movement

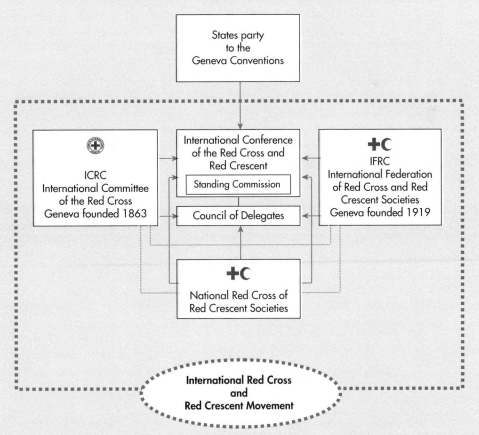

---

[9] IHL (known also as the law of armed conflict or the law of war) is the body of rules which, in wartime, protects persons who are not or are no longer participating in the hostilities. Its central purpose is to limit and prevent human suffering in times of armed conflict.

EXHIBIT II The Fundamental Principles of the International Red Cross and Red Crescent Movement

Humanity

The International Red Cross and Red Crescent Movement, born of a desire to bring assistance without discrimination to the wounded on the battlefield, endeavors, in its international and national capacity, to prevent and alleviate human suffering wherever it may be found. Its purpose is to protect life and health and to ensure respect for the human being. It promotes mutual understanding, friendship, cooperation and lasting peace amongst all peoples.

Impartiality

It makes no discrimination as to nationality, race, religious beliefs, class or political opinions. It endeavors to relieve the suffering of individuals, being guided solely by their needs, and to give priority to the most urgent cases of distress.

Neutrality

In order to continue to enjoy the confidence of all, the Movement may not take sides in hostilities or engage at any time in controversies of a political,, racial, religious or ideological nature.

Independence

The Movement is independent. The National Societies, while auxiliaries in the humanitarian services of their governments and subject to the laws of their respective countries, must always maintain their autonomy so that they may be able at all times to act in accordance with the principles of the Movement.

Voluntary Service

It is a voluntary relief movement not prompted in any manner by desire for gain.

Unity

There can be only one Red Cross or one Red Crescent Society in any one country. It must be open to all. It must carry on its humanitarian work throughout its territory.

Universality

The International Red Cross and Red Crescent Movement, in which all Societies have equal status and share equal responsibilities and duties in helping each other, is worldwide.

Societies must first be recognized by the ICRC. In the same vein, signatory states to the Geneva Conventions[10] and Protocols[11] are obliged to allow the ICRC to monitor the application of International Humanitarian Law (IHL) in conflict situations. In recent years IHL has been challenged especially in respect to non-international armed conflicts, as seen in the detention facilities related to post 9/11.

The International Committee of the Red Cross (ICRC)

History

In 1859, Swiss businessman Henri Dunant, witnessed the War of Italian Unification and wrote his impressions in *A Memory of Solferino*.[12] In a single day, the war between the Austrian and French armies had left about 40,000 dead and wounded. Horrified by the sight of thousands of soldiers from both armies

left to suffer for lack of adequate medical services, Dunant proposed two strategies to limit the suffering of victims of war. They were: 1) the formation of national relief societies to supplement armed forces with medical services in time of conflict; and 2) the development of an international convention to protect the sick and wounded in combat. In 1863, Dunant and four other *Genevois*[13] founded The International Committee for Relief to the Wounded in Time of War which became the ICRC. The Committee supported the development of the first National Societies, and prompted the Swiss government to convene a diplomatic conference which developed the Geneva Convention of 1864.

The Red Cross largely reflects Swiss values such as autonomy, egalitarianism, and consensus-seeking (see exhibit III) shaped by its history. Independent in 1815 (Congress of Vienna), the integration of the then-22 *cantons* (states)[14] implied a continuous effort of balancing the different needs of the cantons and further the cantons' tradition of self-rule with that of central government. Consequently, Switzerland adopted

[10] The four Geneva Conventions of 1949 are applicable in international armed conflicts. They stipulate that persons taking no active part in the hostilities, including those who are suffering and those placed outside the combat, shall be cared for without discrimination. Art. 3, common to all four Conventions authorizes the ICRC to offer its services in the event of a civil war on the territory of one of the signatory States, and accords minimum protection to the victims of such situations.

[11] The Additional Protocols of 1977 supplement the Conventions by developing the protection of civilians in time of war and extending the criteria for the application of humanitarian law to cover the new types of conflict.

[12] The book was published in 1862.

[13] Gustave Moynier, Dr. Louis Appia, Dr. Théodore Maunoir, and Général Guillaume-Henri Dufour.

[14] Currently the Swiss Confederation has 26 cantons : Aargau, Appenzell Innerrhoden, Appenzell Ausserrhoden, Basel-Stadt, Basel-Landschaft, Bern, Fribourg, Geneva, Glarus, Graubünden, Jura, Lucerne, Neuchâtel, Nidwalden, Obwalden, Schaffhausen, Schwyz, Solothurn, St. Gallen, Thurgau, Ticino, Uri, Valais, Vaud, Zug, and Zürich.

- Pragmatism
- Egalitarianism
- Restrained, serious, sense of measure and order
- Perfectionism
- Compromise and consensus
- Prudence and search for security
- Individualism, autonomy, independence
- Strong client orientation

(*Source*: A. Bergmann, 1994)

EXHIBIT IV **Official emblems of The International Red Cross and Red Crescent Movement**

The Red Cross
The Red Crescent
The Red Lion & Sun (not in use since 1980)

The Red Crystal

the use of referendums and a federal constitution in 1848—a central authority existed but the cantons had the right to self-government on local issues.

The early years of the ICRC was dominated by Geneva's "first families." Eventually, Swiss-Italians and Swiss-Germans were accepted under the condition that they mastered oral and written French and conformed to the Swiss-French culture. Today, ICRC is officially bilingual (French and English). But while English dominates both in the field and in certain functions such as public relations, French dominates the HQ and is considered necessary for advancement to top management positions. Furthermore, French remains important to the identity of the ICRC as it differentiates it from other UN and humanitarian organizations.

The ICRC adopted a Red Cross on a white background as its emblem (perhaps an inverted version of the Swiss Flag—white cross on a red background). The adoption of the Red Cross has provoked continuous controversy as the cross also symbolizes Christianity. Despite the adoption of the Red Crescent[15] by Muslim countries, Israel's request in 1949 to use the Star of David was refused. Israel, in turn, refused to use the Red Cross emblem blocking it from being admitted to the Red Cross Movement. Currently over 170 countries use the Red Cross and 30 use the Red Crescent.[16]

It was not until December 2005, after six years of negotiations, that the Red Crystal was adopted as one of ICRC's official emblems[17] (see exhibit IV). This emblem was chosen as it was considered to be a sign of purity and transparency, a neutral symbol free from any religious, cultural or historical reference. Now countries have the choice to use one of the three emblems (the Red Cross/Crescent/Crystal) or up to two emblems together (e.g. the Red Cross inside the Red Crystal). Nevertheless, François Bugnion, the ICRC Director of International Law and Cooperation, proclaimed, "There will not be a Red Crystal on the flag flying above the ICRC in Geneva" (*Il n'y aura pas de cristal rouge sur le drapeau flottant au-dessus du CICR*).[18]

---

[15] In 1876, during the Turkish-Russian war the Ottoman Empire decided to use the Red Crescent instead of the Red Cross as it was taken as an offence to Muslim soldiers.

[16] The Red Lion and Sun (originally a Persian symbol) is another official emblem which has not been in use since 1980.

[17] "Joining the Red Cross and Crescent: A Red Crystal." *International Herald Tribune*, Nov. 26–27, 2005.

[18] Levy, L. "Il n'y aura pas de cristal rouge sur le drapeau flottant au-dessus du CICR." *Tribune de Genève*. Dec. 5, 2005.

ICRC Strategy 2007–10: "Committed to meeting new challenges through action"

In 2006, the ICRC directorate identified key internal and external challenges and raised the following issues: Given increasing competition in the humanitarian sector and the diversity of situations of armed violence, what should be the scope of action or range of ICRC activities? Should the ICRC go for a niche strategy? What type of relationships should they establish with partners and competitors? What should be their role in the humanitarian sector?

After intensive consultations at ICRC, HQ and Heads of Delegation in February and March 2006, the directorate designed its strategy for 2007–10, set management priorities and established action plans.

- As its core mission, the ICRC will keep developing an "all-victims and all-needs approach" in armed conflicts.
- To establish partnerships with National Societies.
- The ICRC confirms its ambition to remain the reference organization for matters pertaining to international humanitarian law.
- The ICRC will continue to assert its identity as a strictly humanitarian, impartial, neutral and independent organization.

Mission

"The ICRC is an impartial, neutral and independent organization whose exclusively humanitarian mission is to protect the lives and dignity of victims of war and internal violence and to provide them with assistance. It directs and coordinates the international relief activities conducted by the Movement in situations of conflict. It also endeavors to prevent suffering by promoting and strengthening humanitarian law and universal humanitarian principles."

The ICRC achieves its mission through three main field activities: Protection, Assistance and Prevention.

Protection includes: 1) protecting the civilians; 2) protecting the detained (e.g. visiting those deprived of freedom in connection with the conflict); 3) tracing (e.g. restoring and maintaining contact between family members separated by conflict, facilitating reunification and keeping track of individuals deprived of their freedom); and 4) finding missing people. In 2008, ICRC visited 2,387 places of detention and collected and delivered some 667,000 messages in order to help maintain contacts between family members.

ICRC takes particular pride in being "first in and last out" of any war zone. For example, when all the NGOs from North Atlantic Treaty Organization (NATO) countries evacuated during the air strikes in Bosnia in 1995, ICRC remained and provided humanitarian assistance to the hundreds of thousands of Serb civilians.

Assistance includes: 1) relief/economic security activities aimed at helping victims meet basic survival needs (e.g. distribution of food and non-food aid, and emergency agricultural and veterinary assistance); 2) water and habitat services; 3) health care services (i.e. caring for war wounded, supporting existing health services, and improving situations for water, sanitations and nutrition that are disrupted by conflict); and 4) physical rehabilitation (for the disabled).

ICRC encourages interventions that improve the economic security of a population. For example, ICRC vaccinated camels in Somalia in order to prevent sickness and/or death of the animals. This, in turn, increased the price of camels thus improving purchasing power and enhancing the local economy. By these actions, ICRC can improve the local economy as well as circumvent war lords which often hijack and redistribute provisions offered directly by ICRC or other NGOs.

Prevention includes spreading the knowledge of the Fundamental Principles of the Movement and International Humanitarian Law (IHL) as mentioned above. The ICRC aims to be seen as the referent and to promote IHL as a means of prevention. Although the ICRC has tended to keep a low profile ("Don't speak too loud or too often!"), it will mobilize the press to bring international attention to violations of IHL (e.g. Rwanda, Guantánamo Bay).

"The ICRC will strive to remain the standard-setting organization in the field of international humanitarian law. It intends to promote the law and to have it recognized and applied as the relevant law in any armed conflict. It will continue to clarify and develop the law taking into account the real nature of conflicts in today's world and working to prevent any erosion of the protection afforded to civilians and persons who are no longer fighting." (ICRC Strategy 2007–2010)

One of the key objectives is to gain access to victims and to engage in dialogue with all parties involved in the conflict. This involves being known, understood and accepted by these different actors. This is sometimes difficult given that the ICRC is identified as a "western" organization and therefore associated with the U.S. or the UN. In order to ensure collaboration particularly in Muslim countries, the ICRC has had to invest more time in explaining who they are, how they work, and how they are different and independent from these other organizations. Furthermore, they stress the link between Islamic principles and IHL as universal rather than western principles.

Funding

The annual budget in 2009 is approximately 1,165.5 million Swiss Francs.[19] ICRC maintains itself based on a double system of compulsory and voluntary contributions. Its revenue come from member states of the Geneva Conventions (governments), supranational organizations (e.g. European Commission), National Societies, and public and private donations (see exhibit V). The *Donor Support Group* was created in 1998 with 11 founding members of the most generous government donors and the European Commission (10%). In 2008 it had 19 members (the same number as in 2007) whose contributions financed 88.3% of ICRC expenditures. Most of the funding comes from voluntary donations making it dependent on the goodwill and generosity of the international community.

The ICRC has progressively worked with the private sector in order to expand the collaboration between itself and the corporate world. In 2005, this initiative has culminated into the creation of the *Corporate Support Group* (a group of Swiss-based companies selected based on strict ethical criteria). These corporate partners are expected to donate a minimum amount of three million Swiss Francs over a period of six years. Donations from the business community account for less than 0.5% of the ICRC's overall expenditure; the organization's objective is to bring this share to 3%.

The ICRC funding process provides it with enough reserves to be able to launch operations without having to appeal to donors first. It is often more effective (and more convincing) to appeal to donors based on past performance and ongoing operations than for "envisioned" projects. This approach—driven by necessity rather than by budgets or resources—means that money *per se* is often not considered as an issue. However, in reality money *is* becoming more of an issue, especially in the last five years as there has been a gradual reduction in the funding of humanitarian activities.

Organization

The governing bodies of the ICRC are the Assembly, the Assembly Council and the Directorate (see exhibit VI). These three bodies along with the Presidency[20] and Management Control[21] make up the decision-making bodies of the organization.

---

[19] From which 996.9 million were for emergency appeals and 168.6 million were HQ appeals. The total contributions received in 2008 was 1.139,4 million Swiss Francs (ICRC emergency appeals and headquarters appeal, 2008).

[20] Jakob Kellenberger is the president of the ICRC as of 2000. The president is assisted by a permanent Vice-President and a non-permanent Vice-President and chairs both the Assembly and the Assembly Council.

[21] Management Control is the body which is responsible for independent operational and financial audit.

EXHIBIT V Contributions by Donor Type & Major Donors (2008)

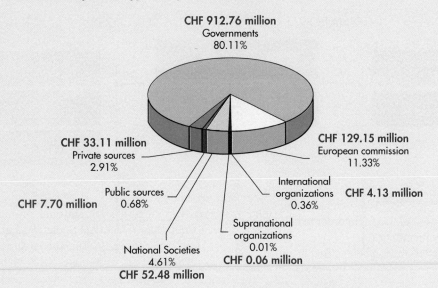

	2005	**2006**	**2007**	**2008**
Governments	72.70%	79.80%	80.13%	80.11%
National Societies	13.10%	8.60%	5.92%	4.61%
European Commission	9.40%	9.00%	11.12%	11.33%
Public & Private	4.80%	2.50%	2.58%	3.59%

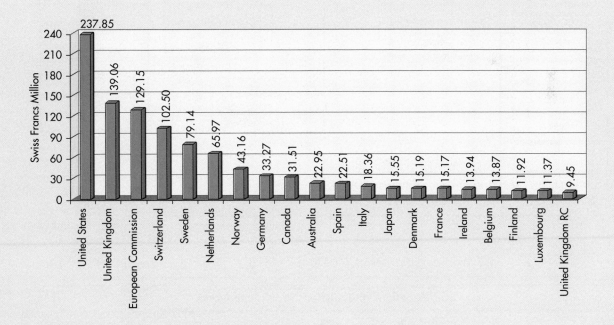

The Assembly meets five times a year and oversees the entire organization's activities (defines general objectives and strategy, formulates policy, appoints directors, and approves the budget and accounts). As stated in Art. 7 (Membership of the ICRC) of the Statutes of the International Committee of Red Cross,[22] the Assembly is composed of 15–25 members, all of Swiss nationality—considered necessary to guarantee neutrality.

The Assembly Council is composed of five members, all Swiss, elected and delegated certain powers by the Assembly. It prepares the Assembly's activities and takes decisions on issues relating to general policy on funding, personnel, and communication. The Assembly Council serves as a link between the Directorate and the Assembly, to which it reports regularly.

---

[22] Art. 7 states "1. The ICRC shall co-opt its Members from among Swiss citizens. It shall comprise fifteen to twenty-five Members."

EXHIBIT VI   Organizational Chart

INTERNATIONAL COMMITTEE OF THE RED CROSS

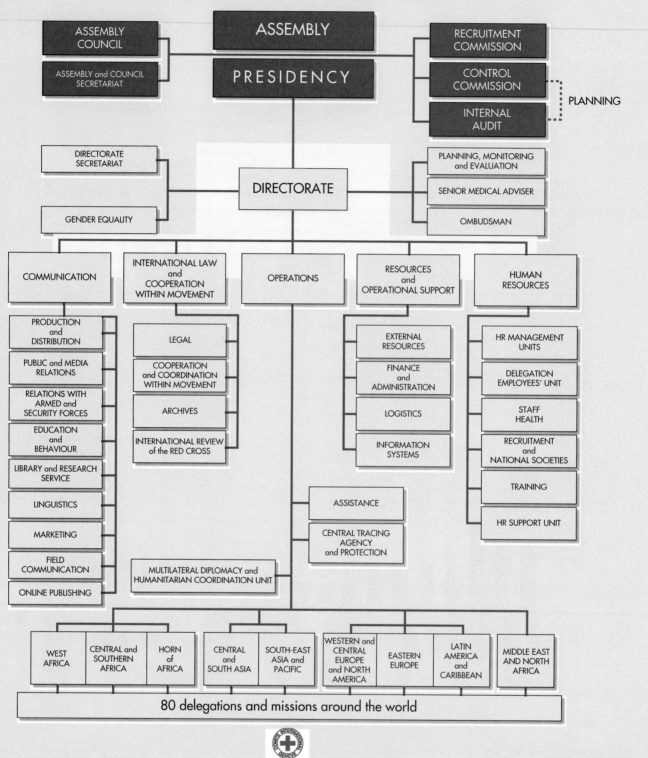

The Directorate is the executive body of the organization responsible for applying and ensuring the application of the general objectives and institutional strategy defined by the Assembly or the Assembly Council. The Directorate is also responsible for the smooth running and the efficiency of the ICRC staff as a whole. Its six members, all of Swiss nationality, are appointed by the Assembly for four-year terms, most recently renewed in 2006.

In the field, operations are managed by "Delegations," numbering around 80 around the world. Country delegations are established in areas of active or recently resolved conflict and are divided into sub-delegations, which usually focus on Protection and/or Assistance activities (e.g. Colombia is considered one delegation but has 12–15 sub-delegations). Regional delegations are established to cover a number of neighboring countries where there are no major active or recently resolved conflicts and are more focused on Prevention activity.

Human Resource Management at ICRC

According to Jacques Stroun, it is often easier to get funding than to find people. By mid 1980, the Swiss labor market could no longer provide the necessary human resources to meet the demands of the ICRC's expanding field operations. Thus they started to recruit foreign staff. The needs were most keen for professionals which were met by seconding staff from the National Societies. Geneva-based contracts were offered to National Society staff that had had a successful two year record of working with the ICRC. This not only eased staff shortages in a cost efficient manner (as the National Societies paid their salaries and benefits), but also improved relationships with them. In 1986, there were 350 expatriates; 10 years later the number quadrupled.

Staff seconded from National Societies is mostly from the developed countries given these were expensive "donations." One famous example is Bernard Kouchner, a medical doctor recruited from the French Red Cross, who later went on to found *Médecins Sans Frontières* (Doctors without Borders) and to become the French Minister of Health (and now Foreign

Policy). Via this route, the number of non-Swiss expatriates increased steadily such that by the early 1990s, 30% of the expatriates were non-Swiss. But although the ICRC recruited both Swiss and non-Swiss professionals, it was only after 1992, with the policy of internationalization, that delegate positions were opened to all nationalities. By 2008, 57% of expatriates were non-Swiss (see exhibit VII).

Delegates are *generalists*, responsible for managing the overall operation in a specific area.[23] They are responsible for negotiations, protection activities, coordination of specialists, and to ensure that different activities are well integrated. The delegate function was, and continues to be, the core function from which the leadership *cadre* (managers) is chosen. The main function of the local staff is that of support. And although an increasing number of local professionals (30%) exist, the number of local managers remains small (5%).

Professionals are *specialists*, hired to do specific/technical jobs defined by their vocational or professional qualifications. Professionals work either in relief or medical activities (e.g. doctor, nurse) or support services (e.g. engineering, IT service, communications). Initially, professionals could advance in the ranks of their own departments, but could not cross into the delegate status until mid-1980.

Although delegates and professionals work for a common objective and share a common set of values, their different perspectives can be a source of conflict. For example, professionals often seek the "best possible way" whereas delegates tend to be more pragmatic. Professionals place more importance on their technical competence and resist being managed by delegates who they think do not understand the technicalities of their

EXHIBIT VII Percentage of Swiss staff

Geneva and field: all expatriate staff

	1998	2003	2008
Swiss	68%	52%	43%
Non-Swiss	46%	48%	57%

Field: Heads of office, heads of sub-delegation, heads of delegation

	1998	2003	2008
Swiss	88%	75%	52%
Non-Swiss	12%	25%	48%

HQ: Directors, general delegates, heads of operation, heads of division

	1998	2003	2008
Swiss	96%	85%	85%
Non-Swiss	4%	15%	15%

[23] Delegates manage the overall operation only when they become managers. In the first two years, delegates have partial responsibility e.g. visiting three prisoners.

specialization. For example, when delegates proposed to build a clinic in a district, the medical staff opposed the initiative because the area did not have the appropriate conditions, e.g. sufficient water supply to build a clinic.

Nevertheless, as delegates are responsible for coordinating activities and negotiation, they tend to have a better grasp of the "big picture," and are more ready to adapt to the local situation and/or constraints. For example, in Uganda, water and sanitation engineers recommended building a well inside the prison as prisoners had to go outside to get water. The act of fetching the water, however, had important consequences that the engineers overlooked as it allowed the prisoners to get exercise and maintain contact with the local population.

Moreover, delegates are convinced of the importance of being "in the field," in order to gain credibility and develop management competencies. Thus, delegates do not necessarily understand the importance professionals give to training aimed at developing technical/professional competencies instead of spending time in the field.

Recruitment and selection

Thirty years ago expatriates in the field would have been young (early twenties), Swiss *Romand* (French-speaking) with similar backgrounds—recruited primarily from universities with degrees in political science, economics, law, or "*letters*" (liberal arts). The new generation of recruits is older (late twenties), more international, speaks more languages, more professional, and often has a more specialized educational background (e.g. degree in humanitarian law). They place a premium on having work that is not only interesting and motivating, but also fulfills their ideals, recognizes their values, and that allows them to express their opinions.[24] For these reasons, the ICRC remains a popular choice not only for those graduating from university as applicants of all ages are increasing (more than 6,000 in 2003).

These new recruits are more concerned with their personal and career development as they are seeking a career at the ICRC and not a short term experience. As such, they are more likely during recruitment to discuss issues of salary, contracts, and vacations. Further, as they tend to stay longer, more and more rotations involve families. Therefore, they are more concerned with seeking work life balance. They also expect internet connections to stay in touch with family and friends on a daily basis.

Recruitment is an important and ongoing activity in ICRC as the demand for expatriates is high. The recruitment procedure is highly centralized and rather intensive in order to maintain a certain degree of homogeneity of profiles. After the first stage of selection based on CV, motivation letter and a personal history form, the candidate is invited to a half-day interview with an HR person. Following this interview, the candidate participates in a recruitment day (*journée de recrutement*) with seven other candidates, making presentations, and engaging in role plays and simulations. Observed by five former delegates, candidates are evaluated on personal qualities (e.g. motivation, resistance to stress, attitude, and maturity), skills (e.g. capacity to analyze, synthesize, negotiate, and initiate), team work performance

[24] Stevens and Michalski (1994) and Reynolds (1994).

(e.g. leadership) and situational reactions (e.g. adaptation to change and managing the unexpected). Thus, they are recruited less for their technical competences but more for their personal qualities, or "soft skills." The organization recruits approximately 450 expatriates per year and has a turnover rate of 9%.

Training and development

One of the most important training events is that provided to the new expatriate recruits. It is a four week intensive Integration Course—two weeks off site and two weeks at HQ—in a group of around 25 people which costs approximately CHF 20,000 to 40,000 per person. General knowledge is gained through documents, museum visits, conferences, and war films. Role plays are used to sensitize cultural differences in communication styles, norms, and behaviors. Informal contacts with experienced expatriates who give briefings help to transmit the ICRC spirit and culture. By the end, all new recruits who begin as strangers end up referring to the ICRC as "us." Once the integration course is finished the new recruit is sent immediately on a mission abroad and continues "learning by doing." Expatriates are expected to become operational and autonomous in a short period of time.

The integration course was originally offered to delegates only, however, in the last ten years professionals have been included. Professionals recruited to work at HQ and who have had no field experience, undergo a very general one week integration course. Integration courses are also given by the regional training units to expatriates or National Society staff with contracts of over 6 months as well as some local staff. Training in the field is also provided for heads of units and professionals every 2–3 years.

Career development

There is no formal career planning in the ICRC for expatriates. However, regular discussions about performance and yearly appraisals are held at the end of each mission for all expatriates. In the last two years, career commissions for middle and top management have been created with the purpose of assessing career prospective. Previously (10 years ago), an Individual Career and Deployment Planning had been introduced to ensure filling management positions and to discuss career possibilities in light of performance appraisals and personal interests. The project was well received but was not fully implemented because the need to urgently fill field positions took precedence. At that time, vacancy rate was over 5 percent; currently it is under 1 percent.

Occasionally there is a shortage of expatriates. Lack of personnel, from the perspective of Operations, is not considered to be a valid reason to forgo planned operations. In order to tackle with this challenge, HR has established a "reserve staff" composed of new recruits (delegates). Currently there are 30 people (1–2 per delegation) who in case of personnel shortage can be transferred immediately. This not only ensures the shortage, but is also a way of giving on-site training to new recruits as they are integrated in the delegations and work with the delegates.

Nevertheless, developing people continues to be a challenge because the nature of the job requires that person be

immediately operational. While the main concern of HR is developing people's competences, Operations need people with competences. New delegates are given much responsibility but their missions can fail due to lack of support. Those that do succeed to high positions are often good at "*se débrouiller*" ("getting around") but may lack more managerial competencies. However, there is little opportunity to discuss how to develop these competencies.

Junior expatriates are managed in a standardized manner during the early years of their career, such that discussions regarding career opportunities are rather limited. Personal preferences are taken more into account at the mid-manager level in discussions between managers and HQ. For local staff, other than a personnel file and a performance appraisal, there is no real career management. In addition, as most local staff is in support roles (60%–70%), few have access to training and opportunities to advance.

Developing local talent may be limited due to political reasons. Those in management positions, delegates or professionals, must be perceived as neutral and impartial. From the perspective of HQ this necessitates expatriates, not locals. In addition, locals cannot take on certain professional roles (for example, as administrators or secretaries) because of issues of trust, especially in handling sensitive information which could put their security in jeopardy. Furthermore, it may be difficult to find local competence in certain countries. Thus, even if both locals and expatriates are "united" by the ICRC's objectives and values, they remain "separated" by their status. From the local perspective, expatriates are often stereotyped as "westerners," and thus considered to be neither sensitive to nor fully understanding of local conditions. Nevertheless there is a growing pool of local professionals or managers who have opportunities for training and advancement as they can now become expatriates.

Problems can arise, however, when locals who have been sent out on *ad hoc* (6 months) missions as expatriates return to their country of origin. This was the case, for example, when a Pakistani who originally worked at Islamabad as a local became an expatriate and then returned to Kashmir. This raised the issue: "Why is a local being treated as an expatriate (i.e. better benefits such as higher salary, insurance, housing, private schooling for children)?" Managing the relationship of locals and expatriates who formerly had local status is an increasing challenge. For these reasons HR defined the status of an expatriate is a matter of mobility—being willing and able to move from one country to another—rather than nationality.

Moving up the hierarchy at the ICRC is based on the "promotion from within" policy. Career paths alternate between the field and HQ where management positions are limited to 2–6 years depending on the post. Experience as a delegate is considered a key factor to access higher posts (at HQ) as credibility largely depends on having had "hands on" experience—having been through the wars together (*Nous avons fait la guerre ensemble*). Thus, it is not surprising that 90 percent of vacancy at HQ is occupied by former expatriates. However, there are often not enough places for those wanting to return from the field.

This brings out two issues. For one, there is a tendency to believe that one can only become manager by having field experience (primarily as a delegate) and that Operations is the only important place to work. Given the high value placed in being "in the field," Operations has a tendency of acting as if it "knows best." As a result, other departments feel less valued. Further, there exists a "field syndrome" by which managers with field experience working at HQ tend to manage HQ as if it were the field. Prioritization of projects is rare as most issues are labeled "urgent." Also, a short term perspective tends to predominate over long term strategy.

However, as more and more professionals gain access to HQ, and as some departments are now being managed by people without field experience, this tradition is being challenged. For example, in the IT department where there were only people with field experience, the current Head of Unit for Information Systems is an external recruit who has no field experience. In HR, the Head of Training has never been in the field, and for the first time an outsider has taken the position as Head of Personnel. Thus at HQ there is a greater need for management based on professional competence rather than on relationships developed in the field, particularly for the upper-echelon positions.

Another issue is that the Operations division remains largely a male bastion. Most Heads of Delegations are men, and most top management positions at HQ are occupied by men. This remains the case even though there are fewer places where women expatriates are not sent (either because they are too dangerous or because of local resistance). Also, there exist places where the delegations are all women. Today, 45 percent of field delegates are women; 32 percent of female are Heads of Sub-delegations while 29 percent are Heads of Delegations (see Exhibit VIII).

The problem of getting more women in higher places is in part due to the problem of dual-careers. Many expatriates meet in the field, have families, and continue to pursue their careers. At some point in time (because there are no two positions open and even less likely at the same level as the previous job), one career (often the man's) is prioritized. Sometimes the woman may also get a job in the new location but often in a lower position. Thus, despite the significant increase in numbers of women recruits and expatriates, the higher up the hierarchical ladder, the fewer there are. Efforts to promote gender equality at ICRC have been ongoing since the late 1980s. The "gender equality policy and strategy framework" adopted in March 2006 has as one objective to achieve parity (a minimum representation rate of 40%) within ten years applicable to all functions and levels of the organization.

- - -

Jacques Stroun returned to his thoughts after talking to his HR team. Stroun himself was convinced that the ICRC culture was crucial to its mission. However, he remained concerned that its very culture could prevent from adapting to the strategic demands of the changing environment. He wondered in what ways the ICRC culture might help or hinder implementing the management priorities and the required HR practices? To what extent would the ICRC culture need to be changed to embrace the growing diversity, but most importantly, to preserve and promote the mission of the Red Cross in a more and more complex world?

EXHIBIT VIII Gender balances

Geneva and field: all expatriate staff

	1998	2003	2008
Women	45%	45%	45%
Men	55%	55%	55%

Field: Heads of office, heads of sub-delegation, heads of delegation

	1998	2003	2008
Women	20%	20%	32%
Men	80%	80%	68%

HQ: Directors, general delegates, heads of operation, heads of division

	1998	2003	2008
Women	16%	26%	29%
Men	84%	74%	71%

Discussion Questions

1. What are some of the challenges facing the Red Cross at this time? (regarding issues of strategy, structure, IHRM, multiculturalism.)
2. Diagnose the ICRC culture.
3. In what ways may the ICRC culture help or hinder implementing the new strategy?
4. What are the implications for Human Resource Management?

Bergmann, A. *The Swiss Way of Management*. Paris: Eska,1994.

HR Executive Forum held at the ICRC on Mar. 6, 2006.

ICRC. *Annual report 2008*. Geneva: ICRC Publications, 2009.

"Joining the Red Cross and Crescent: A Red Crystal." *International Herald Tribune.* Nov. 26–27, 2005.

Levy, L. "Il n'y aura pas de cristal rouge sur le drapeau flottant au-dessus du CICR. » *Tribune de Genève*. Dec. 5, 2005.

Macrae, J. "The New Humanitarianisms: a Review of Trends in Global Humanitarian Action."*HPG Report.* Humanitarian Policy Group, 2002..

Reynolds, A. "Workforce 2005: The Future of Jobs in the United States and Europe," in *OECD Societies in Transition: The Future of Work and Leisure*. Paris: OECD, 1994.

Saner, R. Manifestation of stress and its impact on the humanitarian work of the ICRC delegate. *Political Psychology* 11 no. 4 (1990): 757–65.

Stevens, B., and W. Michalski. Long-term prospects for work and social cohesion in OECD countries: An overview of the issues, in *OECD Societies in Transition: The Future of Work and Leisure*. Paris: OECD, 1994.

www.icrc.org

www.ochaonline.un.org

www.oecd.org

GLOSSARY

affective appeals Negotiation appeals based on emotions and subjective feelings.

appropriability of technology The ability of an innovating firm to protect its technology from competitors and to obtain economic benefits from that technology.

attribution The process in which a person looks for an explanation of another person's behavior.

axiomatic appeals Negotiation appeals based on the ideals generally accepted in a society.

B2B Business-to-business electronic transactions.

B2C Business-to-consumer electronic transactions.

balance sheet approach An approach to the compensation of expatriates that equalizes the standard of living between the host and home countries, plus compensation for inconvenience.

born globals companies that go global from the outset, often through the use of the internet for their operations.

chaebol South Korea's large industrial conglomerates of financially linked, and often family-linked, companies that do business among themselves whenever possible—for example, Daewoo.

codetermination (*mitbestimmung*) The participation of labor in the management of a firm.

collective bargaining In the United States, for example, negotiations between a labor union local and management; in Sweden and Germany, for example, negotiations between the employer's organization and a trade union at the industry level.

collectivism The tendency of a society toward tight social frameworks, emotional dependence on belonging to an organization, and a strong belief in group decisions.

communication The process of sharing meaning by transmitting messages through media such as words, behavior, or material artifacts.

comparative advantage A mutual benefit in the exchange of goods between countries, where each country exports those products in which it is relatively more efficient in production than other countries.

competitive advantage of nations The existence of conditions that give a country an advantage in a specific industry or in producing a particular good or service.

context in cultures (low to high) Low-context cultures, such as Germany, tend to use explicit means of communication in words and readily available information; high-context cultures, such as those in the Middle East, use more implicit means of communication, in which information is embedded in the nonverbal context and understanding of the people.

contract An agreement by the parties concerned to establish a set of rules to govern a business transaction.

control system appropriateness The use of control systems that are individually tailored to the practices and expectations of the host-country personnel.

convergence (of management styles, techniques, and so forth) The phenomenon of increasing similarity of leadership styles resulting from a blending of cultures and business practices through international institutions, as opposed to the **divergence** of leadership styles necessary for different cultures and practices.

core competencies Important corporate resources or skills that bring competitive advantages.

creeping expropriation A government's gradual and subtle action against foreign firms.

creeping incrementalism A process of increasing commitment of resources to one or more geographic regions.

cultural noise Cultural variables that undermine the communications of intended meaning.

CQ - Cultural quotient A person's level of cultural sensitivity and adaptability.

cultural savvy A working knowledge of the cultural variables affecting management decisions.

cultural sensitivity (cultural empathy) A sense of awareness and caring about the culture of other people.

culture The shared values, understandings, assumptions, and goals that over time are passed on and imposed by members of a group or society.

culture shock A state of disorientation and anxiety that results from not knowing how to behave in an unfamiliar culture.

culture-specific reward systems Motivational and compensation approaches that reflect different motivational patterns across cultures.

degree of enforcement The relative degree of enforcement, in a particular country, of the law regarding business behavior, which therefore determines the lower limit of permissible behavior.

differentiation Focusing on and specializing in specific markets.

direct control The control of foreign subsidiaries and operations through the use of appropriate international staffing and structure policies and meetings with home-country executives (as compared with **indirect control**).

distinctive competencies Strengths that allow companies to outperform rivals.

divergence *See* **convergence**.

domestic multiculturalism The diverse makeup of the workforce comprising people from several different cultures in the home (domestic) company.

E-business The integration of systems, processes, organizations, value chains, and entire markets using Internet-based and related technologies and concepts.

E-commerce The selling of goods or services over the Internet.

e-commerce enablers Fulfillment specialists who provide other companies with services such as website translation.

economic risk The level of uncertainty about the ability of a country to meet its financial obligations.

environmental assessment The continuous process of gathering and evaluating information about variables and events around the world that may pose threats or opportunities to the firm.

environmental scanning The process of gathering information and forecasting relevant trends, competitive actions, and circumstances that will affect operations in geographic areas of potential interest.

ethical relativism An approach to social responsibility in which a country adopts the moral code of its host country.

ethnocentric approach An approach in which a company applies the morality used in its home country—regardless of the host country's system of ethics.

ethnocentric staffing approach An approach that fills key managerial positions abroad with persons from headquarters—that is, with parent-country nationals (PCNs).

ethnocentrism The belief that the management techniques used in one's own country are best no matter where or with whom they are applied.

expatriate One who works and lives in a foreign country but remains a citizen of the country where the employing organization is headquartered.

expressive-oriented conflict Conflict that is handled indirectly and implicitly, without clear delineation of the situation by the person handling it.

expropriation The seizure, with inadequate or no compensation, by a local government of the foreign-owned assets of an MNC.

Foreign Corrupt Practices Act A 1977 law that prohibits most questionable payments by US companies to officials of foreign governments to gain business advantages.

foreign direct investment (FDI) Multinational firm's ownership, in part or in whole, of an operation in another country.

franchising An international entry strategy by which a firm (the franchiser) licenses its trademark, products, or services and operating principles to the franchisee in a host country for an initial fee and ongoing royalties.

fully owned subsidiary An overseas operation started or bought by a firm that has total ownership and control; starting or buying such an operation is often used as an entry strategy.

generalizabilty of leadership styles The ability (or lack of ability) to generalize leadership theory, research results, and effective leadership practices from one country to another.

geocentric staffing approach A staffing approach in which the best managers are recruited throughout the company or outside the company, regardless of nationality—often, third-country nationals (TCNs) are recruited.

global corporate culture An integration of the business environments in which firms currently operate, resulting from a dissolution of traditional boundaries and from increasing links among MNCs.

global functional structure Operations are integrated into the activities and responsibilities of each department to gain functional specialization and economies of scale.

globalism Global competition characterized by networks of international linkages that bind countries, institutions, and people in an interdependent global economy and a one-world market.

global geographic (area) structure Divisions are created to cover geographic regions; each regional manager is responsible for operations and performance of the countries within a given region.

globalization The global strategy of the integration of worldwide operations and the development of standardized products and marketing approaches.

global management The process of developing strategies, designing and operating systems, and working with people around the world to ensure sustained competitive advantage.

global management team Collection of managers in or from several countries who must rely on group collaboration if each member is to experience optimum success and goal achievement.

global product (divisional) structure A single product (or product line) is represented by a separate division; each division is headed by its own general manager; each is responsible for its own production and sales functions.

global staffing approach Staff recruited from within or outside of the company, regardless of nationality.

global strategic alliances Working partnerships that are formed around MNCs across national boundaries and often across industries.

governmentalism The tendency of a government to use its policy-setting role to favor national interests rather than relying on market forces.

guanxi The intricate, pervasive network of personal relations that every Chinese person carefully cultivates.

guanxihu A bond between specially connected firms, which generates preferential treatment to members of the network.

haptic Characterized by a predilection for the sense of touch.

high-contact culture One in which people prefer to stand close, touch a great deal, and experience a "close" sensory involvement.

high-context communication One in which people convey messages indirectly and implicitly.

horizontal organization (dynamic network) A structural approach that enables the flexibility to be global and act local through horizontal coordination, shared power, and decision making across international units and teams.

host-country national (HCN) A worker who is indigenous to the local country where the plant is located.

human capital those direct or subcontracted employees whose labor becomes part of the value-added of the firm's product or service. MNCs are increasingly offshoring (outsourcing) that asset around the world in order to lower the cost of human capital

IJV control How a parent company ensures that the way a joint venture is managed conforms to its own interest.

indirect control The control of foreign operations through the use of reports, budgets, financial controls, and so forth. *See* also **direct control**.

individualism The tendency of people to look after themselves and their immediate families only and to value democracy, individual initiative, and personal achievement.

information privacy The right to control information about oneself.

information technology (IT) Electronic systems to convey information.

instrumental-oriented conflict An approach to conflict in which parties tend to negotiate on the basis of factual information and logical analysis.

integration Coordination of markets.

intercultural communication Type of communication that occurs when a member of one culture sends a message to a receiver who is a member of another culture.

internal analysis Determines which areas of a firm's operations represent strengths or weaknesses (currently or potentially) compared to competitors.

internal versus external locus of control Beliefs regarding whether a person controls his own fate and events or they are controlled by external forces.

international business The profit-related activities conducted across national boundaries.

international business ethics The business conduct or morals of MNCs in their relationships to all individuals and entities with whom they come in contact when conducting business overseas.

international codes of conduct The codes of conduct of four major international institutions that provide some consistent guidelines for multinational enterprises relative to their moral approach to business behavior around the world.

international competitor analysis The process of assessing the competitive positions, goals, strategies, strengths, and weaknesses of competitors relative to one's own firm.

internationalization The process by which a firm gradually changes in response to the imperatives of international competition, domestic market saturation, desire for expansion, new markets, and diversification.

international joint venture (IJV) An overseas business owned and controlled by two or more partners; starting such a venture is often used as an entry strategy.

international management The process of planning, organizing, leading, and controlling in a multicultural or cross-cultural environment.

international management teams Collections of managers from several countries who must rely on group collaboration if each member is to achieve success.

international social responsibility The expectation that MNCs should be concerned about the social and economic effects of their decisions regarding activities in other countries.

keiretsu Large Japanese conglomerates of financially linked, and often family-linked, groups of companies, such as Mitsubishi, that do business among themselves whenever possible.

kibun Feelings and attitudes (Korean word).

kinesics Communication through body movements.

kinesic behavior Communication through posture, gestures, facial expressions, and eye contact.

knowledge management The process by which the firm integrates and benefits from the experiences and skills learned by its employees, for example when repatriating managers from the host country.

labor relations The process through which managers and workers determine their workplace relationships.

licensing An international entry strategy by which a firm grants the rights to a firm in the host country to produce or sell a product.

locus of decision making The relative level of decentralization in an organization—that is, the level at which decisions of varying importance can be made—ranging from all decisions made at headquarters to all made at the local subsidiary.

love-hate relationship An expression describing a common attitude of host governments toward MNC investment in their country—they love the economic growth that the MNC brings but hate the incursions on their independence and sovereignty.

low-contact culture Cultures that prefer much less sensory involvement, standing farther apart and touching far less; a "distant" style of body language.

low-context communication One in which people convey messages directly and explicitly.

macropolitical risk event An event that affects all foreign firms doing business in a country or region.

managing environmental interdependence The process by which international managers accept and enact their role in the preservation of ecological balance on the earth.

managing interdependence The effective management of a long-term MNC subsidiary–host-country relationship through cooperation and consideration for host concerns.

maquiladoras US manufacturing or assembly facilities operating just south of the US-Mexico border under special tax considerations.

masculinity The degree to which traditionally "masculine" values—assertiveness, materialism, and the like—prevail in a society.

material culture *See* **object language**.

matrix structure A hybrid organization of overlapping responsibilities.

micropolitical risk event An event that affects one industry or company or only a few companies.

MIS adequacy The ability to gather timely and accurate information necessary for international management, especially in less developed countries.

monochronic cultures Those cultures in which time is experienced and used in a linear way; there is a past, present, and future, and time is treated as something to be spent, saved, wasted, and so on. *See also* **polychronic cultures**.

moral idealism The relative emphasis on long-term, ethical, and moral criteria for decisions versus short-term, cost-benefit criteria. *See also* **utilitarianism**.

moral universalism A moral standard toward social responsibility accepted by all cultures.

multicultural leader A person who is effective in inspiring and influencing the thinking, attitudes, and behavior of people from various cultural backgrounds.

multidomestic strategy Emphasizing local markets, allowing more local responsiveness and specialization.

multinational corporation (MNC) A corporation that engages in production or service activities through its own affiliates in several countries, maintains control over the policies of those affiliates, and manages from a global perspective.

nationalism The practice by a country of rallying public opinion in favor of national goals and against foreign influences.

nationalization The forced sale of an MNC's assets to local buyers with some compensation to the firm, perhaps leaving a minority ownership with the MNC; often involves the takeover of an entire industry, such as the oil industry.

negotiation The process by which two or more parties meet to try to reach agreement regarding conflicting interests.

noise Anything that serves to undermine the communication of the intended meaning.

noncomparability of performance data across countries The control problem caused by the difficulty of comparing performance data across various countries because of the variables that make that information appear different.

nontask sounding (*nemawashi*) General, polite conversation and informal communication before meetings.

nonverbal communication (body language) The transfer of meaning through the use of body language, time, and space.

object language (material culture) How we communicate through material artifacts, whether architecture, office design and furniture, clothing, cars, or cosmetics.

objective-subjective decision-making approach The relative level of rationality and objectivity used in making decisions versus the level of subjective factors, such as emotions and ideals.

open systems model The view that all factors inside and outside a firm—environment, organization, and management—work together as a dynamic, interdependent system.

openness Traits such as open-mindedness, tolerance for ambiguity, and extrovertedness.

outsourcing or offshoring The use of professional, skilled, or low-skilled workers located in countries other than that in which the firm is domiciled.

paralanguage How something is said rather than the content—the rate of speech, the tone and inflection of voice, other noises, laughing, or yawning.

parent-country national (PCN) An employee from the firm's home country sent to work in the firm's operations in another country (*see also* **expatriate**)

parochialism The expectation that "foreigners" should automatically fall into host-country patterns of behavior.

political risk The potential for governmental actions or politically motivated events to occur in a country that will adversely affect the long-run profitability or value of a firm.

polycentric staffing approach An MNC policy of using local host-country nationals (HCNs) to fill key positions in the host country.

polychronic cultures Those cultures that welcome the simultaneous occurrence of many things and emphasize involvement with people over specific time commitments or compartmentalized activities. *See also* **monochronic cultures**.

posturing General discussion that sets the tone for negotiation meetings.

power distance The extent to which subordinates accept unequal power and a hierarchical system in a company.

privatization The sale of government-owned operations to private investors.

projective cognitive similarity The assumption that others perceive, judge, think, and reason in the same way.

proxemics The distance between people (personal space) with which a person feels comfortable.

protectionism A country's use of tariff and nontariff barriers to partially or completely close its borders to various imported products that would compete with domestic products.

questionable payments Business payments that raise significant ethical issues about appropriate moral behavior in either a host nation or other nations.

regiocentric staffing approach An approach in which recruiting for international managers is done on a regional basis and may comprise a specific mix of PCNs, HCNs, and TCNs.

regionalization strategy The global corporate strategy that links markets within regions and allows managers in each region to formulate their own regional strategy and cooperate as quasi-independent subsidiaries.

regulatory environment The many laws and courts of the nation in which an international manager works.

relationship building The process of getting to know one's contacts in a host country and building mutual trust before embarking on business discussions and transactions.

repatriation The process of the reintegration of expatriates into the headquarters organization and career ladder as well as into the social environment.

resilience Traits such as having an internal locus of control, persistence, a tolerance of ambiguity, and resourcefulness.

reverse culture shock A state of disorientation and anxiety that results from returning to one's own culture.

ringi system "Bottom-up" decision-making process used in Japanese organizations.

self-reference criterion An unconscious reference to one's own cultural values; understanding and relating to others only from one's own cultural frame of reference.

separation The retention of distinct identities by minority groups unwilling or unable to adapt to the dominant culture.

stages model *See* **structural evolution.**

stereotyping The assumption that every member of a society or subculture has the same characteristics or traits, without regard to individual differences.

strategic alliances (global) Working partnerships between MNCs across national boundaries and often across industries.

strategic business unit (SBU) A self-contained business within a company with its own functional departments and accounting systems.

strategic freedom of an IJV The relative amount of control that an international joint venture will have, compared with the parents, in choosing suppliers, product lines, customers, and so on.

strategic implementation The process by which strategic plans are realized through the establishment of a *system of fits* throughout an organization with the desired strategy—for example, in organizational structure, staffing, and operations.

strategic planning The process by which a firm's managers consider the future prospects for their company and evaluate and decide on strategy to achieve long-term objectives.

strategy The basic means by which a company competes: the choice of business or businesses in which it operates and how it differentiates itself from its competitors in those businesses.

structural evolution (stages model) The stages of change in an organizational structure that follow the evolution of the internationalization process.

subculture shock A state of disorientation and anxiety that results from the unfamiliar circumstances and behaviors encountered when exposed to a different cultural group in a country than one the person is familiar with.

SWOT analysis An assessment of a firm's capabilities (strengths and weaknesses) relative to those of its competitors as pertinent to the opportunities and threats in the environment for those firms.

subsidiary A business incorporated in a foreign country in which the parent corporation holds an ownership position.

sustainability/sustainable development adopting business strategies and activities that meet the needs of the enterprise and its stakeholders today, while protecting, sustaining and enhancing the human and natural resources that will be needed in the future.

synergy The greater level of effectiveness that can result from combined group effort than from the total of each individual's efforts alone.

technoglobalism A phenomenon in which the rapid developments in information and communication technologies (ICTs) are propelling globalization and vice versa.

terrorism The use of, or threat to use, violence for ideological or political purposes.

transnational corporations (TNCs) Multinational corporations that are truly globalizing by viewing the world as one market and crossing boundaries for whatever functions or resources are most efficiently available; structural coordination reflects the ability to integrate globally while retaining local flexibility; typically owned and managed by nationals from different countries.

transpatriate A term similar to expatriates but referring to managers who may be from any country other than that in which the firm is domiciled, and who tends to work in several countries over time —that is who has no true corporate "home."

turnkey operation When a company designs and constructs a facility abroad, trains local personnel, and turns the key over to local management, for a fee

uncertainty avoidance The extent to which people feel threatened by ambiguous situations; in a company, this results in formal rules and processes to provide more security.

utilitarianism The relative emphasis on short-term cost-benefit (utilitarian) criteria for decisions versus those of long-term, ethical, and moral concerns. *See also* **moral idealism.**

values A person or group's ideas and convictions about what is important, good or bad, right or wrong.

virtual global teams Employees in various locations around the world who coordinate their work and decisions through teleconferencing, e-mail, and so on.

work centrality The degree of general importance that working has in the life of an individual at any given time.

workforce diversity The phenomenon of increasing ethnic diversity in the workforce in the United States and many other countries because of diverse populations and joint ventures; this results in intercultural working environments in domestic companies.

works council In Germany, employee group that shares plant-level responsibility with managers.

World Trade Organization (WTO) A formal structure for continued negotiations to reduce trade barriers and settling trade disputes.

NOTES

Chapter 1

1. Peter Gumbel, "The Meltdown goes global," *Time,* October 20, 2008.
2. *Time,* October 20; Keith Bradsher and Carter Dougherty, "Economic Uncertainty Spreads," www.nytimes.com, October 11, 2008; "World of work 2008: Social Inequality: facts, causes and policies?" International Labour Office, *International Labour Studies,* Geneva: ILO, 2008; http://news.bbc.co.uk/go/pr/fr/-/2/hi/business/7654647.stm, October 10, 2008; Nelson, D. Schwartz, "Economic Puzzles: Suddenly, Europe Looks Pretty Smart," www.nytimes.com, October 19, 2008. Global Competitiveness Report, www.worldeconomicforum.com, 2008; Martin Fackler, "Trouble Without Borders," www.nytimes.com, October 24, 2008; Jeffrey E. Garten, "The Big Bang of Bailouts," *Newsweek,* December 22, 2008; David Barboza, "China Unveils Sweeping Plan for Economy," www.nytimes.com, November 10, 2008; Edmund L. Andrews, "U.S. Plans $800 billion in Lending to Ease Crisis," www.nytimes.com, November 26, 2008; Bettina Wassener, "Japan Moves to Take Stakes in Ailing Companies," www.nytimes.com, January 28, 2009; "Giant Stimulus Plan Proposed for Europe," Associated Press, November 27, 2008; Mure Dickie in Fukuoka and Lindsay Whipp and Robin Harding in Tokyo "Japan unveils emergency measures on economy," December 12, 2008; Justin Fox, "Stimulating the World Markets," www.Time.com, February 3, 2009; "South Korean Exports Fall," *Associated Press,* www.nytimes.com, February 2, 2009; Tara Kalwarski, "World Trade Hits a Wall,"*Business Week,* January 26, 2009; Bob Davis, Carrick Mollenkamp, "Financial Protectionism is Latest Threat to Global Recovery," *Wall Street Journal,* : February 2, 2009; Floyd Norris, "The Upside to Resisting Globalization," www.nytimes.com, February 5, 2009; David Barboza, "China Starts Investing Globally," www.nytimes.com, February 20, 2009; www.worldbank.org, March 21, 2009; Mark Landler and David E. Sanger, "G-20 Pact Has New Rules and Commitments of $1.1 Trillion," www.nytimes.com, April 3, 2009.
3. "World of work 2008: Social Inequality: facts, causes and policies?" International Labour Office, *International Labour Studies,* Geneva: ILO, 2008
4. "Global Breakdown," October 10, 2008. (http://news.bbc.co.uk/go/pr/fr/-/2/hi/business/7654647.stm)
5. J. E. Garten, "The Big Bang of Bailouts," *Newsweek,* December 22, 2008.
6. Floyd Norris, "The Upside to Resisting Globalization," www.nytimes.com, February 5, 2009.
7. *Bob Davis, Carrick Mollenkamp,* "Financial Protectionism Is Latest Threat to Global Recovery," *Wall Street Journal, Feb 2, 2009.*
8. Francesco Guerrera, "The Future of Capitalism, A Need to Reconnect," www.FT.com, March 12, 2009.
9. Mark Landler and David E. Sanger, "G-20 Pact Has New Rules and Commitments of $1.1 Trillion," www.nytimes.com, April 3, 2009.
10. Thomas L. Friedman, *The World Is Flat* (New York: Farrar, Straus and Giroux, 2005): 5.
11. "The Globalization Index 2007," *Foreign Policy* (accessed September 12, 2008).
12. Ibid., 7.
13. H. L. Sirkin, J. W. Hemerling, and A. K. Bhattacharya, *Globality,* Boston Consulting Group, 2008. (New York: Hachette Book Group)
14. Pankaj Ghemawat, *Redefining Global Strategy,* Harvard Business School Publishing Corporation, 2007.
15. www.atkearney.com, accessed September 12, 2008.
16. Fareed Zakaria, *The Post-American World.* New York: Norton, 2008.
17. "World's Largest Corporations," *Fortune,* July 2008.
18. "A Bigger World," *The Economist,* September 20, 2008.
19. P. Stephens, "A Perilous Collision Between Nationalism and Globalisation," *Financial Times,* March 3, 2008.
20. Joseph E. Stiglitz, *Making Globalization Work,* New York: Norton, 2006.
21. Daniel Gross, "Is America Losing at Globalization?" *Newsweek,* September 8, 2008, 66.
22. Peter Coy, *Business Week,* July 31, 2008.
23. Section contributed by Charles M. Byles, Virginia Commonwealth University, April 3, 2009.
24. Europa: European Union institutions and other bodies, "The European Commission," Retrieved March 30, 2009, http://europa.eu/institutions/inst/comm/index_en.htm
25. J. Sapsford and Norihiko Shirouzu, "Mom, Apple Pie and . . . Toyota?" *The Wall Street Journal,* May 11, 2006.
26. David E. Sanger, Jeff Zeleny and Bill Vlasic, "GM to Seek Bankruptcy and a New Start," www.nytimes.com, May 31, 2009.
27. Nanette Byrnes, "Avon: More Than Cosmetic Changes," *Business Week,* March 12, 2007.
28. *The Economist,* September 20, 2008.
29. J. L. Levere, "A Small Company, a Global Approach," www.nytimes.com, January 1, 2004.
30. Ibid.
31. P. Drucker, Interview, in *Fortune,* January 12, 2004.
32. www.wikipedia.org, May 21, 2006.
33. George Parker and Quentin Peel, "A Fractured Europe," *Financial Times,* September 17, 2003, 15.
34. Eric Beinhocker, Ian Davis, and Lenny Mendonca, "The Ten Trends You Have to Watch," *Harvard Business Review* 87, no. 7/8 (2009):,55–60.
35. *James C. Cooper,* "A Resurgent Asia will lead the Global Recovery," *Business Week* 4140 (*2009*): 16.
36. FT Summer School, "China: Rough But Ready for Outsiders," *Financial Times,* August 26, 2003.
37. Sources include: Keith Bradsher, "China Plans to Bolster its Slowing Economy," www.nytimes.com Oct.21, 2008; Jim Yardley and Keith Bradsher, "China, an Engine of Growth, Faces a Global Slump," www.nytimes.com, October 23, 2008; CEQ on FT.com: "Large and in charge," by Arthur Kroeber and Rosealea Yao, July 14 2008; Fareed Zakaria, *The Post American World* (New York: Norton, 2008.); www.worldeconomicforum.gov, accessed October 20, 2008; Thomas Friedman, *The World is Flat* (New York: Farrar, Straus and Giroux, 2005); Tony Fang, Verner Worm, Rosalie L. Tung, "Changing success and failure factors in business negotiations with the PRC" *International Business Review* 17, no. 2 (2008).
38. Keith Bradsher, "China-U.S. Trade Dispute Has Broad Implications," www.nytimes.com, September 15, 2009.
39. Scott Cendrowski, "China Takes the Lead," *Fortune* 160, no. 5 (*2009*): 24.
40. Bradsher, 2009.
41. Friedman, 114.
42. www.worldeconomicforum, accessed October 20, 2008.
43. "A Second-best choice," *The Economist,* September 6, 2008.
44. H. Kumar, "South Asia Looks to Sign Free Trade Pact," www.nytimes.com, December 31, 2003.
45. Elisabeth Malkin, "Nafta's Promise Unfulfilled," www.nytimes.com, March 24, 2008.
46. Ibid.
47. www.wikipedia.org, May 27, 2006.
48. www.cia.gov, September 4, 2008.
49. www.worldbank.org, May 27, 2006.
50. Geri Smith, "Look Who's Pumping out Engineers," *Business Week* (May 22, 2006): 42–43.
    Daniel. Altman, "Managing Globalization," *International Herald Tribune,* March 20, 2008.
51. www.wola.org/economic/cafta/htm, May 13, 2006.
52. "Special Zones Offer Oasis for Investment," Supplement, *Washington Post,* April 29, 2009.
53. Daniel Altman, "Managing Globalization," *International Herald Tribune,* March 20, 2008.
54. Andrew Jack, "Foreign investment in limbo as Putin's Team Backtracks," *Financial Times,* May 1, 2006.
55. Andrew E. Kramer, "BP makes Deep Concessions in Agreement with Russian Partner," *New York Times,* September 5, 2008.
56. Khalid Abdulla-Janahi, Chairman of Ithmaar Bank and Co-Chair of the World Economic Forum on the Middle East.
57. www.statisticssa.gov.za, accessed February 1, 2009.
58. N. Itano, "South African Companies Fill a Void," www.nytimes.com, November 4, 2003.
59. Sources for this section include: www.intel.com; John Boudreau, *San Jose Mercury News,* April 17, 2008; Daniel Altman, "Peeking under the surface of globalization," *International Herald Tribune,* May 4, 2007 (www.Forbes.com, April 2007)
60. World Economic Forum, October 2008.
61. Pete Engardio, "Can the U.S. Bring Jobs back from China?" *Business Week,* June 30, 2008.
62. Friedman, 6.
63. Heather Timmons, "Obama's Plan on Corporate Taxes Unnerves the Indian Outsourcing Industry," www.nytimes.com, May 6, 2009.

64. *Forrester Research Report,* November 2002.

65. J. Fox, "Where Your Job is Going," *Fortune,* November 24, 2003, 84–87.

66. Kerry Miller, "Outsourcing," *Business Week,* June 25, 2007

67. Sol E. Solomon, "India's IT Services Sector reassesses Itself," *Business Week ZD Net Asia,* September 19, 2008.

68. Mehul Srivastava, *Nandini* Lakshman, and Steve Hamm. "Outsourcing Shops Feel The Street's Pain," *Business Week*, October 13, 2008, 80

69. Steve Hamm, "Off-shoring: The sky is not falling: Info from Infosys," *Business Week Asia,* October 10, 2008.

70. "Outsourcing: Make way for China," www.businessweek.com, July 29, 2003.

71. *The Economist,* September 20, 2008.

72. www.A.T.Kearney, accessed September 12, 2008.

73. B. Weiner, "What Executives Should Know About Political Risks," *Management Review* (January 1991): 19–22.

74. "Venezuela is Set to take Control of Cemex Plants," Reuters, in www. businessweek.com (August 19, 2008)

75. David Luhnow and Jose de Cordoba, "Bolivia's President Morales Orders Nationalization of Natural Gas," *Wall Street Journal,* May 2, 2006.

76. Clifford J. Levy, "In Hard Times, Russia Tries to Reclaim Industries," www. nytimes.com, December 8, 2008.

77. Carter Dougherty, "Financial Crisis Dims Hopes for Giant Cross-Border Banks in Europe," www.nytimes.com, January 30, 2009.

78. E. F. Micklous, "Tracking the Growth and Prevalence of International Terrorism," in *Managing Terrorism: Strategies for the Corporate Executive*, ed. P. J. Montana and G. S. Roukis (Westport, CT: Quorum Books, 1983), 3.

79. W. Shreeve, "Be Prepared for Political Changes Abroad," *Harvard Business Review,* (July–August 1984): 111–18.

80. Taoka and Beeman, 112

81. Ibid.

82. Overseas Private Investment Corporation, *Investment Insurance Handbook,* 4, 2000.

83. Schnitzer, Liebrenz, and Kubin, 45–47.

84. B. O'Reilly, "Business Copes with Terrorism," *Fortune,* January 6, 2004, 48.

85. F. John Mathis, "International Risk Analysis," in *Global Business Management in the 1990s,* ed. R. T. Moran (Washington, DC: Beacham, 1990), 33–44.

86. Joseph Kahn, "Dispute Leaves U.S. Executive in Chinese Legal Netherworld," www.nytimes.com, November 1, 2005.

87. Ibid.

88. Rahul Jacob, "Asian Infrastructure: the Biggest Bet on Earth," *Fortune,* October 31, 1994, 139–46.

89. R. J. Radway, "Foreign Contract Agreements," in *Global Business Management in the 1990s,* ed. R. T. Moran (Washington, DC: Beacham, 1990), 93–103.

90. Chris Nicholson, "Bringing the Internet to Remote African Villages," February 1, 2009.

91. Friedman, 176.

92. Jack Goldsmith and Tim Wu, *Who Controls the Internet? Illusions of a Borderless World* (London: Oxford UP, 2006).

93. *Financial Times,* May 17, 2006.

94. Hans Dieter Zimmerman, "E-Business," www.businessmedia.org, June 13, 2000.

95. J. Rajesh, "Five E-Business Trends," Net.Columns, www.indialine.com, February 18, 1999.

96. "Europe's borderless market: the Net," www.businessweek.com, May 17, 2003.

97. "E-Management," *The Economist,* November 11, 2000, 32–34.

98. "E-commerce Report, *New York Times,* March 26, 2001, 7–8.

99. S. Mohanbir and M. Sumant, "Go Global," *Business 2.0,* May 2000, 178–213.

100. A. Chen and M. Hicks, "Going global? Avoid culture clashes," *PC Week,* April 3, 2000, 9–10.

Chapter 2

1. Sources include: "Moral Maze for Retailers Reliant on developing world suppliers," Anonymous. *Financial Times*. July 2, 2008; "Embroidered T-shirt. Price: £4. Cost: Misery, www.news.bbc.co.UK, June 23, 2008; Danny Rogers, "CSR seems to be out of fashion," *PR Week* (London ed.) London: June 27, 2008, 22–23; Maggie Ury, "Primark takes action on child labour," *Financial Times,* June 17, 2008.

2. A. Maitland, "No Hiding Place for the Irresponsible Business," *Financial Times Special Report,* September 29, 2003, 4.

3. Milton Friedman, *Capitalism and Freedom* (Chicago: University of Chicago Press, 1962).

4. T. Donaldson, "Defining the Value of Doing Good Business," *Financial Times,* June 3, 2005.

5. T. Donaldson, June 3, 2005.

6. Ibid.

7. N. Bowie, "The Moral Obligations of Multinational Corporations," in *Problems of International Justice*, ed. LuperFay (New York: Westview Press: 1987), 97–113.

8. Peter Burrows, "Stalking High-Tech Sweatshops," *Business Week,* June 19, 2006, p. 63.

9. Joanna Ramey, "Clinton Urges Industry to Enlist in the War Against Sweatshops," www.labordepartment.com, April 15, 1997.

10. Jem Bendell, "Nike Says Time to Team Up," *The Journal of Corporate Citizenship,* Autumn 2005 i19 p. 10(3).

11. *Business Week,* June 19, 2006, 63.

12. "Sweatshop Police," *Business Week,* October 20, 1997, 30–32.

13. Kathleen A. Getz, "International Codes of Conduct: An Analysis of Ethical Reasoning," *Journal of Business Ethics* 9 (1990): 567–77.

14. "Will the Olympics Boost China's Human Rights," www.businessweek, August 22, 2008

15. Peter Marsh, "Foreign Makers Find Advantages on More Familiar Turf," *Financial Times,* May 8, 2006.

16. *Asian Wall Street Journal,* April 8, 2004.

17. Steven Greenhouse, "A.F.L.-C.I.O. Files a Trade Complaint against China's Labor Practices," *New York Times,* June 9, 2006.

18. Howard W. French, "Despite Web Crackdown, Prevailing Winds Are Free," *New York Times,* February 6, 2006.

19. Ibid.

20. Ibid.

21. B. Einhorn and B. Eglin, "The Great Firewall of China," *Business Week,* January 23, 2006, 63.

22. John Gapper, "Google Is Putting its Own Freedoms at Risk in China," *Financial Times,* January 20, 2006.

23. R. Waters, M. Dickie, and S. Kirchgaessner, "Evildoers? How the West's Net Vanguard Toils Behind the Great Firewall of China," *Financial Times,* February 15, 2006.

24. M. Dickie, "Amnesty Accuses Web Groups over Human Rights in China," *Financial Times,* July 20, 2006.

25. Alison Maitland, "How Ethics Codes Can Be Made to Work," *Financial Times,* March 7, 2005.

26. Swee Hoon Ang, "The Power of Money: A Cross-Cultural Analysis of Business-Related Beliefs," *Journal of World Business* 35, no. 1 (2000): 43.

27. C. J. Robertson and W. F. Crittenden, "Mapping Moral Philosophies: Strategic Implications for Multinational Firms," *Strategic Management Journal* 24 (2003): 385–92.

28. A. Singer, "Ethics—Are Standards Lower Overseas?" *Across the Board* (September 1991): 31–34.

29. Ibid.

30. www.transparencyinternational.org, January 10, 2008.

31. Reena SenGupta, "Trouble at Home for Overseas Bribes," *Financial Times,* February 2, 2006.

32. G. R. Laczniak and J. Naor, "Global Ethics: Wrestling with the Corporate Conscience," *Business,* July–August–September 1985, 152.

33. "How to Respond When Only Bribe Money Talks," *Financial Times,* July 11, 2005.

34. J. T. Noonan, Jr., *Bribes* (New York: Macmillan, 1984), ii.

35. SenGupta.

36. Ibid.

37. M. E. Shannon, "Coping with Extortion and Bribery," in *Multinational Managers and Host Government Interactions*, ed. Lee A Tavis (South Bend, IN: University of Notre Dame Press, 1988).

38. "Oil, politics and corruption," *The Economist,* September 20, 2008, 20.

39. Ibid.

40. P. W. Beamish et al., *International Management* (Homewood, IL: Irwin, 1991).

41. Adapted from Asheghian and Ebrahimi, *International Business* (NY: Harper and Row, 1990).

42. Adapted from R. H. Mason and R. S. Spich, *Management: An International Perspective* (Homewood, IL: Irwin, 1987), 202.

43. www.bbc.co.uk.com, October–November, 2008.

44. R. T. De George, *Competing with Integrity in International Business* (New York: Oxford University Press, 1993), 3–4.

45. György Málovics, Noémi Nagypál Csigéné and Sascha Kraus, "The Role of Corporate Social Responsibility in Strong Sustainability," *Journal of Socio-Economics* 37, no. 3,(2008): 907–18

46. J.A.G. van Kleef and N.J. Roome, "Developing Capabilities and Competence for Sustainable Business Management as Innovation: a Research Agenda," *Journal of Cleaner Production* 15 (2007): 38–51.

47. B. Atkins, "Corporate Social Responsibility: Is it 'Irresponsibility'?" *Corporate Governance Advisor* 14 (2006): 28–29.

48. *Newshour with Jim Lehrer,* PBS news report, November 17, 2008.

49. Ibid.

50. Ibid.
51. S. Tifft. "Who Gets the Garbage," *Time,* July 4, 1988, 42–43.
52. Jang B. Singh and V. C. Lakhan, "Business Ethics and the International Trade in Hazardous Wastes," *Journal of Business Ethics* 8 (1989): 889–99.
53. T. E. Graedel and B. R. Allenby, *Industrial Ecology* (Upper Saddle River, NJ: Prentice Hall, 1995).
54. P. Asheghian and B. Ebrahimi, *International Business* (New York: Harper and Row, 1990), 640–41.

Chapter 3

1. David A. Ricks, *Big Business Blunders: Mistakes in Multinational Marketing* (Homewood, IL: Dow Jones–Irwin, 1983).
2. Carla Joinson, "Why HR Managers Need to Think Globally," *HR Magazine* (April 1998): 2–7.
3. Ibid.
4. J. Stewart Black and Mark Mendenhall, "Cross-Cultural Training Effectiveness: A Review and a Theoretical Framework for Future Research," *Academy of Management Review* 15, no. 1 (1990): 113–136.
5. Geert Hofstede, *Culture's Consequences: International Differences in Work-Related Values* (Beverly Hills, CA: Sage Publications, 1980), 25; E. T. Hall, *The Silent Language* (Greenwich, CT: Fawcett, 1959). For a more detailed definition of the culture of a society, see A.L. Kroeber and C. Kluckholhn, "A Critical Review of Concepts and Definitions," in *Peabody Museum Papers* 47, no. 1 (Cambridge, MA: Harvard University Press, 1952), 181.
6. David Dressler and Donald Carns, *Sociology, The Study of Human Interaction* (New York: Knopf, 1969), 56–57.
7. Lane Kelley, Arthur Whatley, and Reginald Worthley, "Assessing the Effects of Culture on Managerial Attitudes: A Three-Culture Test," *Journal of International Business Studies* (Summer 1987): 17–31.
8. Jangho Lee, T.W. Roehl, and Soonkyoo Choe, "What Makes Management Style Similar and Distinct Across Borders? Growth Experience and Culture in Korean and Japanese Firms," *Journal of International Business Studies* 31, no. 4 (2000): 631–52.
9. E.T. Hall, "The Silent Language in Overseas Business," *Harvard Business Review* (May–June 1960).
10. "One Big Market," *Wall Street Journal*, February 6, 1989, 16.
11. Philip R. Harris and Robert T. Moran, *Managing Cultural Differences* (Houston: Gulf Publishing, 1987).
12. Mansour Javidan and Robert J. House, "Cultural Acumen for the Global Manager: Lessons from Project GLOBE," *Organizational Dynamics* (Spring 2001): 289–305.
13. V. Gupta, P.J. Hanges, and P. Dorfman, "Cultural Clusters: Methodology and Findings," *Journal of World Business* 37 (2002): 11–15.
14. Ibid.
15. Geert Hofstede, *Cultures and Organizations: Software of the Mind* (New York: McGraw-Hill, 1997), 79–108.
16. Elizabeth Weldon and Elisa L. Mustari, "Felt Dispensability in Groups of Coactors: The Effects of Shared Responsibility on Cognitive Effort" (unpublished manuscript, Kellogg Graduate School of Management, Northwestern University).
17. P. Christopher Earley, "Social Loafing and Collectivism: A Comparison of the United States and the People's Republic of China," *Administrative Science Quarterly* 34 (1989): 565–81.
18. H.K. Steensma, L. Marino, and K.M. Weaver, "Attitudes towards Cooperative Strategies: A Cross-Cultural Analysis of Entrepreneurs," *Journal of International Business Studies* 31, no. 4 (2000): 591–609.
19. G. Hofstede, *Culture's Consequences: Comparing Values, Behaviors, Institutions, and Organizations Across Nations,* 2nd ed (Thousand Oaks, CA: Sage, 2001), 500–02.
20. F. Trompenaars, *Riding the Waves of Culture* (London: Nicholas Brealey, 1993).
21. L. Hoeklin, *Managing Cultural Differences: Strategies for Competitive Advantage* (New York: The Economist Intelligence Unit/Addison-Wesley, 1995).
22. SOURCE: J. J. Lawrence and Ryh-song Yeh, "The Influence of Mexican Culture on the Use of Japanese Manufacturing Techniques in Mexico," *Management International Review* 34, no. 1 (1994): 49–66.
23. Hwang Kyu-june at Hanaro Company, Broadband Service Provider, quoted in Andrew Ward, "Love Affair Starts to Grip South Korea's Internet Generation," *Financial Times*, October 14, 2003, 6.
24. Ward, 6
25. Ibid.
26. H. Jeff Smith, "Information Privacy and Marketing: What the U.S. Should (and Shouldn't) Learn from Europe," *California Management Review* 43, no. 2 (2001): 30–34.
27. Ibid.
28. Ibid.
29. "Data Privacy Deal," *Journal of Commerce* (March 28, 2000): 4.
30. R. Howells, "Update on Safe Harbor for International Data Transfer," *Direct Marketing* 63, no. 4 (2000): 40.
31. Smith, 30–34.
32. Sources include: The Indian advantage, November 21, 2008, *by Stefan Stern,* www.FT.com; Mehul Srivastava, "A Backlash Grows in Bangalore Over Tech Revolution: Old-timers and anti-poverty groups are fighting a culture war over the cultural and economic costs of the high-tech boom" www.businessweek.com, November 6, 2008; Anand Giridharadas, "India Calling," www.nytimes.com, November 23, 2008; Jagdeep S. Chhoker, "Leadership and Culture in India: The GLOBE Research Project," www.mgmt3ucalgary.ca/web/globe.nsf/index, November 10, 2001; Emerging Markets: India's Role in the Globalization of IT *Alok Aggarwal. Association for Computing Machinery. Communications of the ACM.* New York: *Jul 2008.* Vol. 51, Iss. 7; pg. 17; India's IT Looks Inward *Anonymous. InformationWeek.* Manhasset: *Mar 10, 2008.*, Iss. 1176; pg. 34, 1 pgs
33. Mehul Srivastava, "A Backlash Grows in Bangalore Over Tech Revolution: Old-timers and anti-poverty groups are fighting a culture war over the cultural and economic costs of the high-tech boom" www.businessweek.com, November 6, 2008.
34. Anand Giridharadas, "India Calling," www.nytimes.com, November 23, 2008.
35. Ibid.
36. Stefan Stern, "The Indian advantage," November 21, 2008, *www.FT.com.*
37. Jagdeep S. Chhoker, "Leadership and Culture in India: The GLOBE Research Project," www.mgmt3.ucalgary.ca/web/globe.nsf/index, November 10, 2001.
38. Mark Landler and Michael Barbaro, "Wal-Mart Finds That Its Formula Doesn't Fit Every Culture," *New York Times,* August 2, 2006.
39. Geert Hofstede, *Culture's Consequences: International Differences in Work-Related Values* (Beverly Hills, CA: Sage, 1980).
40. George W. England, "Managers and Their Value Systems: A Five-Country Comparative Study," *Columbia Journal of World Business* (Summer 1978): 35–44.
41. Philip R. Harris and Robert T. Moran, *Managing Cultural Differences* (Houston: Gulf Publishing, 2004); Lennie Copeland and Lewis Griggs, *Going International* (New York: Random House, 1985); Boye De Mente, *Japanese Etiquette and Ethics in Business* (Lincolnwood, IL: NTC Business Books, 1989); R. L. Tung, *Business Negotiations with the Japanese* (Lexington, MA: Lexington Books, 1984); W. G. Ouchi and A. M. Jaeger, "Theory Z Organization: Stability in the Midst of Mobility," *Academy of Management Review* 3, no. 2 (1978): 305–14; Fernando Quezada and James E. Boyce, "Latin America," in *Comparative Management*, ed. Raghu Nath (Cambridge, MA: Ballinger Publishing, 1988), pp. 245–70; Simcha Ronen, *Comparative and Multinational Management* (New York: John Wiley and Sons, 1986); and V. Terpstra and K. David, *The Cultural Environment of International Business*, 3rd ed. (Cincinnati, OH: South-Western, 1991).
42. Akio Kuzuoka, Forty-year Employee at a Japanese Company, quoted in *The Wall Street Journal,* December 29, 2000.
43. R. G. Linowes, "The Japanese Manager's Traumatic Entry in the United States: Understanding the American–Japanese Cultural Divide," *Academy of Management Review* (1993): 21–38.
44. FT Business School, "Go West for a New Mind-Set," *Financial Times,* October 10, 2004.
45. Ibid.
46. www.ft.com, November 26, 2008.
47. Yumiko Ono and William Spindle, "Japan's Long Decline Makes One Thing Rise—Individualism," *Wall Street Journal,* December 29, 2000, 5.
48. D. Walker, T. Walker, and J. Schmitz, *Doing Business Internationally,* 2ed. (New York: McGraw-Hill, 2003), 188–89.
49. Nicholas Kulish, "The lines a German won't cross," www.nytimes.com, April 4, 2009.
50. Ibid.
51. E. T. Hall and M. R. Hall, *Understanding Cultural Differences* (Yarmouth, ME: Intercultural Press, 1990), 4.
52. Walker et al., 2003, 188.
53. Ibid., 195.
54. John A. Pearce II and Richard B. Robinson, Jr., "Cultivating *Guanxi* as a Foreign Investor Strategy," *Business Horizons* 43, no. 1 (2000): 31.
55. J. Lee, "Culture and Management—A Study of Small Chinese Family Business in Singapore," *Journal of Small Business Management* (July 1996): 17–24.
56. R. Sheng, "Outsiders' Perception of the Chinese," *Columbia Journal of World Business* 14 no. 2 (Summer 2000): 16–22.
57. Henry Yeung Wai-chung, "Debunking the Myths of Chinese Capitalism," May 11, 2005, www.nus.edu.sg/cororate/research/gallery/research30.htm.
58. Ralston et al.
59. http://www.monash.edu.au/news/newsline/story/532
60. Rupa-Pratirupa - Man & Mask Feb 20th.–Apr. 12th 1998, Matighar, IGNCA http://ignca.nic.in/ ex_0032.htm.
61. George B. Whitfield, 2006, Executive Orientation Services of Jakarta (EOS) www.indo.net.id/EOS/.

Chapter 4

1. Kevin J. O'Brien, "Privacy Laws Trip Up Google's Expansion in Parts of Europe," www.nytimes.com, November 18, 2008; Scott Bradner, "Telling Google and Others to do Less Evil," *Network World,* 25, no. 16 (2008): 25; "EU Panel Queries Google on Privacy Concerns," *Wall Street Journal,* May 26, 2007; Laura Smith, "Spotlight on the spy in the surf," Information World Review, Oxford, U.K., November 2007. i.240; Andrew Edgecliffe-Johnson, "Google founders in web privacy warning," www.ft.com, May 19, 2008.
2. E. T. Hall and M. R. Hall, *Understanding Cultural Differences* (Yarmouth, ME: Intercultural Press, 1990), 4.
3. E. Wilmott, "New Media Vision," *New Media Age,* September 9, 1999, 8.
4. Hall and Hall; K. Wolfson and W. B. Pearce, "A Cross-cultural Comparison of the Implications of Self-discovery on Conversation Logics," *Communication Quarterly* 31 (1983): 249–56.
5. H. Mintzberg, *The Nature of Managerial Work* (New York: Harper and Row, 1973).
6. L. A. Samovar, R. E. Porter, and N. C. Jain, *Understanding Intercultural Communication* (Belmont, CA: Wadsworth Publishing, 1981).
7. P. R. Harris and R. T. Moran, *Managing Cultural Differences,* 3rd ed. (Houston: Gulf Publishing, 1991).
8. H. C. Triandis, quoted in *The Blackwell Handbook of Cross-cultural Management,* ed. M. Gannon and K. Newman (Oxford, UK: Blackwell Publishers, 2002).
9. Samovar, Porter, and Jain.
10. Hall and Hall, 15.
11. Adapted from H. C. Triandis, *Interpersonal Behavior* (Monterey, CA: Brooks/Cole, 1997), 248.
12. James R. Houghton, Former Chairman of Corning, Inc., quoted in *Organizational Dynamics* 29, no. 4 (2001).
13. J. Child, "Trust: The Fundamental Bond in Global Collaboration," *Organizaional Dynamics* 29, no. 4 (2001): 274–88.
14. Ibid.
15. World Values Study Group (1994), *World Values Survey, ICPSR Version* (Ann Arbor, MI: Institute for Social Research); R. Inglehart, M. Basanez, and A. Moreno, *Human Values and Beliefs: A Cross-cultural Sourcebook* (Ann Arbor: University of Michigan Press, 1998).
16. Mansour Javidan and Robert J. House, "Cultural Acumen for the Global Manager," *Organizational Dynamics* 29, no. 4 (2001), 289–305.
17. Samovar and Porter; Harris and Moran.
18. M. L. Hecht, P. A. Andersen, and S. A. Ribeau, "The Cultural Dimensions of Nonverbal Communication, in *Handbook of International and Intercultural Communication,* ed. M. K. Asante and W. B. Gudykunst (Newbury Park, CA: Sage Publications, 1989), 163–85.
19. H. C. Triandis, *Interpersonal Behavior* (Monterey, CA: Brooks/Cole, 1977).
20. Harris and Moran.
21. Adapted from N. Adler, *International Dimensions of Organizational Behavior,* 2nd ed. (Boston: PWS-Kent, 1991).
22. D. A. Ricks, *Big Business Blunders: Mistakes in Multinational Marketing* (Homewood, IL: Dow Jones–Irwin, 1983).
23. D. Walker, T. Walker, and J. Schmitz, *Doing Business Internationally* (New York: McGraw-Hill, 2003).
24. P. Garfinkel, "On Keeping your Foot Safely out of Your Mouth," www.nytimes.com, July 13, 2004.
25. Jiatao Li, Katherine R. Xin, Anne Tsui, and Donald C. Hambrick, "Building Effective International Joint Venture Leadership Teams in China," *Journal of World Business* 34, no. 1 (1999): 52–68.
26. Walker et al., 2003.
27. Ibid.
28. R. L. Daft, *Organizational Theory and Design*, 3rd ed. (St. Paul, MN: West Publishing, 1989).
29. Li et al., 1999.
30. O. Klineberg, "Emotional Expression in Chinese Literature," *Journal of Abnormal and Social Psychology* 33 (1983): 517–30.
31. P. Ekman and W. V. Friesen, "Constants Across Cultures in the Face and Emotion," *Journal of Personality and Social Psychology* 17 (1971): 124–29.
32. J. Pfeiffer, "How Not to Lose the Trade Wars by Cultural Gaffes," *Smithsonian* 18, no. 10 (January 1988).
33. E. T. Hall, *The Silent Language* (New York: Doubleday, 1959).
34. Hall and Hall.
35. Ibid.
36. Hecht, Andersen, and Ribeau.
37. Li et al., 1999.
38. Pfeiffer.
39. Hall and Hall.
40. Robert Matthews, "Where East Can Never Meet West," *Financial Times,* October 21, 2005.

41. Hall and Hall.
42. Matthews, 2005.
43. Hecht, Andersen, and Ribeau.
44. Hall and Hall.
45. E. T. Hall and M. R. Hall, *Understanding Cultural Differences* (Yarmouth, ME: Intercultural Press, 1990); Martin Rosch, "Communications: Focal Point of Culture," *Management International Review* 27, no. 4 (1987): 60.
46. M. K. Nydell, *Understanding Arabs* (Yarmouth, ME: Intercultural Press, 1987).
47. Harris and Moran.
48. E. T. Hall, *The Hidden Dimension* (New York: Doubleday, 1966): 15.
49. Hall and Hall.
50. Ibid.
51. Based largely on the work of Nydell; and R. T. Moran and P. R. Harris, *Managing Cultural Synergy* (Houston: Gulf Publishing, 1982): 81–82.
52. Ibid.
53. Hall and Hall.
54. D. C. Barnlund, "Public and Private Self in Communicating with Japan," *Business Horizons* (March–April 1989): 32–40.
55. Hall and Hall.
56. A. Goldman, "The Centrality of 'Ningensei' to Japanese Negotiating and Interpersonal Relationships: Implications for U.S.–Japanese Communication," *International Journal of Intercultural Relations* 18, no. 1 (1994).
57. Jean-Louis Barsoux and Peter Lawrence, "The Making of a French Manager," *Harvard Business Review* (July–August 1991): 58–67.
58. D. Shand, "All Information Is Local: IT Systems Can Connect Every Corner of the Globe, But IT Managers Are Learning They Have to Pay Attention to Regional Differences," *Computerworld* 88 no. 1 (2000).
59. T. Wilson, "B2B Links, European Style: Integrator Helps Applications Cross Language, Currency and Cultural Barriers," *InternetWeek,* October 9, 2000, 27.
60. Shand.
61. Wilmott.
62. *Business Week,* February 1998, 14–15.
63. Wilson.
64. www.Businessfordiplomaticaction.org, retrieved August 19, 2006.
65. R. B. Ruben, "Human Communication and Cross-cultural Effectiveness," in *Intercultural Communication: A Reader,* ed. L. Samovar and R. Porter (Belmont, CA: Wadsworth, 1985), 339.
66. D. Ruben and B. D. Ruben, "Cross-cultural Personnel Selection Criteria, Issues and Methods," in *Handbook of Intercultural Training,* Vol. 1, *Issues in Theory and Design,* ed. D. Landis and R. W. Brislin (New York: Pergamon, 1983), 155–75.
67. Young Yun Kim, *Communication and Cross-cultural Adaptation: An Integrative Theory* (Clevedon, UK; Multilingual Matters, 1988).
68. Ibid.
69. R. W. Brislin, *Cross-cultural Encounters: Face-to-Face Interaction* (New York: Pergamon, 1981).

Chapter 5

1. Sources include: F. Robert Buchanan and Syed T. Anwar (2009). Resource Nationalism and the Changing Business Model for Global Oil, *Journal of World Investment & Trade,* 10(2): (in press). *Corporate Europe Observatory and Platform* (2009). BP case and the Russian bear: A case study, (January): 1–7; *Financial Times* (various issues); *TNK-BP.* (2009). BP, AAR say management team completed for TNK-BP joint venture, (June 20), http://www.tnk-bp.com/press/news/2003/6/22/; *Timesonline.* (2008). TNK-BP: Timeline of events, (July 7): http://business.timesonline.co.uk/tol/business/industry_sectors/natural_resources/article4286033.ece; *Wall Street Journal* (various issues).
2. Clive Thompson, "Google in China: the Big Disconnect," www.nytimes.com, April 23, 2006.
3. John Pfeiffer, "How Not to Lose the Trade Wars by Cultural Gaffes," *Smithsonian* 18, no. 10 (1988): 145–56.
4. Nancy J. Adler, *International Dimensions of Organizational Behavior,* 4th ed. (Boston: PWS-Kent, 2002), 208–32.
5. Philip R. Harris and Robert T. Moran, *Managing Cultural Differences,* 3rd ed. (Houston: Gulf Publishing, 1991).
6. John L. Graham and Roy A. Herberger, Jr., "Negotiators Abroad—Don't Shoot from the Hip," *Harvard Business Review* (July–August 1983): 160–68; Adler; John L. Graham, "A Hidden Cause of America's Trade Deficit with Japan," *Columbia Journal of World Business* (Fall 1981): 5–15.
7. Phillip D. Grub, "Cultural Keys to Successful Negotiating," in *Global Business Management in the 1990s,* ed. F. Ghader et al. (Washington, DC: Beacham, 1990): 24–32.
8. S. E. Weiss and W. Stripp, *Negotiation with Foreign Business Persons: An Introduction for Americans with Propositions on Six Cultures* (New York University Faculty of Business Administration, February 1985).
9. R. Fisher and W. Ury, *Getting to Yes* (Boston: Houghton Mifflin, 1981).

10. S. Weiss, "Negotiating with 'Romans,'" *Sloan Management Review* (Winter 1994): 51–61.

11. John A. Reeder, "When West Meets East: Cultural Aspects of Doing Business in Asia," *Business Horizons* (January–February 1987): 72.

12. Adler, 197.

13. Fisher and Ury.

14. Lennie Copeland and Lewis Griggs, *Going International* (New York: Random House, 1985), 85.

15. Adler, 197–98.

16. Fisher and Ury.

17. Jeanne M. Brett, *Negotiating Globally* (San Francisco, CA: John Wiley and Sons, 2001).

18. G. Fisher, *International Negotiation: A Cross-cultural Perspective* (Chicago: Intercultural Press, 1980).

19. *China Economic Review*. (2007). Danone vs. Wahaha, (September 2007), http://www.chinaeconomicreview.com/cer/2007_09/Danone_v_Wahaha.html; The *Economist* (various issues); *Financial Times* (various issues); Tao, Jingzhou, and Hillier, Edward. (2008). A tale of two companies, *Chinabusinessreview.com*, (May–June 2008): 44–47; *Wall Street Journal* (various issues); *Wikipedia*. (2009). Groupe Danone, http://en.wikipedia.org/wiki/Groupe_Danone; *Wikipedia*. (2009). Wahaha, http://en.wikipedia.org/wiki/Wahaha.

20. Pfeiffer.

21. *Wall Street Journal*, February 2, 1994.

22. Pierre Casse, *Training for the Multicultural Manager: A Practical and Cross-cultural Approach to the Management of People* (Washington, D.C.: Society for Intercultural Education, Training, and Research, 1982).

23. John L. Graham, "Brazilian, Japanese, and American Business Negotiations," *Journal of International Business Studies* (Spring–Summer 1983): 47–61.

24. T. Flannigan, "Successful Negotiating with the Japanese," *Small Business Reports* 15, no. 6 (1990): 47–52.

25. Graham, 1983; Boye De Mente, *Japanese Etiquette and Ethics in Business* (Lincolnwood, IL: NTC Business Books, 1989).

26. Robert H. Doktor, "Asian and American CEOs: A Comparative Study," *Organizational Dynamics* (Winter 1990): 49.

27. Harris and Moran, 461.

28. Adler, 181.

29. These profiles are adapted from Pierre Casse, *Managing Intercultural Negotiations: Guidelines for Trainers and Negotiators* (Washington, DC: Society for Intercultural Education, Training, and Research, 1985).

30. D. K. Tse, J. Francis, and J. Walls, "Cultural Differences in Conducting Intra- and Inter-Cultural Negotiations: A Sino-Canadian Comparison," *Journal of International Business Studies* (3rd Quarter 1994): 537–55.

31. B. W. Husted, "Bargaining with the Gringos: An Exploratory Study of Negotiations Between Mexican and U.S. Firms," *International Executive* 36, no. 5 (1994): 625–44.

32. Pierre Casse, *Training for the Cross-cultural Mind*, 2nd ed. (Washington, DC: Society for Intercultural Education, Training, and Research, 1981).

33. Nigel Campbell, John L. Graham, Alain Jolibert, and Hans Meissner, "Marketing Negotiations in France, Germany, the United Kingdom, and the United States," *Journal of Marketing* 52 (1988): 49–63.

34. Neil Rackham, "The Behavior of Successful Negotiators" (Reston, VA: Huthwaite Research Group, 1982).

35. J. Teich, H. Wallenius, and J. Wallenius, "World-Wide-Web Technology in Support of Negotiation and Communication," *International Journal of Technology Management* 17, nos. 1/2 (1999): 223–39.

36. Ibid.

37. Ibid.

38. A. Rosette, Jeanne Brette, Zoe Barsness, Anne Lytle, "When Cultures Clash Electronically: The Impact of E-mail and Culture on Negotiation Behavior," The Dispute Resolution Research Center, Northwestern University, accessed February 9, 2009.

39. J. A. Pearce II and R. B. Robinson, Jr., "Cultivating *Guanxi* as a Foreign Investor Strategy," *Business Horizons* 43, no. 1 (January 2000): 31.

40. Rosalie L. Tung, Verner Worm, and Tony Fang, "Sino-Western Business Negotiations Revisited—30 Years after China's Open Door Policy," *Organizational Dynamics* 37, no. 1 (2008): 60–74.

41. Joan H. Coll, "Sino–American Cultural Differences: The Key to Closing a Business Venture with the Chinese," *Mid-Atlantic Journal of Business* 25, no. 2–3 (December 1988/January 1989): 15–19.

42. M. Loeb, "China: A Time for Caution," *Fortune*, February 20, 1995, 129–30.

43. O. Shenkar and S. Ronen, "The Cultural Context of Negotiations: The Implications of Chinese Interpersonal Norms," *Journal of Applied Behavioral Science* 23, no. 2 (1987): 263–75.

44. Tse et al.

45. J. Brunner, teaching notes, the University of Toledo.

46. Kam-hon Lee, Guang Yang, and John L. Graham, "Tension and Trust in International Business Negotiations: American Executives Negotiating with Chinese Executives," *Journal of International Business Studies* 37, no. 5 (2006): 623.

47. Joanna M. Banthin and Leigh Stelzer, "Ethical Dilemmas in Negotiating Across Cultures: Problems in Commercial Negotiations between American Businessmen and the PRC," paper presented at 1st International Conference on East–West Joint Ventures, October 19–20, 1989, State University of New York–Plattsburgh; and J. M. Banthin and L. Stelzer, "'Opening' China: Negotiation Strategies When East Meets West," *Mid-Atlantic Journal of Business* 25, no. 2–3 (December 1988/January 1989).

48. Brunner.

49. Pearce and Robinson.

50. Ibid.

51. Ibid.

52. Tony Fang, Verner Worm, and Rosalie L. Tung, "Changing Success and Failure Factors in Business Negotiations with the PRC," *International Business Review*, 17, 2008.

53. C. Blackman, "An Inside Guide to Negotiating," *China Business Review*, 27, no. 3 (May 2000): 44–45.

54. Brunner.

55. Boye De Mente, *Chinese Etiquette and Ethics in Business* (Lincolnwood, IL: NTC Business Books, 1989), 115–23.

56. S. Stewart and C. F. Keown, "Talking with the Dragon: Negotiating in the People's Republic of China," *Columbia Journal of World Business* 24, no. 3 (Fall 1989): 68–72.

57. Banthin and Stelzer, "'Opening' China."

58. Fang et al., 2008.

59. Blackman.

60. Ibid.

61. Lucian Pye, *Chinese Commercial Negotiating Style* (Cambridge, MA: Oelgeschlager, Gunn, and Hain, 1982).

62. Fang et al., 2008.

63. W. B. Gudykunst and S. Ting Tomey, *Culture and Interpersonal Communication* (Newbury Park, CA: Sage Publications, 1988).

64. W. Gudykunst, L. Stewart, and S. Ting-Toomey, *Communication, Culture, and Organizational Processes*. Sage Publications, 1985.

65. L. Copeland and L. Griggs, *Going International* (New York: Random House, 1985), 80.

66. M. A. Hitt, B. B. Tyler, and Daewoo Park, "A Cross-cultural Examination of Strategic Decision Models: Comparison of Korean and U.S. Executives," in *Best Papers Proceedings of the 50th Annual Meeting of the Academy of Management* (San Francisco, CA, August 12–15, 1990), 111–15; G. Fisher, *International Negotiation: A Cross-cultural Perspective* (Chicago: Intercultural Press, 1980); G. W. England, "Managers and Their Value Systems: A Five-Country Comparative Study," *Columbia Journal of World Business* 13, no. 2 (1978); W. Whitely and G. W. England, "Variability in Common Dimensions of Managerial Values Due to Value Orientation and Country Differences," *Personnel Psychology* 33 (1980): 77–89.

67. Hitt, Tyler, and Park, 114.

68. B. M. Bass and P. C. Burger, *Assessment of Managers: An International Comparison* (New York: Free Press, 1979), 91.

69. Copeland and Griggs; M. K. Badawy, "Styles of Mideastern Managers," *California Management Review* 22 (1980): 51–58.

70. N. Namiki and S. P. Sethi, "Japan," in *Comparative Management—A Regional View*, ed. R. Nath (Cambridge, MA: Ballinger Publishing, 1988), 74–76.

71. De Mente, *Japanese Etiquette*, 80.

72. S. Naoto, *Management and Industrial Structure in Japan* (New York: Pergamon Press, 1981); Namiki and Sethi.

73. Harris and Moran, 397.

74. S. P. Sethi and N. Namiki, "Japanese-Style Consensus Decision-Making in Matrix Management: Problems and Prospects of Adaptation," in *Matrix Management Systems Handbook*, ed. D. I. Cleland (New York: Van Nostrand, 1984), 431–56.

Chapter 6

1. www.southafrica.info, accessed February 15, 2009.

2. Ibid.

3. OECD International Direct Investment Database, www.oecd.org/daf/investment/statistics, accessed January 7, 2009.

4. "Business Breaks out the Ax," *Business Week*, January 26, 2009.

5. Bill Vlasic and Nick Bunkley, "G.M.'s Latest Plan Envisions a Much Smaller Automaker," www.nytimes.com, Aprl 28, 2009.

6. Pete Engardio, "Emerging Giants," *Business Week*, July 31, 2006, 41–49.

7. Ibid.

8. Steve Hamm, "IBM vs. Tata: Who's More American?" *Business Week*, April 23, 2008.

9. Ibid.

10. Eric Beinhocker, Ian Davis, and Lenny Mendonca, *Harvard Business Review* 87, no. 7/8 (2009): 55–60.

11. S. Daneshkhu, "U.K. Tops List for Foreign Direct Investment," *Financial Times,* June 29, 2006.

12. D. Kirkpatrick, "A Growing AOL Europe Now Sets Example for U.S.," www.nytimes.com, September 8, 2003.

13. A. MacDonald, A. Lucchetti, and E. Taylor, "Long City-Centric, Financial Exchanges Are Going Global," *Wall Street Journal,* May 27, 2006.

14. David Jolly, "Merck to Buy Schering-Plough for $41.1 Billion," *New York Times,* March 10, 2009.

15. Engardio.

16. A. K. Gupta and V. Govindarajan, "Managing Global Expansion: A Conceptual Framework," *Business Horizons* (March/April 2000).

17. Dean Foust, "Taking Off Like 'A Rocket Ship'," *Business Week,* April 3, 2006.

18. Ibid.

19. "McDonald's goes on the offensive," www.msn.com, Money Blog.

20. Nanette Byrnes, "Avon: More Than Cosmetic Changes," *Business Week,* March 12, 2007.

21. Haig Simonian, "Cement Industry suffers amid global downturn," www.FT.com, November 13, 2008; E. Malkin, "Mexican Cement Company Bids for Australian Concern," www.nytimes.com October 28, 2006; David Oakley and Adam Thomson, "Cemex tumbles as it fails to refinance debt," www.FT.com, December 11, 2008; Joel Millman, "The Fallen: Lorenzo Zambrano: Hard Times for Cement Man," *Wall Street Journal,* December 11, 2008.

22. Joel Millman, "The Fallen: Lorenzo Zambrano: Hard Times for Cement Man," *Wall Street Journal,* December 11, 2008.

23. Ibid.

24. "Special Zones Offer Oasis for Investment," *Washington Post Supplement,* April 29, 2009.

25. Priscilla Murphy, "Companies rush to complete M&A deals in Brazil ahead of uncertainty about tax break after 2009," www.mergermarket.com, February 19, 2009.

26. M. McCarthy, M. Pointer, D. Ricks, and R. Rolfe, "Managers' Views on Potential Investment Opportunities," *Business Horizons* (July–August 1993): 54–58.

27. M. Maynard, "Foreign Makers, Settled in South, Pace Car Industry," *New York Times,* June 17, 2006.

28. Henry Mintzberg, "Strategy Making in Three Modes," *California Management Review* (Winter 1973): 44–53.

29. www.sanyo.com, accessed March 24, 2009.

30. www.siemens.com, accessed March 24, 2009.

31. Helen Deresky and Elizabeth Christopher, *International Management* (Pearson Education Australia, 2008.)

32. Arvind V. Phatak, *International Dimensions of Management,* 2nd ed. (Boston: PWS-Kent, 1989).

33. M. Porter, *Competitive Strategy* (New York: Free Press, 1980).

34. This section contributed by Charles M. Byles, Professor, Virginia Commonwealth University, March 11, 2009.

35. Mike W. Peng, *Global Strategy,* 2nd, Southwestern, Cengage Learning, 2009.

36. Douglass C. North, *Institutions, Institutional Change, and Economics Performance,* New York: Cambridge University Press, 1990; W. Richard Scott, *Institutions and Organizations,* Thousand Oaks, CA, Sage Publications, 1995.

37. Peng, 2009; Mike W. Peng, Denis YL Yang, and Yi Jiang, "An institution-based view of international business strategy: a focus on emerging economies," *Journal of International Business Studies,* 39, no. 5, July–August 2008; *The Economist,* "Order in the Jungle," March 13, 2008.

38. *The Economist,* 2008.

39. Peng, 2009.

40. Ibid.

41. Peng, Yang, and Jiang, 2008.

42. Ibid.

43. www.Mitsubishi.com, January 20, 2009.

44. Diane J. Garsombke, "International Competitor Analysis," *Planning Review* 17, no. 3 (1989): 42–47.

45. C. K. Prahalad and Gary Hamel, "The Core Competence of the Corporation," *Harvard Business Review* (May–June 1990): 79–91.

46. Ibid.

47. Diane J. Garsombke, "International Competitor Analysis," *Planning Review* 17, no. 3 (1989): 42–47.

48. P. Ghemawat, "Distance Still Matters," *Harvard Business Review* 79, no. 8 (2001): 137–47.

49. M. E. Porter, "Changing Patterns of International Competition," in *The Competitive Challenge,* ed. D. J. Teece (Boston: Ballinger, 1987), 29–30.

50. T. Chen, "Network Resources for Internationalization," *Journal of Management Studies* 40: 1107–30.

51. Porter, 1987.

52. P. W. Beamish et al., *International Management* (Homewood, IL: Irwin, 1991).

53. A. Palazzo, "B2B Markets—Industry Basics," www.FT.com, January 28, 2001.

54. "A Bigger World," *The Economist,* September 20, 2008.

55. Ibid.

56. Nick Bunkley and Bill Vlasic, "Chrysler and Union Agree to Deal Before Federal Deadline," www.nytimes.com, April 27, 2009.

57. A. J. Morrison, D. A. Ricks, and K. Roth, "Globalization versus Regionalization: Which Way for the Multinational?" *Organizational Dynamics* 19 (Winter 1991).

58. "Wal-Mart Selling Stores and Leaving South Korea," www.nytimes, March 23, 2006.

59. Beamish et al.

60. Pankaj Ghemawat, *Redefining Global Strategy,* Harvard Business School Publishing, 2007.

61. www.panasonic.net, accessed January 3, 2009.

62. Ghemawat, 2007.

63. Thomas Friedman, *The World is Flat* (New York: Farrar, Straus, and Giroux, 2005).

64. Yoram Wind and Susan Douglas, "International Portfolio Analysis and Strategy: The Challenge of the 1980s," *Journal of International Business Studies* (Fall 1991): 69–82.

65. Daniel J. Isenberg, "The Global Entrepreneur," *Harvard Business Review,* December 2008.

66. Ibid.

67. www.ibm.com, April 10, 2001.

68. Bob Tedeschi, "E-Commerce Report; Sensing economic opportunities, many developing nations are laying the groundwork for online commerce," www.nytimes, November 20, 2008.

69. Sorid, 2008.

70. P. Greenberg, "It's Not a Small eCommerce World, After All," www.ecommercetimes.com, February 23, 2001.

71. Ibid.

72. M. Porter, *The Competitive Advantage of Nations* (New York: Free Press, 1990).

73. S. Butler, "Survivor: B2B Style," www.emarketer.com/analysis/ecommerce, April 13, 2001.

74. "eBusiness Trends," www.idc.com/ebusinesstrends, April 12, 2001.

75. "Online Auctions Free Procurement Savings," BHP Corporate Services, www.bhp.com, April 20, 2001.

76. "eBay Inc. Outlines Global Business Strategy at 2006 Analyst Conference," *Canada News Wire Group,* May 4, 2006.

77. Ibid.

78. Bruce Einhorn, "How China's Alibaba is Surviving and Thriving," *Business Week,* April 9, 2009.

79. M. Sawhney and S. Mandal, "Go Global," *Business 2.0,* May 2000.

80. Ibid.

81. B. Bright, "E-Commerce: How Do You Say 'Web?' Planning to Take Your Online Business International? Beware: E-Commerce Can Get Lost in Translation," *Wall Street Journal,* May 23, 2005.

82. Ibid.

83. Ibid.

84. A. Baxter, "Rewards and Risks of Going Global," *Financial Times,* January 4, 2006.

85. U.S. Department of Commerce, 2005.

86. Peter Marsh, "Play the Home Advantage," *Financial Times,* November 26, 2008.

87. Ibid.

88. Harold L. Sirkin, James W. Hemerling, and Arindam K. Bhattacharya, *Globality: Competing with Everyone from Everywhere for Everything* (New York: Hachette Publishing Company, 2008.)

89. *Dante Di Gregorio, Martina Musteen, Douglas E Thomas,* "Offshore outsourcing as a source of international competitiveness for SMEs," *Journal of International Business Studies.* Washington: *Aug 2009.* Vol. 40, Iss. 6; pg. 969,

90. "Learning to Live with Offshoring," *Business Week,* January 30, 2006, p.122.

91. J. Johnson, "India at Center of Microsoft's World," *Financial Times,* December 8, 2005.

92. William Hoffman, "Trend to IT Outsourcing Slows as Companies Reassess the Benefits," *Shipping Digest,* August 28, 2006.

93. Hewitt Associates Research Press Release, CNBC-TV March 5, 2004.

94. S. Hamm, "Big Blue Shift," *Business Week,* June 5, 2006.

95. Manjeet Kripalani,"Call Center? That's so 2004,"*Business Week,* August 7, 2006, 40–42.

96. Pete Engardio, "The Future of Outsourcing," *Business Week,* January 30, 2006, 50.

97. Manjeet Kripalani, "Five Offshore Practices that Pay Off," *Business Week,* January 30, 2006, 60.

98. S. Zahra and G. Elhagrasey, "Strategic Management of IJVs," *European Management Journal* 12, no. 1 (1994): 83–93.

99. Yigang Pan and Xiaolia Li, "Joint Venture Formation of Very Large Multinational Firms," *Journal of International Business Studies* 31, no. 1 (2000): 179–81.

100. R. Bream and Arkady Ostrovsky, "Merger Leaves Rivals Lagging Behind," *Financial Times,* June 27, 2006.

101. Kenichi Ohmae, "The Global Logic of Strategic Alliances," *Harvard Business Review* (March–April 1989): 143–54.

102. Zahra and Elhagrasey.

103. Bill Vlasic and Nick Bunkley, "Alliance With Fiat Gives Chrysler Another Partner and Lifeline," www.nytimes.com, January 21, 2009.

104. "A Bigger World," *The Economist*, September 20, 2008.

105. "Lenovo to Lay Off 1,000," www.PCWorld.com, March 16, 2006.

106. P. Meller, "Procter and Gamble Gets European Approval to Buy Gillette," *New York Times*, July 16, 2005.

107. Simeon Kerr, Joseph Menn, "Yahoo buys Arabic internet portal," *Financial Times*. London (UK): Aug 26, 2009. pg. 18

108. Richard Milne. "European Business is Changing, One Step at a Time." *Financial Times* (August 14, 2008): 11.

109. L. Miller, "Go East, Young Company," www.businessweek.com, October 22, 2003.

110. Global Competitiveness Report 2009–2010, www.worldeconomicforum.org, September 8, 2009.

111. Global Competitiveness Report 2009–2010, www.worldeconomicforum.org, September 8, 2009.

112. Julia Manea and Robert Pearce, "MNEs' Strategies in Central and Eastern Europe: Key Elements of Subsidiary Behaviour," *Management International Review* 46, no. 2 (2006): 235–55.

113. Ibid.

114. Milne, 2008.

115. N. G. Carr.

116. Ibid.

117. D. Sanger, "Backing Down on Steel Tariffs, U.S. Strengthens Trade Group," www.nytimes.com, December 5, 2003.

118. "EU Renews Browser Dispute with Microsoft; Commission Accuses Software Maker of Stifling Competition," *Reuters*, January 16, 2009.

119. Syed Anwar, "EU's Competition Policy and the GE-Honeywell Merger Fiasco: Transatlantic Divergence and Consumer and Regulatory Issues," *Thunderbird International Business Review* 47, no. 5 (2005): 601–26.

120. Ibid.

121. L. E. Brouthers, S. Werner, and E. Matulich, "The Influence of TRIAD Nations' Environments on Price-quality Product Strategies and MNC Performance," *Journal of International Business Studies* 31, no. 1 (2000): 39–62.

122. Ibid.

123. Excerpted and adapted from *International Management—Concepts and Cases* by A.V. Phatak, 270–75, Cincinnati, OH: South-Western College Publishing, 1997.

124. Yigang Pan and David K. Tse, "The Hierarchical Model of Market Entry Modes," *Journal of International Business Studies* 31, no. 4 (2000): 535–54.

125. Gupta and Govindarajan.

126. Ibid.

127. A. E. Serwer, "McDonald's Conquers the World," *Fortune*, October 17, 1994.

128. G. Hofstede, *Cultures and Organizations: Software of the Mind* (London: McGraw-Hill, 1991).

129. Pan and Tse.

130. Hofstede.

131. Pan and Tse.

132. Hofstede.

133. Pan and Tse.

Chapter 7

1. Mary B. Teagarden and Dong Hong Cai, "Learning from Dragons who are Learning from Us:: Developmental Lessons from China's Global Companies," *Organizational Dynamics* 38, no. 1 (2009): 73–81, copyright 2009 Elsevier, used with permission of Elsevier.

2. B. R. Schlender, "How Toshiba Makes Alliances Work," *Fortune*, October 4, 1993, p. 116–20.

3. D. Lei and J. W. Slocum, Jr., "Global Strategic Alliances: Payoffs and Pitfalls," *Organizational Dynamics* (Winter 1991).

4. Julie MacIntosh and Francesco Guerrera, "Cancelled M&As Close to Eclipsing Takeovers," www.ft.com, December 1, 2008.

5. Dana Cimilluca and Sara Schaefer Munoz, "Lloyds Reaches Deal with U.K. on Bailout," *Wall Street Journal*, March 7, 2009.

6. J. Griffiths, "A Marriage of Two Mindsets," *Financial Times*, March 16, 2005.

7. Ibid.

8. Ibid.

9. Robin Harding and Robin Kwong, "*Abu Dhabi* to take on Taiwan in chipmaking big league," *Financial Times*. London (UK): Sep 8, 2009. pg. 16.

10. J. Tagliabue, "Thomson and TCL to Join TV Units," www.nytimes.com, November 4, 2003.

11. *The Economist*, September 20, 2008.

12. Bill Vlasic and Nick Bunkley, "Alliance with Fiat Gives Chrysler another Partner and Lifeline," www.nytimes.com, January 21, 2009.

13. Micheline Maynard, "Chrysler Bankruptcy Plan Is Announced." www.nytimes.com, April 30, 2009.

14. Ibid.

15. Thomas Friedman, *The World Is Flat* (New York: Farrar, Straus and Giroux, 2005), 144.

16. Heather Timmons, "French Company Joins Indian Utility in a Deal for Nuclear Plants," www.nytimes,com, February 5, 2009.

17. www.covisint.com.

18. "EU Agrees to Rules on Mergers," *Financial Times*, November 28, 2003.

19. Daniel Dombey, "European Takeover Proposals Anger U.S.," *Financial Times*, November 2, 2003.

20. "The Return of the Deal," www.businessweek, November 24, 2003.

21. www.e4engineering.com, January 4, 2001.

22. Tim Burt, "Disney's Asian Adventure," *Financial Times*, October 30, 2003.

23. Ibid.

24. Ibid.

25. Ibid.

26. Ibid.

27. D. Lei, "Offensive and Defensive Uses of Alliances," in Heidi Vernon-Wortzel and L. H. Wortzel, *Strategic Management in a Global Economy*, 3rd ed. (New York: John Wiley & Sons, 1997).

28. Andres Parker and Gerrit Wiesmann, "Cross-border Sensitivities Give Grounds for Pessimism," *Financial Times*, Sep 9, 2009.

29. R. N. Osborn and C. C. Baughn, "Forms of Interorganizational Governance for Multinational Alliances," *Academy of Management Journal* 33, no. 3 (1990): 503–19.

30. Lei, 1997.

31. Steve Lohr, "China Poses Trade Worry as It Gains in Technology," www.nytimes.com, January 13, 2004.

32. Lei, 1997.

33. T. L. Wheelen and J. D. Hunger, *Strategic Management and Business Policy*, 6th ed. (Reading, MA: Addison-Wesley, 1998).

34. Shameen Prashantham and Julian Birkinshaw, "Dancing with Gorillas: How Small Companies Can Partner Effectively With MNCs," *California Management Review* 51, no. 1 (2008), 6-23.

35. Ibid.

36. Dovev Lavie, "Capturing Value from Alliance Porfolios," *Organizational Dynamics* 38, no. 1 (2009): 26–36.

37. Ibid.

38. Lei, 1997.

39. Wheelen and Hunger.

40. Catherine Belton in Moscow, "Foreign investment: Future unclear as perceived risk grows," www.ft.com, September 30, 2008.

41. Andrew Kramer, "Norweigan stake in Russian Joint Venture Seized," www.nytimes.com, March 13, 2009.

42. A. Kramer, "Moscow presses BP to Sell a Big Gas Field to Gazprom," *New York Times*, June 23, 2007.

43. N. Buckley, "Huge Gains but Also a Lot of Pain," *Financial Times*, October 11, 2005.

44. www.transparencyinternational.org

45. Andrew E. Kramer, "Ikea Tries to Build a Case Against Russian Graft," www.nytimes,com, September 12, 2009.

46. Guy Chazan, "GM Venture in Russia Hits Snag Following Kremlin Involvement," *Wall Street Journal*, February 18, 2006.

47. Foreign Investment Advisory Council, http://www.fiac.ru/files/fiac_survey_2008_eng.pdf, accessed January 29, 2009.

48. Ibid.

49. N. Buckley, "An Unmissable Opportunity," *Financial Times*, April 5, 2005.

50. "Special Zones Offer Oasis for Investment," *Washington Post Supplement*, April 29, 2009.

51. N. Buckley, "Huge Gains but Also a Lot of Pain," *Financial Times*, October 11, 2005.

52. M. A. Hitt, D. Ahlstrom, M. T. Dacin, E. Levitas, and L. Svobodina, "The Institutional Effects on Strategic Alliance Partner Selection in Transition Economies: China Versus Russia," *Organization Science* 15, no 2 (2004): 173–85.

53. Garry Bruton, David Ahistrom, Michael Young, Yuri Rubanik, " In Emerging Markets, Know What Your Partners Expect." *Wall Street Journal*, December 15, 2008.

54. A.E. Serwer, "McDonald's Conquers the World," *Fortune*, October 17, 1994.

55. Jack Welch (then CEO of GE) interviewed in *Fortune*, March 8, 1999.

56. Josh Green, *Harvard Business Review*, 87 no. 7/8 (2009): 19.

57. P. Engardio, "The Future of Outsourcing," *Business Week*, January 30, 2006, 50.

58. Ibid.

59. M. Kripalani, D. Foust, S. Holmes, and P. Enga, "Five Offshore Practices that Pay Off," *Business Week*, January 30, 2006, 60.

60. Josh Green, *Harvard Business Review* 87 no. 7/8 (2009): 19.

61. J. M. Geringer, "Strategic Determinants of Partner Selection Criteria in International Joint Ventures," *Journal of International Business Studies* (First Quarter 1991): 41–62.

62. J. M. Geringer and L. Hebert, "Control and Performance of International Joint Ventures," *Journal of International Business Studies* 20, no. 2 (1989).

63. Geringer, 1991.

64. P. Marsh, "Partnerships Feel the Indian Heat," *Financial Times*, June 22, 2006.

65. Ibid.

66. P. W. Beamish et al., *International Management* (Homewood, IL: Irwin, 1991).

67. J. L. Schaan and P. W. Beamish, "Joint Venture General Managers in Less Developed Countries," in *Cooperative Strategies in International Business*, ed. F. Contractor and P. Lorange (Toronto: Lexington Books, 1988), 279–99.

68. Oded Shenkar and Yoram Zeira, "International Joint Ventures: A Tough Test for HR," *Personnel* (January 1990): 26–31.

69. R. Mead, *International Management* (Cambridge, MA: Blackwell Publishers, 1994).

70. R. Duane Ireland and M.A. Hitt, "Achieving and Maintaining Strategic Competitiveness in the 21st Century: the Role of Strategic Leadership," *Academy of Management Executive* 19, no. 4 (2005): 63.

71. R. S. Bhagat, B. L. Kedia, P. D. Harveston, and H. C. Triandis, "Cultural Variations in the Cross-Border Transfer of Organizational knowledge: an Integrative Framework," *Academy of Management Review* 27, no. 2 (2002): 204–21.

72. D. G. Sirmon, M. A. Hitt, R. D. Ireland, in press. "Managing Firm Resources in Dynamic Environments to Create Value: Looking Inside the Black Box," *Academy of Management Review*, in press, 2006.

73. M H. Hitt, V. Franklin and Hong Zhu, "Culture, Institutions and International Strategy," *Journal of International Management* 12, no. 2 (2002): 222–34.

74. I. Berdrow and H. W. Lane, "International Joint Ventures: Creating Value through Successful Knowledge Management," *Journal of World Business* 38, no. 1 (2003): 15–30.

75. Ibid.

76. Ibid.

77. "China's New Restrictions on Deals," *Financial Times*, August 10, 2006.

78. J. Pura, "Backlash Builds Against Suharto-Lined Firms," *The Wall Street Journal*, May 27, 1998.

79. W. M. Danis, "Differences in Values, Practices, and Systems Among Hungarian Managers and Western Expatriates: An Organizing Framework and Typology," *Journal of World Business* (August 2003): 224–44.

80. R. Schoenberg, "Dealing with a Culture Clash," *Financial Times*, September 23, 2006.

81. Ibid.

82. P. Rosenzweig, "Why Is Managing in the United States so Difficult for European Firms?" *European Management Journal* 12, no. 1 (1994): 31–38.

83. Ibid.

84. "In Alabama, the Soul of a New Mercedes?" *Business Week*, March 31, 1997.

85. Ibid.

86. M. Craze and J. Simmons, "Road from Acrimony to Giant Steel Merger: How Mittal and Arcelor Came to terms," *International Herald Tribune*, July 6, 2006.

87. P. Marsh, "Deal Finalised in a Palace, but Sealed in an Airport," *Financial Times*, June 27, 2006.

88. Craze and Simmons, 2006.

89. Ibid.

90. P. Betts, "Steel Deals France a Hard Lesson in Reality," *Financial Times*, June 27, 2006.

91. H. James, "Europe Rediscovers the Tradition of Family Capitalism," *Financial Times*, July 4, 2006.

92. P. Glader and E. Bellman, "Breaking the Marwari Rules," *The Wall Street Journal*, July 10, 2006.

93. Ibid.

94. Ibid.

95. Ibid.

96. J. A. Pearce II and R. B. Robinson, Jr., "Cultivating *Guanxi* as a Foreign Investor Strategy," *Business Horizons* 43, no. 1 (2000): 31.

97. Ibid.

98. www.NextLinx.com, September 10, 2001.

99. Ibid.

Chapter 8

1. Greg Tarr, "Samsung Restructures, Combines Biz Units," *TWICE: This Week in Consumer Electronics* 24, no. 3 (2009): 4–8, Kelly Olsen, "Samsung Electronics Reorganizes to Fight Slump," *www.nytimes*, January 16, 2009. *Evan Ramstad*, "Corporate News: Samsung Overhaul Will Form 2 Divisions," *Wall Street Journal*. (Eastern edition). *Jan 16, 2009*.

2. Kelly Olsen, "Samsung Electronics Reorganizes to Fight Slump," *www. nytimes*, January 16, 2009.

3. R. Foster and S. Kaplan (New York, NY: *Currency*, 2001.)

4. Charles A. O'Reilly III, J. Bruce Harreld, and Michael L. Tushman, "Organizational Ambidexterity: IBM and Emerging Business Opprtunities," *California Management Review* 51, no. 4 (2009): 75–99,

5. Roberto C. Goizueta, (Former) Chairman and CEO, Coca-Cola Company.

6. A. D. Chandler, *Strategy and Structure: Chapters in the History of the American Industrial Enterprise* (Cambridge, MA: MIT Press, 1962); R. E. Miles et al., "Organizational Strategy, Structure, and Process," *Academy of Management Review* 3, no. 3 (1978): 546–62; and J. Woodward, *Industrial Organization: Theory and Practice* (Oxford University Press, 1965).

7. C. A. Bartlett and S. Ghoshal, *Managing Across Borders* (Boston: Harvard Business School Press, 1989).

8. J. M. Stopford and L. T. Wells, Jr., *Managing the Multinational Enterprise* (New York: Basic Books, 1972).

9. "Heinz's Johnson to Divest Operations, Scrap Management of Firm by Regions," *The Wall Street Journal*, December 8, 1997.

10. www.Nestle.com, December 7, 2000.

11. *Financial Times*, February 22, 2005.

12. Ibid.

13. L. Greenhalgh, "Ford Motor Company's CFO Jac Nasser on Transformational Change, E-Business, and Environmental Responsibility (Interview)," *Academy of Management Executive* 14, no. 13 (August 2001): 46.

14. J. Strikwerda and J. W. Stoelhorst, "The Emergence and Evolution of the Multidimensional Organization," *California Management Review* 51, no. 4 (2009): 11–31.

15. H. Henzler and W. Rall, "Facing Up to the Globalization Challenge," *McKinsey Quarterly* (Fall 1986): 52–68.

16. "Petrobras creates 6 companies for Comperj project—Brazil." *Business News Americas*, February 5, 2009,.

17. T. Levitt, "The Globalization of Markets," *Harvard Business Review* (May–June 1983): 92–102; and S. P. Douglas and Yoram Wind, "The Myth of Globalization," *Columbia Journal of World Business* (Winter 1987): 19–29.

18. www.levistrauss.com, accessed April 18, 2009.

19. October. 10, 2006.

20. www.pg.com, News releases, November 22, 2006.

21. "Gillette, P&G Team Up for Doubles," *Knight Ridder Tribune Business News*, January 17, 2006.

22. "P&G Corporate Information: How the Structure Works," www.pg.com, November 22, 2006.

23. Christina Berk, "P&G Is Stronger with Gillette," *Wall Street Journal*, October 11, 2006.

24. "P&G Corporate Information: How the Structure Works," www.pg.com, November 22, 2006.

25. For additional information on emerging markets and relevant Web sites, see Syed T. Anwar, *Marketing and International Business Links: Emerging Markets*, http://www.wtamu.edu/∼sanwar.bus/otherlinks.htm#Emerging_ Markets (retrieved on December 5, 2006); Goldman Sachs, *Dreaming with BRICs: The Path to 2050* (New York: Goldman Sachs, 2003).

26. For more detail, see, *The New Global Challengers: How 100 Top Companies from Rapidly Developing Economies Are Changing the World* (Boston, MA: The Boston Consulting Group, 2006); *Organizing for Global Advantage in China, India, and Other Rapidly Developing Economies* (Boston, MA: The Boston Consulting Group, 2006); Khanna, Tarun and Krishna Palepu, "Emerging Giants: Building World-Class Companies in Developing Countries," *Harvard Business Review* (October 2006): 60–69.

27. See Syed T. Anwar, "Global Business and Globalization," *Journal of International Management* 71 (2007): (in press); "Emerging Giants," *Business Week*, July 31, 2006, 40–49.

28. Raymond E. Miles, Miles Grant, Charles C. Snow, Kirsimarja Blomqvist, and Hector Rocha, "The I-form Organization," *California Management Review* 51, no. 4 (2009): 61–76,

29. Andy Reinhardt, "Philips: Back on the Beam," www.businessweek.com, May 3, 2004.

30. *Financial Times*, February 9, 2005.

31. www.Intel.com, August 18, 2005.

32. S. Ghoshal and C. A. Bartlett, "The Mulinational Corporation as an Interorganizational Network," *Academy of Management Review* 15, no. 4 (1990): 603–25.

33. Mohanbir Sawhney and Sumant Mandal, "Go Global," *Business 2.0* (May 5, 2001): 178–213.

34. J. D. Daniels, L. H. Radebaugh, and D. P. Sullivan, *Globalization and Business* (Upper Saddle River, NJ: Prentice Hall, 2002).

35. "Energizing the Supply Chain," *The Review*, Deloitte & Touche, January 17, 2000, 1.

36. C. A. Bartlett and S. Ghoshal, "Organizing for Worldwide Effectiveness: The Transnational Solution," *California Management Review* (Fall 1988): 54–74.

37. Ibid.

38. Based on models by R. E. White and T. A. Poynter, "Organizing for Worldwide Advantage," *Business Quarterly* 54 (Summer 1989); John M. Stopford and Louis T. Wells, Jr., *Managing the Multinational Enterprise* (New York: Basic Books, 1972); and C. A. Bartlett, "Organizing and Controlling MNCs, " *Harvard Business School Case Study*, no. 9 (March 1987): 365, 375.

39. C. W. L. Hill and E. R. Jones, *Strategic Management: An Integrated Approach*, 3rd ed., 390. Copyright © 1995 by Houghton Mifflin Company. Reprinted with Permission.

40. Business International Corporation, *New Directions in Multinational Corporate Organization* (New York: Business International Corporation, 1981).

41. Based on and adapted from R. Tannenbaum and W. Schmidt; and A. G. Kefelas, *Global Business Strategy* (Cincinnati: South-Western, 1990).

42. Francesco Caio, CEO, Merloni Elettrodomestici, interview in *Harvard Business Review*, January/February 1999.

43. John B. Cullen and K. Praveen Parboteeah, *Multinational Management: A Strategic Approach,* 3ed, (Cincinnati: South-Western, 2005), 281.

44. www.McDonalds.com, February 20, 2001.

45. Andrew Jack, "Russians Wake up to Consumer Capitalism," www.FT.com, January 30, 2001.

46. Ibid.

47. G. Rohrmann, CEO, AEI Corp., press release.

48. W. G. Egelhoff, "Patterns of Control in U.S., U.K., and European Multinational Corporations," *Journal of International Business Studies* (Fall 1984): 73–83.

49. Ibid.

50. Ibid.

51. S. Ueno and U. Sekaran, "The Influence of Culture on Budget Control Practices in the U.S.A. and Japan: An Empirical Study," *Journal of International Business Studies* 23 (Winter 1992): 659–74.

52. A. R. Neghandi and M. Welge, *Beyond Theory Z* (Greenwich, CT: J.A.I. Publishers, 1984), 18.

53. www.Nestle.com, press release, March 21, 2000.

54. Phatak.

Chapter 9

1. www.McKinsey.com/mgi/; "Capturing Talent," *The Economist*, August 18, 2007, 59–61; Douglas A. Ready, Linda A. Hill, and Jay A. Conger, "Winning the Race for Talent in Emerging Markets," *Harvard Business Review* (November 2008); Harold L. Sirkin, "Need Global Talent? Grow Your Own," Business Week Online, September 17, 2008; "Talent Retention: Ongoing Problem for Asia-Pacific Region," *T+D* 61 no. 3 (2007): 12.

2. www.McKinsey.com/mgi/; "Capturing Talent," *The Economist*, August 18, 2007, 59–61.

3. *The Economist,* 2007.

4. Douglas A. Ready, Linda A. Hill, and Jay A. Conger, "Winning the Race for Talent in Emerging Markets," *Harvard Business Review* (November 2008).

5. Sirkin, 2008

6. *Economist,* 2007.

7. Sirkin, 2008

8. Ready et al., 2008.

9. Ibid.

10. Tanya Mohn, "The Dislocated Americans," *New York Times,* December 2, 2008.

11. J. L. Laabs, "HR Pioneers Explore the Road Less Traveled," *Personnel Journal* (February 1996): 70–72, 74, 77–78.

12. Friso Den Hertog, Ad Van Iterson, and Christian Mari, "Does HRM Really Matter in Bringing about Strategic Change? Comparative Action Research in Ten European Steel Firms," *European Management Journal*, in press, 2009.

13. www.kpmglink.com, accessed February 24, 2009.

14. Ibid; "International Assignments Remain On the Upswing Despite Economic Concerns, Says KPMG," Anonymous, *PR Newswire, Dec 3, 2008*.

15. Ibid.

16. C. A. Bartlett and S. Ghoshal, "Matrix Management: Not a Structure, a Frame of Mind," *Harvard Business Review* (July–August 1990).

17. S. B. Prasad and Y. K. Krishna Shetty, *An Introduction to Multinational Management* (Upper Saddle River, NJ: Prentice Hall, 1979).

18. Rochelle Kopp, "International Human Resource Policies and Practices in Japanese, European, and United States Multinationals," *Human Resource Management* 33, no. 4 (1994): 581–99.

19. Updated and adapted by H. Deresky in 2007, from original work by D. A. Heenan and H. V. Perlmutter. *Multinational Organization Development* (Reading, MA: Addison-Wesley, 1979), 18–19.

20. Ibid.

21. Tung, "Selection and Training of Personnel for Overseas Assignments."

22. Dowling and Schuler.

23. S. J. Kobrin, "Expatriate Reduction and Strategic Control in American Multinational Corporations," *Human Resource Management* 27, no. 1 (1988): 63–75.

24. Company information, www.ABB.com, accessed July 26, 2004.

25. Hem C. Jain, "Human Resource Management in Selected Japanese Firms, the Foreign Subsidiaries and Locally Owned Counterparts," *International Labour Review* 129, no. 1 (1990): 73–84; Bartlett and Ghoshal.

26. www.GMACGlobalrelocation.com, accessed March 1, 2009.

27. *Personnel Today,* May 23, 2006.

28. M. Mendenhall and G. Oddou, "The Dimensions of Expatriate Acculturation: A Review," *Academy of Management Review* 10, no. 1 (1985): 39–47.

29. Zsuzsanna Tungli and Mauri Peiperl, "Expatriate Practices in German, Japanese, U.K., and U.S. Multinational Companies: A Comparative Survey of Changes," Human Resource Management, January–February 2009, Vol. 48, No. 1, Pp.153–171 © 2009 Wiley Periodicals, Inc.

30. Theresa Minton-Eversole, "Best Expatriate Assignments Require Much Thought, Even More Planning". SHRMs 2009 Global Trend Book, *HRMagazine* (2009): 74–75.

31. Tye and Chen, 2005.

32. D. Erbacher, B. D'Netto, and J. Espana, "Expatriate Success in China: Impact of Personal and Situational Factors," *Journal of American Academy of Business* 9, no. 2 (2006): 183.

33. www.FT.com, March 5, 2001.

34. Rosalie Tung, "American Expatriates Abroad: From Neophytes to Cosmopolitans," *Journal of World Business* 33 (1998): 125–44.

35. Business Editors, "International Job Assignment: Boon or Bust for an Employee's Career?" *Business Wire, Inc.*, March 13, 2006.

36. R. D. Hays, "Expatriate Selection: Insuring Success and Avoiding Failure," *Journal of International Business Studies* 5, no. 1 (1974): 25–37; Tung, 1998.

37. His-An Shih, Yun-Hwa Chiang, and In-Sook Kim, "Expatriate Performance Management from MNEs of Different National Origins," *International Journal of Manpower* 26, no. 2 (2005): 161–62.

38. *Business Wire*, 2006.

39. J. S. Black, "Work Role Transitions: A Study of American Expatriate Managers in Japan," *Journal of International Business Studies* 19 (1988): 277–94.

40. *Business Wire*, 2006.

41. Tung, "U.S., European, and Japanese Multinationals."

42. Ibid.

43. B. Wysocki, Jr., "Prior Adjustment: Japanese Executives Going Overseas Take Anti-Shock Courses," *The Wall Street Journal*, December 4, 1987.

44. Mendenhall and Oddou.

45. K. Oberg, "Culture Shock: Adjustments to New Cultural Environments," *Practical Anthropology* (July–August 1960): 177–82.

46. Ibid.

47. Ibid.

48. P. R. Harris and R. T. Moran, *Managing Cultural Differences,* 4th ed. (Houston, TX: Gulf Publishing, 1996), 139.

49. Tung, "Selection and Training of Personnel for Overseas Assignments."

50. Ronen.

51. Ibid.

52. Kealey, 81.

53. Adapted from J. S. Black, Mark. E. Mendenhall, Hal B. Gregersen, and Linda K. Stroh, *Globalizing People Through International Assignments* (Reading, MA: Addison Wesley Longman, 1999).

54. R. Peterson, "The Use of Expatriates and Inpatriates in Central and Eastern Europe Since the Wall Came Down," *Journal of World Business* 38 (2003): 55–69.

55. Christopher Tice, Manager, Global Expatriate Operations, DuPont Inc., quoted in Mark Schoeff, "International Assignments Best Served by Unified Policy," *Workforce Management* 85, no. 3 (2006): 36.

56. Ibid.

57. "Living Expenses," www.economist.com, July 22, 2000; "Runzheimer International Compensation Worksheet," www.runzheimer.com, 2000.

58. *Business Wire,* 2006.

59. B. W. Teague, *Compensating Key Personnel Overseas* (New York: Conference Board, 1992).

60. C. Reynolds, "Compensation of Overseas Personnel," in J. Famularo, *Handbook of Human Resource Administration,* 2nd ed. New York: McGraw-Hill, 1989.

61. S. F. Gale, "Taxing Situations for Expatriates," *Workforce* 82, no. 6 (2003): 100.

62. R. B. Peterson, "The Use of Expatriates and Inpatriates in Central and Eastern Europe Since the Wall Came Down," *Journal of World Business* (2003): 55–69.

63. Gina Ruiz, "Kimberly-Clark: Developing Talent in Developing World Markets," *Workforce Management* 85, no. 7 (2006): 34.

64. Martin Fackler, "The 'Toyota Way' Is Translated for a New Generation of Foreign Managers," www.nytimes.com, February 17, 2007.

65. Ibid.

66. Ibid.

67. Company website, www.starbucks.com, accessed March 5, 2009.

68. "Seoul Is Supporting a Sizzling Tech Boom," www.businessweek.com, September 25, 2000.

69. P. Damaskopoulos and T. Evgeniou, "Adoption of New Economy Practices by SMEs in Eastern Europe," *European Management Journal* 21, no. 2 (2003): 133–45.

70. Fay Hansen, "The Great Global Talent Race: One World, One Workforce: Part 1 of 2," *Workforce* Management85, no. 7 (2006): 1.

71. D. Kiriazov, S. E. Sullivan, and H. S. Tu, "Business Success in Eastern Europe: Understanding and Customizing HRM," *Business Horizons* (January/February 2000): 39–43.

72. Ibid.

73. Y. Ono and W. Spindle, "Japan's Long Decline Makes One Thing Rise: Individualism," *The Wall Street Journal,* January 3, 2001.

74. Ingmar Bjorkman and Yuan Lu, "The Management of Human Resources in Chinese-Western Joint Ventures," *Journal of World Business* 34, no. 3 (1999): 306.

75. Ibid.

76. "Personnel Demands Attention Overseas," *Mutual Fund Market News,* March 19, 2001, 1.

77. Mary Ann Von Glinow, Ellen A. Drost, and Mary B. Teagarden, "Converging on IHRM Best Practices: Lessons Learned from a Globally Distributed Consortium on Theory and Practice," *Human Resource Management* 41, no. 1 (2002): 133–35.

Chapter 10

1. Julia Werdigier, "Paychecks and Passports," *New York Times*, April 2, 2008; Doreen Carvajal, "Paid in Dollars, Some Americans Are Struggling in Europe," *New York Times*, December 15, 2007; Alan Paul, "The Expat Life: Clock Counts Down as Decision Weighs: Should I Stay or Go?" www.wallstreetjournal, February 28, 2008; Monica Ginsburg, "Getting Ahead by Going Abroad," *Crain's Chicago Business* 31, no. 50 (2008): 20; Philip Shearer and Abby Ellin, "Foreign from the Start," www.nytimes.com, September 21, 2003; Jad Mouawad, "Total, the French Oil Company, Places It Bets Globally," www.nytimes.com, February 22, 2009; www.GMACglobalrelocationsurvey.com, accessed March 1, 2009; Keith Bradsher and Julia Werdigier, "Abruptly Expatriate Bankers Are Cut Loose," www.nytimes.com March 4, 2009.

2. Werdigier.

3. Bradsher and Werdigier.

4. *Wall Street Journal,* February 28, 2008.

5. www.nytimes.com, February 22, 2000.

6. Ginsburg.

7. Ibid.

8. Shearer and Ellin.

9. Alison Maitland, "Top Companies Value Overseas Experience," *Financial Times*, July 3, 2006.

10. www.GMACglobalrelocationsurvey.com, accessed March 1, 2009.

11. Maitland.

12. "International Assignments Remain On the Upswing Despite Economic Concerns, Says KPMG," *PR Newswire*, December 3, 2008; www.kpmglink.com.

13. M. Lazarova and P. Caligiuri, "Retaining Repatriates: The Role of Organizational Support Practices," *Journal of World Business* 36 no. 4 (2001): 389–401.

14. Rosalie Tung, "Career Issues in International Assignments," *Academy of Management Executive* 2, no. 3 (1988): 241–44.

15. M. Harvey, "Dual-Career Expatriates: Expectations, Adjustments and Satisfaction with International Relocation," *Journal of International Business Studies* 28, no. 3 (1997): 627.

16. Tung.

17. Charlene M. Solomon, "One Assignment, Two Lives," *Personnel Journal* (May 1996): 36–44.

18. www.GMACglobalrelocationsurvey.com, accessed March 1, 2009.

19. Ibid.

20. Solomon.

21. www.GMACglobalrelocationsurvey.com, accessed March 1, 2009.

22. R. Pascoe, "Employers Ignore Expatriate Wives at Their Own Peril," *Wall Street Journal,* March 29, 1992.

23. www.FT.com, March 5, 2001.

24. P. Asheghian and B. Ebrahimi, *International Business* (New York: HarperCollins, 1990), 470.

www.GMACglobalrelocationsurvey.com, accessed March 1, 2009.

N. J. Adler, *International Dimensions of Organizational Behavior*, 4th ed. Boston: PWS-Kent, 2002).

Bonache and C. Brewster, "Knowledge Transfer and the Management of atriation," *Thunderbird International Business Review* 43, no. 1 (2001): 58.

28. Berthoin-Antal, "Expatriates' Contributions to Organizational Learning," *Journal of General Management* 26, no. 4 (2001): 62–84.

29. Mila Lazarova and Ibraiz Tarique, "Knowledge Transfer upon Repatriation," *Journal of World Business* 40, no. 4 (2005): 361–73.

30. Ibid.

31. Excerpted from www.Netscape.com case studies.

32. J. S. Black and H. B. Gregersen, "The Other Half of the Picture: Antecedents of Spouse Cross-cultural Adjustment," *Journal of International Business Studies* (1992): 461–77.

33. T. Gross, E. Turner, and L. Cederholm, "Building Teams for Global Operations," *Management Review* (June 1987): 32–36.

34. www.BritishTelecom.com/cases, February 19, 2001.

35. J. Conger and E. Lawler, "People Skills Still Rule in the Virtual Company," *Financial Times*, August 26, 2005.

36. Based largely on Adler, 2002.

37. T. Gross, E. Turner, and L. Cederholm, "Building Teams for Global Operations," *Management Review* (June 1987), 34.

38. T. R. Kayworth and D. E. Leidner, "Leadership Effectiveness in Global Virtual Teams," *Journal of Management Information Systems* 18, no. 3 (2001–02): 7–40.

39. C. Solomon, "Building Teams Across Borders," *Global Workforce* (November 1998): 12–17.

40. Ibid.

41. Some of this content is based on Kenneth W. Kerber and Anthony F. Buono, "Leadership Challenges in Global Virtual Teams: Lessons from the Field," *SAM Advanced Management Journal* 69, no. 4 (2004): 4–10.

42. J. Cordery, C. Soo, B. Kirkman, B. Benson, and J. Mathieu, "Leading Parallel Virtual Teams: Lessons from Alcoa," *Organizational Dynamics* 38, no. 3 (2009): 204–16.

43. Ibid.

44. Ibid.

45. B. Rosen, S. Furst, and R. Blackburn, "Training for Virtual Teams: An Investigation of Current Practices and Future Needs," *Human Resources Management* 45, no. 2 (2006): 229–47.

46. Michiyo Nakamoto, "Cultural Revolution in Tokyo," www.ft.com, September 17, 2009.

47. Ibid.

48. A. Joshi, G. Labianca, and P. M. Caligiuri, "Getting Along Long Distance: Understanding Conflict in a Multinational Team through Network Analysis," *Journal of World Business* 37 (2002): 277–84.

49. V. Govindarajan and A. K. Gupta, "Building an Effective Global Business Team," *MIT Sloan Management Review* 42, no. 4 (2001): 63.

50. Ibid.

51. Ibid.

52. S. Chevrier, "Cross-cultural Management in Multinational Project Groups," *Journal of World Business* 38, no. 2 (2003): 141–49.

53. Ibid.

54. *Business Wire*, 2006.

55. Jessica Shambora, and Beth Kowitt, "50 Most Powerful Women," *Fortune*. New York: September 28, 2009. 160, no. 6 (2009): 99.

56. Rupali Arora, Blake Ellis, Sarah Kabourek, and Anu Partanen, "International Power 50," *Fortune* (September 28, 2009).

57. Shyamantha Asokan and David Patrikarakos, "Leading Businesswomen in the Arab World: Who's Who: Extended Version of Our List of Personalities," www.ft.com, June 23, 2008.

58. R. L. Tung, "Female Expatriates: The Model Global Manager?" *Organizational Dynamics* 33, no. 3 (2004): 243–53.

59. M. Kaminski and J. Paiz, "Japanese Women in Management: Where Are They?" *Human Resource Management* 23, no. 2 (1984): 277–92.

60. P. Lansing and K. Ready, "Hiring Women Managers in Japan: An Alternative for Foreign Employers," *California Management Review* 26, no. 4 (1988): 112–27.

61. Japan's Neglected Resource – Female Workers," www.nytimes.com, July 24, 2003.

62. Ibid.

63. G. K. Stahl, E. L. Miller, and R. L. Tung, "Toward the Boundaryless Career: A Closer Look at the Expatriate Career Concept and the Perceived Implications of an International Assignment," *Journal of World Business* 37 (2002): 216–27.

64. Patrick Jenkins and Bettina Wassener, "How Germany Keeps Women off the Board," *Financial Times*, June 15, 2004.

65. Alison Maitland, "The North-South Divide in Europe, Inc.," *Financial Times*, June 14, 2004.

66. Ibid.

67. M. Jelinek and N. Adler, "Women: World Class Managers for Global Competition," *Academy of Management Executive* 11, no. 1 (February 1988): 11–19.

68. N. J. Adler and D. N. Izraeli, *Women in Management Worldwide* (Armonk, NY: M. E. Sharpe, 1988).

69. Ibid.

70. Jacob Vittorelli, Former Deputy Chairman of Pirelli.

71. "A New Deal in Europe?" www.businessweek.com, July 14, 2003.

72. M. R. Czinkota, I. A. Ronkainen, and M. H. Moffett, *International Business*, 3rd ed. (New York: Dryden Press, 1994).

73. Rik Kirkland, "The New Face of Labor," *Fortune* (October 16, 2006).

74. C. K. Prahalad and Y. L. Doz, *The Multinational Mission: Balancing Local Demands and Global Vision* (New York: Free Press, 1987).

75. R. J. Adams, *Industrial Relations Under Liberal Democracy* (University of South Carolina Press, 1995).

76. J. S. Daniels and L. H. Radebaugh, *International Business*, 10th ed. (Reading, MA: Addison-Wesley, 2004).

77. Dowling, Schuler, and Welch.

78. Adams.

79. Ibid.

80. D. Barboza, "China Passed Law to Empower Unions and End Labor Abuse," *New York Times*, October 12, 2006.

81. David Barboza, www.nytimes.com, October 12, 2006. Copyright The New York Times Co. Reprinted with permission.

82. Ibid.

83. *Anonymous.* "Asia: Arbitration needed: China's Labour Laws," *The Economist*. London: Aug 1, 2009, 392, no. 8642 (2009): 37

84. B. Barber, "Workers of the World Are Uniting," *Financial Times*, December 7, 2004.

85. International Confederation of Free Trade Unions, www.icftu.org, October 31, 2006.

86. Ibid.

87. M. M. Lucio and S. Weston, "New Management Practices in a Multinational Corporation: The Restructuring of Worker Representation and Rights?" *Industrial Relations Journal* 25, no. 2 (2004): 110–21.

88. D. B. Cornfield, "Labor Transnationalism?" *Work and Occupations* 24, no. 3 (August 1997): 278.

89. R. Martin, A. Vidinova, and S. Hill, "Industrial Relations in Transition Economies: Emergent Industrial Relations Institutions in Bulgaria," *British Journal of Industrial Relations* 34, no. 1 (1996): 3.

90. Daniels and Radebaugh.

91. A. M. Rugman and R. M. Hodgetts, *International Business* (New York: McGraw-Hill, 1995).

92. R. Milne and H. Williamson, "Selective Bargaining: German Companies Are Driving a Hidden Revolution in Labour Flexibility," *Financial Times*, January 6, 2006.

93. Milne and Williamson.

94. Gerrit Wiesmann, "Germans Eye U.K. Listings as a Way Out of Worker Law," *Financial Times*, May 24, 2006.

95. Ibid.

96. "A New Deal in Europe?" www.businessweek.com; *BW Online*, July 14, 2003.

97. Milne and Williamson.

98. Ibid.

99. J. Hoerr, "What Should Unions Do?" *Harvard Business Review* (May–June 1991): 30–45.

100. H. C. Katz, "The Decentralization of Collective Bargaining: A Literature Review and Comparative Analysis," *Industrial and Labor Relations Review* 47, no. 1 (1993): 3–22.

101. Williamson, *Financial Times*, July 22, 2004.

102. www.nytimes.com, July 24, 2004.

103. Adams.

104. www.wallstreetjournal.com, April 24, 2009.

105. "The Perils of Cozy Corporatism," *The Economist*, May 21, 1994.

106. Wofgang Streeck, "More Uncertainties: German Unions Facing 1992," *Industrial Relations* (Fall 1991): 30–33.

107. "Germany's Economic Future Is on the Bargaining Table," *Business Week*, March 30, 1992.

Chapter 11

1. A. Maitland, "Le patron, der Chef and the Boss," *Financial Times*, January 9, 2006.

2. Ibid.

3. M. Kets de Vries and K. Korotov, "The Future of an Illusion: In Search of the New European Business Leader," *Organizational Dynamics* 34, no. 3 (2005): 218–30.

4. Ibid.

5. Maitland.

6. Ibid.

7. R. J. House, *Culture, Leadership and Organizations: The GLOBE Study of 62 Societies* (Thousand Oaks, CA: Sage, 2004).

8. F. C. Brodbeck, M. Frese, and M. Javidan, "Leadership Made in Germany: Low on Compassion, High on Performance," *Academy of Management Executive* 16, no. 1 (2002).

9. R. House and M. Javidan, "Cultural Acumen for the Global Manager: Lessons from Project GLOBE," *Organizational Dynamics* (2001).

10. Mansour Javidan, Peter W. Dorfman, Mary Sully de Luque, Robert J. House, "In the Eye of the Beholder: Cross Cultural Lessons in Leadership from Project GLOBE," *The Academy of Management Perspectives* 20, no. 1 (2006).

11. N. Payton, "Leaderships Skills Hold Britain Back," *The Guardian*, February 22, 2003.

12. S. Michailova, "When Common Sense Becomes Uncommon: Participation and Empowerment in Russian Companies with Western Participation," *Journal of World Business* 37 (2002): 180–87.

13. "Fujitsu Uses Pay Cuts as a Motivational Tool," www.nytimes.com, January 27, 2004.

14. Garry A. Gelade, Paul Dobson, and Katharina Auer, "Individualism, Masculinity, and the Sources of Organizational Commitment," *Journal of Cross-Cultural Psychology* 39 (2008): 599.

15. Ibid.

16. F. Rieger and D. Wong-Rieger, "A Configuration Model of National Influence Applied to Southeast Asian Organizations," *Proceedings of the Research Conference on Business in Southeast Asia*, May 12–13, 1990, University of Michigan.

17. R. M. Steers, *Made in Korea: Chung Ju Yung and the Rise of Hyundai* (New York: Routledge, 1999).

18. Meaning of Work International Research Team, *The Meaning of Working: An International Perspective* (New York: Academic Press, 1985).

19. Ibid.

20. D. Siddiqui and A. Alkhafaji, *The Gulf War: Implications for Global Businesses and Media* (Apollo, PA: Closson Press, 1992): 133–35.

21. Ibid.

22. A. Ali, "The Islamic Work Ethic in Arabia," *Journal of Psychology* 126 (1992): 507–19.

23. Yasamusa Kuroda and Tatsuzo Suzuki, "A Comparative Analysis of the Arab Culture: Arabic, English and Japanese Language and Values," paper presented at the 5th Congress of the International Association of Middle Eastern Studies, Tunis (September 20–24, 1991), quoted in Siddiqui and Alkhafaji.

24. Adapted from Abbas J. Ali, "The Islamic Work Ethic in Arabia," *Journal of Psychology* 126, no. 5 (1992): 507–19.

25. A. Furnham, B. D. Kirkcaldy, and R. Lynn, "National Attitudes to Competitiveness, Money, and Work among Young People: First, Second, and Third World Differences," *Human Relations* 47, no. 1 (1994): 119–32.

26. D. S. Elenkov, "Can American Management Concepts Work in Russia? A Cross-cultural Comparative Study," *California Management Review* 40, no. 4 (1998): 133–57.

27. Abraham Maslow, *Motivation and Personality* (New York: Harper & Row, 1954).

28. R. L. Tung, "Patterns of Motivation in Chinese Industrial Enterprises," *Academy of Management Review* 6, no. 3 (1981): 481–89.

29. Swee Hoon Ang, "The Power of Money: A Cross-cultural Analysis of Business-Related Beliefs," *Journal of World Business* 35, no. 1 (2000): 43.

30. Geert Hofstede, "National Cultures in Four Dimensions," *International Studies of Management and Organization* (Spring–Summer 1983).

31. D. Walker, T. Walker, and J. Schmitz, *Doing Business Internationally*, 2nd ed. (New York: McGraw-Hill, 2003).

32. Ibid.

33. Ibid.

34. Ibid.

35. M. B. Teagarden, M. C. Butler, and M. Von Glinow, "Mexico's Maquiladora Industry: Where Strategic Human Resource Management Makes a Difference," *Organizational Dynamics* (Winter 1992): 34–47.

36. John Condon, *Good Neighbors: Communication with the Mexicans* (Yarmouth, ME: Intercultural Press, 1985).

37. G. K. Stephens and C. R. Greer, "Doing Business in Mexico: Understanding Cultural Differences," *Organizational Dynamics* (Summer 1995): 39–55.

38. Teagarden, Butler, and Von Glinow.

39. Stephens and Greer.

40. Ibid.

41. C. E. Nicholls, H. W. Lane, and M. B. Brechu, "Taking Self-Managed Teams to Mexico," *Academy of Management Executive* 13, no. 3 (1999): 15–25.

42. Ibid.

43. Ibid.

44. Mariah E. de Forest, "Thinking of a Plant in Mexico?" *Academy of Management Executive* 8, no. 1 (1994): 33–40.

45. Ibid.

46. Ibid.

47. Teagarden, Butler, and Von Glinow.

48. Malgorzata Tarczynska, "Eastern Europe: How Valid Is Western Reward/Performance Management?" *Benefits and Compensation International* 29, no. 8 (2000): 9–16.

49. Snejina Michailova, "When Common Sense Becomes Uncommon: Participation and Empowerment in Russian Companies with Western Participation," *Journal of World Business* 37 (2002), 180–87.

50. M. A. Von Glinow and Byung Jae Chung, "Comparative HRM Practices in the U.S., Japan, Korea and the PRC," in *Research in Personnel and HRM—A Research Annual: International HRM*, ed. A. Nedd, G. R. Ferris, and K. M. Rowland (London: JAI Press, 1989).

51. A. Ignatius, "Now if Ms. Wong Insults a Customer, She Gets an Award," *The Wall Street Journal*, January 24, 1989.

52. T. Saywell, "Motive Power: China's State Firms Bank on Incentives to Keep Bosses Operating at Their Peak," *Far Eastern Economic Review* (July 8, 2000): 67–68.

53. A. Maitland, "Le patron, der Chef and the Boss," *Financial Times*, January 9, 2006.

54. A. Morrison, H. Gregersen, and S. Black, "What Makes Savvy Global Leaders?" *Ivey Business Journal* 64, no. 2 (1999): 44–51; and *Monash Mt. Eliza Business Review* 1, no. 2 (1998).

55. D. Walker, T. Walker, and J. Schmitz, *Doing Business Internationally* (New York: McGraw-Hill, 2003).

56. Based on Walker et al. 2003; and Gary P. Ferraro, *The Cultural Dimension of International Business* 5th ed. (Upper Saddle River, NJ: Prentice Hall, 2006).

57. "In the Driver's Seat," *Newsweek*, June 30, 2008.

58. A. Morrison, H. Gregersen, and S. Black, "What Makes Savvy Global Leaders?" *Ivey Business Journal* 64, no. 2 (1999): 44–51; and *Monash Mt. Eliza Business Review* 1, no. 2 (1998).

59. Ibid.

60. R. H. Mason and R. S. Spich, *Management: An International Perspective* (Homewood: IL: Irwin, 1987).

61. Ibid., p. 184.

62. Ibid., p. 186.

63. Mason and Spich.

64. B. M. Bass, *Bass & Stogdill's Handbook of Leadership* (New York: Free Press, 1990).

65. See, for example, M. Mead, *Sex and Temperament in Three Primitive Societies* (New York: Morrow, 1935); M. Mead et al., *Cooperation and Competition among Primitive Peoples* (New York: McGraw-Hill, 1937).

66. D. McGregor, *The Human Side of Enterprise* (New York: McGraw-Hill, 1960). See, for example, R. M. Stogdill, *Manual for the Leader Behavior Description Questionnaire—Form XII* (Columbus: Ohio State University, Bureau of Business Research, 1963); R. R. Blake and J. S. Mouton, *The New Managerial Grid* (Houston: Gulf Publishing, 1978).

67. F. E. Fiedler, "Engineering the Job to Fit the Manager," *Harvard Business Review* 43, no. 5 (1965): 115–22.

68. Den Hartog, N. Deanne, R. J. House, Paul J. Hanges, P. W. Dorfman, S. Antonio Ruiz-Quintanna et al., "Culture Specific and Cross-culturally Generalizable Implicit Leadership Theories: Are Attributes of Charismatic/Transformational Leadership Universally Endorsed?" *Leadership Quarterly* 10, no. 2 (1999): 219–56.

69. Selected data from Den Hartog, R. House et al. (GLOBE Project) *Leadership Quarterly* 10, no. 2 (1999).

70. Ibid.

71. R. House et al., "Cultural Influences on Leadership and Organizations: Project GLOBE," *Advances in Global Leadership*, vol. 1 (JAI Press, 1999).

72. Ibid.

73. Geert Hofstede, "Motivation, Leadership and Organization: Do American Theories Apply Abroad?" *Organizational Dynamics* (Summer 1980): 42–63.

74. Ibid.

75. Geert Hofstede, "Value Systems in Forty Countries," *Proceedings of the 4th International Congress of the International Association for Cross-Cultural Psychology* (1978).

76. Andre Laurent, "The Cultural Diversity of Western Conceptions of Management," *International Studies of Management and Organization* 13, no. 1–2 (1983): 75–96.

77. C. Hampden-Turner and A. Trompenaars, *The Seven Cultures of Capitalism* (New York: Doubleday, 1993).

78. M. Harie, E. E. Ghiselli, and L. W. Porter, *Managerial Thinking: An International Study* (New York: John Wiley and Sons, 1966).

79. C. Hampden-Turner and A. Trompenaars, *The Seven Cultures of Capitalism* (New York: Doubleday, 1993).

80. S. G. Redding and T. W. Case, "Managerial Beliefs Among Asian Managers," *Proceedings of the Academy of Management* (1975).

81. I. Kenis, "A Cross-cultural Study of Personality and Leadership," *Group and Organization Studies* 2 (1977): 49–60; F. C. Deyo, "The Cultural Patterning of Organizational Development: A Comparative Case Study of Thailand and Chinese Industrial Enterprises," *Human Organization* 37 (1978): 68–72.

82. M. K. Badawy, "Styles of Mid-Eastern Managers," *California Management Review* (Spring 1980): 57; various newscasts, 2001.

83. A. A. Algattan, "Test of the Path-Goal Theory of Leadership in the Multinational Domain," paper presented at the Academy of Management Conference, 1985, San Diego, CA; J. P. Howell and P. W. Dorfman, "A Comparative Study of Leadership and Its Substitutes in a Mixed Cultural Work Setting," unpublished manuscript, 1988.

84. D. H. Welsh, F. Luthans, and S. M. Sommer, "Managing Russian Factory Workers: The Impact of U.S.-Based Behavioral and Participative Techniques," *Academy of Management Journal* 36 (1993): 58–79.

85. Alison Maitland, "An American Leader in Europe," leadership interview with Nancy McKinstry, Wolters Kluwer, *Financial Times*, July 15, 2004.

86. Ibid.

87. Ibid.

88. Ibid.

INDEX

Note: The locators followed by 'b', 'ex' and 'n' refer to box, exhibits and notes cited in the text.